A History of West Germany

VOLUME 2

France and Jessica

Democracy and its Discontents 1963–1988

Dennis L. Bark

and

David R. Gress

Basil Blackwell

British Library Cataloguing in Publication Data

A CIP catalogue record for this book is available from the British Library.

Library of Congress Cataloging in Publication Data
Bark, Dennis L.
    A history of West Germany/Dennis L. Bark and David R. Gress.
    p.   cm.
    Bibliography: v. 1.
    Includes indexes.
    Contents: v. 1. From shadow to substance, 1945–1963 – v.
2. Democracy and its discontents, 1963–1988.
    ISBN 0-631-16787-0 (v. 1) – ISBN 0-631-16788-9 (v. 2)
ISBN 0-631-16924-5 (set)
    1. Germany (West) – History.   I. Gress, David, 1953–
II. Title.
DD258.7.B37   1989
943.087 – dc19

Typeset in 10½ on 12pt Ehrhardt
by Joshua Associates Ltd, Oxford
Printed in Great Britain by
T. J. Press, Padstow

Verstandene Geschichte ist nach meinem
Dafürhalten die wahre Philosophie der Geschichte.
Leopold von Ranke

Tot nos praeceptoribus, tot exemplis instruxit
antiquitas, ut possit videri nulla sorte nascendi
aetas felicior quam nostra, cui docendae priores
elaborarunt.
Quintilian, *Inst. Orat.* xii, 11, 22

Contents

PART VIII

The Fourth Chancellor of Germany, Willy Brandt, 1969–1974

PART IX

The Era of the "Macher," 1974–1982

PART X

The Pillar of Central Europe

VOLUME 1
From Shadow to Substance: 1945–1963

PART I
The Beginning and the End

PART II
Reconstruction and Division

PART III

The Establishment of the Federal Republic, 1949–1955

PART IV

Consolidation and Division, 1955–1961

PART V

The End of the Adenauer Era, 1961–1963

Abbreviations

ABM	Anti-ballistic missile
Antifa	Antifaschistischer Aktionsausschuss (Anti-fascist action committee)
APO	Ausserparlamentarische Opposition (Extraparliamentary opposition)
BBC	British Broadcasting Corporation
BBU	Bundesverband Bürgerinitiativen Umweltschutz (Citizens' environmental group)
Benelux	Belgium, Netherlands, Luxembourg
BfV	Bundesamt für Verfassungsschutz (Internal security agency)
BGAG	Beteiligungsgesellschaft für Gemeinwirtschaft
BFW	Bund Freiheit der Wissenschaft (Association for the Freedom of Scholarship)
BHE	Bund der Heimatvertriebenen und Entrechteten (Bloc of Expellees and Disenfranchised)
BLK	Bund/Länder Kommission
BMG	British Military Government
CARE	Cooperative for American Remittances to Europe
CDU	Christlich-Demokratische Union (Christian Democratic Union)
CEEC	Committee for European Economic Cooperation
CFM	Council of Foreign Ministers
CIA	Central Intelligence Agency
CND	[British] Campaign for Nuclear Disarmament
CPSU	Communist Party of the Soviet Union
CSCE	Conference on Security and Cooperation in Europe
CSU	Christlich-Soziale Union (Christian Social Union)
DCV	Deutscher Caritas Verband

DDP	Deutsche Demokratische Partei (German Democratic Party)
DEKT	Deutscher Evangelischer Kirchentag (German Protestant Assembly)
DGB	Deutscher Gewerkschaftsbund (German Trade Union Federation)
DIHT	Deutscher Industrie- und Handelstag (German Assembly of Industry and Commerce)
DKP	Deutsche Kommunistische Partei (German Communist Party)
DNA	Deutsche Nachrichten Agentur (German Press Agency)
DP	Deutsche Partei (German Party)
DVP	Deutsche Volkspartei (German People's Party)
EAC	European Advisory Commission
EC	European Community
ECSC	European Coal and Steel Community
ECU	European Currency Unit
EDC	European Defense Community
EDIP	European Defense Improvement Program
EEC	European Economic Community
EKD	Evangelische Kirche in Deutschland (Evangelical Church in Germany) [Protestant]
EMS	European Monetary System
EPC	European Political Cooperation
EPU	European Payments Union
ERP	European Recovery Program (Marshall Plan)
ERW	Enhanced radiation warhead
EURATOM	European Atomic Energy Community
FCMA	Friendship, Cooperation, and Mutual Assistance [Treaty]
FDP	Freie Demokratische Partei (Free Democratic Party)
FRG	Federal Republic of Germany
GATT	General Agreement on Tariffs and Trade
GCND	German Campaign against Nuclear Death
GDR	German Democratic Republic
GLCM	Ground-launched cruise missile
GSFG	Group of Soviet Forces in Germany
GVP	Gesamtdeutsche Volkspartei (All-German People's Party)
HICOG	[Office of the US] High Commissioner for Germany
HLG	High Level Group
ICBM	Intercontinental ballistic missile

IHK	Industrie- und Handelskammer (Chamber of Industry and Commerce)
IMF	International Monetary Fund
INF	Intermediate-range nuclear forces
IPPNW	International Physicians for the Prevention of Nuclear War
IRBM	Intermediate range ballistic missile
JCS	Joint Chiefs of Staff
Jusos	Jungsozialisten (Young Socialists)
KPD	Kommunistische Partei Deutschlands (Communist Party of Germany)
KVP	Kasernierte Volkspolizei (barracked People's Police)
LDPD	Liberaldemokratische Partei Deutschlands (Liberal Democratic Party of Germany)
MBFR	Mutual and balanced force reductions
Mifrifi	Mittelfristige Finanzplanung (Medium-term fiscal strategy)
MLF	Multilateral force
NATO	North Atlantic Treaty Organization
NORAD	North American Aerospace Defense Command
NPD	Nationaldemokratische Partei Deutschlands (National Democratic Party of Germany)
NPG	Nuclear Planning Group
NSDAP	Nationalsozialistische Deutsche Arbeiterpartei (National Socialist German Workers' Party)
NVA	Nationale Volksarmee (East German Army)
OECD	Organization for Economic Cooperation and Development
OEEC	Organization for European Economic Cooperation
OKW	Oberkommando der Wehrmacht (High Command of the Armed Forces)
OMGUS	Office of Military Government for Germany, United States
OPEC	Organization of Petroleum Exporting Countries
OSS	Office of Strategic Services
PLO	Palestine Liberation Organization
RAF	Rote Armee Fraktion (Red Army Faction)
RIAS	Rundfunk im amerikanischen Sektor (Radio in the American Sector)
RSHA	Reichssicherheitshauptamt (Reich security main office)
SACEUR	Supreme Allied Commander Europe
SALT	Strategic Arms Limitation Talks

SA	Sturmabteilung (Storm Troopers)
SBZ	Sowjetische Besatzungszone (Soviet Occupied Zone)
SD	Sicherheitsdienst (Security Service)
SDI	Strategic Defense Initiative
SDS	Sozialistischer Deutscher Studentenbund (German Socialist Student Federation)
SED	Sozialistische Einheitspartei Deutschlands (Socialist Unity Party of Germany)
SI	Socialist International
SMAD	Soviet Military Administration in Germany
SOFA	Status of Forces Agreement
SPD	Sozialdemokratische Partei Deutschlands (Social Democratic Party of Germany)
SRP	Sozialistische Reichspartei (Socialist Reich Party)
SS	Schutzstaffel (Elite Squad)
UEM	United Europe Movement
UN	United Nations
VDS	Verband Deutscher Studentenschaften (German Student Body Association)
WAV	Wirtschaftliche Aufbau-Vereinigung (Economic Reconstruction Party)
WEU	West European Union

PART VI

Erhard as Chancellor, 1963–1966

To everything there is a season, and a time to every purpose . . .

Ecclesiastes 3:1

And what appears as flickering image now,
fix it firmly with enduring thought.

Goethe, *Faust*

1
Germany in Transition

When Adenauer resigned, the Federal Republic was the same age as the Weimar Republic when it was abolished in 1933. However, the Weimar Republic had been governed by 13 chancellors and the Federal Republic by only one during the same number of years. This dramatic difference in political stability symbolized the degree to which the Federal Republic was a unique state in twentieth-century German history. But it was more than that. It had become a success. Its stability was not artificial, but had been influenced by three powerful factors: first, the international conditions, that produced Western integration; second, the need for alliance in the face of Soviet threat; and third, US protection, which made possible the development of a free market economy.

West Germany's leaders had recognized that Germany could no longer exercise a dominant position in Europe since the old European system had been destroyed, so they replaced it successfully with a positive idea of West Germany's role as a partner in a West European system. At the same time they succeeded in convincing the Western Allies that West Germany could not fulfill this role unless it were free from occupation. They saw also that political stability is very much a function of economic growth. The power of the free market economy made a dramatic and, for many, an unexpected impact. The critics of Adenauer and Erhard, notably the SPD, argued that what happened in 1949 was the restoration of capitalism, which it asserted was incompatible with democratic values. The opposite had proved to be the case, however. The free market led to economic efficiencies and to a tremendous increase in personal affluence, which was the only way that the needy, of whom there were many in 1949, could be helped without the massive intervention of state power, of which there was little. But the recovery also contributed to the development of the welfare state, which came slowly but surely, and which was well underway by 1963.

Despite the country's accomplishments, however, the trade unions remained critical of the CDU-controlled governments, but at the same time avoided open confrontation. Many workers, moreover, could see with their own eyes the power of a social market economy – a free market committed to social responsibility – and saw no interest would be served by conflict. A key to the economic miracle was the astonishing efficiency of German business between 1949 and 1963, largely a result of the fact that the war and occupation had destroyed many of the bureaucratic hindrances that inevitably slow growth. The absence of bureaucratic impediments in the 1950s allowed German firms to operate with almost complete freedom and with a minimum of abuse. But as the focus shifted from the common goal of reconstruction, to many different interests which recovery made possible, legislation, bureaucracy, and regulation grew also in the 1960s and 1970s and contributed to economic slowdown.

When Adenauer departed from active politics, political life, thought, and culture in the Federal Republic were completely different from those of the Weimar Republic. There was almost no anti-democratic extremism. The vast majority regarded liberal democracy as the best and most effective form of government. Strong groups did not, as in the 1920s, despise it as irrational, inappropriate, and inefficient. One of the major reasons for this development was the change in the political party system. In the Weimar Republic there had been a large number of small parties with highly divergent interests, and the larger parties were primarily ideological in nature. In the Federal Republic the smaller parties, comparatively few in number, played unimportant and innocuous roles, and the larger parties saw themselves as parties representing the interests of all people, and not merely as parties for a single class or sectional interests.

The party system, moreover, was closely connected to the principles of the Basic Law and the constitutional framework. This structure strengthened the parliament, and provided the constructive vote of confidence in the Bundestag which prevented the chaos of Weimar, during which governments could be and were easily removed. In addition, abolition of the plebiscite, used as a tool of political decision making, was also instrumental in maintaining stability.

In 1963, as a result of the equalizing effects caused by the war, West Germany's social structure was much less regimented than in Weimar Germany. The old authoritarian German family had been replaced by a family less rigid and more mobile. The gradual liberalization of the educational system also contributed to greater opportunity for a larger number of people, and allowed them to develop their talents and pursue careers in a more imaginative and more flexible way. By 1963 many

Germans had a real stake in their society that served them well in the 1970s, when student rebellion and economic problems, had they occurred in Weimar, might have posed a real threat to stability and, therefore, to democracy.

In 1963 Georg Picht, a theologian and education expert, warned in articles of what he called "the German education catastrophe" (*die deutsche Bildungskatastrophe*), a phrase that became the title of a book he published in 1964 and which became famous because it was serialized in *Stern*. Picht argued for greater understanding by academics of the social and political implications of their work and for closer ties between theoretical and practical activity: "The older generation now governing the universities has suffered such losses through emigration and war, has had its self-confidence shattered by the experience of National Socialism, and has had to spend so much effort on non-scientific tasks in the years of war and reconstruction that it cannot be expected to rebuild the German university."[1] Therefore, Picht continued, the task of renewal fell to the younger and more liberal generation of students and faculty.

Picht's warnings of a "German education catastrophe" appeared just as the first new postwar universities in Bochum (1965), Constance (1966), and Regensburg (1967) were being established. Picht was worried that higher education was still largely reserved for the sons and daughters of academics, *Beamte*, and the rich, and insisted on a "civil right to education" as a means of making German society truly democratic. Others worried that West Germany was faring poorly in international competition and innovation because of its inadequate system of higher education, especially in science, technology, and applied social sciences like economics and business. A third group, including most of the literary intellectuals, transformed the issue of reform into a political issue which the VDS (*Verband Deutscher Studentenschaften*, German Student Body Association) presented in its educational reform proposals for what they called the "Democratization of the University." The members of VDS and other student organizations in the late 1960s led the rediscovery of the ideology of radical Marxism. They were strongly influenced by the "Free Speech Movement" of the University of California at Berkeley and student protests elsewhere in the United States, and by the introduction of a particular form of political science in postwar German universities.

In demanding more political involvement by academics, Picht was picking up the ideas of the anti-nuclear movement of 1957–60 and looking to figures like Carl Friedrich von Weizsäcker as models. Picht

---

[1] Cited in Wilharm, ed., *Deutsche Geschichte 1962–1983*, 1: 231.

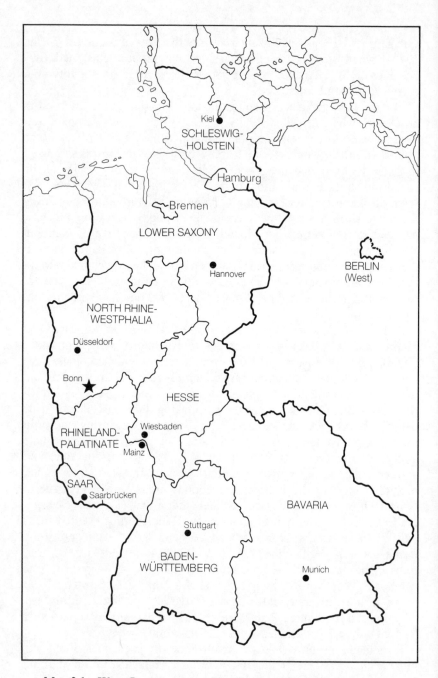

Map 2.1 West Germany today. The borders of the Federal Republic of Germany, as constituted in 1949, remain unchanged forty years later. *Source*: Federal Statistical Office, *Statistical Compass 1987*, 3

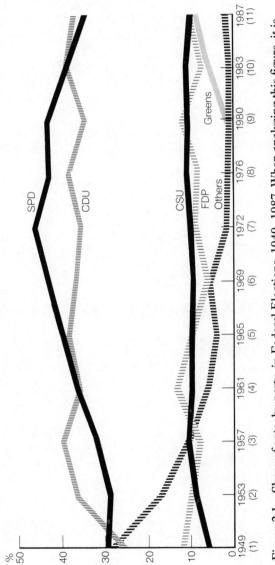

Figure 2.1 Share of vote, by party, in Federal Elections, 1949–1987. When analyzing this figure, it is necessary to add the share of the vote of the CSU to that of the CDU to obtain the total strength of the conservative parties.

Source: Stat. Bundesamt, *Statistisches Jahrbuch 1987*, 89

TABLE 2.1   RESULTS OF FEDERAL ELECTIONS ACCORDING TO *LÄNDER* (IN PER CENT)

	Federal Republic without Berlin	Schleswig-Holstein	Hamburg	Lower Saxony	Bremen	North Rhine-Westphalia	Hesse	Rhineland-Palatinate	Baden-Württemberg	Bavaria	Saarland
SPD											
1949	29.2	29.6	39.6	33.4	34.4	31.4	32.1	28.6	23.9	22.7	–
1953	28.8	26.5	38.1	30.1	39.0	31.9	33.7	27.2	23.0	23.3	–
1957	31.8	30.8	45.8	32.8	46.2	33.5	36.0	30.4	25.8	26.4	25.1
1961	36.2	36.4	46.9	38.7	49.7	37.3	42.8	33.5	32.1	30.1	33.5
1965	39.3	38.8	48.3	39.8	48.5	42.6	45.7	36.7	33.0	33.1	39.8
1969	42.7	43.5	54.6	43.8	52.0	46.8	48.2	40.1	36.5	34.6	39.9
1972	45.8	48.6	54.4	48.1	58.1	50.4	48.5	44.9	38.9	37.8	47.9
1976	42.6	46.4	52.6	45.7	54.0	46.9	45.7	41.7	36.6	32.8	46.1
1980	42.9	46.7	51.7	46.9	52.5	46.8	46.4	42.8	37.2	32.7	48.3
1983	38.2	41.7	47.4	41.4	48.7	42.8	41.6	38.4	31.1	28.9	43.8
1987	37.0	39.8	41.2	41.4	46.5	43.2	38.7	37.1	29.3	27.0	43.5
CDU and CSU											
1949	31.0	30.7	19.7	17.6	16.9	36.9	21.4	49.0	39.6	29.2	–
1953	45.2	47.1	36.7	35.2	24.8	48.9	33.2	52.1	52.4	47.8	–
1957	50.2	48.1	37.4	39.1	30.4	54.4	40.9	53.7	52.8	57.2	54.5
1961	45.3	41.8	31.9	39.0	27.0	47.6	34.9	48.9	45.3	54.9	49.0
1965	47.6	48.2	37.6	45.8	34.0	47.1	37.8	49.3	49.9	55.6	46.8
1969	46.1	46.2	34.0	45.2	32.3	43.6	38.4	47.8	50.7	54.4	46.1
1972	44.9	42.0	33.3	42.7	29.6	41.0	40.3	45.9	49.8	55.1	43.4
1976	48.6	44.1	35.9	45.7	32.5	44.5	44.8	49.9	53.3	60.0	46.2
1980	44.5	38.9	31.2	39.8	28.8	40.6	44.6	45.6	48.5	57.6	42.3
1983	48.8	46.5	37.6	45.6	34.2	45.2	44.3	49.6	52.6	59.5	44.8
1987	44.3	41.9	37.4	41.5	28.9	40.1	41.3	45.1	46.7	55.1	41.2

FDP

Year											
1949	11.9	7.4	15.8	7.5	12.9	8.6	28.1	15.8	17.6	2.5	–
1953	9.5	4.5	10.3	6.9	7.5	8.5	19.7	12.1	12.7	6.2	–
1957	7.7	5.6	9.4	5.9	5.8	6.3	8.5	9.8	14.4	4.6	18.2
1961	12.8	13.8	15.7	13.2	15.2	11.8	15.2	13.2	16.6	8.7	12.9
1965	9.5	9.4	9.4	10.9	11.7	7.6	12.0	10.2	13.1	7.3	8.6
1969	5.8	5.2	6.3	5.6	9.3	5.4	6.7	6.3	7.5	4.1	6.7
1972	8.4	8.6	11.2	8.5	11.1	7.8	10.2	8.1	10.2	6.1	7.1
1976	7.9	8.8	10.2	7.9	11.8	7.8	8.5	7.6	9.1	6.2	6.6
1980	10.6	12.7	14.1	11.3	15.1	10.9	10.6	9.8	12.0	7.8	7.8
1983	6.9	6.3	6.3	6.9	6.5	6.4	7.6	7.0	9.0	6.2	6.0
1987	9.1	9.4	9.6	8.8	8.8	8.4	9.1	9.1	12.0	8.1	6.9

Greens

Year											
1983	5.6	5.2	8.2	5.7	9.7	5.2	6.0	4.5	6.8	4.6	4.8
1987	8.3	8.0	11.0	7.4	14.5	7.5	9.4	7.5	10.0	7.7	7.1

Other parties

Year											
1949	27.9	32.3	24.8	41.4	35.8	23.1	18.5	6.6	18.9	39.5	–
1953	16.5	21.9	15.0	27.8	28.7	10.7	13.4	8.6	11.8	22.6	–
1957	10.3	15.4	7.4	22.2	17.6	5.9	12.5	6.1	7.1	11.8	2.2
1961	5.7	8.1	5.5	9.1	8.2	3.4	7.1	4.4	6.0	6.2	4.6
1965	3.6	3.6	4.7	3.5	5.8	2.7	4.4	3.8	4.0	3.9	4.8
1969	5.5	5.1	5.1	5.4	6.4	4.2	6.7	5.8	5.3	7.0	7.3
1972	0.9	0.8	1.0	0.7	1.2	0.8	1.0	1.1	1.1	1.0	1.6
1976	0.9	0.7	1.4	0.7	1.6	0.8	1.0	0.9	1.0	1.0	1.1
1980	2.0	1.7	3.0	2.0	3.7	1.7	2.4	1.8	2.2	1.8	1.6
1983	0.4	0.3	0.5	0.4	0.9	0.4	0.5	0.6	0.5	0.8	0.6
1987	1.4	0.8	0.7	0.8	1.3	0.9	1.4	1.3	2.1	2.1	1.3

Sources: 1987 figures from Stat. Bundesamt, *Statistisches Jahrbuch 1988*, 88; rest from Rytlewski and Opp de Hipt, *Die Bundesrepublik Deutschland in Zahlen 1945/49–1980*, 233–4.

further argued that much academic research in Germany in the early 1960s was too highly specialized, which he did not consider wise in a healthy democracy. He accordingly demanded reform of the educational institutions.

Adenauer left a legacy of confidence and respect. The country's institutional structure, including the bureaucracy, the legal system, the business community, the military, were all administered according to democratic values. Even the presence of former Nazis in the new German government, which was often used by critics to assert that the Federal Republic was not really democratic, was less important than the fact that the "four d's" – denazification, decartelization, demilitarization, and democratization – had taught a lesson, which was to avoid mixing politics with the institutional system. The bureaucracy in the Federal Republic was the servant of the state, and not a party to the competition of ideas among political parties.

2

Erhard Begins

When Erhard became chancellor in October 1963, he renewed Adenauer's cabinet with only minor changes. The biggest change was that the FDP chairman, Erich Mende, entered as minister for all-German affairs. Schröder continued as foreign minister, Hermann Höcherl (CSU) as minister of the interior, Kai-Uwe von Hassel as defense minister, and Ewald Bucher (FDP) as minister of justice. In his book, *Der Volkskanzler Ludwig Erhard*, Michael Caro quotes a cabinet minister, who served under Adenauer as well as under Erhard, describing Erhard's first cabinet meeting:

> Adenauer was a genius of superficiality and a master of improvisation. He understood the art of suddenly producing an effect with one or two remarks. . . . Erhard is the exact opposite. Because of this, he is much more ready than Adenauer to discuss matters and listen to the other opinion. . . . Adenauer was authoritarian in cabinet: he alone decided the scenario for each meeting. He treated his ministers like students in a seminar. There was never any real discussion among the ministers, except on the rare occasions when Adenauer himself was uncertain. . . .
>
> For Erhard, on the other hand, discussion is the primary process for forming political opinions. He speaks very freely to his ministers, even about diplomatic secrets. Even in his position as federal chancellor he is prepared to learn from others.[1]

Erhard's first formal policy statement did not portend great changes. But his address did draw attention to the end of the most important period of time in postwar German history, which he described as "the path of the German people out of political, economic and social chaos into the present." He added further, addressing Adenauer:

---

[1] Caro, *Der Volkskanzler*, 206–8.

That we could gain a respected place for the free part of our country among the free nations of this world is primarily your doing, and it is thanks to you and your tireless work that our brothers and sisters on the other side of the border [with East Germany] may hope that also for them the hour of freedom will and may ring some day. And it is thanks to your convincing position that we could again find trust and friends in the world.[2]

Change, however, is part of political life, and Erhard's style was very different from Adenauer's. "I stand by the Erhard government – even if I shall again have disagreements with Erhard," Adenauer is reported to have said.[3] The question looming in everyone's mind – very understandably – was whether Erhard could fill Adenauer's shoes, *and* mold the chancellery to suit his own temperament and approach to solving problems. Hans Globke, Adenauer's faithful assistant, the *éminence grise* of the Adenauer era, had announced that he would retire in September 1963, long before Adenauer reconciled himself to leaving. The departure of Globke from the chancellery marked a change within the government, as important as that of Adenauer's departure in the country at large. The style as well as the substance of power was changing; and Globke's successor, Ludger Westrick, while able, never exercised the influence of his predecessor.

Erhard's broader vision was also different from that of his predecessor. He saw Germany as part of the Western world based on the free exchange of ideas bolstered by his economic philosophy. He was an internationalist for whom traditional states were incomprehensible relics, and he never really recognized or conveyed the need for action on behalf of state power, but always assumed that the world was moving inevitably in the direction of a global society. On a domestic level he was unable to articulate clearly the conflict between political parties and always searched for a consensus that sometimes was not possible. These weaknesses were not important when things were going well, but they became fatal during the economic crisis of 1966.

Erhard's main concern, announced in October 1963, was social and economic policy. His basic concept was summed up in the phrase "We must either reduce our expectations or work harder. Work is and remains the basis of wealth."[4] Erhard's speech anticipated a development which would eventually cause very real problems: that precisely when strong economic growth seemed to be achieved, the demand for social spending would increase so rapidly that it would jeopardize that growth. German economic growth in the 1950s had averaged over 4 per

---

[2] Beyme, ed., *Die grossen Regierungserklärungen*, 153.
[3] Kortmann and Wolf, eds, *Die Lage war noch nie so ernst!*, 17.
[4] Hildebrand, *Von Erhard zur Grossen Koalition*, 46.

cent in real terms; in the 1960s, the figure was closer to 2.5 per cent per annum. The crucial change in the rate of growth took place precisely during Erhard's tenure of power, although for reasons over which he had no control. It was the consequence of progress. As postwar German industry developed, and as economic structures and social patterns became established and entrenched, there was less scope for new initiative, new entrepreneurship, and innovations easily transformable into productive energy. Yet Germany continued to grow faster for a longer time than any of her European political and economic partners – at least until the early 1980s.

3

Foreign Policy and Intra-German Affairs 1964–1965

Historians have never quite known how to analyze Gerhard Schröder's foreign policy, which in its apparent ambiguity – forward-looking or sterile – resembled Erhard's chancellorship itself. Though Schröder became the foreign minister under Adenauer in late 1961, scholars have always identified his outlook and tenure with the Erhard administration. He arrived as a transitional figure; Adenauer had already promised to resign, and many observers in 1961 knew that Adenauer put more faith in Charles de Gaulle than in John F. Kennedy. In this respect Schröder and Erhard saw eye to eye: the cardinal elements of German foreign policy must remain alignment with the US and European integration, but not with one country, France, at the expense of another, Britain. Ironically, Erhard's belief in close alliance with the US was one reason for his fall in 1966.

It was in the area of Ostpolitik that the Janus-faced nature of Schröder's foreign policy is most apparent in hindsight. Did he really want to break new ground in relations with Eastern Europe, the Soviet Union, and perhaps even the communist regime in the GDR, or was he merely trying to continue the policy of the Hallstein Doctrine and the claim to sole representation in more flexible ways in a changing world? Neither Erhard nor Schröder, nor their party, nor indeed the CSU, the SPD or the FDP, had yet fully come to terms with the new constellation of forces in the international arena that had emerged after the Berlin Wall. But they were facing a new reality with which they would have to deal in the future. Since 1961 it had become clear that the Western allies no longer supported a policy of reunification through strength, but rather were moving towards the conviction that detente with the Soviet Union must come first, as a basis for any further improvements.

The acceptance of the change had gone further in the SPD, and to some extent in the FDP. Mende, the minister for all-German affairs in Erhard's cabinet, saw the position as a responsibility and opportunity for the liberal party to reassume its traditional role as the guardian of the national interest. In the early 1960s the FDP commissioned studies on the German question which proposed abandoning the Hallstein Doctrine and the entire approach to the question of German unity taken by the CDU/CSU. In Erhard's government, however, Mende was unable to transform these ideas into policy; and the launching of a new Ostpolitik did not fully take place until 1969, when the FDP joined with the SPD whose ideas concerning national policy they fully shared by that time.

The most important development in matters concerning the German question under Erhard was the negotiation with East Germany for the issuance of permits to allow German citizens to pass from West Germany to the GDR, and from West Berlin to East Berlin. The reason for the negotiation was a humanitarian one. In the fall of 1963 the Wall had stood for more than two years, It was clear to Willy Brandt, the mayor of Berlin, "that the Wall could not be eliminated by an isolated campaign."[1] The period between August 1961 and late autumn 1963 produced an increasing number of hardship cases caused by the division of the city; families were divided, and, therefore, in cases of illness or death, it was extremely difficult, if not impossible, for family members to be reunited. The Catholic and Protestant churches were able to be of some assistance, but it was not until shortly before Christmas of 1963 that an indication came from East Berlin, carried by journalists, suggesting that a humanitarian solution might be found in a limited way.

As a consequence of formal discussions between the East Berlin and the West Berlin governments, comprising seven meetings lasting 30 hours, an agreement was produced on December 17. But it was not without a symbolic price: the official "Protocol Governing the Issuance of Passes for West Berliners for Visits to East Berlin during the Christmas Holidays" referred to East Berlin as "the GDR capital," thus breaking an unwritten, but solemn rule that no democratically elected authority, in any Western country, should officially accept the GDR regime's claim that the Soviet sector of Berlin was the capital of East Germany.[2] The protocol took effect the next day and expired on January 5, 1964. For the next 18 days – 28 months after the Berlin Wall had been built – West Berliners were able to visit their relatives in East Berlin and East Germany. As Brandt later wrote, "a referendum conducted with hearts as well as feet" took place, not only from West to East, but including as well relatives and friends from East Germany who travelled to East Berlin. During that period of time approximately 1.2 million

[1] Brandt, *People and Politics*, 94.
[2] Dept of State, *Documents on Germany*, 860.

visits were made to East Berlin. This first effort was followed by agreements which covered All Souls' Day and Christmas 1964, Easter and Whitsun 1965, Christmas and New Year's 1965–6, and Easter and Whitsun in 1966. In succeeding years, however, no pass agreements could be reached. In fact, six years passed until the Quadripartite Agreement on Berlin, implemented in 1972, allowed West Berliners once again to visit East Berlin and East Germany. Brandt expressed the telling effects of the Berlin Wall, and the inhuman consequences imposed on citizens of both East and West, in his memoirs covering this period:

I should have liked, more vehemently than the situation allowed, to confront my critics in the Federal Republic with the fact that we in Berlin – unlike them in their West German haven – were obliged to *live* with the Wall. I should have liked to draw their attention more explicitly to the warring emotions of a Berlin mayor who had to muster the police to "protect" the Wall from the wrath of student demonstrators eager to charge that hated obstacle. Only as the years went by did people seem to grasp that minor steps were better than no steps at all. Furthermore, the realization later dawned that it is sometimes possible to let conflicting legal positions rest.[3]

On June 12, 1964, Erhard was in Washington on the first of several visits to President Lyndon B. Johnson. In their joint communique, Johnson and Erhard repeated the formal position that "so long as Germany remains divided, Europe will not achieve stability." But there were signs in the document that the presuppositions of Western policy had changed since, and because of, the Berlin and Cuba crises, and the growing US involvement in South-east Asia. The communique "stressed the importance of improving relations with the nations of Eastern Europe," a gesture to Schröder in particular, who believed that West Germany could exert influence in Eastern Europe and perhaps draw some Eastern European regimes away from total dependence on the Soviet Union. Finally the communique spoke of the war in Vietnam. In 1964 there was as yet no doubt that West Germany fully supported the US government in Indochina. The president and the chancellor "agreed that the Communist regime in Hanoi must cease its aggression in South Viet-Nam and Laos."[4]

On the same day, June 12, Khrushchev and Ulbricht signed a "Treaty on Friendship, Mutual Assistance, and Cooperation" to complement and expand the provisions of the earlier treaty on basic relations of 1955. Nine years earlier, this treaty had been a response to the Paris Treaties

[3] Brandt, *People and Politics*, 98.
[4] Dept of State, *Documents on Germany*, 867–8.

between the Western powers and Adenauer's Germany. When Bulganin and Ulbricht signed the 1955 treaty the GDR was still an endangered state, with an open border around Berlin which people could, and did, cross quite freely. When Ulbricht signed the 1964 friendship treaty, on the other hand, the character of the GDR was much more permanent. The Berlin Wall had brutally staunched the drain of skilled workers and professionals and crushed the hopes of Germans in the East for reunification and freedom. A first symbol of this consolidation was the SED's "National Document" of March 1962, which declared the victory of socialism in the GDR to be the necessary precondition of solving the national question. In other words, the GDR regime defined reunification in terms of expanding its socialist dictatorship to include West Germany. The "National Document" acknowledged that this might be a distant prospect and declared that, for the foreseeable future, there would be "peaceful coexistence" between the "two German states."[5] The next sign of ideological and political consolidation of the regime was the first party program of the SED, adopted at the sixth party congress in January 1963. It proclaimed that the "epoch of socialism" had begun in the GDR, and that the goal of overcoming capitalism everywhere required that the workers seize power under the guidance of a Marxist-Leninist party. This also meant that there could be no reunification until West Germany was no longer capitalist. Perhaps more important than these ideological claims, however, was the fact that the SED's power grew ever more absolute. Hitherto the fiction that party and government were separate had been rigidly emphasized; the sixth party congress abolished this fiction and announced that SED directives, and the provisions of the party program, should be "the immediate basis of action of organs of the state."[6]

The 1964 friendship treaty marked a further stage of this development. Apart from the usual Soviet-bloc assurances about mutual respect for sovereignty and love of peace, the treaty contained certain clauses that were entirely inadmissible from a Western standpoint. The treaty declared that West Berlin was an "independent political unit," thus implicitly repeating the Soviet contention that the four-power status of Berlin applied only to the Western sectors, and that "in view of the existence of two sovereign German states ... the creation of a peace-loving democratic united German state can be achieved only through negotiations on an equal footing."[7] This was not original either, but simply a repetition of what the Soviet government had asserted on

---

[5] Weber, *Die DDR 1945—1986*, 58.
[6] Ibid., 59–60.
[7] Dept of State, *Documents on Germany*, 871.

numerous occasions since 1955; namely, that reunification could only come about following Western recognition of the GDR and of the 1945 frontiers in and around Germany. Finally, the treaty alluded darkly to the machinations of unidentified "militarist and revanchist forces," a communist codeword for the democratically elected West German government.

Although these propaganda assertions were not new, they did serve an obvious political purpose. The three Western powers felt obliged to respond in a special statement on June 26, in which they made clear that "West Berlin is not an 'independent political unit.' ... Unilateral initiatives taken by the Soviet Government in order to block the quadripartite administration of the city cannot in any way modify this legal situation." Moreover, "the Three Governments consider that the Government of the Federal Republic of Germany is the only German government freely and legitimately constituted and therefore entitled to speak for the German people in international affairs." Finally: "The charges of 'revanchism' and 'militarism' ... are without basis. The Government of the Federal Republic of Germany ... has renounced the use of force to achieve the reunification of Germany."[8]

Several weeks later the US ambassador to Bonn, George C. McGhee, spoke at the same church academy in Tutzing, Bavaria, where Egon Bahr had argued for change through rapprochement one year before. McGhee adressed the thorny question of the Berlin pass agreements and whether the humanitarian impulses of the West Berlin authorities had led them to give up too much – namely, by recognizing the GDR as a negotiating partner. The ambassador was not reticent about stating the implications. By entering into the negotiations the German authorities in West Berlin might find themselves on a long and very twisted road, at the end of which might emerge GDR authority over matters concerning West Berlin and the eventual absorption of the Western sectors via the introduction of a quadripartite status pertaining only to West Berlin, as demanded by Khrushchev and Ulbricht since 1958. In addressing this problem, the ambassador touched on the whole issue of how to define the nature of West German contacts, official or unofficial, with the GDR regime. As the US well knew, this was a question whose resolution many West Germans considered increasingly urgent as time wore on; thus, Bahr's argument, that progress lay in recognizing the status quo, was gaining ground.

We all know ... that there is more to the pass question than the joy of family reunions. The visitations have involved discussions between representatives of

[8] Ibid., 877–8.

the East German regime. This circumstance poses complex and sensitive problems, some of which are of direct concern to the United States. . . . It is from this point of view that we must examine any pass arrangement. Would it undermine the rights and responsibilities of the Allies? Would it tend to alter the status of Berlin to that of a "third German state," independent of Allied control and stripped of political and economic ties with the Federal Republic? . . . The discussions with the East Germans, and their signature at the bottom of protocols . . . raise other far-reaching problems, including the question of the extent to which the Federal Republic and the Senate [of Berlin] should deal with representatives of the Ulbricht regime. This we have felt from the beginning is an area in which German authorities should define the German interest. . . . [A]s Chancellor Erhard and President Johnson stated in their communique of June 12, there can be no stability in Europe as long as Germany is divided. This statement should be a clear answer to those who accuse the United States of believing that a *détente* (a word so vague that I wish it could be eliminated from our vocabularies) exists or can exist until this cause of tension is removed from central Europe.[9]

The last sentence was a barely veiled rebuke to Adenauer and his allies on the CDU/CSU right, like Guttenberg, Hans Graf Huyn, Krone, and Dufhues – the German Gaullists, in short. The ambassador went on to respond to them, and others, who wanted the US to do more for German unity: "It is very easy to say, 'Why haven't you done something about reunification?' It is more difficult to say, particularly in light of the fact that both Americans and Germans have renounced the use of force in achieving reunification, what in fact we should do about it right now." He concluded by reminding the Germans that although they were now stronger and more independent than they had been before, they also bore more responsibilities for the common fate of the free world.[10]

The West German government did not wish to ignore its responsibilities for the Germans living in the GDR. The question was how to deal with the anomalies that Germany's division produced; this often required creative, if questionable solutions. One such issue was trade between East and West Germany, known as interzonal trade. It was not a major factor in the West German economy as a whole, but important to certain German industries, and to West Berlin, which received, for example, extensive quantities of milk and coal from East Germany. In the 1960s this trade grew in size, for two reasons. On the one hand, so argued Egon Bahr in 1963, such trade "should have a relaxing effect in the Zone."[11] On the other hand, it also might contribute, presumably, to a material improvement which would have the paradoxical effect of

[9] Ibid., 879–83.
[10] Ibid.
[11] *Der Spiegel*, no. 35 (1963), 20.

improving the daily lives of the East Germans, but also of improving the stability of the East German government. Interzonal trade, in addition, presented its own paradox in divided Germany. The GDR, because it was not recognized as an independent, sovereign state by the West German government, or by West Germany's allies, did not have to pay customs duties on exports to the FRG, nor to countries of the Common Market, since, as a part of Germany, it was treated as a member of the European Community in the economic sphere. This, in turn, allowed it to sell goods to the EEC members at prices much higher than the GDR would have received in Eastern Europe. On the other hand, this advantage would theoretically cease if the GDR were accorded diplomatic status, recognized as an independent state, and therefore recognized as a country foreign to the EEC; in fact the GDR still enjoyed this special relationship in the EEC in 1988.

Although the SPD was still a long way from power, and many Germans believed that the CDU was on its way to becoming the permanent party of government, there were important reasons for increasing optimism in the SPD that it would one day be the party of the majority. In this regard the Godesberg Program of 1959 became increasingly important as the 1960s developed, as both the symbol and the reality that the SPD accepted what the majority of the German population supported: a social market economy and the rejection of social revolution. A leading figure of this new pragmatism in the 1960s was the economist Karl Schiller, whose ideas and personal manner made him a credible opponent to the CDU in discussions and political debate. In the area of foreign affairs the SPD enjoyed the strong position of being in accord with the main trends of US foreign policy. This attitude became steadily more marked throughout the 1960s, particularly on the question of detente with the Soviet Union and the search for arms control. Western leaders wanted to replace Cold War with efforts to liberalize the Soviet system and achieve some sort of diplomatic movement in Eastern Europe by offering inducement in the form of treaties and economic assistance, and general assurances of peace.

The SPD shared the conviction of leading policy makers in the US that the way to maintain stability in Europe was to reassure the Soviet Union of peaceful intent and to "respect their legitimate security interests." No one clearly defined those interests. Did they include, for example, Western acceptance of the Berlin Wall as a legitimate European border? Ambassador McGhee made clear, in his speech in Tutzing in the summer of 1964, that, in the opinion of the US government, it did not. But, nonetheless, the replacement of the Cold War with a new view of how to deal with the Soviet Union was becoming the philosophical basis for the entire policy of detente as it was practiced by West Germany from the mid-1960s until the late 1970s. Detente was also becoming – Ambassador McGhee's assurances to the contrary – the cornerstone of US foreign policy in Europe.

In the mid-1960s Brandt and Erler reinforced each other, as they argued for detente, and the Atlantic Alliance, at the same time. Their arguments undoubtedly contributed to the official policy that NATO adopted in December 1967 which rested on the Harmel Report – that Western defense represented a combination of detente and deterrence. According to this concept, neither would work without the other: a policy of detente, without sufficient deterrent strength, would tempt the Soviet Union to use its military superiority to put political pressure on Western Europe; but, by the same token, a policy of building up military strength, without pursuing arms control and improved relations with the East, could only provoke Soviet paranoia and fears and therefore increase the likelihood of crisis. Brandt felt strongly that "nothing should be allowed to impair the Federal Republic's links with the Atlantic Alliance in general and the United States in particular, nor its obligations under the EEC treaties signed in Rome." At the same time both the CDU and the SPD agreed "on the cardinal importance of Franco-German reconciliation and cooperation."[12] The difficulty was, simply, how to preserve the Federal Republic's close association with the United States, that had played the major role in Germany's postwar development, and simultaneously build upon the reconciliation with its neighbor, France. Brandt considered the confrontation between the Atlanticists and the Gaullists – or Europeanists – that divided opinion in Bonn, as "unreal and doctrinaire because it did justice neither to Washington's position nor to that of Paris."

The "Europeans," or, as they liked to call themselves, the "German Gaullists," failed to grasp that the General would not pursue their dreams of a European nuclear deterrent (he firmly rejected German participation). They also overlooked the fact that he was engaged in devising a policy of detente which could never have been supported by the Union's [CDU] right wing and was really, in many respects, paving the way for our subsequent Ostpolitik. The "Atlanticists," for their part, chased after the illusion of a "special relationship" between the Federal Republic and the United States for which America, too, lacked what they conceived to be the prerequisites. They refused to acknowledge that some of the political planners and strategists in Washington – probably including President Johnson – paid no more than lip-service to European unity. It was far from certain that they genuinely wished Europe to

[12] Brandt, *People and Politics*, 120.

develop an independent will and a dynamism born of union (if only in a *Europe des patries*).[13]

The foreign minister, Schröder, also shared many of the ideas of the Atlanticist proponents, but not at the expense of recognizing the equal validity of the other ideas:

It is impossible to talk of unification of Europe without referring to the United States of America. With great foresight they have supported the movement for European unity, and they are still supporting it. . . . We must never lose sight of the fact that Europe needs the political, economic and military power of the United States in order to stand firm against the expansionist policy of the communist bloc.[14]

Schröder's opponents were found, as they had been since 1961, and as Brandt recognized, in the CSU and on the right wing of the CDU. Here, the sense of having been betrayed by the US in the Berlin crisis remained strong, and leading figures such as Strauss, Huyn, Krone, Guttenberg, Gerstenmaier, and Adenauer himself, repeated their calls for consolidation of Western European interests to generate political power independent of the US in relation to the East. The Gaullists accused Schröder of seeking to make the Federal Republic into an autonomous national state, acting in and of its own right, and not as a representative of the German nation, temporarily divided, which would one day be unified. The irony was that, if they were right, Schröder was more of a Gaullist than they, because de Gaulle was not interested in German reunification.

Schröder's task, according to Waldemar Besson, a perceptive historian of West German foreign policy, was to understand and act on "the principal challenge to Bonn's foreign policy in the 1960s," which was "to find a German answer to the American desire for detente and at the same time to evaluate what de Gaulle's emphasis on the autonomy of the European states meant for the *raison d'état* of the Federal Republic. . . . Schröder understood de Gaulle's motives better than the German Gaullists, because he systematically tried to understand what the revalued role of the national state could and should mean for the Federal Republic, particularly as it regarded decreasing the level of ideological confrontation with the East."[15] Schröder had the support of Wehner, the chief SPD strategist, in refuting the accusations of Guttenberg and his colleagues. In the summer of 1964 there was, thus, a

[13] Ibid., 123–4.
[14] Schröder, *Decision for Europe*, 192.
[15] Besson, *Aussenpolitik*, 322–3.

cross-party Atlanticist faction, which prefigured the grand coalition that finally came about in 1966.

In July 1964, de Gaulle again visited Bonn, mainly to complain that the Germans were not living up to the principles of the Franco-German treaty, which required coordination of the two countries' foreign policies. If the Federal Republic were not willing to join France in an independent European policy, now that the US was becoming over-extended in Vietnam, the French president argued, then France had no choice but to seek its own policy, which would involve an understanding with the Soviet Union on European security without regard for the interests of the Federal Republic. De Gaulle's typically brutal, albeit honest intervention, brought the domestic German debate to a climax. Indeed, his argument convinced the Atlanticists, led by Erhard, that they must follow the American, not the French lead, including support of the Vietnam War. The German Gaullists, led by Strauss and Adenauer, argued it was precisely Vietnam that was leading the Americans to seek easy agreements with the Soviet Union, in order to reduce their commitment to Europe; therefore, Germany, under the circumstances could even less afford to follow the American lead and must move closer to France.

Erhard had the full support of the FPD and the SPD in arguing that acceptance of the French position would be tantamount to a declaration of hostility toward the US. That was unthinkable. On the contrary, America's worldwide commitments provided even better reason why West Germany should become her strongest ally in Europe, so as to give the Americans a justifiable reason for staying. This argument also had an immediate and very concrete purpose. By the summer of 1964, pressure for greater West German participation in defraying troop costs had mounted to such a degree that the US – largely because of the balance of payments deficit, but not entirely – requested the West German government to contribute to the cost of stationing US troops in Germany. Between 1945 and 1955 the Germans paid occupation costs incurred by France, Great Britain, and the US, a figure which came to $13 billion.[16] Thereafter these costs were paid by the three respective governments. In 1961, military equipment and weapons for the Bundeswehr began to be purchased by the West German government, in order to mitigate or partially offset the dollar deficit.

The summer of 1964 may also have marked the high point of alignment between the SPD leaders and their American counterparts. The friends of the Americans in the SPD were the rising leaders, men like Brandt and Schmidt. They fought strenuously within their party to

---

[16] Treverton, *Dollar Drain*, 32.

secure support for the American proposal for the MLF, against strong opposition from the old guard still influenced by the neutralist and anti-nuclear ideas of the 1950s. At the SPD party conference in November 1964 in Karlsruhe, Fritz Erler won what was to be his last major political victory, when the party officially approved West German participation in the MLF. It was a very significant step for a party that as late as 1960 had categorically refused to consider nuclear armaments for West German forces under any circumstances. The MLF plan endorsed the concept of multinational participation in decision and control and, in case of war, in the use of US-supplied nuclear weapons.

In December 1964, however, Johnson dropped the entire proposal overnight, virtually without warning. Helmut Schmidt commented years later: "We, who had fought for an important strategic interest of the US, were fooled and lost reputation at home. That was the first time I realized that it can be risky, in domestic politics, to commit oneself on behalf of a policy of the leading power of the alliance, if that power is inconsistent and unreliable."[17] The MLF traumatized many of those who had argued, at some cost to themselves, that West Germany owed it to the United States to support their defense doctrine and requirements, even if its wisdom was doubtful. Coming at the same time as the escalation of the Vietnam War, and amid early indications of a revival of left-wing radicalism in university and intellectual circles in West Germany, the way the MLF issue had been handled by the United States did much to sour the pro-Americanism of the new leaders of the SPD. Their loyalty remained strong, but the first élan had gone out of it.

The US dramatically increased its commitment in Vietnam in 1964–5, a commitment that for the next six to eight years shifted much of the focus of US foreign policy to South-east Asia and led to fierce domestic conflict in America. The West Europeans reacted to this shift in various ways. De Gaulle took a critical view of the American involvement in Vietnam, because of the French experience there in the 1950s and because it raised questions about the extent and the nature of the American commitment to Europe. The Germans and the British at first supported the US effort, accepting the argument that it was necessary to prevent a communist takeover. Many Germans saw in Vietnam an analogy to their own country: like Germany, Vietnam had been artificially divided into a communist and a non-communist part. Now, in the 1960s, the rulers of the communist part of Vietnam were trying to gain by force what they had failed to gain by diplomacy. Atlanticist social democrats, like Erler, took special pains to reassure the Americans that they stood behind the US effort. Often they were more pro-American than the Christian

[17] Schmidt, *Menschen und Mächte*, 176.

democrats. A curious example of this occurred in March 1965, when the conservative *Bild Zeitung* editorialized that "the right of peoples to self-determination holds in Vietnam as well, even if the elections there should have results unfavorable to the Americans." The argument that opposition to the US role in Vietnam was justified by the principle of national self-determination was a stock element of propaganda of the Vietnamese communists, and later of their many sympathizers in the West. Two days after the article appeared, Erler complained to Axel Springer, the publisher of *Bild*, that articles like this were very harmful, because they "destroyed the last shred of confidence that our allies have in us as a people". In April, Brandt and Erler visited Washington and gave Johnson official assurances of their support.[18]

Heinrich Lübke (1894–1972) of the CDU was re-elected federal president in 1964 for a second five-year term, during which the presidency reached a low point in terms of its influence or prestige in German politics. This happened partly for reasons beyond Lübke's control. The grand coalition of 1966–9 was so strong, and the internal balance between the SPD and the CDU/CSU so fascinating to watch for observers, that few had any attention to spare for what was mainly a ceremonial office. Further, most of the media saw Lübke's own brand of old-fashioned Christian democratic politics as outdated and irrelevant; they were impatient to see a true "progressive" as president, and got their wish with Heinemann in 1969.

Partly, however, Lübke was responsible for weakening the president's prestige. The office offered tremendous scope for an incumbent who knew how to use its ceremonial function to spread a cultural message about Germany and the German character or to present a strong public image of democratic Germany, as did Theodor Heuss in the 1950s, Gustav Heinemann and Walter Scheel in the 1970s, and Richard von Weizsäcker in the 1980s. By contrast, Lübke was a passive, if well-intentioned politician without a strong vision of his office. Moreover, by common consent he was one of the least dynamic speakers in Bonn, which was not well known for the rhetorical skills of its politicians. Many observers then and since found him awkward, and he appeared as an innocent abroad. For example, on one occasion he translated the phrase *gleich geht's los* (something is just about to start) as "equal goes it loose."

Lübke's re-election itself was less important than the fact that complicated negotiations preceeded it, demonstrating new uncertainty and flexibility between the three major parties. The SPD, led in the negotiations by Herbert Wehner, was for the first time a necessary

---

[18] Grosser, *L'Allemagne en Occident*, 271–2.

partner, because no single party had a majority in the federal assembly. Since the SPD had made considerable electoral gains in various *Länder*, from which one-half of the assembly delegates were drawn, SPD representation was greater than it had been in the past. Therefore, the SPD was able to nominate a larger number of delegates from the *Länder* than from the Bundestag. The structure of the Federal Republic was particularly important in allowing parties that had little power in Bonn to exercise power on a regional level, and thus to be seen by the voters as credible parties of government. Many voters supported a different party locally from the one they supported in federal elections. Long before the question of changing coalitions became important in Bonn, there thus evolved, in the *Länder*, a tradition of coalition government and negotiation that anticipated changes on the federal level.

The practical result of negotiations for Lübke's re-election was that the SPD supported him, and did not insist on the election of its own candidate. The decision to do so represented another important step on the SPD's way to the grand coalition of 1966 with the CDU/CSU. Wehner quietly, but systematically, continued to make the point that as long as the SPD could not be elected as a majority party, coalition with the CDU/CSU, rather than with the FDP which he fundamentally distrusted, was the only way to provide the SPD the opportunity to govern. In turn, this would allow the SPD to present itself to the German voter in future Bundestag elections as a legitimate and responsible party of national government. Within the CDU/CSU there was also developing, slowly, a greater willingness to consider giving up the traditional small coalition with the FDP in favor of a grand coalition. The SPD, for its part, was certainly growing closer to the FDP, especially on issues of foreign policy and on the German question. It did not yet, however, see advantages in a coalition with the FDP, but rather in collaboration with the CDU. The victim of this process was the FDP; but it, too, profited from these changes by re-evaluating its own policy of close alignment with the CDU, and adopting gradually a leftist liberalism indistinguishable from major elements within the SPD. These changes occurred simultaneously with developments in domestic and foreign policy, such as the re-election of Lübke and the MLF decision, and were continually encouraged by the politically important liberal journals of the Hamburg triad, i.e., *Der Spiegel*, *Die Zeit*, and *Stern*.

Schröder's foreign policy and the SPD's role in it was put to serious test in 1964–5 in the Middle East. The basic issue was the morally burdened relationship between West Germany and Israel. Political leaders in the Federal Republic had for a long time discussed establishing diplomatic relations with Israel, but had never done so. Adenauer recognized that the Israeli government had not resolved its own doubts about the moral implications of relations with Germany, and there existed strong Arab opposition to the idea. In May 1965 relations were formally established, but the long and careful preparation and negotiation, particularly with Egypt, that preceeded it, did not prevent leading Arab states from breaking off relations with West Germany. (East Germany never established diplomatic relations with Israel.)

The Federal Republic had been providing Israel with financial assistance as well as arms supplies for some time, but this support had been the source of great irritation to the Arabs. The arms supplies were initially secret, but became public in November 1964, and caused an immediate crisis in relations with Egypt. The West German government halted weapons deliveries to Israel in February 1965, shortly before the East German leader, Walter Ulbricht, made his first state visit to Cairo. Thus, on the one hand, Bonn was seen to have capitulated to Egypt, and on the other hand, sentiment was growing in Bonn to break off diplomatic relations with Cairo.

On May 12, the day after Bonn established formal relations with Tel Aviv, all the Arab states, except Libya and Morocco, broke off diplomatic relations with the Federal Republic. Had Bonn followed the Hallstein Doctrine to the letter it would have been necessary for the Germans, not the Egyptians, to break off relations the moment Egypt had established relations with the GDR in March. But Bonn had not done so, and "world public opinion registered how quickly the federal government had caved in. Nasser had easily been able to turn the weapon of the Hallstein Doctrine around."[19] Egypt, which had accepted a massive aid program from the GDR following Ulbricht's visit, maintained this break with West Germany until the early 1970s. A German historian, Ernst Nolte, judged the opening of diplomatic relations with Israel to be probably the "most unwise" and "most moral" transaction that had ever taken place among states.

The Hallstein Doctrine clearly no longer carried leverage to prevent diplomatic recognition of the GDR, if indeed it ever had. On the contrary, it was an embarrassment. In the case of Egypt Bonn did not want to break off relations, precisely *because* Egypt was moving closer to the GDR. Egypt's dealings with the GDR were thus a compelling reason for Bonn to maintain contacts, not to cut them off. Although the Hallstein Doctrine demanded that Bonn cut the links, the Germans ignored it. To add insult to injury, Egypt took the initiative two months later and broke off relations, after Bonn established diplomatic relations with Israel. The result was the same as it would have been, had Bonn applied the Doctrine – but the point was that Bonn had not chosen to do

[19] Besson, *Aussenpolitik*, 352.

so. The net effect of the outcome was to discredit the purpose of the Hallstein Doctrine and the conduct of West German foreign policy became less credible.

Schröder, and many others, saw this dilemma clearly. On March 4 Schröder had asked, at a cabinet meeting, whether the national interest, which hitherto had been defined as the common desire of Germans East and West for reunification in freedom, might not be better defined in the future as the interests of the Federal Republic, even at the price of having two German representatives in some foreign capitals. The Middle East crisis represented a milestone in a development that led West German politicians to identify "the German interest" with "the interest of the Federal Republic" in its own survival and prosperity. West Germany could, and should act as a state in its own right, and cease pretending that artificial diplomatic positions would prejudice a unity that did not exist, and that lay in the distant future. Only by taking itself seriously, could the Federal Republic, as such, contribute to peace and security in Europe.

This reasoning had been part of the argumentation of Brandt, Wehner, and Bahr in the SPD and of many in the FDP since 1961, or even earlier; it was now spreading to the CDU. It was a traumatic argument for those who felt strongly that if West Germany developed its own concept of state interest, it would betray a moral obligation.

4

Overcoming the Past?

The gradual softening of rigid ideological divisions, and the pronounced and increasing tendency for the main policies of the major parties to converge, meant that there were few counterparts in the 1960s to the great debates on principle between Adenauer and Schumacher, concerning the proper role of government and the proper political direction to be taken by postwar Germany. But if this kind of political excitement appeared absent, Germany's position in the real world of politics among nations was no less than remarkable. The mid-1960s marked the period in which German society, at last, fully entered the modern world, with the stabilization of the party system and the emergence of an astonishingly broad consensus on the main goals of social, economic, and increasingly also foreign policy.

During this period, the West Germans, once again, turned their attention to the persecution of Jews during the Third Reich. The question of how to deal with the Nazi past had been constantly present since 1945, and it posed problems of an almost unfathomable magnitude of a moral and psychological, but also of a political and economic nature. The denazification processes of the immediate postwar years attempted to resolve the political aspects by the means of trial, punishment, and re-education. While the process itself had not worked perfectly, an honest attempt had been made by the occupation powers, and by the Germans, to exact a reckoning in a straightforward and forthright manner, at least in the Federal Republic, for the GDR government denied any responsibility whatsoever for "the past."

Between 1959 and 1964 the Federal Republic paid almost one billion marks to victims of the Nazi regime in twelve Western countries, Luxembourg, Norway, Denmark, Greece, the Netherlands, France, Belgium, Italy, Switzerland, Austria, Britain, and Sweden. In addition to the ongoing payments to individual victims under the Hague Agreements of 1952, the Federal Republic continued to make payments according to the Indemnification Law as revised in 1956, which up to 1984 alone reached the staggering total of 56.2 billion marks; about 40 per cent or 22.48 billion marks of this went to Jewish survivors of persecution. Much of the remainder went to German victims of Nazi persecution who could prove that they had lost income or property for political reasons.[1]

World opinion continued to hold West Germany responsible for financial compensation. This fact reflected the conviction of the West German government, that if it claimed to represent the German people in both parts of Germany, as a freely elected government, it also assumed, indeed, the moral responsibility for the crimes of the Nazi Reich, and the commitment to make whatever restitution was possible. Large majorities in the Bundestag had, since 1952, approved payments to Israel and to Jewish survivors and heirs of victims of Nazi persecution. They had likewise approved the grants to governments of countries which the Third Reich had occupied and, especially since 1956, massive compensation to millions of individuals located in many different countries. The West German government did not always wait for individuals to make claims for themselves but conducted active searches for victims or their heirs in order to make what restitution was possible. Few, if any, argued that money by itself could compensate morally or ethically for Nazi crimes. Some victims, indeed, rejected compensation, since they felt it was adding insult to injury. Most accepted it as not merely welcome aid in itself, but as a sign that the democratic government in West Germany was honest in its desire to atone for the past.

No such will to atone was found in the other Germany, the former Soviet zone. The rulers of the GDR rejected any continuity with the Germany of 1945 and before, whether legal, moral, economic, or political. In their view, the SED regime marked a complete break with the class-ridden Germany of the past. The GDR was the new, classless Germany, representing and incorporating all the good, progressive forces that the old Germany had repressed and persecuted. Therefore, the SED regime did not regard itself as in any way responsible for what Germans had done before 1945, and entertained no claims for restitution. For the SED leaders, West German attempts to assert legal and political continuity – via the claim to sole representation on the one hand, and the restitution to victims of Nazism on the other – were simply proof that West Germany was the Nazi state in new clothes.

Such, at least, was the assertion of the SED. The reality was

---

[1] Rumpf, "Die deutschen Reparationen nach dem Zweiten Weltkrieg," in Willms, ed., *Handbuch*, 1: 346–7, 358.

somewhat different. Both the post-1949 states on German territory were continuations of the past. The Federal Republic brought genuine democracy, equality of opportunity, economic growth, and a remarkable degree of individual and social freedom. It was a continuation of the progressive, democratic elements in German history, of the liberal movement of the 1830s and 1840s, of the democratic socialist movement of the late nineteenth century, and of the pro-democratic currents in the Catholic and Protestant churches. The SED regime in the GDR, on the other hand, was a continuation of the radically anti-democratic KPD (Communist Party) of the Weimar years, of the current of intolerance and repression that was unfortunately also present in German history, and of the totalitarian methods and structures of the Third Reich. The German communists claimed that their denazification was far more thorough than what took place in the West. In fact, the SED was not as concerned with Nazis as it was with anyone who might oppose the dictatorship of the party. The SED removed prominent Nazis not because it had any genuine moral indignation against dictatorial practice, but because Nazis were generally anti-communist and might threaten the power of the new regime. The German communists had their own cadres who were at least as ruthless and efficient as the Nazis in seizing and holding power and in suppressing dissent. The Allies and the West Germans denazified in order to make democracy; the Soviets and the German communists in the east denazified in order to replace one dictatorship with another.

During the 1950s and 1960s, both the federal and the *Land* governments in West Germany sponsored a range of educational and other activities designed to further public understanding of how the National Socialist regime came about and what it did. Most *Land* governments exceeded their normal authority in approving school textbooks on the Third Reich that would teach students of the totalitarian dangers that threaten every democracy, and of the particular problems of Germany in the 1920s that gave Hitler's movement its chance. The governments also converted the sites of the main concentration camps on West German territory into *Gedenkstätten* (memorials) to the victims of the Third Reich. The most famous such sites were at Dachau near Munich and at Bergen-Belsen in Lower Saxony. Under Hitler, these had been concentration camps in the general sense, that is, prison camps for political enemies of the regime. The Nazis had been careful to locate the actual extermination camps (Auschwitz, Treblinka, Belzec, Maidanek, Sobibor, Chelmno), where they did most of their organized killing, outside the Reich, in occupied Poland.

The GDR also turned the sites of camps on its territory into *Gedenkstätten*, but the message to the public there was different from that in the West. In the Federal Republic, people learned to reject Hitler and Nazism as part of their own history and to understand that this matter concerned them directly, as Germans, as democrats, and as Europeans. In the GDR, people were taught that "German fascism," as the official ideology had it, was an alien force that had nothing to do with them directly, but which was still alive and well in West Germany.

Psychological and moral issues, however, were much more difficult to define and to resolve, if indeed a resolution was possible at all. The horror of the Holocaust, and the enormity of the crimes of the Third Reich and responsibility for them, represented burdens for Germany – that is to say for West Germany – that did not disappear. They did not, because the Germans could not forget, nor would the victims of the Nazi tyranny let them forget, especially the Jews, and on their behalf, Israel.

The issue of Nazi crimes, of overcoming the past, came to the fore once again in 1963, when the West German government began a series of trials before German courts, 18 years after the war. Under the Allied occupation during 1945–9 a great number of trials had taken place, and the Allied military government determined that no one who had been tried then could be tried again for the same crime, but that crimes committed by others, that might come to light in the future, could be tried by German courts under German criminal law. The most important of these trials concerned people who had been in charge of persecuting the Jews at the concentration camp set up in 1940 in Auschwitz, located 37 miles west of Cracow, Poland.

The "Auschwitz Trial," as it became known, took place in Frankfurt and found 16 former SS staff members and a former prisoner overseer guilty on charges of mass murder and torture at the concentration camp (six of those convicted received life sentences at hard labor, the highest sentence a German court may impose, the death penalty being prohibited by the Basic Law).

The issues were emotional and sensitive, but the question that received major public attention was whether Germany was on trial, or individuals accused of individual crimes. Henry Ormond, one of the prosecuting attorneys, pointed to the emotion the Auschwitz Trial produced: "One shudders to think that those who now sit on the defendants' bench were for twelve years looked on as the elite of the German people and thought of themselves as such. One is ashamed on behalf of the German nation for having accepted this."[2] But the issue was probably drawn most sharply by the philosopher Hannah Arendt (1906–1975). Arendt, who was Jewish, a student of Martin Heidegger

[2] Naumann, *Auschwitz*, 388.

and Karl Jaspers and later a refugee from Nazi Germany to the United States, wrote:

It would be quite unfair to blame the "majority of the German people" for their lack of enthusiasm for legal proceedings against Nazi criminals without mentioning the facts of life during the Adenauer era. It is a secret to nobody that the West German administration on all levels is shot through with former Nazis. The name of Hans Globke, noted first for his infamous commentary on the Nuremberg Laws and then as a close advisor to Adenauer himself, has become a symbol for a state of affairs that has done more harm to the reputation and authority of the Federal Republic than anything else. The facts of this situation – not the official statements or the public organs of communication – have created the climate of opinion in the "pays réel," and it is not surprising under the circumstances that public opinion says: "The small fish are caught, while the big fish continue their careers."[3]

The president of the court, Hans Hofmeyer, expressed one view of the dilemma posed merely by holding the trial:

The court was not convened to master the past; it also did not have to decide whether this trial served a purpose or not. The court could not conduct a political trial, let alone a show trial. . . . those who followed this trial know that it was anything but a show trial, a trial in which the verdict is agreed on in advance and the trial itself is nothing but a farce designed to give the public a show. The court has tried to search out the truth. . . .

This was an ordinary criminal trial, regardless of its background. The court could reach a verdict only on the basis of laws which it has sworn to uphold, and these laws demand that subjectively and objectively the concrete guilt of a defendant be established.[4]

The frustration of the critics of the trials reflects the terrible paradox that they saw. On the one hand, they sought legal prosecution of individuals who had committed terrible crimes and who they knew were guilty of violating the rule of law, under which a civilized society must live if it is to avoid the abyss of chaos that produced the destruction of moral and ethical values during the Third Reich. On the other hand they were unhappy with the verdicts in some cases, and in others resented the fact that people, who they knew had committed atrocities, had not been brought to trial. They thus had to obey the rule of law of the Federal Republic which had permitted the verdicts to be delivered, but condemned that same society for allegedly failing to reach the proper verdicts – as they saw it – in all cases and for failing to try the

[3] Arendt, Introduction to *Auschwitz*, by Naumann, p. xvii.
[4] Cited in Naumann, *Auschwitz*, 414–17.

guilty in other cases. This reasoning contradicted the very principle of law and civilized behavior which had been violated under Hitler.

This concern undoubtedly underlay Hofmeyer's emphasis on the purpose of the court. But, he too, as millions of Germans and others, felt the anguish of the crimes committed by many – some of whom could no longer be tried because witnesses to those crimes had died in the intervening 20 years, or because some of the guilty had so successfully changed their identities that they had not yet been found. This concern too, raised the question of jurisdiction and how to deal with these cases in a new form, because under German criminal law there was a statute of limitations for murder of 20 years, so that any one who committed atrocities during the Third Reich would not be subject to prosecution if discovered after May 8, 1965. After a long and agonizing debate in the Bundestag, the statute of limitations was extended for five years, by arbitrarily setting the date for the beginning of the statute of limitations at January 1, 1950, three months after the formation of the Federal Republic.

This decision postponed, but did not solve the basic conflict between the argument that limitations are a legal right and should not lightly be given up, and the argument that the Nazi crimes were so grotesque that some sort of legal atonement was necessary irrespective of when former Nazis were found. The debate on the issue culminated in early 1965, involved all shades of opinion in the Federal Republic, and raised profound and strong emotions; but the dilemma was not resolved.

When Hofmeyer pronounced sentence on those convicted in the late summer of 1965, his words reflected the anguish felt not only by Germans, but also by people around the world who remembered World War II, and who, with the Germans, were committed to dealing with the past as a consequence of looking forward to the future:

As to the sentences, it cannot be assessed arithmetically how high the penalty for a single crime was. Even the life sentences, considering the number of victims, could not be considered an even approximately just expiation. For that human life is much too short. . . . There will be some among us who for a long time to come will not be able to look into the happy, trusting eyes of a child without seeing the hollow, questioning, uncomprehending, fear-filled eyes of the children who went their last way there in Auschwitz.[5]

The paradox, which was understandably so painful to Arendt and others, was expressed perhaps best by Bernd Naumann, who covered the trial for the *Frankfurter Allgemeine Zeitung* and who wrote the following:

[5] Ibid., 414–26.

The chief judge, in his oral summation made it clear that the judges and the jury had not conducted an "Auschwitz trial" and had not sat in judgement over Germany's past. The greater insights into the political, legal, and psychological conditions of the National Socialist era undoubtedly gained in the course of the trial could not influence the jury "to depart from its legally mapped-out course and venture forth unto areas closed to it." Its sole task was to establish guilt within the framework of the penal code. Thus justice triumphed over the injustice of Auschwitz.[6]

The Auschwitz Trial contributed to a debate concerning the direction being taken by the Federal Republic. Many Germans opposed the trials, not because they opposed justice, but because the trials once again resurrected shadows of the past they wished to surmount, and because they wished to concentrate their energies, two decades after the war, on the future and not on self-condemnation. But many Germans also felt an obligation to continue the search for, and prosecution of those, who had committed inhuman crimes. An analysis of the complex and conflicting feelings in Germany at this time was that of Emmi Bonhoeffer, whose husband and brother-in-law were killed by the Nazis for their resistance to Hitler. Written as a series of letters to an American friend in Ohio while the trial was being held, they were published as a book, with an introduction by Helmut Gollwitzer, the Protestant theologian, who wrote:

Among the reasons against the trials, as quoted by Emmi Bonhoeffer, the most weighty seems to me the one least often stated: punishment asked for the murderer of a taxi driver is not something that threatens us ouselves; compared to him we are the innocent, the just. But with the atrocities of the Hitler regime, with the gruesome murder of Jews, Gypsies, Poles, Russians, Communists, etc., we are in some way linked. Most of us have at one time or another seen some promise in Hitler's plans; have perhaps ourselves looked down upon the groups he set out to destroy; have looked on or turned away when the atrocities began; have kept the knowledge and the thought of them out of our mind; have, in failing to protest or to help, profited by the fact that we ourselves were not among the persecuted groups; and many of us, if not actively taking part, have had relatives or friends in the service of the Hitler movement, which has now come to be so horribly unmasked.

Therefore, innumerable people feel subconscious apprehension: if everything that happened at that time is still to come to light we may all be linked in many ways to those accused here; the question of guilt, as it is raised in these trials, will reach into our own lives as well. That is why people object to the trials; that is why they want them ended. For their own sake, for the peace of their own conscience, many wish, as they say, that "the curtain finally be dropped."

[6] Ibid., vii.

It is to be hoped, however, that a report such as this one by Mrs Bonhoeffer might show to many that it is necessary, and indeed good and wholesome, that the wish for that dropped curtain not be fulfilled. Only if we are not easy on ourselves, only if we, each one of us, take ourselves to task, only if we look back upon the past with open eyes, will we find the right path toward a future where repetition of such a past is barred and blotted out. And only then can we make full use of the opportunity the present holds for us.[7]

The past and its capture by the present, in 1965, was reflected not only in the trials conducted in Frankfurt. It was also seen in the continued watch, by the four former Allies, over the three remaining Nazi war criminals sentenced at the Nuremberg trials in 1946. Twenty years later Albert Speer, Baldur von Schirach and Rudolf Hess remained prisoners in Spandau prison in the French sector of Berlin. On September 30, 1966, Speer and Schirach were released after serving their sentences in full. For Speer, "the only tangible result of the Spandau years" had been a walk around the world, over a ten-year period in the prison garden, of almost 32,000 kilometers. When he was released at midnight, he received 2,778 Reichsmark, "no longer valid, which had been taken from me in May 1945."[8] On the afternoon that Speer was to be released, the then mayor of Berlin, Willy Brandt, sent Speer's daughter a bouquet of carnations.

[7] Bonhoeffer, *Auschwitz Trials*, 8–9.
[8] Speer, *Spandau, The Secret Diaries*, 445ff.

5

A Government of Contradictions

The result of the fifth Bundestag election in September 1965 at first seemed to rebut the perception that the constellation of political forces in the Federal Republic was changing. It was a victory for the CDU/CSU and a personal triumph for Erhard who was committed to continuing the coalition with the FDP (CDU/CSU 47.6 per cent; SPD 39.3 per cent; FDP 9.5 per cent). The CDU gained ground again after the staggering reverses of 1961 and of the *Land* elections of 1961–2. But the victory was short-lived. One year after the election Erhard was forced to resign as the defeated head of a minority government following the withdrawal of the FDP from the coalition. Among the many reasons for the surprising weakening of Erhard's popularity after his victory was division within his own party. Adenauer, who took an active part in the election, did not give Erhard his wholehearted support, and was surprisingly gentle in his references to the SPD, whose candidate was Willy Brandt. Adenauer still did not have faith in the judgement or the abilities of Erhard or Schröder and had come to the conclusion that a grand coalition with the SPD was the best way to remove them from office.

The new cabinet of 1965 was what Gerstenmaier, in administering the oath of office, termed "a government of contradictions." Among the new additions was Gerhard Stoltenberg (CDU), who became minister of science; a 37–year-old historian from Kiel who was also a member of the board of the Krupp concern. Before 1945, Krupp had been a major producer of armaments. After the war, the occupation authorities dissolved the concern as part of the policy of demilitarization and decartelization. The new Krupp company produced exclusively civilian goods and refused to take part in any armament production, even when it would have been permitted to do so. In an age when government direction of scientific and technical research was rapidly expanding, the ministry of science was a position with a strong future, which Stoltenberg knew how to use. Bruno Heck was another member of the second postwar political generation in the CDU; he became minister for family affairs. Both the FDP and the CSU strengthened their positions in the cabinet. The CSU brought in Richard Jaeger, a skillful and conservative lawyer, as minister of justice. Apart from Mende, who continued as minister for all-German affairs, the most important liberal in the cabinet remained Walter Scheel who, since 1961, as minister for economic cooperation, had expanded this ministry into an important center of foreign policy, particularly toward the Third World.

In his policy statement of November 10 Erhard coined a phrase that became widely known as a symbol of what he believed about his government, and hence of that glaring discrepancy between his vision and reality that was the most characteristic aspect of his tenure. He declared that 20 years after 1945 "the postwar era is at an end!" The foreign policy implications of this assertion were unclear, because of the continuing conflict between the view of the SPD, that West Germany pursue "the interest of the Federal Republic," that is to say, improving relations with the GDR and Eastern Europe – and the view of most Christian democrats, although not of Gerhard Schröder, that one should pursue "the German interest," that is to say, reunification. In many ways, however, Erhard's conclusion did apply to domestic policy; postwar reconstruction was over, and the time had come for a new stage of social development. This stage he called the *formierte Gesellschaft*, a phrase hard to define even in German, but which connoted a rational, "shaped" or "fully formed" society; one in which organized political interests and their struggles did not harm, but rather helped, social and economic progress. Erhard believed – and in this he was surely right – that West German society in 1965 was on the threshold of a new era, one with social and political forces, ideologies, beliefs, and interests quite different from those operating between 1945 and the end of the Berlin crisis. The basis of success in the first era was the social market economy, that of success in the second was to be the vision and, increasingly, the practice of the *formierte Gesellschaft*. He wanted to put his mark on that new era, to make sure it developed to the advantage of a free economy and society for the German people. He was unable to realize his design, but it was nevertheless an impressive and worthy effort.

The notion of the *formierte Gesellschaft* originated in discussions between the economist Götz Briefs, the philosopher Eric Voegelin, and Erhard's advisor, Rüdiger Altmann. Briefs and Voegelin shared a vision of historical development from the society of estates (*Stände*) of early modern Europe, the class society of the industrial revolution, and the postwar modern society which, as yet, had not achieved a durable shape. The main problem of postwar society, in their and Erhard's view, was that organized interest groups and their lobbies – unions, industrial associations, professional groups, bureaucracies of all kinds – were endangering the economic system, the social order, and the constructive operation of parliamentary democracy. They were strong enough to make decisions that had economic and political effects on everyone, not just on their own members. For example, the bureaucracy of the social services had a clear interest in expanding social spending, since that meant more jobs in that bureaucracy, and more power for its officials. The bureaucracies were strong enough to push through the increases in spending, because the politicians had become too weak to resist such claims, even if, as a consequence of political battles, they objectively harmed society by adversely affecting incentive, and diverting funds from other areas. Erhard feared that no one any longer was willing to give anything to the state, whereas everyone, in return, had high demands on it. Where consensus had existed on the need to rebuild Germany during the 1950s, dissension was gradually replacing it as a consequence of new interests and priorities, impossible to consider amid the destruction of postwar Germany.

Despite the best intentions of the free-marketeers of the early years, West Germany was becoming a welfare state. Gerhard Leibholz, a justice of the Federal Constitutional Court from 1951 to 1971 and one of postwar Germany's most respected political scientists, wrote during Erhard's chancellorship:

To an ever greater degree we in the West have achieved such social homogeneity that we are justified in speaking not only of formal but of material democracy, not only of political, but of social democracy, not only of active citizens, but of social citizens in an economic democracy. Despite the social market economy the state has evolved ever more in the direction of a kind of welfare state that encompasses all areas of our life and puts them under public care. Increasingly, anyone who suffers misfortune in life is granted a claim to material compensation. In accordance with this tendency the state has increasingly become a service state, and the earlier administration of intervention (*Eingriffsverwaltung*) is gradually giving way to a service and control administration of planning and distribution.[1]

It was no accident that this vision of a growing anarchy of interest groups, fighting among each other for a bigger share of political power and economic wealth, appeared in Germany in the same year that an American economist, Mancur Olson, produced a brilliant analysis of precisely this phenomenon in the book *The Logic of Collective Action*. It was difficult, indeed, to avoid recognizing the transformation in the

---

[1] In Steinberg, ed., *Staat und Verbände*, 115.

United States as well. Olson argued that the "logic of collective action" was, over time, that large interest groups would emerge in any stable society with the power to make economic decisions in their members' interest that might harm the overall economic growth or political stability of the society. An industrial cartel or powerful union might be able to raise its prices to benefit its members, even though such a price rise might cut consumption in other areas of society, thus causing unemployment and lower growth. There was a conflict, Olson argued, between the narrow interest of an individual as a member of his interest group, and his broader interest in society's prosperity. Olson believed that conflict was inevitable; Altmann's proposal to Erhard of a concept and a strategy to deal with it was the *formierte Gesellschaft*.

The *formierte Gesellschaft*, in Erhard's view, was a strategy to save society as a whole from organized and self-serving interests. This was particularly urgent in West Germany, he believed, because of the country's exposed political situation and because the war and its aftermath had left the Germans with very little ballast, in terms of traditional state authority, to deal effectively with the conflict between disparate interests and the national interests. Because of the war West Germany had lost many of the legitimate social and cultural obstacles to rapid social change; it was in many ways Europe's most modern society.

Erhard's vision, however, was never transformed into reality. By the time he and his aides were ready to make concrete proposals to the Bundestag, and to generate support for his concept with the public at large, his political position was already too weak. Moreover, the left quickly attacked the *formierte Gesellschaft* as undemocratic; a curious irony, since its purpose was to save democracy from the undemocratic influence and effect of special interests.

6

West Germany's Dilemma:
With the West, but in the Middle

E rhard's policy statement announcing the vision of the *formierte Gesellschaft* also contained a design for foreign policy. It was symptomatic of how many people perceived Germany's position at this time, that Erhard found it necessary to state with emphasis that "We do not want LESS but MORE detente." This was directed at the United States. Erhard wanted to provide assurance that Germany was not dragging its feet in developing new policies toward the East. The problem was, given that Bonn was not prepared to abandon the Hallstein Doctrine, that West Germany had no choice but to oppose major aspects of a US concept of detente in Europe which was related to the simultaneous US policy of military activity in Vietnam.

Erhard referred to one of Schröder's main policy concepts when he said: "It will remain the wish of the Federal Government to extend its relations with the countries in the East and South-east of Europe." But he could not explain how to accomplish this without violating the Hallstein Doctrine. His remarks on NATO, however, indicated, that he was *au courant* with the developments in strategy associated with Robert McNamara's tenure at the Pentagon; namely, the emphasis on assured destruction as the foundation of arms control and on the interdependence of deterrence and detente.

Most of the foreign policy remarks in the statement were devoted to Europe. Erhard found that "the policy of European unification which, to begin with, extended to cooperation of national economies, has entered a crisis. We have to state that the sense of solidarity that exists in European peoples does not yet seem capable of political organization." Nevertheless: "Our goal must remain . . . to include in time the whole of free Europe" in the three European communities of the ECSC, the EEC, and EURATOM. That meant Britain above all.[1]

[1] Dept of State, *Documents on Germany*, 902–5.

In early 1966 both the government and the SPD undertook separate initiatives to break the seeming deadlock in Germany's international position. On March 25, the government sent a note to all governments in the world, with the exception of the GDR, on its efforts to improve East–West relations, that became became known as the "Peace Note." One important motive for the note was that the US was pressuring West Germany to sign the nuclear non-proliferation treaty. While not seeking nuclear weapons, Erhard's government nevertheless feared that by signing the treaty, it would lock itself into a position of permanent inferiority vis-à-vis the British and the French, who already had nuclear weapons, and vis-à-vis the Soviet Union with its nuclear and conventional military power.

In the note, Bonn declared that "its aim is an equitable European order on the basis of peaceful agreements," and went on to cite evidence of a bellicose and aggressive mentality in Moscow. Substantively, Bonn proposed agreements limiting and reducing the number of nuclear weapons in a non-aggression treaty with the Soviet Union and other East European states.[2] The ensuing exchange of diplomatic notes produced no result, but did reflect the West German government's frustration with its policy towards the East and its concern to strengthen its own credibility as a responsible power. The note emphasized especially that all efforts to enhance mutual security and pursue a policy of disarmament were inextricably tied to a resolution of the German question in such a way that the German people would be given the right to freely determine their own fate. The note repeated the old assertion that the main cause of tension on the European continent was Germany's division.

The SPD initiative was actually a reaction to another initiative, but as a reaction it was ambitious. In February 1966 the central committee of the communist SED sent an open letter to the SPD party conference in Dortmund proposing an exchange of speakers between the two parties. The SPD responded affirmatively, and spokesmen from the two parties actually met to discuss the proposed visits. These talks constituted what became known as the "all-German spring." For several weeks it seemed as though the exchange might actually occur, without the GDR insisting that the West German government or the SPD explicitly recognize the regime as a legitimate government. The key SPD figure in these discussions was Herbert Wehner, who kept the government informed of the talks and who intended to keep the SPD's activities within the parameters of West German foreign policy that he himself had endorsed in his June 1960 speech.

[2] Ibid., 914–18.

Partially as a result of the SED's open letter in February, the SPD crossed a decisive line in Dortmund concerning how it would deal with the GDR in the future. The conference stated that the four powers, the old wartime Allies, would never solve the German question. Independent action by Germans was therefore necessary. The purpose of West German policy toward East Germany, the party further decided, should be to obtain better living conditions for its population. Willy Brandt, the party's candidate for chancellor, accepted peaceful coexistence with the GDR in a phrase that became a symbol of his own Ostpolitik between 1969 and 1974: he defined the ideal relations between the two parts of Germany (he did not yet refer to two German states) as "coexistence regulated and limited in time." Later he was to drop the reference to a limit of time; coexistence became, from the SPD's viewpoint, permanent.

Later in the spring the SED broke off the talks, using as an excuse the special law on free conduct that the Bundestag had to pass to permit SED members to visit West Germany without being arrested, since, according to West German law, the SED was an illegal organization, because it was identical to the prohibited KPD. The SED claimed that such a law was an insulting denial of its legitimacy and of the sovereignty of the GDR.

The SPD's position in Dortmund found much sympathy among academics and political intellectuals, reflecting a deep-seated unease with what many saw as immobility and lack of imagination in Erhard's foreign policy. In October 1965 the EKD (the Protestant church) had issued a policy paper proposing reconciliation with communist-ruled Poland and acceptance of the Oder–Neisse line. In a response to this paper, Mende's all-German ministry recommended in February 1966 that government policy on the national issue emphasize the idea of unity and de-emphasize the idea of territorial restoration. While this proposal did not proceed further, it was nonetheless still another indication that the establishment of new principles for the conduct of Ostpolitik was only a matter of time.

Other examples of public interest in all and any means of moving forward on the German question abounded throughout 1966. Rüdiger Altmann, the father of the phrase *formierte Gesellschaft*, presented an unlikely, but positive future in a television program that he directed in early 1966. The program (which one of the authors of this book watched at the time) took the form of an imaginary documentary about how West and East Germany were reunited during the period 1966–76. The result of the process was a German Federation (*Deutscher Bund*), a phrase already used by Wehner, and the name of the political organization to which most of the numerous German states belonged from 1815 to 1871. Historically, the term represented a strand, or a movement, of German history that opposed unification as a single national state, but supported pluralism and coexistence. Its popularity in 1966 was highly symptomatic.

A further illustration of the reviving interest in the German question was a provocative article by the political scientist Theodor Eschenburg, who argued that reunification was neither meaningful nor necessary. Would it not bring with it more problems than it solved? A reunited Germany might well have to be neutral; German neutrality would, as Adenauer had always maintained, create instability in Central Europe and pose a threat to the security of freedom and democracy in Germany. Eschenburg, who was old enough to remember the Weimar Republic and who was one of the fathers of constitutional democracy in the postwar south-west of Germany, asked if it would not be better to recognize the GDR than to pursue illusions that only made Germany's friends and adversaries uneasy.

The weightiest intervention into the debate in 1966 was a book by the learned and respected philosopher, Karl Jaspers, entitled *Wohin treibt die Bundesrepublik?* (partial English translation in 1967 as *The Future of Germany*). Jaspers reached the same conclusion as Eschenburg, but by another route. His purpose was to address a moral exhortation to the Germans on the two most important issues of the day as he saw them: the question of guilt for Nazi crimes (and the associated question of restitution), and the question of democracy. His book generated a great deal of attention in Germany, both because it was so highly critical and because many German intellectuals believed that his analysis was correct.

Jaspers argued that Nazi crimes were so great, and the suffering that Germans had inflicted so immense, that no democratic German goverment that sought moral standing had a legitimate right to ask any European government for anything in terms of political or strategic concessions. So, for example, West Germany should recognize the borders of communist Poland as set by Stalin in 1945, including the Oder–Neisse line, and certainly also the existence of the GDR. He further argued that the debate of the early 1960s concerning the statute of limitations on Nazi crimes, as well as a number of other aspects of life in the Federal Republic, were a sign that democracy simply had not yet taken root in West Germany.

In Jasper's view, the failure of some groups in West Germany to recognize their burden of guilt and to act on it by recognizing the status quo in Europe, proved that the country was moving inevitably toward an authoritarian dictatorship that would lead to a third World War. The critique dealt only with the Federal Republic and ignored any danger that the authoritarian dictatorship in East Germany would logically pose, if Jasper's reasoning were correct. He concluded that the only chance for democracy in Germany lay in rejecting any demand or wish for reunification, and concentrating on freedom as the only goal of policy.

In one of the most compelling parts of the book Jaspers picked up and revised a long-standing argument of some German political thinkers; namely, that Germans had been torn since the early nineteenth century between the desire for national unification and the love of freedom. Historically the two had proven incompatible: the unified nation-state was an authoritarian state; the beginnings of democracy in Germany were only found in some of the smaller German states that were ruthlessly absorbed by Prussia in the process of unification. Jaspers implied that the German psyche had not changed: to pursue unification would inevitably mean destroying freedom, because Germans were simply unable to maintain a balance between the two.

The intense discussion of the German question, the Peace Note, and the SPD–SED talks could not change the fact that if the Germans wanted to change the terms of their relationship with the East, they would, sooner or later, have to recognize the GDR. Schröder's strategy was to improve relations with East European states without abandoning the principle of non-recognition of the GDR. But this policy did not result in improved relations with East Germany; indeed, a viable alternative was not possible as long as Bonn maintained that there were not two German states.

In May 1966, the Soviet Union replied to the Peace Note by demanding recognition of East Germany, and in July the governments of all the Warsaw Pact countries repeated the Soviet view of the German question: the impediment to resolving the division of Germany and Europe was West Germany, which was a member of NATO. West Germany must leave NATO, expel foreign troops, promise never to seek nuclear weapons, and recognize East Germany and the Oder–Neisse line. The Warsaw Pact declaration concluded by elaborating on a suggestion the Soviet government had begun to make during the Berlin crisis: at that time, Khrushchev said that the solution to all strategic and security problems in Europe was for the West to recognize something he called "common security," to be achieved by East–West demilitarization. In the 1966 declaration the Warsaw Pact governments went a step further and made a proposal that, unlike Khrushchev's, was destined for a bright future: a conference on security and cooperation in Europe. The Soviet bloc states were right in concluding that such a conference, which finally came about in 1973, would be "a major landmark in contemporary European history."[3]

[3] Ibid., 928–31.

NATO, however, was also attacked from the West. In March 1966 de Gaulle made another surprise assault on Western policy. He declared that France could no longer stay in NATO, since the Soviet threat that was NATO's rationale had, to all intents and purposes, ceased to exist, and because NATO policies and strategies were incompatible with essential French interests. Therefore, France would withdraw from the integrated military structure and planning of the Alliance in June, and would like all Allied personnel and military installations to leave French soil within one year. This development provoked a rare burst of unity in Germany: across the political spectrum all agreed de Gaulle's move was harmful to the West. The German Gaullists were deprived, by de Gaulle, of their last shred of credibility. Erhard's government sent a sharp note to de Gaulle, disagreeing with his conclusion that the Soviet Union did not pose a threat to European security, and asking how the French government proposed to fulfil its obligations to defend Germany under the Brussels and Paris Treaties. De Gaulle's response was to agree to maintain the French troops already stationed in Germany.

In retrospect de Gaulle's reasoning makes much more sense than it did to many at the time. He was worried, with some reason, that America's commitment in Vietnam was leading US policy-makers to neglect Europe, either because they could not afford the commitments, no longer considered them necessary, or because their attention was elsewhere. This might tempt the US to follow inconsistent or unsustainable policies in Europe, and it was imperative that France free herself from dependence on the US in order to follow her own, more consistent, approach to detente. De Gaulle's error may have been his inveterate assumption that the Soviet Union was four-fifths Russian and only one-fifth communist, and therefore harbored no ambitions for ideological or political domination.

7

Signs of the Times

In Berlin the building of the Wall in 1961 had a curious consequence at the university: "in the place of rejection of Marxism came a preoccupation with it." By 1967, there may very likely have been more self-proclaimed Marxists at the Free University in West Berlin than at the old university in the East. One practical reason for this was that the Wall put a decisive stop to the flow of GDR students escaping from dictatorship in the GDR to democracy in West Berlin. The university and city authorities frowned on the so-called *Fluchthelfer* (escape helpers), students who, at great personal risk, continued to help East Germans to escape to West Berlin. Instead of the constant influx of students from the East who had personal experience of a Marxist regime, an increasing number of dissident elements moved to the city from West Germany, including draft dodgers, since there was no conscription in West Berlin because it was not officially a part of the Federal Republic.

Many of Berlin's disenchanted – although by no means the majority – and others dissatisfied with the shape of democracy in postwar Germany for a myriad of reasons, used the freedom of a democratic society to express rejection of their state. They were, however, in the second instance, in search of a means and a vehicle by which to express their own views of society, and they found it in the writings of Herbert Marcuse, Theodor Adorno, and Max Horkheimer, and in a city, in which after the building of the Wall on August 13, 1961, "a new intellectual situation arose."[1] Thus, while the vast majority were far from experts on Marxism – in fact it is questionable how many students in Berlin in the 1960s actually read Marx at all – they nonetheless became members of the movement which espoused Marxist or radical views and put a permanent stamp on the political life of university education.

[1] Deuerlein, *Deutschland 1963–1970*, 105.

The most important organization of the radical students was the *Sozialistischer Deutscher Studentenbund* (German Socialist Student Federation), whose initials SDS coincidentally were the same as those of the American activist organization, Students for a Democratic Society. Originally, the SDS was an offshoot of the Young Socialists of the SPD, but in 1961 it was expelled and membership in it made incompatible with membership in the SPD. At that time the chief concern of the radical left, including the SDS, was opposition to NATO and Western integration. The SDS was, in its beginnings, a part of the old, anti-NATO and anti-Adenauer left of the 1950s. By 1961, this old left was in danger of disappearing completely. Writers and intellectuals, such as Grass and Böll, were critical of the society and culture of the Adenauer era, but were not yet politically active in a major way.

At the universities there were virtually no leftist academics of stature. But of the few, one was a political scientist, Wolfgang Abendroth, born in 1906, at Marburg. In September 1951 Abendroth had delivered a lecture to students from the University of Marburg concerning German unity and European integration and their relationship to the preamble of the Basic Law. He argued that the division of Germany was a tragedy for which no one was to blame, and saw the cause of the division in the diverse interests of the Allied powers; indeed, he saw only "one, single legitimate way" to unify the country, which would be free and internationally controlled elections to create a national assembly.[2] By 1961, however, he had changed his opinion and concluded that Adenauer, the Western powers and the "West German capitalists" were to blame for the division. What had appeared to him as "tragedy" now was "a piece of villainy."[3]

The SPD expelled Abendroth in 1961 for activities incompatible with the aims of the party, including support of the German Peace Union, a front for the then illegal communist party. Abendroth and his disciples were also the chief organizers of the SDS. By 1965, they were beginning to receive a hearing in West Germany, thanks to the new moralism of the *Vergangenheitsbewältigung* (overcoming the past) and the growing impatience with the values of liberal bourgeois society.

In 1965–6, due to intense student demand, a number of German universities began offering courses on the relationship of the universities to the Nazi regime. For example, at the Free University of Berlin the annual university-sponsored lecture series entitled "University Days," was devoted to this subject. It was presided over by the rector of the university, with lectures delivered by professors from Berlin, Heidelberg, Munich, Bonn, Marburg and Giessen.

[2] Nolte, *Deutschland und der Kalte Krieg,* 280.
[3] Ibid., 502–3.

In 1966 there occurred in Berlin the first demonstrations against the Vietnam War, inspired largely by Rudi Dutschke, a young refugee from East Germany, who demanded the creation of an extraparliamentary opposition (*Ausserparlamentarische Opposition*, APO) at the Free University of Berlin. In the brief period from early 1966 to April 1968 he was the leader of the German student movement. As Ernst Nolte wrote: "It was extraordinarily characteristic of the German situation that a young man, Rudi Dutschke [born 1940], should become its most prominent spokesman, who like many other representatives of the movement, was a refugee from the GDR."[4]

As the German sociologist Arnold Gehlen said, many leaders of organized interests by the mid-1960s regarded the state as a milch cow – Rüdiger Altmann referred to it more pungently as a "castrated cat" – big enough to collect taxes, but too weak to resist the demands of special interests. The student movement and its sympathizers among the professoriate constituted one such special interest. Another interest was represented by those demanding increased social spending, made possible by previous economic growth. This latter development was accompanied by an economic recession.

By mid-1966 it was clear that the West German economy was in temporary crisis. Inflation and unemployment were rising rapidly and Erhard seemed unable to control public spending – thus ironically confirming the problems he attempted, unsuccessfully, to address in his vision of the *formierte Gesellschaft*. To many people's amazement Alfred Müller-Armack, the man who had invented the phrase social market economy, recommended in September 1966 increased government intervention, planning, and control, including state support of coal, steel, and other investment and export industries. Müller-Armack had been Erhard's respected state secretary in the economics ministry during the era of the economic miracle, but had resigned in 1963 to take up posts on the boards of various large companies. In his lengthy memorandum to Erhard three years later, he wrote that the time had come to emphasize the "social" aspect of the social market economy: "We must forgo the illusion that the market economy will put everything to rights by itself without a corresponding market-oriented, active economic policy. Social market economy rightly understood does not mean that the competitive economy is fully automatic and requires no servicing, but is rather, as I have often said, semi-automatic and presupposes control by means of an economic policy."[5] This amounted

[4] Ibid., 507.
[5] Cited in Hildebrand, *Von Erhard zur Grossen Koalition*, 208.

to a revolutionary change in the notion of what "social market economy" meant. In the 1940s Müller-Armack, Hayek, Röpke, Rüstow, Böhm, as well as Erhard himself, had argued that the phrase meant that the free market was, in and of itself, "social," since it invariably produced more wealth and a better quality of material and spiritual life for all than any collectivist system. The only role for the state – and it was an important one – was to provide protection against foreign invasion and to assure that competition remained balanced, that organized interests did not corrupt the market. Now Müller-Armack appeared to repudiate this point, and to be arguing that the government should, after all, take an active role in planning the economy and redistributing wealth.

It was largely because of this loss of faith in the free market, whose very success provided its critics the luxury of changing its focus, that West German governments after the mid-1960s began to accelerate public spending faster than the growth of the economy, thus confirming the economic rule known as Wagner's law (named after a famous nineteenth-century German political economist), which states that public spending will always rise faster than the rate of overall economic growth. Until 1965 Germany had disproved Wagner's law. Developments since then suggested strongly that this may have been due to exceptional circumstances; namely, the demands of reconstruction and the unique opportunities for growth and production offered by a society swept virtually clean of strong organized interests through war and occupation, with a stable currency, and with the influx of skilled labor from the East in the late 1940s and 1950s.

Significant social policy initiatives were already in place by 1966, illustrating a philosophy of more aggressive social engineering and a greater burden on the budget. In 1960 the government passed the foreign pension law benefiting mainly expellees and refugees, giving them the same claim to benefits as if they had lived and worked all their lives in West Germany, and the law on housing subsidies for lower-income renters and public housing construction. Also in 1960, the Federal Constitutional Court required every doctor to treat any and all patients covered by the national health insurance system. In 1961, it introduced a law securing welfare payments for lower-income groups. In 1963, Erhard reviewed and revised existing welfare programs; this review was not completed during his tenure or that of the grand coalition and continued into the Brandt government formed in 1969. Finally, in 1964 the Bundestag revised the law on child support. Since 1954 the law provided for payments to families with three or more children in an effort to encourage larger families. In 1961, the government provided for payments to families with two children, and in 1975 to families with only one child. Guest workers, mostly from Turkey, Italy and Yugoslavia, were included in this benefit.

Quite possibly Müller-Armack was influenced by the dire result for the CDU of the North Rhine-Westphalian elections of July, 1966, which indicated that the electorate was very sensitive to signs of economic crisis. His recommendations might thus be interpreted as a warning that the fate of the CDU's political fortunes was clearly connected to the public's judgement of the success of the social market economy. The implication was that perhaps it was necessary to take political steps, in terms of government intervention, in order to assure the CDU's continued popularity. In other words, the CDU must temporarily forsake its principles, in order to keep the power necessary to carry them out in the long term.

In the North Rhine-Westphalia election the SPD for the first time became the largest party, almost winning an absolute majority (49.5 per cent; CDU 42.8 per cent; FDP 7.4 per cent). Catholics were a plurality in the region and many of them obviously voted SPD for the first time. One reason was the effect of the recently concluded Second Vatican Council (1962–5), which began an epoch of liberalism in Catholic theology, culture, and personal behavior that represented a radical departure from the past. The Council had profound repercussions in Germany and coincided with a deliberate policy of rapprochement between the Catholic church and the SPD. In March 1964, Pope Paul VI had received in audience an SPD delegation, led by Erler, a step that disturbed and irritated the German Catholic hierarchy. Its members at that time were far more conservative politically than the pope and were upset at other signs of cultural change in Germany, notably Rolf Hochhuth's 1963 play, *The Deputy*, in which Hochhuth purported to demonstrate that Pope Pius XII had not taken all the steps he had available to prevent the Holocaust.

Political choices were no longer clear-cut; it was not necessary "for one's eternal salvation" to vote CDU if one were Catholic. The bishops of the *Land* issued a much-noted pastoral letter before the election, repeating the Vatican Council's new principles of freedom of conscience and political toleration and indirectly acknowledging the right of a Catholic to vote socialist with a completely clear conscience. The religious factor in the Westphalian vote was a sign of the times. Old patterns and ideologies were breaking up, and the old rule of thumb, that the SPD was only strong in Protestant regions, clearly was invalid.

Another sign of the times was the course of a controversy that occurred over an unexpected subject: the German air force's F-104G Starfighter plane, introduced in 1961. Since 1963 approximately 60 of these US-designed (by Lockheed), but German-built, fighter-bombers had crashed. The reasons for the accidents were technically complex, but the SPD took the occasion to question the military's ability and authority to govern its own affairs, including dealing with a problem such as that of the Starfighter. The immediate target was the minister of defense, Kai-Uwe von Hassel. The public demand for action in the matter led to a conflict concerning the degree of political and military leadership of West Germany's forces, in which the *Angestellte* union organization used the issue as a platform to demand increased influence in the internal structure of the Bundeswehr. This demand, which the minister of defense approved, provoked the resignation of the military chiefs of the Bundeswehr as a whole, and of the air force. The new chief of the Bundeswehr was General Ulrich de Maizière, an influential protagonist of the concept of *innere Führung*, and General Johannes Steinhoff was appointed commander of the air force. De Maizière succeeded in expanding the prerogatives of his position to become the chief subordinate of the minister in all military affairs.

The particular problem of the Starfighter did not end, and by the beginning of 1973, 157 Starfighters had crashed and approximately half of the German pilots had lost their lives. The aircraft was eventually replaced in the early 1980s, and in the meantime General Steinhoff had successfully restored confidence in the air force. But the entire affair was a tragic example of conflict between political interests that had supported purchase of the Starfighter over its competitor, the Mirage, built in France.[6]

[6] See *Der Spiegel*, Dec. 5, 1962, no. 49.

8

Vietnam, US Policy, and the Fall of Erhard

The social democrats, and many other Germans with them, began to reassess their support of the United States' commitment to Vietnam in 1966. One reason was unquestionably growing doubt that the Americans had the moral right, as well as geopolitical reasons, to be there. These doubts were powerfully fueled by the fast-growing domestic US opposition to the war, which spanned all sectors of society and "divided the country as no event in American history had since the civil war."[1] In January 1966, while the number of US troops in Vietnam continued to rise, a Democratic senator, J. William Fulbright, the chairman of the Senate Foreign Relations Committee, began congressional hearings on American policy in South-east Asia. By mid-1967, the Johnson administration clearly indicated that it had surrendered the moral ground to the opposition when Secretary of Defense Robert McNamara declared: "The picture of the world's greatest superpower killing or injuring 1,000 noncombatants a week, while trying to pound a tiny backward nation into submission on an issue whose merits are hotly disputed, is not a pretty one."[2]

Another reason that many Germans were changing their minds about Vietnam was a much more practical fear, namely, that America was becoming so obsessed with South-east Asia that it was neglecting the security of Europe. This fear came into the open in the summer of 1966. In August of that year, the Democratic Senate majority leader, Mike Mansfield, a long-standing opponent of US overseas military involvement, proposed sharp reductions in the number of US troops in Europe. Though Johnson managed to prevent Mansfield's amendment from being voted on, it sent an alarming signal to the Germans. Perhaps West Germany needed to insure its security by a more aggressive detente with

[1] Tindall, *America: A Narrative History*, 1289.
[2] Ibid., 1291.

the East, in case US security commitments to Europe became uncertain. SPD leaders in particular began thinking that they could pursue detente in Europe, as the US clearly wanted, while disapproving of the US role in Vietnam both on moral grounds and on the grounds that it was distracting American attention from what was still the main arena of East–West struggle, namely Europe.

When American political and intellectual leaders themselves began doubting that the US had a legitimate reason to be in Vietnam, it was no wonder that America's allies did the same. By 1966–7, many Americans were losing confidence in their role in the world as guarantor of peace and freedom. The West Germans, who at this time were very sensitive to changes in domestic American public opinion, picked up these signals immediately. As a result, German journalists, writers, political figures, and student movement leaders added the issue of Vietnam to their already furious debates on historical responsibility and guilt for the Third Reich, on university reform, and on the need for a new German foreign policy vis-à-vis the Soviet Union and the GDR. As the younger participants in this debate, as well as growing numbers of SPD and FDP leaders, came to oppose the US involvement in Vietnam in ever more radical terms, the heretofore revered American example of morality, as well as faith in the American nuclear guarantee, sustained lasting damage in the later 1960s. As a later US ambassador to West Germany put it: "Many Germans, particularly younger ones, lost an ideal. The United States, which had been a model during the 1950s, became for many young Germans an anti-model during the 1970s."[3]

Although the Mansfield amendment failed, the US did in fact withdraw some 15,000 troops from West Germany in 1966. Quite apart from worries about Vietnam, this action brought to the surface a crisis in NATO, provoked on the one hand by the threat posed by increasing Soviet nuclear power, and on the other hand by the dominance in Washington of the idea that detente with the Soviet Union should have priority over traditional allied interests. The logical consequence of this line of thought was the idea that a nuclear arms agreement should be made with the Soviet Union, even at the price of solidarity within NATO. This faced the Germans with a choice of adapting to the new US policy, at the price of appearing much weaker in relation to the Soviets, or of becoming isolated.

Erhard's and Schröder's foreign policy was, in a manner of speaking, without clear form due to the fundamental contradiction inherent in

---

[3] Richard Burt, "An affair of similarities and differences: an ambassador looks at two nations," *German Tribune*, October 23, 1988, reprinted in English translation from *Die Welt*, August 31, 1988.

West Germany's international position in the 1960s: on the one hand, the need to remain aligned with the US with the consequent liability of being subject to shifts of US policy, and, on the other hand, the need for West Germany to find its own path forward in European integration and in East–West relations. Some Americans realized this. One of them was Henry Kissinger, then professor of government at Harvard, who cogently discussed US–German relations at hearings of the Senate Foreign Relations Committee in June 1966. His remarks concerning the political psychology of West German foreign policy in this time of transition had relevance far beyond the immediate circumstance of his testimony:

Urged by France to pursue a "European" course and by the United States toward "Atlantic" conceptions, advised to seek unity now by firmness, now by conciliation, pressed to meet balance-of-payments costs, the pillar of everybody's construction and the worry of many, the Federal Republic stands in danger of losing the precarious stability which it has so painfully and so responsibly developed since the war.

For the seeming balance and solidity of postwar Germany – which causes it to be the object of constant wooing – is highly deceptive. Every German over 55 ... has lived through three revolutions. He has known four different regimes each claiming to be morally antithetical to its predecessor. ... Germany has suffered too many breaks in historical continuity and too many shocks to sustain prolonged pressure. Great national prosperity has developed at the same time that national, political, and territorial integrity has been lost. The incongruity of this situation contributes to the insecurity of German leadership groups, the legalism of whose policy prescriptions often hides a lack of inner assurance.[4]

Kissinger's understanding of Germany's psychological as well as strategic problems was not shared by all in the US administration. Helmut Schmidt noted that President Johnson had hurt Erhard and other friends of the US badly by first persuading them to support the MLF at some political cost to them and then suddenly canceling the project. A second case of this type occurred in the late summer of 1966. The occasion was Erhard's fifth and last trip to Washington in September, which observers later recognized as marking the beginning of the end of his government. He went to the US to ask Johnson to permit Germany some degree of direct access to NATO nuclear weapons, but also to seek relief from the payments that the US was demanding for US military supplies to Germany and for stationing of US troops, according to an agreement on this matter concluded between

---

[4] Senate Committee on Foreign Relations, *Hearings on United States Policy toward Europe*, June 27, 1966.

the United States and the Federal Republic in 1964. Before Erhard left Germany he had promised in the Bundestag not to give in to American pressure to raise the agreed ceilings on payments. Schmidt, who by now was the SPD's chief defense and security spokesman since Erler was seriously ill, suggested that Erhard should give in on the question of nuclear "co-determination," as it was called, and in turn demand a reduction, rather than accept an increase, in the amounts paid to the US. The amount involved in 1966 was a cumulative deficit, since the 1964 agreement, of $2 billion.

Public attention was focused on Erhard's trip because by late summer 1966 West Germany was facing an economic crisis. Erhard was therefore under great pressure to demonstrate ability as a firm representative of German interests. When he returned from Washington Schmidt asked him, in the Bundestag, what he had promised to pay the Americans. Erhard could not answer, because in fact he had broken his promise to reduce the claim. By pressuring the German chancellor to fulfill his earlier pledge, Schmidt later argued, Johnson effectively caused Erhard's fall.[5]

Despite the recession of 1966, the mid-1960s were by no means a time of serious crisis in West Germany. The country had enjoyed strong economic growth for 15 years. The unemployment rate was lower than that of West Germany's competitors, and important sectors of society were beginning to enjoy the goods and amenities that had been initially available to only a very few in the postwar years. Paid vacation time in 1965 had increased from 18 to 24 days per year (by 1982 industrial workers uniformly received six weeks of paid vacation). The length of the work week was declining, although most still worked an average of 42–3 hours, and the number of households with electrical appliances and telephones was increasing. Between 1959 and 1965 about 570,000 new apartments were built or old ones reconstructed; and in 1965 about 9.3 million people owned private cars, 11.4 million had television sets and almost 18 million people were in possession of a radio. The Federal Republic now had 59 million inhabitants who, if interested, could listen to one of the 7,000 operas produced or attend one of 18,400 plays or dramas.[6]

The immediate cause of the fall of Erhard was the budget deficit, which he proposed to reduce by raising taxes, whereas the FDP insisted on reducing government spending. On October 27, 1966, the FDP ministers resigned from the cabinet, and Erhard's government was now a minority one. It survived only ten days, until the Bundestag refused to

---

[5] Schmidt, *Menschen und Mächte*, 176–7.
[6] Statistisches Bundesamt, *Statistisches Jahrbuch 1966*, 113ff.

give it a vote of confidence. Erhard resigned as chancellor on November 30, opening the way for the grand coalition that he had always opposed.
Willy Brandt remarked after the fall of Erhard:

Some may call it ironical that Ludwig Erhard should have foundered on the very rock – that of economics – whose avoidance had earned him such acclaim as a successful helmsman, not only within his own party but far beyond its confines. ... Almost naively preoccupied with the maintenance of good relations with the United States and President Johnson, Erhard lacked all sense of the need for a careful adjustment with our partners in Western Europe.[7]

The CDU quickly agreed that their candidate for chancellor of a grand coalition should be Kurt Georg Kiesinger (1904–1988), who had been minister-president of Baden-Württemberg since 1958. In November 1966, as negotiations between the three parties proceeded following Erhard's resignation, the liberals still had a chance to remain in government either with the SPD or the CDU/CSU. The decisive momentum toward the grand coalition came with the Bavarian state elections on November 20, which were a disaster for the FDP, which lost its representation in the Bavarian parliament. The CSU confirmed its absolute majority of seats, whereas the SPD made minor gains (CSU 48.1 per cent, SPD 35.8 per cent, FDP 5.1 per cent). The big winner was the right-wing National Democratic Party (NPD) which received 7.4 per cent. The CSU leader, Strauss, had confirmed his popularity. He was not prepared to accept anything less than a senior cabinet post. The FDP, on the other hand, absolutely refused to join a government of which Strauss was a member. This left the road free for Wehner and Kiesinger to put the final touches on the grand coalition.

Many factors, beyond the problems of the weakening economy and the departure of the FDP, seem to have contributed to the fall of Erhard. There was his lack of strong leadership and the quarrels within the CDU, but also his basic rejection of a Franco-German union in favor of Atlanticism. He was fundamentally an apolitical man, whose ambitions did not rest in the desire for or in the defense of power. By not concentrating on his position of leadership, however, he was unable to counter the negative effects of the centrifugal and factional disputes, which naturally followed the centralist authoritarian style of Adenauer. Power, from Erhard's point of view, was not, ipso facto, a sign of strength; it did not stimulate him, rather it exhausted him. Erhard, the economist, thrown into the turbulence of governing, experimented with the possibilities that were automatically at his disposal in the office of

[7] Brandt, *People and Politics*, 143–4.

the chancellor. This attitude might help to explain why his political fall did not reflect on his personal stature. There was too large a part of his personality that he had never surrendered to politics. His personal popularity among the citizens of West Germany was precisely due to the apolitical tendencies of the skeptical era of the late 1950s up to the mid-1960s. The Federal Republic, which Erhard had helped to build under the motto, "Prosperity for Everyone," did not continue to develop as he, and with him the "reconstruction generation," had hoped. The result of prosperity was not only, as it turned out, greater individual freedom, social institutions more open to citizen involvement, and higher moral standards; rather prosperity by the mid-1960s produced a certain unease and disquiet. Many Germans in 1966 felt a sense of malaise which made it hard to continue carrying out the political, economic and social responsibilities inculcated in the years of reconstruction since 1948.

Erhard did, however, establish diplomatic relations with Israel, attempted a major diplomatic initiative toward detente in the Peace Note of March 1966, and set a new political style, unknown under the leadership of Adenauer. He failed because he did not understand, or did not wish to use power, and therefore let it slip from his hands. The recession need not have produced a change of government. It did so partly because the FDP defected, but that, in turn, was due largely to the public perception that the chancellor was "bankrupt in leadership."[8] Erhard's style and personal belief in a social realm beyond politics, which would increasingly replace politics as the arena of human action in the *formierte Gesellschaft* of his vision, was not in accord with the tendencies of the time and with the increasing intellectual unrest and widespread desire for cultural change.

Those who felt uncomfortable in the postwar affluence of West German society and questioned its value demanded movement, often merely for movement's sake, in both foreign and domestic policy. Movement in foreign policy – and primarily in Ostpolitik – was held back artificially by political constraints, but burst forth all the more vigorously and rapidly in 1969–70 and thereafter. The domestic movement began in 1965–6 in the universities and editorial rooms of the leading magazines and broadcast media, and reached a high point during the grand coalition of 1966–9. The rock-solid stability of the governing majority produced, like an immune reaction, the ideological and revolutionary wave of the New Left.

[8] Hildebrand, *Von Erhard zur Grossen Koalition,* 231–7.

PART VII

The Grand Coalition, 1966–1969

Time present and time past
Are both perhaps present in time future,
And time future contained in time past.

T. S. Eliot, *Four Quartets*

"Greater prosperity," according to my understanding, means the possibility of a richer, better and freer life, thus opening new perspectives to the way we lead our lives. Whatever can be achieved and furthered in the field of general education, special schooling and self-improvement, whatever can enrich us, be that through knowledge or awareness, whatever opens our minds to values and works of art, of culture and of spirit, whatever can help us acquire inner balance through true reflection and recreation — all that belongs to the broad range of human need. And all these things must be incorporated into economic thought, because none of these is simply given to us, but must be achieved through work.

Ludwig Erhard, *Generaltexte zur sozialen Marktwirtschaft*

Introduction

The grand coalition lasted from December 1966 to October 1969 and was the first German federal government since 1930 that included the SPD. Kurt Georg Kiesinger and the CDU/CSU intended the coalition to be a period of consolidation and recovery for the party after the troubles of the Erhard era. They expected that electoral reform, to a system of single constituency voting, would eliminate the FDP and any other smaller parties that might arise from ever achieving representation in the Bundestag. In a two-party system they had reason to hope that the CDU would continue as the permanently predominant party.

The SPD, and in particular its chief strategist Herbert Wehner, saw the grand coalition from a different perspective, as a way by which the SPD could become a party of government, and later *the* party of government. In the crisis of 1966 Wehner faced a choice: he could recommend a coalition with the FDP in which the SPD would be the overwhelmingly dominant partner, or he could advocate a grand coalition. A mini-coalition with the FDP would give the social democrats the power to carry out their agenda. But whether it was wise, was another question. It would have a majority of only six FDP seats until the next election and, given the internal confusion of the FDP and the resulting risk of defections, would be at constant risk of being overthrown by a constructive vote of no confidence. Such an outcome would reinforce the common prejudice that the SPD was after all incapable of governing on its own.

A grand coalition was a slower and more arduous, but by the same token, safer road to power for the SPD, and that was what Wehner recommended. He had worked with great perseverance toward this goal, which was finally achieved over the objections of many in both parties. On the other hand powerful figures on both sides had advocated a grand coalition in Bonn on several occasions since the mid-1950s, and such black-red coalitions had not been uncommon in the *Länder*, notably in

North Rhine-Westphalia in the late 1940s and in Berlin in the 1950s. The governmental crisis of 1966 was the occasion for strategists on both sides – Wehner and Schmidt in the SPD, Gerstenmaier and Guttenberg in the CDU/CSU – to bring about a result they had long sought. Or, as a historian later commented: "In November 1966 things had reached the point where the social democratic efforts to participate in government encountered the CDU's need for relief."[1]

The formation of the coalition provoked irritation and intense political activity both on the extreme right and the extreme left, among the media, political intellectuals, and students. Radical activism had begun at the Free University of Berlin in the summer of 1965 and intensified in the winter of 1965–6. Many observers, not only radicals, considered the grand coalition to be a violation of democratic principles because it virtually eliminated opposition in the Bundestag – the governing parties included 447 voting members against 49 voting members of the FDP who constituted the only opposition. They argued that a governing coalition, that would so effectively control the Bundestag, would undermine parliamentary practice, since, in their view, any democracy, and in particular German democracy, depended for its survival on the existence of a vigorous opposition that was strong enough to provide credible alternatives to government policy. An opposition one-tenth the strength of the governing parties could not possibly be assertive enough to do so.

Others saw the coalition not as an opportunity for the SPD to participate in government for the first time, but as the specter of Weimar, as an unacceptable compromise of political principles and as a "product of fear and weakness" of the SPD.[2] The new government consisted of 19 ministers – ten from the CDU/CSU and nine from the SPD. The chancellor, Kiesinger, had been minister-president of Baden-Württemberg since 1958 and one of the few CDU members in the 1950s to call for a more realistic foreign policy, based on recognition of the status quo in Eastern Europe. As many critics of West Germany were quick to comment, Kiesinger had joined the NSDAP in 1933 and had worked in the Reich Broadcasting Corporation during the war. Others, however, could point out that Kiesinger, who had been a lawyer in private practice before the war, had put himself and his family at considerable risk to help Jews and others persecuted by the regime. In 1947 he began his career in the Swabian CDU, serving in the Bundestag 1949–59 and thereafter in his home state. He was what people in the 1960s still referred to as a learned man, familiar with political thought

[1] Hildebrand, *Von Erhard zur Grossen Koalition*, 247.
[2] Ibid., 241.

and the history of philosophy and able to use the teachings of the classics, like Plato or Descartes, in addressing modern problems. He would have made an excellent foreign minister, but Adenauer chose his devoted associate Heinrich von Brentano for that post until 1961, and then turned to Gerhard Schröder to accommodate the CDU's northern and Protestant wing. That was the main reason Kiesinger left Bonn in 1958 to become head of government in the south-west and to establish his political reputation in that very important state. His abilities were so widely recognized that he thus became his party's candidate for chancellor in 1966 and so it was he, the Swabian, who succeeded the Franconian Erhard in November 1966. When Kiesinger left Stuttgart he left behind him a grand coalition in miniature, led by his fellow Christian democrat Hans Filbinger.

The most dramatic feature of the new government, of course, was precisely the presence of the SPD. Its chairman, undisputed leader, and candidate for chancellor, Willy Brandt, hitherto governing mayor of Berlin, became foreign minister (and vice-chancellor); Brandt was chairman of the SPD from 1964 to 1987, having succeeded Erich Ollenhauer. Schröder became, in turn, minister of defense, a post he hoped would be a springboard for higher office. From retirement, Adenauer and Globke had unsuccessfully opposed Schröder's retention in the government. Kai-Uwe von Hassel, who had held the defense post since the *Spiegel* affair, became minister for refugees and war invalids. In the SPD, two rising leaders, born in the generation of the 1920s, were Georg Leber, a trade union leader who took over the increasingly important ministry of communications, and Hans-Jürgen Wischnewski, a former leader of the Young Socialists who took over Scheel's post of minister for economic cooperation – the ministry in charge of foreign aid and thus an important one for the social democrats with their growing commitment to the Third World.

Carlo Schmid, the SPD's official political philosopher, became minister for federal affairs, a post that suited his constitutional lawyer's mind. It gave him the opportunity to engage in frequent and lengthy discussions with the chancellor, who shared his intellectual concerns, on the subjects of cultural decline, the idea of progress in history, and the concept of the modern state. While no doubt relaxing and stimulating for Kiesinger and Schmid, these excursions into political theory irritated the more concretely and managerially minded members of the cabinet like Karl Schiller and Wischnewski, and embarrassed others whose knowledge of political theory was not strong, like Brandt. Two cabinet ministers who retained their posts through the dramatic change were the minister for agriculture, Hermann Höcherl of the CSU, and the minister for science and research, Gerhard Stoltenberg, of the CDU.

Many considered the recall to government of Franz Josef Strauss to replace the liberal Rolf Dahlgrün as minister of finance as ill-advised if not dangerous, and pointed questions were raised as to whether and how he would be able to work with Schiller, the new economics minister. Wehner became minister for all-German affairs and Heinemann of the SPD replaced Richard Jaeger of the CSU at the ministry of justice. This was a radical change, since Jaeger was a legal and philosophical as well as a political conservative, and Heinemann a religious liberal with very different ideas about using the instrument of the law to change society. The social and cultural changes of the later 1960s were Heinemann's great opportunity to be "the conscience of the SPD," since "to a generation that wanted to have everything and to give nothing, he personified at one and the same time the security of the affluent bourgeoisie and the desire for experimentation."[3] He represented an unusual type of social democrat. Culturally he was anything but a socialist; rather, he was a liberal Protestant whose pacifism and mistrust of capitalist democracy led him to the SPD in the hopes that this party would further his somewhat utopian ideas on peace and justice.

As minister of justice, Heinemann introduced a thorough reform of the German penal system. It replaced older methods and principles with a psychological approach that rejected blame and punishment in favor of rehabilitation and concern with the social sources of crime. Capital punishment had not been in existence in the Federal Republic since it was prohibited in the Basic Law, whereas it was in common use in East Germany. Heinemann went much further to develop the concept contained in the Basic Law, which was that the Federal Republic should be a *Rechtsstaat*. This concept, familiar to students of German constitutional law, included, but was not limited to, what Americans usually understood by the rule of law. The *Rechtsstaat* connoted a system of government and administration permeated by legal rules interpreted impartially as a matter of principle, and not as a matter of justice. Heinemann was influenced by those liberal legal reformers who wanted, on the one hand, to use the law to redistribute resources and power in society and, on the other, to interpret laws in ways that took account of individual circumstances.

Apart from his penal reforms, Heinemann's service as minister of justice marked a commitment to a pluralism of values in which the state would not seek to enforce, via law, a particular type of morality. The old but still valid German civil code of 1900 contained numerous rules on personal behavior and family structure that were remnants of a society in

[3] Ibid., 267.

which a certain morality was not only universally accepted as valid and binding, but in which the state was expected to enforce it. Also, for example, there were still laws on the books in the 1960s forbidding a landlord or head of household to permit unmarried persons of the opposite sex to share a room, and there were still cases in the 1960s where judges enforced these provisions with criminal penalties. Heinemann, to use an American phrase, wanted to "get the law out of people's bedrooms" and use it, instead, to promote the social democratic vision of social justice.

Tragically, Fritz Erler was too ill to see his long struggle to give the SPD a coherent defense, foreign, and military policy, crowned by the reward of a government post. Although still officially head of the party's Bundestag caucus, he entered hospital with leukemia for the last time in late 1966 and died on February 22, 1967. Since the 1965 election Helmut Schmidt had gradually taken over Erler's policy and administrative responsibilities, and so it was natural for Schmidt to succeed his friend, whose outlook he shared completely. Keeping the SPD caucus in line was a particularly important task in a grand coalition with a party that many social democrats still saw as the enemy. Schmidt had his hands full and exercised great influence of a nature very different from that of a cabinet post. To the surprise of many he collaborated very well with his counterpart, Rainer Barzel, head of the CDU/CSU caucus.

Barzel and Schmidt were undoubtedly the most powerful political figures outside the cabinet. Time and again they cooperated in ensuring that the government fulfill its coalition program. On the other hand, Kiesinger's position as chancellor was a powerful one, and not easily assailed by either his own or the SPD caucus. The West German constitution indisputably placed the government over the parliament; postwar Germany never knew the American problem of a legislative branch trying to govern over the head of the executive. Indeed the entire concept of the radical separation of powers is foreign to the traditions on which German constitutional democracy was built. On one occasion during the coalition Schmidt asserted that the government was bound to carry out what the Bundestag had decided. Kiesinger answered politely, but firmly, that if that was Schmidt's view he had better find another chancellor, because the fact was that it was the government's job to lead, and that of parliament to exercise control.[4]

Kiesinger's position as chancellor of a government of two parties of opposite ideological background but almost equal size, was often a difficult but never a precarious one. The Swabian statesman knew that the grand coalition was a temporary phenomenon which, in 1966,

[4] Ibid., 271.

appeared to be in the interest of both the large parties. Kiesinger recognized the limits of his power to pressure the SPD and, by not transgressing those limits, retained his authority and respect. This restraint was the more remarkable because it required Kiesinger, on some occasions, to refrain from the exercise of powers that constitutionally were his. The Basic Law had given the chancellor greater power, both over the parliament and over his cabinet, than any previous German constitution, and Adenauer had used that power to the full. He thus set a standard for the chancellor's authority which all his successors in one way or another either had to live up to or deliberately reject. The danger was that anyone who rejected the Adenauer standard ran the risk of appearing weak.

The most important chancellor's prerogative in the Basic Law was the *Richtlinienkompetenz*, the power to determine policy guidelines and parameters. That meant that the chancellor determined not only the competence and the authority of each minister but also the way in which that authority was exercised. No minister could publicly criticize or act in any way contrary to the stated program or the spirit of the chancellor's policy. This was hard enough to enforce as long as the government consisted of a single party or of a coalition in which the chancellor came from the predominant partner, as had been the case since 1949.

In 1966, however, the two parties were almost equal. As Schmidt put it: "There are no guidelines (*Richtlinien*) to apply against Brandt and Wehner."[5] The SPD leaders were not only ministers under Kiesinger, they were leaders of a powerful political party who were not prepared to accept the constitutional right of a chancellor to determine in detail what policies to execute and how to execute them. It was to Kiesinger's credit that he understood this and adapted his style of leadership accordingly. In doing so he was not only deferring to the reality of a coalition of two nearly equal partners; he was deliberately giving the chancellorship a more open and democratic character. Although himself a conservative and an intellectual, Kiesinger understood that times were changing and that the new Germany, in the 1960s, was maturing and would not tolerate the autocratic style of an Adenauer. He wanted to preserve the dignity and integrity of the office by making it acceptable to Germans of the younger generation. He had few illusions that he could also appease the radicals at the same time, for whom no change would be sufficient.

The grand coalition faced an array of problems. Its mission was to stabilize the economy, pursue detente in ways that would keep Germany aligned with its allies and yet not make it vulnerable to Soviet and GDR

---

[5] Cited ibid., 269.

pressure, to continue the social and welfare reforms of earlier years, to reform higher education, perhaps to institute electoral reform, and to pass amendments to the Basic Law confirming the government's powers in civil emergency. Such powers were part of the normal authority of every government, but in the Paris Treaties of 1954, the former occupying powers had temporarily retained them. Erhard's government had passed most of the necessary individual laws, but had been unable to obtain the necessary two-thirds majority for the amendment to the Basic Law that would complete the legislation.

Kiesinger's government had to accomplish these tasks in an atmosphere of rapidly changing values and assumptions. The changes in German culture and political style in 1966–9 amounted, in the opinion of many, to nothing less than a cultural revolution, one charged, in the case of Germany, with the particular burden of guilt for the Nazi past.

1

The Cultural Revolution

Throughout Western Europe and the United States the 1960s saw the rise of a rigorous and sometimes fanatical political moralism which condemned Western imperialism and oppression, and praised the alleged virtues of totalitarian regimes and their political efforts to control and subjugate their populations. The West German form of this moralism, not surprisingly, was an obsessive concern with the Nazi past, a concern which actually moved away from objective historical understanding and turned the Third Reich into an almost mythological entity of total evil. Public discussion of the Nazi period became, in many cases, strident and hysterical. Even in the late 1980s it remained extremely difficult for German historians to discuss the Nazi regime in public as a historical phenomenon and to try to put it into some sort of ideological context without being accused, by the survivors of the cultural revolution, of attempts at apology and of neo-Nazism.

Who were the leading figures of the cultural revolution? There were two main and overlapping groups: politicians proper and political intellectuals. The latter group represented a social amalgam largely unknown in the United States but more common in European countries. It consisted primarily of ideologically committed academics, journalists, political figures, and writers. The political journalist was an especially significant figure. In West Germany, as generally on the Continent, though not in Britain or the United States, newspapers and the broadcast media had definite editorial positions on political issues which journalists and commentators were expected to follow. There was often little pretense at the American distinction between reporting news and presenting opinion, and the German public recognized this. The media were therefore not so much the vehicle of information, pure and simple, as they were rallying-points for currents of political judgement, and thus exerted an influence and power far in excess of the numbers of people they employed. They exercised, in fact, a representative function

TABLE 2.2   CIRCULATION OF MAJOR NEWSPAPERS AND MAGAZINES

	1951	1961	1971	1981	1988
Frankfurter Allgemeine Zeitung	55,428	230,573	255,778	316,021	353,965
Frankfurter Rundschau	125,082	97,177	147,140	189,108	191,544
Rheinischer Merkur	56,557	49,651	51,475	136,945	106,265
Der Spiegel	110,474	422,190	906,031	938,645	990,170
Stern	464,457	1,435,717	1,583,559	1,688,317	1,391,318
Süddeutsche Zeitung	180,024	201,007	264,355	329,761	372,255
Die Welt	192,845	230,771	218,663	205,076	221,210
Die Zeit	45,350	120,671	290,908	342,939	468,751

Note: Figures are the average number of copies sold of each issue in each year. The jump in sales for *Rheinischer Merkur* (a Catholic weekly) between 1971 and 1981 occurred following its merger with *Christ und Welt*, its Protestant counterpart, in 1978.

Source: Informationsgemeinschaft zur Feststellung der Verbreitung von Werbeträgern (IVW), Bonn, 1988

parallel to that of elected assemblies, but without having been elected and not subject to the will of the electorate. The political media and their role was one reason why opinion polls in West Germany, although they were very numerous, were not necessarily indicative of the state of play and the correlation of forces among political groups in society. The political intellectuals, including the journalists, operated several degrees to the left – in the direction of the cultural revolution – of general public opinion. While it can be argued that this was not the case during the late 1940s and 1950s – indeed, the occupation authorities took measures to prevent it – it was so from the mid-1960s onward.

By the mid-1960s the most influential liberal and left-leaning West German media, those of the Hamburg triad, *Der Spiegel*, *Die Zeit*, and *Stern*, had consolidated their position. Since the *Spiegel* affair of 1962 – one of the starting signals of the cultural and political revolution – the journal had enjoyed a rising prestige and power as the voice of the politically progressive and committed elite. Long before the dissolution of the grand coalition in 1969, Rudolf Augstein and his magazine were proclaiming the need for recognition of the existing borders in Europe and for an activist Ostpolitik. In *Die Zeit*, Marion Dönhoff and Theo Sommer led a group of journalists and commentators who presented the same views in more moderate language. Henri Nannen's *Stern*, for its part, was a sensationalist magazine which, insofar as it had a political position, became increasingly anti-American and sympathetic to Soviet and GDR positions. Nannen seemed to find it easy and financially lucrative to act as a supporter of the New Left, although he appeared to have few political convictions of his own. Like Augstein, he was a member of the FDP and identified strongly with that party's left wing which gained control of the party in 1967–8, replacing the older national liberals led by Erich Mende. Under the Nazis Nannen had worked in a propaganda unit (*Propagandakompanie)* of the NSDAP in the Wehrmacht, where his job was to write favorable reports on the war. He was living disproof of the argument that loyal servants of Hitler necessarily became right-wingers in postwar West Germany. On the contrary, Nannen appeared as the supreme opportunist, and his magazine used news as propaganda for particular interests:

> Nannen personifies everything that has made *Stern* big and that has kept it successfully on the market. When times demanded it, he was a passionate anti-communist, but when the wind turned, he defended detente with the East. . . . He was a representative of the market economy, to the point that Ludwig Erhard could not have wished for a more decisive one, but when it became opportune to think about distribution and to be social-minded, Henri Nannen marched at the head of the line. . . . This has nothing to do with lack of principles, but all the more with the secrets of a successful illustrated magazine.[1]

Stern also led the way in the sexual revolution. Like other aspects of the cultural revolution, this was more rapid and thorough-going in West Germany than elsewhere in Europe, and by 1970 *Stern*, sometimes erroneously compared to *Life* magazine in the United States because of a superficial similarity of format and appearance, regularly presented unclad females on its cover.

The period of the grand coalition was the second major transitional period in West German history, the first being the occupation period. The political shift of dominance from the Union to the SPD was merely one manifestation of a much broader breakthrough to modern civil society. In 1966 Karl Jaspers could still wonder in his widely read book *Wohin treibt die Bundesrepublik?* if West Germany was not on the way to authoritarian dictatorship, full rehabilitation of the Nazi regime, and war. By 1969, such ideas seemed increasingly absurd to reasonable people. If some hierarchical and patriarchal patterns of behavior and social organization had survived World War II and had flourished during the reconstruction of Germany, they succumbed to the changing values of the 1960s. West Germany was, in significant ways, a different

---

[1] *Die Zeit,* May 20, 1983, cited in Brandt et al., *Karrieren eines Aussenseiters,* 229.

country in 1969 from what it was even in 1966. Norms of personal behavior were less disciplined, artistic and cultural standards had changed almost beyond recognition, the universities had become centers of radical activism and not the locus of intellectual reflection and study for which they had been so famous. The social philosophy of the country had changed too: the coexistence of a strongly free-market oriented liberalism on the right and a commitment to a modernized social democracy on the left had given way to a common ground, symbolized by the figure of Karl Schiller, and based on belief in economic planning, interventionist government fiscal policy, and the need and obligation for the state to control economic strategy. The calm and peaceful *Machtwechsel* of 1969 demonstrated clearly, moreover, that constitutional democracy had come to stay.

Underlying and surrounding the change in political leadership that culminated in the two elections of 1969 – for federal president and for the Bundestag and chancellor – were three principal and inter-connected trends, all of which accelerated after 1966. The first was a trend toward more relaxed and less authoritarian personal and group behavior. The second was the growing role and influence of political intellectuals. The third was the change in political culture that made the SPD the only political party that the intellectuals and many prominent academics considered morally acceptable. The other side of this trend was the decline and virtual disappearance, for almost a decade, of conservative thought as a respectable body of opinion in West German culture.

The first trend, influencing the others, was the change reflected in personal style, expectations, and everyday attitudes of West German citizens. The need to build one's life from the ground up was replaced in the mid-1960s by a consumer mentality more typical of the United States. Increasing numbers, especially of young people, no longer accorded work and profession the same priority as the need to survive and rebuild had commanded during the years of reconstruction. The rapid pace of technological and institutional change meant that profes-sional expertise was not simply an automatic or dependable basis for a career. Urbanization, personal mobility thanks to the automobile and airplane, and increasing prosperity, were combined with changes concerning attitudes toward and expectations from work and career, and generated, in turn, a restlessness that sought ever new outlets and satisfactions. Issues which had been of secondary importance in postwar Germany became the focus of increasing attention and debate, and included ecological and environmental concerns, the growth of bureaucracy, university governance, work conditions, use of leisure time, and equality, not of opportunity, but of result – which meant the deliberate violation of rules and traditions, if the cause was declared just, and the distortion of moral and ethical standards.

While these elements of change in personal attitudes were common throughout the West, their effect was exacerbated in West Germany by generational factors that weighed more heavily here than elsewhere. The loss of millions of members of the, by now, middle-aged generation through war and conflict – graphically illustrated in the distorted age pyramid – meant that those born after 1940 were unusually numerous both relatively and absolutely. The generational shift was, in this case, a generational leap. Likewise, the young of the late 1960s no longer had any clear memory of "Zero Hour" and did not share their elders' experience of war and of drastic changes of government. Many senior politicians and public figures were still alive who had lived parts of their adult life under four or five wholly different regimes. The large cohorts of young people had less in common with their parents and grand-parents than any generation before them in German history.

Generational differences did not prevent most younger Germans from performing their service in the *Bundeswehr*, getting jobs, and raising families. This silent majority, however, was unusually silent in West Germany, where the public culture from the later 1960s to at least the mid-1970s was shaped overwhelmingly by adherents or sympath-izers of the student movement that began in earnest in 1966 in Berlin. The student radicals and their sympathizers in political and intellectual circles succeeded in setting the agenda and defining the problems of West German political culture in the broadest sense, and in putting those who opposed their strategies and doctrines on the defensive. Ironically but unsurprisingly, these radicals, who saw themselves as defenders of the workers, were usually the sons and daughters of academics, clergy, or businessmen. Very few, if any, came from working-class homes, and they had nothing to say that interested the silent majority of their contemporaries who did not go to university but were *Lehrlinge* (trainees), learning a manual skill. The media, which also consisted primarily of political intellectuals, gave the revolutionaries a disproportionate amount of friendly attention, especially in Berlin. That city was a focal point of the movement; one of the reasons was that there was no conscription there, since Berlin was not officially part of the Federal Republic but remained under Allied occupation. Thus thousands of young men who did not want to serve in the *Bundeswehr* flocked to Berlin, where some of them entered one of the city's three universities and others simply became hangers-on.

The movement leaders and their sympathizers tried to use the left-wing traditions of the Weimar Republic to create for themselves a legitimate past and to present themselves as the true heirs of what was progressive in German history. However, they were not nearly as original or productive as their predecessors. They usually were content to borrow the Weimar intellectuals' contempt for democracy, without noting that Weimar democracy was flawed in ways that the Bonn democracy was not. It was nothing less than historical fraud for the movement leaders in the 1960s to claim that the Bonn democracy was under imminent threat from neo-Nazis, and was secretly controlled by big business and American imperialists, and to use this paranoid vision as an excuse for anti-democratic agitation. If there was any threat to democracy in West Germany, it came from the student radicals themselves and not from any mythical right-wing conspiracy.

The literary and political intellectuals fomented and shared this contempt for and opposition to the democratic system. In West Germany this group included not merely many leading academics, but also journalists, editors, publishers, leaders of religious and professional associations, and clergy. Most of them were liberal or radical, partly from conviction and partly because they believed that West Germany was as yet imperfectly democratic and needed fundamental change to become a genuine democracy. They saw themselves as leaders in that process of change, which would for the first time in German history bring about the unity of *Geist* (spirit) and *Macht* (power). Many German writers and scholars attributed the repugnant aspects of modern German history, especially Nazism, to the fact that spirit and power had not been united; that the politicians, in short, had not done what the writers and scholars recommended. Few were self-critical enough to see that what they were demanding was a dictatorship by the intellectual class, which would be no less oppressive than any other.

Because of their social position and environment, political intellectuals were particularly sensitive to real or perceived changes in society and in the social forces affecting their own and others' life circumstances. In the early 1960s, the leading figures in this group sensed that West Germany was entering a period of broad and at first ill-defined cultural and political change. Many of them were impatient with the Adenauer regime and wanted some sort of new society, without being able to define it precisely. The intellectuals recognized that education could be one important vehicle of change. That suited them very well, since their control of an educational system that needed change would significantly expand influence for members of their own group, the teaching and writing class. Therefore, far more frequently than in the 1950s, they organized petitions, led demonstrations, and argued for political change. The mixture of activism, agitation, propaganda, and debate was all the more remarkable because it became the characteristic trait of the West German political scene, as compared to its neighbors and allies. So, for example, when Willy Brandt became chancellor in 1969, a conservative was elected president of the United States, Richard Nixon. The objections of writers and other intellectuals to the political system and practices of the Federal Republic were exemplified not so much by Jaspers' book, which represented fears and beliefs that were rapidly being overtaken by events, but by the left-leaning editorials of Rudolf Augstein in *Der Spiegel*.

In a similar vein, the formation of the grand coalition provoked Günter Grass, already on his way to the position of a leading intellectual of the Bonn republic, to write an open letter to Willy Brandt, as the new foreign minister in the grand coalition, on November 30, 1966. In this letter Grass claimed that "general conformism will determine attitudes to state and society. The youth of our country will turn to left- and right-wing extremism, if this miserable marriage [the grand coalition] takes place." He further accused Brandt and the SPD of sanctioning "20 years of mistaken foreign policy" by joining with the CDU/CSU instead of continuing to press for full recognition of the GDR, the postwar borders, and Soviet hegemony in Eastern Europe.[2]

A number of landmark publications and events of the early 1960s, in retrospect, marked the stages of the cultural revolution. In 1961, the historian Fritz Fischer's contention that the German elite had deliberately unleashed World War I in a bid for European domination undermined a cherished image of many Germans that World War I happened by accident. Fischer's work, implicitly questioning the moral value of the entire course of German history in modern times, provoked a flood of similar studies by left-liberal historians throughout the 1960s and 1970s adding to his picture. In 1962 occurred the *Spiegel* affair.

In 1963 the cultural revolution experienced a major step forward in the *cause célèbre* provoked by Rolf Hochhuth's play *The Deputy*. After what appeared to be a superficial study of the available evidence Hochhuth, who was not a historian, concluded that Pope Pius XII knew about the Holocaust, but did nothing to stop it or to influence Nazi policy in any significant way. The play dramatized this interpretation and suggested that the pope kept silent in part because he himself shared some anti-Semitic beliefs, and in part because of his pro-German sympathies. The latter were a fact of historical record, but the insinuation that Pius was anti-Semitic was an unsubstantiated allegation that bordered on defamation. Hochhuth justified his moral indignation against the pope by implying that Pius could easily have done something, for example by making a public statement condemning persecution of the Jews or excommunicating any Catholic who took part

[2] Deuerlein, *Deutschland 1963–1970*, 88–9.

in it. Since Hitler and many of his collaborators, as well as many German soldiers and SS members, were nominally Catholic, such an action might have had positive effect.

The pope's defenders argued in response to Hochhuth that matters were not as simple as he claimed and that the pope had no way of knowing that the Nazis were actually committing the systematic murder of millions of Jews. Documents published since 1963 concerning the Vatican's role in the war tended to support Hochhuth's critics. They also pointed out that it was entirely possible that the only effect of a papal exhortation would have been to permit Hitler to regard all German Catholics as potential traitors.

The Deputy played to packed theaters in Germany for most of 1963, and the printed version of the play sold over 100,000 copies, an extraordinary number for a work of drama. Many people, especially students, journalists, and Catholic intellectuals like Heinrich Böll, accepted Hochhuth's argument. For them it was welcome evidence that a great conservative institution, such as they perceived the papacy to be, was tainted by collaboration with Nazism, and the play confirmed their distrust of all traditional institutions and their demand for a thorough settling of accounts with the past.

The same year saw the publication of *The Three Faces of Fascism*, an exhaustive study of the history and ideology of the radical and anti-democratic right in Italy, Germany, and France. Its author was an unknown historian named Ernst Nolte. The book made him famous almost overnight and contributed to the use of the word "fascism" to describe Hitler's movement, a usage favored by Marxists for whom all non-socialist systems were at least theoretically "fascist" in character. Nolte was later to object to this usage, but the impact had been made. After the mid-1960s it was virtually impossible for German journalists and intellectuals to discuss Nazism without calling it "German fascism," and without at least implying that the root causes of this "German fascism" still existed in West Germany.

In 1964 Georg Picht published his book on education and democrat-ization. In 1964-5, the Auschwitz Trial and the debate on extending the statute of limitations for Nazi crimes stoked the fires of self-examination and criticism. In 1966, Karl Jaspers fought back in his book *Wohin Treibt die Bundesrepublik?* against Erhard's and Strauss' view that "the postwar era is over," and that the time had come to "draw a bottom line" under the balance sheet of Nazi atrocities, of destruction in war, and of the loss of half of Germany to communist domination.

In 1967 two psychiatrists, Alexander and Margarete Mitscherlich, leading figures of the progressive intelligentsia, published *The Inability to Mourn*, in which they described the "mechanism of denial, isolation, reversal, withdrawal of attention and affect" with which the Germans in the Third Reich protected themselves from having to notice and deal with the inhumanities of the regime. The Mitscherlichs argued that the Federal Republic suffered from an extreme case of a neurotic social condition characteristic of modern societies, namely a rejection of the validity of emotions and feelings and an emphasis on "tough," rational behavior. This general condition was, the Mitscherlichs believed, exacerbated by the burden of the Nazi past; a burden which, according to them, was not acknowledged and not permitted to play its proper moral role in public life:

> It is clear that we are dealing here with two distinct psychic processes: the retrospective warding off of real guilt by the older generation and the unwilling-ness of the younger to get caught up in the guilt problems of their parents. The general disintegration of traditional patterns of behavior contributes to this detachment.[3]

Alexander Mitscherlich's explanation for this phenomenon was expressed in an earlier study, *Society Without the Father*, in which he argued that postwar German society was a society without a father, whose members had no positive image of paternal authority. Mitscher-lich concluded that the old-fashioned paternal values of consistency, order, duty, discipline, and structured social life had been so discredited by the abuse of these values under the Third Reich, that they could no longer form the basis of a democratic society in Germany. He argued further that such a society, psychologically and politically, was obliged to turn to some values, as principles by which it guided itself. These were values formally associated with womanhood and the family, such as caring, affection, protecting the weak, and belief in the importance of the individual, rather than in the importance of results:

> We grow up from the power relationships of childhood, which are tied to persons, into an incomprehensible system of power relationships under which we spend our working life, the phases of our life in which our character has been finally formed. Thus we go through two contrasting phases. If we compare this with the uniformity of the paternalistic structure of society – in which the relationship with the father was succeeded by that with teacher, employer, landlord, all the way up to the king – we are entitled to describe contemporary society as a fatherless society. When no identifiable individual holds power in his hands we have a sibling society.[4]

---

[3] Mitscherlich and Mitscherlich, *The Inability to Mourn*, xx.
[4] Mitscherlich, *Society Without the Father*, 277.

Mitscherlich was describing a social psychology that was not unique to West Germany. Everywhere in the democratic West traditionally masculine and martial values were being rejected by the left-wing intelligentsia. Germany presented a particularly sensitive form of this tendency because the Nazis had exalted and abused masculine values. To reject the father in Germany was for many not merely part of becoming fully modern, but a moral obligation.

In fact, however, those who argued that the strong role of the father in the traditional German family was the psychological cause of Nazism were wrong. Nineteenth-century Swedish Lutherans, Scottish Calvinists, and French Catholics often had strong fathers who did not spare the rod. Yet none of these groups attempted to set up dictatorial governments. If the West German Freudian-Marxists had been seriously interested in the reasons for Hitler's power, they might have noted that he drew his strength disproportionately from groups that had lost their religious or cultural identity, or that felt threatened by loss of economic and social status. Hitler himself, and many of his closest supporters, were lapsed Catholics who feared and despised the church and the cultural and spiritual identity it offered. Further, the single largest group of Nazi voters were *Angestellte* (white-collar salaried employees) in the Protestant and urban regions of Germany, who feared unemployment and socialism in about equal proportions. The Nazi movement was weakest in rural Catholic Germany and in working-class milieus of the west and north.

There was a problem with praising the new "sibling society" of greater equality, caring, and femininity that was coming into being. In fact there were two problems. The first was that even a caring society must still, in order to survive internally, maintain some form of hierarchy, institutional structure, and a legal and political system of objective rules. A society is, by definition, more than a large family; to pretend it could be run like a family was to replace political rationality with sentiment and emotions – and, as any family member knows, the emotions engendered by family life can be negative as well as positive. The second problem was that the values of caring, femininity, and peacefulness might all be very well for a society living in happy immunity from all threats from whatever source, but West Germany in the 1960s could not permit itself such a luxury. West Germany had enemies, foreign and domestic, who would not hesitate to exploit the self-inflicted weakness of a society that followed Mitscherlich's recommendations. Without principles of order and hierarchy, his society was destined to degenerate into chaos or to be destroyed by enemies.

Studies of social values carried out in Germany from the late 1940s onward showed that old values did survive and were respected, especially in certain regions such as Bavaria. After Adenauer's retirement, however, the problem of the missing father image became acute. Adenauer himself had performed the impossible feat of being both a father and a determined opponent of militarism and false masculinity. It was no coincidence that people called him "der Alte." The German phrase has much of the colloquial resonance of the English equivalent, "the old man." The leftist critics of the Federal Republic who had attacked Adenauer for what they called restoration of authoritarian social structures and a failure to allow a breakthrough to true democracy, ridiculed the fact that the Germans were without a father figure, while at the same time welcoming the new so-called softer values as appropriate ones. These same people were those who had high hopes for government in a new Germany following 1945, but who became disenchanted with Germany's development, primarily when the decisions to become integrated with Western Europe and to rearm, clearly showed that it would not be possible to become a neutral country.

Mitscherlich was a left-wing Freudian, and much of his social psychology was an attempt to apply the ideas and methods of Freud to a whole society rather than to an individual. Freud himself, however, had a tragic view of life, and never made the mistake of assuming that it was either desirable or possible to create a more perfect society simply by curing individuals of their mental illnesses or by explaining the unconscious reasons for behavior. Mitscherlich and his numerous admirers and students saw themselves, by contrast, as doctors of the spirit of German society. Mitscherlich's most influential collaborator and student, Horst Eberhard Richter (1923–), extended the analysis of *The Inability to Mourn* in the years to come and reached the conclusion that German society was, indeed, sick, and that those few individuals sensitive enough to realize that demonstrated their sensitivity by becoming sick themselves. One of the symptoms of the sickness of Germany was that the German government, and the Germans, believed in defending themselves against Soviet attack; for Mitscherlich and even more so for Richter, there was no Soviet threat, and even if there were, it would be immoral to defend against it. Since, however, there was no threat, those Germans who believed that there was and that they should defend themselves, were in reality covering up their deep fear of their own spiritual weakness. Mitscherlich and Richter had no better evidence for their view than ordinary Germans, who took the threat seriously, had for theirs. Their psychology was, in fact, part of a political effort to make Germany softer and more peaceful, an effort they pushed forward without regard to the effects of such a change on Germany's ability to survive as a democracy.

Much of the left-liberal criticism of the existing institutions and social attitudes of West Germany, which reached tremendous dimensions during the grand coalition, was an attempt to impose a new father image. But this was largely an unconscious process, so the new father figures – the bearded student revolutionaries – were far more tyrannical and authoritarian than the old ones had been. In particular, they had no respect or understanding of the institutional structure and resilience of democracy. Since they believed that the Bonn government represented a morally inadequate state that did not deserve popular support, they sought to undermine its institutions and destroy them, without acknowledging that it is much easier to weaken democratic institutions than it is to create and preserve them. They ignored the fact that democracies are not run like families or collectives. In the 1960s the completion of the major part of reconstruction, and the increase in leisure time and in wealth, allowed people time to think seriously about the implications of the Nazi past, and this served as a stimulus for much of the new wave of attacks against the Federal Republic and its institutions.

If the leaders of the student movement saw themselves as the heirs of the radical intelligentsia of the Weimar Republic, they also had at least as much in common with the Nazi students of the 1930s. The large and powerful Nazi student movement despised institutional democracy in very much the same way and for the same reasons as the leftist students of the 1960s. Both groups saw it as decadent and unexciting. Both contrasted a depraved present with a radiant future. Most important, both blamed present depravity on specific "guilty parties" who had to be eradicated if the radiant future was to became reality. The Nazis pointed to the Jews; the student radicals of the 1960s to American capitalism and its German allies, in particular the CDU/CSU. These extremist ideas were not specifically Hitlerian or even right-wing; they were the common ideological grist of radicals on both sides of the spectrum.

According to Mitscherlich and Richter, Germans had little self-esteem or autonomy, in part because of a system of education and a personal and family morality which was unable to engender balanced self-confidence and social sensibilities. They learned from their environment and its standards that they must be perfect, and that doubt, ambiguity, and ambivalence were signs of weakness, if not failure. This made them unable to form healthy personal attachments and led instead to a perverse love for the Führer, Hitler, and to an inability to feel concern for his victims. The task of the new German society must be to correct these faults via education and by political action:

> The inability to mourn the loss of the Führer is the result of an intensive defense against guilt, shame, and anxiety, a defense which was achieved by the withdrawal of previously powerful libidinal cathexes. The Nazi past was de-

realized, i.e, emptied of reality. The occasion for mourning was not only the death of Adolf Hitler as a *real* person, but above all his disappearance as the representation of the *collective ego-ideal*. . . .

What censorship has excluded from German consciousness for nearly three decades as a memory too painful to bear may at any time return unbidden from the past; it has not been "mastered;" it does not belong to a past that has been grappled with and understood. The work of mourning can be accomplished only when one knows what one has to sever oneself from. And only by slowly detaching oneself from lost object relations – whether these be to other human beings or to ideals – can a meaningful relationship to reality and to the past be maintained. Without the painful work of recollection this can never be achieved. And, without it, the old ideals, which in National Socialism led to the fatal turn taken by German history, will continue to operate within the unconscious.[5]

Mitscherlich did not think that Germans had psychologically rejected Hitler and continued to carry in themselves a regret for the lost past of Nazism. The only evidence he would accept of a genuine rejection of Hitler was a thorough "overcoming of the past," but he defined that task so narrowly and so politically, that it was hard to see how Germany could pass his test without adopting all his political preferences. The "overcoming" that Mitscherlich, and with him the left-liberals of the 1960s, wanted was a process of self-flagellation and public repentance that would at the same time result in a political change toward a more egalitarian, more socialist society. That new society would shed its fear of the East, a fear that Mitscherlich equated with the fear of rejecting Hitler because Hitler believed that Germany needed an enemy to the East. Once Germans fully overcame the past, they would therefore realize that there was no Soviet threat. The result would be peace in Europe. Thus, for Mitscherlich and the many who believed him, historical moralism and self-purification and faith in Soviet peaceful intentions were two sides of the same coin.

The weighty dilemmas posed by a "fatherless society" were, however, mostly the concern of intellectuals, and intellectuals did not comprise the majority of West German society any more than they did in any other society. Indeed, the average German was not preoccupied with political turmoils and philosophical self-indulgence, but with living life in a healthy and constructive way. Part of this life in postwar Germany, as elsewhere, was reading novels of adventure, such as those by author Karl May (1842–1912). His famous characters, among them Old Shatterhand and the American Indian Winnetou, became involved in

[5] Mitscherlich and Mitscherlich, *The Inability to Mourn*, 23, 66.

deeds of daring and his books were read by children throughout the Federal Republic. In the early 1960s more than 25 million copies of May's novels of heroes and their exploits in the American West, in the Sahara, and in the Orient were in print in West Germany, and had been translated into more than 20 foreign languages.[6]

Postwar Germany also produced many popular writers, though the gap between them and what critics considered serious literature was perhaps greater than in the US or Britain. In America, the writings of John Updike or Tom Wolfe were taken seriously as literature while retaining enormous public appeal. In Germany, most writers thought that to be serious you could not be naturalistic or realistic in your fiction. Moreover, the serious writers, like Böll and Grass, were also those who became internationally famous. Therefore it is not surprising that popular postwar German fiction remained largely unknown outside Germany. Perhaps the most popular writer of the 1950s and 1960s was Hans Hellmut Kirst, an East Prussian and war veteran. Returning from Soviet imprisonment, Kirst achieved an instant breakthrough with his war trilogy, *08/15* (1954–57), the first and possibly best attempt at a fictional portrayal of the war as seen by Germans. He went on to produce a long array of bestsellers, of which one, *The Night of the Generals* (1962), was made into a successful Hollywood film. In the 1970s and 1980s, Kirst turned to portrayals of the life of postwar Germany, as in *Der Nachkriegssieger* (The postwar victor), 1979, a cynical but sympathetic portrait of a returning POW who ruthlessly takes over a small town, manipulating both his family and its other inhabitants to make himself a local bigwig. Kirst emphasized what he saw as the greed, cynicism, and opportunism that was a part of the Adenauer era but without sliding into an equally empty posture of leftist criticism. By the mid-1980s, over twelve million copies of his books were in print in Germany and elsewhere.

As the years passed, younger writers emerged willing to try their hand at representing the fate of modern Germany in a naturalistic style. Perhaps the most successful was Walter Kempowski, born in Rostock in 1929 and barely old enough to have been drafted as a *Flakhelfer* (helper at an anti-aircraft battery) in the last year of the war. Both the Nazis and the communists who took over Rostock in 1945 regarded Kempowski as politically unreliable, and in the 1950s he spent eight years in the harsh prison camp at Bautzen in the GDR. After coming to the West he began publishing a series of books which, through the life of his own ancestors and family in Rostock, described German history from the first years of

---

[6] See Raddatz, *Das abenteuerliche Leben Karl Mays*, and Ostwald, *Karl May: Leben und Werk*.

the century to the 1950s. Kempowski's *Chronik des deutschen Bürgertums* belonged to a peculiar genre, hardly known in English literature but well-known and accepted in Germany, which was neither fiction nor history, but a blend of the two in which real people and events become stories told with literary art.

2

The Grand Coalition:
Stabilizing the Economy

As a government, the grand coalition went through three phases, the first through August 1967, the second through August 1968, and the third to the election of September 1969. During the first phase the parties had to accustom themselves to governing together: the CDU/CSU to sharing power, and the SPD to using it. They also had to accept inevitable disagreements in some areas, the most important of which was foreign policy and Ostpolitik. It was clear that Brandt, as foreign minister, had a different philosophy of and approach to foreign policy than the CDU. He wanted to move further along the road of diplomatic recognition and negotiation with the GDR and Eastern Europe than the chancellor, and he encouraged his ministry to take initiatives that went beyond what the government as a whole could tolerate.

Partly to deal with this problem and partly to gain cabinet support for major new fiscal policy initiatives, the chancellor summoned the leaders of both parties to Kressbronn on Lake Constance, where he was vacationing in August 1967. The Kressbronn meetings were so successful that the chancellor decided to form a permanent working group of the senior leaders in both parties, to meet regularly to discuss current problems and issues. The core of the group consisted of the chancellor, Brandt, Wehner, and Schmidt from the SPD, and Bruno Heck, Barzel, Strauss, and Guttenberg from the CDU/CSU. Because the group had first met in Kressbronn it became known as the Kressbronn Circle, even though it met weekly thereafter in Bonn.

The Kressbronn Circle meetings began the second and most stable phase of the coalition, which lasted until the Soviet Union and three of its satellites invaded Czechoslovakia on August 21, 1968, in order to put an end to the liberalization taking place there. This event produced a crisis for the government's Ostpolitik and brought to a head disagreements on domestic and fiscal policy, thus opening the third and final phase of the coalition. Still it was not until the election of Heinemann as federal president in March 1969 that the two parties found themselves definitively opposed. Thenceforth, they prepared to fight the fall election which would decide which of them was to continue in power.

Karl Schiller and Franz Josef Strauss constituted an unlikely team when they first found themselves shoulder to shoulder as minister of economics and of finance, respectively. They quickly found not only that they got along well personally, but that they were able to collaborate effectively on matters of substance. In the public presentation of policy issues Strauss found an unlikely ally in his old nemesis, Conrad Ahlers, the deputy editor of *Der Spiegel* whom Strauss, as minister of defense, had caused to be arrested in Spain, an act that cost him his post and probably his chances of ever becoming chancellor. Ahlers became deputy head of the government's press and information office and was a loyal servant of the grand coalition. While it was being formed he had put together a documentation of Kiesinger's real role in the Third Reich that proved that the Swabian had taken risks in opposing Hitler's racist and imperialistic policies. Coming from a known liberal, this documentation helped to defuse some of the domestic and international resentment that a former member of the NSDAP was now chancellor of the Federal Republic. It did not, however, stifle it all.

Stabilizing the economy had three aspects: stimulation of investment, production, and employment by the government; the "concerted action" of government, interest groups, and economic experts; and the government's own medium-term planning strategy. A fourth element of the government's overall economic plan was a reform of federalism, that is, of the fiscal relationship between the federation and the *Länder*. The first aspect required a balanced budget, which would make it possible to increase investments, promote demand, and reduce unemployment. The government's strategy lay in the hands of Schiller and Strauss, and in those of the president of the Bundesbank, Karl Blessing. Schiller was especially adept at communicating constant optimism, and at explaining complex economic issues in simple terms. He believed that the "naive phase" of the social market economy was over and that the time had come for "the enlightened social market economy."[1] Strauss and Schiller, men from two completely different political orientations, were able to improve economic performance significantly, a remarkable achievement. Their success initially overshadowed the fact, clear in hindsight, that the change of government and policy of 1966–7 marked a caesura in the history of the West German economy. The economic framework from 1948 to 1966 allowed market mechanisms to operate relatively freely, with the government deliberately eschewing a positive

---

[1] Hildebrand, *Von Erhard zur Grossen Koalition*, 294.

role as regulator of growth and stability. The new structure, introduced in 1967, was one in which the government deliberately sought to manage the national economy by direct policy measures, in the belief that economic cycles and periods of growth could be controlled by government action. This belief met its demise in the energy, inflation, and unemployment crisis of 1974.

Initially, however, the new optimism concerning the ability of the state to improve the economy was justified. The problem was to put the 600,000 unemployed back to work, eliminate the 4.6 billion mark budget deficit, raise the capacity utilization rate of industry, fill the order books, and restore optimism as well. The new policy offensive began with a credit financing law of February 1967, according to which federal and local governments would invest funds obtained on credit in infrastructure and research. The first major result of Schiller's and Strauss' joint political effort was the revised budget passed in January 1967, which showed a surplus on paper thanks to projected tax increases, spending cuts, and rescheduling of various benefits. At the same time the Bundestag passed the so-called stabilization law (its full name was the "law to promote stability and growth of the economy," *Stabilitätsgesetz*) that gave the government much greater power in economic planning. Such a law would have been unthinkable to Erhard, at least in his earlier days as economics minister, since it contradicted the whole idea of perfect competition in a free market. But the law increased public confidence and in the short term it fulfilled its purpose. It marked an important change in West German economic policy in a way that was successful at the time, but which in the long term pointed toward a much more collectivist and centralized direction of the economy, contradicting the principles of a social market economy as understood by Erhard.

Following a proposal by Schiller, representatives of the government, of employers and labor unions, and economic experts, began a series of regular meetings in February 1967 to discuss economic policy. The main purpose of this second aspect of the government's strategy, the so-called "concerted action," a phrase coined by Schiller, was to create stability in the economy by discussing wage contracts and industrial planning in advance. The law on stability and growth required the government to present an annual economic program which would include a survey and a plan for the coming year.

The third aspect of Schiller's new social market economy was intermediate-term fiscal planning, in which the responsible ministers in the government would attempt to foresee the course of the economy over a period of several years, and plan budgets accordingly. The German expression for this was *mittelfristige Finanzplanung*, which the

Germans turned into the acronym *Mifrifi*. The government addressed this issue at the hitherto longest cabinet meeting in the history of the Federal Republic, which lasted three full days from July 4 to 6, 1967; because of the summer heat some elements of the session were held outdoors on the lawn of the chancellery. The session approved a second investment program of 2.8 billion marks from federal funds and 1.5 billion marks from *Land* and local funds. It also highlighted the different approaches to economic policy taken by the coalition partners: that CDU members tended to favor measures to increase exports and balance the budget, whereas the SPD was more anxious to stimulate domestic demand and employment. Despite these differing views the meeting produced agreement on how to continue the government's policies.

The *Mifrifi* planned savings of 3.5 to 7 billion marks a year from 1968 to 1971, the four-year period envisaged in the strategy, and additional revenues of 13 billion marks. To enforce such measures, when confronted with powerfully entrenched interests in West Germany, was enormously difficult. The farmers were especially enraged that their subsidies were cut, but they, as well as other pressure groups, found that they had ultimately no leverage in the face of government solidarity: there was no opposition able to take over power, and early elections in 1967 or 1968 were unthinkable before the coalition had a chance to work. Indeed, many feared that the right-wing NPD, which had entered the Bavarian legislature in November 1966, might enter the Bundestag if new elections were held.

The area of defense was particularly sensitive because here the government was dealing not only with its own member, Schröder, who was adamantly opposed to cuts, but with what one might call the most powerful pressure group of all; namely, the US government and NATO, neither of which wanted West Germany to cut its rate of modest growth in defense spending. The *Mifrifi* called for cuts of two billion marks a year or more in Schröder's budget. At a time when the US was pursuing detente with the Soviet Union, cutting the West German military budget was bound to elicit criticism at home and abroad, because the NATO allies had agreed that Western strength was a precondition for success-ful detente. Precisely this was the main point of the Harmel Report (named after Pierre Charles Harmel, who was the Belgian foreign minister) accepted by NATO in December 1967, and which became the basis for the security policy of all members of NATO for the next two decades.

Shortly after the marathon cabinet session in July, the government stated that the *Mifrifi* required a cut in manpower of the Bundeswehr of 60,000. Schröder attempted independently, via the US government, to put pressure on Kiesinger and Strauss. He sent a cable to Washington explaining that the federal budget cuts meant that the Bundeswehr would decline from 457,000 to 400,000 men. In response, the US secretary of defense, McNamara, canceled a planned visit to Germany. Schröder offered to resign, but in order to maintain the strength of his own party in the coalition, Kiesinger did not accept the offer, though both he and the SPD, who openly described Schröder as "not indispensable," would have been pleased to see the minister depart. Fortunately for the German-American relationship Kiesinger was able to reassure the Americans that the manpower cuts would not take place. In September the government announced it would neither reduce troop strength, nor the length of service of 18 months. The result, while not satisfactory to the left, did solve the immediate defense concern. Among the SPD Helmut Schmidt recognized its importance. He followed the domestic and international debate on strategy and military policy closely and was writing his second major book on the subject – a study that appeared in 1969 under the title *Strategie des Gleichgewichts* (published in English as *The Balance of Power* in 1971).

Only a few days before the NATO Council meeting Kiesinger, in a major policy statement, presented the results of the economic stabilization strategy which included reforms in the armed services. The most important was that the army and the territorial defense forces (analogous to the US National Guard) would be amalgamated. Relying on the consultations of the Kressbronn Circle, which were now a routine part of his method of government, Kiesinger assured the public that there were no major disagreements within the coalition. That this was not entirely true became clear a month later, in January 1968, when Schiller failed to persuade the cabinet to agree to the ambitious third stage of his program of structural reform and investment. Schiller wanted to move rapidly along the path of his "new economics," as he described it; but in view of the striking success of the stabilization strategy up to that point, the bare conservative majority of the cabinet regarded what had already been done as sufficient. Schiller then proposed, in the interests of what he called "social symmetry," to recommend significant wage increases in 1968, since there had been virtually no raises in 1967. Again, he was defeated by Strauss and the CDU/CSU, who were concerned with reducing government debt before introducing new measures to stimulate the economy. Schiller was only able to receive approval of additional funds and credits for regional development and special assistance for industry in the coal-producing areas.

In 1968 and 1969 economic growth returned to very high levels of 7–8 per cent per year, while inflation fell to 1.5 per cent. When Brandt succeeded Kiesinger in 1969, the federal budget showed a surplus of 1.5

billion DM, and important reductions in the public debt. The unemployment rate and the number of unemployed fell during the coalition period from 600,000 to 200,000 by the spring of 1969, which contributed to the existing labor shortage. After reaching total employment in 1957–8, and because the flow of refugees was reduced to a trickle after 1961, the West German economy began to rely on foreign workers to an increasing degree in an effort to alleviate the labor problem. By the summer of 1964 they numbered over a million, rising to 1.2 million in 1968. By early 1969 the so-called guest laborers, especially from Yugoslavia, Turkey, and Italy, had reached 1.8 million (or 8.6 per cent of the German labor force). Twelve years later, in 1981 approximately 4.5 million foreigners lived in the Federal Republic, more than 7 per cent of the total population. The majority, however, were not laborers, but members of their families; by 1980 more than half of their one million children had been born in West Germany. The result was that the initial problems of adjustment to the workplace gradually turned into socio-political problems, such as the emergence of ethnic ghettos in major cities and large numbers of foreigners with virtually no knowledge of the German language. In 1973 the West German government sought to reduce the numbers of foreigners and their families by placing an embargo on the employment of new guest laborers by German companies, and later introduced a repatriation program that offered generous financial assistance to those wishing to return to their own countries.[2]

In late 1968 the government finally addressed the politically loaded issue of fiscal reform, i.e. the redesign of the economic role of the federal government versus the *Länder*. This involved farm support and reform of agricultural policy, regional economic planning, education, and research. The latter issue concerned financing the many new universities and educational institutions that were in their early stages of development. The Basic Law had foreseen that the federal government would contribute heavily to investments by the *Länder* in education and housing, and in transportation and health, but there had never been a major reorganization of the federal-state relationship.

In May 1969 the Bundestag added a provision to the Basic Law transferring greater authority to the federal government in the area of fiscal responsibility. Specifically, the amendment gave the federal government the authority to redistribute monies between the poorer and the richer *Länder* as it saw fit. Thus, the law eliminated a previously unambiguous division of administrative responsibility between the federal government and the *Länder*, and created a new area of federal

---

[2] See *Brockhaus Enzyklopädie*, vol. 6, 793.

responsibility and power which was not directly subject to parliamentary control. What this really meant was that the federal government – that is to say, the political parties governing in Bonn – now had the power to distribute tax revenues in accordance with their own political philosophy of government, and could thus direct the expenditure of tax monies for government-funded or subsidized projects which the governing parties supported for political reasons. As long as the grand coalition lasted the desire of the SPD to use this instrument to increase public spending was held in check, but it was widely recognized what an opportunity it would offer should the SPD become the dominant party of government.

The newly created Article 104a (burden sharing by federal and *Land* governments) gives the federal government the possibility, as a result of the so-called investment responsibility, . . . to grant individual states financial assistance for especially important investments, if such investments are necessary to prevent a disturbance of the economic balance, to equalize different economic power in the Federal Republic, or to promote economic growth. This general clause [that was passed following an acrimonious debate] basically gives the federal government the task of establishing economic balance between the *Länder*.[3]

The grand coalition extended the reach of government, not only by passing laws regulating economic policy across a far wider spectrum than any previous government, but also by expanding public spending. This expansion was already taking place on the *Land* and local level. Beginning in the mid-1960s, the welfare state in Germany changed from being a provider of emergency welfare to being a provider of what Rüdiger Altmann, Erhard's advisor, called "collective provision for existence" (*kollektive Daseinsvorsorge*). Looking at the process of industrial, institutional, and cultural modernization of the 1960s as a whole, Altmann commented during the grand coalition that "a new triangle of forces has taken shape, consisting of economic processes, scientific and technological progress, and public assistance."[4]

As the country became richer and the government larger, people asked more of it. By the late 1960s it was clear to many observers that the nature of government was changing. Traditionally – in Europe, this meant until the late nineteenth century – the task of the state was to protect the state religion from heresy and the national territory from invasion or domestic disorder. This was the "negative" or defense state. The next stage of government was the "positive" or welfare state, installed throughout most of the Western world during the 1930s. The

---

[3] Seifert, "Die Verfassung," in *Die BRD,* ed. Benz, 1: 49.
[4] Cited in Hildebrand, *Von Erhard zur Grossen Koalition,* 298.

early welfare state, however, was a government not of permanent activism but of directed, emergency intervention. The third stage, that of the state of permanent care, evolved after World War II and especially during the 1960s. Some economists, particularly those of the so-called public choice school, drew a connection between the increasing rate of public spending that began around 1965, and the decline in rates of economic growth that became obvious after the end of the 1960s. According to that school, a large public sector creates vested interests that pressure government to extract resources from productive sectors of the economy for their own benefit or those of their clients. The cost of these transfers is reduced efficiency and eventually slower growth of income and production. In Germany, as in most of the West before the oil crises of the 1970s, the consensus in favor of expanding public spending (except on defense) was overwhelming; even the conservative parties supported it.[5]

The grand coalition, by accelerating social spending, prepared the way for the ambitious welfare budgets of the Brandt–Scheel coalition of 1969–74. In the short term of 1967–8, however, public expenditures added stability and public confidence in the government's economic and fiscal policy.

[5] Social services comprised 15.7 per cent of the GNP in 1950, and changed as follows: 1953: 15.4 per cent; 1957: 17.0 per cent; 1961: 16.2 per cent; 1963: 16.5 per cent; 1966: 17.8 per cent; 1969: 18.7 per cent; 1975: 25.4 per cent; 1980: 24.0 per cent; 1982: 23.0 per cent; (Zöllner, "Sozialpolitik," Die BRD, ed. Benz, 2: 319).

3

New Ideas on Ostpolitik

K iesinger was prepared to embark on what he called "new Ostpolitik," a concept that received steadily increasing attention after
construction of the Berlin Wall in 1961, both from the SPD and from
Gerhard Schröder as foreign minister between 1961 and 1966. This
concept involved expanding the range of Bonn's relations with Eastern
Europe and the Soviet Union, while continuing to deny the existence of
the GDR. Willy Brandt wanted to go further. Where Kiesinger and
Schröder thought that a policy of "small steps" could bring reunification
closer or at least make life for Germans in the East better without
recognizing the GDR, Brandt, Wehner, Bahr, and Schmidt, the entire
SPD leadership, in fact, believed the opposite, that recognizing the
GDR was a necessary precondition for any other improvements.

In this belief the social democrats enjoyed the nearly unanimous
support not only of the FDP, which was in fact far ahead of them on this
issue until 1969, but, even more important, of published opinion in the
media, whose influence on West German history in the late 1960s was as
great or greater than that of any of the three parties actually represented
in the Bundestag. The *Süddeutsche Zeitung*, the *Frankfurter Rundschau*, *Die
Zeit*, *Stern*, and *Der Spiegel* "ceaselessly repeated ... the image of a
CDU/CSU putting a brake on Ostpolitik and thus appearing to be
negative, whereas they consistently presented the social democrats
positively as the progressive force."[1] The leaders of published opinion
consistently favored the alternative of a small coalition of SPD/FDP,
which they thought (correctly, as it turned out) would move more swiftly
toward recognition of the GDR and broad agreements accepting the
status quo in Central Europe. This position, relentlessly pursued on the
part of the media, led Kiesinger to coin the pejorative term, "party of
recognition," for those individuals and groups who were insisting on

---

[1] Hildebrand, *Von Erhard zur Grossen Koalition,* 325.

recognition of the GDR and the Oder–Neisse line as a legitimate frontier.[2] Ostpolitik was the major, but not the only, area of public policy in which published opinion became a determining force in German politics; others were the cultural revolution and the changes within the structure of German universities.

While the FDP was unable to become a party of government, because of the disparity of power in the Bundestag, the party sought to conduct an active and energetic opposition policy, which produced dramatic changes in its leadership. Between 1966 and 1969, the FDP experienced the defeat of the old national liberal group under Erich Mende, and the rise to power of a more left-leaning group in favor of a new Ostpolitik, supported by the pragmatists of the so-called "Saxon guard," Hans-Dietrich Genscher, Wolfgang Mischnick, and Walter Scheel.

They were unusually able men who were to play roles of major importance. Hans-Dietrich Genscher was born in 1927, held different positions in the FDP, beginning in 1956, and served as minister of the interior between 1969 and 1974. In 1974 he became foreign minister, as well as FDP party chairman. While he relinquished his position as chairman to Martin Bangemann in 1985, he was still foreign minister in 1988. His tenure as foreign minister was the longest in the history of the Federal Republic, or indeed anywhere in democratic Europe. Of his abilities, Ralf Dahrendorf, a former member of the FDP who was head of the London School of Economics and Political Science from 1974 to 1984, wrote: "What he says makes sense. It always stands up and it gets to you."[3] Walter Scheel was born in 1919 and served in the Bundestag from 1953 to 1974, as minister for economic cooperation from 1961 to 1966, as FDP party chairman from 1968 to 1974 and as foreign minister from 1969 to 1974. In 1974 he was elected federal president and served in that capacity until 1979. Wolfgang Mischnick, born in 1921, served in the Bundestag from 1957, as minister for expellees, refugees and war invalids from 1961 to 1963, and later became chairman of the FDP caucus in the Bundestag. All of them well understood the forces of politics. Mischnick expressed their approach clearly: "Politicians do not live from hand to mouth, but from budget to budget and from one election to the next. Therefore their future has already begun, whenever the voter wants it."[4]

The FDP responded to the challenge of being the small, single opposition party by revolutionizing its own position on the German question. That meant recognition of the legitimacy of the GDR and of

---

[2] Besson, *Aussenpolitik*, 406–10.
[3] Introduction to *Deutsche Aussenpolitik*, by Genscher.
[4] Bolesch, *Typisch Mischnick*, 144.

the Oder–Neisse line as an acceptable price to pay for eventual unity. One reason that the liberals were less concerned with the border issue was that many of their leaders came from the German south-west. That region had been the heartland of democratic nationalist liberalism in the nineteenth century and continued to provide a strong influence in the FDP for regional autonomy, and against strong central state authority.

When the liberals lost their foothold as a governing party and went into opposition in 1966, the split between the old nationalists supporting the chairman, Mende, and the radical innovators became obvious. The radicals wanted the party to adopt a new national policy and favored leaping on the rapidly rolling bandwagon of social and cultural change in the Federal Republic. Using the interest awakened by the debate on Ostpolitik, the FDP saw in it the best hope of surviving the opposition period without being swamped either by loss of public support or, more dangerously, by the flight of marginal voters to the new right-wing party, the National Democratic Party (NPD). Thus, "both the forward-looking radical democratic innovators and the pragmatists of the party, who were still cautiously studying the terrain, let themselves be carried by the mighty current of the new age of movement in world politics, of spiritual searching, of radical chic and the happy breaking of taboos, of mini-rebellions and the cultural revolution, of the profound change of values and the abrupt change of climate."[5]

In January 1967 a working group led by Wolfgang Schollwer, a leading liberal publicist, presented an internal policy paper to the party leadership on the German question. It led to a "battle for Germany" between the liberal and socialist leaders of published opinion and the conservative defenders of the official policy, which, since Adenauer, had been followed and shared – until that moment – by all parties, including the SPD. Schollwer was a friend of Egon Bahr and of another progressive social democratic publicist, Peter Bender, but as a liberal he was able to state clearly what the social democrats, bound to some extent by party and government discipline, could only suggest. In a truly revolutionary move, Schollwer abandoned reunification in a single national state and even political federation as a goal. Instead, he proposed *Verklammerung* – "bracketing together" – of the two German states, without either abandoning its sovereignty, as the only reasonable goal. This was the key of the whole proposal, which also recommended accepting the Oder-Neisse line and demilitarization of both German states.

Schollwer and his supporters had chosen sides in the old argument of German liberals since 1848 – should national unity or freedom come

[5] Hildebrand, *Von Erhard zur Grossen Koalition*, 340.

first? They defined a specific understanding of individual and social freedom, an understanding colored by the social and cultural revolution of habits and values then taking place throughout the Western world; and they combined that understanding with a view of the German question that subordinated the goal of reunification to the goal of preserving peace. In short, the radical liberals, who now dominated the party, wanted freedom in the manner of student radicals for West Germans but were unwilling to jeopardize peace (as they understood it) to bring it to East Germans.

Schollwer's study won the immediate and delighted support not only of liberal leaders like Thomas Dehler and Hildegard Hamm-Brücher – who was to become one of the leaders of the FDP left in the 1970s – but also of influential journalists who were members of the FDP, like Henri Nannen and Rudolf Augstein. Following their insistence that the Schollwer recommendations become party policy Genscher, Scheel, and Mischnick joined the new line.

This was the beginning of the end for Mende's chairmanship. Several weeks after Schollwer had presented his study to the public, Nannen visited the party chairman, Mende, and demanded that the FDP adopt an "entirely new opposition policy." This new policy would be based on the Schollwer recommendations and would include recognition of the GDR, acceptance of the Oder–Neisse line as the final and irrevocable eastern border of Germany, and of a confederation of the two German states "in the manner proposed by Moscow and East Berlin." Mende refused, but was soon to discover that fighting the combined forces of Nannen and Augstein was futile. In March, Nannen published excerpts from the Schollwer paper in *Stern* under the headline, "FDP spokesman Schollwer has drafted a radical plan ... No fear of Ulbricht!" A few weeks later the treasurer of the party, Hans Wolfgang Rubin, wrote an article in support of Schollwer, which Nannen likewise gave extensive publicity in *Stern*. Like Schollwer, Rubin recommended recognition of the GDR and called reunification impossible.[6]

The split between the old nationals around Mende and the radical innovators around Schollwer and Rubin, came to a head at the party conference in Hannover in April 1967. Mende insisted that recognizing the Oder–Neisse line should not be FDP policy: "Whoever today is ready to light-heartedly dispose of a fifth of German territory, will tomorrow be forced to deal similarly with West Berlin and the day after tomorrow with the Federal Republic." Genscher, the pragmatist, succeeded in hammering out a compromise formula, and during the rest of 1967 the three Saxon guardsmen – Genscher, Scheel, and Mischnick

[6] Ibid., 346–7.

– conducted a "tightrope walk"[7] between the radical and conservative wings of the party. The question was clear: would "peaceful reunification with Central Germany *and the East German territories* in one *German Reich* with a liberal constitution ... remain our *supreme goal?*" Or would "the overcoming of European and, with it, the German division, as well as the creation of a lasting peace order for all of Europe ... be our supreme goal?"[8]

The question was, in reality, already answered, influenced by the power of published opinion and the eagerness with which not only the radicals but also the pragmatists were embracing "peace." It was also answered by another development: the FDP and the SPD were now clearly working toward a future coalition, the binding force of that coalition to be agreement on the German question and on social policy. Shortly after the Hannover conference Rubin met with Egon Bahr and determined that they were in complete agreement on the issues.

In September 1967 Mende resigned as chairman, and in January 1968 the party conference, held in Freiburg, elected Scheel to succeed him. This conference marked the completion of the change in the party. The star of the conference was the 38–year-old sociologist Ralf Dahrendorf, who, wearing a red carnation (the symbol of socialism) in his lapel, spoke eloquently of the need for radical reforms of administrative, fiscal, and educational policy and attacked the "immobility" of the government. Dahrendorf was to become an influential figure not only of the FDP, but of non-socialist liberals and progressives throughout the Western world. His political and ideological analyses corresponded perfectly to the temper of an age that rejected both old-fashioned collectivism and authoritarian conservatism and restraints on personal freedom.

From the Freiburg conference onward the FDP followed not only a new foreign policy, but an increasingly radical and egalitarian path on social policy, and on what in America would be called civil rights, which in Germany was called *Rechtspolitik* or judicial policy. In this turbulent period for the party Scheel was the man in the middle who had to reconcile the party's new leftward course with the need to keep its older voting base. The signs were set for the future coalition with the SPD, particularly since the social democrats decided, at their own conference in March 1968, to postpone indefinitely consideration of single constituency voting, a plan that would have killed the FDP as a national party.

[7] Ibid., 281.
[8] Ibid., 348, emphasis in original.

4

Official Ostpolitik 1966–1968

Inspired by Bahr, whom he made head of the policy planning staff in the foreign ministry between 1967 and 1969, Brandt had decided by 1962 that West Germany could make no progress at all toward the East without first recognizing the status quo, including the existence of the GDR, although he did not state this unambiguously until he became chancellor in 1969. Nevertheless he sent clear messages even though, as foreign minister, Brandt was technically obliged to follow the government's jointly approved foreign policy. Kiesinger complained early on in the coalition of the "trickles" that were coming from the foreign ministry – that is, from Bahr's office, and in October 1967 the chancellor went so far as to describe Bahr confidentially as "a really dangerous man."[1]

Speaking on the German issue in January 1967, Brandt declared in an interview that "we ... shall not shy away from contact with the authorities in the other part of Germany, if it serves the people and helps our case. This means we shall take initiatives so that the people in both parts of our fatherland will not drift apart any further; although I am well aware of the fact that we cannot make any progress if the other side builds walls."[2] "The other part of Germany" remained the official way of referring to the GDR until 1969; but it replaced reference to the GDR as "the Zone" or the "SBZ" (*Sowjetische Besatzungszone*) and foreshadowed a dramatic change in the language used to define the issues resulting from Germany's division.

Brandt's excuse in occasionally going beyond what the government as a whole could support was that, as SPD chairman, he had the obligation and responsibility to advance SPD goals irrespective of whether this conflicted with his cabinet obligations. He shared the view later formulated by Marion Dönhoff, when she wrote that the "Hallstein

---

[1] Cited in Hildebrand, *Von Erhard zur Grossen Koalition*, 327.
[2] *Welt am Sonntag*, January 7, 1967.

Doctrine was no longer an effective instrument for keeping other nations on their best behaviour," and that West Germany had little clout as long as it "clung to its claim to speak for the whole German people."[3] Brandt, Bahr, and Wehner agreed that maintaining legal and moral claims, that were not going to be realized, was doing more harm than good both to West Germany's standing and to the people of Central Europe. The social democratic leaders believed that the communist regimes to the east were basically nationalistic regimes who were looking for opportunities to break away from Soviet domination. West Germany could help them by diplomatic recognition, trade, and political concessions. Schmidt formulated SPD foreign policy in June 1967 in this way: "Just as in the final analysis we need all of these three Western powers, so we need the Soviet Union just as much, that is the ABC of German foreign policy, as the social democrats spelled it out in the early 1950s here in the Bundestag. . . . We are simply coming back to recognizing the old outlines of the power structure as it exists in Europe."[4]

Wehner's ultimate goals and methods were and remained obscure. His critics believed that he had always hoped for some kind of socialist reunification which would transform both Germanies, and the few indications he ever offered of his personal vision of the future might be interpreted in that direction. On the other hand, he was always fiercely loyal to the memory of Kurt Schumacher, who was a determined anti-communist, and it is unlikely that Wehner entertained a vision that involved the self-abandonment or dissolution of the SPD. During the grand coalition, in any event, Wehner found in Kiesinger, Guttenberg and others, "useful temporary partners" in ultimately advancing the social democratic program for Ostpolitik, chiefly by letting the SPD prove itself in power so that, when the time came, it could put its policies into practice alone.[5]

During most of the grand coalition there was outward harmony between the two parties on the issue of Ostpolitik, based to a great extent on the efforts of Schröder. He had done much to reorient the "policy of strength" of the Adenauer era. While he had not been able to develop a coherent and convincing strategy for dealing with Central European questions, his practical approach and his desire to formulate a pragmatic *West* German national interest, even if this meant indirect recognition of the statehood of East Germany, was the necessary and important precondition for the national policy of the coalition. It

[3] Dönhoff, *Foe into Friend*, 116.
[4] Cited in Hildebrand, *Von Erhard zur Grossen Koalition*, 327.
[5] Ibid., 332.

enabled Willy Brandt to move much more rapidly than otherwise would have been the case.

As the mayor of West Berlin when the East Germans stopped free movement within the city and built the Wall, Brandt had witnessed at first hand the action and inaction that defined the limits of Western commitment to German unity and self-determination and the possibilities for promoting freedom in Central Europe. In 1961 it had finally become clear that article 7, clause 2 of the treaty of 1954 on relations between the three Western powers and Germany, in which the three powers declared support for the democratic unification of Germany, would not produce reunification in the foreseeable future. The premise of Brandt's Ostpolitik was that the status quo was intolerable and needed changing. But, whereas Adenauer, the CDU, and even more so the CSU, maintained that detente was without value if it implied even indirect acceptance of the dictatorial behavior of the Soviet and East German regimes, the Brandt Ostpolitik introduced the idea that change would follow from an acceptance of the status quo, would serve as means to improve the *Lebensbedingungen* (quality of life) of Germans in the East and would contribute to detente in Europe generally.

The basic position of the grand coalition on the German question was defined in Kiesinger's inaugural policy declaration of December 13, 1966, as follows: "That peace may be preserved is the hope of all nations, and the German Nation desires this no less than others. The will to preserve peace and to promote international understanding is, therefore, the first word and the primary concern of this Government's foreign policy." In this statement Kiesinger (and with him Brandt, who stood behind the declaration as well) signaled a new departure. He did not begin by asserting the right to reunification and denouncing the GDR regime for preventing it. On the contrary, the main theme was peace and detente, and therefore Kiesinger turned to the subject of the Soviet Union. The chancellor reminded the public that "I was one of those who strongly advocated the establishment of diplomatic relations between the Federal Republic and the Soviet Union" in 1955. He went on to say that "Germans harbored neither ill-will nor hatred towards the peoples of the Soviet Union; that, on the contrary, they wanted to live side by side with them."

He went on to discuss relations with Eastern Europe, and used a phrase that became more common later: "Germany was for centuries the bridge between Western and Eastern Europe. We should like to fulfill this mission also in our time." He expressed his desire for reconciliation with Poland and Czechoslovakia and touched only lightly on the atrocities inflicted by the Czech and the communist Polish regimes on the German populations they came to control in 1945. He stated that

Germany wanted a united Europe and in particular desired to develop Franco-German cooperation under the 1963 treaty.

Turning to the GDR, which he still referred to by its official designation as the "East Zone," he took further steps away from the old policy of rejection. After repeating the claim of sole representation he said:

> This does not mean that we want to treat in a patronizing manner our countrymen in the other part of Germany. . . . We wish to do our utmost to prevent the two parts of our nation from drifting apart as long as the country is divided; . . . we wish to bridge the gulfs, not deepen them. That is why we wish to do all we can to encourage human, economic and cultural relations with our countrymen. . . . Where this requires the establishment of contacts between authorities of the Federal Republic and of those in the other part of Germany it does not imply any recognition of a second German State.[6]

This was the first time a West German chancellor had referred, even indirectly, to the fact that there might be a government in the GDR with which one might have to deal. Perhaps in order to reaffirm his government's basic position, he went on to state that "the Federal Government will do everything in its power to make sure that Berlin remains a part of the Federal Republic" – a position denied by both the Soviet Union and the Western powers, as the latter found occasion to state in an aide-mémoire of April 18, 1967.[7]

In his statement Kiesinger signaled that the former official position of the West German government, maintained since its formation in 1949, was to be replaced by a new and more flexible approach to the issue of German unity. The goal of reunification remained a national policy of the grand coalition, but was set in the context of a "general European peace order." An end to Germany's division was no longer a precondition for detente, and, thus, became a goal to be achieved as a result of detente. Though Kiesinger insisted that his outstretched hand to the GDR did not imply that Bonn was abandoning its legal position, many – both left and right, and in East and West – rightly saw his statement as foreshadowing future recognition of the GDR.

In a further statement of policy on January 18, 1967, Kiesinger declared, for the first time, that he wanted to pursue a "new Ostpolitik," which he defined as "a far-ranging policy of peace and understanding, with its goal a happy future for all Europe."[8] In accordance with his

---

[6] Dept of State, *Documents on Germany*, 935–40.
[7] Ibid., 940, 960.
[8] Ibid., 943.

expressed desire for improved relations with the Soviet Union, Kiesinger also proposed talks with the Soviet government on a treaty on the mutual renunciation of force. Kiesinger and Brandt felt that such a treaty could not be injurious, since NATO, of which West Germany was a member, was in any case a defensive alliance, and might be productive. On February 7, 1967, Bonn transmitted to Moscow a draft declaration on renunciation of force and in April sent a longer statement to the UN Disarmament Committee that was meeting in Geneva. In this latter statement, the German government stated that it had no intention of acquiring or requesting nuclear weapons.

One reason for the April statement was the nuclear non-proliferation treaty which the US government had been pressing Bonn to sign since 1966. Relations with the US were temporarily damaged in 1967 over this issue and over the issue of German payment for the cost of stationing American troops in the Federal Republic, the same problem that had provoked the governmental crisis leading to Erhard's fall. In February 1967 Kiesinger made an unprecedented public critique of US foreign policy and announced that US and German interests were not inevitably identical, and that the time of unquestioning acceptance of US leadership was over:

General de Gaulle blames us Germans for being – well, he says it politely – too obedient toward the Americans; all of us, including Adenauer. Now I'd like to answer him: I cannot accept that on the part of my government. Of course, also we know that American policy in Europe exclusively pursues American interests. There are some Germans who think that there exists a special friendship or friendly arrangements. This always leads to deep disappointments later on. In politics, there exist different interests between peoples. American policy here is pursuing American interests. The task is to determine to what extent American interests coincide with our own, with German and European interests, and to what extent they do not or no longer do so.[9]

Kiesinger was reacting to US pressure to sign the non-proliferation treaty, but wanted to indicate in an unambiguous manner that West Germany wished to be treated as an equal, and to shake the complacency of those in Washington who took West German acceptance for granted. One of the main sources of concern in West Germany was that the treaty would be used by the Soviet Union as a means to discriminate against West Germany, thereby preventing it from ever becoming a nuclear power. Another reason was that the Soviets claimed the right to force Bonn to sign it on the basis of clauses 53 and 107 of the UN

[9] Cited in Hildebrand, *Von Erhard zur Grossen Koalition*, 310.

Charter, the enemy states clauses. Under these clauses any member of the wartime United Nations could intervene to prevent Germany from becoming a new threat to world peace. The Soviets chose, at least in their propaganda, to regard West Germany's potential access to nuclear weapons as a threat to peace. Kiesinger was thus also concerned that, by signing the treaty, Bonn would appear to be accepting this Soviet assertion which might set a precedent for future intervention by the Soviet government in West German affairs.

The US government, under President Lyndon Johnson, was alarmed by Kiesinger's statement. It sent none other than the well-respected former High Commissioner, John J. McCloy, on a special mission to Germany. He succeeded at least in calming German fears on the non-proliferation treaty. He also worked out an agreement concerning transfer payments by which West Germany would cover part of the cost of stationing US troops in Germany and secure future German purchases of US matériel. In addition, the West German government agreed to use the strong German mark to support the dollar, which was starting to lose its value as inflation and foreign deficits, caused by America's overseas obligations, began troubling the US economy.

Kiesinger met with President Johnson when the latter attended the funeral of Konrad Adenauer in April, and continued this "frank and far-reaching" conversation in Washington in August, as their joint communique at that time indicated: "We share the view that a policy of relaxation of tensions . . . can remove the causes of existing tensions. . . . It is only by following such a policy that the division of Europe and the division of Germany can be ended."[10] Since the Soviet Union demanded preliminary recognition of the status quo as a precondition for relaxation of tensions, Kiesinger, representing the coalition of the major political parties of Germany, effectively abandoned the last vestiges of the old Ostpolitik, albeit without being able to admit it.

In the April 1967 statement to the UN Disarmament Committee, Kiesinger and Brandt proposed general nuclear disarmament as a policy superior to nuclear non-proliferation, which by definition bound only those states which did not have nuclear weapons. The statement was, however, a political maneuver rather than a serious proposal for disarmament. The offer of renunciation of force, made to the Soviet Union in February, was intended more seriously and negotiations dragged on for over a year with no final result. But they did serve to emphasize the concept of conciliation in Kiesinger's "new Ostpolitik."

In 1965 Schröder had already taken the first step away from the Hallstein Doctrine when he declared that the East European commun-

---

[10] Dept of State, *Documents on Germany*, 963.

ist regimes were "born" with diplomatic relations to the GDR. They had no choice in the matter and so could not be expected to honor the Hallstein Doctrine, which said that West Germany would deny or withdraw diplomatic recognition from any government that recognized the GDR. This "birth defect theory" permitted West Germany to establish relations with Romania in January 1967 despite the obvious fact that, as a communist regime, Romania recognized the GDR. Brandt was actually somewhat skeptical about the wisdom of continuing Schröder's example set with Romania. From the viewpoint of the Soviet Union and the East European regimes, the policy merely proved that the West German government was beginning to accept the status quo in Eastern Europe, and recognized that it could not isolate the GDR or successfully bring pressure to bear for reunification. The reaction of Moscow, and of GDR leader Walter Ulbricht, therefore, was to continue their hard line.[11] Although Bonn successfully concluded an agreement in August 1967 to exchange trade missions with Prague, it did not prove possible to establish new diplomatic relations with any other East European states.

In April 1967 representatives of all communist parties of both Western and Eastern Europe met at Karlsbad in Czechoslovakia. In the final statement of the conference, the communist parties reiterated the Soviet demand, made since the late 1950s, for a system of "collective security" in Europe, recognition of the Oder–Neisse line as the frontier of Poland, recognition of two German states, renunciation by the Federal Republic of any claim to obtain nuclear weapons, and a universal European treaty renouncing the use of force.[12] The communist parties suggested that the Western Europeans not renew the North Atlantic Treaty when it expired in 1969, a proposal they had made in 1966 as well.

In the same month Kiesinger publicly announced a series of proposals to improve communications between the Federal Republic and East Germany. They were not only positive in intent, but practical as well:

1 improved travel possibilities for Germans in Germany;
2 easing the receipt of medicines and gift parcels sent to the GDR;
3 permitting the joining together of families;
4 expansion of internal German trade;
5 joint development of new transport facilities, e.g. road, and rail, and barge traffic;

---

[11] Brandt, *People and Politics*, 170.
[12] Dept of State, *Documents on Germany*, 961–3.

6 improved postal and telephone connections;
7 contacts between universities, research institutions and scientific associations;
8 "step-by-step" exchange of books, magazines, and newspapers;
9 athletic contacts.[13]

Kiesinger's statement coincided with the seventh party congress of the SED, to which the SPD addressed an open letter suggesting talks. Ulbricht responded haughtily that since Kiesinger "failed to take cognizance of the German Democratic Government" (a curious phrase in Western ears, since it would seem to describe the Bonn government and not the totalitarian GDR regime) and still pursued "an ostrich-like policy," there was no reason for discussion. "Unity of the German nation under the leadership of the imperialists is impossible," Ulbricht concluded, because "the nation consists essentially of the sovereign peoples (*Staatsvölker*) of two independent German states, the socialist GDR and the imperialist and militarist West German Federal Republic, whose rulers are bent on restoring the irretrievable past and on new aggression. ... If the two German states are to be united, then a democratic transformation in West Germany ... and the curtailment of the power of the monopolies by the strength of the working people are the first and foremost requirements."[14]

Further in this vein, the chairman of the East German Council of Ministers, Willi Stoph, wrote to Kiesinger in May proposing "to normalize relations between the two German states" as the only way of doing justice to "the elementary interests of the citizens of both German states." He also demanded payment of money, using the long-standing GDR argument that West Germany was exploiting the East to its economic detriment and was obliged to perform financial restitution. Kiesinger's response in June was to deplore the East German insistence on all or nothing, and to repeat his own earlier desire to improve life in Germany.[15]

The debate stirred by this official exchange of correspondence continued throughout the year. In June Kiesinger made yet another conciliatory approach describing "our new policy in the East," which sought "a gradual overcoming of differences" in Europe. "Germany, a reunited Germany, is of a critical size," the chancellor continued, picking up a favorite theme of philosophically inclined historians and

---

[13] Ibid., 955-7.
[14] Ibid., 958-9.
[15] Bundesministerium für innerdeutsche Beziehungen, *Dokumente zur Deutschlandpolitik* ser. 5, 1: 909, 922, 1115-7.

geopoliticians: "It is too large not to play a role in the balance of forces and too small to keep the forces surrounding it in equilibrium. Therefore it is truly hard to conceive that, if the present political structure of Europe continues, a complete Germany would be able to join one side or the other just like that. That is precisely why one can only conceive a coalescence of the divided parts of Germany in the process of overcoming the East–West conflict in Europe."[16] Wehner welcomed this speech and referred to it with respect. In fact the underlying message – conciliation and a view of reunification that saw it as a part of, and not a precondition for, a general European settlement of the East–West conflict – was identical to the long-term view of the social democrats.

In August 1967, Brandt was Germany's first foreign minister to refer, albeit indirectly, to East Germany as the GDR. At the SPD party conference in Nuremberg in 1968 he emphasized that "we could not regard the GDR as a foreign country," and that since reunification "did not figure in the current international agenda," it would be necessary "to regulate the coexistence and cooperation of the two parts of Germany in the interests of people and of peace."[17]

The exchange between Bonn and East Berlin continued to September 1967, when Stoph provided the draft of a treaty to "normalize" relations, to renounce the use of force, and to remove all nuclear forces from both the GDR and the FRG. Kiesinger's response emphasized the right of all Germans to determine their own government, and, therefore, their destiny, irrespective of where they lived. Brandt and Wehner, on the other hand, called for unconditional negotiations, and stressed that "we do not assert the right to exercise official authority (*behördliche Macht*) in the other part of Germany." This was a rebuke, on Brandt's part, to the position advocated by the CSU leaders Guttenberg and Strauss. They argued that any policy not designed and perceived to lead to liberalization of the regime and ultimately to extension of the civil rights of the West German constitution to East Germany was immoral and a violation of the Basic Law itself. This disagreement covering what constituted the most effective direction of Ostpolitik posed a real dilemma. On the one hand, those sharing the views of Strauss and Guttenberg had a good case. On the other hand, the new direction given Ostpolitik by Willy Brandt and the grand coalition, separately and together, had yet to succeed or to fail.

The Bonn-GDR exchanges of 1967 had no immediate consequences. The SED regime was simply not willing to make what it regarded as

[16] Cited in Hildebrand, *Von Erhard zur Grossen Koalition*, 332.
[17] Brandt, *People and Politics*, 186.

concessions to Bonn. The response of the SED to the grand coalition's approaches was a "reverse Hallstein Doctrine" practised by Ulbricht. The GDR would do what it could to penalize East European or Third World states that recognized both Germanies. This policy was viable because of the rapid growth in the 1960s of the so-called nonaligned movement, a forum of political agitation and consultation made up of at first about 30, later more than 70 states mostly in Africa, Asia, and Latin America. Their governments claimed they were not aligned either with the US or the Soviet Union, and held their first major conference in Havana in communist-ruled Cuba in 1966. In practice, the nonaligned movement was anti-Western and friendly toward the Soviet bloc, and the GDR found many countries in the movement that were willing to support Ulbricht's reverse Hallstein Doctrine.

In his annual statement on the state of the German nation in March 1968 Kiesinger summed up the first year of the grand coalition's Ostpolitik and foreign policy generally, and looked to the future in the spirit of conciliation:

> Without abandoning the indestructible right of our Nation to live in one state, we are attempting to pave the way towards a European peace order which is also to overcome the division of Germany. . . .
>
> Strong as our links in the Atlantic Alliance, as our relations with the United States may be, we should not seek our own future and, we believe, that of a United Western Europe within the firm framework of a North Atlantic Imperium. Such a solution would turn the demarcation line dividing Germany and Europe into a permanent frontier wall. Such a solution could also dramatically increase the danger of a major world conflict.
>
> Since the end of the Second World War, the United States has always advocated a policy of European unification. A strong, united Europe could take part of the burden off America's shoulders and could assume a greater share of the responsibility for its own security. Such an independent Europe, linked in friendship with America, could render a major service to peace in the world and could help to build a bridge between West and East.

Turning to the GDR, he said:

> The overlords in the other part of Germany have exploited the division of our nation, imposed on us by international developments, forcibly to cordon off our fellow-countrymen. . . .
>
> With a few exceptions . . . it is only old-age pensioners who are allowed to travel to the Federal Republic. Last year, they numbered approximately a million. Visitors from the Federal Republic are generally only allowed into the other part of Germany if they want to visit first or second-line relatives. In 1967 they numbered about 1.4 million. To West Berliners even this is denied. . . .
>
> There is no separate German Democratic Republic (GDR) nation. It is true

that the Germans in the other part of Germany have experienced their own difficult lot during the postwar period and developed from this a consciousness of their own which we respect. . . .

I repeat once again the offer that I made in the Government Declarations of December 13, 1966 and April 12, 1967, as well as in my two letters to Herr Stoph. The Federal Government adheres to the intention of easing the lot of the people in divided Germany. It is prepared to negotiate with the Government in East Berlin about all practical questions concerning the living together of Germans. It hereby expressly extends the list of proposed topics by adding the subject of the renunciation of the use of force. We are prepared to talk about all these topics if the other side abandons its attempt to tie up these talks with its demand for international recognition.[18]

In comparison with the formulations of the 1950s and early 1960s, this was a remarkable exercise in conciliation. Kiesinger spoke of "East Berlin," not Pankow, as the seat of "government" of the GDR, admitting that there was a government and that it was located in Berlin. Hitherto official Bonn usage spoke of "Pankow," a suburb of Greater Berlin, since the Federal Republic followed Allied legal practice in refusing to recognize the division of Berlin and the Soviet transfer of authority over the Eastern sector to the GDR, and therefore referred to Pankow where the East German leaders lived. Though he only used the phrase "GDR" in denying that there was such a thing as a GDR nation, even that went beyond previous practice. Speaking of the division of Germany as caused by "international developments" and not due solely to the machinations of the Soviet Union and the German communists was also unprecedented for a CDU chancellor. Times were indeed changing, even though the SED was not yet ready to test the new soft West German line.

Instead of continuing the communications with Bonn in 1968, however, the GDR regime presented new demands for "normalizing" relations, presumably in an effort to see how conciliatory the West German government was prepared to be. At the same time, Ulbricht resumed his harrassment of West Berlin in the spring and summer of 1968. In April the GDR forbade members of the federal government to use road and rail routes between West Germany and West Berlin. On June 11, claiming a need to respond to the amendment to the Basic Law granting the West German government special powers in the event of civil emergency, passed in the Bundestag on May 30, the SED regime introduced a requirement for passports and visas for travel to the GDR and between West Berlin and West Germany. In his response, Kiesinger was again conciliatory: "Our policy of the relaxation of

[18] Dept of State, *Documents on Germany*, 991–6.

tensions and cooperation with the East European states will be continued. Our offer of conciliation continues to include the other part of Germany."[19]

Two weeks later, on June 24, Brandt, attending the NATO Council of Ministers meeting in Reykjavik, repeated his famous description of the goal of West German foreign policy as "a controlled, peaceful co-existence." In his statement, however, Brandt took another step forward, ahead of what Kiesinger had been willing to say publicly, when he outlined the terms on which inner-German relations should be conducted. Using virtual synonyms for the word "state" to describe the GDR, and rejecting the hitherto accepted official West German formulations, such as "the Zone" or "the other part of Germany," Brandt concluded:

> The special relations of both German systems are characterized by:
>
> a   the residual rights of the Four Powers with reference to Berlin and Germany as a whole;
>
> b   the continued application of Four Power Agreements on the future of the German people. . . .
>
> c   the statement of both German parties that they respect the unity of the nation and are working toward peaceful unification.
>
> Accordingly, the aim of discussions . . . should be reciprocal declarations . . . in which both sides agree:
>
> a   to seek a solution of the national problem only by peaceful means. . . .
>
> b   not to make any attempt to alter by force the social structure in the other part of Germany respectively.[20]

Brandt's phrasing was tantamount to a distinct revaluation of the status of the GDR by a member of the Bonn government. His starting point was that the two states had an equal right to exist and should negotiate on that basis. He was presenting, as foreign minister, the position reached by the SPD at its party conference in Dortmund in June 1966, when the party decided that the four powers would never solve the German question and that Germans – which meant West Germans – should take the initiative.

The same NATO meeting issued a broad communique on arms control and East–West relations which indicated how far the West had moved, since the Berlin crisis of 1958–62, toward accepting the Soviet bloc's proposal for a general European security arrangement. Until the

[19]   Ibid., 1012.
[20]   Ibid., 1012–13.

early 1960s, the West rejected Soviet bloc suggestions for disarmament or demilitarization in Central Europe on the grounds that they were transparent covers for a unilateral weakening of Western security. The West's position was that the threat to peace in Europe came not from armaments as such, but from the political strategy of the Soviet Union. By 1968, the West was in the process of abandoning that view and accepting the notion that arms control as such might help preserve peace.

After condemning the GDR activities in restricting traffic to and from Berlin, the NATO foreign and defense ministers

> recognized that the unresolved issues which still divide the European Continent must be settled by peaceful means. . . . Mindful of the obvious and considerable interest of all European states in this goal, Ministers expressed their belief that measures in this field including balanced and mutual force reductions can contribute significantly to the lessening of tension. . . .
>
> Ministers agreed that it was desirable that a process leading to mutual force reductions should be initiated. To that end they decided to make all necessary preparations for discussions on this subject with the Soviet Union.[21]

Brandt's (and to a lesser extent the chancellor's) conciliatory approaches and statements were met by measures to further emphasize the sovereign identity of the GDR as a legitimate and independent state. In the later 1960s, the Ulbricht regime introduced measures designed to give the GDR an identity uniquely different from that of the Federal Republic. Until the mid-1960s the official communist position had been that national division was caused by the monopoly capitalists and imperialists in the West, and the GDR was, in fact, the true guardian of German unity. During 1967-8, however, the SED regime severed the last formal ties to the unified German past and accelerated its efforts to create an ideology supporting the concept of a "GDR nation." The first step in this direction was passage of a law in the GDR in February 1967 which abolished the old citizenship law of 1913 as the basis for determining German citizenship. This was an important legal issue, because one basis of the West German claim to represent all of Germany was that West Germany recognized only one form of German citizenship, as defined in the 1913 law, so that all Germans in the GDR were German citizens and could, if they escaped from the GDR, immediately enjoy all the rights of citizens who were already in the Federal Republic. The systematic denial of those rights – especially the freedoms of belief, expression, assembly, organization, and movement – by the communist regime was thus not only a violation of international

[21] Ibid., 1015-16.

human rights, but of the national rights of Germans as guaranteed by the Basic Law.

The second step was the new penal code of the GDR, introduced in January 1968, which put an end to what remained of legal unity between the two Germanies. Hitherto large parts particularly of the criminal legal code were still identical, since they antedated 1933. In early 1967, the minister of justice of the GDR, Hilde Benjamin – known in the West as "Red Hilde" – made the first public announcement that the new code was in preparation. Its preamble declared that the purpose of criminal law was to strengthen the GDR in all directions, and to promote "the systematic construction of socialist law as an instrument of state direction of society."[22] Many harsh clauses of the old German criminal code were abolished; on the other hand, the range of political crimes was broadened and penalties increased up to and including the death penalty.

An expression of the Federal Republic's principle that the behavior of the GDR regime was criminal because that regime's subjects did not enjoy the rights of all Germans was the *Zentrale Erfassungsstelle Salzgitter*, a federal office established after the building of the Berlin Wall and charged with collecting information and keeping records of acts committed by the GDR that were considered crimes under German criminal law as enforced in West Germany – for example, shooting to kill persons attempting to cross the inner-German border. The Salzgitter monitoring agency was a standing denial of the legitimacy of the GDR regime. After the inauguration of Brandt's Ostpolitik in 1969–70, the significance of the agency declined because Bonn no longer asserted that German law, and in particular the citizenship law and the Basic Law, should apply to the GDR. Still it was maintained, even though the SPD, from the mid-1980s onward, joined the GDR in demands for its abolition.

A third step toward consolidation of a new state ideology was the new constitution of the GDR, passed in April 1968. Unlike the old constitution of 1949, the new one openly defined the communist party, the SED, as the ruling force in state and society, and declared that the GDR, as a "socialist state of German nationality," was in the process of "realizing socialism" under the leadership of the working class "and its Marxist-Leninist party."[23]

Were two nations, in fact, being created in Germany by the late 1960s? The evidence was unclear. In West Germany public opinion polls and statements indicated that, by 1970, the sense of a community

---

[22] Weber, *Die DDR 1945–1986*, 68.
[23] Ibid., 69.

of national feeling had by and large disappeared. But this was the reflection of a process that had been underway for many years. In 1956, for example, a doctor from East Berlin visiting General Gerd Schmückle in West Germany had already drawn that conclusion:

Even today we have two German armies, two different school systems, two interpretations of history, two currencies. One day we shall also have two German states. Even our languages will develop in different directions. On both sides people are being declared incapacitated, are being made into foreigners towards each other. The division is being reinforced. By ourselves. But there is one chance: here as well as there lives a group of people who have more in common than the powers-that-be suspect.[24]

On the other hand, some of the more subtle studies of public opinion in the Federal Republic, such as those of the Allensbach Institute, indicated that if there was weak public interest in the national issue – as differentiated from the interest of the West German government – the reason might be that it was *so* sensitive that people preferred not to talk about it or to pretend that it did not exist. Elisabeth Noelle-Neumann, of the Allensbach Institute, concluded in her study "Who Needs a Flag?" that nations did need a flag, as a symbol of national identity and pride, and of the ability to survive. But at a conference in Marl, near Gelsenkirchen in North Rhine-Westphalia in 1963, a different view was clearly expressed to her by participants such as the writers Erich Kuby, Jens Feddersen and Ernst Glaser. They referred to a flag as "a piece of cloth," but Noelle-Neumann emphasized its value as "a symbol, a signal for an idea, comprehensible to all and publicly visible," and she considered her colleagues to be "ignorant of social psychology." But writing about it 20 years later, in 1983, she concluded that "their main concern was the fear of a new German nationalism," and that this manner of thinking was also consistent with those ". . . who fought for eliminating the playing of the national anthem at the end of every radio-broadcasting day" in Germany.[25]

The GDR regime was certainly afraid of national feeling, as its policy of *Abgrenzung* – delimitation and rejection of West German influence – established in response to the new Bonn Ostpolitik made clear. The more steps Bonn took to be conciliatory toward East Berlin, the more the regime under Ulbricht's leadership refused to join in any steps that might, however indirectly, raise the issue of unity or common nationality. This reaction disproved the thesis of Egon Bahr and Peter Bender,

[24] Schmückle, *Ohne Pauken und Trompeten,* 127.
[25] Noelle-Neumann, "Who Needs a Flag?" *Encounter* 60, no. 1 (January 1983): 72–80.

that an Ostpolitik of respect for the communist regimes would lead to their liberalization and to the gradual breakdown of the Iron Curtain.

This thesis received a further rude shock on August 21, 1968, when forces of the Soviet Union, Poland, East Germany, and Hungary invaded and occupied communist-ruled Czechoslovakia. Since early 1968 the regime of Alexander Dubcek had loosened the reins of power, giving more freedom of expression and activity to the people, and even going so far as to indicate that civil and economic rights might be expanded. The GDR regime attacked this "Prague spring" on several occasions and was eager to join with the Soviet government when it decided to put an end to the Czech experiments in August. After occupying Czechoslovakia and installing a strictly orthodox and loyal regime, Soviet leader Leonid Brezhnev propounded the "Brezhnev Doctrine" in October 1968, according to which the Soviet Union had the right and the obligation, vis-à-vis the world communist movement, to intervene whenever a regime within the "socialist commonwealth" (as defined by the Soviet Union) deviated from the Soviet political line or from the geostrategic role assigned to it by Moscow.

The invasion of August 21 and the Brezhnev Doctrine put a brief stop to Western efforts at detente and reintroduced some of the old realism. It was brief because all Western governments, nonetheless, agreed that there was no alternative to a vigorous pursuit of detente and arms control. In particular, it was also what the US, still embroiled in Vietnam, favored.

Two weeks after the US voters had elected Richard Nixon to succeed Lyndon Johnson in November, the NATO foreign and defense ministers met in Brussels to condemn the Soviet action and put it in the context of German and NATO efforts at detente:

> Applied to Germany the policies which the USSR derives from its doctrine of a so-called "socialist commonwealth" raise new obstacles to the rapprochement and ultimate unification of the two parts of Germany. Moreover, they would be contrary to the letter and spirit of the four-power agreements relating to Germany as a whole. . . .
>
> [T]he ministers confirm the support of their governments for the declared determination of the three powers to safeguard Berlin's security and to maintain freedom of access to the city.[26]

In Bonn, Brandt emphasized that efforts toward detente must continue, despite the fact that the Soviet invasion might raise doubts about the wisdom of detente with the Soviet Union.

[26] Dept of State, *Documents on Germany*, 1023.

[W]e regard our entire foreign policy as a consistent and effective peace policy. To preserve peace is also the task the Atlantic Alliance has set itself. . . .

At the Brussels Ministerial Meeting it was not a question of altering the policy of the Alliance and seeking refuge in the barren phraseology of the cold war. It was rather a question of defining how the Alliance could fulfill its task of preserving and safeguarding peace in a situation changed by the Czechoslovakia crisis. . . .

In Brussels I emphasized on behalf of the Federal Government that the Federal Republic . . . is particularly aware that a mere military response is not enough. I said that we could not afford to relax our efforts to find political solutions and that the Alliance must not relent in its search for openings for creating a system that will ensure peace and security and include our continent in terms of an all-European peace order. . . .

[S]ome voices can be heard from time to time in this country advocating the conceptions of by-gone days and accusing us of succumbing to illusions. . . . One does not need to be very far-sighted to foretell that the two world powers will open a new dialogue. This is an objective fact. Our aim . . . is to ensure that the still outstanding central European and German problems are not left out of any future East–West dialogue.[27]

Brandt's statement indicated a growing divergence between the SPD and the CDU/CSU on how far and how fast to move in Ostpolitik, and marked the transition to the third stage of the grand coalition, the stage of internal struggle leading up to the elections of late 1969.

In its relations with its Western European allies, the grand coalition moved beyond the Atlanticist-Gaullist controversy of the Erhard years. Schmidt expressed the government's position exactly when he called France "our second most important ally."[28] Kiesinger tried, without success, to persuade de Gaulle to accept Britain's second application to join the Common Market, which the Labour prime minister, Harold Wilson, communicated to the Council of Ministers in May 1967. Later that same month the heads of government of the Six met in Rome and decided to combine the three communities – the ECSC, the EEC (Common Market), and EURATOM – into a single entity, known henceforth as the European Community (EC). The Rome meeting took place in the shadow of crisis in the Middle East. Gamal Abdel Nasser, the president of Egypt, had demanded and obtained the withdrawal of the UN peacekeeping force from the demarcation line between Egypt and Israel. With the UN soldiers gone war appeared imminent. It broke out June 5, 1967, and ended six days later in an overwhelming Israeli victory. The Six Day War set in motion a number of changes in the

---

[27] Ibid., 1024–6.
[28] Cited in Hildebrand, *Von Erhard zur Grossen Koalition,* 315.

Middle Eastern Arab countries which led, in turn, to greater influence of the Organization of Petroleum Exporting Countries (OPEC) and of the Palestine Liberation Organization (PLO) and, by 1973, to a dramatic change in the political balance in the area. The Israeli victory provoked de Gaulle to embark on an extremely pro-Arab foreign policy which served to isolate him still further within Europe. In December 1967, over German objections, he vetoed, for the second time, British membership in the Common Market. In 1968 he took up proposals for a European peace system, including the neutralization of Germany, which were indistinguishable from the Karlsbad proposals of the European communist parties of April 1967.

As early as 1968, however, de Gaulle began revising his negative view of British membership. He appears to have recognized the growing strength and size of the West German economy, and that it might be useful for France to have Britain in the EC as a counterweight. The stimulus to French reconsideration came from the currency crisis of 1968, which culminated in a conference of the chairmen of the central banks of the "Group of Ten" countries, namely Belgium, Germany, France, Britain, Italy, Japan, Canada, the Netherlands, Sweden, and the US, in Bonn in November 1968. The background to the conference was the weakness of the dollar, the French franc, and the pound sterling due to balance of payments deficits, and the resulting steady pressure throughout late 1968 on West Germany to revalue the mark in order to make German exports more expensive and so reduce the German current account surplus. The US, Britain, and France, Germany's main trading partners, all had deficits on their current accounts. But Schiller and Strauss refused to revalue the mark; and Schiller especially irritated his Western colleagues by lecturing them on economic policy and export management. This was the first time that the Federal Republic had taken on its major foreign allies and refused to bow to their wishes in a matter of national interest. Schiller's perceived arrogance at the conference provoked anti-German reactions in Paris and London. It also led Kiesinger and Strauss to worry that the price of the German victory on the currency issue might be high in terms of Western resentment of a Germany that, in international economic policy at least, was becoming increasingly independent.

5

Domestic Policy in the Era of the New Left

The grand coalition faced four major problems in domestic policy in addition to the need to stabilize the economy: electoral reform, the amendment to the Basic Law granting the government emergency powers, reform of higher education, and a spreading and intense wave of demonstrations, agitation, and propaganda of the so-called New Left. The problems were related to each other as well as to the German question and foreign policy. But before they could be dealt with in earnest, the Federal Republic had to deal with the formal end of the first phase of the history of West Germany, symbolized by the death of Adenauer at the age of 91 on April 19, 1967.

Adenauer left Germany a legacy of freedom, of respect, and of hope which had been almost non-existent in 1945. His policies laid the foundations for the maturity of postwar Germany: the republic's ties to the West, the rapprochement with France, the "economic miracle" of the social market economy, and the structure of a constitutional government that was becoming one of the most stable in the world. He did not achieve reunification, but he established the basis of peace with freedom from which it might one day develop and receive the support from Germany's neighbors that would be essential if it were ever to succeed. Adenauer was, in the words of the former British prime minister, Anthony Eden, "a firm believer in patience and in the healing properties of time." His accomplishment reflected the courage of his conviction. At the base of it all rested his belief that to succeed, as he emphasized in his last public speech in 1967, "the decisive factor is love of one's neighbour and love of one's people."[1]

Until his death he continued to follow the course of German politics and did not hide his anxiety over the future security of the West German

---

[1] Rudolf Bauer, *Rheinische Post*, April 18, 1987, as reprinted in the *German Tribune*, May 3, 1987.

state and the declining will to resist Soviet encroachment and totalitarianism in Eastern Europe. He was buried with state ceremony and pomp unprecedented in the Federal Republic. Among the many present at the funeral were the former Israeli prime minister, David Ben Gurion, and the former chairman of the Jewish Claims Conference, Nahum Goldmann, who had negotiated the issue of restitution with Adenauer. The old chancellor undoubtedly would have looked askance at the unusual gesture made by the federal president, Heinrich Lübke, following the formal state ceremony in the Bundestag, who joined together the hands of his French and American counterparts, Charles de Gaulle and Lyndon Johnson. But it was, nevertheless, a symbol of unity – and Atlanticism – whose importance Adenauer had always recognized.

The funeral services were held in the cathedral of the city of Cologne, where he had been mayor from 1917 to 1933 and again in 1945. No one who witnessed the chancellor's last trip on the river Rhine thereafter would ever forget it:

After the funeral service in Cologne Cathedral, Adenauer's coffin was taken in a solemn procession to the banks of the Rhine river, passing through huge crowds of people, then placed aboard a ship of the federal navy, in order to be transported to Rhöndorf [his residence across the river]. When the ship was halfway across the river, other boats of the federal navy as well as French, Belgian, Dutch and British boats joined in the escort and, in the light of the setting sun and the evening haze of the stream, they moved slowly up the Rhine. Presumably never in its long history has this river seen a more overpowering funeral march; Europe, for which he has done so much, could not possibly have given this statesman a more magnificent escort; and a more appropriate funeral road for this man, who always thought of himself as a "Rhinelander," is unimaginable.[2]

Adenauer's own wish concerning his legacy was simple and to the point: "Sometime in the future, when people are able to look beyond the fog and the dust of this period in time, I wish that they can say about me that I did my duty."[3]

Following Adenauer's death, the parties returned to the debate on electoral reform. A majority of the CDU/CSU favored a system of majority voting for all seats in the Bundestag, and one intention of the grand coalition was to introduce this change. It would mean the end of the FDP as a Bundestag party, since the liberals could not hope to win a single constituency on their own and relied entirely on the proportional distribution of seats for their representation.

[2] Lahr, *Zeuge von Fall und Aufstieg*, 461.
[3] Adenauer, *Nachdenken über die Werte*, frontispiece.

The SPD's position was more ambiguous. Many on the center-right of the SPD favored the majority vote system; others, notably the left wing which feared that most of its members would not be elected under such a system, were against it. Wehner, the master strategist, had one aim: the SPD as the dominant party in power. Prior to formation of the grand coalition, he indicated to the CDU/CSU that he would work to get his party to support electoral reform, but he did so because he knew that such a promise would open the door to the grand coalition, and a grand coalition remained the high road to a government dominated by the SPD. The CDU/CSU thought it had the SPD's promise to help pass a reform of the electoral system by 1969 and to organize the first national elections under the new system in 1973. In his first policy declaration of December 1966 Kiesinger presented the argument for this goal: "The strongest guarantee against a possible abuse of power is the firm will of the partners of the grand coalition to set a time limit, namely the end of this legislative period, for its continuation. . . . During this period of cooperation, according to the opinion of the Federal government, a new system of electoral law should be put into place which, for future elections to the German Bundestag after 1969, will make possible clear majorities."[4] The chancellor added that he hoped to introduce a transitional electoral system for the 1969 elections, and that progress toward establishing a new system would create an institutional barrier to the continuation of the grand coalition as well as to any future need for coalitions.

Since Wehner regarded a government dominated by the SPD as the best solution for the Federal Republic and for Germany as a whole, he was willing to do whatever was tactically necessary to bring that result closer – and in 1966, what was necessary was to promise to support electoral reform:

In this respect the socialist Herbert Wehner resembled the bourgeois Konrad Adenauer and was to that extent an exceptional phenomenon. Because he pursued his concept of acquiring social democratic power with a view into the future, the demand for a new electoral system did not constitute a fundamental problem for him. Rather it was a versatile and useful means of political struggle – against the critics of the grand coalition in his own party, against the partner in government, and finally against the FDP, who, since the formation of the grand coalition, did not pose an immediate threat, and against whom the cruel garrote of electoral reform might well turn out to be an attractive sacrifice for subsequent collaboration.[5]

---

[4] Cited in Hildebrand, *Von Erhard zur Grossen Koalition,* 358.
[5] Ibid., 356.

Wehner, in other words, used electoral reform tactically to bring about the grand coalition and later to woo the FDP with the promise that he would stop electoral reform from ever coming to pass. Since the CDU/CSU had declared itself in favor of electoral reform it was unable to use the promise to drop it as a way of attracting the FDP back into a coalition. Once again, Wehner had seized the tactical high ground in the great game of power that preceded and accompanied the grand coalition.

Wehner's tactics, and the fact that the SPD was not at all as safely committed to electoral reform as Kiesinger and others were led to believe, became clear as the SPD delayed action on the matter through 1967. In December of that year Kurt Schmücker of the CDU, the budget minister, asked for resolution of the issue, warning that delay would play into the hands of those in the SPD who wanted a small coalition with the FDP: "If these discussions continue for too long into the next year, we may stumble and force the FDP and the SPD into collaboration."[6] A few days earlier a committee of experts in constitutional and electoral law appointed by Paul Lücke (CDU), the minister of the interior (responsible for administering elections), had issued a statement strongly recommending single constituency voting. Its chairman was Theodor Eschenburg, the distinguished political scientist who had played an important part in the constitutional debates of 1945-9 and in formulating the constitution of Baden-Württemberg, the southwestern state. The committee opposed a transitional election system for 1969 and recommended proceeding forthwith to single constituency voting.

Reform, therefore, depended on the SPD. Wehner recognized that the left wing of the SPD, which was rapidly growing in influence and confidence as student and intellectual radicalism swept the country, was against the majority system. He knew that the FDP was justifiably terrified of it. He also suspected, or at least feared, that the majority vote system might condemn the SPD as a whole to permanent opposition, given the electoral geography of West Germany. Though this assumption was not necessarily justified, it received strong support in a study on the subject published by the Institute for Applied Social Research in Bad Godesberg that appeared in January 1968. The report, deliberately issued at this time, claimed that the SPD would suffer a disastrous defeat if elections were held under a system of majority voting. While Wehner said little in public, the coalition partners agreed in January that the SPD would hold a special party conference in November to consider the specific issue of electoral reform.

[6] Cited ibid., 358.

In March 1968 the SPD held a party conference in Nuremberg, which had already been scheduled, to discuss the party's position on the pending legislation concerning emergency powers. The conference, however, also took up the question of majority voting on March 21, and postponed fuller discussion of the issue to a later party conference, with the implication that this would not be until after the next elections. The SPD's March 21 decision was effectively the end of the matter, and the agreement to convene a special conference in November became void. Paul Lücke resigned his cabinet post in protest. He was convinced that electoral reform was essential to the democratic process of the Federal Republic. He regarded the failure of the SPD leadership to fight for the issue at Nuremberg as a betrayal of the SPD's coalition promises, and that of Kiesinger to insist on pursuing the matter, as a betrayal by the CDU as well. After listening to his impassioned arguments, Kiesinger coolly answered that if he, Lücke, had so little faith in the democratic values of the German people that he thought the future of German democracy depended on a constitutional reform, then he had better retire from politics at once. Wilhelm Hennis, a colleague of Eschenburg's on Lücke's advisory committee and a supporter of majority elections, commented sarcastically that Kiesinger's faith in the judgement of the masses suggested that the chancellor had been reading the writings of the radical philosopher, Herbert Marcuse.[7] Lücke's successor as minister of the interior for the remainder of the grand coalition period was Ernst Benda, a lawyer who later became chief justice of the Federal Constitutional Court.

Both left and right argued that the grand coalition was part of a plot, in both the major parties, to control political life permanently and deny any outlet for heterodox and radical ideas. On the right, the National Democratic Party (NPD), founded in Hannover in November 1964, gathered a number of votes of neo-Nazis, former Nazis, and many others who were discontented with what they considered unacceptable compromises with liberals and socialists by the CDU. During the entire grand coalition the NPD was a source of concern to many politicians and public intellectuals, but also a provocation for the left who used it as an argument to defend and justify its own extremist activities. In November 1966, the NPD gained 7.9 per cent in Hesse and 7.4 per cent in Bavaria in elections which took place while the CDU/CSU and SPD were still negotiating for the grand coalition. During the coalition the NPD scored even greater successes: 8.8 per cent in Bremen in October 1967, 9.8 per cent in Baden-Württemberg in April 1968 – the last *Land* election to take place during the fifth Bundestag.

---

[7] Ibid., 364.

Observers had every reason to expect that the NPD would vault into the Bundestag in 1969 with somewhere around 7–8 per cent of the seats, perhaps causing the FPD to lose its representation. Such considerations played a part in the debate on electoral reform, as well as helping to create a climate of hysteria on the left, whose members saw an imminent threat of a neo-Nazi mass movement. While the NPD did not gain entry to the Bundestag in 1969, almost all of its voters were eventually absorbed by the Christian democrats. The CDU/CSU made a great effort to achieve this end, but this led to accusations from the left that the CDU/CSU was an authoritarian right wing party sharing the ideology of the NPD. Indeed, the campaign to absorb the NPD became a factor in the defeat of the CDU/CSU in 1969.

On the left the grand coalition conjured up images of a one-party state, in which the ideals of the SPD would be forfeited by compromise with the conservative elements in West Germany. The grand coalition was thus an important element in fueling the student movement and the broad wave of leftist intellectual criticism of the Bonn republic which began at this time. Many intellectuals at West German universities shared the left's belief that the Bonn republic would not be able to withstand a coalition and they foresaw the collapse of the democratic political system, thus leading many to question whether Bonn would not indeed become Weimar. Their role grew during the later 1960s because the number of students as well as universities was rapidly increasing.

Both electoral reform and the emergency powers issue – the latter more than the former – were grist for the mill of the New Left, who saw in them attempts by the established interests to suppress new thinking and new forms of political action. The New Left itself was a disparate combination of the leaders of published opinion, journalists, intellectuals, and academics, and its shock troops were the growing numbers of students attending institutes of higher education. Because it was composed largely of intellectuals, students, journalists, and other public figures with close ties to the institutions of higher education, the New Left was intimately involved with the politics of educational reform.

The universities had been, until the *Spiegel* affair, for the most part, quiet backwaters. Their administrative structure was essentially unchanged since the nineteenth century, with all power in the hands of the tenured professors, the *Ordinarien*. The *Spiegel* affair, however, began to crystallize student opinion against this authoritarian framework, a development much hastened by the swelling numbers of students. Initially the centers of this activity were the political and social science departments and related institutes, at the universities of Berlin and Marburg. By 1966, alliances had been formed between leftist political organizations of students and progressive and radical faculty, and they focused their attention on university reform and on West Germany's policy toward the GDR, the countries of Central Europe, and the Soviet Union. They were particularly critical of US foreign policy, and this criticism was fueled by the developing conflict in Vietnam.

The activist student groups and left-liberal professors justified their demands for greater influence and more resources by pointing to the relatively low level of scientific research and educational spending in Germany compared to other Western countries. Thus the political demands of the reformers for a new ideology of education merged with a feeling shared by many across the political spectrum, that science and university research were essential factors of production in a modern society and that society in general should therefore have greater control over the substance of academic life. These were two distinct issues, however: one group, the revolutionaries, wanted to use higher education as a lever to change society in a radical way; the other, educational analysts and politicians who were genuinely concerned with German economic and scientific capacities, wanted to restructure higher education to make Germany more productive within the framework of a democratic capitalist society.

The main organization to carry the spark of the revolution was the *Sozialistischer Deutscher Studentenbund* (SDS), expelled from the SPD in 1961, and by 1966 safely in the hands of the authoritarian left. In 1967–8 the SDS made its great effort to bring revolution to the streets of West Germany; after it failed to do so, it died a slow death. Its leaders dissolved it in 1970 and joined either the established SPD or the more radical and ruthless communist, Maoist, Trotskyite or other organizations.

The student and academic New Left, the influence of the SDS, and the creation of the extraparliamentary opposition *(Ausserparlamentarische Opposition,* APO) by Rudi Dutschke, cannot be clearly understood without reference to the process of social and institutional reform, the growth of the welfare state, and the value changes of the mid-1960s. The concentration on social and economic policy, as well as the fact that the universities were under the exclusive jurisdiction of the *Länder,* not the federal government, meant that the character and form of higher education had proceeded at a different pace from the political development of West Gemany. Thus, by the mid-1960s, there were genuine grounds for complaint regarding university conditions, administrative policies, and relationships between professors and students, which were atypical of West German society as a whole.

In 1913, out of a population of 67 million, 79,557 were students; in

1965 there were 384,400 students in a population of 60 million, and by 1970 the number had risen to 510,500. It was clearly necessary to undertake the institutional and organizational transformation of higher education from an elite pursuit to an essential complement of West German society. Yet the universities had survived the intervening 50 years with probably less change than any other public institution; indeed one observer called them "highly feudal institutions."[8]

The rise of the New Left in the universities, therefore, took place against a background of rapidly expanding student bodies and faculties and in the context of an excited and sustained debate on educational reform in general. Following Georg Picht's warnings in 1963-4 of an imminent "German education catastrophe," the debate began quietly with the establishment in 1965 of a committee of experts called the *Bildungsrat* or Educational Council. Although education and research remained, according to the Basic Law, prerogatives of the *Länder,* progressive politicians in all parties increasingly called for greater centralization and coordination of policy to serve the perceived needs of a changing society as the 1960s progressed. On April 10, 1968, the standing conference of *Land* ministers of culture (who, individually, were responsible for educational policy) released a document on the structural reorganization of the universities, which became the formal signal for reform.

April 1968 was, for many Germans in positions of responsibility, indeed "the cruelest month." The SPD had just decided that it would not support electoral reform, thus issuing a challenge to the CDU/CSU and looking ahead to the elections due in late 1969. The ministers of culture of the *Länder* had responded to the call for university reform. The NPD was going from victory to victory in *Land* elections. And most dramatically, in April and May the Bundestag was due to review and pass the amendments to the Basic Law giving the government its emergency powers and thus completing the transition to full sovereignty that began in 1949. The emergency powers debate crystallized the broad opposition of the New Left and led to the largest and most violent demonstrations since the last days of the Weimar Republic.

When the occupation powers approved the Basic Law, they retained emergency powers, that is, the right to decide what action to take in case of war, civil war, or the imminent threat of either. The purpose of the proposed change in emergency authority was to provide the German government with the ability, in case of crisis, to exceed its regular authority in securing order and the survival of the state. Obviously,

---

[8] Roellecke, "Entwicklungslinien deutscher Universitätsgeschichte." *Aus Politik und Zeitgeschichte,* B 3-4/84, (January 21, 1984). See part II, chapter 9.

given the history of Nazi Germany, there were many, both in Germany and abroad, who were concerned how the West German republic would deal with this legislation. Not only the New Left and the leaders of published opinion, but most of the unions and large parts of the SPD were opposed to emergency powers of any kind. Nevertheless, the moderate majority of the SPD agreed that such powers were necessary, and one of the reasons they agreed to enter a grand coalition was to help provide a government with a majority large enough to pass the necessary amendment to the Basic Law.

On March 10, 1967, the cabinet had approved the draft of the "17th law to amend the Basic Law" which changed or added 18 clauses to the Basic Law granting the government the power, in case of war or civil war, to pass laws, draft citizens, employ police, override *Land* authority, and take other measures as it might deem necessary. The CDU/CSU believed a sitting government should have the right to determine when to invoke the emergency powers without necessarily consulting the Bundestag, and sought to include serious civil disturbance as a justification. The SPD successfully resisted these demands, so that the amendments, as finally passed, provided that only the Bundestag or an emergency parliament could declare a state of emergency, which was moreover restricted to the event of actual foreign invasion. These SPD stipulations made it virtually impossible for any future government to use civil unrest as a pretext for invoking emergency powers. The Bundestag passed the resulting law on May 30, 1968, with 384 votes against 100, the latter consisting of the votes of the FDP, of the left wing of the SPD, and one CSU member. The German government's emergency powers were thus rather modest by international standards, a fact which was ignored by the rabid opposition of the student left to the proposed amendments.

In December 1966 the radical student leader Rudi Dutschke had responded to the grand coalition by calling on progressive students to form the APO, the extraparliamentary opposition, without a formal structure and closely allied to the SDS. Dutschke's call reflected his hostility to "the existing party structures, pluralistic democracy and the institution of parliament" as incapable of providing the kind of opposition the APO endorsed.[9] Dutschke's own description of the APO, however, best speaks for itself:

When we say: extraparliamentary, we mean that we aim for a system of direct democracy – indeed, democratic councils permitting people to vote directly for their current representatives or to vote them out of office, should they [the

---

[9] Chaussy, "Jugend," in *Die BRD*, ed. Benz, 2: 54.

people] consider it necessary on the basis of critical awareness in opposition to every form of control.[10]

The logical consequence was not the formation of a political party or organization in the conventional sense, but the achievement of the transformation of society and, therefore, power as a consequence of continual agitation. Dutschke and the self-proclaimed members of the APO presented, as the model for political engagement and behavior, the phrase "the long march through institutions," which over the long term produced considerable support for the left wing of the SPD in the 1970s and 1980s.

The Berlin APO published a newspaper, the *Berliner Extra Dienst*, from 1967 to 1970, as well as numerous pamphlets and monographs, including one published in 1967 entitled *The Transformation of Democracy*, written by Johannes Agnoli, a teaching assistant at the Otto-Suhr Institute (the department of political science at the Free University of Berlin, named after the second postwar mayor of West Berlin) and Peter Brückner. The book was abstruse, confused, basically a third-rate attempt at political philosophy, and almost incomprehensible. It appealed, however, as did so much of the literature published in the late 1960s, to the sense of romantic revolution, held by the readers who were almost exclusively students and who, in West Berlin, purchased much of this material at tables set up in front of the university's student union.

A more important source of New Left ideology was a paperback published in 1968 by Rowohlt near Hamburg, a commercial publishing house with a long-standing sympathy for the left. Its authors were Dutschke and three other leaders of the APO, Uwe Bergmann, Wolfgang Lefevre, and Bernd Rabehl. The book was called *Die Rebellion der Studenten oder die neue Opposition* (Student rebellion or the new opposition). In it, Dutschke and his comrades presented the whole gamut of arguments of the New Left concerning the universities, West German society, and modern democracy as a whole. The universities, they contended, were the place where true radical freedom might come about, following suppression of the established forms of governance and condemnation of all professors unwilling to join the revolution. Once the APO was in secure control of the campuses, it would have a strong base from which to disrupt and eventually take over the vital functions of the state, thus exploiting the democratic system.

Dutschke and those associated with him justified their program of revolution by denouncing the West German democratic state as an oppressive and exploitative system, permeated with old and new Nazis

[10] Cited ibid.

and their numerous sympathizers. Events of 1966–8, they argued, showed that the forces of reaction and oppression in Germany were about to put an end to what little democracy in fact existed. This apocalyptic view that fascism was about to return explains why Dutschke and his comrades were so determined on immediate and direct action, and to some extent also explains why some of his followers turned to terrorism when their political projects failed.

Dutschke advocated what represented a new version of Marxism that rejected the state socialism of the East as an incorrect or degenerate form of Marxism. He and his supporters, therefore, flatly denied that their revolutionary activities against the democratic West German state in any way served the interests of the Soviet Union or the GDR. It is ironic that some of the most radical leftists, some of whom later became terrorists in the 1970s, were refugees from the communist part of Germany.

While German students had a legitimate concern with the rigidity of the German university system which had changed little in the twentieth century, this positive interest was shared primarily by those students who were the followers and not the self-proclaimed leaders of the APO. The leaders themselves pursued a very different agenda, and used dissatisfaction with the structure of the university as the means to achieve other goals. Recognizing quite correctly that the university was the easiest institution to exploit and misuse for their own purposes, the leaders employed methods that smacked of Hitler's Germany, methods which were repressive, violent, and vicious; for example, wives of university professors were threatened by anonymous telephone callers, their children were harrassed, professors themselves were shoved and kicked, and their seminars disrupted so that it was impossible to teach – all in the name of democratizing society.

Initially the students used the condemnation of fascism to justify their behavior, as they smeared classroom walls with slogans condemning "the browns" (a reference to the brown uniforms of Nazis) and authoritarianism. They recognized that no one in good conscience could defend Nazis, and that this misuse of language would allow them to demonstrate, violate laws, and shut down classes. They expected little resistance on behalf of the professoriate and, indeed, found little, for most professors were ill-equipped, either physically or psychologically, to deal with students storming into their classrooms.

Protest demonstrations against internal university conditions began in 1966–7, but soon turned to address political, social and economic issues. The first explosive confrontation occurred on June 2, 1967, during the visit to West Berlin by the Shah of Iran. Demonstrators, both pro and anti Shah, gathered in front of the Berlin opera house, where the

Shah was attending a performance of *The Magic Flute* in his honor. The subsequent riot and confrontations between demonstrators and the West Berlin police resulted in the accidental and fatal shooting of a student, Benno Ohnesorg, by a policeman in an apartment building courtyard. Following a funeral march for Ohnesorg on June 8, during which hundreds of students from Berlin travelled unimpeded through the GDR to Hannover, more than 4,000 students gathered to discuss "University and Democracy," and were urged by Dutschke to mount coordinated "political actions" in the coming weeks and months throughout the entire Federal Republic. The *Frankfurter Allgemeine Zeitung* concluded that "the Ohnesorg case . . . was the spark which has ignited the passion for engagement. . . . The spark will spread from Berlin."[11]

The crisis provoked by the Ohnesorg shooting lasted through Easter of 1968 and led to frequent interruptions of seminars and lectures at universities throughout West Germany. The APO and the SDS were thus given life and grew, clearly fueled also by widespread fear of the emergency laws – the *Notstandsgesetze*, which the left referred to jeeringly as the "Enabling Acts" passed in the Third Reich – and rejection by students and their sympathizers of the apparent power monolith of the grand coalition. In April 1968, while preparing for nationwide demonstrations against the emergency laws, Dutschke was seriously wounded in Berlin by a right-wing assassin, a 23–year-old house painter, Josef Bachmann. (Dutschke never really recovered, and his death in December 1979 was attributable to the effects of the wound.) This attempted assassination led to the biggest demonstrations and clashes between demonstrators and police in many cities during the Easter week that Germany had witnessed since 1932, and resulted in two deaths in Munich. A particular target of the vandals was the "Springer Press," since many believed that Bachmann had been provoked into shooting Dutschke by reading the sometimes inflammatory and right-wing *Bild Zeitung* published by Axel Springer.

There was a great deal of sincerity, as well as cynical manipulation, in the student movement. Many participants believed with absolute conviction that they were struggling for "the abolition of the domination of man by man." Their mental world was both utopian and paranoid, a mixture entirely characteristic of radical intellectual movements throughout modern European history. They saw the possibilities of human development in a truly liberated society as infinite and thus shared what Thomas Sowell has called the "unconstrained" vision of man and of human potential. On the other hand, they believed that the

[11] Deuerlein, *Deutschland 1963–1970,* 106.

state and society in which they actually lived, namely the Federal Republic, was dominated by a sinister conspiracy of capitalists, Americans, and neo-Nazis. In other words, their optimistic view of human nature and their faith in human goodness extended only to the unreal future, and not at all to the real present. After the attack on Dutschke, when the Bundestag was debating the emergency laws, thousands of students in Berlin and West Germany "took to the streets ... in turbulent and violent demonstrations, determined to make a final statement of their will to resist before they might be imprisoned in the concentration camps of the authoritarian emergency state before the year was over."[12] This exaggerated fear that the Bonn government was on the verge of shedding its democratic facade was absolutely real and had great force in the minds not only of students, but of a sizable number of left-wing politicians and journalists.

I remember exactly, when I began to study, that the SDS was rampant with fantasies of fear. Our man [Strauss] was intent on making himself into the dictator of West Germany, possibly even with the help of the Bundeswehr!

Not least because of that, we had to fight desperately hard against passage of the emergency laws: he wanted to have a legal basis for his seizure of power, we were dealing with his "Enabling Acts" [*Ermächtigungsgesetze*] and nothing less! And now, exactly as was true then [in 1933], most people had no idea, or closed their eyes willingly to the catastrophe.[13]

On April 30, 1968, the Bundestag officially debated the condition of the country, a euphemism for a discussion taking place in the wake of the riots, demonstrations, and widespread disruption of normal university life, and interminable student meetings in smoke-filled auditoriums characterized by harangues as well as by physical searches by students of those people attending who seemed "suspicious." The minister of the interior, Benda, reported that the five Easter holidays had seen demonstrations in 27 cities, with the arrest of 827 people.[14]

It was a sad but typical symptom of the paradoxical and rapidly changing political and ideological atmosphere of the grand coalition era that Heinemann, the minister of justice, gave a speech full of "forward-looking tolerance" on Easter Sunday, in response to the demonstrations, in which he seemed to be condemning those citizens who wanted law and order and excusing the demonstrators:

[12] Nolte, *Deutschland und der Kalte Krieg*, 508.
[13] Rutschky, "Neues aus der Strauss-Forschung." *Merkur* 41 (January 1987): 78.
[14] Deuerlein, *Deutschland 1963–1970*, 107.

Anyone who points a finger and puts general blame on presumed instigators or manipulators ought to consider also that the hand with the index finger outstretched also includes three fingers that point back at himself. By this I mean that all of us have to ask ourselves what we, in the past, may have done to contribute to a situation where anti-communism can reach the point of leading to attempted murder, and where demonstrators can lose themselves in violent destruction and arson.[15]

The New Left and the radical activists were not communists or even friendly to communism in any traditional sense, although the reconstituted communist party later tried, with some success, to infiltrate and control New Left groups and organizations. The Soviet Union had long insisted that West Germany, if it wished for better relations, should prove its commitment to peace by lifting the 1956 prohibition on the communist party. On July 4, 1968, a former deputy of the KPD, Grethe Thiele, met with Heinemann who was in favor of legalizing the party. One problem was that since the prohibition, in accordance with the Basic Law, stemmed from a verdict of the Constitutional Court and not from an act of the Bundestag, which had no power to forbid or permit political organizations, the government had no power to overrule the Court. The conclusion of the discussion was that the party would reconstitute itself under a slightly different name – *Deutsche Kommunistische Partei* (DKP) instead of *Kommunistische Partei Deutschlands* (KPD). The reconstitution took place on October 27, 1968, and the DKP held its first conference in Essen in April 1969.

Chancellor Kiesinger did not consider the DKP a subversive threat, and was not impressed by those who wanted to petition the Court for a new prohibition against the right-wing NPD as well. "The real danger comes from the extreme left," he told the Bundestag in January 1969. "All of the big hullaballoo of struggle between the CDU and the SPD, or between Adenauer and Schumacher and so forth should not distract us from seeing that we are on one side and that on the other there is what now calls itself the APO. . . . Communism is not the danger! . . . The real enemies of our contemporary society and order are not so much communists or their agents, the real danger arises from the depths of a people that has to overcome a difficult history: nihilism and anarchism."[16]

The Easter demonstrations of 1968 were the high point of this New Left anarchism, but by no means the end of the movement. APO adherents continued to attack the SPD for capitulating to capitalist interests, and the CDU/CSU for allegedly not having settled accounts

[15] Cited in Hildebrand, *Von Erhard zur Grossen Koalition,* 381.
[16] Cited ibid., 373–4.

with the Nazi past. This latter accusation received national and international attention, because Kiesinger had been a member of the Nazi party and had been involved in radio propaganda for the regime. Heinrich Böll called Kiesinger an "insult" to the German people, and Karl Jaspers likewise referred to his election as a *Beleidigung* (insult). The attacks on Kiesinger culminated in a scene in which Beate Klarsfeld, a German-born woman living in Paris, boxed the chancellor's ear in Berlin at a CDU meeting in November 1968. She had gained entrance to the meeting by pretending to be a newspaper reporter:

> The huge hall was full. . . . Chancellor Kiesinger sat in the center, flanked by the former chancellor, Ludwig Erhard, Bruno Heck, the secretary general of the party, and Defense Minister Gerhard Schröder. Kiesinger was writing; he appeared to be putting the finishing touches on the speech he would deliver in about an hour. . . .
> I slipped behind the dignitaries. As I got behind Kiesinger he sensed my presence and half turned around. My nerves tensed agonizingly. I had won. Shouting "Nazi! Nazi!" at the top of my lungs, I slapped him. I never even saw the expression on his face.[17]

"The Slap," as it came to be known, generated enormous publicity. Klarsfeld's purpose was to focus attention on her claim that "Kiesinger and his colleagues are turning Germany into a revengeful expansionist nation that ignores the consequences of world war and demands atomic weapons. So long as Kiesinger and his accomplices remain in power, all the people who suffered under Nazism, especially those in the East, will have good reason to be wary of the Germany governed from Bonn."[18] Klarsfeld was given a suspended sentence of one year that same day, and was defended in court by Horst Mahler, an attorney who acted as defense counsel for a number of left-wing groups in Berlin during the late 1960s and early 1970s, together with such others as Otto Schily and Hans Christian Stroebele. Thirty-six hours after "the Slap" Klarsfeld was again in Paris. To her apartment *Interflora* delivered a bunch of red roses with a card that read: "Thanks – Heinrich Böll."[19]

The criticism by Böll, Grass, and Jaspers once again exemplified the attitude of those who felt they were not responsible for German history during the Third Reich. They believed that they were morally obligated to declare this loudly and clearly, and to distance themselves from all those political forces which did not share what they perceived to be their picture of a bad Germany and a good Germany. They took for

[17] Klarsfeld, *Wherever They May Be*, 55–6.
[18] Ibid., 50–1.
[19] Ibid., 63.

themselves the sole right to level praise and criticism because they alone claimed the purity of motive and a clean conscience obtained by having left Hitler's Germany. In the case of Böll and Grass they had not gone into self-imposed exile. Grass was only a boy during the war and Böll had served in the army, but he was one of those for whom 1945 was a liberation and not a defeat. The problem was put by Böll indirectly in 1985, when he was quoted in *Die Zeit* as saying that when he returned to destroyed Cologne in 1945 he could not imagine that there would ever again be a Germany. There was indeed a Germany, but not one in which his ideas prevailed.

The leaders of the radical left of the later 1960s despised the political, economic, and social liberties enjoyed by West Germans. To them, democracy and economic growth were not privileges which the Germans since 1945 had won for themselves by dint of hard work, but rather a form of camouflage of oppression. In the radical world-view, oppression was total and ubiquitous. The prosperity of postwar Germany was a direct result of oppression and exploitation of the workers both in Germany and abroad. Moreover, the radical argument continued, the Germans were oppressing themselves by wanting material goods like cars, appliances, paid vacations, and decent food, and by demanding an ever-rising material standard of living. The radicals saw the wish for prosperity not as a natural human impulse but as an evil perversion which found expression in "consumption terror" – their phrase for the alleged psychological pressure to buy and to consume which Germans, as well as all other inhabitants of the West, faced every day on the streets and in the shops of their affluent societies.

The German radicals related the notion of consumption terror to another, more general condemnation of Western democracy. This was the concept of "structural violence." It was coined by the Norwegian political scientist and "peace researcher" Johan Galtung, who enjoyed a considerable following among West German political scientists from the late 1960s onward. Galtung argued that modern industrial societies, and especially the United States, by their very nature exercised violence against the rest of the world. Some of this violence took the form of open aggression. Like most radicals, Galtung regarded the Vietnam War as the prime modern example of Western aggression against the Third World. But the most insidious form of violence engendered by modern Western democratic capitalism, Galtung argued, was "structural" rather than overt. Structural violence, according to Galtung, was anything that kept a human being from exercising his full mental and physical potential. Any perceived hurt or injury, any discrimination, whether felt or real, was evidence of "structural violence" and hence of injustice. It was typical not only of Galtung and his followers, but of the entire radical tradition of the 1960s, that they conceived of life as an incessant series of demands for material and mental pleasure. If others did not or could not meet these demands, this was evidence of fundamental injustice.

A German student of Galtung's, Dieter Senghaas, became one of the leading spokesmen for the radical view of international politics. As a "peace researcher," he claimed to have the explanation for war and conflict, but in fact his works consisted largely of direct and indirect denunciations of Western democracies and especially of the United States. His works found an eager audience among leftist academics both in Germany and the US, who used the notion of structural violence to argue that the democratic West was engaged in systematically exploiting the Third World, and that the only cure for this disease was for Western nations to disarm and embrace socialism. Senghaas, for his part, conducted a very successful "march through the institutions" (the radical prescription for the long-term takeover of society); by the 1980s he was a respected and successful director of one of several important government-sponsored peace research institutes and in command of a widespread network of influence both in scholarship and in the SPD.

Those who believed that Western society was permeated by structural violence clearly were unable to admit that prosperity and democracy in Germany were the fruit of much serious effort and would survive only thanks to continued effort. They were not amazed and happy at what their parents had accomplished, but petulant and impatient because Paradise did not exist now. Their hedonism found a powerful prophet in another and even more influential thinker, Herbert Marcuse. Marcuse (1898–1979) belonged to the Frankfurt School of German social thought. Beginning in the 1920s, this group of mainly Jewish scholars had sought to combine the political and social theories of Karl Marx with the psychology of Sigmund Freud to produce a general inter-pretation of the ills of modern society and culture. Like the other members of the School, Marcuse left Germany when the Nazis took power and emigrated to the US. Unlike the other members, however, he did not return to Germany soon after the war but continued to reside in the US, where he taught a generation of American radicals. In 1964, he published his most important work, *One-Dimensional Man*, in which he denounced the citizens of modern democracies as programmed by their environment, oppressed and exploited by the capitalist ruling classes, and unable to live a life of true freedom according to the doctrines of Marx and Freud.

One-Dimensional Man found easy resonance among those young West Germans who were discontented with what they saw as the materialism and short-sighted conservatism of their peers and elders. Marcuse gave them a justification for their own hedonism and demands for instant gratification. Together with the idea of structural violence, the Marcusean idea of freedom as gratification swept German university campuses in 1966–70.

In adopting and propagating the idea of structural violence and "democratization," one part of the New Left indirectly demonstrated its own true vision of society, which was an opportunistic and hedonistic *Lustgesellschaft* (pleasure-oriented society), diametrically opposed to the *Leistungsgesellschaft* (achievement-oriented society), that characterized the real world. This image was, however, not universal. There was also a New Left which was strictly political and which concentrated on the political subversion of what its members regarded as an oppresive state. The pleasure-seeking attitude was illustrated by the "Commune I" founded in Berlin in 1967, one of whose members, Dieter Kunzelmann, expressed the philosophy well: "The Vietnam War is not what interests me, but difficulties with my orgasm do."[20]

The era of the grand coalition was not an era only of demonstrations, high left-wing seriousness, and worry about "German fascism." Another name for the period was "the sex wave," succeeding the earlier "waves," the "eating wave" of the early to mid-1950s and the "travel wave" of the late 1950s and early 1960s. Klaus Rainer Röhl, the husband of Ulrike Meinhof, the former anti-nuclear activist and later terrorist, wrote a paean to the new age in his magazine, *Konkret*, which was read not only by the radical left but by numerous university and high school students across the land:

In a society overfed by butter-cakes and fried chickens, Germany's high school students, undernourished in regard to love, are rehearsing revolution. But the girls and boys who have joined forces to do battle against the prudery of the school system and society's double standards, in the process might possibly discover other wrongs and begin to reflect on questions other than those concerning their love life. That sex and politics, Vietnam protests and contraceptive pills, love and political struggle – against the emergency laws for example – might not be mutually exclusive at all, but rather fit together very well ("make love not war"), is something that has been rumored throughout Germany for some years now. New, entirely new forms of political resistance are coming into being. The left, which has been powerless and unimaginative for far too long, really needs some fresh blood. The dusty style of the Easter marches imported from England and reminiscent of the Salvation Army or of the Youth Movement [of the 1910s] corresponds rather to the taste of Stalinist youth functionaries and Christian boy scouts than to that of the new young masses interested in rock'n'roll and sex. Whether we are giving information about the Vietnam War or about the Pill, whether we are using journals, the

[20] Langguth, *Protestbewegung*, 22–3.

SDS, or the Union of Humanists, the key word is enlightenment. And we are not surprised to find the opponents of the student enlightenment campaign in the ranks of the darkest counter-enlightenment.[21]

The single-minded focus on self-indulgence, and the insistence that anything unpleasant was an irrational and intolerable imposition, contributed powerfully to confuse the understanding of the real and genuine threats to West German liberty and security in the public mind. Thus the New Left of the late 1960s and the early 1970s was both the direct and indirect forerunner of the neutralists and the pacifists of the 1980s:

Today's peace movement, the entry of the Green party into the German Bundestag, the appearance of Alternatives, the battle over squatters' rights to occupy housing – all of these forms of today's protest movements – are often met with helplessness and lack of understanding. Without the primarily student-run protest movements around 1968, they would be unthinkable. The new "social movements" of the present are in the tradition of the 1968 protest movements. . . . No event, however, has so intensely influenced the domestic political atmosphere in the Federal Republic, in the medium, and in the long term, as the student revolts of that time – a phenomenon of the entire Western world.[22]

In that same year, 1968, Berlin and Baden-Württemberg led the way in passing laws that completely altered the inherited structure of the universities. Instead of the *Ordinarienuniversität*, where all decisions were made by tenured professors, there arose the *Gruppenuniversität* where decisions were made according to a system of "tri-parity" by the professors, the junior faculty and staff, and the students, each group occupying one-third of the positions in all organs of university government. Since the junior faculty – the *Assistenten* – were often as radical and politicized as the students, especially in the humanities and social sciences, this reform represented an open door to leftist control of institutes and entire faculties at many universities. Respected standards of competence and achievement were abandoned, with negative effects that were still making themselves felt in the mid-1980s.

In Berlin, the law was strongly influenced by the radical student movement and the effects of the attempted Dutschke assassination, but in Baden-Württemberg it was approved by the CDU as well as the SPD; it was not, however, applied at all German universities. In 1968 there were still many in the CDU who agreed with the general principle that a

---

[21] Cited in Hildebrand, *Von Erhard zur Grossen Koalition*, 377–8.
[22] Langguth, *Protestbewegung*, 11.

thorough reform of higher education was overdue and desirable. That position, however, was soon to change, and the following years saw acrimonious struggles for control of educational policy, in which the SPD-ruled *Länder* (and the Bonn government) fought to impose guidelines that encouraged "emancipation," whereas the Union parties sought to impose guidelines guaranteeing functional competence and objective standards. Support for such standards, in turn, was denigrated by the New Left as an example of bourgeois oppression.

It would be unfair to say, however, that there was a clear line drawn between the SPD and the CDU concerning their attitudes towards discipline and authority at the German university. The German universities were subject to the governments of the *Länder* in which they were located, and, therefore, to the political parties governing. But student unrest, demonstrations, and violence were belittled or condoned by many political figures, by much of the West German press, with some exceptions including the newspapers published by Axel Springer (*Die Welt* and the boulevard paper, *Bild Zeitung,* among others), as well as by much of the German professoriate. German working men and women, however, as well as business professionals, did not condone indiscriminate violation of the law, destruction or demonstrations; but it was not they who were responsible for providing students with constructive role models which they could emulate. The professors, however, were so charged, particularly in the schools of humanities throughout West Germany, and few carried out their responsibility well or with conviction.

The main vehicle by which New Left ideology entered the SPD was educational policy. The way to change society in the future, however, was not to introduce Marxist schemes for state control of production, but to change individual and mass consciousness. The way to do this was via control of educational policy, and in particular of the curricula of the schools and universities. Since these were under *Land* control, the success of radical educational reform was directly proportional to the degree of SPD control in any given *Land.* But the effects did not become dramatically clear until after 1969 when the SPD, at both the *Land* and the federal levels, exerted increasing influence on educational policy. This resulted not only in the restructuring of the secondary school system in a more "democratic" manner, but also produced new textbooks which glossed over or distorted various aspects of twentieth-century German history, and also contained unambiguous anti-American sentiments and views.

Helmut Schmidt summed up the feelings of many moderate social democrats in a letter he sent to all SPD parliamentary representatives in January 1969, commenting on what was increasingly recognized by many as the "new totalitarian challenge:"

I believe there is no way to ignore the fact that the demolition of university presidents' offices, or of department stores or labor union buildings or [political] party offices – no matter how ideologically legitimized this may be – is in no way different from the behavior of the SA troops of 30 or 35 years ago.[23]

Concurrent with the breakdown of academic standards was the movement of the extraparliamentary opposition toward open endorsement of terrorism as a "necessary" countermeasure to the "consumer terror" allegedly incorporated in West German society. As early as March 1967, following a winter of hectic demonstrations and mass rallies at the Free University of Berlin, Rudi Dutschke called for extraparliamentary opposition, not merely to the grand coalition, but to bourgeois society in general. The attempted murder of Dutschke in April 1968 led to a split in the student movement, with a small, intense faction moving toward terrorist measures. Leading figures in this shift, all in their late twenties and thirties, were Andreas Baader, Gudrun Ensslin, and Ulrike Meinhof, who, with their followers, committed murder and acts of violence until they were finally arrested and, in prison, chose, one by one in 1976 and 1977, the violent end which they had for so long desired to impose on others.[24]

They graduated from members of the student movement to a full-fledged terrorist gang, bent not on robbery for their own purse, as the famous Bonnie and Clyde of the 1930s, but on destruction for the sake of sowing terror in the hearts and minds of West Germany's population. To fund this enterprise they committed theft and armed robbery. Like many other members of the student movement of the 1960s, they came from middle- or upper middle-class families, grew up in a society of increasing prosperity, enjoyed its benefits but shirked its responsibilities, and indulged and cultivated their resentment, for whatever reason, by keeping company with others of the protest movement.

Ulrike Meinhof, born in 1934, the year after Hitler came to power, was the daughter of an art historian and later museum director in Jena, today East Germany. Her mother was a junior lecturer at the University of Jena. Meinhof studied education, German literature and philosophy at the Universities of Marburg and Münster and became involved in the late 1950s with the German Campaign against Nuclear Death. As a result of her participation in this movement she began to write for the student newspaper *Konkret*. Eventually she married its publisher, Klaus Rainer Röhl, with whom she had twin daughters, and served as editor-in-chief and columnist from 1960 to 1964. In the late 1960s she became

[23] Cited in Hildebrand, *Von Erhard zur Grossen Koalition*, 380.
[24] See J. Becker, *Hitler's Children*.

involved with Andreas Baader, Gudrun Ensslin and others, and participated in bank robberies and bombings. Arrested and sentenced to eight years in jail, she committed suicide in prison in May 1976 by hanging herself.

Andreas Baader, born in 1944, was just five years old when the Federal Republic was founded. His father, a historian, was killed on the Russian front during the war, and the handsome Baader grew up as the son of an adoring mother, who worked hard to keep him supplied with all he desired. Baader went to Berlin at the age of 20, where he was exempt from military service, to study art and work as a journalist. He lived with Elly Michel, an artist, and they had a daughter, Suse, born in 1965. Later he met and married Gudrun Ensslin, who introduced him to her student friends in the SDS in Frankfurt and Berlin. In 1968 he was convicted of arson, served a partial sentence and fled the country while on parole. When he returned to Germany and was imprisoned again, he was freed in an armed raid by Ulrike Meinhof and others in 1970. Caught again in 1972, he was tried together with Meinhof and Ensslin, and was sentenced to life imprisonment; he committed suicide by shooting himself in 1977.

Gudrun Ensslin, born in 1940, was the daughter of a Lutheran pastor and the fourth of seven children. She studied philosophy, and English and German language and literature, at the University of Tübingen with the aim of becoming a school teacher. At Tübingen she met Bernward Vesper, with whom she moved to Berlin, to study German and English at the Free University. In 1967 she gave birth to a son, Felix Robert, about the time Benno Ohnesorg was shot. It was at this point that she emotionally proclaimed: "They'll kill us all – you know what kind of pigs we are up against – that is the generation of Auschwitz we've got against us – you can't argue with the people who made Auschwitz. They have weapons and we don't. We must arm ourselves."[25] That same year she met Baader, they fell in love, left their respective partners and children behind, and went to Frankfurt in 1968.

Ensslin, who became the actual leader of the Red Army Faction (RAF) – as the group became known – was arrested for arson in 1968, together with Baader. She served part of her sentence and fled the country while on parole. Returning to Germany in early 1970, she was rearrested in 1972 and tried with Baader, Meinhof, and Jan-Carl Raspe (born in 1944) for murder, bank robbery and related criminal activities. She also committed suicide (by hanging) in 1977.

The activities of these four, as well as their friends, were not simply pranks or political demonstrations. They were deliberate acts of

[25] Ibid., 72.

violence and terror. In April 1968 Ensslin and Baader set fire to two apartment stores in Frankfurt. Ensslin's analysis of the meaning and purpose of arson, together with instructions for building bombs, was found in her notebook: "A burning department store with burning people gives us, for the first time, the exciting Vietnam feeling that we have had to miss in Berlin thus far."[26] This sentence was not composed by Ensslin, but was lifted from a leaflet distributed in Berlin by Fritz Teufel and Rainer Langhans (members of Commune I) several days after an arson fire in a department store in Brussels in May 1967, which killed 251 people. But it illustrated the perverted conclusions of a young woman, in her late twenties. And the subsequent trial illustrated the well-intentioned efforts of their elders to help Ensslin, Baader and their two accomplices who had been convicted of arson. Ensslin's father, with the assistance of his friend and minister of justice, Heinemann, succeeded in providing this group with a permanent address at a social welfare home, necessary for their bail while appeal was pending.

Baader's own defense sought to justify his actions by citing Herbert Marcuse's conclusion that the repressed minority had a "natural right" to oppose, with violence, the existing government structure, which it considered necessary to destroy. After the trial, three of the four, including Ensslin and Baader, pretending to be remorseful, volunteered to form a group to assist juvenile delinquents, called the "Staffelberg Group," a name taken from its street location in Frankfurt. Eventually this group contributed to more than 1,500 violations of the law, primarily robbery, but also theft of blank identity cards for the purpose of name changes.[27]

The historian Karl Dietrich Bracher, one of the foremost students of modern ideological movements, later made the point that in its utopianism and faith in the possibility and benign consequences of radical change, the German student movement of the late 1960s was the final expression of belief in progress. The radical leaders and their sympathizers in the ranks of published opinion believed that they were moving West Germany forward in the direction of a better society – one with more freedom and more autonomy. And they believed that such historical movement was possible. Their faith had its roots in the radical vision of the eighteenth-century Enlightenment, particularly in the utopian thought of Jean-Jacques Rousseau. This radical belief in social and political progress has led to great achievements as well as great violence and destruction. The critical difference between the German left in general and the radicals who believed in physical or psychological

---

[26] Bundeskriminalamt, *Der Baader-Meinhof Report*, 12.
[27] Ibid., 22–24 ff.

intimidation, or even in outright terror, was that the former remained grounded in democracy, whereas the latter were convinced that they were engaged in a civil war with people whom they had to destroy if they were not themselves to be destroyed. If one believed that, then one was morally obligated to destroy the enemies of progress, and for the student revolutionaries the enemies were the Bonn government and the capitalist system.[28]

In this perspective there could be no greater contrast than that between the ruthless, but optimistic revolutionaries of the Dutschke generation and those of the later 1970s and 1980s. As a participant in the movement of the 1960s, Winfried Vogt, wrote in 1979: "Probably none of us who, at the emergence of the late 1960s, were filled with so much hope of progress for an enlightened, liberal-socialist movement, can now, at the sober ending of the 1970s, avoid a sense of resignation. The abolition of the domination of man by man has not moved one step further, and just to mention it today has a rather embarrassingly pathetic and romantic sound."[29]

[28] Bracher et al., *Republik im Wandel, 1969–1974*, 346–53.
[29] Cited ibid., 312.

6

The Fate of the Grand Coalition

In April and May 1968 the Bundestag and governmental system of the Federal Republic successfully survived the challenge of the streets and passed the amendments giving the government its emergency powers. In June, Brandt stated in Reykjavik, Iceland, that he was ready to discuss terms of coexistence with the other "German system," the GDR. Between August and November, he was making every effort to assure that the Soviet bloc invasion of Czechoslovakia did not harm the process of detente. All of the events and tendencies of this period marked the initiation of the final phase of the grand coalition, which began in earnest at the turn of the year when attention was given to the first of the two important national elections, that of the federal president.

It is not surprising that the student movement, and its social and political consequences, influenced West Germany's political parties. No party was untouched, but the SPD was especially affected, as its left wing began to incorporate the ideology of the New Left into its own thinking. The result of this effort was a cross-contamination of ideas and programs. Much of the New Left began "the long march through the institutions" by which it hoped eventually to decisively influence German society by actively participating in it. The net effect of the rapprochement of the SPD and the student movement, which began in 1968-9, eventually resulted in the transformation not of society, but of the SPD, a development that culminated in the 1980s with the rejection by the increasingly influential left wing of the SPD of the basic principles of Western security policy.

The cultural revolutionaries rejected the inherited political and moral ballast of the Adenauer years – the belief in the moral superiority and sole legitimacy of the Federal Republic as representative of the aspirations of all Germans; the belief that wartime and postwar suffering and repentance had, more or less, counterbalanced Nazi atrocities; the faith in a conservatively colored, somewhat authoritarian capitalism; and a set of social and cultural mores which still bore, to a diminishing extent, the heavy imprint of the prewar, even pre-Weimar past. In contrast to these beliefs, which sustained the consensus that reached from the CSU on the right well into the SPD on the left in the 1950s and early 1960s, the cultural revolution of the late 1960s generated a new set of beliefs and norms. They did not supplant the older ones, but developed alongside them, and gradually became powerful enough to form the basis of a second, new political consensus in West German society and politics from the late 1960s onward and which, in crucial respects, even survived the second *Machtwechsel* in 1982 and the return to power of the CDU/CSU.

The consensus that emerged by the end of the grand coalition period consisted of six elements. First, a growing number of Germans believed that a policy of detente was more likely than a policy of confrontation to lead to better conditions for Germans in the East. They accepted the Soviet-imposed communist regime in the GDR as a fact of life. Second, they came to believe that the Federal Republic should abandon the role of a frontline NATO state and instead become, as a prominent spokesman of the new consensus, Peter Bender, put it, "a Western state in Central Europe." Third, a growing number of public figures argued successfully that the Soviet Union felt genuinely threatened by a resurgent West Germany and that the way to security in Europe was to assuage these supposed Soviet fears by favoring detente and trade over defense and cold war. Fourth, many, especially journalists, students, and academics, argued the need for "overcoming the Nazi past" (*Vergangenheitsbewältigung*) by means of sometimes moralistic analysis and, in particular, the revelation of supposed quasi-Nazi traits in West German society. Fifth, the same circles successfully spread the notion that a thorough "democratization" of West German society and a rejection of alleged hierarchy, authoritarianism, elitism, and inherited patterns of behavior and culture, was overdue and necessary if democracy were to survive. Sixth, progressive intellectuals argued that the time had at last come to introduce genuine enlightenment into German culture and politics. These intellectuals, who drew their inspiration from the combined Marxism and Freudianism of the Frankfurt School of Max Horkheimer, Theodor Adorno, and Herbert Marcuse, believed that they were the true heirs of the eighteenth-century Enlightenment. In their view, the existing political system was authoritarian and not truly democratic. The way to change it was to introduce genuine "critical thought," usually of a Marxist coloration, into the practice of politics and social policy.

An illustration of how the left-liberal press and intelligentsia exploited emotional issues of the past for political purposes was the case of the speaker of the Bundestag, Eugen Gerstenmaier. Because he was a staunch anti-communist Protestant from south-west Germany, and had been involved in the resistance movement that on July 20, 1944, attempted to assassinate Hitler, he was unpopular at a time when the focus was increasingly on leftist resistance to Hitler and not on conservative opposition; and also at a time when anti-communism was not compatible with general faith in detente and the attitude of goodwill toward the Soviet Union. In early 1968 *Stern* published an article claiming that in the previous decade Gerstenmaier had illegitimately influenced the writing of an amendment to the laws relating to indemnification and speeded up its passage. As a consequence of this amendment he was paid compensation of 281,000 marks, for a chair in theology which he had been denied in 1938 for political reasons. *Stern* claimed that he had received personal gain from the quick passage of the law. The article generated enough suspicion of scandal for Gersten-maier to resign as speaker of the Bundestag in January 1969. The allegations were never proven, but his party did not give him support, nor did the sympathy of Helmut Schmidt, who believed in his innocence, help him. He had become a difficult and awkward figure, and he resigned to the general relief of his party and was succeeded by Kai-Uwe von Hassel. Ironically, his legacy to the Bundestag, and to the political landscape of Bonn, was the home of the new Bundestag offices, constructed in 1969, which towers over the bank of the Rhine river, and which was named the "Tall Eugen" (*Der lange Eugen*).

The fall of Gerstenmaier was the first of the major political transitions of 1969. Negotiations for the election of a new federal president were already underway, since the CDU did not renominate the incumbent Lübke, who announced in October 1968 that he would step down in the spring of 1969, rather than in September, in order to avoid holding the presidential and Bundestag elections at the same time. The real reason, however, was that Lübke was 75 years old, and had frequently been criticized by those who considered him awkward or clumsy. Beginning in 1966, when he was an important figure in the negotiations producing the grand coalition, the GDR propaganda machine began spreading disinformation to the effect that Lübke had been involved in building concentration camps during the Third Reich. In fact, he had not; he worked for a construction company which built workers' barracks at the Peenemünde rocket testing site, and some of these workers were forced laborers. The facts of the case were less important than the effects of the rumors spread by the GDR, which were very willingly repeated in the Federal Republic. The reaction to the unsubstantiated rumors about Lübke's past, however, illustrated an emotional shift in judgement about the Third Reich; namely, that alleged association with it sufficed to condemn opponents of the left for political reasons. A point had been reached where the older generation was being forced, in a manner of speaking, to apologize just for having lived during the time of the Third Reich.

The CDU/CSU had a hard time deciding whom to nominate for the post of president. Kiesinger favored a choice between the social democrat Georg Leber, the minister of communications, and Richard von Weizsäcker, the chairman of the Protestant Assembly (DEKT) and brother of the physicist and critic of nuclear strategy, Carl Friedrich von Weizsäcker. In the event, neither party chose the candidate supported by the chancellor. Richard von Weizsäcker was to have his chance much later, when he was elected federal president in 1984. The CDU/CSU selected Gerhard Schröder to be its candidate and the SPD nominated Heinemann.

The resignation of Lübke led to the most intensely contested election of a federal president in the republic's history, but it also had other dramatic aspects. It was held (for the last time) in Berlin, which enraged the GDR and the Soviet government who regarded the presence in Berlin of the Federal Assembly – the electoral college responsible for choosing the president – as illegal. "In the interests of peace and security" the GDR decreed that "members of the Federal Assembly ... cannot be allowed to travel through the sovereign territory of the German Democratic Republic." The SED regime further forbade "the transport of working material for the planned West German Federal Assembly" and the transit of members of the Bundeswehr and any other government employees.[1] Since the GDR, however, could not interfere with air traffic to and from Berlin, it harassed overland travelers to Berlin by creating delays at the border checkpoints on the autobahn.

Only at the very last minute did the FDP leadership, after a closed session in the hotel where the election took place, declare that they would support Heinemann. Three rounds were necessary to elect Heinemann by a vote of 512 out of 1,023, a one-vote majority. The results produced a serious rift in the grand coalition. Indeed, the one-vote majority electing Heinemann was nearly as significant as the one-vote majority by which the first Bundestag elected Adenauer chancellor in 1949. Heinemann, as head of state, represented the victory of the new moralism and the new faith in atonement and guilt as the way to pursue reconciliation and a just society. Schröder's candidacy symbolized the sensible pragmatism and political realism of the forces that had carried

---

[1] Dept of State, *Documents on Germany*, 1027–8.

the Federal Republic to the position it had reached, but which were now competing with political forces of a different color and temperament. The support of the FDP for the SPD candidate was also the first act in the history of the little coalition, even though that coalition did not become a reality until after the next Bundestag election in the autumn.

The rift in the grand coalition over the election of the federal president in 1969 meant that the period preceding the Bundestag election in September became a time of political paralysis. The two different visions of the future course of the Federal Republic were becoming clearly defined, and the question was who would prevail and why. Immediately after his election Heinemann summarized the philosophy of the SPD's view of modern Germany, as he saw it, in an interview with the *Stuttgarter Zeitung*. He spoke of those who had supported the development of the Federal Republic thus far, and said they "had to get used to the fact that there are people other than conservatives in this Federal Republic." Concerning foreign policy his position represented a similar view:

Then as now, I regard my opposition to the actions of the federal chancellor, Dr Adenauer, in the summer of 1950 as well justified. . . . The old opposition against the former policy of Dr Adenauer, however, did not achieve its goal, as is well known. As a result, certain facts have emerged: the fact of armament, the fact of military treaties and the fact of Western integration. Only when bearing these facts in mind, can one take political action today. The question is in which direction. . . . That is to say that any kind of Bundeswehr must, in principle, be prepared to place its existence in question, if a better political solution can be found.

Also, membership in NATO, as I have often pointed out in the past, cannot be the final destination of German policy [*Deutschlandpolitik*], because it is impossible to achieve restoration of our national community within NATO, just as it is impossible to achieve it within the Warsaw Pact. In principle we must be prepared to get out of these blocs.[2]

The election was, in a general sense, a confirmation of Kissinger's prediction in his Senate testimony of 1966 (testimony which he had in the meantime elaborated upon in his book *The Troubled Partnership*, a book that added significantly to his reputation prior to his being appointed national security advisor by President Nixon in January 1969). Kissinger had said in 1966 that unless the US clearly stated its own foreign policy goals and its own desires for the future of Europe, the Germans would become ever more insecure and ever more prone to dangerous experiments either in the direction of nationalism or of

---

[2] Cited in Hildebrand, *Von Erhard zur Grossen Koalition,* 398.

neutralism – or both. The fears and uncertainties of the summer of 1969, and the nervous haste with which the new West German government of Brandt and Scheel gave substance to their Ostpolitik, following their election in September, demonstrated that Kissinger was right to worry about the direction this policy would take. In Kissinger's view,

> [t]he best hope to prevent a latent nihilism in Germany from again menacing the West is to give the Federal Republic a stake in something larger than itself. The future of the Federal Republic depends on two related policies by the West: (1) recognition of the psychological and political dilemmas of a divided country and (2) the ability to make the Federal Republic part of a larger community. These policies are interdependent; to pursue one without the other is to defeat both.[3]

Just before 1968 ended another event signaled a change in the international climate, namely the election of Richard Nixon to the presidency of the United States. The New Left and the SPD were alarmed; they knew of Nixon's past in the House Un-American Activities Committee and regarded him as an unrepentant anti-communist. They did not believe his promises that he would end the war in Vietnam, an issue that did more than anything else to estrange the German New Left from an America that many of its supporters regarded as a land of democratic promise.

Nixon paid his first visit, with Kissinger at his side, to Germany in February 1969. In his memoirs Kissinger describes how he at first was suspicious of Brandt and those in the SPD, like Bahr, who wanted to push far and fast in Ostpolitik. After visiting Bonn and talking to the social democratic leaders Kissinger came away with a high opinion of them and convinced that an SPD-led government would not lead Germany on the path of neutralism.

Nixon's official message to Germany was in the same tradition that began in September 1946, when Secretary of State Byrnes first told the Germans that America supported a democratic Germany. Speaking in Berlin, he reiterated the American promise: "No unilateral move, no illegal act, no form of pressure from any source will shake the resolve of the Western nations to defend their rightful status as protectors of the people of free Berlin. . . . Berlin must be free." On the other hand, the West had no intention any longer of demanding that the East yield what it had wrongfully seized: "We reject any unilateral alteration of the status quo in Berlin. . . . Let us set behind us the stereotype of Berlin as a

---

[3] Kissinger, *The Troubled Partnership*, 224.

'provocation.' Let us, all of us, view the situation in Berlin as an invocation, a call to end the tension of the past age here and everywhere."[4]

One month later the Soviet Union showed that it had received the Western message that the West did not intend to see the invasion of Czechoslovakia as an obstacle to development of detente. On March 17, 1969, the Warsaw Pact regimes issued a collective call for a conference on European security, as they had done in July 1966. A precondition of the proposed conference was that the West, including West Germany, recognize "the inviolability of the frontiers existing in Europe, including the frontiers on the Oder and Neisse and also the frontiers between the German Democratic Republic and the Federal Republic of Germany" and that West Germany renounce "its claims to represent the entire German people" and "the possession of nuclear weapons in any shape."[5] The statement concluded by suggesting that representatives of all European governments meet for a preparatory conference. This, in fact, took place in 1973, with US participation.

In his statement on the state of the German nation in June 1969, Kiesinger summarized the somewhat ambiguous result of the two and a half years of grand coalition Ostpolitik. His speech was also a commemoration of the twentieth anniversary of the founding of the Federal Republic. Although well aware that not merely the FDP, not merely the journalistic and academic leaders of published opinion, but even and especially his coalition partners in the SPD had already moved beyond what he, the conciliator, could accept in terms of Ostpolitik, he spoke gravely and seriously about what had been achieved, and about what, in his view, could not be achieved without sacrificing essential elements of West Germany's legal and moral standing and self-respect.

> The fundamental political orders in the two parts of Germany today differ in their structure and aims more than ever. Our Basic Law which became effective 20 years ago created a free democratic and social state based on the rule of law. It has made human dignity and human freedom the highest principle for any governmental action and embodied them in basic rights, the essence of which even the legislator cannot encroach upon. This Basic Law enabled a vigorous social and governmental system to develop here which has secured for every citizen a life in freedom and for the nation prosperity and social justice.
>
> In contrast to this, developments so far in the other part of Germany, and especially the new constitution of the GDR of April 1968, leave no room for the existence of a free and social community. The [East German] legal and social

[4] Dept of State, *Documents on Germany*, 1032–3.
[5] Ibid., 1036.

system is based solely on the political standards of the Communist Unity Party. . . .

The enforced division of our country and of our nation is bitter enough. But bitterest of all is the fact that our countrymen over there are compelled to live in a coercive social and political organization without any possibility of making a free decision. The theory proclaimed by the Soviet Union in connection with its forcible intervention in Czechoslovakia, which shocked the whole world, purports that a country, once it has become part of the Socialist camp, never again has the right to leave it. . . .

This should give food for thought to those appeasers and euphemists among us who are advocating recognition of the GDR. . . .

Such recognition would confirm injustice to be justice and would violate the generally accepted principle of self-determination. This the 60 million Germans living in the free part of our fatherland, their legislative bodies and their government, have no right to do. . . .

[T]he Federal Government has once again solemnly professed the binding preamble of the Basic Law which calls upon the whole German people to accomplish the unity and freedom of Germany in free self-determination. It harbours no illusions whatsoever that it will be very difficult to attain this aim by peaceful means – for it is peaceful means only that we will employ – and that long perseverance and unremitting energy will be required to this end. In the last resort, the success of our efforts for unification depends essentially on an overall European understanding, on the gradual establishment of that European peace arrangement within the framework of which there will also be a possibility of overcoming the partition of Germany.[6]

A few weeks earlier Bonn had taken note that Iraq, Sudan, Syria, and Cambodia had recognized the GDR. These governments were informed that Bonn regarded their action as an "unfriendly act," in accordance with the Hallstein Doctrine, but Kiesinger chose not to apply the full version of the doctrine, which would have required him to withdraw West German recognition of those countries. No observer could seriously doubt that the Doctrine was without substance – whether or not the "party of recognition," that is, a SPD/FDP coalition, came to power in Bonn.

In late June, with election fever already in the air, the Bundestag managed to pass one last symbolically very important law, the law abolishing the statute of limitations for acts of genocide. The statute of limitations for murder in West Germany was 20 years. In 1964 the Bundestag decided to postpone a final decision on the issue by deciding arbitrarily that acts of genocide – mass atrocities committed or ordered by servants of the Third Reich – could be prosecuted for 20 years after the founding of the Federal Republic, that is, until the end of 1969. In

[6] Ibid., 1039–42.

1969 it was clear that a majority of public opinion was against extending the limitation; in a common phrase of the time, most Germans who paid attention to the issue wanted to "draw a final line" under the past. But a majority of both parties in the grand coalition, bearing in mind West Germany's international reputation, decided on June 26, 1969, to abolish all limitations on the prosecution of acts of genocide, and to extend to 30 years the period for prosecuting any crime punishable by life-long imprisonment. The required law – officially, it was the ninth amendment to the criminal code – passed with the votes of the CDU and SPD against those of the CSU and FDP. Under the new provision all Nazi crimes could be prosecuted until 1979, and genocidal acts as long as the perpetrators lived.

One month before the Bundestag election in August, Helmut Schmidt led the leaders of the SPD caucus on a trip to Moscow to discuss European relations, and it was clearly an attempt to demonstrate to the German voters that the SPD was a respected party of foreign affairs. The Soviet Union had found Kiesinger to be a conciliatory partner, but the chancellor also recognized that West Germany had little leverage with the Soviet government in the expanding atmosphere of detente. Still, from the Soviet viewpoint a government led by Brandt, with Bahr as advisor, was clearly preferable; it promised more favorable and faster results. Thus, Schmidt's trip was carefully planned in coordination with Brandt, the SPD chairman and foreign minister.

Schmidt had visited Moscow as a tourist in 1966, but on this occasion his interlocutors were more important than they had been then. The SPD delegation spoke with the foreign minister, Gromyko, and with the foreign policy strategist Valentin Falin, who later became Soviet ambassador to Bonn. Schmidt outlined Brandt's proposed Ostpolitik to Gromyko: "I made it clear from the beginning that the Germans would never give up the hope of living in *one* house; they were convinced that they had this historic right. In view of the prevailing circumstances, however, we were prepared to enter into agreements with the GDR on the basis of equality, including a legally valid treaty on the renunciation of force, which would include guarantee of all the GDR's borders."[7]

The CDU/CSU approached the elections with considerable optimism. It had done well in the *Land* elections during 1967 and 1968, regaining much of the loss suffered in the Erhard years. At the same time the SPD was plagued by constant turbulence on its left wing. Some people, grumbled Wehner, "seem to want to conduct a permanent plebiscite within the party."[8] After the disastrous defeat in Baden-Württemberg in

[7] Schmidt, *Menschen und Mächte*, 25–6, his emphasis.
[8] Cited in Hildebrand, *Von Erhard zur Grossen Koalition*, 384.

April 1968, when the SPD lost over eight percentage points, Schiller charged his comrades to rediscover their "sense of political power," insisting that they would achieve no success if they pretended not to like power.[9]

Schiller need not have worried. The social and political, national and international, visions of Heinemann and Brandt represented ideas that were re-emerging after ten years of hibernation, and they appealed to many voters who were discontented with what they saw as passivity in the national issue on the part of the CDU/CSU. The SPD conducted its campaign in the Bundestag election on the claim that it was a more modern, more sophisticated, and simply a more competent party of government than the CDU/CSU. The implication was that the CDU/CSU was too old-fashioned and inflexible and not really in touch with the times, whereas the SPD was capable of dealing with all the problems of international security, relations with the East, progress on the German question and European integration, and all domestic issues as well. Karl Schiller was the guarantee that the SPD was not in the grip of the extreme left, that it was not only the party of compassion, but the party of competence. During the campaign Schiller broke with Strauss on the currency issue, having changed his mind since the meeting of the Group of Ten in November 1968. Schiller now argued that West Germany should have revalued the mark in the spring of 1969.

The economics minister reassured the moderates, whereas Brandt and Heinemann mobilized the left, the intellectuals, and the leaders of published opinion, many of whom for the first time considered it chic to support the SPD. This appeal was enough to bring the SPD, for the first time, to above the 40 per cent mark; the party received 42.7 per cent of the votes versus 46.1 per cent for the CDU/CSU. Since the FDP received 5.8 per cent, a disastrous result, but still enough to enter the Bundestag, the two parties were able to form the hoped-for coalition. The NPD failed to clear the 5 per cent hurdle, and whatever appeal it had originally enjoyed was clearly diminished.

In hindsight most Germans regarded the SPD's gains in 1969, and the resulting coalition of socialists and liberals, which lasted until 1982, as an inevitable sea-change in postwar German politics, a new beginning after 20 years of conservative domination. There is some truth to this judgement. Since 1962–3, the year of the *Spiegel* affair and of Hochhuth's play *The Deputy*, sharply critical of the pope's behavior in the war and indirectly of the powerful Catholic establishment of postwar West Germany, a revolution of attitudes, personal values, behavior, and political expectations had affected a significant proportion of Germans,

---

[9] Cited ibid., 385.

especially those under 30. Those affected by the revolution ranged from the ideological extremes of the revolutionary New Left to more moderate and pragmatic groups such as the Jusos (Young Socialists), led from 1969 to 1972 by Karsten Voigt, who was to become, in the 1980s, his party's chief foreign policy spokesman in the Bundestag. To a varying degree, they rejected the perceived authoritarianism, hierarchical values, and subordination of pleasure to work of the Adenauer and Erhard years. They wanted a "different republic," as their sympathizers later put it, a society of compassion and collectivism, not of industrial efficiency and individualism. During the grand coalition, the cultural revolution spread fast and far, capturing the allegiance of a critical mass of journalists, writers, and other public figures. They regarded the victories of Heinemann and Brandt as victories for their vision of Germany and for them, it was a long-overdue correction.

On the other hand, the CDU/CSU in 1969 was in no conceivable sense a spent force in German politics. It remained the largest party grouping with a leadership fully capable of governing and willing to govern. Its problem was a fundamental and growing lack of credibility with precisely those groups that set the agenda for public debate in Germany, namely the journalists, anchormen, political academics, and writers. The very fact that the CDU/CSU had held power since the beginning of the Federal Republic – and, in the Economic Council, since 1947 – had exposed the party to all the general misfortunes of office, as well as the particular burdens of the German past. No doubt an SPD government in the 1950s would also have had to hire former high-ranking members of the administration of the Third Reich, like Hans Globke. But the fact was that it was the CDU/CSU that had done so. Their loss of power in 1969 was, in some respects, a result of their successful tenure since 1949. They paid the price of success, leaving West Germany in new, but eager hands.

PART VIII

The Fourth Chancellor of Germany, Willy Brandt, 1969–1974

I see myself as the Chancellor of a liberated, not a defeated, Germany. Our partners in the world will be dealing with a loyal government but not always an easy one.

Willy Brandt

Introduction

The Bundestag election of September 28, 1969, did not produce a clear majority for either party of the grand coalition. The CDU/ CSU lost less than two percentage points (46.1 per cent); the SPD gained just over three (42.7 per cent). But the FDP suffered a four point loss (5.8 per cent) that represented 40 per cent of its strength at the 1965 election. To the relief of the German public the right-wing NPD failed by 300,000 votes to enter the Bundestag, receiving 1.4 million (4.3 per cent) of the valid votes cast. Despite the strong SPD campaign, fully supported by the leaders of published opinion, and the widespread popular excitement at the prospect of a breakthrough in Ostpolitik under a social democratic government, the CDU/CSU had done well and remained the larger party. But this was not decisive. Brandt, Scheel and their advisors were to seize the initiative and produce a dramatic change. In foreign policy, the change would mean treaties with the communist regimes by which Bonn recognized the status quo and offered economic aid and diplomatic support. The SPD's agenda for fiscal and social policy would maintain the centralization of economic power in the federal government begun in Adenauer's last years and continued under Erhard and Kiesinger. While the SPD was the innovator in foreign policy, the CDU, in opposition, campaigned for innovation in domestic policy; namely, to reverse that trend toward centralization and to return economic power to the *Länder*. In foreign policy, the SPD was the party of change, but on fiscal and budgetary issues it wanted to preserve and expand the foundation of the welfare state of the 1960s.

From the SPD's election victory emerged a new group of German leaders. They had waited for a quarter of a century for the chance to determine Germany's future, an opportunity which they felt, under the guidance of Kurt Schumacher, had been unjustly denied them in 1949. New leadership marked the most momentous change in German politics since Adenauer, and it was to have far-reaching consequences. Out of the period of 1969 to 1974 arose the modern, expanded German welfare state, as well as a basic change in foreign policy vis-à-vis the GDR, central Europe and the Soviet Union. No matter how far the grand coalition had moved in Ostpolitik, it had not taken the decisive steps. But without the groundwork it laid, the direction of Ostpolitik under Chancellor Brandt would have been impossible.

During the first hours after the election, Kiesinger and the CDU's leaders were convinced that they had won. They believed they would be able to form a coalition with the FDP, even though the FDP had been toying with the idea of a coalition with the SPD for almost a decade and had moved sharply to the left during the grand coalition. The FDP leader, Walter Scheel, had committed himself to a coalition with Brandt in the event that the SPD and the FDP obtained a majority. Shifting political judgements within the party gave Scheel the confidence to state publicly, three days before the election in 1969, that he hoped for a coalition with the SPD "if the figures allow it," and that the task of the FDP was to "push the CDU into opposition." The harbinger of this shift had occurred in the spring. The FDP had voted with the SPD to elect Gustav Heinemann federal president in March and this action was understood by the FDP, and the public at large, as advance notice of what might happen if the SPD and the FDP together could muster a majority of seats in the new (sixth) Bundestag.

While Kiesinger and his government were still debating how to attract the FDP, Brandt had already taken action. As soon as the results were in, he told Scheel that he intended to lead the new government. A friend of Brandt's, the journalist Hans Ulrich Kempski, was present on the election night and later claimed that he had given Brandt the final encouragement by handing him a note that read simply: "Now or never!"[1] Brandt, as Kempski reported, "appeared as relaxed as though he had already been chosen chancellor. All his worries and doubts seemed to be gone. Never before in two decades had I seen him in a comparable mood, this mood of suggestive confidence."[2] The momentous "change of power" (*Machtwechsel*) from the CDU/CSU to the SPD/FDP coalition was due not to the verdict of the voters, but to the decisive action of Willy Brandt. The hours and days following the election were his finest moment. He acted with strength and determination and with what for him was an unusual serenity and belief in his own ability.

Brandt, who had lost two bids for the chancellorship, in 1961 and 1965, was a changed man. No doubt the unequivocal support of Scheel

---

[1] Baring, *Machtwechsel*, 172.
[2] Bracher et al., *Republik im Wandel, 1969–1974*, 16.

– and the encouragement of Heinemann from the presidential palace on the Rhine, the Villa Hammerschmidt – was a help. Brandt encountered difficulty, however, in convincing his own colleagues in the SPD leadership, Wehner and Schmidt. They remained leading spokesmen in the SPD for majority voting which would have produced a Bundestag of only two parties, with alternating stable majorities. Perhaps more importantly, they doubted Brandt's perseverance and personal stability. Wehner in particular, the party strategist, disliked the idea of a government dependent on FDP votes, because he regarded the FDP as fundamentally unreliable, since it could in theory return to a coalition with the CDU at any time. In particular, Wehner feared that a few liberal deputies might not vote for Brandt when he presented himself to the Bundestag. If only five members of the FDP voted against Brandt in the parliament, he would not get a majority and would not become chancellor. Wehner was shocked that Brandt and Scheel were prepared to run that risk.

Wehner's long-term goal was to see the SPD as the permanent party of government. He was deeply convinced that an SPD government in Bonn was the best thing for Germany – by which he specifically meant the GDR as well as the Federal Republic. Anything that tended to make that goal more difficult was to be rejected, and he preferred not to have to rely on the FDP. He also did not trust Brandt's abilities as a parliamentarian and head of a coalition government. In his detailed chronicle of the Brandt–Scheel government, the historian Arnulf Baring – who counted among his friends left-leaning social democrats such as Günter Gaus, Kurt Sontheimer, and the writer Günter Grass, as well as members of the CDU – wrote that Wehner regarded Brandt as an excellent *candidate* for chancellor, but not as a potential head of government. In Wehner's eyes Brandt was "not diligent enough, much too easy-going, never in bed on time."[3] Put differently, one might say that, in Wehner's opinion, Brandt had great ambitions but neither the personal character traits nor the political support to carry them through. Wehner was terrified that Brandt would try to climb too high from too narrow a base – namely, the slim majority of the SPD and FDP. If he failed, it would discredit the SPD for many years.

Not only might some or all members of the FDP Bundestag group defect, but Wehner and Schmidt also feared that the liberals might, at some point in the future, not receive the minimum 5 per cent of the vote required for representation in the Bundestag. In such a case, it would be possible that another party, such as the ultra-conservative NPD or an ultra-left group, might have its representatives elected to the Bundestag.

[3] Baring, *Machtwechsel*, 173.

Wehner considered the FDP an "irresponsible partner" because it was internally weak, and because it did not share the same political and economic goals.

Schmidt also had other doubts about Brandt. He did not believe that Brandt and his associates from Berlin had the skills or the patience to manage government on a large scale. He was concerned that running the SPD in Berlin or the city government of Berlin was not good training for managing the Federal Republic as a whole. Furthermore, in his view and in that of many others, the Berliners had no notion of responsible fiscal management. Since 1949, Bonn had demonstrated its commitment to West Berlin by special grants and subventions, thus relieving the city government of the need to balance its budgets. As a result, Brandt and his supporters in Berlin were used to spending freely without regard to the effects of high public spending on taxation or employment. Schmidt, who believed in the need for more social reforms and a bigger role for government, was afraid that the Berliners would spoil the chances for such reforms by over-ambitious spending in Bonn, which would undermine the economy and produce a backlash against the SPD.

Other senior members within Brandt's party, however, supported his position. The main architect of domestic policy reform was Schiller, who continued as economics minister and in 1971 became minister of finance as well, thus combining the jobs he and Strauss had held under the grand coalition. Schiller enjoyed wide respect in international financial circles and among centrist-oriented SPD members. But more decisive, given Brandt's own personal inclinations, was the fervent support of the party's youth organization, the Young Socialists (Jusos). They were led by Karsten Voigt, director of an institute of adult education, who was especially interested in foreign affairs (born 1941, chairman of the Jusos from 1969 to 1972, and elected to the Bundestag in 1972), the journalist and political scientist Johano Strasser (born in 1939, deputy chairman of the Jusos from 1969 to 1975), and an economist, Wolfgang Roth (born in 1941, chairman of the Jusos from 1972 to 1974, and elected to the Bundestag in 1976). They were excited at the prospect of power and determined to translate their ideas for a leftward shift in domestic and foreign affairs into real policies. And this could only be done if the SPD was the dominant partner in a coalition, not the junior partner as would be the case if the grand coalition continued.

Most FDP leaders, however not Scheel, had not wanted to bind the party definitely to a coalition with the SPD before the election, partly because the internal struggle was not over, but mainly to avoid alienating the important conservative element in the FDP electorate. This element had dominated the party from its formation in the 1946–9 period to 1966, and its natural leader was the former party chairman, Erich Mende. Mende had resigned in 1967 when he was no longer willing to head a party that did not share his view on Ostpolitik and the German question. His successor, Walter Scheel, led the group that also included Genscher and Mischnick. These pragmatists did not insist on a specific position concerning Ostpolitik, but realized that the power in the liberal party lay with the radicals. For the sake of the party they took charge of the radical platform to try to make it palatable to more voters and to give the FDP the necessary veneer of seriousness. Mende's departure reflected the increasing influence of the new generation of younger members who supported a revision of policy vis-à-vis the GDR: namely, an effort to overcome the division of Germany and Europe and to create a lasting, all-European peace order. What this meant in practice was the adoption of a new approach to East Germany, by calling for diplomatic recognition of the GDR and the Oder–Neisse line as East Germany's eastern border prior to signing a peace treaty and acceptance of a confederation of both German states, as proposed by the Soviet and East German governments.

The leading figures of the radical liberals were the sociologist Ralf Dahrendorf and the journalist Hildegard Hamm-Brücher. Dahrendorf was concerned with opening a dialogue with radical youth. He served as secretary of state in the foreign ministry and member of the Bundestag from 1969 to 1970, and as a member of the party's executive committee from 1968 to 1974, after which he left Germany, disenchanted with the FDP, to become director of the London School of Economics until 1984. Hamm-Brücher called for radical reform of the West German educational system in the direction of more student participation and control. She served as state secretary in the federal ministry of education and science from 1969 to 1972 and in a similar position in the foreign ministry from 1976 to 1982.

The CDU, however, did not give up easily in its efforts to woo the FDP. In curious anticipation of a similar situation in 1982, it was Helmut Kohl, minister-president of the Rhineland-Palatinate and a candidate to succeed Kiesinger as CDU chairman, who had the best contacts in the FDP and who worked hardest for a coalition. But the decision was not Kohl's to make. It was made by Brandt and Scheel, and there was no conceivable offer from the CDU attractive enough to halt the trend of the *Zeitgeist*, the atmosphere of the time.

By October 3, it was clear how the wind was blowing. The FDP was not interested in serious negotiations with the CDU. In great bitterness, Kiesinger threatened the FDP with revenge and promised every effort on the part of the CDU to "hurl the FDP out of the *Land* parliaments" in the six *Land* elections scheduled for 1970. That remark poisoned CDU–FDP relations for more than a decade.

Thus, on October 21, it was possible, for the first time in the history of the Federal Republic and for the first time in German history since 1928, for the SPD to become the major governing party, supported by the FDP. The new chancellor was Willy Brandt. FDP chairman Walter Scheel became foreign minister, and Hans-Dietrich Genscher became minister of the interior. Karl Schiller remained minister of economics, and the leader of the SPD caucus in the Bundestag, Helmut Schmidt, became minister of defense. Herbert Wehner assumed leadership of the caucus in the Bundestag, a position he retained until 1983. Two other figures were also given influential positions, and they came to typify the "Brandt revolution" in politics, government, and culture of the Federal Republic. One was Horst Ehmke, a rising figure on the SPD left wing, who had taken over Heinemann's post as minister of justice when Heinemann became federal president, and who now became head of the chancellery with the rank of minister without portfolio. Ehmke had expressed his revisionist views on the grand issues as early as 1949 at the age of 22, when, as a student of the University of Göttingen, he analysed the founding of the Free University of Berlin in the student newspaper:

We do not want to deceive ourselves about the fact that the anti-communist crusade of the West, in which the Free University functions as the academic ensign, stems to a great extent from the insecurity and helplessness of the West.[4]

The other figure was Conrad Ahlers, a handsome man with silver hair, formerly deputy editor of *Der Spiegel* and regarded as a prominent victim of state power in the *Spiegel* affair. Ahlers was deputy director of the federal government's press and information office during the grand coalition. Brandt made him the head of that office, a post of increasing importance in an era characterized by the growing power and influence of the media. In this case it was a particularly significant appointment because Ahlers, as a respected liberal journalist, maintained excellent connections with the press, as did his successor during the second Brandt government, Rüdiger von Wechmar (who later became West German ambassador to the United Nations, and subsequently to Italy and Great Britain).

The formal election of the chancellor in parliament on October 21 was for some a traumatic occasion, for others an emotional triumph.

---

[4] Bergmann et al., *Die Rebellion der Studenten*, 9.

For the first time since the Weimar Republic the German chancellor was a social democrat. Many, particularly among the political intellectuals and the Jusos, regarded the election of Brandt as the overdue correction of a historical injustice and as the merited recognition of SPD achievements and power in postwar German society. Writers, intellectuals, academics and journalists who had kept their distance from what they saw as the conservatism or even revanchism of the Adenauer and Erhard eras, hailed the election of Brandt as a historic watershed. And it was. The fact that Brandt, the illegitimate son of a sales clerk and an unknown father and a refugee from Nazism, could become head of government, was, to them, thrilling. The writer Heinrich Böll described Willy Brandt as the first German chancellor to lead the German people "out of the master race tradition" and wrote in 1972:

> Willy Brandt's life provides material for a legend, almost for a fairy tale come true. The man who became chancellor in 1969 was not the legitimate, aggressive Catholic from Munich [i.e., Strauss], but the illegitimate Herbert Frahm from Lübeck, who even managed to aggravate this blemish – the idiotic original sin – in the eyes of bourgeois society, by becoming a socialist and an emigré.[5]

Brandt himself (who had taken that name in 1933 to avoid possible discovery and assassination by the Gestapo) regarded his victory as the final end of World War II. Many of his followers saw the *Machtwechsel* as the chance to give the Federal Republic a new form of legitimacy, the legitimacy of a morally renewed and liberated state rather than one reconstituted for political reasons by the Western Allies between 1946 and 1949. As the political scientist Wilhelm Hennis wrote in 1983, Brandt's supporters believed that 1969 was a "second *Stunde Null* (zero hour)," the chance for a true reconstruction unlike the ramshackle and imperfect "emergency reconstruction" of 1945.[6] Brandt's first formal policy statement to the Bundestag on October 28, 1969, which included his appeal to "dare more democracy," strongly encouraged these notions. But the sense of triumph and of a new beginning also fueled antagonisms and conflicts on both sides of the political spectrum, which ultimately led to Brandt's fall and the retreat from radicalism on the governmental level – but not the local or internal party level – under the leadership of Helmut Schmidt.

Brandt's program was ambitious. First, he announced his intention

[5] Cited in Bracher et al., *Republik im Wandel, 1969–1974*, 24.
[6] Cited ibid.

to make far-reaching domestic reforms in economic, social, and industrial policy and in the educational system. Second, and most important, Brandt insisted on continuity as well as renewal in foreign policy, and announced an effort to loosen the *Verkrampfung* (tension) in the German question. As late as September 1968, both parties in the grand coalition, the SPD and the CDU/CSU, had declared that "there can be no question of recognition of the other part of Germany as foreign territory or as a second sovereign state of German nationality." In his policy statement to the Bundestag Brandt specified that "the policy of this government will be one of continuity and renewal." He went on to present a posture which retained many elements of the Ostpolitik of the grand coalition, notably the reference to a "European peace order." Curiously, although this was a phrase that Kiesinger had often used and which undoubtedly represented his thinking, it became afterward associated in the public mind exclusively with his successor. Brandt added dramatic new emphasis, however, when he picked up elements from his Reykjavik declaration of June 1968 offering talks on a basis of equality with the GDR, and even more when he mentioned "two states" in Germany – the first time any free German speaking in an official capacity had done so:

[T]his government works on the assumption that the questions which have risen for the German people out of World War II and from the national treachery committed by the Hitler regime can ultimately be answered only in a European peace order. . . .

Twenty years after the establishment of the Federal Republic of Germany and of the GDR we must prevent any further alienation of the two parts of the German nation; that is, arrive at a regular modus vivendi and from there proceed to cooperation. . . .

The Federal Government will continue the policy initiated in December 1966 by Chancellor Kiesinger and his government and again offers the Council of Ministers of the GDR negotiations at government level without discrimination on either side, which should lead to contractually agreed cooperation. International recognition of the GDR by the Federal Republic is out of the question. *Even if two states exist in Germany* [emphasis added], they are not foreign countries to each other, their relations with each other can only be of a special nature.

Following up the policy of its predecessor, the Federal Government declares that its readiness for binding agreements on the reciprocal renunciation of the use or threat of force applies equally with regard to the GDR.

The Federal Government will advise the United States, Britain, and France to continue energetically the talks begun with the Soviet Union on easing and improving the situation of Berlin.[7]

[7] Dept of State, *Documents on Germany*, 1049–50.

The CDU/CSU objected strenuously to Brandt's public statement that two states did, indeed, exist in Germany, and interpreted it as a renunciation of the long-established policy vis-à-vis the GDR, without a quid pro quo that would help improve the lives of those in East Germany. The objection was stated most forcefully by Guttenberg: "There is only one sovereign who can decide ... whether one or two states exist on German soil, and that sovereign is the German people."[8] The problem was that no one, since 1955 at least, had any idea how to establish the sovereignty of the German people, that is, how to liberate East Germany.

The Brandt–Scheel government and its supporters believed that the idea of bringing freedom to the East, and the associated notion that only the Bonn government was the legitimate representative of all Germans, was not only provocative and out of touch with the realities of international politics – specifically, with US–Soviet detente – but also a liability. Instead, they argued, one could begin to overcome the division of Europe by demonstrating that West Germany had no desire to try to change the political system of the GDR or to deny the legitimacy of Soviet security interests. Only after establishing this equality of respect by each side for the other's legitimacy, they thought, could one, by negotiation and concession, help improve the human rights and living standards of Central Europeans. Instead of demanding that the East change before there could be serious talks, the Bonn government now offered to talk as a means of obtaining change.

This policy was nothing more, nor less, than what the leaders of published opinion had advocated since the mid 1960s, exemplified early on by Karl Jaspers in 1966 in *Wohin treibt die Bundesrepublik?* Jaspers believed German responsibility – for war, for inflicting death and destruction on Central Europe, and thus for the division of Europe itself – to be so great that he regarded German apologies and German professions of guilt as the minimum precondition for making any demands at all on the Eastern regimes. The Ostpolitik that took shape in 1966–9, and reached its full force in 1969–72, was the foreign policy equivalent of the internal rebirth and the sense of a true "new beginning" that characterized the feelings aroused by Brandt's assumption of power. But it had a logical flaw. On the one hand the leaders of published opinion and the SPD rejected the idea that the Federal Republic could speak for all Germans. On the other hand they asserted that the West Germans, in West Germany, should atone for Germany's crimes and seek reconciliation with Eastern Europe – thus ignoring the East German government's refusal to do so.

[8] Cited in Bracher et al., *Republik im Wandel, 1969–1974*, 167.

It was fortunate for Brandt's design of Ostpolitik that relations with France and the United States also took a turn for the better after the uncertainties of the grand coalition. In April 1969 Charles de Gaulle unexpectedly declared he would resign if a majority of the French electorate did not support the government in a referendum he had called on a law to reform the administrative structure of France. The government's proposal lost by a small margin, and de Gaulle accordingly stepped down after eleven years in power. His successor, Georges Pompidou, announced that France no longer objected to British membership in the European Community, an issue that had been a source of serious disagreement between Paris and Bonn since 1963; in so doing he thus gave Brandt greater flexibility in pursuing his concept of Ostpolitik.

In relations with the United States there was also a difference between Brandt's government and the governments of Erhard and Kiesinger: whereas the earlier governments had adapted to a US course that was already defined, Brandt deliberately took on the role of providing initiative in East–West relations, and defining specific German goals that potentially went far beyond the concept of Nixon and Kissinger. In 1966 Kissinger had warned publicly that unless there was movement in the German question, the loyalty of West Germany to the West might weaken, and that he understood the negative consequences of such developments. As national security advisor in January 1969, following Nixon's election in November 1968, and later as secretary of state, Kissinger was faced with a Germany that certainly achieved change in the German question, but not perhaps in the manner and direction he had hoped.

Just prior to Brandt's public statement of October 28, the Brandt–Scheel government had taken its first foreign policy initiative by raising the value of of the mark by 8.5 per cent against other major currencies (this was the second time the mark had been revalued; the first time was in 1961, and the third and fourth revaluations took place in 1971 and 1973). Schiller had spoken forcefully for revaluation in the campaign, having changed his mind since late 1968, when he absolutely refused to revalue, although Germany's trading partners begged him to do so. The CDU opposed revaluation because it would adversely effect exports by making them more expensive abroad. But the new government, by allowing the mark to rise in value, acknowledged the existence of an export and dollar surplus of the Federal Republic. Schiller was trying to re-establish a foreign trade balance which would allow Bonn to use its currency reserves more productively; this included financial support of underdeveloped countries, and it made it less expensive for foreign countries to sell goods in Germany. But it also meant that maintaining

American forces in Germany became more expensive for the United States, and the cost of living correspondingly increased for the families of American soldiers stationed in Germany.

The strength of the German economy, however, took second place to Brandt's first priority, which was his policy vis-à-vis the GDR and Eastern Europe. A figure of continuing importance in this area was Egon Bahr. As head of the policy planning staff in the foreign ministry under Brandt from 1966 to 1969, he had prepared the positions for a rapid start of negotiations with the East to produce what he and Brandt saw as a "normalization" of relations leading to a "European peace order" – Kiesinger's phrase from his state of the nation speech in 1967 in which he had proposed a "grand design for a European peace order" to be realized through a political reorganization of Europe and a reduction of tensions between the two alliances leading to "inescapable collaboration." Bahr described himself as a German nationalist who believed that the way to maintain the German nation was through conciliation of and concessions to the regimes in power in the GDR and the Soviet Union. He had defined this policy as one of "change through rapprochement" since 1963. To those who argued that such a policy harmed the "German interest" or went beyond what Germany's allies would like or tolerate, Bahr could point to the new direction that two former US presidents, John F. Kennedy and Lyndon Johnson, had advocated stronger East–West relations, and in particular to Kennedy's call in 1963 for more contacts between states and peoples in Western and Eastern Europe.

Schmidt, the SPD's defense expert and head of the Bundestag caucus from 1966 to 1969, was sympathetic to this approach. Although skeptical of Bahr's and Brandt's far-reaching vision of East–West reconciliation in Europe, he had played a vital part in opening channels between the SPD and the Soviet government during the grand coalition. On two trips to Moscow in the summer of 1966 and in August 1969 Schmidt confirmed, as he informed his party colleagues, that the Soviet Union was, indeed, a status-quo power that had no interest in German reunification, a conclusion already held by Bahr. While Franz Josef Strauss called Schmidt's 1969 trip a "senseless pilgrimage to Moscow" and the CSU newspaper, *Bayernkurier*, published in Munich, referred to the SPD as "the party of the East,"[9] Schmidt's impressions of that trip influenced the design of Brandt's Ostpolitik. The main lesson was that in order to obtain improvements in the daily lives of those living in Eastern Europe, the Federal Republic would have to recognize the status quo as defined by the Soviet government. This meant that

[9] Lehmann, *Öffnung nach Osten*, 110.

Brandt's government embraced a concept of detente which included bilateral dialogue with the GDR, the Soviet Union, and with other Eastern European countries. In turn, the FRG would establish itself as a serious and reliable member of the European political system and a credible partner in East–West dialogue.

In a different but related area, Schmidt was very aware of developments in military and security matters in the United States and within NATO. In 1969, before the election, he published the German edition of his study on *The Balance of Power.* The book was a defense of the NATO strategy of flexible response discussed by the defense ministers of the Alliance in 1967 and officially approved by the North Atlantic Council at the same time as the Harmel Report. Schmidt argued that the advance of the Soviet Union to effective nuclear parity with the West combined with Soviet conventional superiority was changing the political equations in Europe. In the future no Western promise or hope of liberating Eastern Europe would be credible. The US, under Johnson, had officially introduced the strategy of flexible response in NATO in 1967, which threatened possible nuclear use to compensate for the conventional inferiority of NATO in the case of a Soviet attack. The US, under President Nixon, was, moreover, prepared to recognize Soviet global parity in the arms control talks that were in the planning stages in 1969. Under those conditions the only way to preserve peace and security in Europe was by pursuing a policy of equilibrium of military force and political claims. This meant detente, mutual troop reductions, and, in turn, the predictability of the status quo. For Schmidt, peace and stability now depended on recognizing and maintaining the existing division of Europe and parity of military force, not on making unrealizable demands for change. Schmidt's goal – a goal he had pursued from the late 1950s, when he opposed the nuclear arming of the Bundeswehr, and which he continued to pursue as chancellor between 1974 and 1982 – was to establish a durable arms control regime in Europe.

In 1968 Bahr and his staff had outlined three strategies that could be followed in talks with the East in an attempt to define "the German interest in the discussions on the form of a European security."[10] One was to pursue detente through disarmament on the basis of the existing alliance systems in East and West, but not to try to overcome or undermine those systems. The second was to create new organs composed of both East and West European states. These new organs would at first merely supervise disarmament, but would eventually replace the existing alliances. The third was to replace the alliance

---

[10] Bracher et al., *Republik im Wandel, 1969–1974,* 171.

systems with a pan-European security system including all European states and guaranteed jointly by the US and the Soviet Union, who would, however, not themselves be members. Bahr rejected the middle option because it would hinder, not help, German reunification, and he realized that the third option was unrealistic, because it was unacceptable to both the US and the Soviet Union. Nevertheless, he was emotionally committed to the third option and to the design of a Central European security system, that is to say, to a "kind of European house."

Bahr's design for Europe was not made public until 1973, but was presented to an American scholar in an interview in 1969 (published in 1973), as a response to a hypothetical question. The concept consisted of a four-stage plan that proposed starting within the first option and then moving to the third: (1) recognition by the Federal Republic that there were two states in Germany followed by mutual acceptance by the Federal Republic and the GDR of a special relationship between them, different from normal state sovereignty; (2) renunciation of the use of force and the recognition of all existing borders; (3) large-scale reductions of the numbers of Soviet and US troops in Germany; and (4) development of a collective security system in central Europe to be guaranteed by both super powers, and the dissolution of NATO and the Warsaw Pact.[11]

Bahr believed that the nation-state remained the necessary and inescapable emotional focus of political loyalty among peoples both east and west of the Iron Curtain. He hoped to achieve a new political and strategic order in Central Europe by appealing to the nationalism of the Central European peoples under communist government, but in a way that did not question the communist parties' right to rule. At the same time, this vision was not easily compatible with the general and deeply anchored West German commitment to a supranational West European economic and political union, a commitment that Brandt and Scheel reaffirmed. Bahr, however, saw West European supranational integration as an obstacle to an opening to the East European regimes and people, whereas Brandt, who believed that the first of Bahr's three strategic options was the only viable one, saw no conflict.

Even before his inaugural statement on October 28, Brandt had dispatched Bahr to Washington to inform, not consult with, the White House, Kissinger, and the National Security Council of the new government's revolutionary Ostpolitik:

> Bahr was a man of great intelligence and extraordinary confidence in his ability to devise formulas to overcome a diplomatic impasse . . . Though Bahr was a man of the left, I considered him above all a German nationalist. . . .

[11] See Hahn, "West Germany's Ostpolitik." *Orbis* 16 (1973): 859–80.

So I met Bahr with the attitude of establishing a cooperative relationship . . . The Brandt government was asking not for our advice but for our cooperation in a course to which its principal figures had long since been committed. . . .

My contact with Bahr became a White House backchannel by which Nixon could manage diplomacy bypassing the State Department.[12]

One of Brandt's first acts in his redesign of Ostpolitik was symbolic. On October 28, 1969, he announced that he was changing the title of the ministry that dealt with issues of divided Germany. Hitherto its name had been the ministry for all-German affairs (*gesamtdeutsche Fragen*). Henceforth, according to Brandt's decision, it would be known as the ministry of inner-German relations (*innerdeutsche Beziehungen*). The former title presupposed the claim to sole representation, which was that the Bonn government, as the only democratically elected German government, was the only legitimate representative of the *entire* German nation, including that part of it controlled by the dictatorial and illegitimate SED regime. By changing the title, the Federal Republic de facto abandoned the claim to sole representation and accepted the SED regime as a legitimate and equal partner in diplomatic intercourse.

At the NATO ministerial meeting in Brussels in December 1969, the foreign and defense ministers of the Alliance gave support to the German initiatives:

A just and lasting peace settlement for Germany must be based on the free decision of the German people and on the interests of European security. The Ministers are convinced that, pending such a settlement, the proposals of the Federal Republic for a modus vivendi between the two parts of Germany and for a bilateral exchange of declarations on the non-use of force or the threat of force would, if they receive a positive response, substantially facilitate cooperation between East and West on other problems. . . .

The Ministers would regard concrete progress in both these fields as an important contribution to peace in Europe. They are bound to attach great weight to the responses to these proposals in evaluating the prospects for negotiations looking toward improved relations and cooperation in Europe.[13]

Brandt and many others, including Bahr, assumed that the US was planning to withdraw some, or perhaps all, of its troops from Germany, in view of growing pressures in the United States to reduce overseas commitments as a result of the continuing war in Vietnam. The SPD vision of a European peace order was therefore partially designed to create new options to protect German security interests in the expected

[12] Kissinger, *White House Years*, 410–11.
[13] Dept of State, *Documents on Germany*, 1054.

event of a reduction of US forces. Brandt and Bahr wanted to protect Germany from potential threats should United States troops no longer be stationed on German soil by cultivating, within a European security pact, potential enemies as well as friends.

It was in large part due to Bahr's preliminary work that the new government was able to move swiftly to show its goodwill to the Soviet government. On October 30, 1969, Scheel welcomed a Soviet offer to resume the talks on a treaty of non-aggression and mutual renunciation of force which the grand coalition had pursued in 1967–8 without result. The result of these talks led not to a non-aggression treaty, but to the much broader Moscow treaty of August 1970. On November 28, the Federal Republic signed the nuclear non-proliferation treaty, thus fulfilling a long-standing demand of the Soviet Union and a wish of the United States. And on January 30, 1970, Bahr began a first round of negotiations in Moscow with the Soviet government for the purpose of concluding a treaty which would recognize the status quo in Europe.

1

At Last: The New Ostpolitik

The Brandt–Scheel government pursued several roads simultaneously in order to establish its Ostpolitik as an internally coherent grand diplomatic strategy – negotiations with the Soviet vnion, with Poland, with Czechoslovakia, and with the GDR. These four strands, but especially the first and fourth, were intimately connected; successes and delays along one strand immediately made themselves felt along the others. They were also more generally linked to the state of the talks on Berlin between the Western Allies and the Soviet Union that began in early 1970. The four strands of Ostpolitik were related, in turn, to the state of arms control talks between the US and the Soviet Union which Kissinger had initiated in the spring of 1969.

If Brandt was waiting to decide how to set in motion the talks with the GDR, he did not have to wait long. Realizing that a new, and from the GDR viewpoint, more conciliatory government, was in charge in Bonn, Ulbricht sent the West German government a draft treaty on December 18, 1969, "concerning the establishment of equal relations."[1] Since it assumed not merely two German states, but that these two states had no more, or no less, in common than any two other sovereign states in the world, the Brandt government could not accept it. Ulbricht's proposal, however, began the process of mutual exchanges that led, first, to the visits of Willi Stoph, the head of the SED government, to West Germany and of Brandt to East Germany, and ultimately to the inner-German treaties of 1971–2.

In his first "State of the Nation" address of January 1970, Brandt returned again to his view that since German actions, namely, Hitler's war of aggression, had led to the division of Germany, it was up to Germans to take the lead in moving toward a settlement with the communist regimes. He also sounded a theme that would become

---

[1] Dept of State, *Documents on Germany*, 1055.

commonplace in his vision of the purpose of Ostpolitik, the idea of the nation as a cultural and emotional, and not a political fact, and the concept of sacrificing legal positions to retain as much of that national idea as possible. The speech was one of Brandt's most impressive efforts. It was a *tour d'horizon* of his political vision for Europe in the German perspective that displayed the vigor and enthusiasm of a new beginning:

Some 25 years after the unconditional surrender of the Hitler Reich the concept of the nation forms the tie in divided Germany. In the concept of the nation, historical reality and political will are combined. The word "nation" encompasses and means more than common language and culture, more than state and social system. The word "nation" is based on the continuous feeling of belonging together held by the people of a nation.

Nobody can deny the fact that in this sense there is and will be one German nation as far as we can think ahead. ... We must ... have a historical and political perspective ... if we confirm the demand for self-determination for the whole German people. History which has divided Germany through its own faults – at any rate not without its faults – will decide when and how this demand can be implemented. Yet as long as the Germans muster the political will not to abandon this demand the hope remains that later generations will live in one Germany in whose political system the Germans in their entirety can cooperate.

The national components will also have their place in a European peace settlement. We have, however, a long and tedious way to go to reach self-determination for the Germans. ... The length and difficulty of this road must not prevent us from arriving at a regulated coexistence between the two states in Germany. ... What matters is the German contributions in an international situation in which, to quote President Nixon, a transition from confrontation to cooperation is to occur. ...

[T]he opinion expressed under the term "convergence theory" is wrong and correct simultaneously – wrong because the two states in Germany do not automatically develop toward each other, and correct, because the necessities of modern industrial society in East and West demand measures ... regardless of what political and social conditions exist. ...

The Federal Republic and the GDR are not foreign countries to each other ... recognition of the GDR under international law is out of the question for us. ... Whoever has a minimum of self-respect and sense of realities will have to reject East Berlin's attempts to press conditions on everybody which would not improve European conditions. ... There are ... on our part indispensable orientation points.

1 The right of self-determination,
2 The desire for national unity and freedom within the framework of a European peace order,
3 Close ties with East Berlin. ...

4 [T]he rights and responsibilities of the three powers for Germany as a whole and for Berlin. . . .

What are the objectives toward which German policy in this context should be oriented?

The first answer is that we must preserve freedom in those parts of Germany where it exists today or – as was said – that the Federal Republic must voice its own recognition. The second answer is that we wish to and must solve all our problems only peacefully. The third answer is that we must contribute to the granting and implementation of human rights. . . .

The Federal Government proposes to the GDR Government negotiations on the exchange of declarations on the renunciation of force on the basis of equality and nondiscrimination. Having entered into an exchange of views with the Soviet Union on this issue . . . we consider it a practical step to enter negotiations also with the GDR Government. . . . In the near future, I shall make an appropriate proposal to the chairman of the Council of Ministers [of the GDR]. In this proposal, the Federal Government will proceed from the following principles:

1 Both states are obligated to maintain the unity of the German nation. They are not foreign countries to each other.

2 In other respects, the generally recognized principles of international law must have validity. . . .

3 . . . [T]he obligation not to try to change by force the social structure prevailing in the territory of the other partner.

4 . . . [N]eighborly cooperation. . . .

5 The existing rights and responsibilities of the four powers with regard to Germany as a whole and to Berlin. . . .

6 Efforts of the four powers to make arrangements for an improvement of the situation in and around Berlin are to be supported. . . .

[T]he Federal Government enters into negotiations with the Soviet Union, with Poland, the GDR, and others guided by the serious desire for serious negotiations. . . . The Federal Government is testing itself and the other governments mentioned here to see if efforts for detente and peace are serious.[2]

The terms of reference of Brandt's Ostpolitik were new, though much of the language was not. According to Henry Kissinger, "the Soviet leaders and their East German proteges were clearly intrigued by the prospect of dealing for the first time since the 1930s with a Social Democratic government in Germany."[3] Stephan Thomas, an aide to Brandt and former director of the *Ostbüro* (Eastern Office) of the SPD in West Berlin, pointed to the price Brandt and Bahr were willing to pay to make their Ostpolitik

[2] Ibid., 1059–64.
[3] Kissinger, *White House Years*, 529.

attractive to the East bloc regimes. After Brandt's election the SPD, at Wehner's behest, closed the *Ostbüro*, which maintained contact with the clandestine SPD in the Soviet zone, on the grounds that it was a typical cold war institution. In October 1970 Thomas, in a seminar at the Hoover Institution at Stanford University, defined the "new element" in West German foreign policy as the fact that Brandt enjoyed a better *esprit de corps* – had more in common, in short – with the socialist governments of Eastern Europe than his CDU predecessors.

Whether or not this affinity between socialists in the West and in the East really represented a bridge between Eastern and Western Europe, that had heretofore not existed, was in some ways beside the point. The significant issue was that under Brandt and Scheel the SPD/FDP coalition initiated a concerted and systematic effort to improve relations with Eastern Europe. Thus began, in early 1970, a series of negotiations with the Soviet Union, Poland, the German Democratic Republic, Czechoslovakia, Hungary, Romania, and Bulgaria with the aim of reducing tension and achieving detente between East and West. They thus occurred simultaneously with negotiations, for the first time in eleven years, between France, England, the United States and the Soviet Union on the Berlin problem – and parallel to the discussions between the Soviet Union and the United States concerning the limitation of strategic arms and anti-ballistic missiles.

One of the first results of the new Ostpolitik was not an official government treaty at all, but an economic arrangement for the delivery of oil and gas via pipeline to West Germany from the Soviet Union. The oil and gas agreements resulted from three-cornered negotiations between the Bonn government, West German industry, and the Soviet Union. On February 1, 1970, Soviet and German representatives signed three agreements in Essen. The USSR undertook to supply, over a period of 20 years, 52 billion cubic meters of natural gas, valued at DM 2.5 billion in 1970 prices to Ruhrgas in West Germany. If requested, the Soviet Union promised to increase the amount of gas to be delivered to 80 billion cubic meters. Deliveries were to start in 1973. The gas would be supplied through an extension of the existing pipeline, which ran from the gas fields in Siberia to Bratislava (formerly Pressburg), the main city in eastern Czechoslovakia, located on the Danube river near the junction of the Austro-Hungarian border. The extension was to terminate at Marktredwitz on the Bavarian-Czech border.

The West German Mannesmann group, the largest manufacturer of steel piping in Europe, undertook in return to supply the Soviet Union with 1.2 million tons of large-diameter steel pipes and other equipment during 1970–2. A consortium of 17 West German banks, led by the Deutsche Bank, granted the Soviet Foreign Trade Bank (Vneshtorgbank) credit for the full amount of 1.2 billion marks at an interest rate of 6.25 per cent to finance the sale of pipes, to be repaid, they hoped, within eleven years from the proceeds of the Soviet gas supplies. The loan was ultimately guaranteed by the Bonn government, and therefore by the West German taxpayers.

The agreements were signed by Soyuzneftexport and Promsyrie-export for the Soviet Union and by Ruhrgas, Mannesmann and Deutsche Bank for the West Germans, with Schiller, the German economics minister, and Patolichev, the Soviet foreign trade minister, present at the signing ceremony.

A second set of Soviet-West German agreements, similar to those signed in February 1970, was signed in Düsseldorf in July 1972, whereby a further 1.2 million tons of large-diameter steel pipes would be supplied during 1972–5 to the Soviet Union by Mannesmann of Düsseldorf in return for the supply of natural gas to Ruhrgas. As in the 1970 agreements, a consortium of West German banks, led again by Deutsche Bank, granted a credit of DM 1.2 billion to the Soviet Foreign Trade Bank to finance the pipe supplies, this credit being repayable by 1983, again principally from the proceeds of the Soviet gas supplies. This latter arrangement was concluded at the same time that the Soviet and West German governments signed a major treaty on long-term trade. This accord included West Berlin. It was the first agreement to do so and was seen as introducing a new era in trade development, but West Berlin still was not included in the gas and pipeline agreements (and was not so included until 1981).[4]

These economic and trade negotiations supplied the Soviet economy with needed high technology, while the concurrent political negotiations led to recognition of the Soviet-imposed status quo in Central Europe. Thus, the Soviet Union benefited on both counts, economic and political. Its success was a tribute to persistence and perhaps even more to its underlying military power. In its own view, the Soviet government regarded its developing commercial, industrial, and political gains as simply reflecting the fact that the West had come to a realistic assessment of the strategic balance in Europe.[5] The West German government arrived at its own realistic assessment of what the status quo in Europe required. It concluded that to improve relations between the two parts of Germany the status quo should be defined in a series of treaties. The result was the set of agreements affecting both parts of Germany concluded between 1970 and 1973. They fell into four groups, three of them directly concerning Germany and one concerning East–West relations as a whole:

[4] *Relay from Bonn*, July 6, 1972.
[5] See Ulam, *Expansion and Coexistence*, 751–5.

I   West German treaties with East bloc states:

  1   The Bonn–Moscow Treaty, signed August 12, 1970.

  2   The Bonn–Warsaw Treaty, signed December 7, 1970.

  3   The Bonn–Prague Treaty, signed December 11, 1973.

  4   Treaties establishing diplomatic relations between Bonn and Hungary
       and between Bonn and Bulgaria, concluded in December 1973.

II   Treaties on Berlin:

  1   The Quadripartite Agreement on Berlin, signed September 3, 1971,
       but not put into effect until the foreign ministers of the four powers
       signed the Final Protocol in Moscow on June 3, 1972.

  2   A series of inter-German follow-up agreements in addition to the
       Quadripartite Agreement, regulating postal issues (signed September
       30, 1971), transit to and from West Berlin and from West Berlin to the
       GDR (signed December 17 and December 20, 1971) and exchanges of
       territory in Berlin (signed December 20, 1971), to be put into effect
       together with the Quadripartite Agreement on Berlin on June 3, 1972.

III   Treaties between the two Germanies:

  1   The Inter-German Traffic Accord (*Verkehrsvertrag*), the first agree-
       ment between the governments in Bonn and East Berlin, signed May
       26, 1972.

  2   The Treaty on the Basis of Relations between the Federal Republic
       and the GDR (*Grundlagenvertrag*), signed December 21, 1972.

IV   Arms Control between the Superpowers: SALT I, the first agreement on
     limiting strategic arms, concluded between the United States and the
     Soviet Union, signed in Moscow May 26, 1972.

The treaties in the first three sets, the German treaties, were interrelated
so that progress on each one of them depended on progress on the
others. Since some negotiations were carried on by Bonn and others, on
Berlin, by the three Western powers, this interdependence required
close consultation between Bonn and its Western allies in order to
achieve progress and in order to prevent the Eastern side – which did
not have the same problems of cohesion – from playing West Germany
against its allies and vice versa in order to obtain results more favorable
to itself.

One problem that concerned the United States government, as well as
some Germans, was what direction Ostpolitik might take if and when
the treaties were successfully concluded. Kissinger expressed his
concerns in a letter to President Nixon on February 16, 1970:

The most worrisome aspects of "Ostpolitik," however, are somewhat more long-range. As long as he [Brandt] is negotiating with the Eastern countries over the issues that are currently on the table – recognition of the GDR, the Oder–Neisse, various possible arrangements for Berlin – Brandt should not have any serious difficulty maintaining his basic pro-Western policy. . . .

But assuming Brandt achieves a degree of normalization, he or his successor will discover before long that the hoped-for benefits fail to develop. . . .

Having already invested heavily in their Eastern policy, the Germans may at this point see themselves as facing agonizing choices. It should be remembered that in the 1950s, many Germans not only in the SPD under Schumacher but in conservative quarters traditionally fascinated with the East or enthralled by the vision of Germany as a "bridge" between East and West, argued against Bonn's incorporation in Western institutions on the grounds that it would forever seal Germany's division and preclude the restoration of an active German role in the East. This kind of debate about Germany's basic position could well recur in more divisive form, not only inflaming German domestic affairs but generating suspicions among Germany's Western associates as to its reliability as a partner.[6]

[6] Kissinger, *White House Years*, 529–30.

2

The First Phase of Negotiations

These cross-cutting concerns and hopes provided the political and diplomatic context of the negotiations. In January 1970, Egon Bahr began his discussions with Soviet leaders, and in February the three Western powers announced that, after consultation with Bonn, they accepted the Soviet Union's proposal of quadripartite talks on Berlin. The Brandt government regarded an arrangement with the GDR as the centerpiece of its Ostpolitik but acted on the assumption that the preconditions of such an arrangement were, in the first place, an agreement with Moscow, and, in the second place, a satisfactory Berlin agreement between the four powers. Therefore, Bonn's negotiations with the GDR did not make serious progress until after the Moscow treaty was signed and the quadripartite talks well on their way to a successful conclusion. In Moscow, Bonn received the Soviet Union's agreement to the outlines of the planned arrangement with the GDR. This meant that when, in late 1970, talks between Bahr and the East Germans began in earnest, Bahr assumed that the GDR would have to accept, because he had a Soviet promise to that effect. On March 10, Gromyko told him not to worry about the attitude of third parties – Poland or the GDR – because "the Soviet Union will have a word with them."[1]

Although Bahr was not able to make progress in his talks with the SED representatives until after the Moscow treaty was signed, the most spectacular event in the intra-German relationship in the Brandt era in terms of public effect, took place much earlier, while the Moscow talks and the quadripartite talks were still barely underway. That was Brandt's visit to Erfurt in East Germany in March, the first visit of a West German head of government to what many Germans in the West still called "the Zone."

---

[1] Bracher et al., *Republik im Wandel, 1969–1974*, 215.

Willy Brandt's interlocutor in Erfurt, and later on a return visit to Kassel in West Germany in May, was Willi Stoph, the chairman of the Council of Ministers and thus the formal head of government of the GDR. The real, hidden interlocutor, however, was the aging SED party chief Walter Ulbricht. As head of the communist party, the SED, and therefore also as actual (although not formal) head of state and government, he had not only presided over the transformation of the postwar Soviet zone of Germany into a socialist state subject to Soviet control, he had also, at every step of the way, guided, encouraged and supported the division of the country and of Berlin. The beginning of detente in 1969 posed potential difficulties for the stability of his regime. A genuine relaxation of tensions might very well undermine his authority, given the emotion-laden atmosphere that Ostpolitik was generating.

After building the Berlin Wall in 1961, Ulbricht had introduced incentives to rejuvenate the GDR economy and had tried by various other means to accelerate economic growth. Since the Wall had sealed the border he no longer needed to worry about losing educated professionals and skilled workers to the West. Ideologically Ulbricht took an increasingly independent course, reflecting the new self-confidence of the regime following the Wall. This was astounding to those who remembered his slavish loyalty to Stalin and his use of terror to destroy all rivals, including anyone who advocated even minimal independence from Moscow. In 1968, he announced a theme that was bound to cause alarm in Moscow: he declared that socialism was not merely a stage on the road to achieve communism, but a long-lasting social formation in its own right, and he announced that the GDR was becoming a "socialist human community." In doing so, he implicitly rejected the Soviet Union's claim that communism was the goal and that the Soviet Union was the most advanced socialist society.

The new Ostpolitik in Bonn appeared to have frustrated, if not also confused, Ulbricht. He probably did not expect so rapid a change. In 1963, at the sixth party congress of the SED, Ulbricht had reiterated that "on the way to the establishment of normal relations between the two German states, we want to achieve a confederation that stops the people from drifting further apart and that will free the way to reunion."[2] Faced with the offer of talks and with a new, more friendly Federal Republic that could not easily be depicted in the GDR as an imperialist aggressor state with plans to attack and annex the GDR, Ulbricht and Stoph initially retreated to a maximum position, demanding full diplomatic recognition by Bonn. (Willi Stoph served as chairman of the

[2] Cited in Weber, *Geschichte der DDR*, 505.

Council of Ministers from 1964 to 1973, became chairman of the Council of State from 1973 to 1976, and returned to his post on the Council of Ministers in 1976, a post he continued to hold in 1988. He was born in 1914 and was a construction worker by trade. He joined the KPD in 1931, and first served the GDR as minister of the interior and as minister of defense.)

The East–West German treaties, both those concerning Berlin required by the quadripartite agreement and the general treaty on the basis of relations, resulted from a process of expanding contacts and talks. This process began when Ulbricht, in December 1969, sent a letter to Heinemann, the federal president, with a draft treaty on basic relations founded on the full and unconditional diplomatic recognition of the GDR by Bonn as a sovereign state – a demand Bonn could and would not fulfill. Heinemann's reply did not refer to the draft and proposed, instead, negotiations on the mutual renunciation of force and on humanitarian relief and named Bahr as chief negotiator. In February 1970, therefore, the GDR temporarily dropped the demand for immediate and unconditional recognition and invited Brandt to come to East Berlin – without passing through West Berlin – to discuss the proposed treaty with Stoph and the foreign minister, Otto Winzer. Bypassing West Berlin was unacceptable to Brandt. Therefore the GDR agreed to change the venue to Erfurt and accepted a return invitation for Stoph to come to Kassel in West Germany. The GDR invitation came shortly after Bahr had first gone to Moscow and after the beginning of the quadripartite talks on Berlin. Thus, the course of the intra-German talks was constantly affected by, and in turn affected, the conduct of Ostpolitik on other levels, as well as the Western Allied negotiating position in Berlin.

The meeting in Erfurt was a historical event of the first magnitude. Brandt's trip to the GDR meant that the Federal Republic recognized the existence of "the other Germany." It was the first time that the heads of both German governments had met with one another, a quarter of a century after the war. It raised the hopes of Germans in both East and West that this first meeting might be the beginning of a detente which could result in a much closer relationship between the states in the future, although no one was able to foresee what form it might take.

From the East German viewpoint the meeting was a formal one between two sovereign states. Thus, Stoph was accompanied by his foreign minister, Otto Winzer, as well as by several other officials. Brandt, on the other hand, was joined by his minister for inner-German relations, Egon Franke, in addition to other officials, including his press spokesman, Conrad Ahlers.

Erfurt itself was not without its own meaning. It was one of the birthplaces of the Lutheran Reformation of the sixteenth century and an important economic and cultural center from that time onward. Here, in 1808, Napoleon had said to Goethe that "politics is destiny." For members of the social democratic party Erfurt was also significant for another reason. As Brandt declared in his opening statement to Stoph in the hotel Erfurter Hof:

> For a Social Democrat, it is also natural to think of the role that was played by the Erfurt Programme of 1891, and what it meant for the rising German workers. Wherever one may choose to place this programme in the history of ideology – how much misfortune would the German people, would Europe, would the whole world have been spared, had the will to democracy, the will to broader social justice and the will to peace promptly enough carried the day![3]

Brandt and his entourage traveled to Erfurt by special train from Bonn and arrived at 9:30 a.m. on March 19, a cold and gray morning. Erfurt became "the secret capital of the German nation for this one day." But its appearance was drab and the railway station looked "as if it were put together out of a stone construction set in the thirties."[4] The hotel in which the meeting took place was on the town square, but the square itself was almost empty of people and there were no flags flying. The people of Erfurt were roped off from the square.

> Only as one begins to hear the voices [of the spectators] one half hour before the arrival of the chancellor's train, does it become clear that the barriers, kept especially inconspicuous, were evaded by the masses and now proved to be insufficient as well. Women, trapped by the masses, are screaming, and the crowd grows and grows. . . . Then the Vopos [People's Police] march in – too few too late – they are greeted by howling, irreverent, fearless protest. . . . The howling noise must, also in their ears, sound like stone throws and beatings and falling debris.[5]

In Brandt's own words, when he arrived he "heard chants of 'Willy!' They could have been directed at either of us [Willy Brandt or Willi Stoph]. Then came confirmation: my full name. . . . Apparently, thousands of people risked life and limb by bursting through the flimsy barriers. We covered the 50 yards between the station and the Erfurter Hof Hotel before order temporarily broke down altogether." Once

---

[3] Press and Information Office, *Erfurt March 19, 1970*, 35. The Erfurt Program marked the SPD's emergence as a major political force in nineteenth-century German politics.

[4] *Der Spiegel*, no. 13 (1970), 33.

[5] Ibid.

Christmas in divided Germany. In 1949 the Glienicke Bridge was rebuilt for the use of Allied military vehicles passing between West Berlin and the Western Allied military missions in the Soviet zone, which were (and are) located in Potsdam, immediately outside the southwestern city limits. The GDR authorities renamed it "The Bridge of Unity." On the West Berlin side is mounted a sign that reads: "Those who gave it the name 'The Bridge of Unity' also built the Wall, spread barbed wire, created death strips and thus prevented unity." [*Source*: German Information Center (GIC), New York]

Erhard (center), his foreign minister, Gerhard Schröder (CDU, left) and the American secretary of defense, Robert S. McNamara, during Erhard's first visit to the US in June 1964. McNamara's insistence on increased German offset payments for US troops in Germany contributed to Erhard's domestic and foreign policy difficulties in 1965 and 1966. [*Source*: GIC]

In May 1965, the British royal couple paid a state visit to West Germany. Picture shows Queen Elizabeth II being escorted to dinner in the Petersberg by the federal president, Heinrich Lübke (CDU), who succeeded Theodor Heuss. [*Source*: GIC]

In December 1963, the GDR authorities permitted West Berliners to make day trips into East Berlin during the Christmas season. For the first time in 28 months, some of the families sundered by the Wall were briefly reunited. The price was implicit recognition by the West of GDR sovereignty in the Soviet sector of Berlin. [*Source*: GIC]

Two pro-NATO socialists: the SPD's defense expert, Fritz Erler (right), greeting the British prime minister, Harold Wilson (left), during the latter's visit to Bonn in 1965. Along with Wehner, Erler turned the SPD from opposition to defense in the 1950s to support for NATO and the social market economy in the 1960s. Though he died in 1967, Erler was one of the architects of the SPD victory of 1969. [*Source*: GIC]

In October 1966, the former US High Commissioner, John J. McCloy (right), came to Bonn as special envoy to discuss offset payments. By that time, the question of these payments had already sealed Erhard's fate as chancellor. One reason for McCloy's visit was the worrying report on West Germany's political future given by a Harvard professor, Henry A. Kissinger, in US Senate hearings in June 1966. [*Source*: GIC]

A Franconian nobleman: Karl Theodor Freiherr von and zu Guttenberg (center, with his children) was the foreign policy spokesman of the CSU and an eloquent critic of detente with the GDR, a policy evident in outline by the mid-1960s. What others saw as the only way of alleviating national division, he saw as pointless surrender to communist demands. [*Source*: GIC]

Dignitaries at the memorial service in the Bundestag for Konrad Adenauer, April 1967. From top US President Lyndon B. Johnson; Heinrich Lübke, federal president of Germany; Charles de Gaulle, president of France; Kurt Georg Kiesinger, chancellor of the Federal Republic; Adenauer's eldest son, also named Konrad. [*Source*: GIC]

In 1968, the federal government raised a second monument (*below*) to the victims of Nazism in the grounds of the former concentration camp at Dachau near Munich. Such monuments were an official expression of repentance and the search for reconciliation. [*Source*: GIC]

The revolution in full swing: the radical student leader, Rudi Dutschke (left), in early 1968, debating the sociologist Ralf Dahrendorf (FDP), author of *Society and Democracy in Germany*, a book that enjoyed great influence both inside and outside Germany and made him one of the leading representatives of the progressive (but not radical) intelligentsia. [*Source*: GIC]

One sign of the cultural and political change of the 1960s in West Germany was a new wave of moral concern about the Nazi past and its effects in the present. The new moralists often acted as if they were the first to take the problem seriously. The playwright Rolf Hochhuth fired one of the opening shots of the cultural revolution in his play *The Deputy* (1963), which portrayed Pope Pius XII and the Catholic hierarchy as accomplices of the Third Reich. [*Source*: GIC]

In his 1966 bestseller *Ende oder Wende*, Erhard Eppler, a leader of the SPD left wing, offered a very different solution to the world economic crisis, namely that the West must radically reduce its consumption and transfer its wealth to the Third World. Eppler, who also advocated close ties to the GDR, stood for a politicized version of the moralistic Protestantism of his south-west German homeland. [*Source*: GIC]

Annemarie Renger (SPD), personal secretary to Kurt Schumacher, member of the Bundestag 1953–87 and president 1972–76. One of the first prominent women politicians in West Germany. [*Source*: GIC]

At the height of the demonstration season in the spring of 1968, Andreas Baader (left), a high-school dropout, and Gudrun Ensslin (right), a school teacher, set fire to a department store in Frankfurt, thereby committing the first of a long series of terrorist acts that plagued West Germany through the 1970s. Baader and Ensslin, here shown at their first trial, committed suicide along with several other imprisoned terrorists in 1977. [*Source*: Ullstein/AP]

Terrorism reached its first climax during the 1972 Summer Olympics in Munich, when a Palestinian group killed two Israeli trainers and took nine athletes hostage. The photograph shows one of the terrorists on a balcony of the Israeli quarters in the Olympic village. When Bavarian police tried to free the hostages, the nine Israelis, four terrorists, and one policeman were killed in the gun battle. [*Source*: Süddeutscher Verlag]

The Brandenburg Gate and the Wall in 1969, looking south towards the Potsdamer Platz (left background, behind trees). Since 1961, the GDR authorities have completely razed the Pariser Platz, just east of the Gate, where before the war stood the British and French embassies and two of Berlin's most fashionable hotels, the Adlon and the Bristol. [*Sources*: UPI/Bettmann newsphotos; BBC Hulton Picture Library]

During his visit to Warsaw in 1970 to sign the treaty normalizing relations with communist Poland, Willy Brandt, chancellor since 1969, knelt at the memorial to the 1943 Jewish uprising in the Warsaw ghetto against Nazi occupation. The picture went round the world and shaped an image of Brandt as a German leader seeking reconciliation. *Le Figaro* of Paris commented on December 8, 1970: "The only picture that history will preserve of this day will be that of Brandt before the memorial for the victims of the Warsaw ghetto." [*Source*: GIC]

With militarism and Nazism in vivid memory, the West German government based its armed forces firmly within the framework of the democratic constitution, educating its officers to be genuine citizen soldiers, animated by firm moral principles and commitment to democracy. Helmut Schmidt (SPD, right), who had long been a member of the SPD's pro-defense wing, took over as minister of defense in 1969. This photograph was taken in 1970 at the conclusion of a question and answer meeting with 250 servicemen. [*Source*: GIC]

Leonid Brezhnev, the Soviet party leader, welcomes Brandt at his dacha in the Crimea in September 1971 to discuss further steps in detente after the Bonn–Moscow treaty of August 1970. [*Source*: GIC]

Brandt with Yigal Allon, a leader of the Israeli Labor Party and a famed military commander, in the Ginnossar kibbutz, Israel, in the summer of 1973. A few months later, during the October War, Brandt took a neutral stand that the US and Israel regarded as pro-Arab but which satisfied the growing pro-Third World and anti-American sentiment on the SPD left wing. [*Source*: GIC]

Brandt with a principal aide, Günter Guillaume, in April 1974, just before Guillaume was arrested as an East German spy. While dissatisfaction with Brandt's leadership had been mounting, this affair was the straw that broke the camel's back and led to his resignation. [*Source*: Bundesbildstelle Bonn]

Walter Ulbricht, the communist ruler of the GDR (right), was not convinced that talks with Bonn were useful to his regime. He was therefore ousted in 1971 by Erich Honecker (left), with the full approval of Soviet leader Brezhnev (center), who understood that negotiations would bring far greater diplomatic and economic gains than confrontation, and at no cost to the communist position in Germany or in Europe. In 1969 Ulbricht was still in power as he presided over the twentieth anniversary celebration of the founding of the GDR. [*Source*: GIC]

"As long as we are dealing with negotiating partners such as these, it [the negotiations] can't be too bad." So Michael Kohl (left), the GDR negotiator, described the talks with Egon Bahr (right) that led to Bonn's recognition of the GDR in the treaty of 1972. For the GDR, the treaty was political victory in a long struggle for power in Germany; for Bahr (SPD), it was a triumph for peace and stability. Taken on June 20, 1973, this photograph shows the exchange of notes formally confirming ratification of the Basic Treaty between the two German states. [*Source*: GIC]

Another use for the Berlin Wall, circa 1977. [*Source*: GIC]

In 1977, *Der Spiegel* took a poll of French views of the Germans. This cover shows the result in humorous form: a fat German eagle, perched on a Mercedes with a wad of hundred-mark notes in its claw. In the foreground a bomb with a burning fuse, a reference to terrorism which had reached its apogee a few weeks earlier with the hijacking of a Lufthansa airliner. The handcuffs symbolize the fear of many liberals that the authorities, in responding to terrorism, might violate civil rights. [*Source*: *Der Spiegel* cover, November 21, 1977]

inside the hotel the chancellor heard cries of "Willy Brandt to the window!"

I hesitated, then went to the window and looked down at the excited and expectant people who had claimed the right to hold this spontaneous demonstration. . . . I reminded myself that this was not the first time I had visited a Germany deprived of freedom. Then, I could not help feeling an enemy in my native land. Here it was different. I was moved, but I had to consider the fate of these people: I would be back in Bonn next day, they would not. . . . I made a gesture urging restraint, and my point was taken. The crowd fell silent. Turning away with a heavy heart, I noticed that many of my aides had tears in their eyes. I was afraid of kindling hopes that could not be fulfilled, so I adopted a suitably low-key manner. (The authorities later sent in People's Police reinforcements and squads of loyal factory workers who chanted Stoph's name and demanded "recognition.")[6]

This was what people remembered – the chanting, excited Erfurters, the chancellor hesitant to encourage them. The meeting with Stoph itself, of great symbolic importance, was devoid of concrete result. Sessions were held in the morning and afternoon, and concluded with a visit to the former concentration camp, Buchenwald, by Brandt and Winzer, the GDR foreign minister. The meetings also included two private discussions, without third parties present; as Stoph said, "We both speak German."[7] The meeting served the purpose of allowing the leaders to exchange views on what divided them, as well as on their hopes for peace in Europe. Brandt rejected Stoph's proposal that both governments agree on immediate and joint application for membership in the United Nations, but listened to Stoph's conclusion that Bonn had pursued a "hostile policy of interference" prior to building of the Berlin Wall:

The citizens of the GDR were "relieved" of more than 100,000 million marks. To demonstrate the full extent of this economic war with its enormous damage, let me say that the sum given is nearly as high as the national income of the GDR in 1956 and 1957 taken together. . . . While Bonn spoke of "poor brothers and sisters in the East," everything was done to make them really poor. We assume the Government of the Federal Republic will understand that in our view payment of the debts to the GDR and the fulfilment of all obligations to make good the damages are indispensable.[8]

Stoph insisted that any talks must be based on the GDR draft treaty that Ulbricht proposed in December and, in a cold, arrogant tone, repeated

---

[6] Brandt, *People and Politics*, 371–2.
[7] Ibid., 378.
[8] Press and Information Office, *Erfurt March 19, 1970*, 24.

old GDR propaganda clichés to the effect that the Federal Republic was a militaristic, expansionist state waiting to annex the GDR. In his response, Brandt repeated the six points of his January state of the nation speech. Unlike Stoph, however, he moved beyond his own earlier position, thus setting a pattern that would become familiar over the next years, a pattern of Eastern intransigence and Western concession. Brandt had unequivocally indicated, as had Kiesinger, that the West German government would not attempt to overthrow the GDR by force. In Erfurt, he expanded on this point: "Neither of us can act for the other, neither can represent the other part of Germany abroad. . . . No one must try to subject the other to overweening influence. I have not come here to demand the liquidation of any ties of the GDR or of any social order."[9] This was a significant conclusion. Brandt was saying, in effect, that West Germany would do nothing that might be construed as threatening the sovereignty of the GDR. This was a broad concept, and the GDR in future years made full use of this policy to restrain West Germany from pursuing policies it did not like.

Shortly after the Erfurt meeting, the US secretary of state, William Rogers, was asked at a press conference whether he was worried that the two Germanies might be reunified. His reply was that the US had always hoped there would be a unified Germany. He also stated that he was not worried by Bahr's Moscow talks. Klaus Bölling, who represented the first German television network (ARD) in Washington, and who was later to become Helmut Kohl's press spokesman, asked Rogers whether he feared "special arrangements between Germany and the Soviet Union," arrangements that might conjure up memories of the Soviet–German Rapallo treaty of 1922. (Rapallo was the first foreign treaty signed by the fledgling Soviet Union, which became a symbol of a German tendency to seek security by arrangements with the great power to the east at the expense of general European security.) Rogers replied that he was not worried: "We don't think there is anything at all inconsistent about a strong NATO and an attempt to improve the relations between Western European countries and Eastern European countries. . . . The Federal Republic is just trying to get to the same position that some of the other Western European countries are in presently."[10]

The meeting in Kassel was held in the Schlosshotel, in which Emperor Napoleon III had been imprisoned a century before, and where Hitler had stayed. The meeting in Kassel, however, occurred under the shadow of demonstrations by both right-wing and left-wing

[9] Dept of State, *Documents on Germany*, 1079–80.
[10] Ibid., 1083–4.

extremists. Such disorder existed that Brandt and Stoph had to postpone their visit to the memorial for victims of fascism until the evening, and the GDR flag was pulled down by three demonstrators and torn to pieces.

At Kassel, Stoph reiterated that the GDR draft treaty must be the basis of talks, while claiming, somewhat sanctimoniously, that the GDR insisted on no preconditions. Brandt for his part proposed 20 points as the basis for a treaty between both states.

1   The FRG and the GDR . . . will conclude in the interest of peace and the future and cohesion of the nation a treaty which arranges the relations between the two German states and Germany, improves contacts . . . and contributes to the elimination of existing difficulties. . . .

2   The treaty is to be submitted in the forms laid down by the Constitution through the legislative bodies of both sides.

3   The two sides are to . . . arrange their relations on the basis of human rights, equality, peaceful coexistence, and non-discrimination.

4   Both sides will refrain from any threat of use of force. . . .

5   Both sides will respect the independence and separate status of each of the two states in matters concerning their internal sovereign authority.

6   Neither of the two German states can act for or represent the other.

7   The contracting sides declare that never again must a war arise from German territory.

8   They undertake to refrain from any actions which are likely to disturb the peaceful coexistence of nations.

9   Both sides . . . support all efforts aiming at disarmament and arms control, serving to increase European security. . . .

10   The treaty must proceed from the consequences of World War II and the special situation of Germany and the Germans who live in two states and yet feel as members of one nation.

11   Existing obligations toward . . . the United States . . . and the USSR which are based on special rights and agreements between those powers regarding Berlin and Germany as a whole will remain untouched.

12   The four-power agreements on Berlin and Germany will be respected. The same holds true for the bonds which have arisen between West Berlin and the FRG. Both sides undertake to support the efforts of the four powers to normalize the situation in and around Berlin.

13   Both sides will study those areas in which there are incompatibilities between the legislation of the two German states. . . .

14   The treaty is to . . . expand . . . free movement.

15   The problems which arise from the separation of families are to be brought to a solution.

16   Districts . . . along the common border should . . . solve problems existing there in a neighborly manner.

17   Both states . . . affirm their readiness to . . . expand cooperation in . . . the fields of transport, post and telecommunications, exchange of information, science, education, culture, and questions of environment and sports. . . .

18   Existing agreements . . . and trade contracts . . . will continue to be valid.
. . .

19   The two sides will appoint plenipotentiaries with ministerial rank and establish offices for the permanent representatives of the plenipotentiaries.
. . .

20   The FRG and the GDR will . . . regulate their membership and cooperation in international organizations.[11]

The main points were similar to those of Bahr's 1968 paper: unity of the nation, equal status of the German states, renunciation of the use and threat of force, and continuation of the four-power responsibility for Berlin and Germany as a whole, the promise of cooperation in a wide range of political and economic areas, and joint membership in international organizations. The GDR, however, was still not ready for any of these proposals, and continued to insist on full diplomatic recognition as a precondition for future talks. An American scholar summed up the GDR viewpoint as follows:

These recommendations must have spelled out for the SED in a concrete way the practical implications of regularized contacts with the FRG. At once, the GDR would become permeable. Its boundaries would be opened to routine traffic and travel, and at the same time, through a flood of resuscitated family ties, friendships, and everyday contacts between the two systems, the hearts and minds of the East German citizenry would be exposed to a panoply of new ideas, sentiments, and expectations.

With some candor, Stoph assured Brandt that he, too, was aware that many people had suffered hardships under Germany's division. But, he stressed, his government was not about "to raise false hopes" in the minds of its citizenry. The GDR had already had "bitter experiences" dealing with these issues, "especially before 13 August 1961," and it was not about to repeat them. On this basis, Stoph broke off the talks, arguing that the West Germans (and not his government evidently) needed time to reconsider their views.[12]

In his reply to Stoph, Brandt noted that "you insist on a position of all or nothing. You have not said one word about what positive consequences would ensue for our nation and the people in the two German states. . . .

---

[11]   Ibid., 1087–8.
[12]   McAdams, *East Germany and Detente*, 104.

You have not said one word about the hardships imposed on the German people by their division. . . . You did say that the GDR Government is guided by the interests of the people, but concrete information on this from your side is lacking." Stoph concluded the session by repeating that the GDR draft treaty, which demanded full diplomatic recognition and included no references whatever to the German people, must be the basis of talks. "We have encountered a negative attitude of the FRG Government in all basic questions," he insisted, which was true given the communist position that any objection to any demands was a "negative attitude." He recommended a "time to think" (*Denkpause*).[13] On this at least the two sides were agreed; nothing further took place on the intra-German level until October. Meanwhile, the Bonn–Moscow talks reached their conclusion in a treaty.

Hope and uncertainty weighed equally on the judgement of political leaders on all sides of the political spectrum in West Germany as Bahr negotiated in Moscow in the late winter and spring of 1970. When he concluded 50 hours of talks with Gromyko in Moscow on May 22, he drafted a memorandum setting out the basis for official negotiations. The Bonn government informed its NATO allies of the results of the talks as reported in the Bahr memorandum (not to be confused with Bahr's 1968 policy paper setting forth his overall strategic conception of Ostpolitik, which was made public in 1973) and leaked parts of it to the press. In early June the *Bild Zeitung* obtained a complete copy and published it. It then became clear that the memorandum, later known as the "Bahr Paper," was in reality nothing less than the draft of the proposed treaty itself, and not merely a report of negotiations. Many Germans felt that Bahr had gone too far too fast, and that he had made promises on behalf of the Bonn government that by no means all Germans wished that government to make.

The Bahr Paper contained ten points, the first four of which became parts of the final treaty and the last six of which were declarations of intent regarding other aspects of Ostpolitik. It stated that the Federal Republic and the Soviet Union would work for detente, would be guided by the principles of the UN charter, and "are in agreement . . . that peace in Europe can only be maintained if no one infringes present borders. . . . They regard . . . the borders of all states in Europe as inviolable . . . including the Oder–Neisse line . . . and the border between the FRG and the GDR." In the second part of the paper, the two sides agreed that the proposed West German Ostpolitik vis-à-vis the GDR, Poland, Czechoslovakia, and the Soviet Union must be "a single whole" – this was an essential Soviet demand to demonstrate

---

[13] Dept of State, *Documents on Germany*, 1092–3.

Bonn's acceptance of the status quo. West Germany must reject the *Alleinvertretungsanspruch* (claim to sole representation); both German states must join the UN; Bonn must expand economic, technical, and cultural cooperation with the Soviet Union; and Bonn must join the Soviet call for a European security conference – the plan that in 1973 became the Conference on Security and Cooperation in Europe (CSCE).[14]

Recognizing the existence of the GDR constituted, in effect, the abandonment of the claim that only the Federal Republic had the right to represent the German people. It was also interpreted by Brandt's critics as the tacit abandonment of the claim that the goal of West German policy regarding the German nation must be to obtain political reunification via free elections in the East. While the preamble of the Basic Law calling on all Germans to work for unity was not alluded to, the fact was that political reunification was being abandoned as a national policy. It was replaced by a new goal, particularly important to Brandt and Bahr, that of creating a new idea of German commonality (not unity) as a *Kulturnation*; that is, a "cultural nation" whose bonds would not be official, political ones, but ones based on a common heritage and common hopes for peace in Europe. Brandt and Bahr sought to move toward the *Kulturnation* via humanitarian improvements in the living conditions of Germans in the GDR, and these would be obtained by lending the regime money, by buying goods on terms favorable to the GDR, and by creating an atmosphere of detente.

The Bahr Paper implied West German acceptance of Soviet rule in Central and Eastern Europe, since its negotiation in Moscow directly acknowledged that Soviet approval was needed for any negotiations or treaties with East European states. This was also a change in a policy of 20 years, which held that the Soviet Union had no right to control or speak for the East Europeans, and especially for the East Germans. It also renounced any West German claim, so argued Bahr's critics, on the Western allies to act on their promises in the Paris Treaties of 1954 to work for German reunification. Further, Bonn undertook to reject, once and for all, the Hallstein Doctrine by which the Federal Republic regarded recognition of the GDR by third parties as an unfriendly act that could aggravate the division of Germany. Instead, from 1970 to 1972, Bonn adopted an interim position that became known as the Scheel Doctrine. Under the Scheel Doctrine, Bonn no longer regarded recognition of the GDR as a hostile act, but requested friendly states to delay such recognition until after a basic treaty between the Federal Republic and the GDR was concluded.

[14] Ibid., 1101–3.

The final negotiations on the treaty were conducted by Scheel and Gromyko in Moscow. The treaty was signed in the Catherine room of the Kremlin on August 12, 1970, by Brandt and the chairman of the Soviet Council of Ministers (and thus formal head of government), Aleksei Kosygin, as well as by the foreign ministers, Scheel and Gromyko. But the trip did not occur without incident. While Brandt's stay in Moscow was smooth, his departure from Bonn was delayed by a bomb threat. Thus he expressed the symbolism of his, and therefore Germany's late arrival in Moscow, by greeting Kosygin with the words, "We have come late, but we have come – 15 years after Adenauer."

The treaty repeated the provisions of the Bahr Paper. A careful but sympathetic analyst of the Eastern treaties, Benno Zündorf (a pseudonym concealing the name of a high-ranking foreign ministry official, Antonius Eitel, an aide of Bahr's) argued in 1979 that the Soviet government accepted Bonn's aim of German unity in the treaty preamble, which incorporated by reference the exchange of identical letters between Adenauer and Soviet prime minister Bulganin in 1955 which established Soviet-West German diplomatic relations. Those letters expressed the hope that "the establishment and development of normal relations ... will contribute to the solution of outstanding problems concerning the whole of Germany and will thus contribute also to the solution of the main common national problems of the German people – the establishment of a united democratic German state." In addition, on the same day, August 12, one day before the ninth anniversary of the Berlin Wall, the West German government delivered to the Soviet government a "Letter regarding German Unification" stating that the federal government continued to endorse the "political objective" of German reunification in "free self-determination."[15]

In the Moscow treaty, the Federal Republic recognized the existing realities in Europe in 1970; that is, the prevailing status quo. Brandt's critics argued that the treaty meant renunciation of the commitment to pursue a policy aimed at reunification of Germany. But Peter Bender, an outspoken supporter of Ostpolitik, wrote that because the Soviets agreed to accept the letter on German unity, "Moscow cannot denounce Bonn's efforts at reunification as impermissible."[16] In fact supporters and critics both had to acknowledge that the letter was not legally binding. It was simply a letter. It did, however, state clearly Bonn's commitment to German unity. From West Germany's viewpoint, this commitment, publicly stated, was of both real and symbolic importance. From the Soviet Union's viewpoint the treaty, because it represented

[15] Ibid., 456, 1105.
[16] Bender, *Neue Ostpolitik*, 172.

West German recognition of the status quo in Europe, contributed to political stability in Central Europe. But from the perspective of the future, neither Brandt's critics nor his supporters were correct. Inclusion of a similar affirmation of Bonn's concern with German unity in the Soviet-West German treaty of 1955 had never prevented the Soviet government from denouncing any policy it chose to interpret as an effort at reunification on Bonn's part.

Other aspects of the negotiations, however, attracted criticism of a different kind. Some faulted the haste with which they had been concluded, and others asserted that Egon Bahr had been allowed to exert too much of his own influence on the discussions. These concerns were of enormous importance. Rolf Lahr, a senior foreign ministry official, who was serving as West German ambassador to Rome in 1970, outlined them in a private letter to a colleague in Bonn. He criticized Bahr for placing Scheel in the position of negotiating in Moscow when there was nothing left to discuss. He also believed that "dilettantism was at work" since the Bonn–Moscow treaty was signed prior to an agreement on Berlin. But he recognized that the outcome might not have been different had Bahr been given less flexibility in his discussions and had he taken more time to negotiate. What really worried him, however, was that the "Eastern euphoria" made it difficult to judge the long-term consequences and that Ostpolitik might distract attention from what Lahr called "European and Atlantic policy."[17]

The Americans, by August well engaged in quadripartite talks on Berlin and in arms control talks bilaterally with the Soviet Union, greeted the Moscow treaty favorably, noting that "the treaty cannot affect our continuing rights and responsibilities for Berlin and Germany as a whole."[18] Scheel had in fact declared to Gromyko on August 6 that the treaty they were about to sign had no relevance to four-power rights, and Gromyko had responded with a similar declaration.

In a speech to the German Foreign Policy Society on October 20, 1970, the US ambassador to Germany, Kenneth Rush, provided an assessment of the completed first stage of Ostpolitik, of which the Moscow treaty was only a part, albeit an essential part.

Regarding the *Ostpolitik* of the Federal Republic, I would make three points.

First, because the problem of Germany remains the key to East–West problems in Europe, we have welcomed movement toward a normalization of relations between the Federal Republic and its neighbors to the East. We support the objectives of the Federal Republic in this effort, and we have full

---

[17] Lahr, *Zeuge von Fall und Aufstieg*, 549–50.
[18] Dept of State, *Documents on Germany*, 1106.

confidence in Chancellor Brandt and his government. We also have welcomed the treaty which was signed by the Federal Republic and the Soviet Union in August. With the Federal Republic, we hope that it is a first step toward a general improvement in East–West relations.

Second, we have been fully satisfied with the close consultations which we have carried on with the Federal Republic on this subject. . . .

Finally, with respect to the treaty between the Federal Republic and the Soviet Union, we share the hope . . . that its signature will now be followed by progress in the negotiations on Berlin.[19]

Ambassador Rush went on to refer to the SALT talks, progress in which he hoped would stimulate progress in Germany's negotiations, and to the Warsaw Pact call for a conference on European security. At that point, in October 1970, the US view was that such a conference would be meaningless because the subject, security in general, was too abstract. A conference without precise objectives would merely be a forum for Soviet bloc peace propaganda. Finally, he reiterated NATO's call in May 1970 for East–West talks on mutual and balanced force reductions (MBFR) in Europe.

Two months later, in December of 1970, a political analyst in the United States drew a conclusion that emphasized a different aspect of the treaty's significance:

. . . Treaty is not detente. . . . As Chancellor Brandt recently observed, West Germany needs both "cooperation and consultation" with the West and also, "understanding" with the East. But Bonn's need for "understanding" does not excuse equivocation on the definition of realities. . . . The minefields still divide Germany. The Wall still cuts across Berlin, dividing families and serving as an altar for the death of refugees. The political borders dividing Europe remain. Soviet goals have not changed. Peaceful coexistence has not become detente. It is obviously folly to predict the future course of history. But it is dangerous error to ignore the lessons of the past. As we look toward the East, it is also well, as Aeschylus wrote some 2,400 years ago, to observe the flight of crook-taloned birds, marking which are of the right by nature, and which are of the left, how they consort together, and the enmities and affections that are between them.

East–West relations in Europe are changing. But sometimes the more things change, the more they remain the same, as *Neues Deutschland* . . . recently observed in reference to this treaty. The following citation demonstrates a reality that should be as clear as the difference between detente and cold war . . . "The imperialist wolf appears to some as a generous grandmother. But in reality it is here as in fairy tales. Wolf remains wolf!"[20]

[19] Ibid., 1109–10.
[20] Bark, *Congressional Record,* vol. 117, no. 1 (January 21, 1971).

3

Poland

In February 1970 negotiations between West Germany and Poland also began, and led to an agreement which was concluded in December 1970, but not ratified until June 1972. Like the other Eastern treaties, this settlement consisted of a main treaty text and a series of supplementary documents addressing the contested issues. These issues were the ones most important to Bonn, since they concerned human rights. But addressing them in documents that were not part of the treaty itself allowed Poland to imply that such concerns were peripheral.

The preamble referred to the war "of which Poland became the first victim and which inflicted great suffering on the nations of Europe." It went on to promise mutual renunciation of force and cooperation, but the most important elements were the West German recognition of the Oder–Neisse line as the Western frontier of the Polish People's Republic (that is, of the currently constituted Polish state and not of Poland as it had existed prior to the war): "The Federal Republic . . . and the People's Republic of Poland state . . . that the existing boundary line the course of which is laid down in Chapter IX of the decisions of the Potsdam Conference . . . shall constitute the western State frontier of the People's Republic of Poland."[1] Since West Germany had no common border with Poland, this guarantee by West Germany of a border between two third parties, communist Poland and the GDR, was an indirect acknowledgment by the Polish regime that the Bonn government, to some at least, was a representative of united Germany and could speak for united Germany in the border question. Other provisions promised aid and trade, and in return the Polish government promised to permit the remaining Germans, approximately 300,000, still living in the former Eastern territories of Germany, to emigrate to

[1] Dept of State, *Documents on Germany*, 1125–6.

the Federal Republic. This last provision was the source of permanent wrangling and of successful attempts to extort money from Bonn, because the Polish regime at first claimed that there were only 60,000 persons who could even be considered for emigration permits. Warsaw made the issuance of further permits dependent on economic concessions by Bonn.

As in the case of the Moscow treaty, the Polish agreement signaled the general acceptance by the Bonn government of the position of the Polish regime. No rights were secured for the last remaining Germans in the old Eastern territories, now a part of Poland, and there was no question of *Wiedergutmachung* (restitution) or apology for the expulsion of several million Germans from their ancestral homelands. Instead the Polish government placed the full burden of guilt on the West Germans. Brandt accepted this burden and it strengthened his image of a good German burdened with guilt by the sins of his country.

Brandt's visit to Warsaw in December, to sign the treaty, produced the second of the great symbolic images of the Brandt era, the first being his reaction to the spontaneous demonstration in Erfurt in March. After the signing ceremony, Brandt visited the memorial to victims of the Warsaw ghetto uprising of early 1943, when primarily unarmed Jews rose in hopeless revolt against the German occupiers. Without warning Brandt fell to his knees at the memorial, producing a pictorial image that went around the world. Brandt himself commented:

I went down on my knees before the memorial to those who died in the Warsaw Ghetto. Despite malicious comments in the Federal Republic, I was not ashamed to have done so. This gesture, which attracted worldwide attention, was not "planned." ... Oppressed by the memories of Germany's recent history, I simply did what people do when words fail them. My thoughts dwelt not only on the millions who had been murdered but also on the fact that, Auschwitz not withstanding, fanaticism and the suppression of human rights persisted. My gesture was intelligible to those willing to understand it, and they included many in Germany and elsewhere.[2]

The treaty was criticized by the opposition, particularly the CSU, who claimed that it "represents a gloomy climax of the government's policy pursued behind the backs of those affected by it." However, the writer Günter Grass, a native of Danzig – a former German city in Poland – who, as a private citizen, had accompanied Brandt to Warsaw, said on a television program after the signing: "After the war's end, I realized that I had lost my native city. ... Today I watched how a courageous political

---

[2] Brandt, *People and Politics*, 399.

leader succeeded in breaking a chain of injustices and paying off part of the mortgage of a war launched and lost [by Germany]."[3]

The treaty guaranteed the Oder–Neisse line, although formally it stated that it could not bind any future unified German government, which in theory would be entitled to renegotiate the German-Polish border in a future peace treaty. Despite Bonn's correct legal reservations, however, both friends and adversaries of West Germany regarded the treaty as tantamount to abandonment of all claims to the Eastern territories, a quarter of a century after the Potsdam Conference.

One important symbolic expression of this attitude was that the Vatican, which under Pope Paul VI was conducting its own active Ostpolitik vis-à-vis the communist regimes, abandoned its formal position that diocesan borders in the Oder–Neisse territories could be changed only as a result of a postwar peace treaty with a German government. This position depended on the *Reichskonkordat* of 1933, the treaty between the German government and the Vatican defining the mutual rights and obligations of church and state. One of the concordat's provisions was that any change of ecclesiastical administrative structure must be approved by the German government, and changing the borders of dioceses and church provinces (archdioceses) clearly was such a change. After 1949, the Vatican, the CDU-led governments of 1949–69, and the German Catholic hierarchy, all had an interest in preserving the concordat, mainly because it guaranteed the Catholic church considerable influence on the public school system. The Christian democratic state in West Germany, moreover, was in the 1950s the Vatican's ally against communism. German Catholics were relatively prosperous and provided the Church with more contributions than any other Catholic population outside the US.[4] The CDU government, for its part, wanted to maintain the *Reichskonkordat* not only to preserve religious instruction for Catholics in the public schools, but because it was one of the legal proofs of the continuity of the German state.

The Vatican, accordingly, had refused until 1970 to transfer the province (archdiocese) of Ermland (East Prussia) and those portions of the provinces of Berlin and Breslau that were east of the Oder–Neisse line, to Polish prelates. The German diocesan structure remained intact, but the Polish communist regime did not allow the German bishops and priests to reside in their dioceses. Instead, the Polish cardinal, Hlond, had in 1945 placed administrators in the prelacies of the Oder–Neisse territories. When the social-liberal coalition came to

---

[3] *Relay from Bonn*, December 8, 1970.
[4] Spotts, *Churches and Politics in Germany*, 217.

power in 1969 and indicated that it was prepared to recognize the Oder–Neisse line as a legitimate state border, the Vatican abandoned the fiction that the terms of the *Reichskonkordat* required it to wait for the restoration of a united German government to make changes in provincial administration and boundaries. The German Catholic hierarchy, which since the Vatican Council of 1962–5 had been, in the main, notably more conservative politically than the pope, resisted but could not overcome the combined forces of the new Bonn government, the Vatican, and public opinion. In June 1972, Rome appointed Polish bishops to the former German dioceses.[5]

[5] Ibid., 229–33.

4

The Berlin Agreement and European Security

S ince the building of the Berlin Wall in 1961 travel between West
Berlin and West Gemany had become subject to frequent harassment by East German police. At the borders cars and trucks usually had
to wait in long lines to receive a visa giving them the right to pass
through East German territory. Automobiles with foreign license plates
had to exchange them for East German plates for the length of the trip,
which was a very unpleasant experience for drivers in the dead of winter,
who had to remove the old plates and screw on new ones in extreme
cold, and then reverse the process when they got to the GDR checkpoints at the edge of Berlin. Automobiles and trucks were searched for
newspapers and magazines, and waiting for a visa could take as long as
one or two days if the East Germans deliberately slowed down the
process.

In early 1969, as Richard Nixon assumed office, the Soviets and
East Germans stepped up pressure and threats against the access
routes to West Berlin because of the West German practice of electing
the new federal president in the city. In April, Brandt, then foreign
minister, recommended at the conference of NATO foreign and
defense ministers in Washington that the three Western powers
approach the Soviet government for an exchange of views on Berlin. In
response to the initiative taken by the three Western powers in August,
the Soviet government proposed in an aide-mémoire of February 10,
1970, quadripartite negotiations on Berlin. On the 25th, Brandt
reported to the Western Allies on the first stage of Bahr's Moscow
talks, and said pointedly that his government placed particular value
"on a speedy start of four-power talks on Berlin on the basis of an
agreed Western position."[1] Two days later the Western Allies stated
that, following "consultations with the Government of the Federal

---

[1] Cited in Bracher et al., *Republik im Wandel, 1969–1974*, 198.

Republic," they would open discussions on the ambassadorial level in Berlin.[2]

These discussions were held in the Air Safety Control Center in the American sector of Berlin. The building served as the headquarters for the control of air traffic to and from Berlin, monitored by representatives of the four powers, and was formerly the headquarters of the Allied Control Council. (See part I, chapter 6, "The Potsdam Conference," p. 49.) The Western position, according to Klaus Schütz (SPD), the governing mayor of (West) Berlin at that time, included three essentials: first, informal affiliation of West Berlin with the institutions of the Federal Republic; second, free movement between the Federal Republic and West Berlin; and third, unimpeded access for West Berliners to East Berlin and the GDR. At the first meeting on March 26, the four ambassadors agreed "that the meetings will be confidential and that there will be a minimum coverage on their course."[3]

After Brandt and Kosygin signed the Moscow treaty in August, the Soviet interest in moving forward in the Berlin talks waned. Scheel announced in October 1970 that the federal government would not ratify the Bonn–Moscow treaty until West Berlin was safe. Brandt made his view of the interdependence of the quadripartite talks and Bahr's talks with the GDR, which had begun in October, even clearer in a statement of December 1. He distinguished the issue of traffic between the two Germanies from the issue of access to Berlin.

When the Four Powers reach agreement on the subject – I emphasize, not until then – the German Federal Government will be prepared to talk with the German Democratic Republic on a supplementary agreement ... Thus we differentiate between general traffic questions between the two states, which can be discussed soon, and questions relating to Berlin traffic, on which the Four Powers must reach a settlement of basic principles. ...

Without detente in and around Berlin there can be no detente in Europe.[4]

Strong and openly declared support from the West was an essential component of Brandt's Ostpolitik in all its stages. Conversely NATO, and in particular the US, wanted to make very sure that the Brandt-Scheel-Bahr Ostpolitik did not weaken Germany's ties to the West, and in particular Germany's defense contribution. German soldiers and payments to the US were more important than ever in the early 1970s, when the US Congress initiated a seven-year period of severe, even drastic, cuts in the American defense budget. Mike Mansfield, the

[2] Dept of State, *Documents on Germany*, 1070.
[3] Ibid., 1081.
[4] Ibid., 1116–7.

Democratic majority leader in the Senate, called repeatedly for a reduction of US troop strength overseas. Mansfield spoke for many who wanted not only to get the US out of Vietnam, regardless of the consequences, but who would even consider withdrawing from Europe. Schmidt, the defense minister, knew that the US had effectively reduced its strength in Germany by 20 per cent between 1967 and 1970. *Der Spiegel*, whose editor Rudolf Augstein favored the prospect of the American troops leaving Germany, reported on April 13, 1970, that Brandt's government believed that "starting in 1972, the Americans will reduce their troop strength in Germany, whether by multilateral or bilateral agreement," and that this belief was the chief motive for Ostpolitik. According to this view, Brandt hoped to secure Soviet agreement to maintain the status quo and not to use its military might to dominate Western Europe even in the event of an American withdrawal. The chancellor desired "to come closer to a European peace order that might last beyond the time when the Americans may turn their backs on Europe."[5]

Der Spiegel's fears – or Augstein's hopes – were unfounded, which was undoubtedly fortuitous, since there was no evidence for the belief that the Soviet Union would be restrained by treaties once the counterweight of American forces was gone. At the NATO ministers' meeting of December 1970 in Brussels, the US promised to "maintain and improve its own forces in Europe" and not to reduce them "except in the context of reciprocal East–West action." The "ministers expressed their profound satisfaction at the reaffirmation of Alliance solidarity expressed in this statement," welcomed the Moscow and Warsaw treaties and hoped for progress in the talks on Berlin.

In a separate document on "Alliance Defence for the Seventies" the NATO governments reported that, pursuant to the Harmel Report of 1967, they had conducted "a full and candid exchange of views . . . on their common defence over the next ten years." This exchange resulted in the decision to begin a European Defense Improvement Program (EDIP), a five-year program of improving defense readiness and efficiency, as agreed between the members of NATO's Eurogroup, the European members of the Alliance. They further reported that "NATO's approach to security in the 1970s will continue to be based on the twin concepts of defence and detente," while noting "certain disturbing facts in the international situation. . . . [T]he USSR, intent on extending and strengthening its political power, conducts its international relations on the basis of concepts some of which are not conducive to detente." This referred to the Brezhnev Doctrine that a

[5] Cited in Bracher et al., *Republik im Wandel, 1969–1974*, 176–7.

socialist state must not be permitted to defect from the socialist camp, and perhaps as a consequence the Soviet Union had been increasing its military capabilities, both nuclear and conventional, at a far higher rate than NATO. "Whether East–West relations can in these circumstances be significantly improved," the ministers concluded, "will depend mainly on the actions of the USSR and its Warsaw Pact allies. . . . Progress toward a meaningful detente in an era of negotiation will . . . require the maintenance of a strong collective defence posture."[6]

In response to the repeated calls by the East bloc for a conference on security in Europe, the NATO governments made preparations for such a conference contingent on a satisfactory Berlin agreement and favorable progress in the SALT talks. Just two days before the NATO statement, on December 2, the Soviet bloc regimes demanded immediate action to prepare for the security conference since "sufficient pre-conditions for . . . such a conference" existed thanks to the success of the Soviet Union in obtaining West German recognition of the status quo in the Moscow treaty. The East bloc states also noted that the neutral government of Finland had offered to host the conference.[7] In fact the preparatory talks for the Conference on Security and Cooperation in Europe (CSCE) did begin in Helsinki in 1972, and the conference itself – which turned out to be merely the first in a continuing series – was held there from 1973 to 1975.

In his annual report to Congress on US foreign policy on February 25, 1971, President Nixon confirmed the US position that the CSCE should not take place until the concrete issues – "the German question, Berlin, mutual force reductions" – were decided.

We see little value in a conference whose agenda would be unlikely to yield progress on concrete issues, but would only deflect our energies to drafting statements and declarations the interpretation of which would inevitably be a continuing source of disagreements. . . . Any lasting relaxation of tension in Europe must include progress in resolving the issues related to the division of *Germany*.

The German national question is basically one for the German people. . . . But as Chancellor Brandt has emphasized, it is the strength of the Western coalition and West Germany's secure place in it that have enabled his government to take initiatives which mark a new stage in the evolution of the German question. The reshaping of German relations with the East inevitably affects the interests of all European states, as well as the relationship between the US and the Soviet Union. . . .

I emphasized in my talks with Chancellor Brandt in Washington and in

---

[6] Dept of State, *Documents on Germany*, 1121–5.
[7] Ibid., 1119.

intensive Allied consultation in 1970 that we support West Germany's objective of normalizing relations with its eastern neighbors.[8]

The Berlin talks proceeded throughout the winter until a common basis for a settlement was reached in the spring of 1971. This involved three parts: a quadripartite agreement, agreements pursuant to the latter between the two Germanies and between West Berlin and the GDR on communications, traffic between West Berlin and West Germany, visits by West Berliners to the GDR, the exchange of enclaves of territory around Berlin, and a final protocol incorporating the intra-German agreements and putting the whole treaty package into force. The first part, the "Quadripartite Agreement on Berlin," was initialed by the representatives of the four powers in Berlin on September 3, 1971.

The treaty was the first four-power agreement on Berlin since the end of the Berlin blockade, four months before the creation of the Federal Republic in 1949. It was a milestone in the history of divided Berlin and of divided Germany. The Soviets, for the first time, acknowledged the three essentials which were of such critical importance to the economic and political viability of the Western sectors of Berlin.

In exchange for *Zugang* – unimpeded civilian traffic between West Berlin and West Germany – the Western powers agreed to reduce the demonstrations of federal presence (such as convening the Federal Assembly for the purpose of electing the federal president in West Berlin every five years). They declared that the Western sectors of Berlin were not a legal part of the Federal Republic, but subject to the status determined in the wartime agreements of 1944. The status of the Soviet sector was not mentioned, nor was the quadripartite status of Berlin altered in any way.

The West obtained *Zuordnung* – the recognition of West Berlin's ties with West Germany – in exchange for reducing the demonstration of federal presence and for the implicit acceptance of East Berlin as the capital of the GDR. In view of the limited concessions the West could offer the Soviet Union in exchange for assurances of unimpeded access and recognition of West Berlin's ties with the Federal Republic, the elimination of the Federal Assembly, for example, seemed an acceptable compromise. The maintenance and development of West Berlin's economic, political, cultural and military ties with the Federal Republic was of great political and psychological significance to the citizens of West Berlin. Without further development of these ties it would be extremely difficult to generate sufficient confidence in the future of West Berlin to attract investment and residents.

---

[8] Ibid., 1134–5.

Finally the agreement also established the principle of *Zutritt* — West Berlin citizens would be permitted to visit the Soviet sector and the GDR "under conditions comparable to those applying to other persons entering these areas." What this meant in actual fact was that for the first time since the expiration of the holiday pass agreements in 1966, negotiated under Erhard's government, West Berliners could travel to East Berlin and to East Germany just as freely as persons from other countries.[9]

One almost insuperable obstacle was that the Soviet Union insisted, as it had done since the mid-1950s, that West Berlin was a separate entity with no connection whatsoever to East Berlin, which was the capital of the GDR. Therefore, no treaty on Berlin could have any bearing at all on the status of East Berlin, which as far as the Soviet government and the GDR regime were concerned, had been settled long ago. The Western position, on the other hand, was that the four-power responsibility for Berlin as a whole, and therefore Soviet jurisdiction in the old Soviet sector (East Berlin) had never been abrogated. The Western representatives therefore wanted at least some reference in the treaty text indicating that it had relevance for Berlin as a whole. The Soviet government refused to mention Berlin as a whole in the treaty, but permitted references to "the relevant area" which the West took to mean all of Berlin and the Soviets to mean West Berlin only. Most important, they agreed to a formula that the authority for concluding the treaty was "their quadripartite rights and responsibilities, and . . . the corresponding wartime and postwar agreements and decisions of the Four Powers, which are not affected."

Part I of the treaty further stated that "the four Governments will strive to promote the elimination of tension . . . in the relevant area," that they "agree that there shall be no use or threat of force in the area," that they "will mutually respect their individual and joint rights," and that, "irrespective of differences in legal views, the situation which has developed in the area [i.e. Berlin as a whole] . . . shall not be changed unilaterally."[10] In that way both sides could claim that they had upheld their positions. The Soviets could say that "the relevant area" meant West Berlin, and the West could say, with justification, that the Soviet government acknowledged that the joint responsibility for Berlin as a whole continued.

Did the West conclude a good or a bad agreement? As always concerning a subject about which there exist strongly held opinions, it depends on how you look at it. For the Berliners, life promised to be less

---

[9] Ibid., 1137–9.
[10] Ibid., 1136.

hectic in the future, and "the city in crisis" atmosphere was certain to abate. It could not completely disappear, however, as long as the city remained divided and a wall continued to separate West Berliners from East Berliners. In addition, West Berlin would continue to be a potential hostage for the Soviet Union, as long as it remained free. Harassment of automobile traffic, or of trains, or of airplanes, could be resumed at any time – and for those caught at the West Berlin-East German border, waiting in their cars to drive to West Germany, it could mean waits of up to 24 hours or more. But an arrangement had been reached, and it did augur well for the future, at least on paper. By 1969, when the talks began, the question was no longer whether harassment was illegal, but how to stop it. This situation was a serious matter. Between 1949 and 1969, the Soviet Union had transferred its authority in the Soviet sector to the GDR. It then refused to discuss this violation of the four-power status of Berlin. By degrees, the division of Berlin became permanent, and transformation of the Soviet sector into the capital of the GDR so complete, that negotiations with the Soviet Union on restoring unity to the city were not possible. The West sought, therefore, to gain Soviet assurances that it, and therefore East Germany, would respect *Zugang* (access), *Zuordnung* (ties) and *Zutritt* (entry). This goal was achieved but, as one CSU member of the Bundestag, Guttenberg, observed, what really had taken place was this: "that which is characterized as concessions of the Soviet Union ... is in reality the partial return to the West of rights that have been pilfered in the past years."[11]

Kenneth Rush, the American ambassador who conducted the talks, cabled Henry Kissinger after the agreement was initialed: "It is still difficult for me to believe that it is as favorable as it is. It is still subject to the final approval of you, Gromyko and Brandt respectively. ... We yesterday secured from Falin [Soviet ambassador to West Germany] practically everything we wanted."[12] In his remarks to the press Rush stated what was to become the official Western view: " One thing is clear about this agreement. It does not represent a triumph for one country or the other, or indeed for any of the negotiating countries themselves. It is an agreement whose purpose is, through practical improvements, to benefit people, not national interests."[13]

In another, less formal address, the ambassador reviewed the entire history of the talks, starting with President Nixon's visit to Berlin in February 1969. On the area covered by the treaty, he stated unequivo-

---

[11] Cited in Bark, *Agreement on Berlin*, 109.
[12] Kissinger, *White House Years*, 830.
[13] Dept of State, *Documents on Germany*, 1151.

cally that "the agreement pertains to all of Berlin and not, as some have said, only the Western sectors." He was right, but the fact remained that the treaty did not lead to the dismantling of the Wall or to any steps toward a reunification of the city. On the question of *Bundespräsenz*, the demonstrative presence of the Bonn government in Berlin, the ambassador seemed somewhat disingenuous. He argued that since the Soviets, in the treaty, had recognized the ties between West Berlin and West Germany, "this demonstrative presence becomes less important," and the prohibition on meetings of the Federal Assembly and committees and caucuses of the Bundestag or Bundesrat was therefore insignificant. One can be sure, however, that if it had been insignificant the Soviet government would not have insisted on including it. Indeed, federal presence was a demonstration of enormous symbolic and psychological importance that Berlin was free and democratic.

Concluding his analysis, Rush reminded his listeners that the Quadripartite Agreement was "only the first phase of a three-phase process." The second phase began on September 6, when East and West German officials met to start working out the details governing access to and from Berlin and within Berlin. The final phase was to be examination by the four powers of the results, that would prescribe how the Quadripartite Agreement would be implemented. Overall, Rush judged, "I think it is fair to predict that the successful conclusion of the entire Berlin agreement should have a positive effect on other East–West negotiations, including the inner-German talks on the overall relationship between the two German states, the preparation of a conference on European security, and even on the envisaged negotiations on mutual balanced force reductions." He ended his talk with a reassurance: "I have heard it suggested that conclusion of this agreement means that the United States can now withdraw its troops from Europe. I can assure you that nothing could be further from the truth. . . . A strong defense will be even more necessary in this changing period than it was during the era of hard positions which preceded it."[14]

Kissinger shared Rush's optimistic view:

Whereas before there had existed no legal basis for civilian access at all, procedures for it were spelled out in meticulous detail . . . Whereas before the Soviet Union had washed its hands of Berlin access, claiming that it took place at the sovereign discretion of the East Germans, it now guaranteed it. The Federal presence in Berlin was slightly reduced – especially with respect to activities that had never been recognized by the allies, such as the quadrennial election of the Federal President. But the Soviet Union had accepted the

[14] Ibid., 1156–66.

principle that ties between the Federal Republic and Berlin could be "maintained and developed. . . ."

The unsentimental approach to Soviet relations was now clearly beginning to pay off. We were beginning to demonstrate that calculations of national interest were better solvents of East–West deadlocks than appeals to a change of heart. Linkage was working even if rejected by theorists; we had kept SALT and Berlin in tandem and substantially achieved our goals. And, of course, the Soviets were reasonably satisfied by Brandt's concessions; only amateurs believe in one-sided deals.[15]

The signing itself, as the negotiations, took place in the Air Safety Control Center. (As this book was written the French, British, Soviet and American flags were still raised each morning on the four flagpoles in front of the building. See part I, chapter 6, "The Potsdam Conference," p. 49.) The Soviet ambassador to East Berlin, Pyotr Abrasimov, concluded that "we have come to an understanding on one of the most complicated international problems over which frictions and tensions often have arisen during a quarter of a century."[16] Whether this understanding would continue in the future was a matter of debate in West Germany. But Brandt believed that the "true meaning" of the agreement

lies in the fact that there are to be no Berlin crises in the future. One must proceed from the situation as it is, in order to mitigate and, as I hope, to overcome, in a laborious effort, the consequences of the division of Europe and of our fatherland. The Berlin Agreement is, I am convinced, an important step along this road.[17]

Peter Bender reported that many people, especially in the Federal Republic, had tried to discourage the US from entering into talks on Berlin because they feared that the result could only be a "status quo minus;" that is to say, a settlement in which the West would officially recognize conditions that were illegal in terms of Allied occupation rights, specifically, the division of the city and the incorporation of the Soviet sector in the GDR.

Looking back in 1985, Bender discounted these fears and announced that the settlement was a great triumph because it provided stability.[18] This was also Brandt's view and the view of Benno Zündorf, the pseudonymous foreign ministry official who helped design Brandt's

---

[15] Kissinger, *White House Years*, 830–3.
[16] *Relay from Bonn*, September 3, 1971.
[17] Ibid., September 7, 1971.
[18] Bender, *Neue Ostpolitik*, 188.

Ostpolitik. Zündorf pointed out that the Quadripartite Agreement of 1971 was the first such since 1949. Further, although the Western position at the outset of the talks in August 1969 was weak and without leverage, still the Soviet Union came to realize, according to Zündorf, that it could not obtain movement on the issues of detente and arms control unless it gave guarantees on West Berlin. Because of its vital interest in Berlin, moreover, the Federal Republic, which had no official status in the talks, obtained a great deal of unofficial leverage vis-à-vis the Soviet Union.[19]

Critics of the settlement, like the historian Andreas Hillgruber, focused less on the Soviet promise of stability in and around West Berlin and more on the fact that, for the first time, the West had legally approved and guaranteed the illegal acts of the GDR and the Soviet Union and had accepted the division of the city as final. He argued that, contrary to what Brandt and his supporters thought, the settlement *was* confirmation of a "status quo minus." In particular, he pointed out that the agreement itself was vague, and therefore so were its guarantees. The parties could not even agree on verbal definitions and the text thus referred merely to "existing conditions in the relevant area." Further, the West now for the first time gave the East formal promises that it would limit ties between the Western sectors and the Federal Republic. Another significant Western concession was to allow the Soviet government to establish a consulate general in West Berlin which implicitly acknowledged the Soviet claim that West Berlin was a separate city. In turn, when the United States granted diplomatic recognition to the GDR in 1974, a US embassy was established in the Soviet sector of Berlin and the US ministry in West Berlin became a consulate.[20]

The Quadripartite Agreement was less than two weeks old when Willy Brandt and Egon Bahr made a semi-official visit to the Soviet Union for private talks with Leonid Brezhnev in mid-September 1971. The visit took place at Brezhnev's summer house in Oreanda in the Crimea. In Brandt's own view and that of many observers, the Oreanda meeting was of decisive symbolic as well as diplomatic importance, marking the age of maturity of Brandt's Ostpolitik and turning West Germany into a legitimate Western partner of the Soviet Union. Brezhnev had proposed the trip in June as soon as it was clear that the four powers were going to reach an agreement on Berlin. Brandt did not ask permission of the US to go, he simply informed the Americans that he was going. In handwritten notes at the time Brandt summarized the new self-confidence of the Federal Republic, noting that "improving

[19] Zündorf, *Ostverträge*, 174.
[20] Hillgruber, *Deutsche Geschichte*, 117.

relations" with the Soviet Union was having favorable effects on the US–Soviet relationship, and that West Germany would no longer accept any Allied right to veto its foreign policy.[21] For Brandt, Oreanda was an occasion to present his vision of Ostpolitik to the Soviet leader at a vital stage in the process of negotiations between the two Germanies.

The two leaders agreed that the evolving diplomatic reordering in Central Europe must be complemented by progress in arms control. Without promising anything Brezhnev gave Brandt the impression that the Soviet government might be amenable to mutual and balanced force reductions (MBFR). Brandt and Bahr went home determined to push their NATO allies towards MBFR.

Not all observers found the visit to Oreanda, or the peculiar atmosphere of trust that Brandt claimed developed between him and the Soviet autocrat, reassuring. Some in Europe found it distasteful that the leading representative of democratic socialism in Europe was visiting, at his summer house, the man responsible for destroying the attempt to liberalize state socialism in Czechoslovakia in 1968. Others went further and argued that Brandt's fervent personal wish for a European peace order had led him to believe that such a peace order was possible, and to place excessive good faith in Soviet purposes.

On Brandt's return from Oreanda, he supported, as proposed by Brezhnev, and in the Bahr Paper, the Soviet demand for a conference on security and cooperation in Europe. Brandt also conceded to Brezhnev that the West German government would regard the DKP, the reconstituted communist party in West Germany, which had re-established itself in 1968, as permanently legitimate and would not seek a court order for its dissolution. This concession was warmly welcomed by the predominantly left-liberal media in West Germany and illustrated the unusually close connection between foreign and domestic policy in West Germany. Domestic support for Brandt in these circles increased further when he received the Nobel Peace Prize in 1971 for these efforts and for his direction of Ostpolitik.

The new year of 1972 saw Brandt's popularity at home, and respect abroad, at a pinnacle. He enjoyed mounting prestige as one of the leading statesmen of Europe; for he was credited with the vision to recognize that "change through rapprochement" was the preferable alternative to continued cultivation of the illusions of the past, according to his supporters. He was only the fourth German recipient of the Nobel Peace Prize (the most recent before Brandt was Carl von Ossietzky, who in 1934 was put into a concentration camp by Hitler and was not permitted to accept his prize in 1936).

[21] Bracher et al., *Republik im Wandel, 1969–1974*, 225.

Brandt's conduct of a foreign policy of reconciliation and detente had restored to West Germany – in the eyes of Europeans and many others – the respect earned through exercising the political initiative in a responsible manner. The Nobel Committee, when announcing the award to Brandt, concluded: "In a spirit of good will he has achieved extraordinary results in paving the way for peace in Europe. Political and military detente between East and West Europe are prerequisites for peaceful development."[22]

Indeed, Brandt was *Time* magazine's "Man of the Year" for 1970. The magazine wrote that "Willy Brandt is seeking to end World War II by bringing about a fresh relationship between East and West. . . . He has projected the most exciting and hopeful vision for Europe since the Iron Curtain crashed down." This vision, however, was not solely Brandt's own creation. As *La Nation* in Paris observed the day following the award of the Nobel Peace Prize: "Willy Brandt truly deserves this award. . . . In him all of Germany is honored – hardly a quarter of a century after the end of World War II. Since then Germany has gone a long way, and while Mr Brandt is the beneficiary of this development, he will admit, at least to himself, how much he owes to his predecessors, especially Konrad Adenauer."[23]

At this same time that Brandt was enjoying great prestige, he made an announcement at Harvard University on June 5, 1972, where, a quarter of a century before, Secretary of State George C. Marshall had announced the Marshall Plan, on the same date, at the same university. West Germany had not forgotten it. Brandt presented a gift of 147 million marks from the German people to the United States as an expression of gratitude for the decision made by the Americans in 1947, and as a contribution to a closer understanding between the countries on both sides of the Atlantic in the coming decades.

[22] *Die Zeit*, November 2, 1971.
[23] *Relay from Bonn*, October 21, 1971.

5

1972: The Year of Decision

S oon after the Moscow treaty, the GDR took the initiative in re-opening talks with Bonn at the junior ministerial level. On October 29, 1970, the GDR and the Federal Republic agreed "to carry out by official channels an exchange of views concerning matters whose settlement would serve detente in Central Europe and which are of interest for both states." Bonn's representative was Egon Bahr, whose long-awaited hour had come when he finally sat down in Bonn face to face with his East German counterpart, Michael Kohl, secretary of state to the GDR Council of Ministers. The Bahr-Kohl talks, held alternately in Bonn and East Berlin, led to the implementation of agreements pursuant to the Quadripartite Agreement as well as to the treaty on the basis of relations between the two states which was finally concluded, after much controversy in West Germany, in the autumn of 1972. From one viewpoint:

The East Germans' readiness to pursue talks with the FRG without, however, giving an inch on the preconditions for improved relations lends credence to the view that East Berlin's primary concern was simply to avoid isolation by remaining a partner to the ever-widening scope of discussions on East–West questions.[1]

That was a view that did not credit the SED leadership in the GDR with a well conceived long-term political and ideological strategy on the German question. A diametrically opposed view of the purposes of the SED regime in entering into talks and concluding agreements with the Bonn government came from a man who for much of his working life was part of the SED power elite. The lawyer and political economist Wolfgang Seiffert was in the early 1970s a member of the small group of people advising the SED leadership on its strategic plans. He assessed the SED's "long-term strategy" as follows:

[1] McAdams, *East Germany and Detente,* 104.

First, to establish the GDR state, then to get international recognition for it on the one hand, and on the other to separate the Federal Republic from the US and the Western Alliance, then to obtain complete equality with the Federal Republic, and finally to make the claim to be the force that will truly bring German history to its perfect conclusion.[2]

In the standard Western view, the Soviet government put pressure on the GDR to negotiate since it wanted to coordinate Eastern strategy for the conduct of detente and to meet Bonn's Ostpolitik on a broad front. The quadripartite talks in Berlin were progressing satisfactorily from Moscow's perspective, as were its talks with Bonn on the basis of the Bahr memorandum. The signing of the Bonn–Moscow treaty in September 1970 was another reason for the GDR to move.

Zündorf, along with almost all West German commentators, assumed that the GDR acted independently out of a fear of being left behind both by the imminent Quadripartite Agreement on Berlin and by Bonn's developing relations with the Soviet Union, Poland, and Czechoslovakia. The question, however, is to what extent the idea of an independent GDR had any meaning. The GDR had the same interest as the Soviet Union, namely gaining Western promises not to seek changes in the status quo and, in the more distant future, making detente, and hence Eastern leverage on Western policies, so attractive to West German political and public opinion that it could not be rejected. But the GDR did not have the flexibility to pursue major foreign policy initiatives without Soviet approval, nor did it possess enough leverage to influence significantly the direction of Soviet initiatives. According to some observers the Bonn–Moscow treaty was a clear indication that the USSR was prepared to put its own interests ahead of those of its satellites. Thus, reacting to the GDR claim that the treaty obligated Bonn to accord full diplomatic recognition to East Germany, the Soviet newspaper *Pravda* indirectly criticized the rigidity of the GDR position:

Those who for many years have been accustomed to viewing the Federal Republic as merely the tool of aggressive international blocs now find it hard to reconcile themselves with the fact that West Germany, like any other sovereign state, has its own interests and wishes to pursue a policy line that takes into consideration the real situation and real possibilities.[3]

In 1970–1, while the talks were under way, the GDR repeatedly humiliated and tested the Bonn government by killing persons trying to escape to West Germany and by other provocative acts along the

---

[2] Seiffert, *Das ganze Deutschland,* 108.
[3] Cited in McAdams, *East Germany and Detente,* 105–6.

inner-German border. Domestic pressure to break off the talks grew in West Germany, but the GDR regime correctly judged that Bonn had no such option, given Brandt's and Bahr's commitment. Wolfgang Seiffert recalled speaking to Michael Kohl in the GDR foreign ministry after a session with Bahr and asking Kohl how the talks were going. "He answered: 'Tough and difficult, but probably it has to be that way, because we are not dealing with a laughing matter, but rather we are fighting for our respective power positions.' Looking pensive, he added hesitantly: 'In any event, as long as we are dealing with negotiating partners such as these, it can't be too bad.'"[4]

The GDR provocations were without risk, while at the same time they showed that Bonn was no longer willing or capable of serious protest against acts of harassment, intimidation, and murder. It was thus easier for the CDU/CSU, from its position of opposition in the Bundestag, to criticize both Bahr's conduct of the negotiations and the policies of the GDR. In the long run, however, Rainer Barzel, who was elected CDU party chairman in October 1971, succeeded in persuading his party to abstain rather than vote against the treaties, an accomplishment for which the media gave him little credit.

During that first winter of negotiations the GDR also introduced an element that became a permanent accompaniment of East–West German relations; namely, the repeated attempt to negotiate matters pertaining to West Berlin, even though the GDR had no responsibility or jurisdiction for the questions of Berlin. The purpose of this effort was clear: if the West Germans, by whatever means, could be made, even for a moment, to permit discussion of West Berlin issues, then the GDR would have reached a major strategic goal, namely, the indirect recognition by Bonn that Berlin was legally divided and that the GDR had some right, however vague, of interference in the affairs of the Western sectors.

The Bonn delegation successfully withstood these attempts, and Bahr managed to restrict the talks to traffic matters until September 1971. At that time the four powers transmitted the text of the Berlin agreement to Bonn and East Berlin. In order to be completed, signed, and put into force, the settlement required the two German governments to complete agreements regulating transit between West Germany and West Berlin, transit within Berlin and between West Berlin and the GDR, and telecommunications between West Germany and the GDR. Bonn was anxious to emphasize that the transit agreements depended legally and logically on the Quadripartite Agreement, and ultimately on occupation rights, whereas the GDR was just as anxious to avoid such an emphasis

---

[4] Seiffert, *Das ganze Deutschland*, 95.

because any reference to four-power occupation rights implicitly denied the absolute sovereignty of the GDR.

The transit agreements were supposed to prevent unilateral obstruction by the GDR of traffic and communications to and from West Berlin. As in the case of the provisions of all the other treaties concluded under the concept of Ostpolitik, however, Bonn had no way of enforcing them or of penalizing petty or major violations. The GDR regime was therefore always able to use the threat of violations as effective leverage on Bonn to refrain from policies it saw as objectionable.

At the same time, the GDR could not maintain a position of intransigence indefinitely vis-à-vis Soviet pressure to conclude the necessary agreements following the Bonn–Moscow treaty and the Quadripartite Agreement on Berlin. The Ulbricht regime was having internal economic problems and failures in its planned economy which damaged the leadership's claim to be the guarantor of more rapid growth. The decisive factor in Ulbricht's fall in May 1971 was the Soviet strategy of detente – of ideological struggle by means of peaceful coexistence instead of by means of the cold war – which required that the GDR adhere to Soviet policy initiatives.

For Ulbricht, as probably for Brezhnev, the difference between peaceful coexistence and cold war was mainly cosmetic. Both phrases meant the conduct of foreign relations by peaceful means. But the words peaceful coexistence sounded more soothing and conciliatory. They also suggested a safer way to conduct foreign policy which appeared to be based on reason rather than on the threat of force. What undoubtedly worried Ulbricht, and therefore caused him to resist or at least slow down the movement of detente, was that the concept – and the hopes for peace it engendered – seemed to be developing a momentum of its own. He must have feared that his control over the SED and thus over the population in the GDR could weaken. He was consequently forced from power and leaders with more attractive public images replaced him.

The new leadership under Erich Honecker was confirmed at the eighth party congress of the SED held in East Berlin in June 1971 which, according to official GDR statements, marked "the transition to a new stage of society." The Ulbricht era, its propaganda, methods, and aims, were consigned, more or less, to oblivion, but the Berlin Wall remained. Ulbricht himself was not present at the congress and was granted the honorary position of "chairman of the SED" which he held until his death in 1974. The significance of his disappearance from official life can be judged by the fact that his name was mentioned frequently in the 1970 edition of *Politisches Grundwissen* (Basic political information), the standard text used for ideological schooling in the

GDR, but not once in the 1972 edition. In particular, his statements about the need for German unity were erased wherever possible.

The first agreement was signed on September 30, 1971, and prescribed improvements in postal and telephone communications between East and West Berlin and between East and West Germany. On December 17, Bahr and Kohl initialed the agreement on transit traffic between West Germany and West Berlin. It covered "traffic by road, rail and waterways through the territory of the German Democratic Republic of civilian persons and goods between the Federal Republic of Germany and the Western Sectors of Berlin. ... Transit traffic shall be facilitated and unimpeded."

The transit agreement covered all persons traveling to and from Berlin, whether living in West Germany, Berlin, or anywhere else. Thus in concluding this treaty the GDR directly acknowledged Bonn's right to conclude an agreement of immediate relevance to Berliners. On the other hand, although the treaty obligated the GDR to use "international practice" as a guide for its actions, Bonn was forced to agree to conditions that certainly did not correspond to any "international practice" of civilized states. Under the treaty, transit travelers were forbidden to disseminate or pick up material – newspapers or written messages, for example – while in the GDR, a provision that could be extended to punish anyone who, deliberately or not, left so much as a scrap of paper in a trash can. Further, transit travelers were forbidden to pick up persons or deviate from the designated transit routes.[5] From the time it entered into force in June 1972, the first ten months saw an increase of 37.3 per cent in the number of travellers (an increase of 1,239,826).

On December 17, 1971, a similar agreement was concluded between the GDR and the West Berlin government granting West Berlin residents a basic right to spend up to 30 days per year in East Berlin or the GDR. The resulting improvements in tourist and visitor traffic under this agreement saw an increase in visits of West Berliners to East Berlin and the GDR of more than two million during the first year.

Three days later the Senate of West Berlin signed a third agreement concerning the exchange of enclaves of territory that historically belonged to West Berlin but were surrounded completely by the GDR. Since the GDR claimed that it was giving more territory to West Berlin than it received in return, the West Berlin government paid the GDR four million marks in connection with this exchange. The total area exchanged was minute, no more than about 33 hectares, or a little more than an eighth of a square mile.

[5] Dept of State, *Documents on Germany*, 1170–6.

Following their conclusion the three agreements were returned to the four powers to be included as annexes to the protocol putting the Quadripartite Agreement into effect. Before the protocol was signed in June 1972, however, Brandt's government had to face at home the most serious challenge to its authority. The challenge came from the opposition in connection with the debate on ratification of the Moscow and Warsaw treaties and culminated in an attempt to replace Brandt with Barzel by a constructive vote of no-confidence.

The Bundestag began the ratification debate on the Moscow and Warsaw treaties – usually referred to collectively as the Eastern treaties – on February 23. At Oreanda, Brezhnev had told Brandt that final Soviet approval of the Quadripartite Agreement and the implementation agreements would depend on prior ratification of the Moscow treaty by the Bundestag. This undermined an important part of the opposition's earlier strategy in 1970-1, which had been to accept the Berlin agreements and the Warsaw treaty but to reject the Moscow treaty. After Oreanda, the Soviet Union had put the CDU/CSU in a very awkward position, because to reject the Moscow treaty now meant to destroy the Berlin treaty package, which would have been so unpopular a measure in Germany as to ensure defeat for the opposition in any election. Rainer Barzel, who since 1971 was not only caucus leader, but also chairman of the CDU/CSU, then took the line that his party could accept the entire treaty package – Moscow, Warsaw, Berlin – if the Soviet Union in turn would recognize the European Community as a legitimate partner in economic and political relations, and would acknowledge in principle the German right of national self-determination.

On March 20, 1972, Brezhnev stated in a speech that he accepted the existence of the European Community as a fact of life and that the Soviet government agreed that West Germany's note on self-determination could be included in the ratified Moscow treaty. In early April Barzel and most of his party were still generally skeptical of the wisdom of the treaties and wanted to take power in order to prevent them from coming into force if at all possible. Moreover, the conservatives in the CDU/CSU, led by Strauss and the deputy chairman of the CDU, Helmut Kohl, were pressing for a decision. The opposition could count on the defection of national conservative FDP members. On October 9, 1970, Erich Mende, the former chairman, had left the FDP and joined the CDU along with two other liberal members of parliament, Siegfried Zoglmann and Heinz Starke. That reduced the government's majority to six, and Barzel could hope for further defections. The first such from the SPD was Herbert Hupka, like Mende and the other FDP defectors, a Silesian. Unlike Mende, however, Hupka left the SPD in January 1972 on the issue of the Eastern treaties. Mende, Zoglmann, and Starke left because they disagreed with the leftward drift of the party and feared that the result would be that the FDP would lose votes and disappear from the Bundestag. Hupka went to the CDU because, as a Silesian, he rejected what he considered the government's capitulation to Polish and Soviet interests.

On March 10, 1972, Barzel spoke for the first time in public of the possible use of the constructive no-confidence vote. By early April he was convinced that such a motion would be supported by more than the 249 (out of 496) votes needed to pass. Two other liberal deputies, Knut von Kühlmann-Stumm and Gerhard Kienbaum, privately assured Barzel that while they would not leave the FDP, they would vote for a motion of no-confidence. On April 23, Wilhelm Helms, a liberal deputy from Lower Saxony, announced that he was moving to the CDU. That gave Barzel a total of 249 votes, which was a majority.

Helms announced his defection on the same day that the CDU won an astonishing victory in the Baden-Württemberg *Land* elections. In order not to influence the election, Helms waited to announce his defection until after the polling stations were closed but before any results were announced.

By April 1972 the CDU/CSU had gained absolute majorities in Bavaria, in Rhineland-Palatinate, and Schleswig-Holstein, and even in the traditionally leftist state of Hesse the CDU had increased its vote in the November 1970 election by an amazing 13.3 points to 39.7 per cent. Finally, on April 23, the *Land* election in Baden-Württemberg gave the CDU under Hans Filbinger an enormous gain of 8.5 points for an absolute majority of 52.9 per cent. This result also meant that the government lost its majority in the Bundesrat or upper house, which had the veto power on most important legislation. There had been elections in all eleven *Länder* and in Berlin since the election of the Brandt–Scheel government, and in each one the opposition had made gains. These *Land* elections were heavily influenced, in favor of the CDU/CSU, by the voters' opinions of the government's domestic reform policies. But this support was by no means a guarantee of support for the CDU/CSU in a national election. Ostpolitik was supported by 82 per cent of the population according to polls in early 1972. Therefore, if the opposition wished to come to power to revise Ostpolitik, it would have to be done via the constructive no-confidence vote and not via early elections.

Nor did Barzel want to end Ostpolitik, even though in later years the general impression existed that the no-confidence motion was also a motion on Ostpolitik. This was not the case. Barzel and the CDU/CSU were in favor of an opening to the East, but they thought that Brandt and Bahr were too hasty, too eager, and gave the Soviet Union and the GDR too many concessions. They believed that they could make a better agreement that would more securely safeguard West German political, legal, and national interests. The Soviet government seemed to have agreed that Barzel was likely to be chancellor very soon, for in April it opened channels of communication to him. So certain was Barzel of victory that he booked tickets to Moscow on April 29 so that his aides could open negotiations immediately on behalf of the new CDU-led government.

Speculation about the outcome of the vote, and about the procedure itself, created enormous pressure, and it was therefore a relief when the opposition finally, on April 24, submitted the following motion to the Bundestag: "The Bundestag declares that it has no confidence in Chancellor Willy Brandt and elects deputy Dr Rainer Barzel as chancellor of the Federal Republic. The federal president is requested to dismiss Chancellor Willy Brandt." The decision to proceed with the motion was taken by the CDU/CSU presidium over the opposition of Richard von Weizsäcker, a leading moderate in the party who had failed to obtain the nomination for federal president in 1969 (he became governing mayor of Berlin in 1981 and federal president in 1984), and Gerhard Stoltenberg. The vote was set for April 27.

Brandt's cause looked hopeless. By April 23 Barzel justifiably assumed he would get at least 249 votes for the motion. Another social democrat, Günther Müller of Munich, was wavering. He belonged to the moderate wing of the party and had been rudely shunted aside by the radicals in the Munich SPD. On April 20 he declared that he could not recommend a vote for the SPD in the local elections to be held in Munich in June. As he saw it, moderate social democrats were losing influence and power in the party to the Marxist and radical left with their ideas of revolutionary social reform.[6] Should Müller decide to vote for Barzel, it would give the opposition a majority of two.

Public excitement was heightened as labor and student organizations demonstrated in support of Brandt. Throughout Europe, the majority of the influential media supported Brandt and regarded Barzel's candidacy as little short of an attempted coup. Pressure from street demonstrations did lead some deputies to conclude that the freedom of action of the Bundestag was in peril. Many members of the Bundestag were shocked that the voters and the media did not seem to understand that the Federal Republic was a parliamentary and representative democracy, in which the deputies voted according to their personal convictions and had the right to choose a government without asking the electorate. Barzel's attempt to change the government was perfectly constitutional,

[6] Baring, *Machtwechsel*, 414.

but was nevertheless regarded as a low, shady, and questionable attempt to overthrow a stable government and a noble leader.

Brandt's government, understandably, made the most of this feeling that the CDU/CSU motion was immoral, if not actually illegal. Scheel, for example, declared:

Today every single representative is called upon to make a decision which will have far-reaching political consequences. We are faced with an attempt to alter the political majority without allowing the electorate to participate. Whether or not this is technically legitimate, it is an act which strikes at the nerve of our democracy. If it becomes the rule for parliamentary majorities to be altered by changing the party in power without consulting the electorate, then parliamentary democracy will lose its credibility.[7]

No one knows what would have happened had the motion passed – the unions threatened a general strike – but to everyone's amazement, especially Brandt's, it failed by two votes. Given the known defectors from the SPD/FDP coalition, the only explanation for the result was that two CDU deputies had voted against the motion. In 1973, one of them, Julius Steiner, claimed that he had been bribed with 50,000 marks by Karl Wienand, the secretary of the SPD Bundestag group, to abstain on the motion.[8] Steiner presumably acted for both economic and political motives. He had been sympathetic to Brandt's Ostpolitik since sometime in 1970, partly because he hoped to do business with the East through an associate, the Stuttgart businessman and financier Hans Liebherr. In May 1973, thanks to Ostpolitik, Liebherr was able to sign a contract to deliver equipment worth 300 million marks to the Soviet truck plant in Kama. Steiner's daughter worked for Liebherr's firm.[9]

Steiner, for whatever reasons, struck a pathetic figure. He had entered the Bundestag for the CDU in Baden-Württemberg on a fluke, by happening to win a seat that the party had already written off. He was chronically ill and alleged to be an alcoholic. He was an undistinguished politician and an unsuccessful businessman who, at the age of 47 in 1973, had few prospects either in politics or business. Years later, Arnulf Baring reported SPD members as saying that "of course payments were made; given the risks, an escape at 50,000 marks was cheap."[10] Social democrats considered that the way in which the CDU wooed Wilhelm Helms away from the FDP seemed suspiciously close to bribery as well. The FDP deputy Walter Peters claimed in June 1973 that he had

[7] Dönhoff, Foe into Friend, 148.
[8] Baring, Machtwechsel, 583; Bracher et al., Republik im Wandel, 1969–1974, 112.
[9] Baring, Machtwechsel, 581.
[10] Ibid., 422.

offered Helms, whose farm was in serious financial trouble, 100,000 marks to keep him from joining the CDU. Apparently, Peters concluded, "the other side had made a more generous offer," because Helms did in fact defect.[11]

Steiner's claim led to an exhaustive and inconclusive investigation. Karl Wienand, whom Steiner named as the man who paid him, told a journalist that the CDU had turned five coalition members into defectors; he, Wienand, had brought one of them back and moreover won four CDU/CSU members, thus leaving Barzel with only 247 votes at the decisive moment.[12] The contact between Wienand and Steiner was apparently made by Hans-Joachim Baeuchle, an SPD deputy from Baden-Württemberg who became a close friend of Steiner's, frequently commuting with him between Bonn and Ulm. Baeuchle expected rewards from the party for his services; when they were not forthcoming, he disclosed his story immediately after Steiner's own revelation in June 1973. This put the spotlight on Wienand, who ultimately, in late 1974, had to resign both his seat and his post as secretary of the SPD Bundestag group.

Years later, in 1980, Wehner, who was in charge of tactics as well as strategy for the SPD, admitted that "people were paid" to preserve Brandt's government. And he added: "A caucus leader has to know what is happening, what is being attempted, in order to pull the rug out from under the feet of the government. The government itself doesn't have to know." He went on to indicate that the SPD found itself obliged to use similar tricks: "I . . . always knew it would be difficult. Someone has to be the stupid one, and I was it. . . . I know two people who carried it out. I'm one of them, the other [Wienand] is no longer in the parliament."[13] Wehner, of course, was acting as his conscience as party strategist dictated. He believed that it was essential for Germany – both Germanies – that Brandt and the SPD remain in power. To achieve that end all means were permissible in an emergency. It was highly characteristic of the European attitude toward political intrigue that the affair had no repercussions for Wehner or the SPD, unlike the Watergate scandal in the United States that resulted in President Nixon's resignation in August 1974.

Despite his victory on April 27, Brandt's position remained precarious. On the same day that the opposition's motion failed, Brandt and Scheel negotiated with Barzel on the budget and on further steps to be taken in Ostpolitik. Barzel demanded a roll call vote on one item of the

[11] Ibid., 588.
[12] Ibid., 422.
[13] Ibid., 422–3.

budget, namely the budget of the chancellery. The vote, taken on April 28, resulted in a stalemate, 247 votes for and 247 against, and the budget item was thereby rejected. The stalemate gave Brandt every reason to fear that the opposition might be able to muster enough votes to deny ratification of the Moscow and Warsaw treaties. To prevent this he established a commission with the purpose of preparing a statement on the meaning of the treaties that all parties in the Bundestag could support, and which would be voted on in conjunction with the ratification of the treaties themselves. On May 17, the Bundestag issued the declaration. It included a number of formulations that, while made by the government, corresponded more closely to the ideas of the CDU/CSU. Thus, in a sense, the May 17 declaration was the Bundestag's answer to the Bahr Paper:

1 One of the determinant aims of our foreign policy is to preserve peace in Europe and the security of the Federal Republic of Germany. The treaties with Moscow and Warsaw . . . serve those aims. . . .

2 . . . The treaties do not anticipate a peace settlement for Germany by treaty and do not create any legal foundation for the frontiers existing today.

3 The inalienable right to self-determination is not affected by the treaties. The policy of the Federal Republic of Germany aiming at the peaceful restoration of national unity within the European framework is not in contradiction to the treaties which do not prejudice the solution of the German question. By demanding the implementation of the right of self-determination, the Federal Republic of Germany does not make any territorial claim nor does it claim any alternation of frontiers.

4 . . . the continued validity of [the Paris Treaties] as well as the continued validity of the agreement concluded on 13 September 1955 between the Federal Republic . . . and the Union of Soviet Socialist Republics are not affected. . . .

5 The rights and responsibilities of the four powers relating to Germany as a whole and to Berlin are not affected by the treaty. In view of the fact that the final settlement of the German question as a whole is still outstanding the German Bundestag considers as essential the continuance of those rights and responsibilities.

6 As regards the significance of the treaties, the German Bundestag furthermore refers to the Memoranda which the Federal Government has submitted to the legislative bodies together with the bills for the ratification of the treaties of Moscow and Warsaw.

7 The Federal Republic . . . is firmly embedded in the Atlantic alliance which continues to form the basis of its security and freedom.

8 The Federal Republic . . . will . . . pursue the policy of European unification . . . [and] proceeds on the understanding that the Soviet Union . . . will enter into co-operation with the EEC.

9 The Federal Republic ... reasserts its firm resolve to maintain and develop the ties between Berlin (West) and the Federal Republic ... in accordance with the Quadripartite Agreement and the German supplementary arrangements. ...

10 The Federal Republic ... advocates the normalization of the relationship between the Federal Republic ... and the GDR.[14]

All parties agreed to the statement, but the CDU/CSU abstained. The treaties were therefore ratified, on the same day, with the votes of the coalition alone. The declaration was included in the ratification document transmitted to the Soviet Union, but the Soviet government made it clear that it was not an integral part of the treaty.

Nine days later, President Nixon and Leonid Brezhnev, the general secretary of the communist party of the Soviet Union, signed the Strategic Arms Limitation Treaty (SALT I) in Moscow. A week following, on June 3, the foreign ministers of the US, France, Britain, and the Soviet Union signed the final protocol in Berlin, and the entire settlement came into force, as did, on the same day, the Moscow and Warsaw treaties.

In a joint communique of May 29, the US and Soviet governments welcomed the imminent implementation of the Quadripartite Agreement as a step toward improving "the European situation." They also welcomed the Moscow treaty. Probably most significant was the promise that both powers "are in accord that multilateral consultations looking toward a Conference on Security and Cooperation in Europe could begin after the signature of the Final Quadripartite Protocol." Nixon and Kissinger could congratulate themselves that the Soviet Union agreed the CSCE should "concretely consider specific problems," and that the US would be an active participant in the process. Meeting in Bonn on May 31, the NATO foreign and defense ministers "agreed to enter into multilateral conversations concerned with preparations for a ... CSCE."[15] Considering that the CSCE proposal began as an East bloc propaganda effort designed to extract Western recognition of the Brezhnev Doctrine and to drive a wedge between the US and Europe, it was remarkable that the Nixon administration had in fact succeeded in turning this unpromising beginning into something acceptable to those concerned with Western security.

With the Berlin transit agreements pursuant to the quadripartite settlements concluded in December 1971, Bahr and Michael Kohl

---

[14] Dept of State, *Documents on Germany*, 1189–90.
[15] Ibid., 1201–2.

resumed their fortnightly meetings in January 1972, which now turned to the general issue of East–West German traffic and communications. At the time, trade and travel by West Germans to the GDR were subject to a variety of complicated ad hoc agreements. By moving directly from the talks on transit to Berlin, to general talks on East–West German traffic, the GDR hoped again to give the impression that inner-German communications were the sovereign prerogative of the two German states without reference to any four-power occupation rights. Bonn for its part sought easier access to the GDR for its own citizens, and this could only be achieved through talks with the GDR regime.

The result was the first state-to-state treaty between the Federal Republic and the GDR, the *Verkehrsvertrag*, or Traffic Treaty, of May 26, 1972. In it, both sides promised to promote "normal good-neighborly relations" by permitting "mutual exchange and transit traffic" between the two German states.[16] If the phrase meant that the GDR was now obligated to permit its own citizens to move freely in and out of its territory, it was a cruel irony. The main significance of the treaty was that it was the first concrete example, according to the design of Ostpolitik, of recognition of the GDR. In its public propaganda, the GDR regime associated the treaty with the Berlin transit settlement, to give the impression that both were granted by its own sovereign authority, whereas Bonn correctly regarded Berlin transit issues as subject to the jurisdiction of the four powers.

Once the Moscow and Warsaw treaties were safely ratified on May 17, Brandt sought to break the political stalemate in the Bundestag by proposing new parliamentary elections. Ostpolitik as such was popular, and Brandt hoped that by presenting the elections as a request for a vote of confidence by the electorate in his person, as provider of peace and reconciliation with the East, he could return to power with a safe majority. The Basic Law permitted early elections in two cases: if a chancellor resigned and no majority in the Bundestag could be found for any candidate in two weeks, or if a sitting chancellor requested the Bundestag to express its confidence in him and the motion failed. The opposition preferred the first method, since in that case the government would be seen to have failed. Brandt was just as determined to use the second method.

The opposition was not as interested in national elections as it was in trying to change the government without elections, and Brandt delayed action through the summer holidays until September. On September 20, Brandt put the motion of confidence to the Bundestag with the express desire that it fail and that elections be called. This device, which

---

[16] Ibid., 1191.

was used again by Helmut Kohl eleven years later in 1983, was clearly not intended to be applied in this way by the framers of the relevant clause in the Basic Law, but was perfectly constitutional. To ensure the desired result the members of the cabinet did not attend the vote, so the count was 248 to 233 against the motion. Following the vote, Brandt recommended to Federal President Heinemann that elections be scheduled for November 19.

Political uncertainty pervaded the summer heat and the autumn of 1972. The growing expectation of early elections was the backdrop against which the inner-German negotiations on the last and most important part of the Ostpolitik treaties, namely the *Grundlagenvertrag* or Treaty on the Basis of Relations between the Federal Republic and the GDR, took place.

The treaty complex fell into three unequal parts. First there was the Basic Treaty itself with associated protocols and notes dealing with property rights, citizenship, and border formalities. Some of these protocols were agreed upon by both sides and others, such as the "Letter on German Unity" (identical to the one given to Moscow) which Bahr handed to the GDR representative at the signing ceremony, stated the position of one side on an issue on which no agreement was possible. Second, there were documents concerning the accession of the two Germanies to the UN and of the GDR to the International Postal Union and the International Telecommunications Union. The four powers jointly declared on November 9, 1972, that they would support applications of the Federal Republic and the GDR for membership in the UN once the Basic Treaty was signed. Third, there were the so-called "relief documents," statements by both sides requesting and promising to ameliorate the hardships of family separation and to support the work of West German journalists in the GDR.

The main treaty began with a preamble in which Bonn accepted the extensive use of phrases from Ulbricht's draft treaty of December 1969, specifically in referring to the two sides as "the High Contracting Parties," the highest form of mutual recognition in international diplomatic vocabulary. The bulk of the treaty promised good-neighborly relations in language largely identical to that found in the 20 points Brandt made in Kassel; for example, neither state would claim to represent the other internationally – a phrase denoting Bonn's rejection of the *Alleinvertretungsanspruch*. Bonn now recognized that there were two sovereign German states on the territory of the former Reich, and that East Berlin was the capital, and an integral part, of the GDR. In so doing another of the many paradoxes of the German question was highlighted; in Berlin both the Western allies and the West Berlin authorities continued to distinguish between East Berlin (the Soviet sector) and the GDR. In practice, this refusal to acknowledge the division of the city meant, among other things, that the West Berlin authorities posted no guards at the sector crossings. Not only did this lay the Western sectors completely open to entry by agents from the East, but in the 1980s the GDR also used this lack of control to undermine the Berlin economy by funneling Asian refugees into West Berlin, hoping that the Western authorities would be forced to start turning people back at the sector crossings. Doing so could be interpreted as recognizing that the crossings constituted a state border and hence the legitimate division of the city.

The two sides skirted contentious issues or pushed them into annexes, protocols, and agreed statements. One issue that proved impossible to resolve, even by use of vague language, was the issue of nationality, stemming from the fact that West Germany defined Germans by the 1913 law on citizenship and the GDR by its law of 1967, establishing "GDR citizenship." The West German side stated on record: "Questions of nationality have not been regulated by the Treaty," whereas the GDR stated on record that it "proceeds from the assumption that the Treaty will facilitate a regulation of questions of nationality."[17]

The treaty, with the supplementary protocols and statements, was initialed on November 8, eleven days before the elections, and signed on December 21, 1972. Some observers thought that the political atmosphere surrounding the talks gave the GDR undue leverage on Bonn and put pressure on Bahr to make concessions to the GDR to conclude a treaty in time for the elections. A West German historian (who was actually born in the part of East Prussia seized by Poland in 1945), commented that the treaty

determines the relationship between the two German states for a very long time, and, at first glance, seemingly promises humanitarian relief; but it nonetheless appears, in many ways, immature. The fact that the initialing of this treaty complex did occur, can, no doubt, be seen in connection with the upcoming elections. At that moment and under such conditions the parties were not able to have a thorough debate. For the opposition to argue against the treaty, even if it was well-founded from a factual viewpoint, was next to impossible, considering that humanitarian improvements had been moved into the limelight.[18]

On the other hand, Zündorf argued that the Soviet Union and the GDR offered the best treaty possible under the circumstances. They wanted

[17] Ibid., 1219.
[18] Hillgruber, *Deutsche Geschichte*, 130.

the government to win the election and interfered quite openly and crudely in the campaign, denouncing the opposition as enemies of detente and praising the Brandt–Scheel coalition as guarantors of peace. If the government had said to the voters that no treaty was possible due to the intransigence of the GDR, the voters, according to Zündorf, would have understood that. Bonn, in his view, could have broken off negotiations at any time, even up to the last minute. The GDR, therefore, chose between offering Bonn a good treaty or getting no agreement at all. However, Zündorf's argument depended on the assumption that Brandt and Scheel would in fact have rejected a less desirable treaty. This was highly questionable. The domestic atmosphere in West Germany, charged by the strong personal convictions held by Brandt and Bahr and by Brandt's growing prestige as a statesman of the first rank, was one of expectancy. The GDR government recognized this emotionally laden atmosphere and sought to use it as leverage to gain more concessions from Bonn, and to offer less, something that might not have been the case under calmer conditions. From this standpoint, there was a lack of reciprocity. Bonn received no guarantees from the GDR that it would, in fact, improve humanitarian conditions, and had no way to enforce promises. In addition, the GDR continued to follow a policy of "delimitation," arguing that there existed two independent, sovereign German states, but no German nation.

But, as always in such agreements, there was another way to interpret the treaty's meaning. A sympathetic analyst noted:

Bonn could get away with formally recognizing the equality, the inviolability, and even the sovereignty of the GDR, and still preserve the *special* character of relations between the Germanies. Additionally, like the Berlin accord before it, the *Grundvertrag* also provided for a whole set of practical measures that tended to reinforce the unique bond between the GDR and the FRG – the easing of transit regulations, the facilitation of journalistic activities, the reunification of families, and the improvement of communications between the two states. . . .

Most likely, there were those in the GDR (presumably including Ulbricht himself) who viewed many of these developments with displeasure, sensing that their government could have done better in its negotiations with the FRG. Hence on 16 November . . . Honecker defended the treaty . . .:

"Comrades, such transparent talk about a 'better' treaty is of no help at all. There is no such thing as a better *Grundvertrag*. This treaty, which was negotiated through a harsh and difficult exchange of views, takes into account both the interests of the socialist GDR and those of the FRG and its citizens – otherwise, it would never have been brought about."[19]

[19] McAdams, *East Germany and Detente*, 125.

The broader international situation was another source of pressure on Bonn. When President Nixon went to Moscow to sign the SALT I treaty in May, he brought with him his own and NATO's promise to Brezhnev that the US would join in the CSCE that was now scheduled to begin in 1973. The US also accepted the Soviet demand that the GDR be a full and equal partner in the CSCE. Moreover, in the quadripartite Berlin settlement the Western powers had, for the first time officially, referred to East Germany as the German Democratic Republic. And when the conference to prepare the CSCE began in the fall of 1972, the GDR was represented. Mounting pressure to recognize the GDR, also evident among West Germany's allies, was clear and had been for some years. The Scheel Doctrine, by which other countries were asked to withhold diplomatic recognition of the GDR pending an inner-German settlement, could only be upheld as long as that settlement was seen to be approaching. If negotiations became stalled or broke down entirely, the doctrine would almost certainly fail. All in all, the pressures on Bonn to come to an agreement quickly were, in retrospect, more significant than any reverse pressure on the GDR to make concessions in order to help the Bonn coalition win the election. If the opposition had won the election and had broken off the talks, Bonn would have cut itself off from the mainstream of Western allied policy and from detente, with unforeseeable, but certainly dangerous consequences. The environment in which the talks were completed, therefore, heavily favored the GDR.

On December 21, immediately after Brandt's victory in the elections, the government sent the draft law for ratification of the treaty to the Bundesrat, whose concurrence was required, along with a lengthy memorandum arguing that the treaty "does not resolve the German question but rather keeps it open." The Bundesrat, consisting of representatives of the *Land* governments, was controlled by the CDU/CSU and was expected to look at the treaty very critically, to make certain it was not, in fact, what some critics said it was, namely a "treaty of division."[20]

The Bundestag ratified the treaty on May 11, 1973, with the votes of the coalition and against the votes of the majority of the opposition. The technical form of ratification was the passage of a law accepting the treaty which entered into force following an exchange of instruments of ratification between the two governments on June 20, 1973. On May 28, however, the Bavarian state government applied to the Federal Constitutional Court in Karlsruhe for a declaratory judgement that the law concerning the treaty – the ratification law – was incompatible with the

[20] Dept of State, *Documents on Germany*, 1221.

Basic Law and therefore void, a judgment that would *eo ipso* invalidate the treaty. Bavaria's argument was that "the Treaty denied German national unity and perpetuated the division of Germany by recognizing the German Democratic Republic as an independent state and the inter-German boundary as a national frontier."[21] The West German government rejected Bavaria's claim and would not wait for the court's decision to put the treaty into force. On May 22 and again on June 13, Bavaria applied to the court for an injunction to restrain the government from putting the treaty into force until the case could be decided. The court refused to grant the injunction, thus permitting the treaty to come into force as planned, but declared that it would publish its decision on the case on July 31.

The West German government faced almost irresistible pressure to activate the treaty, despite the Bavarian effort to postpone it and eventually persuade the court to invalidate the treaty's provisions. Indeed, the court might invalidate the treaty for West Germany, but it could not do so for the GDR. And the GDR had at least two good reasons to activate the treaty on June 20. One was that its application to join the UN was to be debated in the UN Security Council on June 21, and the four powers had promised to support that application in a joint statement of November 1972.[22] If the treaty were not ratified in Bonn, West Germany would not be able to apply together with the GDR, thus giving the Eastern regime a unilateral advantage. The other reason was that the foreign ministers' preparatory conference for the CSCE was to begin in early July. Again, if the treaty were not in effect for Bonn, the two German states would be appearing at the conference without their special relationship being defined, and this would accrue to the advantage of the GDR.

There was a great risk that the GDR, having obtained diplomatic recognition, membership in the UN and representation at the CSCE preparatory discussions, would take the excuse of a delay in West Germany to invent some reason of its own to rescind its decision to put the basic treaty into force on June 20. Not only would the GDR then not be bound by any agreement to accept any special relationship, but it could also legitimately refuse to be bound by the humanitarian relief provisions of the treaty. If the treaty unravelled in such a way, the consequences would be unpredictable and extremely serious.

In its decision, on July 31, 1973, the court rejected the Bavarian claim and ruled that the treaty did not violate the commitment contained in the Basic Law to seek reunification. The court also provided an

[21] Ibid., 1248.
[22] Ibid., 1213.

extensive analysis of the German problem that set precise boundaries for Bonn's interpretation of the treaty in the future:

> The Basic Law – and not merely a doctrine of international and constitutional jurisprudence – assumes that the German Reich outlasted the collapse of 1945 and perished neither with the capitulation nor with the exercise of foreign governmental authority in Germany by the Allied Occupation Powers nor at any later time. . . .
>
> Accordingly, the German Reich continued to exist and to have legal capacity, although it lacked the capacity to act for want of institutional organs. . . .
>
> The Federal Republic of Germany thus is not a "legal successor" to the German Reich but, as a state, is identical with the state "German Reich" – to be sure, as regards its territorial extent, "partly identical," so that in this respect identity carries with it no claim to exclusivity. Thus the FRG, as regards its population and its territory, does not embrace all of Germany, without prejudice to acknowledging a unitary population of the international legal subject "Germany" (German Reich), to which its own people belong as an inseparable part, and a unitary territory "Germany" (German Reich), to which its own territory belongs as a likewise inseparable part.
>
> The GDR belongs to Germany and cannot be regarded as a foreign country in its relation to the FRG.[23]

How the German Reich could be incapable of acting despite being "identical" with the Federal Republic, which was certainly capable of acting, the Court did not say, nor did it spell out the notion of an identity which is not exclusive. The Court went on to insist:

> The Treaty can be interpreted in such a fashion as to come into conflict with none of the affirmations of the Basic Law as here set forth. No official statement within the FRG can be understood in a sense that it did or does depart from this constitutional ground in interpreting the Treaty.[24]

On the issue of "the national question," namely reunification, the court held that "the treaty does not endorse the division of Germany and that it does not prohibit the Federal Republic either today or in the future from doing whatever possible to regain national unity."[25] The treaty "was not a treaty of partition, but could be a first step toward some variant of confederation and ultimately toward reunification"[26] Andreas Hillgruber commented as follows:

[23] Doeker and Brückner, eds, *FRG and GDR in International Relations*, 1: 408.
[24] Ibid., 409.
[25] *Relay from Bonn*, August 1, 1973.
[26] Doeker and Brückner, eds, *FRG and GDR in International Relations*, 1: 410.

Reunification is required under constitutional law. However, the political organs of the Federal Republic have the prerogative of deciding what means they will regard as politically correct and appropriate to bring about reunification. ... The preamble of the treaty contains the phrase: "Without prejudice to the differing views of the Federal Republic and the GDR on fundamental questions, among them the national question." Concretely, for the Federal Republic of Germany the "national question" is a constitutional requirement of the Basic Law to seek reunification. ... Read in this way, the preamble is of fundamental importance in interpreting the treaty as a whole; it does not conflict with the Basic Law's command to seek reunification. ... The treaty is no treaty of partition. ...[27]

Not only the Eastern bloc states, however, but even states friendly to West Germany effectively regarded the treaty as an admission by Bonn that Germany's division was, if not permanent, at least an existing reality, just as they had regarded the 1970 Warsaw treaty as tantamount to ceding the Oder–Neisse territories to Poland. The Vatican took this view when it appointed administrators for areas in the GDR that were part of West German dioceses. In the Eastern territories, the appointment of administrators had been the first step toward formal reorganization of the dioceses under Polish bishops.

The court found that the inner-German border was "a state border similar to those separating the *Länder* of the Federal Republic," and that "the current practice at the border . . . that is, a wall, barbed wire, death zones, and the command to shoot to kill persons trying to cross, is entirely incompatible with the treaty," which "provides a legal basis for the Federal Republic to fulfil its duty under the Basic Law by doing everything possible to change . . . these inhuman conditions." The court was, of course, morally right, but was treading on legally thin ground in claiming that the treaty, which expressly "restricts the jurisdiction of each state to its own territory," was "incompatible" with internal practices of the GDR.[28]

[27] Hillgruber, *Deutsche Geschichte*, 131–2.
[28] Ibid., 132.

6

The Third Eastern Treaty

The last of the major documents of the new Ostpolitik to be concluded was the Prague treaty with Czechoslovakia. The two governments began discussions in October 1970 but made no progress for over a year, despite the climate induced by the ratification of the Moscow and Warsaw treaties and the talks with the GDR. In February 1973 Brandt and the Czech communist party leader Gustav Husak started new negotiations. They progressed so swiftly that the resulting treaty could be initialed on June 20, the same day that Bonn and East Berlin exchanged the notes putting in force the Basic Treaty. Disagreements over the Czech position on Berlin delayed signature of the treaty until December 11. The opposition, which despite serious misgivings had not opposed the other treaties in the Bundesrat, including the Basic Treaty, now chose the Prague treaty to make a stand in the Bundesrat, where it had the majority. The Bundesrat, however, could only delay, not veto, the ratification measure. The Bundestag rejected the Bundesrat's objections and ratified the treaty on July 10, 1974. The notes activating the treaty were exchanged in Bonn on July 19.

The reason the opposition objected to the Prague treaty, which included guarantees of existing borders and the renunciation of force, was the Czech demand that Bonn denounce the Munich settlement of September 1938 as null and void from the beginning. The Munich settlement was the agreement, designed by Britain and France and accepted triumphantly by Germany and under protest by Czechoslovakia, by which the German areas of Czechoslovakia, the Sudetenland, were ceded to Germany. In 1945, the German population of about 3.5 million was expelled by the returning Czechs with extreme brutality and much loss of life. In 1967, Kiesinger declared that "the Munich settlement, which was brought about by the threat of force, is no longer valid." That, however, was not the point. The point of the Czech demand, which had been accepted by all East bloc states, was to accord the Czech regime the right to deny the German citizenship of the approximately 10,000 ethnic Germans still living in the former Sudetenland. Had Bonn accepted this demand, the validity of acts performed under German law – such as marriage licenses and wills – when the Sudetenland was part of Germany between 1938 and 1945 would have been subject to question; and, implicitly, acceptance would have exposed Sudeten Germans to prosecution for treason for acts in support of Germany, including involuntary acts like bearing arms, during those same years. Although almost all former Sudeten Germans were now living in the Federal Republic, and not in the GDR which accepted the Czech demand in 1950, the issue was a valid concern.

The negotiations ended in a compromise. Bonn accepted that the treaty would refer to the Munich agreement, and the Czechs accepted that the treaty simply stated that the two parties deemed the agreement "void with regard to their mutual relations." On the thorny issue of the validity of German law in the Sudetenland from 1938 to 1945, the treaty stated that it would "not affect the legal effects on natural or legal persons of the law as applied in the period between 30 September 1938 and 9 May 1945." In short, acts under German law remained valid. In a separate letter, the Czech authorities declared that they would permit emigration by Czech citizens of German nationality.[1]

---

[1] Dept of State, *Documents on Germany*, 1256–8.

7

Domestic Initiatives

M embers of Brandt's government, and the SPD itself, made it clear in 1969 that they wanted to move from democratic politics to a more democratic society, according to their definition of democracy. Jürgen Habermas, a social philosopher with tremendous prestige and influence on the democratic left in Germany, in 1969 defined democracy as "the self-determination of mankind. Only when that has been achieved does true democracy exist. Political participation will then become identical with self-determination."[1] In this view the representative and hierarchical system established under Adenauer was undemocratic, because there were clear differences in authority and power. The New Left wanted what they called "transparency" of political and economic relations, more power to smaller groups, less authority and hierarchy. In fact these ideals were never realized. Instead, the result of the progressive legislation and other reforms of the early 1970s was in many cases to make power relationships less, not more transparent, and to permit small groups motivated by radical ideologies to push through their own agendas without democratic control.

Ralf Dahrendorf, the left-liberal sociologist, began with high hopes for the Brandt era which he later modified severely:

The great slogans of Willy Brandt's government (in which I, as did some of its members, believed as much as most Germans) – "internal reforms," "daring more democracy," – remained slogans, paper promises and never became serious social objectives. There is not only no major position to agree with; there is not even one to disagree with – unless one wants to disagree with everything, with "the system," which is, of course, exactly the sentiments which the terrorists are trying to exploit.[2]

[1] Cited in Bracher et al., *Republik im Wandel, 1969–1974*, 314.
[2] Cited in Hartrich, *Fourth and Richest Reich*, 275.

The domestic policies of the Brandt–Scheel government were characterized, as was Ostpolitik, by a determination to move far and fast, to
"dare more democracy" and to create a more compassionate, more open,
less authoritarian, and more generous state and society. The change in
tone from the preceding CDU-controlled governments was striking,
with the partial exception of the grand coalition, which during the last of
its three years was effectively unable to undertake major initiatives.
There were significant accomplishments in the areas of education,
welfare, taxation, regional and land use planning, environmental protection, law, and on how to combat terrorism and subversion of the free
political order of the Federal Republic. However, the reforms were
expensive. They led to inflation and fiscal strains and left West
Germany less well prepared than it might have been for the first oil
shock, the oil embargo imposed by the oil-exporting Arab states, that
since the early 1960s had been organized into OPEC, and the resulting
price explosion of late 1973. The devaluation of the dollar that
culminated in 1971–3 and the end of the Western economic system
established at Bretton Woods in 1944 were not, in the main, harmful to
West Germany. The economic shifts did, however, introduce major
shocks to Western Europe just as the EEC (with the ECSC and
EURATOM) – officially referred to since 1967 as the EC or European
Community – was regaining some momentum toward more complete
West European economic and political integration after Britain,
Ireland, and Denmark joined in 1972. Beginning in 1970–1, moreover,
a growing section of the student protest movement fell under radical
left-wing domination, while terrorism escalated.

The *Machtwechsel* of 1969 took place in the context of a widespread
feeling of accelerating social, cultural, and political change in all
Western countries. One result, or corollary, of this sense of change was
the growing belief in the need for planning in public policy. Even
liberals (in the European sense, that is, advocates of the free market)
were, by the later 1960s, arguing that no modern economy or society
could escape the need for extensive planning. In West Germany, the
belief in planning had taken hold quite rapidly among the political elite
following the economic troubles that had led to the fall of Erhard and
the formation of the great coalition. One result of this belief was the
Konzertierte Aktion (concerted action) of unions, public and private
employers, and government, designed to keep the peace in the labor
market. Another was the stabilization law of 1967 which sought to
maintain full employment, price stability, balance in international trade,
and economic growth by means of "global control" of the national
economy and medium-term planning. Global control meant, in the first
instance, that all government departments plan their spending internally

and coordinate these plans, and that the total government budget then be integrated, in its turn, into an overall strategy. The medium-term plan introduced by the stabilization law was based on five-year periods; the first plan ran from 1967 through 1971.

Looking back in 1980, the pro-SPD journalists Hermann Rudolph and Michael Naumann summarized the belief in the need for planning in this way: "In order to meet the challenges of industrial society with its constant changes, politics must ... *plan*, set priorities, consciously set developments in motion, understand the large-scale connections, in short: no longer just govern, but be creative as well. Scientists in general, but particularly social scientists, have an essential contribution to make."[3]

The medium-term plan, conceived largely by the leading prophet of planning for a mixed economy, Karl Schiller, was constrained by the need to recover from the recession of 1966. By the time of the *Machtwechsel* there was much pent-up demand, especially on the SPD left, for broader use of the tools of planning. The center of design and execution for the new, broader type of planning was the *Bundeskanzleramt* (chancellery), which expanded from 125 to 389 employees under Brandt's minister, Horst Ehmke. In a sense the chancellery became a "superministry" with executive powers and directly subordinate to the chancellor. When Ehmke took charge, a special planning staff had just been set up; Ehmke transformed it into a central directorate of overall policy. Each ministry was assigned a planning officer who reported all spending projects and decisions directly to the central planning staff in the chancellery, where they were collected, put on computer, and redistributed to all departments who were thus informed monthly of the overall position and projects of the entire federal government.

Experienced politicians regarded this "early coordination system" as a recipe for chaos. Ehmke, they thought, believed far too much in the political utility of technical innovations and social-scientific theories which he had learned as a student of political science in the US in the 1950s and as professor of public law at Freiburg from 1961 to 1967. In reality his ambitious plans resulted mainly in the proliferation of paper. Even the sympathetic Walter Scheel remarked humorously that "our colleague Ehmke manages to solve almost all the problems he himself has created."[4] Others pointed to the smooth operation of the chancellery under Hans Globke (and later, during Helmut Schmidt's government, under Manfred Schüler) and argued that Globke did more for government efficiency with a staff one-third the size of Ehmke's.

[3] Cited in Baring, *Machtwechsel*, 522.
[4] Ibid.

The planning euphoria – for that is what it was – and the high hopes of reform and state expansion in all areas collided in 1971–2 with hard economic and fiscal reality and in 1973–4, with the oil shock and with rapid (for West Germany) price and wage inflation. The result was a *Katerstimmung* (hangover feeling) that contributed greatly to the resigned, cynical, or even depressed public attitude of many West Germans in the latter part of the 1970s.

Yet everything had begun well. The Federal Republic was in the best financial health in 1969, with the economy growing at a rate of 7.5 per cent. To control prices in the prevailing conditions of full employment and high demand it was necessary to control public (and private) spending, and this was not done. During 1970 and 1971 spending by public authorities – not so much by the central government as by *Länder* and municipalities – exploded, as cities and regions vied with one another in promoting educational, welfare, and cultural reforms. Inflation grew from 2 per cent in 1969 to 5.3 per cent in 1972. And this was before the dramatic increase in oil prices in 1973 sent inflation soaring.

The unions, whose members had received wage increases below the value of actual economic growth, demanded "compensation to restore social symmetry" in 1970–1, when the growth rates were far lower. This drove inflation up. Another powerful factor was the inflow of billions of dollars into West Germany, stimulated by high West German interest rates and by the perception that the mark – despite its 8.5 per cent revaluation in October 1969 – was still undervalued and therefore a good investment. Finally, on May 9, 1971, the Bundesbank allowed the mark to float, thus recapturing some monetary freedom of movement, and on August 15, President Nixon suspended the convertibility of the dollar to gold at $35 an ounce (in reality, the market price of gold had been far above that figure for some years). The dollar, which had remained steady from 1950 to 1961 and again from 1961 to 1969, fell

TABLE 2.3   COMPOSITION OF LABOR FORCE, 1950-1985 (BY PERCENTAGE)

Economic sector	*1950*	*1960*	*1970*	*1980*	*1985*
Farming, forestry and fishing	24.7	13.6	8.5	5.5	5.4
Manufacturing	42.6	47.7	48.8	44.1	41.0
Services	18.4	21.2	25.2	31.9	35.3
Trade and transportation	14.3	17.5	17.5	18.5	18.3
All economic sectors	100.0	100.0	100.0	100.0	100.0

Source: Statistisches Bundesamt, *Lange Reihen zur Wirtschaftsentwicklung, 1986*

TABLE 2.4 ECONOMIC STRUCTURE OF LÄNDER, 1960–1985

Year	Federal Republic	Schleswig-Holstein	Lower Saxony	North Rhine-Westphalia	Hesse	Rhineland Palatinate	Baden-Württemberg	Bavaria	Saarland	Hamburg	Bremen	Berlin (West)
1 Population (in thousands)												
1960	55,433	2,295	6,588	15,694	4,729	3,381	7,591	9,387	1,051	1,823	695	2,199
1965	58,625	2,390	6,872	16,527	5,101	3,550	8,314	9,978	1,120	1,849	728	2,197
1970	60,651	2,494	7,082	16,914	5,382	3,645	8,895	10,479	1,120	1,794	723	2,122
1975	61,829	2,584	7,252	17,176	5,564	3,678	9,194	10,830	1,100	1,726	721	2,004
1980	61,566	2,605	7,247	17,044	5,589	3,639	9,233	10,899	1,068	1,650	695	1,899
1985	61,024	2,614	7,205	16,687	5,532	3,619	9,254	10,963	1,048	1,586	663	1,853
(a) Population (by percentage)												
1960	100	4.1	11.9	28.3	8.5	6.1	13.7	16.9	1.9	3.3	1.3	4.0
1965	100	4.1	11.7	28.2	8.7	6.1	14.2	17.0	1.9	3.2	1.2	3.7
1970	100	4.1	11.7	27.9	8.9	6.0	14.7	17.3	1.8	3.0	1.2	3.5
1975	100	4.2	11.7	27.7	9.0	5.9	14.9	17.5	1.8	2.8	1.2	3.2
1980	100	4.2	11.8	27.7	9.1	5.9	15.0	17.7	1.7	2.7	1.1	3.1
1985	100	4.3	11.8	27.3	9.1	5.9	15.2	18.0	1.7	2.6	1.1	3.0
2 Employment												
(a) Employed (in thousands)												
1960	26,080	919	2,963	7,109	2,265	1,505	3,935	4,565	457	951	364	1,015
1965	26,769	965	2,994	7,111	2,425	1,511	4,195	4,797	446	970	375	980
1970	26,570	960	2,994	6,931	2,441	1,470	4,233	4,834	435	957	370	945
1975	25,266	936	2,803	6,560	2,333	1,374	4,099	4,623	421	897	363	855
1980	26,278	987	2,879	6,915	2,415	1,447	4,236	4,839	442	888	357	871
1985	25,482	957	2,756	6,552	2,364	1,405	4,190	4,819	420	836	323	860

(b) *Employed* (by percentage)

1960	100	3.5	11.4	27.3	8.7	5.8	15.1	17.5	1.8	3.8	1.4	3.9
1965	100	3.6	11.2	26.6	9.1	5.6	15.7	17.9	1.7	3.6	1.4	3.7
1970	100	3.6	11.3	26.1	9.2	5.5	15.9	18.2	1.6	3.6	1.4	3.6
1975	100	3.7	11.1	26.0	9.2	5.4	16.2	18.3	1.7	3.6	1.4	3.4
1980	100	3.8	11.0	26.3	9.2	5.5	16.1	18.4	1.7	3.4	1.4	3.3
1985	100	3.8	10.8	25.7	9.3	5.5	16.4	18.9	1.6	3.3	1.3	3.4

3 Mining and manufacturing

(a) *Number of plants**

1960	56,156	1,489	4,566	16,116	4,604	2,902	10,223	10,561	705	1,532	477	2,978
1965	59,168	1,565	5,127	16,657	5,157	3,229	10,803	11,453	653	1,393	505	2,622
1970	56,219	1,560	4,917	15,894	4,940	3,005	10,579	10,969	680	1,218	431	2,022
1975	52,756	1,548	4,745	14,744	4,650	2,783	10,254	10,399	583	1,043	383	1,655
1980	48,777	1,660	4,803	11,655	4,134	2,899	10,406	10,036	597	991	408	1,188
1985	44,570	1,554	4,317	10,757	3,630	2,655	9,445	9,464	585	818	342	1,003

(b) *Plants* (by percentage)

1960	100	2.7	8.1	28.7	8.2	5.2	18.2	18.8	1.3	2.7	0.8	5.3
1965	100	2.6	8.7	28.2	8.7	5.5	18.3	19.4	1.1	2.4	0.9	4.4
1970	100	2.8	8.7	28.3	8.8	5.3	18.8	19.5	1.2	2.2	0.8	3.6
1975	100	2.9	9.0	27.9	8.8	5.3	19.4	19.7	1.1	2.0	0.7	3.1
1980	100	3.4	9.8	23.9	8.5	5.9	21.3	20.6	1.2	2.0	0.8	2.4
1985	100	3.5	9.7	24.1	8.1	6.0	21.2	21.2	1.3	1.8	0.8	2.3

* From 1960 to 1975: Plants of companies with 10 and more employees, not including trade, electricity, gas and water companies and construction industry. From 1975 to 1985: Plants of companies with 20 and more employees.

Source: Institut der deutschen Wirtschaft, *Wirtschaftstruktur der Bundesländer*

from 3.40–3.60 marks in mid-1971 to 2.90 in early 1973 and then slowly but steadily to 1.80 in 1979.

Blaming the government for inflation became the favorite weapon of the opposition, especially since Ostpolitik was either too complicated for day-to-day political battles or too popular. In September 1970 as the finance minister, Alex Möller (SPD) presented the budget for 1971, a CDU deputy interrupted him in the Bundestag and declared that Möller and his government were preparing the "third German inflation" (after the inflations of 1921–3 and 1945–8). Möller, furious, lost his usual composure and retorted: "Those who were responsible for those world wars and the inflations that followed are closer to you [CDU/CSU] spiritually than they are to the SPD." At that, the entire CDU/CSU delegation left the chamber.[5]

Möller was an extremely conscientious man who tried to remain loyal to Brandt and to the demands placed on him by the various ministries. His position was therefore very difficult, because he was put in the uncomfortable situation of balancing his loyalty to the SPD against the need to be a fiscally responsible minister of government. For about a year after the Brandt–Scheel government took office in 1969 the economy continued to boom. The man who received credit for this, however, was not Möller but his intensely proud and egotistical colleague, Karl Schiller, who continued in the post as economics minister that he had first obtained in the grand coalition in 1966.

Schiller personified the optimism and confidence in the power of economic planning that so many politicians and public figures shared in the first years of SPD rule. His stabilization strategy of 1966–9, his impressive-sounding phrases – "global control," "medium-term fiscal strategy," "goal projection" – seemed to many a kind of "friendly magic" by which the age-old cycle of boom and bust, growth and recession, could be broken.[6] In 1969–70 Schiller had convinced most friends of the government, and many others, that politicians need no longer fear the economy. He, Schiller, knew how to manage things so there would never again be serious inflation, unemployment, deficits, or recession.

This, of course, was what the ambitious but economically untrained reformers of the SPD and FDP wanted to hear. Advised and encouraged by Brandt and Ehmke, they began spending freely, keeping the goal of a vastly expanded, caring state firmly in view. As late as early 1971, they were still following this policy. Möller had warned in early 1970 that even without unforeseen problems arising, tax receipts for the years 1971 to 1975 might be 35 billion marks or almost 4 per cent lower than

[5] Bracher et al., *Republik im Wandel, 1969–1974,* 49.
[6] Baring, *Machtwechsel,* 648.

planned or than required by the spending proposals. In early 1971, however, it was clear that the federal and *Land* budgets would show a surplus for 1970. This seemed to contradict Möller's warnings.

Unfortunately for Möller and indeed for the West German economy, these pleasant figures appeared just as the government was planning the second term of the *Mifrifi* (medium-term fiscal strategy), which was to run from 1972 through 1975. Accordingly, Möller's warnings went unheeded, and Brandt gave him no support against the other powerful ministers. Chief among the latter was Schmidt, who adamantly refused to consider a single one of Möller's demands for cuts in the spending proposals. In early May of 1971, internal memoranda of the ministry of finance showed that public spending either already approved or demanded by the ministers would result in an increase in the federal debt in the four years from 1969 to 1973 of 32 billion marks. By comparison the entire debt incurred by the Bonn government in the twenty years from 1949 to 1969 was only 40 billion marks. Brandt's ministers, that "gang of spendthrifts," as Schmidt (ironically, in view of his behavior toward Möller in early 1971) later called them,[7] were planning almost to double the public debt in their first term in office.

The inflow of dollars aggravated the situation. By early 1971 there were 50 billion "homeless" dollars available in Europe beyond the control of the US or any other government. These "Eurodollars" were available to private banks and corporations, who could flood the economies of Western Europe with easy credit, thus undermining any spending restraints by government. When the Bonn government decided on May 9, 1971, to let the mark float, it hoped to create more control over credit and borrowing, and to force investors out of the mark and back into dollars, thereby reducing the Eurodollar overhang. Möller, however, argued that floating was not enough. In order to send a serious signal to the credit markets and the economy at large, the government must immediately follow up the decision to float by significant cuts in spending. As Möller later wrote in his memoirs:

We could not wait until the fall, for on May 9 we had freed the exchange rates and thereby signaled a decision for stability which had absolutely and as soon as possible to be followed by measures to stabilize spending in the domestic economy. It was necessary that there be no sign of inflated spending by government, because otherwise the newly-won freedom of maneuver would be lost and because one had to consider that the autonomous groups in the total economic process would follow the government's lead in their concern for stability. I

---

[7] Cited ibid., 651.

therefore came to realize that I could do something to help, but only by resigning.[8]

Möller resigned on May 12 after his colleagues, with Schmidt in the lead, had refused to moderate their spending plans.

The winners of this internal battle were Schiller and Schmidt. Whereas Möller, as finance minister, had the primary budgetary responsibility and therefore was always in the role of the nay-sayer and pessimist, Schiller, as economics minister, had the responsibility for managing and planning growth. Both men were touchy and egocentric, "one egg as raw as the other," as Arnulf Baring later wrote.[9]

Schiller, however, was Brandt's favorite. His appointment as "super-minister" of finance *and* economics in May 1971 was the culmination of a phenomenal career that was already well under way in 1935 when the 24-year-old economist completed his PhD as the head of a research group at the Institute of World Economics at the University of Kiel. After war service he returned to academic life as a full professor of economics, first at Kiel and from 1947 at Hamburg. That same year Ludwig Erhard, as economic director of the Bizone, asked Schiller to become a special advisor, a position he continued to hold with the economics ministry after the Federal Republic came into being in 1949. He rose to the top level of public life in West Germany in 1961 when Brandt invited him to Berlin as senator for economic affairs in the city and brought him to Bonn as economics minister in the grand coalition in 1966. "I really liked him," Brandt recalled in 1981.[10] Brandt, who deliberately refused to understand economic principles, favored Schiller in cabinet meetings and tacitly allowed him to insult and ridicule Möller. When Möller resigned, Brandt did not hesitate to accept his resignation and combine the two ministries under Schiller, who welcomed this unprecedented combination of financial and economic responsibility.

Unfortunately for Brandt and his government, Möller was right and Schiller wrong. If Brandt had listened to Möller and ordered his ministers to cut their spending proposals and reduce the deficits, it is unlikely that the economic crisis of 1973–4 would have been as severe, and it is unlikely that the public would have blamed Brandt for the weakened state of the Federal Republic's finances at the time that the oil crisis struck in October 1973. Schiller himself later admitted that even his monumental talents were insufficient to handle the problems of the

[8] Cited ibid., 653.
[9] Ibid., 654.
[10] Ibid., 655.

"superministry" in the conditions of deficit spending and increasing inflation of 1971–2. After he resigned in July 1972, Schmidt, who succeeded him, spoke of Schiller's tenure as "an endless drama in 27 acts."[11] The problems began after the budget for 1972 had been presented in the Bundestag. Tax reform was a major project of the SPD, and in November 1971 the party called a special party conference to discuss the issue. The chairman of the party's tax reform commission was Erhard Eppler, minister for development aid, and a man who had a great future as one of the leaders of the SPD's radical, pacifist, and environmentalist wing. Eppler and Schiller incorporated the two opposing tendencies that, whether or not they realized it, were battling to control the agenda, the orientation, and the future of the SPD. Schiller, a man of the world, skilled at rhetoric, but also professionally brilliant, was the perfect domestic and fiscal policy complement to Brandt's new vision of foreign policy: responsible, committed to a modernized, socially conscious mixed economy, and aware that welfare and social programs depend on economic growth and a strong private sector. Eppler, on the other hand, was a south-west German intellectual, who in the early 1950s belonged to Gustav Heinemann's *Gesamtdeutsche Volkspartei* (GVP) that fought rearmament and capitalism. He was a church minister by education and committed to a moralistic view of the tasks of West German society. He had absorbed the lesson that Jaspers had provided in 1966, the lesson that Germany's task in the world was to be a beacon of moral rectitude as atonement for past sins. Ironically, Eppler had not liked Jaspers' book at all when it appeared, but a few years later became committed to its message. For Eppler, capitalism was fundamentally immoral and wasteful, economic growth was a cause of environmental disaster as well as of personal extravagance. He viewed the task of social democratic politics as establishing in West Germany "another republic," a republic of virtue, equality, and peace – a republic which the left wing of the SPD had been waiting to create since 1949.

The tax reform commission of the SPD, which Eppler chaired, recommended a draconian increase in direct taxes to alleviate "the public poverty" that threatened to hamper the Brandt government's ambitious welfare and social policy reforms. Schiller warned that if these proposals were implemented business confidence and investments would collapse, and the SPD would lose many of the moderate voters who had been attracted to the party in 1969 by Schiller's own brand of pro-market social welfare. His warnings went unheeded. The special party conference overwhelmingly approved Eppler's and the left's proposals for tax and related economic policy. At that moment, in

[11] Cited ibid., 664.

Baring's words, "what was desirable appeared more important than what was possible."[12] Although Schmidt agreed with Schiller that the "longing for renewal" of the radicals was foolish, he refrained from opposing the decisions of the conference, merely appearing at the end and asking Schiller in a jocular tone, "Well, have they decided a lot of nonsense?"[13] After the special conference, the left-leaning *Frankfurter Rundschau* observed that Schiller had "lost all contact with the party base;" when he rose to speak, the delegates demonstrated their lack of interest by walking out on him.[14]

In May 1972, against the backdrop of the coalition's dwindling majority in the Bundestag and the opposition's attempts to seize power, Schiller engaged his own internal party opposition frontally, demanding cuts of 2.5 billion marks in the current (1972) budget. He pointed out that the government's spending plans exceeded expected revenue by 17 billion marks in 1973 and about 20 billion in each of the following three years. This, he said, was "irresponsible from the point of view of a policy of stabilization."[15] In order to make his point he circulated 131 copies of his objections, which naturally meant that they leaked to the public and dramatically confirmed the opposition's argument that Brandt's government was driving the country toward fiscal disaster.

Ironically, the opposition to Schiller's demands for moderation came not from the left-wing ministries like Eppler's, but from the defense ministry under Helmut Schmidt, who stood to lose DM 800 million. Schmidt's conflict with Schiller was different from, but no less serious than, Eppler's. Whereas Eppler represented the left wing who would never understand Schiller's justifications of capitalist democracy, Schmidt was, ideologically, Schiller's ally, with some exceptions: he supported the unions' demand for *Mitbestimmung*, or full co-determination by employers and employees in industry, an equal distribution of property, and a more balanced tax system (which meant for the SPD the passage of tax legislation that would redistribute income, and thereby indirectly also property, by placing heavy tax burdens on the wealthy). Schmidt also was co-author of the party's strategic framework (*Orientierungsrahmen*) that set forth the SPD's vision of a more planned, more egalitarian West Germany to be achieved by 1985.

Schmidt's essential outlook reflected Schiller's philosophy – in contrast to that of Eppler or the Jusos – and was the very reason they could not be in the top party leadership together. Schmidt was

---

[12] Ibid., 666.
[13] Cited ibid.
[14] Cited ibid.
[15] Cited ibid., 668.

determined that he, not Schiller, should lead the fiscally responsible wing of the SPD, and he won. But there was also another reason for the support Schmidt received. Many in the SPD believed that he was, next to Brandt, the most popular leading figure of the party, and that he should not remain in the political shadows as minister of defense. Schiller, in the meantime, was being increasingly often accused of inflationary policies, despite the fact that it was the cabinet's inflationary budgetary policy that was contributing to it. Within the party itself, however, Schmidt was more popular and a much more sophisticated politician, despite the fact that his experience in matters of economic and financial policy was not as broad as Schiller's. In 1973, after Schmidt had won the political battle, Conrad Ahlers commented: "The permanent conflict between Helmut Schmidt and Karl Schiller was conducted, particularly by the present minister of finance [Schmidt], in such a disagreeable manner (partly explained by Schmidt's thyroid disease), that the chancellor more than once left the cabinet room in despair and considered resigning. Karl Schiller was Helmut Schmidt's superior in economic matters but was defeated politically."[16]

In June, Brandt convinced his ministers to accept most of Schiller's proposed cut of 2.5 billion marks, but it was a pyrrhic victory for the minister. The entire cabinet was now against him and took the next occasion to provoke his fall. The occasion arose in late June when the cabinet discussed the rapidly accelerating inflow of foreign exchange due to the depreciation of the pound sterling and the Italian lira. To curb this influx of capital the chairman of the Bundesbank, Karl Klasen, recommended foreign exchange controls. He thereby reopened a struggle that had been going on between Schiller and the Bundesbank since 1967 over who had the authority to change the exchange rates of the mark – the Bundesbank or the minister of economics. At a meeting of the cabinet and the Bundesbank chairman on June 28 Schiller deployed all of his rhetorical skills to convince his colleagues to turn down Klasen's request for controls. Schiller argued that exchange controls would undermine the very foundations of West German prosperity, namely free trade and the free convertibility of the mark. Klasen argued in return that the controls would only last until after the election which the government had already planned for November. When it became clear that the cabinet was going to vote for controls, Schiller declared that he would resign. The next day the cabinet voted to impose the controls with Schiller the only one opposed. His successor in both his posts, as minister of economics and finance, was none other than Helmut Schmidt.

[16] Cited ibid., 669.

The fact that every single member of the cabinet voted against Schiller demonstrated his unpopularity. A large proportion of the SPD and FDP leadership wanted him out. On the evening of June 28, Horst Ehmke summed up the feelings of many when he suggested that the cabinet not miss the opportunity to let Schiller resign: "We'll never again get rid of Karl that cheaply."[17] On July 2, Schiller sent Brandt his official letter of resignation which ran to more than 4,000 words and was a detailed reckoning with what he saw as the errors and dangers of the government's economic policies. After complaining about the manner in which Klasen raised the exchange control issue at a cabinet meeting, without informing Schiller, who was the minister responsible, beforehand, he went on to state that he had to resign because he found no support in the cabinet for a sound economic and fiscal policy.

Schiller withdrew from national politics. He was a man whose character was abrasive to many, and who expressed his opinions in a manner which his colleagues, as well as the general public, often considered to be arrogant and condescending. As Brandt explained it, "the fact was that he had managed to alienate nearly all his cabinet colleagues. My mistake lay in appointing him minister of finance as well as minister of economic affairs when Alex Möller resigned in 1971."[18] For his part, Schiller was so disgusted with the leftward drift of the SPD and with what he considered to be fiscal irresponsibility of the party, that he resigned from the SPD in 1972 and supported the CDU in the election campaign of the autumn (he rejoined the SPD ten years later), and became a member of the prestigious Mont Pelerin Society, of which Ludwig Erhard was a member.

Once he had assumed Schiller's mantle, Schmidt did not hesitate a moment to enforce Schiller's policies. In August 1972 Schiller asked Brandt what had happened to the 800–million-mark cut that he, Schiller, had proposed for defense, and which Schmidt had opposed. Brandt smiled and replied that the problem was solved since Schmidt was now minister of finance and economics. Of course the cut had been passed.[19] This more than anything else demonstrated that Schiller's problem was primarily one of personality and not of policy. On the issue of policy Schmidt was Schiller's ally; in terms of the internal power struggle, they were enemies.

[17] Cited ibid., 672.
[18] Brandt, *People and Politics*, 438.
[19] Baring, *Machtwechsel*, 684.

8

Equality of Opportunity or Equality of Result: The Economy and Education

For the SPD left, economic and social democracy primarily meant equality of results rather than of opportunity. To achieve this end, two areas were of critical importance: the relationship between employer and employee, and the country's educational structure. The question of what role employees should or could play in the management of enterprises in which they worked had been an issue since 1951, when the labor unions in the coal and steel industry obtained the right of co-determination. This meant that the employees shared responsibility with the employer in the company's decision-making process. The Brandt–Scheel government, however, envisaged participation on a much broader scale, in accordance with its philosophy of decentralizing decisions – or at least appeared to do so. Lowering the voting age to 18, for example, was part of the effort to broaden participation in the democratic process. But the most important, and the most far-reaching element in this general effort, was the passage of major changes in the *Betriebsverfassungsgesetz* (Works Organization Act) in November 1971. When this law was first passed under Adenauer in 1952 the SPD refused to accept it because, in its view, it did not go far enough. Thus, when the SPD enjoyed a strong majority coalition in the Bundestag it passed what basically amounted to an entirely new version of the old law.

The result greatly strengthened the role of the employee councils (*Betriebsräte*), which were bodies elected by the employees to represent them, together with the labor unions, in negotiations with employers on the multitude of problems that concern any normal business. The SPD, and Germany's labor unions, demanded full parity of employee and employer representatives on the board of directors. The purpose of the laws, from Brandt's standpoint, was to establish and, by law, guarantee "more democracy in the companies, more humanity in working life, more freedom for the individual employee, and more social justice."[1] The employers, however – that is to say, the owners and managers of the companies – regarded co-determination, as well as the expanded rights of workers contained in the revised *Betriebsverfassungsgesetz*, as a threat to property rights and to the right of the employer to direct and to take responsibility for the operations of their companies. The demand for co-determination caused great debate, and the differing views were not reconciled in law until 1976 with the passage of the *Mitbestimmungsgesetz* (Law of Co-determination) which affected 650 publicly held companies with more than 2,000 employees, with some of the employee seats reserved for union representatives. Thus, it was under the chancellorship of Helmut Schmidt that this issue was resolved.

Educational reform was another, and very important goal in the "democratization" of society envisaged by the Brandt–Scheel government, for the simple reason that control of the structure and content of education was a powerful instrument of political influence. Consensus on the need for reform existed, although not on the form it should take, primarily because vastly increased numbers of students were placing a major burden on the educational system. The number of students in secondary (high) schools rose from 958,000 in 1965 to 2.2 million in 1970. In the same period the number of university students increased from 384,400 to 510,500. Per capita expenditure on education rose from DM 264 to DM 453 and educational costs as a proportion of public spending rose from 11.2 per cent to 14.1 per cent.[2] Measures to broaden educational opportunities included the Federal Education Promotion Act (*Bundesausbildungsförderungsgesetz* or *Bafög* for short) of 1971. It guaranteed the right of everyone to receive state support for the education of his or her choice, and enabled students to borrow money from the government to finance their education.

On the purpose and goal of reform, however, consensus did not exist. The left-wing of the SPD saw education in all its stages, from kindergarten through university, as a means to bring about social change via equality and form of education. Since 1945 the decision-making authority in cultural affairs, which included educational policy, was vested in the *Länder*, and in 1969 this remained unchanged. The moderate progressives wanted to make higher education, at the high school and university levels, available to a larger part of the German population. The radical progressives wanted to use educational reform as tool of "democratization," that is, of radical social change in accordance with their view of democracy.

---

[1] Brandt, *Zum sozialen Rechtsstaat*, 323.
[2] Regierung der BRD, *Gesellschaftliche Daten*, 83, 95.

Map 2.2   Universities. In the 1980s, educational institutions, including theological seminaries, were widely spread throughout the Federal Republic.

Source: Bertelsmann Lexikon-Institut, *Facts about Germany* (1988), 343

The first major initiatives in this area were taken in mid-1963, when Erhard compared the importance of restructuring the educational system with the efforts to deal with the inequalities of social justice in the nineteenth century. In 1964 Georg Picht published his *Deutsche Bildungskatastrophe* (The German education catastrophe), and a few years later Ralf Dahrendorf his *Bildung ist Bürgerrecht* (Education is a civil right). Both of these volumes pointed in different ways to the lack of equal opportunity for education that existed in the Federal Republic, and emphasized that education was not a privilege, but a right. The *Land* ministers of culture themselves, who met on a regular basis in an effort to coordinate and design basic guidelines for educational policy, although they had no collective authority to enforce their recommendations, concluded in a declaration published in Berlin in March 1964 that educational policy must be based on the needs of industrialized society now that the reconstruction of Germany had been concluded.[3]

The mid-1960s also saw the creation of two influential organizations. The first was the Max Planck Institute for Educational Research (established in 1963 in Berlin), and the second was the German Educational Council, established in 1965. It was this latter group that produced a "structural plan" (*Strukturplan*) for educational reform in 1970 that, in turn, was to be given substance by a commission of federal and state representatives charged with designing a general educational plan (the *Bund/Länder Kommission* or BLK).

The primary goal of the structural plan was to achieve "unity of theoretical and practical education," which meant abolishing distinctions between different types of schools in favor of establishing *Gesamtschulen,* or a comprehensive school for all students. This would eliminate different kinds of schools aimed at providing education for different social levels of German society, in an effort to establish equality of opportunity for all students. The federal government went further in a report on educational policy in June 1970. Under the leadership of Hildegard Hamm-Brücher of the FDP the government directly confronted the CDU/CSU-governed *Länder* with the demand that they introduce *Gesamtschulen* in the name of equality and democracy. The CDU/CSU opposition initially indicated its willingness to cooperate in the effort to reform the educational structure, but rejected Hamm-Brücher's proposal. They feared that her plans were part of a broader strategy designed not only to introduce socialist ideology as part of primary and secondary education, but also to abolish constitutional

---

[3] Massing, "Die Bildungspolitik," in *Die Bundesrepublik in den siebziger Jahren*, Glaessner et al., eds, 201.

authority of the *Länder* in this area, and, therefore, to increase the centralized power of the federal government.

The work of the commission responsible for designing a general educational plan also encountered opposition. The BLK consisted of eleven members from the federal government and one from each *Land*, a total of 22. Decisions required a two-thirds majority , but were binding only for the *Länder* whose representatives supported them. Since the federal members and the members of the SPD/FDP-ruled *Länder* together numbered 17, enough for the two-thirds majority, they were able to overrule the five members from the CDU/CSU *Länder*. The result was a split between "*A-Länder*", ruled by the SPD and FDP, which accepted the government's proposals for *Gesamtschulen* and greater student participation in administrative and curricula decisions at the university level, and "*B-Länder*," ruled by the CDU or, in Bavaria's case, the CSU, and committed to maintaining a differentiated school system based on merit. This distinction reflected the dissolution of a fragile political consensus concerning the need to reform the educational system in general terms, and placed "educational reform specifically in the service of an all-embracing reform of society (more equality, more democracy, more emancipation . . .)."[4] As a consequence, educational reform became "the object of political and ideological controversy" and could not be achieved lacking a broad consensus. This dilemma outlasted the Brandt period and, given the crucial importance of education in forming cultural and social identity and values, marked a permanent cultural division in the Federal Republic that continued to exist in the 1980s.

At the university level the student movement, initially focused on reforms within the university system, developed into protest concerning broad social, political and economic issues; it met with virtually no serious and competent intellectual opposition. The radical leaders, and their followers in organizations like the SDS, continued to strengthen their position and influence in the late 1960s. In November 1970 a group of critical academics and scholars joined together to form the *Bund Freiheit der Wissenschaft* (BFW; Association for the Freedom of Scholarship) on the national level, which was a more comprehensive version of the very effective Emergency Society for a Free University, formed in Berlin somewhat earlier.

The BFW, via its publications as well as the writings of its members, warned of politicization of the university and the resulting decline in the standards of higher education. It thus became associated with CDU educational policy, although its membership was bipartisan. It was,

[4] Ibid., 212.

however, vilified by the left as a conservative, if not authoritarian, organization trying to stifle academic freedom and turn back the clock of revolution. In fact, the contrary was the case. The student revolution had come with such speed and force that Germany's professors were simply not prepared to deal with gross abuse of privilege and use and misuse of power by the radicals. Their initial reaction was one of abhorrence, but, beyond condemnation of violence as a means with which to conduct debates, they seemed unable to form any kind of cohesive, consistent defense of educational purpose and standard. The BFW was an attempt to do so, albeit several years too late, and it did succeed, to some degree, over the long term. It focused attention on how perilously fragile academic standards really were; they could be destroyed quickly, but it took years to re-establish them, and years to regain the respect the professors had lost as leaders of Germany's scholarly intellectuals. Eighteen years later, in 1988, the BFW had developed into the kind of respected organization, on a national level, whose absence in the late 1960s had been so sorely missed. It provided the stability of standards that was seldom found two decades earlier, to serve the purpose of "promoting the freedom of research, teaching and learning . . . [and] to oppose every subservience to the claims of power of single groups or interests . . . [and] to insist on a policy that combines a continual expansion of educational opportunities with the maintenance of standards and performance."[5]

The educational battles of the Brandt–Scheel government ended in stalemate, with the *Länder* reasserting their authority vis-à-vis the federal government. The grandiose plan for wholesale reform, announced by Brandt in 1969, included increased compensatory education for the disadvantaged, emphasis on learning by discovery, a great reduction in the degree of streaming according to ability in the higher grade levels, continued expansion of university level education, and transformation of the traditional university organizational structure. The final result, on the federal level, was the introduction in 1971 of the *Hochschulrahmengesetz* (Law on the Framework of Higher Education), a federal law which set the framework for the *Länder,* who were respons-ible for the universities within their states. It proved impossible to pass this law over the objections of the CDU majority in the Bundesrat (whose concurrence was required for measures affecting the authority of the *Länder*), and the bill that finally became law in 1975 was no longer a pathbreaking agenda, but merely a codification of the existing pluralism.

[5] Statement of purpose, *Freiheit der Wissenschaft,* no. 6 (July 1985), 2.

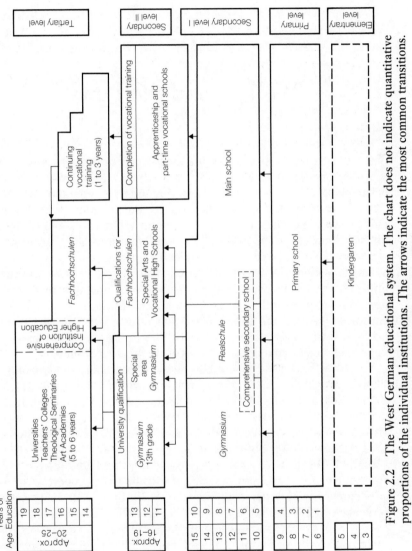

Figure 2.2   The West German educational system. The chart does not indicate quantitative proportions of the individual institutions. The arrows indicate the most common transitions.
Source: Katzenstein, Policy and Politics in West Germany, 301

9

Welfare and the Law

In the area of social security the most significant measure was the *Rentenreformgesetz* (pension reform act) of 1972, which made payments largely independent of contributions. By separating pension rights from what the recipient had paid in while employed the law not only created a new demand on the government but a serious additional financial burden on the budget. The pension reform act ensured that workers would not suffer financial hardship and could maintain an adequate standard of living after retirement.[1] Other reforms included improved health and accident insurance, better unemployment compensation, rent control, payments to families with children, subsidies to encourage savings and investments, and measures to "humanize the world of work" such as better medical care for on-the-job illnesses or injuries and mandated improvements in the work environment.

The SPD/FDP government also hoped to centralize and streamline all welfare policies in a uniform social security act and established a commission of experts in 1970 for that purpose. This was a significant step, consistent with the planning ideology of the Brandt era, but it proved impossible to execute. By the end of the SPD/FDP coalition in 1982 the new bill was not yet ready.

In the 1970s the cost of social services took a sharp turn upward, as in many other industrial countries. Social spending as a proportion of the GNP grew by 21.4 per cent between 1970 and 1981. In terms of percentage of GNP it increased from 25.7 in 1970 to 31.2 in 1981.[2] The easiest way to pay for this increase was via taxes. Therefore, the government proposed a major tax reform, which was, in principle, very much needed since the existing tax laws were numerous and complex, and many of them pre-dated World War II. It proved impossible to

[1] Bertelsmann Lexikon-Institut, *Facts about Germany* (1979), 266.
[2] Ellwein and Bruder, eds, *Ploetz — Die BRD*, 134.

achieve this, however, although the three tax laws that finally were passed during 1974–5 took many lower-income people off the tax rolls and increased child benefit payments.

Another area of bustling activity was reform of the law, particularly criminal and consumer protection law. As minister of justice in the grand coalition, Gustav Heinemann had absorbed the new international currents of opinion concerning criminology and jurisprudence, according to which the purpose of criminal sanctions was not to punish or to express society's condemnation of certain acts. Rather, abandoning the notions of "guilt," "retribution," and "deterrence," liberal views of the law purported that lawyers and judges should focus on the social and environmental causes of crime and rehabilitate, not penalize violators. Criminal law itself should be reformed so as to lessen the severity and the social stigma of criminal penalties.

This was accomplished in a series of acts revising the German penal code that were passed, to a great extent with the concurrence of the CDU/CSU between 1969 and 1976; however, not all revisions of the code met with unanimous approval. One of the most acrimoniously debated measures was the proposal to revise clause 218 of the German criminal code, the clause forbidding abortion under any circumstances. Since 1927 judges had permitted abortion only for medical reasons, but by the late 1960s feminists and progressive lawyers were demanding approval of abortion if requested within the first three months of pregnancy. Initially the SPD favored liberalizing the medical criteria to permit social and ethical concerns to justify abortion, rather than supporting the concept of abortion on request, but changed its view under pressure from the FDP, where feminists were influential. In 1974, the coalition accordingly proposed a revision of clause 218 of the criminal code permitting abortion on request in the first trimester. The revision was enacted over the votes of the opposition in the Bundestag.

The debate caused major public demonstrations for and against, and produced agitated public discussion. After the act had become law, the CDU-governed *Länder* requested a declaratory judgement from the Federal Constitutional Court that the revision of clause 218 was unconstitutional. The court found, on February 25, 1975, that the revision "fails to do justice to the constitutional duty to protect developing life." The court specifically referred to the contempt for life in Nazi Germany as a precedent that should count heavily against any effort to restrict the definition of human life. The government was compelled to return to some form of medical criteria, and in 1976 a large majority of the SPD/FDP joined with a number of CDU members to pass a bill permitting abortion for medical reasons, including that of "social emergency" – in the opinion of the bill's critics, a weak justification for sympathetic doctors to perform abortions on request.

Another contested measure was the modification in 1970 of the law regarding disturbing the peace (*Landsfriedensbruch*), which had hitherto been widely interpreted so as to include passive participation or even mere presence at demonstrations. As the incidence of terrorism increased in the 1970s, however, the coalition tightened the sanctions on promoting or encouraging violence – sanctions that were again lifted in 1981, as the ability to deal effectively with terrorist incidents became more sophisticated.[3]

The broad gauge of social programs of the Brandt government had no impact on one social process of critical importance. It was the declining birthrate, which caused increasing alarm as the decade progressed. Whereas in 1965 the number of children born amounted to 1.04 million, the number decreased to 811,000 in 1970. Despite government financial support for families with children, revised under the Brandt government to include families with only one child, the number of children born in 1975 had declined to 601,000, and reached an all-time low in 1978. The fertility rate reached a postwar high in 1964 with 87 children born per 1,000 women of child-bearing age (15–45 years of age) and declined to 67 in 1970 and to 48 in 1975.[4] Other reasons for the falling birthrate, in addition to the expense of raising children, were the newly emerging attitudes of the younger generations. Some thought it immoral to bring children into a capitalistic society while awaiting the arrival of "the revolution." Others, in a classic example of self-indulgence, did not want to accept the responsibilities that children and families entailed. Still others argued that the future was so threatening that it would be irresponsible to bring children into such a world.

Real income and personal wealth increased during the Brandt government. The average work week, which until the late 1960s was 42 hours, came close to the 40–hour norm. The number of paid holidays per year was 37 days, almost two full months. These changes and reforms by no means satisfied the left which pointed out that income distribution was far from equal. They advocated not equality of opportunity, but equality of result, with little regard to ability, performance, and commitment, and demanded large-scale redistribution of productive capital. They did not achieve significant redistribution, but after the departure of Karl Schiller their influence within the SPD increased until the resignation of Brandt in 1974.

Brandt considered the results of his social policy to be "our most visible

[3] Brandt, *Zum sozialen Rechtsstaat*, 216–9.
[4] Regierung der BRD, *Gesellschaftliche Daten*, 23.
[5] Brandt, *People and Politics*, 232.

and impressive achievements."[5] The changes included increases in pensions for war victims, old-age pension rights for groups that had previously not qualified, the adoption of a flexible retirement age in 1972, increased health insurance benefits, and legislation affecting marriage and the family, in addition to the changes in penal and civil law and in education policy. His domestic policies left a legacy that was in some areas very respectable and in others, such as educational reform, problematic. Marion Dönhoff considered "his vision . . . too bold: he wanted to reform the state and society from the very bottom and create a 'modern Germany.' His motto was more democracy, especially more social democracy; more justice, more tolerance, more neighbourly love."[6]

One could argue that the reforms did not constitute major new initiatives, but were in reality improvements of already existing entitlements and institutional arrangements. From this standpoint the changes were, in fact, less dramatic and certainly far less significant for the daily lives either of ordinary Germans or of the republic itself than the fundamental legislation of the Adenauer era – co-determination in heavy industry, the indexation of pensions in 1957, or the public housing laws of the 1950s. But at the same time, the reforms of the Brandt–Scheel government did have a powerful effect on the public's view of the first SPD government in postwar German history. "People were seized by a completely new feeling about life," wrote Dönhoff in 1982. She continued: "A mania for large-scale reforms spread like wildfire, affecting schools, universities, the administration, family legislation. In the autumn of 1970 Jürgen Wischnewski of the SPD declared, 'Every week more than three plans for reform come up for decision in the cabinet and in the assembly.'"[7] It is fair to conclude that "in retrospect one can say that an important part of the reform proposals was realized, and today we cannot imagine being without it."[8] But many others required a broad political consensus that a social democratic chancellor was not capable of producing; by 1972, at the end of his first term in office, Brandt was called a weak chancellor.

[6] Dönhoff, *Foe into Friend*, 144.
[7] Ibid.
[8] Ellwein and Bruder, eds, *Ploetz – Die BRD*, 135–6.

10

Domestic Stability – Domestic Security

Next to Ostpolitik and "more democracy," the major policy debate of the first social-liberal coalition concerned domestic security. This meant terrorism and subversion. The right-wing NPD had failed in 1969 to breach the 5 per cent barrier required to elect representatives to the Bundestag and it declined rapidly thereafter. On the left, however, Hans-Dietrich Genscher, the interior minister and hence responsible for domestic security, reported to the Bundestag in 1971 that there were in the Federal Republic 392 extreme left-wing organizations with a total membership of 67,000. Since 1969 there had been a distinct tendency to concentration and growth of radical groups; by 1975 there were 279 organizations with 105,000 members. The organizations ranged from orthodox communist groups (including the DKP, the reconstituted communist party, which Brandt had promised Brezhnev he would not touch), via self-proclaimed Trotskyites and Maoists, to anarchists and genuine terrorists.

The original extraparliamentary opposition (APO) of 1966–8 was, in the main, anarchistic, anti-authoritarian, and deliberately anti-hierarchical. The emergency powers legislation of May 1968 provoked on the extreme left a sharp turn to strict organization and, in the case of the terrorists, to belief in the primacy of action over theory.

The acts of violence and terror themselves were not condoned by responsible German citizens of any political persuasion. But vague arguments justifying opposition to an assertedly "oppressive" state were heard from the intellectual left, including such individuals as the writer Heinrich Böll. Despite the bloody nature of the terrorists' deeds, the numbers of sympathizers and apologists were large enough to give the terrorists, at least for a time, a network of friends and helpers who would not turn them in and would provide them with money and resources. That was perhaps not surprising given that the West German intellectual and academic left was extremely sensitive to and uncomfortable with the use of police force, even if it was used to combat terrorism. The memory, whether genuine or assumed, of the abuse of police authority by the Hitler regime was strong, and this led many people not only to give the terrorists the benefit of the doubt in judging their actions, but also to doubt the state's right to act decisively against them.

The first wave of terrorism during 1970–2 led to considerable improvements in police procedure and to a certain amount of centralized organization. This result was difficult to achieve because law enforcement was deliberately decentralized in the Federal Republic. It was not until the second wave of terrorism, in 1974–7, that the government reformed the system of judicial procedure to speed up trials and sentencing.

In the midst of this domestic turmoil West Germany faced the first act of international terrorism on a major scale, transported from the Middle East to Munich. In September 1972 Germany hosted the Summer Olympics for the first time since 1936, when Adolf Hitler presided over them in Berlin (and refused to shake the hand of the Olympic track and field champion Jesse Owens, a black American, who won several gold medals for his athletic performance). In the early morning hours of September 5, 1972, eight Arab terrorists, heavily armed, broke into the quarters of the Israeli athletes in the Olympic village. When the German police arrived one Israeli trainer was already dead in front of the entrance, another lay dead inside, and nine athletes were tied up with rope and were held hostage by the terrorists.

The kidnapping was traumatic for everyone, but particularly for Jews and Germans. Not only were Olympic athletes being murdered, but they were Jews and they were dying in Munich. The terrorists demanded that Israel release 200 Arab prisoners, otherwise the hostages would be killed. The Israeli government refused to make any concessions and after consultations with them the German authorities attempted a rescue. The terrorists refused an offer to substitute German officials for the hostages, including the former mayor of Munich, Hans-Jochen Vogel, who became chairman of the SPD in 1987. When German police finally took action, nine Israeli athletes died as the helicopters in which they were sitting blew up, and one German policeman and four terrorists were killed.

The deaths in Munich were not the fault of the Germans, as the secretary general of the Central Council of Jews in Germany acknowledged at the time. But it was both a human and psychological tragedy of enormous magnitude, and it reinforced Germany's commitment to fight terrorism in every way. The federal president, Gustav Heinemann, was deeply shaken when he spoke for Germany on September 6:

Where happiness and joy reigned only a short while ago, the signs of power-lessness and shock mark the faces of men. . . . Who is guilty of this monstrous deed? In the foreground it is a criminal organization which believes that hatred and murder could be means of a political fight. But those countries who do not hinder these men in their actions also bear responsibility. . . . What matters now, especially in the face of the new victims, is to set our will for an understanding against fanaticism as it roused and frightened the world. The Olympic idea has not been refuted.[1]

The majority on the radical left did not turn to terror, but continued their "long march through the institutions;" that is, the attempt to occupy positions of influence, mainly in education and the media, in order to change political consciousness and the ideology of Germany's citizens in a socialist direction.

On January 28, 1972, the chancellor and the minister-presidents of the *Länder* issued a declaration that became notorious, although it created no new law and was simply an attempt to coordinate existing policies. This was the "extremist directive" (*Radikalenerlass*). It reminded all those in charge of recruiting *Beamte* of a decision taken by Adenauer's government on subversion in 1950, of the civil service law of 1953, and of the civil service rights law of 1957. According to these statutes no person could enter public employment – a category that in West Germany included the entire educational sector as well as the broadcast media – who could not promise to support the free and democratic order as laid down in the Basic Law. The purpose of the "extremist directive" was to establish common ground rules for use in all *Länder* in enforcing the civil service laws. Instead, the result was fear and anger on the left and chaos in practice, with many left-leaning regional administrations refusing to apply the "extremist directive."

The left, including large parts of the SPD and FDP, denounced the directive as tantamount to *Berufsverbot*, that is, forbidding employment to categories of people suspected of subversive behavior or beliefs. The critics pointed to a passage in the directive stating that membership in "an organization pursuing aims hostile to the constitution . . . is reason for doubting" that the person in question would defend "the free and democratic order." (In West Germany this phrase was used semi-officially to describe the political system). "These doubts in general justify rejection of an application for public employment."[2] The SPD and the FDP's Genscher wanted to restrict the prohibitions to indivi-duals guilty of specific and concrete acts, whereas the CDU/CSU

---

[1] *Relay from Bonn,* September 6, 1972.
[2] Bracher et al., *Republik im Wandel, 1969–1974,* 84.

tended to assume that membership in certain organizations was prima facie evidence of hostility to democratic order.

In 1975, the Federal Constitutional Court, responding to a complaint lodged by radical groups, reaffirmed that behavior which could justify rejection of a position as *Beamte* might include "joining or membership in a political party that pursues aims hostile to the constitution, regardless of whether that party has been found unconstitutional by decision of this court."[3] That affected primarily members of the legally reconstituted DKP. An attempt to pass new legislation on the basis of the directive in 1976 failed, and that same year the SPD/FDP-governed *Länder* decided unilaterally to stop enforcing the laws quoted in the directive and issued new guidelines of their own. According to these guidelines, mere membership in any organization was not enough to justify rejection for government employment. Perhaps more important, the authorities of these *Länder* refused to carry out security checks of applicants. The emotional debate continued. In fact, it was a tempest in a teapot because very few individuals were affected. From January 1973 through mid-1975 only 235 persons were rejected for political reasons out of a total of 454,000 applicants for public service jobs.[4]

[3] Ibid., 85.
[4] Ibid., 86.

11

1972: Victory in the Bundestag Elections
1973: Chancellor Brandt's Popularity Wanes

The election campaign of the fall of 1972 was the most emotional and polarized one since 1949. Some observers called it a "plebiscite for Brandt and Ostpolitik."[1] The SPD/FDP majority in the Bundestag had been gradually whittled down by defections in the course of the year, and thus the outcome of the election was of critical importance to the future of the coalition and for Brandt himself. One important defector was Erich Mende, the former chairman of the FDP, who joined the CDU. His itinerary illustrated how far German political culture had moved in a few short years. In the late 1950s he was definitely on the left wing of his party, interested in social and economic reforms and, in his view of Ostpolitik, much closer to Brandt than to Adenauer. He and other younger liberals at the time advocated recognizing the GDR and accepting the Oder–Neisse line. By 1972 his own party had moved so far to the left, in pursuit of radical chic ideas, that he found the FDP unrecognizable.

At the same time, Ostpolitik had generated great support among West Germany's intellectuals, actors, artists, and writers – the leaders of published opinion, in short. Led by Augstein in *Der Spiegel*, Nannen in *Stern*, and Theo Sommer and Marion Dönhoff in *Die Zeit*, they supported Brandt with renewed vigor. They shared the conviction of the writer Günter Grass that Brandt represented the image of a "moral politician."[2] Shortly before the campaign began, Grass published a diary of his participation in the 1969 election – *Aus dem Tagebuch einer Schnecke*

---

[1] Bracher et al., *Republik im Wandel, 1969–1974*, 86.
[2] Ibid., 86–7.

(From the diary of a snail) – in which he described the political efforts which had produced victory for the SPD in 1969, and which were symbolic for the current campaign. Grass believed that although the SPD was moving toward a socialist utopia at a snail's pace, this progress was better than no movement at all. Indeed, Brandt's supporters could point to a great deal in terms of achievements in both domestic and foreign policy.

Adopting a phrase of John F. Kennedy's, Brandt spoke constantly of "the ability to feel compassion". The converse of the intellectuals' glorification, almost sanctification, of Brandt was the demonization of Barzel, the CDU chairman from 1971 to 1973. Augstein's *Spiegel*, drawing freely on the rhetoric and prejudices of its former deputy editor Conrad Ahlers, Brandt's press spokesman, characterized Brandt as a "man of firm principles whose purity is not doubted even by his enemies" and Barzel as "the unattractive prototype of a slick, ambitious man . . . the kind of man whose rich aunt leaves him the least she can get away with."[3]

The barrage of media support for Brandt and vilification of Barzel, coupled with the opposition's lack of a clear campaign focus – Ostpolitik was popular, and few people saw inflation as a serious threat to prosperity – led to the highest voter turnout in the Federal Republic's history (91.1 per cent) and to a triumph for the coalition. The SPD won 45.8 per cent of the vote, and the FDP dramatically improved its position to 8.4 per cent (up from 5.8). For the first time the SPD became the strongest party in the Bundestag. With 44.9 per cent the CDU/CSU had its worst result in 20 years. The SPD's victory was due to what some called the "chancellor effect" – the bonus of incumbency, traditionally strong in West Germany, and enhanced by the award to Brandt of the Nobel Peace Prize for 1971 – and above all to the lowering of the voting age to 18; estimates concluded that almost three-fourths of the 2.5 million 18 to 20–year-olds voted for the coalition.

The SPD left was delighted and saw the vote as confirmation that the public wanted more radical reforms and wanted them fast. Rudolf Schöfberger, the new chairman of the Munich SPD, stated after the elections: "With this result we can begin to build the socialist Germany. We can proceed more directly than before against certain circles of big capital."[4] Arnulf Baring estimated that the radical group included 50 deputies, but "their self-confidence was several times greater."[5] Before the elections the left-leaning deputies and their associates had organized themselves loosely in the so-called Leverkusen circle headed

[3] Ibid., 87.
[4] Cited Baring, *Machtwechsel*, 535.
[5] Ibid.

by Björn Engholm who, in 1988, became minister-president of Schleswig-Holstein, Karsten Voigt, and the radical lawyer Rudi Arndt, from 1964 to 1971 minister of public works in Hesse. The Leverkusen circle demanded a distinctive socialist set of policies for West Germany and was specifically opposed to the long-term economic and political program for the years 1972–85 which Helmut Schmidt had largely drafted and which was to be approved at the party conference in April 1973.

The position of the FDP was strengthened in the new government. After long discussions Brandt and Scheel agreed to divide Schmidt's superministry into its two original components. Schmidt remained minister of finance, while the economic ministry went to a leading FDP moderate, Hans Friderichs. The liberals also took over the office of press spokesman, since Conrad Ahlers had won a seat in the Bundestag; his successor was Rüdiger von Wechmar, who in 1974 became West Germany's first ambassador to the UN. The FDP left was represented by a fifth liberal minister, Hans Maihofer, who joined Bahr in the rank of minister without portfolio.

In tough negotiations with Scheel and his deputy Genscher, Schmidt expanded the authority of the finance ministry to include credit and currency policy, which were normally the prerogative of the economics minister. One reason that the FDP did so well in bolstering its stature in the new government was that Brandt was physically not well. This not only gave Scheel and Genscher more influence, but contributed to a general weakening of the chancellor's authority that became steadily more pronounced as time went on. At the same time Schmidt's prestige continued to grow.

In his statement of policy to the new Bundestag in January 1973 Brandt emphasized the priority of domestic reforms, now that the active phase of Ostpolitik was nearing its conclusion. But his speech was drawn in generalities. It did not reflect the decisive direction that his speeches had provided in 1969 and 1970. He spoke of "the quality of life," but not the qualities that are necessary to forge successful leadership. He emphasized that "modern social policy," in the view of the SPD, "strives for greater justice and aims to ensure that more true freedom prevails in our society."[6] But as he later wrote in his memoirs, he and his party "failed . . . to secure parliamentary enactment of the realistic reforms which both coalition partners should have supported."[7] The fact was that Brandt never really took charge of his second government, and it was plagued by problems and conflicts over both

---

[6] Brandt, *People and Politics*, 446.
[7] Ibid.

domestic and foreign policy, which undermined Brandt's image as a firm leader.

In the spring of 1973 Scheel decided to run for the office of federal president when Gustav Heinemann's term expired in 1974. He believed that the leftward drift of the SPD party apparatus and the chances of serious splits in the SPD would certainly harm and might destroy the coalition, and he did not want to be a member of government when it happened. On the other hand, his prestige as foreign minister and co-author with Brandt of Ostpolitik and of the social reform policies was immense, and the liberals were in despair at the prospect of replacing him.

The internal divisions of the SPD came to the fore at the annual party conference held in April 1973 in Hannover. The leftists of the Leverkusen circle and their supporters demanded "effective change of power relationships in society and simultaneously improvements in the social quality of life."[8] The Jusos held their own conference in Bad Godesberg in March to prepare their agenda for the party conference. They demanded a three-stage transformation of West German society. In the first stage, the government would analyze existing power relationships and the extent to which concentrations of economic power affected the actions of the state. In the second stage, the state would expropriate banks and key industries. In the third stage, the state would socialize all middle-sized and small businesses. After capitalism had thus been destroyed, government planning would determine production and consumption. Most Jusos appeared to believe that these measures would not endanger or destroy political democracy; only a minority, which soon left to join the DKP, argued that political democracy was unnecessary and undesirable.

The opposition and the conservative German press had since 1969 accused Brandt of failing to stand up to the left or even of being secretly in sympathy with its aims. In early April Brandt responded to these charges and to the leftists themselves in a *Spiegel* interview in which he demonstrated once again that he was at his best with his back to the wall. Testily he told the interviewer: "Look at the Godesberg Program. There you will see it stated as a social democratic belief, for example, that private property deserves to be protected and promoted." Asked about the Jusos draft program he stated: "I have said that the election program of October 1972 must not be abandoned. I could not take responsibility for anything that contradicts the program for which I and others found the broad support of the voters on November 19."[9]

[8] Cited in Baring, *Machtwechsel*, 542.
[9] Cited ibid., 546–7.

At the party conference, the left controlled 40–45 per cent of the delegates and had high hopes of turning their agenda into official SPD policy. Voigt, the former head of the Jusos and since 1972 a Bundestag member, arrogantly prophesied that, although the Jusos had formerly hoped to become the SPD of the 1980s, it now seemed they might come to power sooner than that.[10] In the event, the conference decisions, which determined the shape of SPD policy and ideology for the rest of the decade, represented a partial victory for both sides – radicals and moderates.

Schmidt, as deputy chairman, and Brandt opened the proceedings by insisting on the essential value of the SPD/FDP coalition for the health of German democracy. It was a pity, Schmidt argued, that socialists and liberals had not found common cause 100 years earlier; that might have saved Germany from the authoritarian rule of Bismarck and the policies that led to the two world wars. Now that the alliance had finally come about, it must not be abandoned. Schmidt directed these words at the party left, many of whom resented the liberals and wanted the SPD, controlled from the left, to rule alone and unchallenged.

In one of the few occasions when the leading *troika* of the party functioned well together, Schmidt, Wehner, and Brandt had agreed beforehand on the rhetorical strategy to adopt. Schmidt was deliberately provocative in order to draw the fire of the left. Brandt, on the other hand, played the role of the fatherly conciliator, sympathetic to all, but firm on principle. In his opening address, he began by stating his sympathy for those on the left who wanted more rapid change. But practical politics demanded a combination of theory and practice, which in the current case meant collaboration with the FDP and respect for the rules of democracy. He repeated the words of Kurt Schumacher, that he did not care how someone became a social democrat – whether out of belief in Marxist economic analysis, for philosophical reasons, or from belief in the Sermon on the Mount. What mattered was fidelity to the principles of the party. Brandt addressed this reference to "those who again say theory and really mean ideology, that is, a closed system of attitudes to the world and to life as a sort of *ersatz* religion; excited preachers who are still looking for . . . their congregation . . . To be clear: if there are still those here and there who think they can defend the theses of the DKP or the SED, we must make it clear to them that they must look for other places in which to agitate than in our party."[11]

The conference decisions gave some satisfaction to both sides. The left approved the foreign policy line of the party leadership and hid its

[10] Ibid., 543.
[11] Cited ibid., 551–2.

anti-Americanism and neutralism for the time being. They were more successful in fighting the draft program for long-term economic and political development, which in their eyes was no more than a defense of existing "bourgeois" institutions. As Baring later commented, many social democrats quite simply regarded the social market economy and private property as the basis of a system that they wanted to change.[12] The party leadership compromised by sending the program back to a committee for further refinement.

The main defeat of the pragmatists and moderates, the *Kanalarbeiter*, led by Egon Franke, came in the area of appointments to positions in the party. During the conference the leftists succeeded, by skillful use of argument and by abstaining from radical rhetoric and confrontation in getting the support of a critical number of centrists when it came to voting on appointments. As a result the party apparatus was transformed from a bastion of the moderates to a bastion of the New Left. In the old directorate, 28 of 34 members belonged to the center-right of the party; in the new one elected in Hannover, 26 belonged to the left or the center-left. Even as prominent a moderate as Carlo Schmid, one of the fathers of the Basic Law, failed to obtain reappointment. Three leading moderates, Alex Möller, Karl Wienand, and Karl Schiller resigned (Schiller had already formally left the party). Among the leading leftists elected were Peter von Oertzen, Rudi Arndt, and the Juso chairman Wolfgang Roth.

This was a fateful development, since it meant that the pragmatist Schmidt, as chancellor from 1974 to 1982, did not have the support or the sympathy of the leaders of his own party apparatus. There is no doubt that his ultimate failure and fall in 1982 was due as much to this internal resistance as to the defection of the FDP.

In May 1973, Brezhnev returned Brandt's trip to Oreanda of September 1971 and paid his first visit to Bonn. He came to continue the talks that began at Oreanda, when he had convinced Brandt of his sincerity and desire for peace. In 1973, he was concerned particularly with expanding commercial relations with the Federal Republic, and Brandt was concerned with including Berlin in a new trade agreement. On May 19 Brandt and Brezhnev signed a ten-year accord on the development of economic, industrial and technological cooperation, as well as agreements on cultural exchange and air traffic. As in the agreement of 1972, the Soviet government agreed to the inclusion of West Berlin, and Brandt publicly endorsed the Conference on Security and Cooperation in Europe (CSCE), scheduled to begin in Helsinki later that summer.[13]

[12] Ibid., 555.
[13] *Relay from Bonn*, May 18, 1973.

Berlin's inclusion in the agreement was considered a major accomplishment by Brandt's government. As the *Financial Times* of London wrote, "the political situation surrounding the city has been considerably clarified."[14] In another sense, however, if the politics of Berlin were clarified, they now also attracted less attention. The euphoria focused on Ostpolitik between 1969 and 1973 was beginning to wane, and to be replaced by skepticism. Egon Bahr's effort to counter this change in attitude did not prove as successful as Brandt undoubtedly hoped. In July 1973 Bahr interpreted the results of Ostpolitik in a speech at Tutzing, ten years after his sensational speech in the same town when he proclaimed "change through rapprochement." Bahr admitted that Soviet suppression of the Czech reform movement of 1968 and the suppression of the Polish workers' uprising of 1970 had shown that there would be no convergence of a more liberal communism with a more socialist Western Europe. The conclusion he drew from this, however, was that one could not work for relaxation of tensions through undermining the Soviet bloc, but only by a policy embracing treaties between the great powers and between individual states. He did not make it clear how such a policy would serve the interests of the East Europeans as opposed to the interests of their rulers, and that contradiction was, in fact, never resolved.

Concerning Germany Bahr claimed that peaceful coexistence could prevent the further growing apart of the two Germanies. The essential elements of this coexistence, he stressed, must be predictability and stability, but he knew that in practical terms neither he nor anyone else in the West could force the Soviet Union or the GDR to be either stable or predictable. The real meaning of Bahr's philosophy was that the Federal Republic must abandon any policy which could be interpreted – by the Soviets or the SED regime – as demanding greater freedom for the population of the GDR. A logical consequence of this conclusion was Bahr's conviction that in the interest of stability and in the interest of moving from conflict to cooperation, it was not realistic to demand that the GDR abolish the order to shoot on sight persons trying to leave its territory. To insist that the GDR stop killing people who wanted to leave was, in Bahr's view, an aggressive and unreasonable demand that Bonn must not make. A final element in the Bahr doctrine was that the Federal Republic must do everything in its power to maintain stability in Eastern Europe. This meant no support or encouragement of movements aiming at a reform of totalitarian regimes, because such movements were doomed to failure in any case and could cause instability, if the Soviet government had to intervene to suppress them.

[14] *Relay from Bonn*, May 21 and May 24, 1973.

Bahr painted a picture of realities in Central Europe, and especially in the GDR, that was far from optimistic, and that seemed to confirm the predictions of many of Brandt's critics that Ostpolitik had ratified the status quo in Central Europe without clear benefits for Germany and the Germans.

If the public felt Brandt's leadership by late 1973 to be weak, it was in part because Helmut Schmidt was emerging as a powerful SPD figure. As finance minister, he helped to bring about the abolition of fixed exchange rates in March 1973, which immediately resulted in quick export growth and a fall in inflation. Beginning in October, however, the first oil crisis occurred. While the ensuing economic crisis did not help Schmidt, it was even more damaging to Willy Brandt.

The Arab states attacked Israel on October 6, 1973. After eight days of desperate fighting the Israelis counterattacked. To give weight to their political demands, the oil-exporting Arab states, organized in OPEC, declared on October 17 that Western states pursuing a pro-Israel policy would have their oil supplies cut. On October 19, OPEC declared a complete embargo of supplies to the United States and the Netherlands. The United States had been resupplying Israel, and were shipping arms and military supplies from stocks located in the Federal Republic. Bahr explained to the US ambassador to Bonn that West Germany was neutral in the Middle East conflict and would not allow the US to send supplies from Germany to Israel. The US responded on October 25 in a sharply worded note, that it believed "for the West to display weakness and disunity in the face of a Soviet-supported military action against Israel could have disastrous consequences."[15] On October 30, 1973, President Nixon, in a letter to Brandt, wrote in terms that would become familiar in transatlantic disputes over the next decade and a half:

> We recognize that the Europeans are more dependent upon Arab oil than we, but we disagree that your vulnerability is decreased by disassociating yourselves from us on a matter of this importance. Such disassociation will not help the Europeans in the Arab World. The Arabs know that only the US can provide the help to get a political settlement. . . .
> You note that this crisis was not a case of common responsibility for the Alliance, and that military supplies for Israel were for purposes which are not part of the Alliance responsibility. I do not believe we can draw such a fine line when the USSR was and is so deeply involved, and when the crisis threatened to spread to the whole gamut of East–West relations. It seems to me that the Alliance cannot operate on a double standard in which US relations with the USSR are separated from the policies that our Allies conduct

[15] Cited in Kissinger, *Years of Upheaval*, 714.

toward the Soviet Union. By disassociating themselves from the US in the Middle East, our Allies may think they protect their immediate economic interests, but only at great long term cost. A differentiated detente in which the Allies hope to insulate their relations with the USSR can only divide the Alliance and ultimately produce disastrous consequences for Europe.[16]

The oil shock and its effects, such as the temporary banning of auto traffic on Sundays, made a profound impression on most Germans. It undermined the faith in economic growth which had inspired even those on the left of the SPD who called for radical change and a "different republic." It introduced concerns with the limits of growth, with threats to the environment and with German economic dependence and independence. These concerns had not existed prior to 1973 in the same magnitude, a point well illustrated by the government's commitment to large-scale social as well as physical engineering. In 1970 the SPD-led government proposed to accelerate the construction of autobahns (freeways) from 4,400 to a total of 20,000 kilometers. It was only after the first oil shock that these plans were scaled down to a much more modest 8,000 kilometers. In 1974 the government began favoring public over private transportation in its economic planning.

The winter of the oil shock was also a winter of inflation, which, as in most industrial countries, was already quite high in 1973. In 1974 West Germany had to spend 17 billion marks more on oil imports even as consumption fell by 6 per cent. Due largely to the impact of the oil price increases on the individual pocketbook after a year of generally high inflation, the public-sector unions demanded wage increases for the 1974–6 round of wage talks of 15 per cent, an outrageous figure in any, but especially in the German context.

The climate on the labor market had already been damaged during 1973 by a work slow-down of the air traffic controllers from May to November of 1973 which had seriously inconvenienced transportation. During the fall employee councils (*Betriebsräte*) in the metalworking, sanitation, and funeral industries staged wildcat strikes. Even before the oil crisis began, food prices in Germany were 15 per cent above the levels of late 1972. The Jusos denounced the employers as "wage-thieves" and "price-gougers" and called the strikes "legitimate measures."[17] Brandt was unable to call them to heel; the authority he enjoyed at the Hannover conference in April seemed gone.

Genscher, who as interior minister was the employer with whom the *Angestellte* unions had to deal, had to give in and promise virtually the entire package of benefits and wage increases demanded. On January

[16]   Cited ibid., 715–6.
[17]   Baring, *Machtwechsel*, 593.

27, 1974, the day before negotiations began, Schmidt, as finance minister, warned that double-digit raises were absolutely out of the question, since there were already half a million unemployed due to the energy crisis. At first the government held firm, and on February 11 strikes began on a broad front throughout the public sector, among federal, *Land*, and municipal workers. On February 13, however, the *Länder* and the municipalities surrendered. Brandt, who as SPD chairman should have been able to exert some leverage on the unions, failed so ignominiously to moderate the demands of the *Angestellte* unions that even the usually sympathetic *Die Zeit* condemned his weakness and warned that "the unions have the power to restrict the authority of the state."[18] And once the public authorities had conceded such generous increases, the private employers were in no position to do otherwise. The stage was set for 8 per cent inflation and high unemployment.[19]

The internal conflicts and uncertainties stemming from Brandt's failure to take proper charge of his government and his party after the 1972 election now dominated the political landscape. The labor market problems of the summer and fall of 1973 completed the image of a chancellor who was either floundering helplessly or so absorbed in grandiose matters of world policy that he had ceased to be an effective head of government. The public "was no longer interested in him" by late 1973, Baring reported.[20] On September 15, Brandt gave an important speech on the theme of "The SPD and the State." Its author, Günter Gaus, an aide of Brandt's who was soon to take up the post of permanent representative of the Federal Republic in East Berlin, tried in vain to persuade a major newspaper to publish it. A year earlier any newspaper would have leaped at the chance to publish a speech given by the chancellor. This time, there was no interest: "Brandt was completely out."[21] In cabinet meetings, Schmidt would pound the table and demand that the chancellor take charge. To no avail.

That same month, in September – before the oil shock and the disastrous round of wage negotiations – Herbert Wehner led a bipartisan delegation, that included Richard von Weizsäcker of the CDU, to Moscow for informal discussions on Soviet–German relations. Brandt was at that moment in the US, where on September 26 he delivered the first speech ever given by a German chancellor to the UN. On his way to Aspen, Colorado, where he was to receive a prize for his

---

[18] Cited ibid., 699.
[19] Bracher et al., *Republik im Wandel, 1969–1974*, 115.
[20] Baring, *Machtwechsel*, 594.
[21] Ibid.

work for peace, word came to Brandt that Wehner had made derogatory comments in public to journalists accompanying him to the Soviet Union about Brandt's inability to lead. Wehner had never trusted or respected Brandt, and by the fall of 1973 he was extremely irritated by what he considered the chancellor's lackadaisical leadership style which was threatening the coalition and hence the power position of the SPD. For Wehner, party commitment was primary, whereas he suspected that Brandt wanted to escape the pressure of politics, a desire that Wehner regarded as both incomprehensible and immoral.

Wehner's comments were biting in the extreme: "Number one is distant and lazy."[22] The most notorious accusation, however, was reported in *Der Spiegel* of October 8: "What this government needs is a leader." The sentence made headlines, although both Wehner and the *Spiegel* journalist later confirmed that this quotation was not completely accurate. Wehner at that moment was not talking about Brandt in particular, but there was plenty of other evidence that the phrase expressed his feelings precisely. Brandt was understandably distressed, but there were by now too many in the SPD leadership who agreed with Wehner.

Public opinion polls supported the depressing picture: public support for the SPD declined to 34 per cent and increased to 52 per cent for the CDU/CSU in the spring of 1974. In the Hamburg elections of March 4, 1974, the SPD slipped from 55.3 to 44.9 per cent. Two days later, Helmut Schmidt said on television that to save the government, the cabinet should be reshuffled; but that "we may have to go beyond just replacing one or two people." The social democratic mayor of Munich, Hans-Jochen Vogel, blamed the government's unpopularity largely on the irresponsibility of the Jusos and the radical left: "Have we become first and foremost a socialization committee, in charge of educating a few crazy sons of the upper-middle classes, who originally – rightly so – protested against the material excesses of their families, or are we a political party concerned primarily with maintaining the majority and political power, in order to bring change in the interest of the broad majority of the people?"[23]

By March 1974 Schmidt was moving toward open confrontation with Brandt. Many people read his frequent criticisms during early 1974 as elements of an ultimatum to Brandt: either resign and let me, Schmidt, take over, or I will leave the party, like Schiller. Later, Schmidt claimed that he had told Brandt as early as 1972 that he intended to leave the party before Brandt let the left take over completely. In a lengthy

---

[22] Ibid., 619.
[23] Bracher et al., *Republik im Wandel, 1969–1974,* 116.

television interview on March 6, Schmidt provided his own analysis of the evolution of the SPD since 1968, one that directly contradicted Brandt's optimistic view. The SPD, in Schmidt's view, had neither a clear public image nor clear policies. He concluded that the battle between the radicals of the New Left and the moderates that began in 1966–7 had ended, at the Hannover conference in April 1973, with a victory for the left. The conference, in fact, had been "an important stage in the decline of the SPD, mainly because the party chairman failed forcefully to oppose leftist errors and prevent fatal decisions."[24] Brandt regarded the New Left's revolutionary enthusiasm as a sign of hope and renewal. For Schmidt, the New Left was a "movement of half-baked academics" full of elitist jargon and foolish, theoretical ideas. In a meeting of the party leadership on March 8, Schmidt poked further fun at the New Left. They were demanding, he said, that "the SPD should ensure that we leave NATO and do all kinds of other marvelous things – and those responsible are ever so happy if the Springer press makes a full report, because then at least they get in the paper for the first time."[25]

Marion Dönhoff explained what contributed to the crisis of Brandt's chancellorship in this way:

> Never had relations between those in power and the intellectuals been so easy or so naturally amicable and positive as under Willy Brandt – a man who was always more interested in ethical initiatives than in power politics. He led not by authority but by persuasion, with lengthy discussions in which he showed infinite patience: his tendency to philosophize on politics, to favor broad designs and inspiring visions was what attracted the intellectuals to him.
>
> But it was perhaps those very qualities that eventually became his undoing. In the everyday business of government and administration his style gradually became a liability.[26]

At the party leadership meeting on March 8, Brandt seemed finished, attacked from the right by Schmidt and on the basic issue of competence by Wehner. Surprisingly, however, Brandt succeeded in convincing Wehner to support him against Schmidt. After five and a half hours of private talks, Wehner and Brandt agreed that Schmidt had gone beyond the bounds of what was permissible. Both men found the finance minister "arrogant, intolerably disloyal" and moreover insatiable in his demands whether as minister of defense in 1969–72 or as minister of finance since then.[27] It was clear to both that Schmidt wanted Brandt's

---

[24] Paraphrased in Baring, *Machtwechsel*, 705.
[25] Cited ibid., 704.
[26] Dönhoff, *Foe into Friend*, 150.
[27] Baring, *Machtwechsel*, 713–4.

job and obviously regarded himself as vastly more suited to it than Brandt. This was precisely the kind of attack that would rally Wehner's basic loyalty to the party system and to its chairman, no matter what his faults. Wehner, moreover, did not think Schmidt would make a good chancellor with his brusque tone of command and a "notion of solidarity that seemed to originate in the officers' clubs of the Third Reich."[28] Schmidt, in short, would destroy more than he would build. On March 17 Wehner made a brief public statement: "Not only do I not have anything against Brandt . . . there is no replacement for him . . . he is irreplaceable."[29]

Faced with this obstacle in his path, Schmidt too saw the virtues of party loyalty and ceased his attacks. On April 1, Brandt, Wehner, and the two deputy chairmen, Schmidt and Heinz Kühn, issued the April theses, the key phrase of which ran: "Without the center there can be no majority in a democracy. Whoever abandons the center abandons his ability to govern. Social democratic decisiveness means commanding the center."[30] The April theses were not only a tactic in the leadership struggle, they were also yet another move against the Jusos, who in late March broke another taboo when they denounced the Godesberg Program as "an offer of alliance to big capital" and demanded a committed "anticapitalist policy." In response, the April theses insisted that the SPD was not a "debating club" but "responsible for the fate of a large industrial state. . . . There can be no double strategy directed against one's own party and its policies. . . . Democratic socialism seeks identity with the majority of the people."[31]

The April theses and Schmidt's moderation encouraged the FDP, whose leaders were discouraged by the state of the economy and by Scheel's firm decision to run for the office of president. The liberals had decided that Genscher would succeed Scheel as foreign minister, but Genscher, while well known and well liked in political circles, did not have Scheel's immense national and international prestige nor his experience in international politics.

[28] Ibid., 714.
[29] Cited ibid., 715.
[30] Cited ibid.
[31] Cited ibid., 717.

12

Brandt's Resignation

The April theses may have restored faith in the SPD's stability and in the coalition, but they could not save the German chancellor. Despite their show of solidarity, Schmidt, Wehner, and the FDP remained dissatisfied with Brandt's apparent lack of control, and his resignation appeared to be just a matter of time. On April 24, the events that triggered it began.

The proximate cause of Brandt's resignation was, in some ways, an accident. In May 1973, the *Bundesamt für Verfassungsschutz* (BfV), the internal security agency, had told Genscher, the interior minister, that one of Brandt's personal aides in the chancellery, Günter Guillaume, was an agent of the East German secret political police, the *Staatssicherheitsdienst*. Genscher at once told Brandt, who refused to take the warning seriously, because, as he said, he did not want to believe it. In any event he took no action to stop Guillaume's access to classified documents. It was not until almost one year later, on April 24, 1974, that Guillaume was finally arrested. He immediately identified himself as an officer of the *Nationale Volksarmee* (NVA), the East German army but refused to admit that he was also an agent of the *Staatssicherheitsdienst*.

At first Brandt did not consider resigning, but the affair was the straw that broke the camel's back. Lack of confidence in Brandt, as well as rumors concerning his philandering, particularly on the campaign trail, contributed to mounting criticism of his leadership. On May 6, Brandt offered his resignation to President Heinemann. Ten days later, Heinemann appointed Helmut Schmidt chancellor. He formed his new cabinet with Genscher as foreign minister, Hans Apel as finance minister, and Georg Leber as defense minister. One day earlier the sixth Federal Assembly elected Walter Scheel federal president to succeed Heinemann.

Helmut Schmidt was the right man to rescue the government after the debacle of Brandt's leadership. He did not possess utopian and romantic optimism, but he had proved himself in politics and government as a man comfortable with difficult decisions and without excessive illusions concerning the realities of East–West detente. So the coalition government survived the fall of Brandt with much less damage than might otherwise have been expected. There emerged a man, in Helmut Schmidt, who became in the following eight years, from 1974 to 1982, the strongest and most respected leader of post-war Germany since Konrad Adenauer. Under his leadership West Germany became, undisputedly, a pillar of Europe.

But it was not to be an easy or comfortable road. One of the major reasons was the fact that the SPD was losing its traditional base of support. Economic success, political self-confidence, social justice, expanded opportunities in cultural and social areas were continuing to change the complexion and fabric of West German society. The times of great differences between workers and employers were altering too, and the walls which had so clearly separated classes within Germany for decades were coming down. In postwar Germany the efforts of all political parties had contributed to this development, and the domestic policies of the CDU/CSU in the 1960s, as well as those of the SPD since 1969, represented a major contribution. But this also meant that the SPD had to find ways to appeal to broader segments of society, and to interests which it had ignored or criticized in the past. The debate on educational policy had clearly emphasized the importance of political consensus, and also illustrated the frustrations caused by its absence. As Brandt very accurately put it, "German social democracy was engaged in the most difficult remodelling process in its hundred and more years of existence." And Brandt went further, to describe a change that eventually played a decisive role in Helmut Schmidt's resignation in 1982, and that split the party into left and right wings in the 1980s:

[The SPD's] membership was being restratified by a process of sociological change corresponding to the growth of the so-called *Dienstleistungsgesellschaft* [service society]. Its internal climate was also being modified by an influx of young and restless recruits. Within a single decade transformation and expansion had accounted for the remarkable fact that only one-third of the membership was "old" while two-thirds were new recruits, very many of them academics, students and white-collar workers. The successful assimilation of this greatly altered body of support was not a foregone conclusion. Many feared – and others hoped – that a substantial left-wing socialist group would diverge from the mainstream of the party.[1]

The Hannover party conference of April 1973 represented a temporary culmination of trends that meant that the "left-wing socialist group"

[1] Brandt, *People and Politics,* 438.

remained within the party, as Brandt wanted. Whether this was in the true interests of Germany, of the SPD, or of its new chancellor, Helmut Schmidt, was to become one of the main issues of the next eight years. Schmidt's immediate challenge was the world economic crisis caused in large part by the Arab oil embargoes and price increases of 1973–4. In dealing with that crisis he, his government, and the West German public at large came to realize, some with elation and others with dismay, that West Germany was no longer the orderly, cohesive society it had been until at least the mid-1960s. From the time of Brandt and Scheel onward there were, roughly speaking, two Germanies within the Federal Republic – a more conservative Germany of producers and workers, and a sometimes colorful, sometimes abrasive new Germany of self-styled progressives and revolutionaries. Their struggle would determine the future course of Germany's political fortunes for the remainder of the decade.

PART IX

The Era of the "Macher," 1974–1982

Clear judgement for the possible is the most important quality of which German policy — pitched as it is between the two Super Powers — has need.

Helmut Schmidt – 1969

A democratic community needs a minimum of basic shared conviction in order to exist. And, in equal measure, it needs to be offered alternative political concepts. Only when the alternative positions have been clearly presented, is one allowed to proceed to the necessary compromise. Anything else would be mere opportunism.

Helmut Schmidt – 1969

The observance of tradition does not mean keeping the ashes. The observance of tradition means keeping the torch alight. The torch signifies love of mankind and respect for the dignity of everyone. The torch signifies the supreme value of our Basic Law: human dignity and human freedom.

Helmut Schmidt – 1978

Justice, freedom and the dignity of man — these are the common values and principles which also form the basis of German-American friendship and solidarity. We are not of one spirit because we are allies — it is the other way round: we are allies because we are of one spirit, because we have the same moral standards.

Helmut Schmidt – 1980

Introduction

The Federal Republic celebrated its twenty-fifth birthday in 1974. It was, in a manner of speaking, over the age of majority, and its leaders had spent one-quarter of a century participating in the sophisticated world of postwar politics. They were giving color to the fabric of Western European politics; and one of them, Helmut Schmidt, had earned a reputation as "the Doer" *(der Macher)* – a man who could get things done. As Don Cook described him in his book *Ten Men and History:*

> He is rooted in "the art of the possible," and he also knows that "power begets power." He is a political fighter and does not leave it to others to fight his battles for him. He has been called *"Schmidt die Schnauze"* since his early days in the Social Democratic Party – roughly "Schmidt the Lip" – for his pugnacious way of always telling people off. . . . Since he became chancellor . . . his well-known combativeness has become more controlled, and his style has matured, even mellowed. So, too, has his effectiveness increased. He is less of a *schnauze* and more of a *macher*.[1]

The political problems of the 1970s would tax all of Schmidt's abilities to forge sound policies on a basis of compromise, both within his own party and among the West German electorate as a whole. The currents of popular feeling and intellectual opinion often conflicted with political and economic concerns in this decade. Germany's economic and political strength demanded strong leadership, and her Western European neighbors wanted Germany to function as an economic locomotive without, however, translating economic into political power.

In Western Europe and abroad Germany's economic power was respected and appreciated, but was also seen as part of the growing strength of the continent. Europeans looked to Germany as a partner in

[1] Cook, *Ten Men and History,* 450.

sharing the responsibilities of maintaining stable and peaceful relationships in Europe. But the Germans themselves were uncertain what the country's proper role should be on the world stage. Many, perhaps most, believed that Germany's record during the Nazi period should forever restrain its leaders from trying to make Germany the pivot of Europe. Others, like Schmidt, believed that Germany's past created psychological fears of German leadership and strength in other countries, notably the Soviet Union and France. Although Schmidt was personally committed to Germany as a nation whose people had much to give in a complex world, he believed that Germany should not permit itself to become the dominant power on the continent, but an influential and respected member of the European community.

These uncertainties gave rise in the 1970s, when Germany was Europe's economic powerhouse, to doubt and an undefined anxiety about what Germany's responsibilities should, or could be vis-à-vis her neigbors in Central and Western Europe, and vis-à-vis East Germany. It was an attitude less than unrest and more than natural questioning. It was a question of "where are we?" and it gnawed, slowly, at Germany's intellectuals, at the leaders of published opinion, and at political leaders. It was less disturbing to Germany's population as a whole, which had a much clearer idea of where Germany was: namely, in Europe, with a thriving economy, and, though burdened by a growing welfare state, nonetheless respected as a nation whose people dealt with the same kind of daily problems, joys, and sorrows as her neighbors.

The Schmidt-Genscher government practised and symbolized stability and predictability. It took office in May 1974 and lasted eight and a half years, until October 1982. It became the longest continuing coalition in the history of the Federal Republic.

At the outset the new chancellor faced three major issues: first, to restore confidence in financial and social structures that were reeling from the quadrupling of oil prices in 1973–4 (and which staggered later, unexpectedly, from the second oil shock and resultant global recession of 1979–82); second, to continue Ostpolitik and participation in East–West detente without jeopardizing West Germany's security, a process critically challenged when both US and Soviet policies, in the late 1970s, seemed to undermine the very premises of detente; and third, to assure the stability of domestic order, a task radically and mercilessly challenged by the resurgence of violent terrorism in 1974–7, and less radically, if none the less urgently, by the rise of the so-called new social movement of environmentalists and pacifists.

Of these three tasks, most observers outside the radical left, regardless of personal opinion on the issues, gave the government high marks for its treatment of terrorism, good marks for its economic and fiscal policies, and middling-to-poor marks on its handling of West German security, foreign policy, and *Deutschlandpolitik* in the era of disappearing detente.

The government took office in the wake of two experiences particularly traumatic for West German political culture, wedded as it was to the need for stability and predictability: the oil shock and the disintegration of Brandt's leadership. These discouraging events helped weaken confidence in the promises of new beginnings and new vistas spawned by the great debate on democratization and dismantling of authoritarian structures that had begun in the mid-1960s and reached a frenetic culmination in 1969, between the election of Heinemann as president and Brandt as chancellor. At the same time, Ostpolitik and social reforms – West Germany's bid to fulfil its version of the American liberal vision of the great society – continued, and, as in America, the liberal dreams turned out to have paradoxical and unexpected effects when put into practice. On the mood at the time of Schmidt's takeover, the historian Karl Dietrich Bracher wrote:

Two major tendencies overlap in the mid-1970s: an immense and continuing change of social and moral behavior patterns and value systems, which, more rapidly than ever before, affect large parts of the population, and are succinctly labeled "value change" or even "silent revolution" by social scientists; and, a few years later, a perceptible reversal from the sense of progress and a new beginning which marked the year 1969, to a continuously growing awareness of crisis with its external (social) and internal (psychological) traits. And after a few years the great expectations are replaced by great anxieties.[2]

[2] Bracher et al., *Republik im Wandel, 1969–1974*, 338.

1

Two Germanies in the West

The process of changing values, that is to say of what seemed important in a continually changing world, was long underway by 1974. Prior to the Brandt government of 1969, when one spoke of the two Germanies, one always meant the Federal Republic and East Germany, "the Zone." In the Brandt era, one could say that the phrase "two Germanies" acquired new meaning. In this sense, it referred to two Germanies within West Germany: one represented by the defenders of the constitutional state and social order and of the inherited principles of foreign and domestic policy, and the other by the moralistic and often utopian critics of that social order and its principles. To understand the narrative of events that lead to this conclusion, one must look at the emergence of two Germanies, in West Germany, in the 1970s and early 1980s.

The symbolic phrase of the Brandt government was *democratization*; with equal accuracy, one may say that the symbolic phrase of the Schmidt-Genscher era, and to a lesser extent of the Kohl era that followed, was *fear* (*Angst*). Not only did growing numbers of prominent German writers and intellectuals declare they were frightened – frightened of environmental pollution, of repression by an imaginary authoritarian state, of domination by fathers, teachers, or employers, and last, but by no means least, of nuclear weapons and US nuclear policies – but, to a surprising degree, they took pride in being afraid. The *furor teutonicus*, Germanic fury, as described by ancient Roman historians, was being replaced by the *timor teutonicus*, the German fear. Feeling afraid, and congratulating one another on the moral maturity signified by feelings of fear, slowly became a socially and intellectually accepted norm. *Not* to feel and display fear in this most frightening of worlds was to be insensitive and psychologically stunted. The writer Peter Schneider taunted his readers with this conclusion, powerfully expressed but also equally presumptuous. Writing in 1983, he lamented that everything had become unimportant for mankind, and especially for Germans, except surviving a nuclear disaster, and stressed: "Whoever has no fear in Germany is an idiot or has no imagination." He continued:

But if we do not name the conditions for this peace we wish for, then we are already the victim of nuclear blackmail which we are fighting. Whoever, like me, is in favor of unilateral disarmament, must also declare which liberties he will not give up under any circumstances and how, in an emergency, he will defend them.[1]

Some might say that Schneider's conclusion was a contradiction in terms, for if one unilaterally disarmed, one would not have the luxury of choosing to defend any freedoms against a foe with weapons. But the obsession with fear, and the resulting adverse effect on logical thought processes, did not disturb Schneider and the many members of what the left called "the other republic" who thought like him. Nor did it seem to bother another articulate defender of the need to feel fear, the psychiatrist and social critic Horst Eberhard Richter. He was a typical and eloquent example of that other Germany that emerged victorious from the cultural and intellectual battles of the 1960s. To understand Richter and what he was saying was to understand an essential part of the changing temper of West German society outside the ruling circles in Bonn in the 1970s and 1980s. And as Richter's values and way of thinking spread throughout academic, cultural, and professional circles, the associated attitudes and judgements gave birth to significant political effects as well, as one could see in the Green movement and the left wing of the SPD, the FDP, and even the CDU/CSU, in the later 1970s.

In 1966, Richter was offered the opportunity to succeed Alexander Mitscherlich as director of the Psychosomatic Clinic at the Medical School at Heidelberg. But he refused the position in order to remain in Giessen, a city which had been badly bombed during the war, and rejected "conservative," "idyllic," and "whole" Heidelberg with "its castle lighted at night" and "the dream of every American tourist."[2] Just as Mitscherlich had accused West Germans in the 1960s of being "unable to mourn," so Richter in the 1970s and 1980s wrote popular books claiming that West Germans had one great psychological problem: namely their "God complex," their refusal to admit vulnerability and imperfection, a refusal displayed in aggressive drives and

[1] Schneider, "Der Sand an Baaders Schuhen," in *Bewegung in der Republik*, eds Karsunke and Michel, 2: 268, 276.
[2] Richter, *Die Chance des Gewissens*, 158.

feelings of contempt for others, and politically, in the refusal to engage in unilateral disarmament.

This was one man's opinion, but it was a powerful one. Richter advocated an ideal psychological type of personality, of which, for him, Willy Brandt was a model; namely a personality that reacted with nervous tension, anger, fear or even illness to injustice, oppression, and the threat of war. If only all people everywhere would emulate this type and give its representatives greater influence, Richter argued, the world would be a better place. He shared with numerous psychologists and physicians in the Western world the notion that world conflicts, especially the East–West conflict, were largely a product of unconscious and bellicose compulsions of Western leaders and not of any objective facts of historical development, such as the nature and purposes of Soviet foreign policy.

In the 1980s, Richter helped to found the West German physicians' peace movement, which was affiliated with the International Physicians for the Prevention of Nuclear War (IPPNW). It never bothered Richter – or perhaps he preferred to ignore it – that the Soviet co-chairman of this organization, Yevgeny Chazov, was a minister in the Soviet government under Brezhnev. Given Richter's starting-point it was logical that the way to peace was to give up what, in his view, promoted war, and this meant, concretely, the means for defense. In his very successful memoirs, *Die Chance des Gewissens* (The opportunity of conscience), he wrote:

> We men [i.e. males], for example, must learn to liberate our suppressed sensibility and overcome the militant image of "masculinity" that has been drummed into us. All of us, women and men, must learn to endure our fears, to talk about them, instead of "heroically" fighting them. We must deal with our depressions and feelings of impotence instead of always wanting to conquer them. . . . As long as we maintain our inner repressions we cannot convincingly work toward dismantling the repression and the militarism in society. . . . We doctors [in the peace movement] insisted that, contrary to the official propaganda, which defamed fear, it should not be our goal to deny fear, but to eliminate its actual political-military causes and the thoughts of threat (*Bedrohungsdenken*). . . . It was a natural development that our physicians' initiative moved closer to those peace groups which – like most of our members – were in search of unity between their inner life and a foreign policy of understanding and security partnership.[3]

The phrase "security partnership" was one that would become the very symbol of the ideas and illusions, not only of the left, of Brandt,

[3] Ibid., 252–54.

Bahr, and the Greens, but eventually of such centrists as Hans-Dietrich Genscher himself. In all his writings Richter never acknowledged that he was advocating two political principles that directly contradicted the liberal democracy he also professed to admire. First, he refused to recognize that there might in reality be something to defend against, that the threat of aggression from the Soviet Union and subversion from the GDR was not just the figment of sick imaginations but a threat based on historical facts, which a liberal democracy should not ignore if it wished to survive. Second, he came very close to advocating authoritarian compulsion to secure the advance of the sensitive, nervous, anxious personality type that he regarded as socially, politically, and morally superior and better adapted to survival than the strong type he claimed was in power throughout the Western world. In his memoirs and else-where, he wrote of and eloquently condemned the authoritarian suppression of unorthodox thought characteristic, according to him, of West German universities. His vaunted psychological insight ignored his own fierce authoritarianism, and his demand that others should be like him in order to make a better world.

Richter, and by extension those who admired him and felt like him, were latter-day representatives of what the sociologist Max Weber called the "ethics of conscience," people who advocated and followed anti-democratic policies, but couched their advocacy in moral language. Richter did not acknowledge that there might be any consequences other than good ones, and in so doing he was less honest than many moralists before him.

If "the other republic" – the Germany that voted with fervor for Brandt, read the novels of Böll and Grass, and believed Richter's national psychoanalyses – was at one pole of the political-moral spectrum of the 1970s and 1980s, the other pole was occupied by the proponents of Weber's other kind of ethics, the "ethics of responsi-bility." The paramount example was the chancellor himself. Helmut Schmidt was the product of north German Protestantism and the ethics of Immanuel Kant. Schmidt, speaking as chancellor, said in 1978 that he regarded Weber's distinction between the ethics of conscience and of responsibility as "illuminating, useful, and eminently political." But Schmidt's analysis also revealed a thoughtful as well as realistic assess-ment of the principles that guided the Federal Republic in the 1970s:

It is my understanding that politics is pragmatic action for moral purposes, but political action is, by no means, solely justified by morality or ethics; just as little as, conversely, politics could be justified by a theoretical predicament of an inevitable development. Indeed, Max Weber is right: "A politician is respon-sible" – he says – "for the consequences of his actions." One might also say: he must take responsibility for the consequences of his actions, and not merely for his own good intentions.[4]

Schmidt appreciated that the consequences, for the politician, of taking responsibility was "not always a very pleasant task." He pointed out the particular dangers of being in charge of economic and fiscal policy, where exact target figures must be announced far in advance, but which never correspond to the actual results in practice (what national economists call the "outturn"). He concluded that however unpleasant it might be, a politician must take responsibility for his decisions, and that those decisions must always be in accordance with "fundamental values." Some fundamental values, Schmidt believed, were specified in the Basic Law; for example, the principle of equality before the law and of equal rights, and the dignity and freedom of man. Others might not be specifically enumerated, although they were just as fundamental. As a social democrat, but also as a leader, Schmidt considered the right to work and the obligation to seek peace as values basic to a democratic society, a conviction he strove to translate into practical politics.

Schmidt's counterpart in his own party was Erhard Eppler, the former minister for development assistance. Eppler, a South-westerner, was trained as a minister in the Protestant church. In his theology and political philosophy he was a distant follower of Gustav Heinemann and Martin Niemöller, who opposed Adenauer and NATO on moralistic grounds. Like them, he believed that the democratic and capitalist political and economic system of the Federal Republic was morally flawed, that Germans bore a great burden of guilt not merely for the past, but because they were materially successful and prosperous in the present while other countries were not. In Eppler's view affluence and prosperity were undeserved. The Germans were therefore guilty of material abundance and this required atonement. In turn, atonement required reduction of consumption at home and a redistribution of West Germany's wealth, in the form of foreign aid, to the lesser-developed countries on the continents of Africa, Asia, and Latin America. Like Horst Eberhard Richter, Eppler averred that West Germany's greatest enemy was not the Soviet Union or the SED regime in East Germany, but evil forces of greed and selfishness in West German society itself. The politician Eppler embodied the ambitions and aspirations of many who were influenced by Richter's bitter, emotional attacks on West German democracy as it actually functioned. The confrontation between Schmidt and Eppler typified and symbolized the political and

---

[4] Schmidt, *Der Kurs heisst Frieden*, 14–5.

cultural struggle for power and, in particular, the power to set the political agenda in the Federal Republic after 1974.

If the Brandt era of 1969–74 was a period, real or imagined, of new beginnings and new possibilities, the Schmidt era of 1974–82, which began and ended under the shadow of recession amid two oil crises, was one of strenuous and successful attempts to keep afloat. In the Schmidt era, West Germany took the political and economic initiative in areas of vital national importance: the German question, detente, expansion of the European Community, and the currency revaluations that emancipated the West German economy and West German foreign trade from the strains caused by the dollar surplus and the weakening US economy. What German strategic thinkers used to call the *Gesetz des Handelns* (the power to act) lay with Bonn, and in a form that relied less on drama and more on substance.

The oil shock of 1973–4 brought an abrupt end to the era of experimentation in social and economic reform. In his first policy statement on May 17, 1974, Schmidt declared: "The social-liberal coalition has since 1969 been the engine of progress in the Federal Republic" and went on to enumerate the main areas of reform: taxation, child benefits, codetermination, land use controls, environmental protection, pensions, protection of renters, and education.[5] He was careful to promise no new great visions, however. In the Schmidt era, West German leaders often found themselves reacting to, rather than creating the international conditions of policy. Possibly, and even plausibly, West German domestic and foreign policies were better managed by Schmidt than they had been by Brandt, but these superior skills and potential were largely used up in fighting problems, not in creating new opportunities. Thus, the achievements seemed less dramatic; nevertheless, the American historian Fritz Stern had a point when he wrote, in 1980, that the performance of the West German economy and political system in the 1970s, faced with continuing international problems, was in some ways more impressive than in the 1950s, when international conditions were extremely favorable.[6] It was at least ironic, if not tragic, that Schmidt was forced by dissent in his own party and by the defection of Genscher's FDP to resign in 1982, at the very moment that the economic upswing based on what he had argued for throughout his chancellorship was finally beginning throughout the industrial world.

When he took office in 1974 few could have imagined the historically unprecedented degree of international agreement on the need to hold down inflation and combat protectionism that had resulted by 1982.

---

[5] Cited in Wilharm, ed., *Deutsche Geschichte 1962–1983*, 2: 38–42.
[6] Stern, *Dreams and Delusions,* 207.

True, that agreement was not only Schmidt's work; it was also caused by the disastrous second oil shock of 1979–80 and by the tough monetary and fiscal policies of the US Federal Reserve Bank under Paul Volcker, as well as by some of the policies of the Reagan administration. But without Schmidt, it is unlikely that the shock would have taught the salutary lesson that it, in fact, did.

2

Dealing With Economic Crisis

In 1972 West Germany spent 10.8 billion marks to import 140 million tons of oil; in 1974, the same amount cost 32.8 billion marks – three times as much. In 1979 the amount of oil imported by West Germany had risen to 148 million tons, and the cost to 49 billion marks. Then the second oil shock took prices through the roof: 64.8 billion marks on oil imports in 1980, and roughly the same in 1983. But behind the last two figures lurks a vitally important fact, namely that the *amount* imported was finally dropping, and dropping fast: 134 million tons in 1980, and a mere 107 million tons in 1983.[1]

These figures illustrated two points. One was the dimension of the task facing West Germany in 1974 in making up, through other exports and with reduced growth in domestic demand, for what was in effect an outright transfer of wealth to OPEC. The other was that the task of reducing domestic oil consumption was difficult and slow to achieve. The sharp fall in the amounts of imported oil in 1980 and thereafter was not due simply to the second oil shock. Measures to reduce consumption had been under way throughout the 1970s, but were only beginning to take effect when OPEC decided, for the second time, to bring pressure on the economies of the West. The most obvious of these measures, the ones that people noticed, were the short-term regulations of 1973–4 such as prohibition of driving on Sundays and cuts in gasoline supplies. Such interim measures had little effect. Some people argued that a national speed limit – West Germany was the only European country without one – would significantly reduce gasoline and hence oil consumption. *Länder* controlled by the left did introduce such limits, as could still be noted in the late 1980s by anyone driving through, for example, Hesse or the Bremen area. In fact, forcing the drivers of fast cars to travel at 100 rather than 160–180 kilometers an

[1] Thränhardt, *Geschichte der BRD*, 204.

hour would have had only marginal effect on oil consumption. The argument over speed limits – "free speed for free citizens," as the CDU/CSU argued, versus the moralistic demands of the left – had more to do with psychological compulsions. One might venture to say that the more careful and cautious West Germans became in their foreign policy, rejecting above all any action that might be condemned by the Soviet Union or the GDR, the more eager some of them became to express aggressive impulses in super-fast driving or, conversely, to forbid such fast driving in the name of safety and energy conservation.

The real, as opposed to illusory, reduction in oil consumption came from one ultimate reason only. It was that Germany did not (as the United States did) hold down, through government measures, the price of petroleum products. In turn this meant that the high price of oil represented the most powerful incentive for the German marketplace to redesign the devices and procedures that used oil – automobiles, industrial machines, and industrial processes – so that less oil would be required for the same or better performance; these market forces were not allowed to operate in the United States to the same degree until after the election of Ronald Reagan in 1980. German cars in 1983 produced more power and speed with less fuel than in 1974, but this change was simply not one that could be made from one week to the next. It took, in fact, all of the six to seven years from the first oil shock to midway into the second before the new machines and processes were fully on-stream. To have accomplished this retooling and rethinking in a period when new investments and industrial reorganization were far more difficult to manage than in the 1950s was a considerable accomplishment.

In complicated negotiations with the employers and the labor unions, as well as with the FDP and the CDU throughout 1974, the SPD demanded more public investment to create jobs and support industry. The opposition and the FDP questioned this strategy and called for an incomes policy of persuading employers to hold back wage inflation in return for tax relief for industry. In the late summer of 1975, all parties voted for an economic stabilization program which was aimed especially at the construction industry. Soon thereafter, the government passed a number of spending cuts to reduce the budget deficit of 15 billion marks. Nevertheless, the turnaround was very slow in coming, and in the first half of 1976 it was clear that all the measures taken had exerted only a modest effect. Still, the Federal Republic was faring relatively better than most of its competitors. Real income grew by 4.4 per cent in 1975, while consumer prices rose by only 5.4 per cent. The discussion on how to deal with the crisis illustrated two conflicting basic principles: on the one hand the belief in increasing private consumption and restraint in wage increases; on the other hand the belief that no single part of the

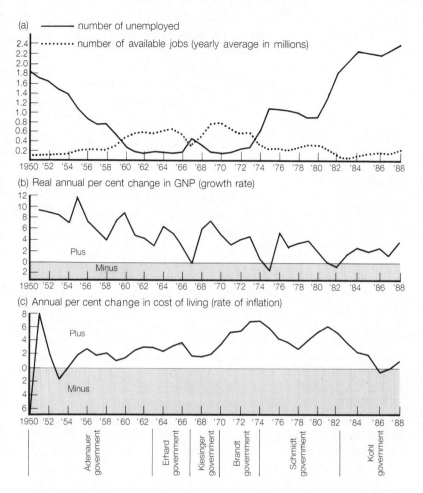

(a) —— number of unemployed
········· number of available jobs (yearly average in millions)

(b) Real annual per cent change in GNP (growth rate)

(c) Annual per cent change in cost of living (rate of inflation)

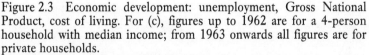

Figure 2.3 Economic development: unemployment, Gross National Product, cost of living. For (c), figures up to 1962 are for a 4-person household with median income; from 1963 onwards all figures are for private households.
Source: Statistisches Bundesamt, Wiesbaden

economy could be helped without involving all the others, and that wide ranging, new international effort was required.

Apart from a range of concrete improvements in social and welfare policy, initiated under Brandt, and designed to ward off the worst effects of the crisis, a major social policy action of Schmidt's first government was the law on co-determination of 1976. This issue had been a major initiative of Brandt's government, but did not become law during his tenure as chancellor, because it generated intense differences of opinion. The co-determination law that passed the Bundestag in 1976 called for the establishment of supervisory bodies in each company composed of equal numbers of representatives of owners and employees. In case of a deadlock, the chairman, who could not be elected without the consent of the shareholders or owners, exercised the deciding vote. The employers' association, arguing that the law would curtail property rights, filed suit with the Federal Constitutional Court in Karlsruhe, which rejected the complaint in 1979, and only then did the law take effect.[2]

Another important area of social policy concerned the rights of women to abortion and divorce. West Germany in 1974 had a no-fault divorce law, which had been a long-standing demand of the SPD, but was not regarded as sufficient by the left. In West Germany the status of women had been the subject of legal regulation far more than in Anglo-Saxon countries, and it was, therefore, an important step when, in 1976, a law on family rights and marriage was passed which officially stated that spouses could determine distribution of household tasks in complete freedom. In this way, social developments which had been going on for decades were recognized in law, since earlier the German civil code had stated that the management of the household was the responsibility of the wife, and that she could only take paid employment if it did not interfere with her duties as wife and mother.[3] Although this clause was outdated, it nevertheless represented an element of traditionalism that the left despised, and whose symbolic importance was far greater than its real significance.

During 1974–5 it became clear that oil prices, if not artificially regulated, would fluctuate according to demand, and that West Germany's trading partners were tempted to take measures to make it more expensive for them to import West German goods in the belief that such protectionist measures would preserve jobs in their own countries. Thus, Bonn adopted a more aggressive strategy in its international economic policies aimed at overcoming the crisis by international cooperation. None of the elements of this strategy was new, but in the post-oil-shock conditions of 1974 they took on increased importance.

There were three main elements. The first was exchange-rate stability. This had two interrelated aspects: the value of the US dollar and the mutual strength of the European currencies within the EC

---

[2] Lampert, *Wirtschafts- und Sozialordnung*, 241–3; Brandt, *Zum sozialen Rechtsstaat*, 48–9.

[3] Ibid., 181–2.

(European Community), which from January 1, 1973, included Britain, Denmark, and Ireland in addition to the original Six. In March 1973, the Council of Ministers of the EC decided to float the most important European currencies (except the pound) against the dollar. It was, in reality, a "dirty float" since government intervention did occur from time to time. The United States, for its part, did not experience a period of true floating until 1981 when the Reagan administration instructed the Federal Reserve Bank and the US treasury to cease interventions in the exchange rate; this policy continued until 1986 when US Treasury Secretary James Baker reversed the policy, a reversal that some observers, including the economist Milton Friedman, considered a major mistake. This so-called "bloc float" marked the final end of the system of pegged currency exchange rates established at Bretton Woods in 1944. Under the Bretton Woods system all major convertible currencies were linked to the dollar, which was therefore a universal reserve currency. The immediate reason for the bloc float was the "dollar overhang" – the surplus of dollars exported by the US to pay for imports and overseas investments. As the dollar was overvalued in terms of European currencies, speculators began to purchase those currencies in the expectation of a dollar devaluation. In August 1971, the Nixon administration, represented in this instance by the secretary of the treasury, John Connally, and his deputy for exchange rate questions, Paul Volcker, had abolished the convertibility of the dollar into gold. In December 1971, the Smithsonian Agreement between the US and the nine most important industrialized countries led to a regulated devaluation of the dollar of about 10 per cent. This change in the pegged exchange rate did not, however, solve the problem of the surplus of dollars on world markets. The Bundesbank was still obligated to buy dollars at the Smithsonian rate.

In late 1972 Schmidt, as finance minister, met in the library of the White House with George Shultz, who had succeeded Connally as US secretary of the treasury, and their French, British, and Japanese colleagues. The five finance ministers called their informal working association the "Library Group" after the place where they first met, and for some months they tried to manage the explosive international currency and financial situation. Their go-between was Paul Volcker, then an assistant secretary of the treasury. The US government had given Volcker an airplane to use which had no windows and which Schmidt therefore dubbed "the flying U-boat."[4]

The float of March 1973 and the repudiation by the Bundesbank of the obligation to buy dollars at any specific rate did not stop speculation, but did provide a general framework for dealing with it. In June 1973

[4] Schmidt, *Menschen und Mächte*, 194.

there had already been a new crisis during which the value of the dollar fell from 2.82 to 2.28 marks. On one memorable day, July 6, 1973, there were no buyers at all for dollars in Frankfurt at a price which sellers were willing to take. During the first oil shock the dollar firmed to 2.87 marks only to fall again in 1975 and much more drastically in 1978–9.[5]

The European currencies, except for the pound sterling and the Italian lira, but including the non-EC Norwegian and Swedish currencies, were linked in the so-called "snake" since January 1973 in an effort to keep their values in balance to one another. Within this system currencies were not supposed to fluctuate more than 2.25 per cent relative to each other, hence the term "snake." While periodic re-valuations of the mark sometimes occurred, the snake functioned reasonably well as a framework for West German foreign trade – 44 per cent of it was with countries which were members of the snake.[6] In fact, the most rapid expansion of world trade in the postwar period occurred between 1972–3 and 1980 when there existed the closest approximation to freely floating rates. In 1976 France left the snake, at a time when the West German economy and international position was improving rapidly. Schmidt, committed to progress in unification of the European currencies, pressed hard for a better system to replace the snake. This system, the European Monetary System (EMS), was worked out after long negotiations in 1977–8, primarily by Schmidt and the French president, Valéry Giscard d'Estaing, who was Schmidt's preferred partner in Europe.

The EMS came into operation in January 1979, just in time for the second oil shock. Unlike the snake, the EMS intended that its members would coordinate their monetary and, inevitably, their general fiscal and economic policies in an effort to achieve exchange rate stability. Because of the high degree of interdependence of the EC economies, the goal of exchange rate stability was designed to represent a big step forward in the direction of integration of policies across the entire EC, but in fact the necessary coordination did not occur. Further, any change of agreed parities between any two currencies in the EMS would have required unanimity of all members of the system. The result was mixed. Revaluations did occur within the EMS following its estab-lishment, and it remained a system of pegged exchange rates. But nonetheless the results were, though debatably, beneficial for both types of European economy – the trade surplus type of economy represented by West Germany and the deficit, inflationary economy represented by France and Italy.

---

[5] See Emminger, *D-Mark, Dollar, Währungskrisen,* esp. 190–210, 240–51, 304–10.
[6] Ibid., 357.

The second element of Schmidt's strategy was to secure access to raw materials and energy. Concerning energy, there was not much that West Germany or any other Western country was able or willing to do to reverse the actions of OPEC in 1973. Instead, West Germany concentrated on absorbing the effects of the oil price increase by strengthening the institutions of international economic cooperation. In Europe, that meant the snake and, later, the EMS. On the global level, it meant the International Monetary Fund (IMF) and the World Bank. Schmidt's government supported the efforts of the IMF to stabilize the prices of commodities produced by Third World countries but was opposed to any effort to arrive at a global agreement on prices for raw materials. The economics minister, Hans Friderichs (FDP), a close ally of Schmidt, stated at the fourth UN Conference on Trade and Development in Nairobi in 1976: "We continue to reject the idea of indexation and, then as now, do not believe that artificial intervention in pricing and in the structures of production and trade will lead to growth of the world economy, or will increase the developing countries' share in world trade."[7]

The third element of Schmidt's effort to achieve international stability was to prevent protectionism and to convince other Western leaders that only cooperation based on the intrinsic strengths of each nation's economy could bring about a return of sustained growth. As finance minister from 1972 to 1974 Schmidt had established good relations with his American counterparts Connally and Shultz. He was, however, never comfortable with what he, and most other leading Germans, including the Bundesbank president, Otmar Emminger, regarded as the inability of American leaders to conduct a coherent and consistent international trade or monetary policy. Particularly after the dollar became relatively free-floating in 1973, economic relations with the US were often more difficult than fundamental political and military relations. One consequence was that the Federal Republic increasingly sought closer ties with its European partners, especially France.

In late 1974 Giscard, who was elected president of France after the death of Georges Pompidou in May, suggested a summit meeting of the heads of government of the leading industrial countries to coordinate policy in the face of persistent economic problems. Schmidt agreed that the problems were serious and fundamental enough that they should be addressed by the heads of government and not just by economic ministers or experts. There was a precedent for this sort of summit in the "Library Group." When Schmidt raised the issue with the Americans in 1975, however, they felt that the US was so weakened by the Watergate

[7] Cited in Haftendorn, *Sicherheit und Stabilität*, 59–60.

affair and the resignation of President Nixon that they would not be able to offer a coherent contribution to any summit and would be exposed to Japanese and European pressure on the currency issue. During the Conference on Security and Cooperation in Europe at Helsinki in the summer of 1975, Schmidt managed to convince the Americans that this need not be the case. President Ford visited Germany in late July, immediately before going to Helsinki to sign the CSCE Final Act. Schmidt later described how he convinced Ford that a system of economic summits between Western leaders was a useful idea:

> Two things leaped to the eye during the days in Finland: the casual and natural way in which the US acted as a European power and was accepted as such, and the withdrawn natural dignity of Gerald Ford. Even more important was the relative ease with which the agreement was made in Helsinki between Ford, Giscard d'Estaing, Wilson, and myself to have a world economic summit meeting of the heads of government of the major industrial democracies. The thought had originally arisen in a conversation between Giscard and myself; we thought of a sort of continuation of the old Library Group on a higher level. But Washington at first had hesitated; since de Gaulle's time its relations with Paris were characterized by caution, occasionally also by a measure of distrust. In Bonn, Ford and I had worked out a common conception, and meanwhile a good personal relationship had also developed between Ford and Giscard. So it was that at a garden table in Helsinki on a beautiful summer afternoon we decided to have the first summit conference; in order that it would not fall into the hands of the bureaucrats we agreed that it would be prepared by personal representatives. We quickly agreed that Japanese participation was necessary – it seemed very desirable to me so that Germany would not be the only defeated country to sit at the table.[8]

Since then, economic summits have taken place regularly:

1 Rambouillet, France: November 1975;
2 San Juan, Puerto Rico: June 1976;
3 London, England: May 1977;
4 Bonn, West Germany: July 1978;
5 Tokyo, Japan: June 1979;
6 Venice, Italy: June 1980;
7 Ottowa (Montebello), Canada: July 1981;
8 Versailles, France: June 1982;
9 Williamsburg, United States: May 1983;
10 London, England: June 1984;
11 Bonn, West Germany: May 1985;
12 Tokyo, Japan: May 1986;

---

[8] Schmidt, *Menschen und Mächte*, 213–4.

13   Venice, Italy: June 1987;
14   Toronto, Canada: June 1988.

The first world economic summit conference was held at Rambouillet in France. The participants at this meeting were Ford and five other heads of government: Giscard, Schmidt, and the British, Japanese, and Italian prime ministers Harold Wilson, Takeo Miki, and Aldo Moro respectively. Thanks to the intensive preparations made by each leader's expert advisors – the so-called "sherpas" (real sherpas guide mountain climbers up the Himalayas) – the meeting was a success. Giscard had invited the heads of government and their personal aides to live at Rambouillet, just as de Gaulle had done, to impress foreign visitors with French *grandeur*, and he sought to keep the meeting informal. His efforts produced what the former director of Chatham House in London, the late Andrew Shonfield, called the "Rambouillet effect," defined as galvanizing "national officials, and also some departmental ministers, who are inclined in present circumstances to become obsessed by the minutiae of narrowly conceived national interests."[9]

The participants committed their governments to exchange-rate stability and to fighting protectionism. The latter commitment was no empty undertaking but it did not produce the intended results. This was an area where there were serious conflicts of interest between, on the one hand, West Germany and Japan, and on the other the US, Britain, and Italy, with France somewhere in the middle. In the latter four countries there were powerful constituencies in favor of measures their leaders believed would protect their own economies, such as taxing imports or establishing import quotas – a problem that remained unsolved a decade and a half later. Nevertheless, the participants at Rambouillet continued their efforts to stop or discourage some protectionist measures, even when these were unpopular in their own parties. The positive atmosphere at Rambouillet encouraged the Western leaders to repeat the experience, and the world economic summit became an annual institution in which, starting in 1976, Canada also participated, thus bringing the number of participating countries to seven. As members of the summit the leaders involved were sometimes referred to as the Group of Seven or "G-7."

In his memoirs, Schmidt estimated that "the three great summit conferences of 1975 – in the Alliance framework in Brussels in May, in July/August on the occasion of the CSCE conference in Helsinki, and in November in Rambouillet – showed the West, in my opinion, at the peak of agreement. There was no doubt about the common 'grand

---

[9] Putnam and Bayne, *Hanging Together*, 37.

strategy,' there was no mutual bitterness or suspicion, and there was confidence in a moderately exercised de facto leadership by the Americans, who refrained from emphasizing their role publicly."[10]

The second summit was held in Puerto Rico in June 1976, under the shadow of the American presidential campaign. Between the first and the second summit the economic picture in the Western world had changed considerably. Most countries were enjoying rapid growth, the US, West Germany, and Japan all had trading surpluses, and the principal danger seemed to be inflation. The 1976 summit concluded that a more restrictive fiscal policy was necessary. In West Germany, the government had shifted its emphasis from pump-priming of growth to restraints on public spending, a shift incorporated in the Law on the Structure of the Budget (*Haushaltsstrukturgesetz*), passed in the spring of 1976, which reduced public sector growth. During the summer and fall, however, it became clear that the growth spurt of 1975–6 was unsustainable, at least outside West Germany. Bonn's partners in the G-7 group began to sink back into that pit of combined inflation, unemployment, and high interest ("stagflation") from which most of them had briefly emerged in 1975, but from which they did not re-emerge until the early to mid-1980s.

In 1976 inflation was also growing again in West Germany, and it was the subject of Schmidt's election campaign against Helmut Kohl and the CDU/CSU that year. Schmidt's conclusion was that "we are better able to tolerate an unemployment rate of 5 per cent than an inflation rate of 5 per cent."[11] For him it was absolutely essential for domestic stability that inflation remain under control; even the prevailing rate of 4.6 per cent was very high by post-1948 standards. Schmidt was determined that West Germany was going to compensate for the oil price rises by increased exports. The export surpluses of West Germany, however, meant that capital was flowing into the country and, among other things, driving up the value of the mark. To keep its exports competitive inflation had to be low, because otherwise prices would rise even faster in foreign currencies. Exports grew throughout the period between 1975 and 1979; in 1977 West Germany achieved a record surplus on the trade balance of 43.3 billion marks.[12] Thus, the growth in exports reflected an undervalued mark and resulted in repeated revaluations of the mark in the currencies of West Germany's chief trading partners. Had these not occurred, other countries would have been driven to even more extreme measures of protection and export/import controls. Schmidt's policy that

---

[10] Schmidt, *Menschen und Mächte*, 215.
[11] Cited in Haftendorn, *Sicherheit und Stabilität*, 55.
[12] Ibid., 67.

oil price rises should be made good in exports and not in inflation was successful when, in 1977 and 1978, West Germany even managed the feat of achieving a surplus on exchanges with the OPEC countries – the value of goods, mostly equipment and machinery of all kinds, going from West Germany to the OPEC countries was greater than the value of the oil going from OPEC to West Germany.

At the summit of 1977 in London, which was the first attended by the newly elected American president, Jimmy Carter, Schmidt was faced with insistent demands by his fellow heads of government to stimulate the West Germany economy. In their view, there was easily enough latent public and private demand in West Germany to increase West German imports and investments abroad and thus to speed up activity in the more sluggish Western economies, notably Britain, France, and the US. Schmidt rejected this argument on the grounds that any more stimulus in West Germany would reignite inflation. Turning to the British prime minister, James Callaghan (formerly chancellor of the exchequer), who had decided to accept an emergency loan of hard currency from the IMF in 1976 and who was battling with inflation rates in the 18–30 per cent range, Schmidt made his point: "I do not believe that the French or the President of the United States will ask us in London to make more inflation. The English might like to see others make a bit more inflation, but I think it would be desirable for the rest of us to help them, as we have been doing until now, to come down from their inflation rate of 18 per cent."[13]

The London summit concluded with the recommendation that the Group of Seven should work for non-inflationary growth and should try to reduce the disparities in their trade balances – a demand made by deficit countries against the surplus countries (West Germany and Japan) with depressing regularity over the next ten years. It was always easier to make this demand at the summits than for the deficit countries to do anything themselves to solve their problems; and in fact rapid inflation followed.

Relations between Schmidt and President Carter were never good, since Schmidt had publicly supported Gerald Ford in the 1976 US elections. The London summit was their first sustained meeting, and it was a disaster. Each profoundly irritated the other. From the West German perspective Schmidt regarded Carter as superficial, incoherent, and an "amateur ... 'just not big enough for the game.'"[14] Carter's national security adviser, Zbigniew Brzezinski, put the blame squarely on Schmidt:

[13] Putnam and Bayne, *Hanging Together*, 72.
[14] Carr, *Helmut Schmidt*, 124.

If the president and I admired the same people, we also shared similar dislikes. Among them the Chancellor of Germany, Helmut Schmidt, took the undisputed first place. This need not have been the case, for Carter's initial attitude toward Schmidt was one of respect and even deference. He knew that Schmidt had a better grasp of world economics, not to speak of the advantage of having inherited from his predecessors a healthy domestic economy. I had known Schmidt for a least a decade and a half prior to my going to the White House, and I had briefed Carter on Schmidt, presenting a most attractive and favorable picture. Prior to their first meeting Carter was eager to learn from, and to work closely with, the German Chancellor. That attitude was unfortunately not reciprocated. Schmidt, almost from the very first encounter, adopted a patronizing attitude, mixed with less than persuasive protestations of friendship. Invariably there followed nasty behind-the-scenes gossip to sundry American and German journalists. . . . His inability to keep his tongue under control soured American-German relations to an unprecedented degree and lent respectability to the increasing German propensity to be highly critical of the US president and of US policies more generally.[15]

Schmidt's opinion of Carter and Brzezinski was equally uncharitable, although the German was somewhat more restrained in stating it. In his memoirs, Schmidt sarcastically called Brzezinski "Carter's know-it-all security adviser." He wrote further:

His [Carter's] equipment consisted . . . of a great supply of good will, considerable intelligence, and an unmistakable personal sense of having a mission. . . . Of course an American moralist and idealist can imagine a world-wide pressure campaign on the Soviet Union waged with all America's political and economic means. He may also enjoy illusions about the chances of success of such a campaign. . . . But he should know that the Kremlin has the sovereign authority over millions of human beings and that the Kremlin can tighten the screws of ideological, police, and military force whenever it seems appropriate. . . .

I saw Carter as well as Vance [the secretary of state] several times during 1977. Clearly Brzezinski's influence on the president was growing during that time. . . . In the course of this growing influence Brzezinski paid me two visits in 1977; he acted undisguisedly as the self-confident representative of a world power. Probably he regarded himself as a realist politician; undoubtedly, however, he was a hawk as far as policy toward the Soviet Union was concerned.[16]

Schmidt's implied view that a "hawk" could not be a "politician of realism" was in itself an indication of his own world view, that detente with the Soviet Union was not only desirable but possible. The clash of

[15] Brzezinski, *Power and Principle*, 26, 291.
[16] Schmidt, *Menschen und Mächte*, 222–9.

the two approaches, personified by Schmidt and by Brzezinski, dominated US-German relations from the economic summits of the late 1970s onwards.

Whatever the exact truth and the motives behind Brzezinski's account, he was right in pointing out that Schmidt's lack of respect for Carter, and the atmosphere of general contempt for the US which Schmidt thereby legitimized in Bonn policy-making circles had wider and unfortunate effects both in West Germany and Europe. Most important, it tended to justify anti-Americanism and contempt for alleged American primitiveness and stupidity across the entire West German left, especially in the peace movement that was soon to emerge from the citizens' initiatives and other radical groupings. Thus, distrust at the top produced tensions and accidents in the relationship between Bonn and Washington during the Carter years, 1977–80, which fed into and foreshadowed the much broader clash between Washington's international security policies of 1979–83 and strong interests in the Federal Republic.

The perceived American failure, or reluctance, to reduce the trade deficit, government spending, and oil imports led to a collapse of the dollar in 1978–9. On March 1, 1978, the dollar fell below two marks for the first time. As in 1972–3, the main reason for the dollar crisis was a higher rate of inflation in the United States than in West Germany which produced massive capital flows into West Germany, and downward pressure on the dollar. These flows were even greater than during the earlier crisis and reached proportions which indicated that many international businesses and even some governments now regarded the mark as a reserve currency next to the unreliable dollar. After a relative improvement over the summer the dollar began falling rapidly again in October, reaching a new low of 1.73 marks, a total depreciation of 28 per cent since the beginning of the sustained slide in the spring of 1977.[17] At that point a change set in. The US government had passed several measures to discourage inflation and speculation; the Federal Reserve raised interest rates above the inflation rate, thereby making credit very expensive; and the US trade balance improved in 1979 and 1980, since the increased dollar prices of West German products made their importation to the United States less desirable.

In West Germany, most bankers, including Emminger, the Bundesbank president, had long argued that the crucial element of stability was the money supply, and that interest rates were secondary. At a momentous meeting with the newly appointed Federal Reserve chairman, Paul Volcker, in October 1979, Emminger, after much argument, convinced

---

[17] Emminger, *D-Mark, Dollar, Währungskrisen*, 376–90.

the former of this point. Volcker returned to Washington and, in a single meeting of the Federal Reserve Board, introduced a revolution in US fiscal and economic policy that completely changed the picture of the global economy. The Board approved a statement announcing that it had decided to control the money supply, regardless of the effects on interest rates. This decision reflected the conviction that drastic steps had to be taken in order to stop inflation. Although the money supply over the next several years was very erratic, the new policy did bring inflation down sharply. It had the political merit of avoiding a specific decision by the Board to raise interest rates sharply; but it also produced a severe recession. Had the Board announced it was raising interest rates, it would have been politically a very unpopular decision.

The new policy was indeed a revolution, but it was not a conscious decision to embrace monetarism. As soon as the meeting was over, at 6 p. m. eastern time, October 6, 1979, Volcker called Emminger, who was attending a meeting of the IMF and the World Bank in Yugoslavia. The local time there was 4 a.m. as Volcker told his German colleague: "I did it, and wanted you to be the first to know." Emminger later commented: "This decision of October 6, 1979, made economic history, not only for the United States, but for the entire world. For it signified the beginning of the American policy of deflation, which turned the world economy upside down."[18]

The American reversal of policy took place under the shadow of the second oil shock, which occurred as a result of the Islamic fundamentalist revolution in Iran in 1978–9. Even before the fall of the Shah, OPEC had announced new price increases from the prevailing price of $12.70 a barrel, arguing that the continuing fall in the value of the dollar had reduced the real price of oil for the West to less than what it was in 1974, after the first wave of increases. This decision was taken in December 1978, even as strikes in the Iranian oil fields were already disrupting production and creating the first signs of panic on the spot market. By late January the oil companies were collecting $22 a barrel on the spot market. At the next OPEC meeting, in March 1979, the radical view prevailed. The oil producers decided to permit each member country to charge as much as the market would bear. By late 1979 the spot market price had reached $40 a barrel for Arabian light crude, while the official OPEC marker price was $24 a barrel. No oil, however, was available at that market price. This extraordinary price explosion was entirely due to the international panic caused by the Iranian revolution and not to any shortage of oil; by late 1979, the supply to the market was higher than in late 1978. There was, moreover, something very significant in the fact

[18] Ibid., 397.

that the West, as in 1973, accepted the dictates of OPEC without any significant attempt, military or diplomatic, to secure supply at a lower price. The view that the West was decadent and subject to indefinite blackmail supported the position of the OPEC radicals and encouraged them to apply a maximum of pressure, since there was no risk of retaliation.

The effects of the second oil shock were similar, but not identical to those of the first. West Germany at first escaped more lightly than its trading partners because the mark remained high in relation to the dollar (DM 1.70 in January 1980), which reduced somewhat the effect of the $12.70 to $40 price explosion in terms of marks. In 1980, however, the monetary revolution introduced by Volcker began to affect the exchange rate and drive up the dollar – a process that did not end until the economic summit of September 1985, at which point the dollar was above three marks. As a result of this effect, which, originally, was unrelated to either OPEC or the Iranian revolution, West Germany (and the EC in general) suffered two serious blows from the second oil shock: the initial tripling of prices, plus the price inflation in terms of their own currencies, generated by the rise in the value of the dollar, the currency in which oil prices were set. In 1979 and 1980 the cost of oil imports to West Germany rose by 45 per cent each year, and West Germany's trade balance moved from a surplus of DM 18.5 billion in 1978 to a deficit of DM 9.5 billion in 1979 and of DM 29 billion in 1980.[19]

At the economic summit in Tokyo in June 1979, Schmidt accused the Americans of having provoked the oil crisis by their Middle East policy, that is, by their uncompromising support of Israel which, in the view of some Europeans, had fueled the political and religious radicalism that underlay both the Iranian revolution and the refusal of the Arab states to recognize Israel. In 1977, Egypt had made peace with Israel, thus earning the rejection and opprobrium of the vast majority of Arab states. The Egyptian president, Anwar Sadat, was assassinated by an Islamic radical in September 1981 because of his relatively democratic, secular, and pro-Western policies.

For economic reasons, directly related to oil, the Europeans therefore took a decisive political step to redress what they considered an American foreign policy imbalance vis-à-vis the Middle East. At the same time as the economic summit in June 1980, the European Council met in Venice. This Council consisted of the heads of state or government of the EC member countries meeting from time to time to conduct business of importance to the EC and, in particular, to lead the process known as European Political Cooperation (EPC), a framework of agreed

---

[19] Haftendorn, *Sicherheit und Stabilität*, 80–1.

policies between the members of the EC. The Council, not to be confused with the Council of Europe established as part of the United Europe Movement in 1948, was first organized by Giscard in 1974. At the Venice meeting, led by Giscard, Schmidt, and the British prime minister, Margaret Thatcher, the European Council made one of its most significant political – as opposed to economic or administrative – statements. This was the Venice Statement in which the EC states declared they would enter into discussions with the various parties to the Middle East conflict and, following those discussions, would take an initiative to secure peace in the region. The declaration's political effect was that of a gesture of appeasement to these Arab states that rejected a peace settlement with Israel. It showed that Western Europe was willing to give up long-held political positions for oil; it was not nearly strong enough to satisfy the Palestine Liberation Organization (PLO) or the rejectionist Arab states, and it irritated and alarmed the Americans and the Israelis by its implied acceptance of the PLO and Arab position in the Middle East. The Venice Declaration of the European Council of June 1980 on the Middle East, however, was one, and, in the view of many, an unfortunate example of what came to be formally known as EPC. In the 1980s it became an officially designated arm of the EC, managed by the heads of state or government acting as the European Council.

The Bundesbank foresaw an improvement in West Germany's foreign trade position in 1981, but this did not come about, because the rest of the West remained in deep recession. In the wake of Volcker's new monetary policy severe inflation occurred during 1979–80, but this was the after-effect of the monetary policy of 1978 and early 1979. Invariably a sharp slowdown in monetary growth produces first a slowdown in the economy, which is temporary, and then a rebound. This, in fact, took place in 1981–2. At the same time the dollar began to rise, the result of encouraging imports to the United States and of the new monetary policy. By mid-1982, this was beginning to improve the picture for West German trade with the US. Domestically, the coalition government was unable to agree on the proper measures to reignite growth and to reduce the public sector deficit. These disagreements were root causes of the defection of the FDP which led to the fall of Schmidt in October 1982.

3

Combatting Euro-Pessimism

The Brandt–Scheel Ostpolitik had aligned West Germany with its allies. From being a potential loser in the detente game, West Germany became a winner, albeit at the price of modifying essential legal and moral positions concerning self-determination and the right of the Germans to a peace treaty and to national unity. Schmidt continued the detente policy begun by Brandt without fundamental change. In relation to the rest of Western Europe, however, Schmidt added a new and major dimension: he revived the Franco-German relationship that had blossomed intermittently under Adenauer, but had always failed to develop in a stable way because of French fears that the Germans were insufficiently independent of the Americans and not committed to the European interest.

Some regard Schmidt's cultivation of France, and the resulting "Paris–Bonn axis," as the most important and lasting achievement of West German foreign policy in the 1970s. It certainly reversed the uncertainties of the 1960s, following the failure of the French–German friendship treaty of 1963 to produce real results. In that decade France distrusted West Germany as an American puppet and West German leaders feared that any attempt to move closer to France would arouse American suspicions without bringing any real benefit to West Germany. In the 1970s, Schmidt sought, in a low-key way, to promote the idea of a common Franco-West German responsibility for basic stability, predictability, and rationality in West European monetary, fiscal, and trade policies, a responsibility that might even, with time, extend to the military or diplomatic spheres (although this was not emphasized by Schmidt or by Giscard, at least not as long as either was in office).

Since 1972, Schmidt, as finance minister, had developed a close working relationship with Giscard d'Estaing, at that time his French counterpart. Both moved to the top position in their countries at about the same time – mid-1974 – and their relationship developed into a true political friendship. They turned the biannual summits mandated by the 1963 treaty into an impressive feature of European politics as long as they remained in power; Giscard until May 1981 and Schmidt until October 1982. The close collaboration between Paris and Bonn in this period was an essential feature of the European political scene as well as an important factor in giving new impetus to the movement for European integration, although this new impetus did not make itself felt until after both leaders had been turned out of office.

This entente initially depended almost exclusively on personal trust, but by the early 1980s it had become an assumption of the political elites of both countries, so that it continued under Helmut Kohl and François Mitterand. Why was it so successful? The main reason was that both Schmidt and Giscard saw the world in generally the same way. The elements of this world-view – shared until the late 1970s by most American leaders as well – was that detente was both desirable and irreversible; that the Soviet Union was genuinely interested in and committed to peaceful relations with the West and not to its destruction; that the division of Europe was an element, not of tension, but of stability, and that no Western power should pursue policies that might provoke or upset the communist regimes to the East. On the contrary, they should do all they could to promote economic development of those regimes on the assumption that this would lead to gradual, peaceful liberalization. In practical terms, these views were put into effect with great skill by foreign minister Hans-Dietrich Genscher, who entirely shared them.

Another important factor in bringing France and West Germany closer together was the perception of American weakness after the oil shock and the Watergate affair. On the one hand most Europeans, including the political leaders, shared the American majority view of the early 1970s that the Vietnam War was a mistake and therefore approved in some vague and undefined sense of the victory of Ho Chi Minh. But on another level the blithe violation by US leaders of promises made to their South Vietnamese allies, and the apparent lack of understanding in the US that the conclusion of the Vietnam War was a geopolitical and diplomatic defeat of the first magnitude, shook the confidence of West Europeans in American reliability. The first seeds of the doubt that came into full bloom in the mid-to-late 1980s – the fear that the US was not fundamentally committed to protecting Western Europe and no longer had the will or the strategy to defend its own interests sensibly anywhere in the world – were sown by the events in Indochina in 1968–75 and by the reaction to them in the American media and in the US Congress.

Since Giscard and Schmidt did not see the world in terms of an East–West confrontation, but rather in terms of East–West detente and continuing stability, they did not, at first, regard themselves as called upon to compensate for declining US power in Europe. Nevertheless, the inherent logic of the Paris–Bonn axis meant that the security question eventually surfaced in the early 1980s. In the 1970s, the main task was to coordinate economic policy in the face of the oil shock and to promote European integration, particularly in view of the new diversity of the EC after the accession of Britain, Denmark, and Ireland – and, later, of Spain, Portugal, Greece and Turkey.

At the beginning of 1974, Spain, Portugal, and Greece were under authoritarian rule. Spain and Portugal were old dictatorships of interwar vintage, where the social and political tendencies were strongly and clearly toward liberalization and eventual democracy. Greece had been democratic for some years in the 1950s and 1960s and the dictatorship there was an authoritarian military reaction to democracy, not an anticipation of it. Helmut Schmidt regarded it as an important task of common European interest to bring democracy to these three relatively poor southern countries. They should be brought into the circle of democratic European states, since this would not only help their own people but serve the common interest of stability. In this, as in other cases, Schmidt demonstrated what to outside observers seemed to be a contradiction in his thinking. On the one hand, he shared the classical liberal (in America: conservative) view that constitutional democracies are by nature peaceful and that therefore the more democracy (or, as he would prefer, social democracy) there is in the world the more peaceful world politics are likely to be. On the other hand, he regarded undemocratic communist rule in Central Europe as a factor of stability, not conflict, which should therefore not be disturbed by demands for democratization or national self-determination.

The Portuguese regime collapsed without resistance when faced with an uprising of left-wing army officers discontented with the burden of fighting in Portugal's African colonies of Angola, Mozambique, and Equatorial Guinea. Portugal was the last major colonial power and had always been by far the poorest. The "revolution of the carnations" of 1974 toppled the ramshackle regime of Augusto Caetano like a house of cards. Portugal risked slipping rapidly from inefficient right-wing rule to efficient left-wing rule. Within months the communist party had infiltrated the revolutionary government and won many adherents in the officer corps: "Some of the officers who represented Portugal in Alliance or NATO committees expressed surprisingly naive, sometimes vulgar-Marxist views. That was particularly the case for the head of government,

Gonçalves, and for the head of state, Costa Gomes."[1] Faced with this spectacle of self-styled communist ideologues in charge of Portugal, Henry Kissinger, the US secretary of state, was prepared to retaliate by cutting American aid to Portugal. Schmidt's view was the opposite, that the cause of democracy in Portugal was not lost and that democracy might survive if one gave the Portuguese socialists financial and other aid to enable them to counter the relentless communist propaganda offensive and the skillful communist attempts to take over the country's media and political institutions.

At this point Schmidt took action. In 1974–5 the SPD, and to some extent the Socialist International, supplied the Portuguese Socialist Party under Mario Soares with financial and moral support, enough to permit the party to escape destruction by the communists and their sympathizers in the military. The salvation of democracy in Portugal by the SPD was one of the major successes of Schmidt's foreign policy.

In the late 1970s Turkey faced an equally serious situation of large-scale public violence verging on civil war. The socialist government received aid from Germany, but this did not prevent the military coup of September 1980 which almost overnight put an end to the violence at the cost of suspending Turkish democracy. Most of Turkey's European allies reacted with horror, some of them threatening to expel Turkey from NATO. These governments appeared to minimize the extreme danger posed by extended public violence, which was an open invitation to Soviet interference in a country that not only bordered on the Soviet Union but was the linchpin of NATO's south-eastern flank. They also appeared to beg the question that the Turkish army was perhaps the most progressive and pro-Western institution in the country, that it had repeatedly taken steps to preserve political stability in Turkey, and that the military rule of 1980–3 was not therefore a typical military dictatorship. Schmidt, however, did recognize Turkey's strategic importance and therefore courted considerable unpopularity among his European government colleagues by continuing economic aid and rejecting calls for the denial of aid or expulsion of Turkey from NATO.

In August 1974 the Greek military regime fell, and in late 1975 the Spanish dictator Francisco Franco died. Within a few years both countries experienced a cultural revolution, as the elements supporting secularization and relaxation of social standards and mores broke free. One aspect of this delayed and therefore particularly forceful and thorough transformation was anti-Americanism, because many in the new political elites saw the US as a supporter of the old regimes.

---

[1] Schmidt, *Menschen und Mächte*, 208.

Schmidt was an advocate of admitting the new southern European democracies to the EC, partly on the grounds that this would appease and eventually temper the anti-Western and even anti-democratic focus of the new leftist elites.

In June 1979 the European Parliament was elected by popular vote for the first time. Interest in this election was not great, particularly since the European Parliament had little authority in managing the affairs of the EC. The important institutions of the European Community were still the European Commission, the Council of Ministers, and the European Council, located in Brussels. In all three, the West German position favored more integration. This would institutionalize 'European Political Cooperation' (EPC) and create a forum in which the Western European countries could coordinate a common approach toward international issues. This joint approach was used to develop a position on the Middle East, which turned out to be basically pro-Palestinian, and a position on economic aid to the Third World. In both areas the European position was at variance with that of the US, and this too caused a certain amount of tension.

Starting in 1979 the European Community adopted a new currency, the European Currency Unit (ECU), to serve as an easier means of accounting for and determining the costs and benefits of trading and services between countries. West Germany was the second largest contributor. In 1970 West Germany paid two billion marks into the EC, by 1975 the amount had more than tripled, and six years later, in 1981, West Germany contributed DM 14 billion.[2] This gave West Germany considerable weight in the discussions on reform of agricultural policy and general policies of intervention and support for the other industries of member countries.

The world economic summits of the Group of Seven that began in 1975 strengthened Franco-German collaboration and enhanced West Germany's standing in Europe. As the 1970s drew to a close in the economic chaos of the second oil shock, the Iranian revolution, and the collapse of the dollar, Schmidt believed more than ever in the vital importance of restoring faith in the future of Western Europe both as a force for stability in the world and as a guarantor of detente in Europe itself.

Another, more promising example of West European common action was the proposal by Hans-Dietrich Genscher and his Italian colleague, Emilio Colombo, first presented in 1981, to achieve a large measure of political, as opposed to merely economic and fiscal, integration of the

---

[2] *The Week in Germany*, January 22, 1982. See also Bundesbank's *Monthly Report* for January 1982.

EC in the immediate future. Leading circles in the original EEC (the Six) greeted the Genscher-Colombo plan enthusiastically, the newer members less so. The perceived unwillingness of Britain and Denmark in particular – both countries were receiving far more in financial support from the EC than they were paying in – to abide by the spirit of their accession to the EC by committing themselves to European integration caused many in West Germany to speak of the need for a two-tier Europe: a fully integrated economic and political powerhouse of the old Six, and a second tier of slower-moving obstructionists who would have to remain outside, since they clearly did not want to be part of the new political efforts to coordinate common policies. Although the governing bodies of the Community never formally adopted the Genscher-Colombo plan, its basic elements represented the continuation of efforts toward greater political coordination. Its aim was to streamline decision-making and to strengthen the European Parliament, via such methods as increased reliance on majority voting. Opposition to it reflected the concern shared by Western Europe's smaller nations, that the proposal was a "device for advancing supranational objectives."[3] While no resolution was found for the dilemma of whether the majority could pass legislation and take decisions binding on the EC's smaller members, the debate also showed a dilemma of a broader nature: how to achieve political and economic power for the EC as a whole, which would benefit its members vis-à-vis larger countries, such as the United States or the Soviet Union or Japan, but which would simultaneously protect national sovereignty?

On February 25, 1982, the 39th Franco-German government meeting took place in Paris between Schmidt and François Mitterrand, who had been elected president of France in May 1981. For the first time both governments declared that they had decided to expand these regular talks to include security policy. This was a difficult step to take since France was not a member of NATO, but both Schmidt and Mitterrand considered that the time was overdue for the two leading continental powers to begin discussing their common security requirements. Although both supported the Reagan administration's restoration of American military strength, they also believed very strongly that Europeans should take greater responsibility for their own security, and both agreed that this could only be done on the basis of Franco-German understanding.

[3] *Keesing's Contemporary Archives*, August 13, 1982.

4

Fighting for Detente

Schmidt was less given to grand visions of a "European peace order" than Brandt, but shared the fundamental belief that detente was a moral obligation and should also become a fact of political and diplomatic life in Europe. That the Soviet government might not share the Western view of detente as necessary for peace in Europe, or that Soviet acts of repression might demonstrate the limits of detente, was not a vision that Schmidt welcomed, and he never came to accept it. For him, the new Cold War of 1980 and after was the result of mutual, not merely of Soviet actions.

The narrow European view of detente in Europe during 1974–9 stressed stability, and little occurred to disturb it. Indeed, Schmidt and most Europeans regarded the signing of the Helsinki Final Act in 1975 after two years of negotiations among delegations from 35 European states, communist as well as democratic, in the CSCE, as a triumph and confirmation that detente was permanent. Looking back in 1987, Schmidt wrote:

> The Helsinki conference of midsummer 1975 was the high point of the phase of relaxation of tensions between East and West. This policy had begun very slowly and at first hesitantly in the second half of the 1960s; starting in 1976 a gradual decline set it, and the Soviet Union's invasion of Afghanistan in December 1979 as well as the Western reaction in 1980 put an end to it.[1]

The governments attending the CSCE comprised four distinct groups: the Soviet bloc, the US, the EEC countries, and those not associated with it at all, including West European neutral states. For the Soviet Union, the Final Act was a promise that the political and territorial status quo of 1944–5 was inviolable and an element of, and not an obstacle to, peace. The conference had been a Soviet demand for years,

[1] Schmidt, *Menschen und Mächte*, 73.

because the USSR saw in it the means to obtain a de facto European peace treaty, codifying its position and laying the basis for an era of so-called peaceful coexistence. In the Soviet vocabulary this concept of peace meant ideological conflict with the West, but not open warfare. The Soviet government reserved for itself the right to conduct activities aimed at undermining the power and stability of Western nations, but any comparable actions by Western nations were forbidden by this principle. By convening the CSCE the leaders of the Soviet government hoped to establish these ground rules, which they themselves had devised, and as such the conference constituted one of the major political victories gained by the Soviet Union since World War II.

Formally the Final Act repeated demands made by the Soviet bloc since 1967. The signatories promised to

> respect each other's sovereign equality and individuality ... including in particular the right of every State to juridical equality. ... They will also respect each other's right freely to choose and develop its political, social, economic and cultural systems. ...
>
> They will respect each other's right to define and conduct as it wishes its relations with other States. ...
>
> They will ... refrain from any form of armed intervention or threat of such intervention against another participating State.[2]

In the Western view, passages such as these forbade the Soviet Union from carrying out actions like the invasion of Czechoslovakia in 1968. In the Soviet view, the invasion of 1968 was necessary to prevent counter-revolution and took place at the request of orthodox communists within Czechoslovakia; it was therefore not armed intervention, but friendly military assistance.

In the Final Act, the 35 governments also agreed on a series of "confidence-building measures," chiefly prior notification of major military maneuvers. The purpose of the act, in the Western view, was to promote good relations and increase mutual confidence and respect. Specifically relations were to be non-violent and not burdened by the existence of threats. Contrary to Soviet expectations, however, the Western nations focused especially on the so-called "Basket III," which included endorsement of freedom of movement and communication between East and West and guaranteed the human rights of citizens throughout Europe. Since these documents had been signed by the Soviet Union, they were used by the democratic opposition movements in Eastern Europe in ways that the Soviet Union had not foreseen and did not welcome.

[2] Dept of State, *Documents on Germany*, 1287, 1289.

In response to the world economic crisis provoked by the oil price explosion, Helmut Schmidt, chancellor since 1974, suggested regular meetings of the heads of government of the industrial countries. He made this suggestion to his colleagues (from left to right) Harold Wilson of Britain, Gerald Ford of the US, and Valéry Giscard d'Estaing of France, at the CSCE meeting in Helsinki in 1975. [*Source*: GIC]

Two who agreed: Helmut Schmidt and US President Gerald B. Ford. In his memoirs, Schmidt maintained that he got along better with Ford than with any other president, and that the world was notably "better governed" by the leaders of the mid-1970s than either before or since. This photograph was taken in November 1980 in Washington, DC, just after the election of Ronald Reagan. [*Source*: GIC]

US–West German governmental relations reached a low point during the presidency of Jimmy Carter (left), primarily because of great personal difficulties between the two leaders. Photo shows Schmidt on his first visit with Carter in July 1977. [*Source*: GIC]

Rainer Barzel, the only CDU chairman who was never chancellor, failed by two votes to unseat Brandt in 1972. In 1984, he resigned as president of the Bundestag in connection with the Flick affair, in which leading politicians illegally raised money from large corporations for their parties. [*Source*: GIC]

Two who emphatically disagreed. Schmidt found the Polish-born Brzezinski (left) intolerably arrogant and "all-knowing" and accused him of irrational suspicion of both Germans and Russians. The dislike was entirely mutual. [*Source*: GIC]

President Carter speaking in Berlin in July 1978. Seated from left to right: Zbigniew Brzezinski, Carter's National Security Advisor; Peter Lorenz (CDU), president of the Berlin parliament; Amy Carter; Schmidt; Rosalynn Carter; French officer; Dietrich Stobbe (SPD), governing mayor of Berlin. [*Source*: GIC]

Henri Nannen (seated at table, left), an extraordinarily adept publisher, gave the mass magazine *Stern* a distinctly leftish and anti-American tilt in the 1960s. In 1978 the magazine was sued by the left-wing feminist Alice Schwarzer (left foreground) on the grounds that its many pictures of nude women constituted sexual exploitation and violated women's rights. In the 1980s *Stern* purchased and published diaries purported to be those of Adolf Hitler; they later turned out to be forgeries. [*Source*: GIC]

Marion Gräfin Dönhoff (right), longtime editor of *Die Zeit* and herself born in East Prussia, was a leading advocate of expanding political and cultural ties to East Central Europe. She is seen here with the Russian emigré writer Lev Kopelev (left), who was imprisoned in the Soviet Union for helping German civilians during the war, and the Czech playwright Pavel Kohout. [*Source*: GIC]

One of the authors lays a wreath in January 1981 at the memorial to Peter Fechter whose murder he witnessed in August 1962. [*Source*: Dennis L. Bark]

The inner-German border between the *Länder* of Hesse and Thuringia separating two historically connected villages, Kleinensee (foreground) and Grossensee (background). Note the interrupted road. The hundred yards behind the barrier on the east is a death zone; the GDR border guards will shoot to kill anyone entering it. [*Source*: GIC]

The German-born Henry Kissinger (right) retained an interest in his native land, which he expressed in his somber report to the Senate in 1966 and during his government service 1969–77. He came to support Ostpolitik, particularly as practiced by Schmidt, while warning the Germans of its risks. In this photograph Kissinger is calling on Chancellor Schmidt in his home in Bonn in 1979. [*Source*: GIC]

In his last years as chancellor, Schmidt found he often had more in common with realistic conservatives like Britain's Margaret Thatcher than with many in his own party. [*Source*: GIC]

The chairman, the strategist, and the chancellor: Brandt, Wehner, and Schmidt in a moment of harmony at an SPD election rally in 1980. [*Source*: GIC]

The *Spiegel* affair of late 1962 forever destroyed Franz Josef Strauss' chances of becoming federal chancellor. Though he returned to Bonn as minister from 1966 to 1969, he concentrated increasingly on his home *Land* of Bavaria, where he was uncrowned king for almost two decades. Here he is seen with his daughter Monika at an *Oktoberfest* (harvest beer festival) in Munich in the 1980s. [*Source*: GIC]

Two German socialists: Schmidt visiting the communist leader, Erich Honecker, in the GDR in December 1981. The two issued an agreed statement that war must never again begin from German soil. Critics said that Schmidt had gone too far in conceding legitimacy to a regime that persisted in denying its citizens rights. [*Source*: GIC]

The old-timer and the newcomer. Foreign Minister Hans-Dietrich Genscher (FDP, left) was the longest-serving foreign minister of any Western country in 1982, when he took his party out of the coalition with the SPD, thereby enabling Helmut Kohl (CDU, right) to become chancellor. Genscher was still in office at the decade's end. [*Source*: GIC]

Violating the Hippocratic oath. In the fall of 1983, 5,000 doctors and medical personnel joined the protests against the double track decision, declaring that they would not support efforts to provide medical care in case of nuclear attack and demonstratively taking off their medical gowns. [*Source*: GIC]

Anti-military demonstrations (*below*) continued throughout the 1980s, many of them directed against the troops of Germany's allies stationed in the Federal Republic. The photograph was taken during a demonstration in September 1984 against the British exercise "Lionheart," which involved 131,000 troops and was the largest since World War II. [*Source*: Süddeutscher Verlag]

In June 1982, in the largest demonstration (*above*) in the history of the Federal Republic, 350,000 persons met near Bonn to protest the NATO double track decision of December 1979 to deploy nuclear missiles in Europe. The placard reads "Atomic death threatens us all". The demonstrators showed remarkable faith in the peaceful intentions of the Soviets and an equally remarkable degree of suspicion of Western policies. [*Source*: GIC]

From left to right: Chancellor Helmut Kohl; Hannelore Kohl; Barbara Bush; Vice President George Bush; the governing mayor of Berlin, Richard von Weizsäcker (CDU), and his wife looking across the Berlin Wall at the Potsdamer Platz in January 1983. The small mound in the distance behind the vice president marks the site of the Führerbunker where Adolf Hitler committed suicide on April 30, 1945. [*Source*: GIC]

Kohl with his minister of defense, Manfred Wörner (center background, in belted coat) at a Bundeswehr maneuver in 1983. Behind the smiles both soldiers and civilians worried that the army would be unable to maintain its strength in view of the rapidly falling birth rate. [*Source*: GIC]

ELECTION POSTERS FROM 1972 AND 1983.

1972. In 1972, the Federal Republic was 23 years old, and the posters reflected the dramatic change in political, social, and economic conditions. *Left* Top row, left to right: The SPD poster displays a photo of Willy Brandt, who had been chancellor for three years, and proclaims, "Germans! We can be proud of our country. Elect Willy Brandt." The CDU poster displays its candidate, Rainer Barzel, assuring the voter that "We build progress on stability." Bottom row: The FDP poster shows a common traffic sign indicating the right of way, with the slogan "Right of way for reason." The CSU's basset hound is saying, "I won't survive another three such dog years. The SPD must go!" [*Sources*: CDU−Bundesgeschäftsstelle der CDU; SPD−Archiv der sozialen Demokratie; FDP−Bundesgeschäftsstelle der FDP; CSU−Hans-Seidel-Stiftung]

1983. By 1983, election posters had become increasingly sophisticated. The Federal Republic was 34 years old. Top row: The CDU poster assures the voter that Chancellor Kohl generates trust, and that the party is "safe, social, and free." The CSU poster quotes Franz Josef Strauss as follows: "We are concerned for our fatherland. Now we must put Germany in order with sensible and honest policies." The FDP poster reminds voters that "Freedom requires courage" and that "Germany needs the FDP−the liberals." [*Sources*: CDU, SPD, FDP, CSU− as above; Greens−Bundesbildstelle]

Axel Springer (right) published *Die Welt*, a conservative paper that warned repeatedly of the dangers of moving too far too fast in granting concessions, money, and legitimacy to the communist regimes of Eastern Europe. Springer, seen here with Henry Ford II, was also the head of a vast media empire with interests in many countries, and a great defender of the freedom of West Berlin and of reconciliation with Israel. [*Source*: GIC]

The Federal Republic was in a key position to support these movements, but was hampered in its ability to do so by the dominant attitude in the government represented by Genscher. His position was that the West should do nothing which might undermine the stability of communist regimes, since that would make things worse than they already were. Instead one must try to soften the rigors of communist rule, but one must not directly support people whom the communist regimes considered their enemies, namely their own citizens. In this way West German foreign policy, vis-à-vis Eastern Europe, may have emerged from one dead end with the abandonment of the Hallstein Doctrine, but soon found itself in a new dead end, where there was no choice but to continue with the policy of political concessions and economic aid to the GDR and other communist regimes. This Ostpolitik was not the flexible tool of liberalization and gradual transformation that had been foreseen by people like Waldemar Besson, professor of political science at the University of Constance, who had hoped that the changes of 1969 and thereafter might lead to a new and positive role for West Germany in the development of Eastern Europe. The most important concrete results of the new Ostpolitik after 1974 were the continued attempts to improve contacts among individuals, although these attempts were often at the mercy of Eastern pressure and blackmail.

The effects of President Nixon's resignation in August 1974 (Watergate), and, notably, the efforts of Congress to limit presidential power in the War Powers Act and similar measures paralyzed the conduct of the United States foreign policy. The Clark Amendment of 1975 prohibited aid to anti-communist guerrillas in Angola, thus effectively granting immunity to the Cuban troops who, on behalf of the Soviet Union, were engaged in destroying the incipient democratic opposition led by Jonas Savimbi. In Europe, no great importance was attached to these signs that the US–Soviet conflict remained fundamental and irresolvable. Support for detente was bolstered by the Helsinki talks, and, as Schmidt pointed out, did not wane until 1979.

The left wing of the SPD, and allied political forces on the left wing of West German society and culture in general, saw detente as a belated rejection by the West of outdated and dangerous imperialist attitudes vis-à-vis not only the communist regimes, but the new socialist elites in the Third World. The SPD party apparatus contained a number of people, primarily former Brandt protégés and younger members such as Karsten Voigt, who subscribed to this pro-Third World view of the world as dominated by the opposition of the rich, exploitative North and the poor, victimized South. This group found a spokesman close to Schmidt in his assistant in the chancellery, state secretary Hans-Jürgen

Wischnewski, who had been minister of economic cooperation (foreign aid) in the grand coalition. Formerly a moderate social democrat, Wischnewski became under Schmidt an activist whose work on behalf of anti-Western Third World causes, initially in the Arab Middle East and later in Nicaragua, earned him the pseudo-Arab sobriquet "Ben Wisch." The social democratic argument for helping these forces was that if the social democrats of Europe did not show active sympathy for leftist movements, they would drift into the arms of the Soviet Union or of Soviet proxies. The flaw in the argument was that these groups, such as the PLO or, later, the Sandinist Nicaraguan regime, were never genuinely interested in the democratic process that governed political change in Western Europe.

Equally important, however, the SPD's foreign policy in southern Europe itself was generally conducted in the interests of NATO and the Western democracies. The most striking examples of this foreign policy were the Schmidt government's economic and organizational assistance to the Portuguese socialists in 1974–5 and to Turkey in the late 1970s and early 1980s. In both cases, Schmidt and his aides acted to help democratic forces and combat Soviet influence in two NATO countries that were at risk of sliding into anarchy or civil war.

In the area of development aid in general, Schmidt continued the policies advocated by Brandt's minister for economic cooperation, Erhard Eppler, the parliamentary leader of the party's left wing. In the Schmidt cabinet, Eppler was replaced by Egon Bahr, the architect of the Ostpolitik of recognition and appeasement. In his new position, Bahr advocated an analogous line: no attempt should be made to force the socialist Third World economies to become more liberal, more efficient, more prosperous, or more useful to their own people. Rather, the asserted interests of the Third World countries themselves – in practice, this meant the narrow interests of their ruling elites – should govern Western aid policies. Not surprisingly, this prescription for passivity reinforced the prevailing tendencies for West German aid to support the destructive economic and political practices of most Third World regimes, particularly in black Africa.

In September 1973 the two German states had become members of the United Nations, and this status was another reason for the new maturity and confidence with which West Germany now engaged itself in international issues. In 1974 West Germany was the fourth largest contributor to the UN budget. The most important area of West German activism was contact between industrial states and the Third World. The West German government hoped for social and economic progress, improvements in international human rights, and self-determination through the UN. The UN was also the scene of confrontation with the GDR, in which the two states would present their opposing views on the German question; other members of the UN referred to this ritual as "the German lesson."

In Third World development policy West Germany and the GDR were also totally opposed, since the GDR as a Soviet satellite supported the Third World's so-called national liberation movements. In October 1975, the Soviet Union and the GDR signed a new treaty of friendship and mutual assistance to replace that of June 1964. In it, the GDR undertook "to support countries liberated from colonial oppression in their striving to consolidate their national independence and sovereignty."[3] In clear language, that meant that the GDR promised to provide military assistance to further world-wide Soviet strategic goals. In the later 1970s and 1980s, the GDR became noted particularly for the role played by its ministry of state security (political police, corresponding to the Soviet KGB) in organizing the secret police forces of Third World Marxist regimes, such as those in Ethiopia and Nicaragua. West Germany, by contrast, felt itself strictly bound by the NATO rule that European NATO members should not act outside the North Atlantic area, and to an even greater degree by the continuing shadow of the past, which meant that any West German activity must be peaceful, and that West German military forces could not take an active role anywhere outside Western Europe.

The completely civilian nature of West German foreign policy, especially in the Third World, led to an asserted belief in liberal West German political circles that all West Germany's international policies must be necessarily peaceful. They ignored the fact that the defense of freedom by force might sometimes be necessary, and, because they exalted "peace" into an absolute principle, they often behaved as though this was the way things not only ought to be, but, in fact, also were.[4] The idea that the primary purpose of foreign policy should be the survival of the state was not given as much credence under Genscher as it had been given in earlier years.

Schmidt's tendency to see security in economic terms, and to minimize the importance of the ideological dimension of the East–West conflict and hence its fundamental nature, did not mean that he did not consider the Soviet Union a potential threat. What distinguished his view from that of American conservatives who, in 1976, were starting very modestly to raise their heads again in the Committee on the Present Danger (among the founding members were Dean Rusk, Paul Nitze,

---

[3] Ibid., 1299.
[4] See Schwarz, *Die gezähmten Deutschen*.

Richard V. Allen, General Andrew Goodpaster, Max Kampelman, George McGhee, and David Packard), was that he did not clearly acknowledge that the Soviet Union regarded the West, and in particular the United States, as its enemy; and that Soviet leaders, whatever their shading or immediate policies, did not accept the permanent existence of other centers of power in the world. It was difficult for Schmidt, and indeed for almost all West European leaders, to recognize, at least publicly, that no matter what they did they could not permanently appease or satisfy the Soviet Union, that no lasting peaceful coexistence was possible, and that a consistent defense effort must be made.

Schmidt, however, did agree with the emphasis of the 1967 Harmel Report, that detente and deterrence were two equally important elements of security. In 1976-7 he recognized that almost a decade of detente in Europe and the post-Vietnam tendencies toward isolationism and defense cuts in America had now brought things to such a pass that even a peaceful Soviet Union could be tempted to attack. In 1977, he began, with regret, to insist that NATO redress the balance sufficiently to restore credible deterrence.

In retrospect, Schmidt believed that the election of Jimmy Carter as president of the United States in November 1976 was the end of the era of a common Western "grand strategy." Speaking about the harmony of views between Ford, Giscard, and himself displayed in the economic summits of 1975-6, he wrote:

After the next change of president in Washington all of that was not completely lost, but it started to crumble. When today, Valéry Giscard d'Estaing, Jim Callaghan, and I still meet, every now and then, at Jerry Ford's invitation in Vail in the Colorado mountains, then sometimes the conversation in the evening, as we sit with our whiskies, may turn nostalgically from the problems of the day to the middle of the 1970s. Somewhat wistfully – and a bit arrogantly – one of us may say, "Of course, the world was governed better in those days. . . ."

The end of the Nixon-Ford-Kissinger era was also, one can see now, the end of that successful period of Western common strategy as it had been formulated ten years earlier, in December 1967, by Pierre Harmel in his report on "Future Tasks of the Alliance."[5]

In 1974, the Soviet Union began deploying a new intermediate-range missile, code-named the SS-20 by NATO. Each missile carried three warheads and the initial rate of deployment was approximately three per

[5] Schmidt, *Menschen und Mächte*, 215.

month, rising to more than one a week by 1980. The SS-20s were targeted on Western Europe and not the US. Since the US was, moreover, rapidly losing – and accepting the loss of – its strategic superiority over the Soviet Union, the role of the SS-20s in Soviet military and diplomatic strategy was clear: it was to intimidate the Europeans by threatening limited war in which the US might not intervene, because of the deterrent effect of the Soviet strategic arsenal, and thus in the medium term to decouple Western Europe from the US and play upon fears engendered by massive Soviet military strength.

James Schlesinger, the American secretary of defense in 1974, had taken account of approaching Soviet parity with the US in his recommendation that US nuclear-war-fighting plans should aim at deterring escalation to higher levels, by giving the president and military commanders "limited nuclear options" to replace the no-longer-credible threat of massive retaliation. In the European theatre, Schlesinger, and his successor Donald Rumsfeld, recommended a long-term program of improvement not only of NATO's theater nuclear forces, but of conventional forces as well. Based on these American recommendations, NATO in 1976–7 developed plans for long-term force improvements. At their regular summit meeting in May 1977, the heads of government and defense ministers of NATO approved a long-term defense improvement program and commissioned member governments to draw up plans for its implementation. One of the elements of the program was an undertaking by each member country to increase real defense spending by 3 per cent per year. Ten years later only the US had consistently met that target; Britain, West Germany, and Norway had come close. France, which was not a member of the military organization of NATO but merely of the political alliance, also increased its spending by above 3 per cent annually for most of the 1980s.

Schmidt, and other Western European leaders, were not entirely pleased with the Schlesinger Doctrine and with the apparent course of events it suggested concerning "limited nuclear options." To them, the purpose might mean that the Americans hoped to confine a nuclear conflict to Europe, and American demands for increased conventional strength might mean that Europe was becoming, once again, "safe" for conventional war. Schmidt was also worried by the apparent willingness of the Carter administration in Washington to accept restraints in shorter-range weapons in the SALT II arms control negotiations that began in 1977. An example was the cruise missile, a slow, low-flying unmanned aircraft capable of penetrating Soviet air defenses (as they then existed). The Europeans did not want the US to give up the option of deploying cruise missiles in Europe because they were a good replacement for the aging bomber fleets which were incapable of penetrating Warsaw Pact air defenses.

It was against this background that Schmidt developed the argument for a qualitative improvement in American nuclear forces in Europe to prove the political will of the Alliance, and to recouple European security to the US, in the event an arms control agreement to deal with the issue of SS-20 missiles was not possible. He presented this idea in his Alastair Buchan Memorial Lecture to the International Institute for Strategic Studies in London on October 28, 1977.[6] In that lecture, Schmidt repeated his fundamental conviction – which he had expressed in his books published in Germany in 1961 and 1969 – that predictability and reliability in East–West relations were essential foundations of security. This emphasis on predictability tended, in the real world of the East–West conflict, to constrain the West while allowing the Soviets to act aggressively in the knowledge that the West would do nothing "unpredictable." Reliability of the system and of the members of the system required balance, and that balance was now being upset by the SS-20s and other new Soviet weapons and deployments. Schmidt believed: "SALT codifies the nuclear strategic balance between the Soviet Union and the United States. To put it another way: SALT neutralizes their strategic nuclear capabilities. In Europe this magnifies the significance of the disparities between East and West in nuclear tactical and conventional weapons." He called for progress in the MBFR (mutual and balanced force reduction) talks that had been going on in Vienna between the US and the Soviet government since 1973: "Today we need to recognize clearly the connection between SALT and MBFR and draw the necessary conclusions. . . . Until we see real progress on MBFR, we shall have to rely on the effectiveness of deterrence," by which he meant deployment of US intermediate-range nuclear forces – cruise missiles or other types – to underscore the US commitment to defend Europe, in Europe, and to demonstrate to the Soviets that an attack on Europe with the SS-20s would immediately involve the US.[7]

The main part of the lecture in London was devoted to general economic and social policies, and included a number of more or less direct reprimands to Washington for not setting its own fiscal and monetary house in order before demanding more defense efforts from the West Europeans, as American representatives had done during

---

[6] Published in *Survival* 20 (1978): 2–10; also in *Helmut Schmidt: Perspectives on Politics*, 23–37.

[7] *Helmut Schmidt: Perspectives on Politics*, 26–7; see also Haftendorn, *Sicherheit und Stabilität*, 20–8, 97–105.

President Carter's visit to London in May to attend the world economic summit and the NATO summit immediately following. Despite what many later asserted, Schmidt did not argue at that time that Western Europe needed new intermediate-range nuclear forces (INF) – weapons with short- or intermediate-range striking ability as opposed to intercontinental missiles. He pointed instead to the gray area at the theater nuclear force level where the Soviets had a monopoly, which could be made permanent, if SALT II were to codify parity at the strategic level of intercontinental forces, without controlling Soviet size and character of theater nuclear forces (that is to say, nuclear weapons located in or targeted on the continent in Europe): "The intermediate-range nuclear rockets constituted a 'gray zone' insofar as they were neither included in the SALT negotiations nor in the MBFR talks, but were rather exempt from any arms control negotiations."[8] This issue was potentially extremely serious and complex, and posed, in Schmidt's view, a problem not fully recognized by the Carter administration:

Already in the first six months of the Carter administration differences of opinion became obvious. ... In the summer of 1977, differences of opinion concerning the answer to the Soviet SS-20 armament added [to the problems]. In September I spent much time trying to make Brzezinski understand the strategic situation of my country and of the divided German people. In that context the political threat to the Federal Republic of Germany by the rapidly growing SS-20 armada of the Soviets played the main role. My efforts did not meet with much success. Brzezinski said that all of this was not really a matter for Bonn, but for the US. If the Federal Republic were ever put under pressure by the Soviet Union with their SS-20s, then the US would be able to counter that threat with their strategic nuclear forces. Carter at first agreed with his security adviser – like Brzezinski, he too had no understanding of my concerns; at least he remained friendly and cordial. Fifteen months later, a very different result came about – although only after a series of considerable additional differences of opinion, and only after I had made my worries plausibly public in a talk to the International Institute for Strategic Studies.

This talk ... has later been described as the real point of origin of the so-called double decision. ... In fact ... I did not pursue the goal of replying to the Soviet armament with a Western counter-armament, but I demanded that the Eurostrategic nuclear weapons as well as conventional forces in Europe be included in the SALT II arms control agreement which both superpowers wanted.

In any event, the talk mainly dealt with the current problems of the world economy. In this connection a range of themes were mentioned on which Bonn and Washington had differing opinions, for instance on energy policy and East–West trade.

---

[8] *Helmut Schmidt: Perspectives on Politics*, 89.

   In Washington the reaction was first surprise, then anger, finally embarrassment. Following that there occurred in the course of 1978 a change of thinking in the White House concerning Soviet Eurostrategic weapons. They realized that what we called the "gray zone" really could not be neglected.[9]

Many Americans read the lecture of October 1977 in London as a demand for INF, even though the secretary of state, Cyrus Vance, stated as the US official position that existing forward-based nuclear weapons were adequate for theater deterrence. The administration had decided, earlier in 1977, to go ahead with production of the enhanced radiation warhead (ERW), publicly known as the neutron bomb. This was a nuclear artillery shell of low explosive yield but with a high, local radiation effect, and thus a convincing deterrent against massed armor or infantry forces, which were precisely the chief conventional threat to Western Europe. The ERW was useless as a counter-city or offensive weapon.

   Although the decision to produce this weapon did not at first cause concern in Europe, left-leaning journalists on both sides of the Atlantic conducted a scare campaign against this "symbol of the perversion of thought," that "kills people but leaves buildings intact."[10] Some questioned the motives behind this campaign since it so obviously served the interests of the Soviet Union in preventing the West from adopting effective and less expensive solutions to the Soviet conventional and theater nuclear threat. Egon Bahr led the campaign against the neutron bomb in West Germany, so that when the US suggested that this might be the answer to Schmidt's proper concern with the gray area, it was politically very difficult for Bonn to say yes. Eventually, however, Schmidt insisted on, and received, the support of his cabinet for agreement to let the US deploy enhanced radiation warheads. A NATO decision to request the ERW was imminent when President Carter, in a gesture almost without parallel in American diplomatic history for its ineptitude, and in response to mounting criticism of the neutron bomb, decided in April 1978 to postpone – in effect, cancel – production of the ERW. The gesture accomplished three things: it destroyed any chance of a relatively simple solution to a large part of the European security problem; it undermined what little faith pro-security West European leaders might still have in American strategic and diplomatic responsibility and sophistication; and it told the left that battles against NATO security plans could be won, and were also worth fighting if only for the divisions and distrust they could

---

[9] Ibid., 230–1.
[10] Egon Bahr, cited in Jäger and Link, *Republik im Wandel, 1974–1982,* 314.

cause within NATO countries. In an interview on April 8, 1978, Franz Josef Strauss, the prospective candidate for chancellor of the CDU/ CSU at the 1980 elections, emphasized these concerns:

Doubts about [US] capacity to lead are not only permitted ... but are unfortunately justified.... I admit that the Europeans have adopted a miserable attitude in the question of introducing the neutron weapon. ... Brandt and Bahr have clearly taken Moscow's position. When the federal government finally pulled itself together enough to approve this weapon, the American president withdrew. In my knowledge of American history since World War II this is the first time an American president has openly and recognizably bowed to a Russian czar.... On the one hand the Americans have decided to stop producing the neutron bomb, on the other they also neglect to insist that the Soviets stop their strategic offensive in Africa.[11]

Public opinion in general still reflected little understanding of these issues. But some leading Western European figures began to wonder if the US was about to decouple its own nuclear-defended security from Western Europe. In order to counter these fears, Carter's defense secretary, Harold Brown, proposed in the summer of 1977 that a working group (known as Working Group 10), which had been set up in NATO under the Nuclear Planning Group (NPG), should be made independent as a "High Level Group" (HLG). The US assistant secretary of defense for international security affairs, David McGiffert, became chairman of the HLG, which was composed of special envoys from each NATO member, and not of NATO bureaucrats already present in Brussels. Brown's original idea was that the HLG would take the nuclear issue out of the general discussion on the long-term improvement program and function as a conduit to and from the national governments, and reassure them that the US was not going to decouple. However, it took on very much a life of its own and, even before the neutron bomb debacle, the HLG had already produced an idea that was eventually adopted, namely, the deployment in Western Europe of a number of new intermediate-range nuclear missiles (INF) to present an effective deterrent to Soviet nuclear power. By February 1978, the HLG had agreed that INF deployment, rather than an increase of the total number of NATO nuclear weapons in Europe, was a desirable and qualitative improvement; that the new INF should be targeted on the Soviet Union to make clear that an isolated attack on Western Europe would be met with retaliation by US weapons on the enemy homeland; that they should be land-based for political effect vis-à-vis the Soviet government; and that they should not be regarded as a counterweight to the SS-20, but as a qualitatively new type of deterrent with its own rationale.

In August 1978, the US administration, in an attempt to show determination and leadership, accepted the HLG recommendations and called for a qualitative improvement of INF. During the following winter, the HLG addressed the question of what the specific weapons should be and recommended a mix of land-based systems: cruise missiles and Pershing II. The total number should be small enough – less than 600 – so that it would be clear (it wasn't, at least not to the opponents of deployment) that these weapons could not, by themselves, be used offensively or in a way that would limit a war to Europe; but that, on the contrary, their very purpose was to recouple the threat of war in Europe to the US strategic deterrent. Finally, the HLG recommended that the decision to deploy be taken at the NATO summit in December 1979. At a meeting on the Caribbean island of Guadelupe in January 1979, the heads of government of the US, Britain, France, and West Germany discussed economic and security policies and agreed that theater nuclear force modernization in Europe was desirable.

The fact that high-ranking civil servants could blithely assume that the small number of weapons would be interpreted by the public as defensive, designed only to show the Soviet government that a theater nuclear attack would involve the US, and that there was no decoupling, tells volumes about the continuing unworldliness of strategic debate as late as 1978, especially after the American experience of Vietnam and the foretaste of developing Europacifist hysteria in the neutron bomb debate of 1977–8. There were evidently still many intelligent people in high places who had not realized that the old world of strategic decision-making was gone forever because West European, and particularly West German, society had changed fundamentally. Any new decision to improve security was going to be contentious in an era of detente, because large parts of the articulate public no longer accepted the logic of security – the logic that there was a threat, that deterrence was possible and necessary, and that the West had something to protect, namely, freedom and peace, that should not be surrendered even at the risk of nuclear war.

Helmut Schmidt, normally a realist, compounded the significance of the unworldly nature of nuclear weapons debate when he insisted, in accordance with his hopes for arms control and the Soviet will to peace, that the decision to deploy be accompanied by an offer to the Soviet government that there would be no deployment if the Soviet government would dismantle its own new theater nuclear forces, primarily, but not exclusively, the SS-20s. Schmidt's proposal was both practical and curious. First, it rested on the assumption that the Soviet Union would give away something for nothing; that is, that it would agree to discuss removal of its own missiles without the West having deployed anything at all. Second, it also ignored the impossibility, in the prevailing political climate of polarization in West Germany between supporters and adversaries of the democratic constitutional state, of carrying out such a diplomatic balancing act. The pressures to negotiate, but never actually to deploy would be, and became, phenomenal. But he must also have viewed this approach as the only realistic way to deal with opposition within his own party, as he sought to muster support for what became the "double track" decision of December 1979. Indeed, he would only remain chancellor as long as his policies received the approval of a large majority of his party.

Schmidt's apparent confusion, or contradictory position, was in part due to domestic politics. At a closed meeting on January 31, 1979, his cabinet agreed that any decision to deploy INF had to be unanimous; that West Germany must not be the only continental country to receive the new missiles; that the decisions to produce and deploy must be taken by the US president; that Bonn would not seek even partial control of any new warheads capable of striking the Soviet Union; and that any deployment decision be accompanied by an offer to negotiate. This meeting took place in an atmosphere of increasing acrimony between government and opposition. Wehner and Bahr, both powerful elder statesmen of the SPD, with an important following among the younger and more leftist members like Eppler or the mayor of Saarbrücken, Oskar Lafontaine, insisted that any Soviet deployments were purely "defensive" (it is unclear what this meant, since no Western European state was capable of attacking the Soviet Union) and that Bonn should use its influence in NATO to promote disarmament and not new Western armaments. Manfred Wörner (CDU), the opposition defense spokesman, warned that the West must first deploy to remain credible and restore the Eurostrategic balance before new arms control talks were in order.[12]

By the end of January Schmidt had succeeded in convincing the opposition leaders to cooperate in trying to lower the emotional level of debate. From then on, the battle was no longer mainly between SPD and CDU/CSU, but within the SPD. The struggle within the SPD over the double track decision of December 1979 was also a struggle over the broad orientation of the party in foreign policy, Ostpolitik, and inner-German relations. A growing current of the SPD no longer supported American proposals and decisions and saw the way to peace and security in more, not fewer, negotiations with the Soviet and Central

[12] Haftendorn, *Sicherheit und Stabilität*, 124–7.

European communist rulers and in a separation of West Germany from what they considered as American militarism and cold war thinking. This rising faction had strong support from Willy Brandt and Herbert Wehner, who together with Schmidt made up the leading *troika* of the party, but also from Egon Bahr. The leaders of this faction were Karsten Voigt, former Juso leader and a Bundestag member since 1972, Gerhard Schröder (not to be confused with his namesake, the former foreign minister of the CDU), Voigt's successor as Juso leader, and Oskar Lafontaine.

The epic battle for control of the foreign and security policy agenda of the SPD, which was also a battle for or against Atlanticism – the belief that West Germany's interests were best served by close alliance with the US – passed through three stages between 1979 and 1987. The first stage lasted from 1979 to late 1981, the second, from early 1982 to the elections of 1987, and the third began in the autumn of 1987. The outcome had momentous consequences for Schmidt and for the future direction of the SPD. In the first stage, Schmidt succeeded, by various means, in quieting opposition to INF deployments and confirming his control of the party. The most important means was to insist, constantly and loudly, that the arms control part of the double track decision was at least as important as the deployment part, while still upholding Bonn's promise to its allies to deploy if negotiations failed.

By such insistence Schmidt managed to persuade the party conference of December 1979 to accept the SPD leadership's binding policy statement of three months earlier. In this statement, the SPD took note of the disparity in intermediate-range nuclear forces and called for its abolition, preferably through negotiations, but if necessary through "defensive options" which would "become effective in the event that arms control efforts fail."[13] So far, he had bought the silence of Brandt and Wehner, and thus deprived the younger revisionists of their support at the top. His good fortune was not to last: as hostility to the Reagan administration and its commitment to strengthening its military forces – denounced as militarism – grew in the SPD in 1981, the revisionists' willingness to support Schmidt declined proportionately. The second stage of the battle for the party was ultimately won by the revisionists and marked the seemingly total defeat of the pro-American, pro-defense, and Atlanticist forces. In 1986–7, there were some slight signs that the Atlanticists were reviving, though what direction the future defense policy of the SPD would take remained highly uncertain.

At their regular meeting in December, 1979, the defense and foreign ministers of NATO took a number of measures resulting from the

---

[13] Ibid., 130.

preparatory work of the HLG and other activities pursuant to the 1978 decision on force modernization. The most important of these was the so-called double track decision to deploy new INF, 572 warheads in all, in West Germany, Britain, and in at least one other continental NATO country, and to propose simultaneously negotiations with the Soviet government on limiting precisely such forces; that is to say, if the Soviet Union would remove its SS-20 missiles, the United States would not deploy its own intermediate-range nuclear missiles. In this decision, the recommendation to deploy was largely due to American initiative, whereas the insistence on negotiations "showed the hallmark of the federal German government."[14] The critical aspect was the timing, because the American missiles would not be available for deployment until 1983. Thus, the negotiation track of the decision would receive immediate priority, since public pressure to negotiate would be enormous.

The decision caused immediate and predictable uproar on the European left. The critics, equally predictably, failed to take note of another decision made at this NATO meeting, namely, to reduce the number of NATO's existing nuclear warheads (primarily tactical missiles and artillery ammunition) by 1,000. Later, in 1983, at their meeting in Montebello near Ottawa, Canada, the NATO ministers decided to remove another 1,400. The decision in 1979 to unilaterally withdraw 1,000 short-range warheads from Western Europe passed virtually without notice in the turmoil of public opposition to the double track decision which, even if the deployment occurred, would only add 572 warheads, a far smaller number. Moreover, the withdrawals were an example of unilateral disarmament – no Soviet quid pro quo was expected or required, or taken.

Two weeks after the NATO governments took the double track decision, the Soviet Union invaded Afghanistan. The US reacted with an embargo and with statements that the Persian Gulf was now directly threatened by the Soviet Union, and that the US would defend it with arms if necessary. In West Germany the events resulted in a dramatic conflict of foreign policy views, which, along with the double track decision, led to the rise of a peace movement, directed primarily against US and NATO policies, and to a split in the SPD between Atlanticists and neutralists. The former were those who still saw the Soviet Union as a threat, and for whom the strengthening of Western defenses was most important. The neutralists were those who believed that the Ostpolitik treaties of the 1970s and including Berlin, SALT I and CSCE, had stabilized relations in Europe, and that whatever the Soviets

[14] Ibid., 124.

did elsewhere should not be allowed to disturb European detente. They believed it was possible to maintain relations between the Soviet Union and Western Europe without danger to themselves, and that the Soviet leaders would regard their position not as weakness, but as strength. They denied that Soviet activity outside Europe was a part of a global Soviet strategy.

Clearly, the factors influencing West German foreign policy were changing once again. The US belief in and commitment to detente, which had prevailed at least since 1963, was disappearing. The changes of the 1970s had meant that, whereas earlier it was the US that had taken the lead in detente, it was now the West Germans who were most reluctant to abandon the belief that detente was the right way to assure security and peace in Europe. The peace movement was only the most extreme manifestation of a more general confusion between hope and reality in West German politics.

Following the Afghanistan invasion, Carter withdrew the SALT II treaty from consideration by the US Senate. Shortly thereafter he declared that the US would not participate in the Summer Olympics to be held in Moscow. Schmidt suppressed his misgivings about the ultimate wisdom of this decision and issued a similar recommendation to the West German Olympic team. These developments were, in some ways, dominated by another event that plagued Carter's final year as president of the United States in a tragic way. In November 1979 the American embassy in Iran had been occupied by Iranians, and in April of 1980 an American attempt to rescue the American hostages ended in catastrophic failure, as well as in great embarrassment to the Carter administration. As a consequence the United States government did not look with pleasure at the prospect of embarking on the negotiating track of the double track decision. While this was, from an American point of view, a very understandable attitude, Schmidt became anxious about the American commitment to pursue both tracks of the double track decision, and to initiate negotiations with the Soviet government.

In May and June 1980 the US-German relationship reached a low point, due largely to mutual misunderstandings: Schmidt's hopelessly poor relationship with Carter, and what Schmidt regarded as Brzezinski's anti-German machinations. In mid-June Schmidt received a letter from Carter, which the White House leaked to the press. In it, the president claimed that, according to press reports, Schmidt had proposed a freeze on deployments of INF by either side. The US, Carter went on, would under no circumstances agree to a freeze, but was prepared to explore the possibilities of limiting INF deployment by both countries. Schmidt, understandably, was annoyed; he knew that the White House had copies of all his public statements and did not have to rely on "press reports" to find out what he thought. He assumed that the true author of the letter was Brzezinski, "who never had been able to decide whether the Germans or the Russians were the main enemy of the Polish people, to which he himself belonged."[15] He was angry that the letter emphasized INF deployments and not the offer to negotiate which was one half – the Schmidt-inspired half – of the double track decision. The result was that Schmidt became even more determined to make an all-out effort on his trip to Moscow in July to persuade the Soviet government to agree to stop their own deployments. Given his view of the Soviets, he had some reason to hope he might succeed; had he done so, he would have been hailed as the statesman of the decade.

Before going to Moscow, he met Carter at the economic summit in Venice in late June. In a conversation with Carter, Schmidt stated:

That your letter has influenced the German-American partnership is regrettable. . . . Perhaps I may remind you that you pressured me to reflate the German economy by 1 per cent of our gross national product. I pointed out at the time [1979] that this could lead to a German balance of payments deficit; that has in fact happened. But since I gave you my word, I have also kept it. No reasonable purpose is served by insulting an ally who keeps his promises. . . .

I have experienced discussions between the US and my country for decades; for example on the Radford Plan, for example on the MLF, that President Johnson later dropped. . . . But since the Alliance decisions on INF there have been no differences of opinion between us on the issue . . . these weapons should be deployed on European soil . . . and we agreed that you would negotiate with the Soviet Union on mutual limitation of INF. . . . In the ideal case, then, a zero solution is conceivable, requiring no deployment. . . .

Now it's clear that you cannot deploy at all *before* the fall of 1983. On this basis I have proposed that both sides, knowing this fact, should refrain from deploying more INF for the next three years. [Schmidt was proposing, in effect, a moratorium.][16]

Schmidt went on to point out that since NATO could not deploy until 1983, the delay would affect only the Soviets, who would in fact be asked to undertake a unilateral moratorium. "Now however I am in doubt whether the American side wants to negotiate with the Soviets at all!" Schmidt concluded. Later in the discussion he obtained Carter's and Brzezinski's agreement to a set of basic principles he could use in presenting the Western position in Moscow: "We will confirm: the Soviets have no opportunity to drive a wedge between us Germans and our Allies. . . . The Soviets must understand that the Federal Republic . . . holds fast to its principle that an equilibrium is necessary in Europe

[15] Schmidt, *Menschen und Mächte*, 254.
[16] Ibid., 257–8.

and the world, and is, indeed, a precondition of any cooperation with the Soviet Union. . . . The Soviets must understand that we, therefore, will comply with the INF alliance decision." Schmidt's final verdict on the Venice summit was "ambiguous." On the one hand "Carter and Brzezinski had backed down." On the other, "the American president had no intention of actively promoting the second part of the double decision. . . . Carter clearly only thought of demonstrating toughness vis-à-vis the Russians because of the election. . . . He was deceiving himself; for he was not prepared to actually put effective pressure on the Soviet government over Afghanistan."[17]

In Moscow in July Schmidt discussed trade and economic relations, notably the execution of the 1978 agreement for trade and scientific exchanges which was to run for 25 years, until 2003, but mentioned INF in an after-dinner speech in the Kremlin. "I blamed the Soviets for the Afghanistan crisis and insisted on the complete withdrawal of Soviet forces. I also blamed the Soviet Union for the situation that had made NATO's double decision of December 1979 necessary, and appealed to my Soviet hosts to agree to begin negotiations without preconditions. At the end, naturally, I spoke of the German desire for peace, of the horrors of the last war, and of our desire for cooperation with the Soviet Union." The next day the Soviets appeared to accept Schmidt's proposal: "The Soviet leaders declared themselves ready to negotiate bilaterally with the Americans on the limitation of intermediate-range nuclear forces . . . without waiting for the ratification of SALT II and before starting SALT III."[18] Schmidt left Moscow in a mood of optimism, but soon became dismayed when the US did not, or could not respond before the presidential election in November.

[17] Ibid., 261, 263.
[18] Ibid., 116, 118.

5

Ostpolitik

Schmidt expressed his faith not only in the possibility of improving stability and securing peace through cooperation with the Soviet Union, in the areas of detente, arms control, and modernization of Western defense, but also in his conduct of relations with the Soviet Union and the communist regimes of Central Europe; in other words, in his Ostpolitik. During Schmidt's tenure and in the first years after his retirement, many critics argued that Schmidt had toned down Brandt's high expectations for a "European peace order," that would flow inevitably from Bonn's opening to the East and acceptance of the Soviet-dominated status quo. There were differences of style and accent. Schmidt did follow the direction Brandt and Bahr had chosen, but with fewer ambitious statements and high-sounding goals.

In his Ostpolitik, Schmidt continued Brandt's effort to establish cordial relations with the Soviet leader, Leonid Brezhnev, and with the SED chief of the GDR, Erich Honecker. Brezhnev went to Bonn twice during Schmidt's tenure, in 1978 and 1981, and Schmidt visited Brezhnev in Moscow during 1974 and 1980. The first meeting, in 1974, followed Brezhnev's successful visit to Bonn in 1973 and bore the heavy imprint of detente or, rather, of Schmidt's and Genscher's faith in it. The second meeting, in 1978, already showed signs that detente was at risk. Schmidt pointed out that the Soviet deployment of SS-20s was incompatible with equilibrium. He succeeded in persuading Brezhnev to endorse a joint declaration stating that both governments "perceive . . . no reasonable alternative to peaceful cooperation between States in spite of differences in several of their basic positions." The declaration endorsed the CSCE Final Act and the ongoing CSCE process. Further, they agreed that "no one should seek military superiority" and that "approximate equality and parity suffice to safeguard defence."[1] By the

---

[1] Dept of State, *Documents on Germany*, 1311–2.

next year, however, it was clear that the Soviet Union was not slowing down its buildup of theater nuclear and conventional forces, but accelerating it. According to an observer close to the SPD, Helga Haftendorn, Schmidt supported the double track decision in part as a signal to the Soviet Union that the West would not tolerate the Soviet INF buildup without taking countermeasures.

Apparently, so Haftendorn suggested, Schmidt naively believed the Soviet government was simply unaware that its buildup was incompatible with detente and had no intention of using this power to weaken the West. At his final meeting with the aging Brezhnev, in Bonn in November 1981, Schmidt "did not succeed in convincing the Soviet leader that the introduction of SS-20s had, in the Western view, tilted the balance of forces in Europe."[2] But there was also another interpretation of Soviet policy vis-à-vis West Germany during 1974–82. It was that the Soviet leaders knew very well what they were accomplishing with the SS-20s and their conventional and chemical arms; namely, building up a tremendously powerful military machine that would, by its mere presence, bring about Soviet geostrategic dominance over Western Europe and prevent the West Europeans from ever undertaking any policy hostile to Soviet interests. Schmidt, so the supporters of this argument held, never recognized the nature and purposes of Soviet policies during his tenure.

Schmidt supported the concept of Brandt's and Bahr's Ostpolitik toward the regimes of Central Europe and the GDR as well. Schmidt was particularly concerned with the political fortunes of Edward Gierek, the first secretary of the Polish communist party, and effectively the head of the Polish government, whom he called "a reliable partner."[3] Gierek received 2.3 billion marks in credit and economic aid in 1975, in return for the Polish government's agreement to allow 125,000 Germans to emigrate to West Germany.[4] Schmidt and the SPD right wing argued that aid for the Central European communist regimes would make the regimes more secure, consequently less inclined to repression and unrestrained violence against their own people, and therefore, eventually, more liberal and less authoritarian. Insofar as the SPD left had any clearly defined Ostpolitik at the time, it was a policy of accommodation and appeasement in the belief that this would speed up the decline of control by "both superpowers" in both halves of Europe; the implication was that American presence in Western Europe was morally and strategically equivalent to Soviet domination of the East.

[2] Haftendorn, *Sicherheit und Stabilität*, 152.
[3] *Die Zeit*, May 15, 1987.
[4] Lehmann, *Öffnung nach Osten*, 189.

In the mid-1970s the general attitude in West Germany on foreign affairs was that the treaties with the East concluded between 1970 and 1974 had brought the Federal Republic forward from the dead end of the Hallstein Doctrine and had opened the way to a more flexible relationship with the GDR, Eastern Europe, and the Soviet Union, and positive aspects did develop. At the same time these treaties by no means expressed the legal and moral acceptance of the status quo in Europe, although that was precisely how the Soviet Union saw them. In the Soviet view the Federal Republic was the last major Western country to recognize Soviet hegemony in Eastern Europe and the de facto existence of two German states. The Eastern treaties were, in effect, understood in the Soviet Union as peace treaties, accepting and guaranteeing the status quo.

In May 1974 the first permanent representatives of the two states started their work in Bonn and in East Berlin. The West German representative was Günter Gaus, who remained in East Berlin until 1981, and the East German representative was Michael Kohl, who had been the negotiating partner of Egon Bahr in 1971–2. The number of trips made from West Germany to the GDR grew from 1.1 million in 1969 to 1.5 million in 1972, and then to 2.3 million in 1973. In addition, as the transit agreement included provisions for day trips by residents of West Berlin to East Berlin and adjacent areas of the GDR, West Berlin residents made use of this possibility on 3.8 million occasions during 1973. One recurring problem affecting visits to East Berlin and the GDR was the GDR's requirement that visitors exchange a certain amount of currency at official rates. This was particularly burdensome for West Germans and visitors from West Berlin, who were required to exchange one West German mark for one East German mark, even though the East German mark had an actual value of anywhere from 2 to 14 to one West German mark on the black market. On semi-official currency exchanges in West Berlin the West German mark had a value of approximately 1 to 2.4 in 1957 and by 1987 had moved up to 1 to 14 vis-à-vis the East German mark.[5] However, the general trend showed that the supply of East German marks much exceeded their demand. Those GDR citizens who happen to be in possession of large amounts of East German marks much preferred to travel from East to West Berlin prior to 1961 in order to exchange thousands of East German marks against precious West German marks, even though this exchange was always officially illegal. In the winter of 1973 the East German government doubled the minimum currency amount each West German visitor to the GDR was required to exchange, from DM 10 to DM 20

---

[5] *Die Zeit*, February 6, 1987.

(and from DM 5 to DM 10 for day visitors to East Berlin and adjacent areas), which resulted in a decrease in the number of visitors. It rose again in 1975 to 3.1 million (plus 3.2 million visitors from West Berlin), after the GDR reduced the obligatory amount to be exchanged.

In the other direction, in 1975, 1.3 million Germans from the GDR visited the West. Almost all were old-age pensioners. Only 40,400 persons of other categories received permission to go to West Germany, and then only for family emergencies. This latter figure did not change much during the following years. However, the total number of trips made by West Germans and residents of West Berlin crossing into the GDR in 1976 had reached 6.3 million and remained at that level until 1980. In October 1980, the GDR announced stringent new currency exchange regulations, just days before Erich Honecker, the head of state of the GDR and general secretary of the SED, delivered a speech in the GDR calling for improved neighborly relations with West Germany. The compulsory minimum amount to be exchanged was again doubled, this time from DM 13 to DM 25 (and from DM 6.50 to DM 25 for day visitors). Senior citizens and children, who had so far been exempt, now also had to exchange currency: senior citizens, DM 25, children, DM 7.50. The total number of trips made decreased rapidly and by 1983 was down to a total of 3.7 million.[6]

Another result of the Basic Treaty was the "swing," which had started in 1968 during the grand coalition and which was renegotiated in 1974. Its purpose was to create an interest-free line of credit available for use by the GDR in West Germany. Over the five-year period 1975 to 1980 the amount available was 850 million marks, described as *Verrechnungseinheiten* (accounting units), solely for the purpose of intra-German trade, so as to avoid giving the East and West German marks equal value for other purposes. The "swing" was again renegotiated in 1982 at reduced levels, at the same time that the West German government began to seriously consider, and finally implement, direct credit lines to the GDR.

Economic assistance to the GDR had little impact on the stringency with which the GDR guarded its borders against those who sought to escape. Between 1961 and 1988 East German border guards killed over 175 persons trying to escape, at least nine of them after the GDR government signed the Basic Treaty. As pointed out by Egon Franke, the minister for inner-German relations in Schmidt's government, the violence on the frontier was a factor that belied the claims of the GDR

---

[6] Bundesministerium für innerdeutsche Beziehungen, *DDR Handbuch*, 202–3; Bender, *Neue Ostpolitik*, 279.

that it desired a policy of good neighborly relations. In the same period from 1961 to 1988, about 200,000 persons successfully escaped from the GDR.

The insurmountable problem adversely affecting a more "flexible relationship" was that the GDR, from the moment the prospect of a de facto recognition by West Germany seemed within reach, intensified its policy of "delimitation" (*Abgrenzung*), which means "isolating" or "fencing off" the GDR from West German influence, that is to say, from democratic ideas. The more West Germany tried to normalize relations and expand contact, the more the East German regime responded by insisting on the enormous difference between the Federal Republic and the GDR and stressing the existence of two completely sovereign and independent states. The official position was that the Federal Republic, as part of the imperialist Western camp, was trying to subvert the GDR which, therefore, had to maintain particular vigilance and protection of its own interests. Dissidents were harshly punished. In 1975 there were 6,500 political prisoners in the GDR out of a population of 16.7 million, and any attempt at disloyal or unorthodox behavior was met with severe sanctions, such as the loss of jobs or student status, and other measures designed to reduce objections, including imprisonment.

The obvious refusal of the GDR regime to support greater liberalization and a more relaxed attitude toward its own citizens and toward West Germany led to new controversy in the Federal Republic over Ostpolitik. The opposition charged that the GDR policy of *Abgrenzung* was evidence that the SPD had seriously misjudged the character and intentions of the GDR. Wolfgang Seiffert, a professor of law in Potsdam who worked closely with the East German regime and who defected to the West in 1978, later supported this argument when he wrote:

Whoever has lived and worked under this regime [the GDR] is shocked to see the carelessness, naivete, insecurity, and the lack of self-confidence with which the political elite of the Federal Republic encounters the elite of the GDR.
This impression corresponds with the impression that leading SED representatives have gained as far as their Western negotiating partners are concerned. . . .
Indeed, the Social Democrats of that era could not deal with the difficult and problematic nature of ideological conflict and the simultaneous need for dialogue at the highest level with the government of the GDR, when their leading representatives proceeded from the premise that only an approach that "recognized the other as equal" would lead to political success. This political trivialization confuses the necessary legal equality, namely the recognition of

facts, with the recognition of communist dictatorship and its inherent suppression of self-determination of the people.[7]

Despite the on-again, off-again nature of relations with the GDR,
Schmidt's government generally considered them to be satisfactory and
progressing favorably. During the 1970s, Bonn and East Berlin followed
up the major treaties of 1971–2 with various subsidiary agreements. In
1974, each of the two states undertook to provide free medical and
hospital treatment for visitors from the other. In 1976, they concluded a
separate postal and telephone agreement. Between 1973 and 1977 a
special border commission met to adjust the demarcation line at points
where it was contested. The two sides could not agree on where the
border should be along the Elbe river. The GDR, which regarded the
demarcation line as a border in the full international legal sense, insisted
that it ran in the middle of the river, since that is the usual practice with
river frontiers between sovereign states. The West German government
regarded the demarcation line as simply the border between two *Länder*
of Germany, and maintained that the border by the Elbe ran along the
east side of the river, as it was defined when the Allies occupied
Germany after the war. In 1978, the two states agreed on the exact
demarcation of the inner-German border with the exception of about 60
miles along the Elbe river in the north.

In 1974, 1978, and again in 1983, both governments signed agreements concerning non-commercial payments, such as inheritances. In
1975, 1978, and 1980 they followed up the 1972 treaty on traffic
questions with agreements on land and water transport. In the 1978
accord, they agreed to improve the highways and canals carrying traffic
between West Berlin and West Germany, subject to four-power
approval. In addition to the annual transit fees that Bonn paid to the
GDR under the 1972 treaty, and which by 1980 were about 500 million
marks a year, the Federal Republic promised to finance a new autobahn
on East German territory running from West Berlin in the direction of
Hamburg to the East–West German border, but which would be built
and maintained by the East German government. Maintenance costs,
however, for the new autobahn as well as for existing transit autobahns
were to be assumed by West Germany.

There were three existing transit autobahns: one running west from
Berlin to Helmstedt on the border with Lower Saxony, carrying traffic
for the Hannover area, the Ruhr district, and points further west, and
another, part of the prewar "Müleiberl" (Munich–Leipzig–Berlin) link,
carrying traffic for Nuremberg, Stuttgart, Munich and points south

---

[7] Seiffert, *Das ganze Deutschland*, 94–5.

across the Bavarian border with the GDR at Rudolphstein. At Herms-
dorf near Jena, the latter crossed a third prewar autobahn running east
to west, and this highway entered West Germany (Hesse) at Herles-
hausen, carrying traffic for the Frankfurt area.

The agreements – and financial support – were made with the GDR
as part of an Ostpolitik aimed at maintaining national identity despite
political division. Few commented on the official policy of the GDR, the
denial of any national identity with West Germany. In 1974, the GDR
regime issued a revision of the constitution which removed the word
"German" from clause 1, which had read: "The German Democratic
Republic is a socialist state of the German nation." It now read: "The
German Democratic Republic is a socialist state of workers and
farmers." Also stricken from the text, for the same reason, was a passage
of the preamble that alluded to "the historical fact that imperialism, led
by the USA in collusion with monopoly capitalist circles in West
Germany, has divided Germany . . . which contradicts the vital interests
of the nation."[8] The West German government responded to this
change by declaring: "A nation, like the German nation, cannot be either
created or eliminated merely by the stroke of the lawmaker's pen. The
German nation . . . has a right to national self-determination. . . . The
Federal Government reconfirms the political goal of the Federal
Republic of Germany to work towards a state of peace in Europe in
which the German people will regain its unity through free self-
determination."[9]

From 1974 until the beginning of the 1980s, the GDR responded to
Bonn's attempts to obtain more frequent personal contact and easier
permission for East Germans to visit the West with increased efforts to
fortify the border and assure instant and horrible death in the minefields
for anyone attempting to escape from the East, and with rhetorical
insistence that the German nation was a thing of the past. Nevertheless,
the name of the East German communist party remained "Socialist
Unity Party of Germany," the party news organ was still called *Neues
Deutschland* (New Germany), the state railroad was still called the *Deutsche
Reichsbahn* (a real curiosity, that), and, somewhat to East Berlin's
annoyance, the official designation of the 600,000 or so Soviet troops in
the GDR remained the "Group of Soviet Forces in Germany" (GSFG).
And all East Berlin license plates still carried the letter "I," which was the
old letter, standing for Berlin, that had been used before 1945.

In December 1976, Schmidt reported on the state of intra-German
relations to the Bundestag. He listed the many areas of improvement in

[8] Hildebrandt, ed., *Die deutschen Verfassungen*, 234–5.
[9] Dept of State, *Documents on Germany*, 1276.

personal contacts, travel and visits, exchanges of information about property questions, and better telecommunications. "The Federal Government notes with satisfaction ... that intra-German trade has more than doubled since 1969;" the volume of trade in 1976 was about eight billion marks. He also pointed out that the Quadripartite Agreement on Berlin seemed to be working well and promised continuing federal support for the economy and culture of the old capital. And he stressed that his government had "no illusions" about the GDR. "The GDR leadership pursues as its long-term goal the replacement, the defeat of our political system. We know this – and we can stomach these ideas of the Socialist Unity Party. On the other hand, the GDR leadership will have to stomach the fact that we remain committed to the unity of the nation." [10]

In May 1977 the three Western powers and West Germany issued a joint declaration on Berlin, their first on this subject. Expressing satisfaction with the "positive effect" of the Quadripartite Agreement, they reaffirmed that the Soviet Union and the GDR could not unilaterally change the status of Berlin. They went on to affirm "that the ties between the Western Sectors of Berlin and the FRG should be maintained and developed."[11]

In October of 1980, Erich Honecker announced in a speech in Gera (a city of approximately 120,000 citizens, located in Thuringia, the south-western part of the GDR, not far from Erfurt) his conditions for continued good neighborly relations with the Bonn government. He demanded that Bonn recognize the sovereignty and citizenship of the GDR – although Bonn had hitherto refused to recognize more than one German nationality. Further, the two permanent missions in East Berlin and Bonn should be turned into proper embassies, with an exchange of ambassadors, as was customary between independent sovereign states. Third, Bonn also must accept the middle of the Elbe river as the border, according to international law concerning river boundaries. Finally, he demanded that Bonn dissolve the monitoring office in Salzgitter which recorded violations of West German law by GDR officials, usually border guards.[12] These were old demands, but Honecker repeated them with emphasis and seemed to be making their fulfilment a precondition of progress in relations with Bonn.

The SPD-led government, in particular its representative in East Berlin, Günter Gaus, had no desire to emphasize the national issue. This very reticence on Bonn's part, however, may have encouraged

---

[10] Ibid., 1304–6.
[11] Ibid., 1309.
[12] *Neues Deutschland*, October 14, 1980.

Honecker to revive the national issue, this time in the form of the argument that the GDR represented the true, progressive German nation, a higher stage of socialist nationhood to which West Germany must still aspire. In a much-quoted passage reported on the front page of *Neues Deutschland*, Honecker said at a party conference in 1981: "When ... the workers take in hand the socialist transformation of the Federal Republic of Germany, then the question of unification of both German states will have to be asked completely anew! There should certainly be no doubt in anyone's mind as to how we shall decide at that point." According to the paper, the remark was greeted with "prolonged applause."[13]

The new self-confidence of the GDR regime in relation to the national issue was displayed in this same period – 1980 and thereafter – in approaches to matters of national German history.[14] In 1981, the East German Academy of Sciences, which, like all public institutions in communist states, was an arm of the regime, issued an intriguing statement: "The GDR is deeply rooted in all of German history. As the socialist German state, it is the result of centuries of struggle by all the progressive forces of the German people for social progress. Everything progressive and all who have contributed to it are indispensable parts of the traditions that shape the national identity of the GDR."[15]

The 1980s provided a number of occasions for the GDR to display its new-found concern for German historical traditions. One was the centennial of the death of Karl Marx in 1983. Perhaps surprisingly, the Marx centennial was overshadowed by the five-hundredth anniversary of the birth of the religious reformer, Martin Luther, in the same year. The GDR used the occasion for an intense ideological offensive to win recognition and respect from scholarly and political-intellectual circles in the West. The *Frankfurter Allgemeine Zeitung* warned in that connection: "The regime of the GDR has, as its main goal, the elimination of the special nature of inter-German relations. When not only church officials, but also those holding state office – even the highest representatives of the constitution – go to the GDR in order to demonstrate that the Reformation included all of Germany, then the schemers of the atheist state will turn this intent upside down and use the Luther Year further to destroy any German sense of community."[16]

---

[13] Cited in Seiffert, *Das ganze Deutschland*, 105. See also Weber, *Geschichte der DDR*, 459.

[14] See various articles by Ron Asmus, e.g. "The GDR and Martin Luther," *Survey* 122 (Autumn 1984), 124–56; also Seiffert, *Das ganze Deutschland*, esp. 93–114.

[15] Cited in Asmus, ibid., 132.

[16] Cited ibid., 141.

The warning, issued by one of West Germany's most respected news-papers, drew attention to a real peril inherent in West German policy vis-à-vis the GDR. The East German government recognized in the position of the Bonn government an opportunity to assume the mantle of the defender of national unity. Thus Honecker created a reverse claim for sole representation (*Alleinvertretungsanspruch*) for the GDR, which he viewed as the heir to all that was good in German history. This struggle over symbolism and memory was an aspect of the ideological battle in Europe largely unrecognized in the United States or indeed, anywhere outside Germany. And it was not always given the attention it deserved within West Germany.

Schmidt's German policy reached its apogee – or nadir – when he visited Honecker for talks at the Werbellinsee in Mecklenburg from December 11 to 13, 1981. Three weeks before, in Bonn, Schmidt had assured Brezhnev of West Germany's commitment to peace, still in the belief that such assurances were useful. The two German heads of government stated that relations between the two German states must not, in themselves, give rise to tensions in the East–West relationship. The meeting took place in an atmosphere of tensions which the GDR did much to exploit. Among the elements of tension were statements by President Reagan in November concerning a hypothetical nuclear confrontation in Europe, which many Western Europeans of the left and the right, as well as Americans, chose to interpret as expressing an American policy of confining an eventual nuclear war to Europe.

Another element was Poland, where the Solidarity workers' move-ment rose to prominence in August 1980 and wrung the right to exist and organize from the communist regime. In March 1981 Solidarity's leaders found themselves pressured by activists in the movement to take a stand which, in effect, amounted to a demand that the Polish com-munist party surrender its power and that Poland become a constitu-tional democracy. This demand, reasonable and even modest on the face of it in a democratic society of Western Europe, was incompatible with the realities of power in Central Europe, and by making it, Solidarity contributed to its temporary demise (until 1988). The demise followed the regime's declaration of martial law in Poland on December 13, 1981, an action ordered, but not carried out, some months before-hand by the Soviet Union.[17] In West Germany the position taken by Schmidt's government, "political condemnation of the military regime but continuation of limited economic cooperation – brought the Federal Republic into contradiction with the hard line of Washington policy, yet

[17] See Ash, *The Polish Revolution*.

was unable to revive detente policy."[18] The result was justified doubt about Bonn's sense of proportion and agreement with Western principles in Washington. In Germany Bonn's response did not satisfy the West German left, which was already intent on undermining Schmidt's political basis of support.

[18] Haftendorn, *Security and Detente,* 251.

6

The End of Detente

Quite independent of any actions by Schmidt, the detente of the early 1970s, which culminated in the visit of President Nixon to Moscow in June 1972 to sign the SALT I treaty and the Berlin Accords, died during 1979–80. Its death had several causes. One was the relentless ideological offensive against the West which the Soviet Union maintained throughout the 1970s, despite or perhaps because of the CSCE process (the Helsinki Conference and Final Act of 1975 and the follow-up conferences at Belgrade and Madrid in 1977–8 and 1980–1983). As Soviet bloc spokesmen never tired of repeating, detente ("relaxation of tensions") in no way meant or implied the relaxation of ideological or class warfare against the "class enemy." Soviet ideology still did not and could not admit the right to exist of independent, democratic, constitutional states such as West Germany or its allies. The principle of ideological warfare meant that the Eastern regimes could never really permit national self-determination, an opening of their borders, or genuine domestic democratization – ideas which, in the Western view, were at the very heart of true detente. Thus detente, as many in the West understood it, was never realistic or possible.

These considerations were indirect causes. The direct causes were the Soviet invasion of Afghanistan in December 1979 and the subsequent genocidal warfare waged with utter ruthlessness by the Soviet and Afghan communist forces against the national resistance movement, and the US reactions to this invasion. President Carter said in early January 1980 that he had learned more in the past week about the Soviet Union than in his entire previous career. This statement merely confirmed Schmidt, Giscard, and others in their belief that Carter was an amateur on the international scene. Schmidt later wrote that Giscard and he "were no less outraged at the rape of Afghanistan than the Americans in Washington ... but we thought little of Carter's notion of 'punishing' the Soviets, a notion with no recognizable strategic concept behind it."[1]

Carter and his secretary of defense, Harold Brown, had been doing what was politically feasible to increase US defense spending and restore morale in the US armed forces for two years already; but in fact, due largely to Carter's own policies, little had been accomplished. In the new American public climate of suspicion of the Soviet Union following the invasion of Afghanistan, however, attitudes began to change. Soviet policy did not help Carter win re-election, largely because of his perceived failings in economic policy – US inflation in 1980 reached 18 per cent and the dollar exchange rate went down to a low of DM 1.7 – and because of his failure to deal effectively with Iran for its acts of war against US diplomats.

One beneficiary of these problems was the Republican presidential candidate, Ronald Reagan, who won an overwhelming victory in November 1980, based primarily on domestic policy considerations, but also influenced by America's declining prestige abroad and increased Soviet military power. During the campaign, Reagan and his advisers had stated clearly that, in their view, detente had primarily benefited the Soviet Union and that it was not in the American or Western interest to continue it on present terms. In particular, the SALT II treaty, signed by President Carter in 1979, should not be ratified by the US Senate, since it codified US inferiority in strategic nuclear weapons. These positions alarmed many West Germans greatly. They considered that "detente was divisible," that even though the Soviets might be aggressive in Afghanistan or elsewhere, in Europe only one policy was viable, namely one of conciliation and appeasement. Some of them, such as the social democratic political journalist Peter Bender, spoke of the collapse of detente as being caused equally by the Soviet Union and the US, which he described as "two neurotic giants," fixed on weaponry and military competition.[2] In May 1981 Schmidt visited Washington, where he and President Reagan declared that they regarded "arms control and disarmament, along with deterrence and defense," as an "integral part of Alliance policy."[3] Willy Brandt travelled to Moscow in the summer of the same year and discussed Soviet proposals to freeze deployment of nuclear weapons in Central Europe.

Brezhnev, the first Soviet leader to visit West Germany, came to Bonn for the third time in November 1981. At this point he was already quite ill and was unable to take a forceful lead in the talks, which were there-

[1] *Die Zeit*, May 15, 1987.
[2] See Bender, "Zwei neurotische Riesen." *Merkur* 34 (1980): 529–41.
[3] *Relay from Bonn*, May 29, 1981.

fore conducted mainly by his aides. Following Brezhnev's visit to Bonn, the West German government press spokesman referred to West Germany as an "interpreter" of each superpower to the other, the closest any official of the Bonn government came, at that time, to taking an overtly third party or neutralist position as mediator.[4] Schmidt viewed his position as that of an "honest interpreter of *Western* policy" (emphasis added). He described himself to a gathering of West German newspaper publishers on November 10, 1981, as "a firm believer in military balance . . . a balance of mutual deterrence. This balance at the lowest possible level and – as regards medium-range weapons – preferably at zero level, along with economic, political and cultural cooperation between East and West, secures peace."[5]

The Soviets were playing to West German public opinion in an attempt to appear peaceable and non-threatening and to turn the Germans against the double track decision. The final communique of the visit declared the economic relationship to be satisfactory and called for progress in arms control. As on the first occasion, in May 1973, Brezhnev's immediate purpose was to confirm existing bilateral trade agreements and conclude new ones.

On November 20, 1981, the Soviets signed a fourth agreement on steel pipe deliveries (following the agreements of 1970, 1972, and 1974) with German steel producers and banks. This time both governments agreed that the Soviet Union, in 1984–5, would begin delivering 40 billion cubic meters of natural gas annually to seven European countries over a period of 25 years, and that it would connect West Berlin to the gas pipeline and supply 700 million cubic meters a year to that city. The Soviets undertook to supply the gas to the Czech-GDR border, but the two German governments were responsible for planning and constructing the pipeline across the GDR. To build the 3,000–mile pipeline from the Siberian fields to the GDR border the Soviet Union needed six million tons of large-diameter steel pipes from Western Europe, of which the West Germans were to supply half. The West Europeans also undertook, in separate agreements, to build the pumping stations and all other necessary installations. The Soviet government would pay for the entire project in gas, calculated at 1981 prices, estimated to cost the West European suppliers about 20 billion marks. The price, moreover, was fixed. By 1986 the world price had fallen by more than 50 per cent, much to Soviet benefit.[6]

The Americans raised several objections to this project, economic,

---

[4] Haftendorn, *Sicherheit und Stabilität*, 142, 150.
[5] *Relay from Bonn*, November 13, 1981.
[6] "The Soviet Pipeline Lesson," *Wall Street Journal*, June 6, 1986.

strategic, and moral. At the world economic summit in Ottawa in July 1981 Reagan expressed concern to Schmidt about the implications of the proposed pipeline deal, which was already well known. The Americans considered it dangerous to provide the Soviet Union high technology on terms which would never be given in the open market. In general, his new administration believed economic agreements with the Soviet government should follow normal business principles; there should be no special deals for political reasons. In particular, the West, in 1981, should not appear weak or anxious for agreements, but should present a strong and united front in the face of Soviet violations of the principles of detente in Afghanistan, Africa, Central Europe, and elsewhere. The US government was also worried that the Soviet Union would gain military advantages it would not otherwise have gained so easily, from some, if not all, of the products to be delivered under the agreement.

Specifically, the electronic equipment in the remote-controlled pumping stations might be turned to uses that would fill significant gaps in Soviet military technology. The Soviets, moreover, had shown themselves in the past capable of deriving military advantage from almost any advanced technology they could obtain from the West. In addition, the West European governments were all increasing their natural gas consumption in order to reduce oil imports, but by promising to take such a large amount of natural gas the West Europeans were making themselves hostage to Soviet demands for political concessions. The International Society for Human Rights in Frankfurt and other Western groups reported that the Soviet government was using forced labor, including political prisoners from the concentration camp system, in the Siberian gas fields and in the construction that was already taking place under the earlier agreements. According to reports, these forced laborers were living and working under conditions that were likely to kill many of them. The human rights groups pointed out that by giving the Soviet Union the means to increase gas production and by promising to receive the gas, the West European countries were aiding and abetting the Soviet forced labor and prison camp system.

Only three weeks after Schmidt and Brezhnev signed the pipeline agreement, the Polish communist regime imposed martial law and suppressed the Solidarity workers' movement. On December 29, in retaliation against the Soviet Union, as the real power behind the actions in Poland, President Reagan declared economic sanctions against the USSR. The sanctions included stopping the supply of certain oil and gas drilling equipment, which US firms were to provide as part of the pipeline agreement. The US was not a partner in the agreement, since it had been concluded solely between the Soviet Union and seven West European countries, but there was some equipment that was only produced in the US, and American firms had undertaken to supply it.

Schmidt had first met Reagan in Washington in May 1981 and gained a very positive impression. "At the end of our discussions . . . I was relieved and thought that after four years of uncertainty I was now again dealing with a steady and therefore predictable American president. Reagan had the firm intent to consult intensively with his allies and to avoid surprises."[7] In January 1982, one month after the Polish regime introduced martial law, Schmidt stopped in Washington on his way home from Christmas vacation in Florida. The US administration had gained the impression that the Europeans were "soft" on the Polish regime and wanted the allies to support demonstrative gestures which Schmidt regarded as useless:

Certain people in the White House had quietly given the media to understand that hard and clear language would be used with Schmidt, also concerning the "possibly serious consequences for the Western Alliance that might result if the European reaction remained as weak as it has been so far." At the same time they fed to the media the suggestion that the American side might try to undermine the natural gas pipeline agreement which was being negotiated between a European consortium and Moscow. The high point of these threats spread by irresponsible aides of Reagan was the indication that American banks might be asked to call in loans they had made to Poland, which, in turn, would make waves in Western European financial circles.

I decided to remain tough on the issue. Two points of view were decisive for me which apparently no one in the US was willing to put forward publicly. The whole world had experienced the Soviet invasion of Budapest in 1956 and of Prague in 1968, just as it had witnessed the invasions of Laos and Cambodia and the occupation of Afghanistan. These rapes of other people by the Soviet Union . . . had in each case provoked world-wide indignation – just as the building of the Wall through the middle of Berlin had done in 1961. I had experienced all of that and was just as shocked as everybody else. But I had also understood that the US . . . did not have any effective instruments of power at its disposal, with which to reverse these rapes.

I also had a specifically German motive. . . . I was moved by the wish for a reconciliation of Poles and Germans. . . . Reconciliation was a decisive motivation for Willy Brandt's and my own Ostpolitik. We were fully aware that we had to accept the communist rule established under Soviet control in the People's Republic of Poland as a fact. . . . Any West German attempt to drive a wedge between the Polish people and its government, to say friendly words to the former but to deny aid to the latter, must fail; it would also give the communist propagandists in Warsaw arguments against an alleged "German

---

[7] Schmidt, *Menschen und Mächte*, 293.

revanchism. . . ." Finally, economic sanctions hit the little man in Poland much harder than the people at the top of the party.[8]

Schmidt spoke with most important members of the administration and was satisfied that they understood and agreed with the German position. Alexander Haig, the secretary of state, said that the comments in the American media criticizing Bonn for weakness vis-à-vis the Soviets and the Jaruzelski regime in Poland had surprised him; "they had not been stimulated by his ministry (which I believed), nor by the White House (which I did not believe)."

Five months later, at the economic summit in Versailles, Reagan suggested that the European allies join in the embargo of drilling equipment, but found that they were distinctly uninterested. They wanted to separate economic agreements from political gestures and did not agree with the Americans that the two were inseparable – and that to continue fulfilling agreements, no matter what the Soviets did, was in itself a political gesture, a gesture of appeasement. Schmidt, of course, saw it differently: "Neither the bulk of the American media nor the administration ever admitted to themselves that the division of Central Europe at Yalta [in 1945] into two spheres of influence (or into a Western sphere of influence and an Eastern power bloc) could not be abolished through television speeches, grandiose gestures, and related small gestures."[9]

On June 18, 1982, President Reagan extended the sanctions to include all equipment produced abroad under license from US firms or by subsidiaries of US firms. Given that the Europeans did not want to join the sanctions, this led to a legal imbroglio. Margaret Thatcher of Britain joined Mitterrand and Schmidt in taking the position that the US had no jurisdiction to tell foreign subsidiaries or licensees of US firms what to do. Schmidt averred that "the decision does not accord with the principles of international law and is unacceptable to the European Communities. We and our European partners will be firm about the pipeline . . . The maintenance of the open world trade system would be seriously jeopardized by unilateral and retroactive decisions on international trade . . . We don't want a trade war with the Soviet Union."[10] On August 12, the EC presented a formal protest to the US, calling the attempted extension of the sanctions "a unilateral breach of contract."

There was a reason why Schmidt, as virtually all leading figures in the Federal Republic, took such a serious, even solemn, view of international law. It was the memory of the lawless Third Reich and the

[8] Ibid., 305–7.
[9] Ibid., 310, 313–14.
[10] *Relay from Bonn*, June 25, 1982.

disasters it brought on Germany and Europe. In the first years of West German independence, two jurists, Walter Hallstein and Wilhelm Grewe, rebuilt West German diplomacy on a new basis, that of respect for law. In later years critics argued, with some justification, that the Germans had forgotten that power is at least as important as international law for survival and independence.

Schmidt and the EC won the intra-Western struggle. On November 13, 1982, the US lifted the economic sanctions against the Soviet government. Many felt that the sanctions should never have been imposed if they were going to be lifted for merely political reasons. The US originally imposed them to retaliate for what was happening in Poland, yet they were lifted without any improvements having occurred in that unfortunate country.

The decision was preceded by the US president's visit to West Germany in June 1982 to attend a conference of the heads of government of NATO countries. In his speech to the Bundestag he emphasized that the US government was searching for a viable program for arms control, and that the threat of Soviet missiles against Western Europe must be countered. Schmidt later wrote that the president's speech "was a political and a psychological masterpiece. He achieved what no German federal chancellor has ever achieved: a standing, long-lasting ovation from both the left and the right for a speech on security policy . . . Although there had been serious doubts in the Bundestag vis-à-vis Reagan – and by no means only on the left – he succeeded in his speech of little over half an hour in convincing the Bundestag, whose three caucuses interrupted him with their joint applause at least 20 times."[11] Schmidt, indeed, compared the effect of Reagan's speech as an affirmation of the German-American alliance to that of Kennedy's "Ich bin ein Berliner!" speech in Berlin in June 1963.

The president began by speaking of the roots of democracy in German history and its success in the present: "Over the past 30 years, the convictions of the German people have built a cathedral of democracy – a great and glorious testament to your ideals." He greeted with satisfaction an agreement signed in April 1982 on wartime host support, that is, an arrangement by Bonn to provide resources and manpower to the US in crisis or war, with the cost, about $570 million, to be shared equally by the US and West Germany. He went on to warn:

I don't believe any reasonable observer can deny that there is a threat to both peace and freedom today. . . . Without a strengthened Atlantic security, the possibility of military coercion will be very great. . . . For almost 40 years, we

[11]   Schmidt, *Menschen und Mächte*, 338.

have succeeded in deterring war. Our method has been to organize our
defensive capabilities, both nuclear and conventional. ... Deterrence has
kept that peace. ... We also are resolved to maintain the presence of well-
equipped and trained forces in Europe, and our strategic forces will be
modernized and remain committed to the Alliance. ...

Those who advocate that we unilaterally forgo the modernization of our
forces must prove that this will enhance our security and lead to moderation by
the other side – in short, that it will advance, rather than undermine, the preser-
vation of the peace. The weight of recent history does not support this notion.
... And those who decry the failure of arms control efforts to achieve substantial
results must consider where the fault lies. ... To those who've taken a different
viewpoint and who can't see this danger, I don't suggest that they're ignorant,
it's just that they know so many things that aren't true. ...

The West has established a clear set of goals. We, as an Alliance, will press
forward with plans to improve our own conventional forces in Europe. At the
same time, we propose an arms control agreement to equalize conventional
forces at a significantly lower level.

We will move ahead with our preparations to modernize our nuclear forces in
Europe. But, again, we also will work unceasingly to gain acceptance in Geneva
of our proposal to ban land-based intermediate-range nuclear missiles.[12]

While he was speaking, more than 200,000 demonstrators marched
peacefully outside the Bundestag and protested against the arms race
and, in particular, against the proposal to station new medium-range
missiles in Western Europe. "To those who march for peace, my heart is
with you," Reagan said, "I would be at the head of the parade if I
believed marching alone could bring about a more secure world."[13]

[12] Dept of State, *Documents on Germany*, 1346–50.
[13] Ibid., 1348–9.

7

The Greens

The Greens represented, culturally and sociologically, the continuation of the views espoused by the student radicals of the late 1960s, and reflected in the citizens' initiatives that began with the organization of the anti-nuclear *Bundesverband Bürgerinitiativen Umweltschutz* (BBU) in 1972. Brandt had, in 1969 and 1972, captured what later became the Green vote. Schmidt disappointed the ecological and egalitarian left by refusing to enact its agenda. This gave the affected groups no option but to form their own party with political goals which conflicted with one another.

It was the first new party to achieve representation at any level since the mid-1950s, with the exception of the NPD which appeared briefly in the late 1960s in Baden-Württemberg, Bavaria, Bremen, Hesse, Lower Saxony, Rhineland-Palatinate and Schleswig-Holstein.

The Greens – so named because of the emphasis on the environment – were not so much a party as a movement made up of a wide range of components, with a platform calling for ecological, anti-nuclear, basic democratic and non-violent policies, and opposing industrial growth. There was a hard core of communist-dominated groups who used the new movement for propaganda purposes. There were also a few right-wing environmentalists, but most of the elements came from the New Left of the 1970s, especially conscientious objector groups, urban squatters, and intellectuals. Opinion polls indicated that many of the Green ideas had the support of as much as 20 per cent of the population. In districts close to nuclear power plants, Green candidates often obtained that same degree of support. It was, therefore, logical for the Greens to run candidates in the federal election in 1980.

The Greens were able to build their popularity on legitimate concerns about the environment. The Rhine was virtually a dead river north of the Mannheim-Ludwigshafen region. From the mid-1970s forests throughout Germany, particularly at higher elevations, began dying. Acid rain, the result of chemical reactions in the atmosphere provoked by industrial emissions, plagued lakes, waterways, and agricultural land across Germany. Pollution of the environment was even worse in East Germany. There, the main fuel was lignite (brown coal), which produces more toxic and corrosive fumes than ordinary coal or oil. Also, machinery and industrial plants in the GDR were generally more old-fashioned, requiring more energy and producing far more waste than comparable machinery in the West. Moreover, the GDR regime's first priority was industrial output and thereafter came environmental concerns.

Ironically, the Greens radically opposed the only energy source that promised a practical solution to the problems caused by fossil fuels, namely nuclear power. Thus their policy was not one of efficiently and effectively dealing with the issues of environmental deterioration, but a political program aimed at turning modern German industrial society back in time, with an emphasis on bucolic images of rural society. Yet the environmental problems of Germany in the 1970s and 1980s were so pronounced that voters supported or sympathized with the Greens without recognizing the logical consequences of their real political agenda.

Gerd Langguth, an expert on protest movements and their history since the early 1960s, noted three stages in the development of the Green movement. The first stage was that of the citizens' initiatives of 1972–7; by the latter year, there were 1,000 such groups with a total membership of over 300,000. They were mainly concerned with opposing the construction of nuclear power plants; the names of the villages of Wyhl and Brokdorf (near Freiburg and Hamburg respectively) became common in headlines due to the demonstrations and blockades that were constantly occurring there. Anti-nuclear citizens' initiatives coordinated by the BBU continued to exist alongside the Green party proper; the federal environmental agency estimated that in 1980 there were over 11,000 regional groups with over five million participants.

Although many of the participants were apolitical or romantic conservatives, communists and committed radicals of various types controlled the organizations from an early date. They had an agenda that went far beyond stopping nuclear power; in fact, doing so was merely an element in their campaign to transform society. They provided the momentum that led to the second stage, that of regional organization on the state level. This stage began in 1977–8 when various political groups with the word "Green" in their names entered candidates in state elections, for the first time in Lower Saxony in December 1977. In early 1978, the Stalinist Communist Association organized anti-nuclearists, homosexual activists and other radical groups for the state elections in Hamburg. At this stage, there were often several groups competing in the same election, with the result that none gained representation.

The third stage was that of consolidation into a single movement on the federal level. This took place during 1978–9 as a result of endless debates and ideological arguments in the existing *Land* groups, and because of the need to provide a single umbrella organization to participate in the elections to the European Parliament which were held for the first time in June 1979. The umbrella organization was formed in March 1979 and called itself the Greens. One of its leaders was the German-born but American-educated activist, Petra Kelly. She was the stepdaughter of an American officer, Lt Col. John E. Kelly, and was educated at American University in Washington, DC. At the time the Greens were being formed she was an assistant on the staff of the Economic and Social Committee of the EEC in Brussels. Her job and her background made her a typical member of what some sociologists, 30 years after Milovan Djilas' famous book of that title written in Yugoslavia, called "the new class" – people dealing with the manipulation of information, knowledge, and opinions.

The theory of the new class was originally developed by people trying to explain the nature of power in advanced bureaucratic societies. One of the earliest exponents *avant la lettre* of new class theory was the German-born economic philosopher Joseph Schumpeter, who predicted in *Capitalism, Socialism, and Democracy* that capitalism necessarily engendered its own destruction in the shape of an intellectual class hostile to the principles of capitalism itself. The three most important of these principles were free enterprise, economic inequality as an engine of change and innovation, and limited government. Capitalism needed this class of knowledge-manipulators (teachers and administrators) to survive, but as this group grew, it would begin to develop a class interest separate from that of the capitalists, and to avow that this interest is in fact the interest of society as a whole. As a result, the new class would become in the main leftist or even revolutionary. Schumpeter's theory seemed borne out by the triumph of university radicalism in the 1960s and in a different sense by the Greens, who overwhelmingly drew their strength from young people (under 35) with university degrees, and among them from the so-called "caring professions:" social workers, doctors, administrators in the welfare state apparatus, and educators.

Ronald Inglehart, an American sociologist, revived and revised Schumpeter's new class theory in his book *The Silent Revolution*. Inglehart argued that the wealth and opportunities created by postwar economic growth in the West had produced a "silent revolution" in the attitudes of a majority of young people, so that they no longer shared their parents' preoccupation with material wealth and the work ethic, but rather held to what he called "post-materialist" values, such as pacifism, rigid control of growth in the interests of the environment, and feminism. He was able to document this revolution with considerable evidence from opinion polls.

Petra Kelly shared the beliefs of the new class to an extreme degree. From 1979 to 1984 she was the dominant figure in the movement, which constituted itself as a party for purposes of participating in *Land* and federal elections in January 1980. Their first successes were in Bremen and in Baden-Württemberg. In the federal elections of September 1980 they obtained only 1.5 per cent. The main reason for their rapid growth in 1981–3 was the controversy over the NATO double track decision and the widespread fear of nuclear war, not because of a Soviet attack, but as a result of "the whole apparatus of nuclear weapons in some way 'getting out of control'."[1]

By 1983, the Greens had developed a reasonably coherent set of policies based on four pillars: non-violence, ecological activism, unilateral disarmament, and social transformation. The actual commitment of the Greens to non-violence was somewhat dubious given that several prominent members of the movement had close ties to the terrorist network, and that the Greens sympathized with the terrorists and generally approved of violence in the name of what they considered just causes – against South African apartheid, for example, or against US missile deployments. In general, the four pillars were interpreted according to a rigid and moralistic code which had no place for freedom and individual liberty, and which condemned Western industrial society, its legal and political institutions, its individualism, pluralism and faith in the rule of law, and its commitment to self-defense.[2]

[1] Howard, *The Causes of Wars*, 257.
[2] On the Greens see Langguth, *Green Factor in German Politics*.

8

The Peace Movement

The hundreds of thousands of Germans who demonstrated against the double track decision from 1980 to 1983 were part of that loosely defined phenomenon known as the peace movement. It included, most broadly, all those opposed to the double track decision or other NATO plans for arms modernization, but was also, as a social and ideological phenomenon, a part of the general opposition to industrial society that was also found, for example, in the movement against nuclear energy. The peace movement included the Greens, but extended beyond the confines of the Green movement to include many social democrats, free democrats, and even some Christian democrats. The organizers of the peace demonstrations sought the broadest possible support. They therefore were careful to ensure that the slogans and the banners carried by demonstrators were as innocuous and as seemingly apolitical as possible. In this way the leaders of the movement, who had the specific goal of disrupting German security policy and making the US presence in Germany as uncomfortable as possible, gained the temporary support of thousands who by no means shared that agenda.

The peace movement first took official form at a meeting of prominent opponents of the double track decision. The result was the "Krefeld Appeal," initiated in November 1980 in Krefeld near Düsseldorf, which demanded that the German government rescind its support of the double track decision. The appeal, which gathered 2.7 million signatures by April 1982, was drafted by left-wing groups, including members of the German communist party (DKP), and was worded in such a way that it did not appear to be overtly anti-American. It generated, however, heated debate, which prompted Schmidt to threaten his resignation if support for the double track decision was not forthcoming from the SPD. He made his conviction clear in a speech in Wolfratshausen in Bavaria in May 1981: "For once and for all don't let anybody tell you that the Americans are our enemies and the Soviets are our friends."[1] Later in the year a similar appeal emerged, the "Bielefeld Appeal;" however, it came from the SPD itself, had a similar basis to the Krefeld Appeal, but became submerged in the growing cacophony surrounding the arguments, pro and con, on NATO policy. The chancellor's support for the decision was upheld in parliament by a vote of 254 to 234 in May, with 17 members of Schmidt's own party abstaining. But while the chancellor won the debate, he indicated in a speech to the Bundestag in October 1981 that the peace movement consisted of more than naive pacifists with illusions about the role of force in the world:

We politicians and parliamentarians of the German Bundestag do not want to put the majority of the demonstrators into the same category as those persons who use violence as a political instrument, or who condone it or even ask for it. ... But please be aware of the fact that some very shady characters have attached themselves to you. Do not let them misuse you.[2]

The "shady characters," described by Schmidt, were real and substantive. A report to the Bundestag on youth involvement in the peace movement concluded in May 1981 that more discussion was the only way to make security policy more comprehensible to younger people. But the problem was not merely one of comprehension. Complicated and sensitive issues and choices concerning defense strategy and weapons had become subject to public debate by people who knew little about the issues, and in a climate of fear of the future and hence emotional uncertainty. It was easy for agitators to use scattered facts and legitimate concern to build up an emotional appeal which had little to do with actual conditions and needs. In addition, the peace movement was not particularly peaceful in its treatment of opponents. The euphoria of the movement with its failure to provide realistic solutions for real problems made it a danger to democratic stability. Those, like Willy Brandt, who treated it as a sign of health, either ignored or overlooked the fact that certain groups within the peace movement were being exploited by the Soviet Union, the DKP and extremist groups in West Germany for political purposes.

The demonstrators against Reagan in Bonn in June 1982 did not believe that the negotiations going on between the US and the Soviet Union on intermediate-range nuclear forces (INF) were going to succeed, and they were already blaming the US, rather than the Soviet government for the suspected outcome. They had recently received some support from four American former government officials,

---

[1] *Relay from Bonn,* May 22, 1981.
[2] *Archiv der Gegenwart,* October 10, 1981.

McGeorge Bundy, George F. Kennan, Robert McNamara, and Gerard Smith. These four had written an article in *Foreign Affairs* arguing that NATO should adopt a declared strategy of "no first use" of nuclear weapons in response to a Soviet conventional attack in Europe.[3] They believed that it was within the means of the NATO governments to improve their conventional forces to such an extent that these alone could deter attack, and there would be no need to threaten possible nuclear retaliation. The prevailing NATO strategy since 1967, known as flexible response, assumed that the best deterrent was uncertainty. If the Soviet government never knew how the West would respond it would be less likely to attack than if it knew that the West had promised "no first use" of nuclear weapons. The "Gang of Four," as the authors came to be known, questioned this argument.

The "no first use" debate continued for years, and it upset many West Germans, especially those in official or semi-official circles who had dealt with defense and strategy for a number of years. Four of them, two social democrats and two members of the CDU/CSU, responded in the next issue of *Foreign Affairs*. The two social democrats were Karl Kaiser, the respected director of the German Foreign Policy Society, and Georg Leber, who served as minister of defense from 1972 to 1978. The two Christian democrats were Alois Mertes, a scholar and analyst of defense and foreign policy, who became secretary of state in the foreign ministry under the CDU-led government of Helmut Kohl, and Franz Josef Schulze of the CSU, a security specialist and consultant to Franz Josef Strauss. They argued that flexible response remained a viable strategy, but only if NATO remained able to threaten nuclear use in response to an attack. They explained that NATO might be able to repel an attack conventionally, but that it was very risky to change the existing strategy at a time when Soviet strength, both nuclear, chemical, and conventional, was fast growing. In any event, why should the Soviets believe a "no first use" promise? If they believed it, they might be tempted to attack, since they had good reason to think they could easily defeat NATO's conventional forces alone. If they did not believe it, the whole idea was pointless to begin with.

In some respects the "Gang of Four" were simply expressing the tendency of the time. Few doubted that in the real political world NATO already was bound to "no first use." No one could realistically conceive of a NATO commander firing the first nuclear weapon in a war. Many sophisticated observers, including most European politicians, outside the narrow circle of strategic specialists, believed that

---

[3] Bundy et al., "Nuclear Weapons and the Atlantic Alliance." *Foreign Affairs* 60 (1981–2): 753–68.

once a nuclear weapon, any weapon, was fired the war would inevitably escalate to a total holocaust. Few West Germans saw any real purpose in NATO's complicated system of defenses, ranging from conventional to battlefield nuclear weapons, to short- and intermediate-range missiles and bombers, to the US strategic arsenal. No one, moreover, knew for certain what Soviet attack doctrine actually was. The best evidence was that the Soviets intended, if war came, to attack with "combined arms," probably using chemical and small-yield nuclear weapons from the outset. The whole "no first use" debate, therefore, was an academic exercise.

The official Soviet position was that the Warsaw Pact, of course, had a "no first use" policy and that it would be conducive to stability if the West would follow suit. Moreover, the proposed new Pershing II missiles to be deployed in West Germany were capable of hitting targets in the USSR, and very accurately too, so that, in the Soviet view, they were first-strike weapons, symbolizing an alleged offensive strategy of NATO. This argument, that the Pershing IIs were offensive first-strike weapons, became popular in the West German peace movement.

9

Combatting Terrorism

One important issue of the Schmidt era, namely the largely successful struggle against terrorism, adds perspective to the growth of the Federal Republic under Schmidt's leadership. After an initial series of attacks in 1968–70, when the leading terrorists were simply at one end of the continuum of student radicalism, a hard core – the Red Army Faction (RAF), whose most important members were known as the Baader-Meinhof gang – continued to plunder and kill with increasing sophistication and effectiveness, in no small part thanks to training given, sometimes at Soviet expense, in the Middle East or in Eastern Europe. Following the arrest of Andreas Baader and some of his henchmen in 1972, the rate of attacks declined for almost two years. In late 1974 one imprisoned terrorist, Holger Meins, starved himself to death. The next day members of the RAF assassinated the president of the Berlin superior court, Günter von Drenkmann, in his home. Early in 1975, they kidnapped the head of the Berlin CDU, Peter Lorenz, and demanded the release of their imprisoned associates. The government gave in and Lorenz was released. The humiliation of the authorities was great and was the primary reason why the opposite course was adopted when the occasion arose again in 1977. In the Lorenz case all parties agreed that the value of one life was great enough to justify the abandonment of the principle that crimes should be punished. Those who believed that giving in once would lead to further terrorism were unfortunately proved right in April 1975, when West German terrorists occupied the German embassy in Stockholm, killed one staff member, and destroyed the building after their demands were rejected. The terrorists depended for resources and organizational support on domestic sympathizers, but above all international support was provided by the PLO and by a shadowy network of organizations and channels which, during the 1970s, was built up throughout Europe, and which had clear connections to Eastern Europe and to the USSR.

Terrorism was only the most extreme manifestation of the so-called new consciousness that had been produced by the radicalization of the late 1960s. In 1975, Schmidt and other leaders were not yet willing to publicly condemn surrender to terrorist demands as simply encouraging more violence. Learning this lesson was the main psychological result of the terrorist wave of 1974–7. But there were other results, seen in the legal system and in moral and political attitudes of Germany's citizens.

Five of the six terrorists released as a result of kidnapping Lorenz demanded to be flown to South Yemen, a Soviet satellite, and to prevent being stopped en route, they took a hostage, Heinrich Albertz, a prominent figure of the SPD religious left, a former mayor of Berlin, and a close friend of Willy Brandt. Following occupation of the West German embassy in Stockholm in June 1975, the RAF occupied a hotel in Geneva in December 1975 where the oil ministers of OPEC were meeting, probably in the belief that moderate Arabs could be forced to take a more hostile stand against the West. In June 1976 an Air France airplane bound for Israel was hijacked and its Jewish passengers kidnapped, but later released.

In April and August 1976 the Bundestag passed amendments to the criminal code and other laws. The amendments made it easier for the state to prosecute people inciting others to break the law, spreading false and malicious rumors, or spreading propaganda designed to undermine the security of the republic. Other measures made it illegal for groups of persons charged with acts of violence to share defense counsel, something that, in the past, had made it very difficult to obtain convictions. The laws were aimed not merely at terrorists, but at the sometimes violent demonstrators against nuclear power plants. Judges – who in general had a much more prominent position in German law, with its Roman law influence, than in English or American law – were given the right to exclude defense attorneys from certain proceedings. The number of attorneys permitted to each defendant was limited, and each attorney could defend only one prisoner. Further, in certain cases the judge could assign a particular attorney against the defendant's will.

These measures outraged the left, which felt betrayed by the SPD. But this outrage was only one reason why much of the intellectual left began to withdraw its support of the SPD between 1979 and 1982 and instead gave its energies to the new party, the Greens, and to the peace movement. Throughout the period following 1974 there was in West Germany a continuous, and sometimes hectic, discussion of whether the *Rechtsstaat* – state under the rule of law – was being safeguarded or violated, and if so, in what direction. The conservative view claimed that the state, in particular the SPD state, was too weak in its own defense and not confident enough in its prosecution of subversion. The left asserted that the state was authoritarian in any case, and that the legal system in particular had never been purged of Nazis, any more than of authoritarian procedures; that, therefore, measures of the 1970s to combat extremism and subversion were simply excuses invented by the right to conceal the re-establishment of the apparatus of state coercion and oppression. Leftist critics, like Uwe Wesel, a professor of the history of law at the Free University of Berlin, pointed to the revisions of criminal procedure just cited, and to the law to protect civil peace of 1976. This act made "unconstitutional advocacy of violence" into a crime, a phrase which, the left argued, could be used to sanction any expression of opinion unfriendly to the powers that be. In 1981, the law was repealed, with little effect on the number of prosecutions for disturbing the peace.[1]

As was often the case, this leftist fear ascribed to government authorities the kind of oppressive behavior and violence that radicals themselves would have liked to indulge in, had they been in power. There was, indeed, ample evidence to support this view. In 1968, one of the members of the academic new left, Oskar Negt, wrote openly that "the majority of student actions is justified." They were justified because "'demonstrative violence' to enforce a public attitude defined by a political interest in enlightenment may include the violation of rules which themselves are used repressively." In clear language, Negt was arguing that the radicals were entitled to use force to prevent the expression of ideas hostile to them and to enforce public support of their own ideas and ideology.[2] Throughout the 1970s, as the radical activism of 1966–70 lived on in the form of "citizens' initiatives" at the one end of the spectrum and terrorism at the other, Negt's words appeared prophetic.

In 1977 the wave of terrorism reached its peak. In April a terrorist gang murdered a federal lawyer, Siegfried Buback, in Karlsruhe, the seat of the Federal Constitutional Court. He had been a supporter of stricter measures to control imprisoned defendants and their lawyers and had defined the free communication between terrorists in prison and their lawyers as providing "the best protected location for conspiracy that we have in the Federal Republic."[3] Schmidt's response to the murder was a policy statement on combating terrorism, that the CDU/CSU considered begged the question:

[1] Wesel, *Juristische Weltkunde* 139–40.
[2] Negt, "Studentischer Protest – Liberalismus – 'Linksfaschismus'," in *Bewegung in der Republik,* eds Karsunke and Michel, 1: 163.
[3] Cited in Wilharm, *Deutsche Geschichte 1962–1983,* 2: 148.

There must not be a special legal process for terrorists. The violent murderer and the terroristic murderer must be brought to court under the same law, even under the same procedure. . . . But I also repeat: we cannot get rid of terrorism by legislation only. We must destroy the spiritual soil that nourishes it. To do that it will be necessary to bring to our citizens, particularly the young generation . . . a more direct experience, a greater awareness of the unique character, in our national history, of the liberal state under the rule of law. . . .

The intellectuals in our society should help those in positions of political responsibility in the task of enlightening those young Germans who still do not have a clear picture and judgement about terrorists, their motives, and their alleged justification. I direct this call to those university professors, scientists, philosophers, and writers to whose voices the young generation listened so intently back then, in the later 1960s, in the era of the APO.[4]

The opposition leader, Helmut Kohl, insisted that the social democratic governments themselves bore a share of responsibility for the climate of culture and opinion within which terrorism and sympathy for terrorism had grown:

Unfortunately we have to admit that certain circles within social democracy [i.e., the social democratic party] still have a disturbed relationship to that exercise of power by the state under the rule of law which is necessary to guarantee the future of the state. State power appears as something immoral to these circles. They suffer from the misconception that only the state can be a threat to liberty and security. Here the utopia of a social order without domination still prevails. . . . The soil from which this sort of cultural attitude was able to grow was not solely prepared within the current criminal milieu. Rather, it is inextricably connected to developments in school and educational policy, with the higher education policy of certain *Länder*, with conditions at certain German universities. . . . So, for example, the Hessian "Guidelines for Civics Courses on Level I" recommend "to examine whether there were and are situations in which it has to be clarified whether formally democratic rules and rights should temporarily be abolished in order to improve or secure democratic conditions." In another place they recommend "learning to examine historical and contemporary forms of violence . . . with regard to whether they serve the exercise of domination or whether they might be understood as counter-violence to combat political, economic, or military oppression."[5]

Shortly thereafter, following a five-year trial and investigation, the terrorists Baader, Ensslin, and Raspe were sentenced to life in a prison built specially for them in Stammheim, a suburb of Stuttgart. In reaction, terrorists in July murdered Jürgen Ponto, the chief public relations officer of one of West Germany's three big commercial banks,

[4] Cited ibid., 145.
[5] Cited ibid., 146–7.

the Dresdner Bank. In September, the president of the Employers' Association and of the Federation of German Industry, Hanns Martin Schleyer, was kidnapped and his four companions killed. On September 30, the Bundestag finally passed a law forbidding contact between convicted terrorists in prison. The kidnappers of Schleyer demanded the release of Baader, Ensslin, and several other leading RAF members. To press their claim, the RAF also hijacked a Lufthansa 747, the "Landshut," on October 13, 1977. After 24 hours of flying from one airport to the next, the airplane landed on the tarmac at Mogadishu, Somalia (East Africa). Schmidt sent Hans-Jürgen Wischnewski to negotiate with the Somalis and stall the terrorists. Wischnewski accomplished both tasks. He persuaded the Somalis to allow the special anti-terrorist squad, the *Grenzschutzgruppe 9*, to come to Mogadishu. While waiting for its arrival, Wischnewski kept the terrorists busy from the airport tower with negotiations and offers. The passengers were freed and the captors themselves killed or captured.

Of great importance, however, was that the German government maintained a clear position. An editorial in the *Stuttgarter Zeitung* read:

> The strategy of international terrorism has been condemned to failure in the psychological sector, too. It would indeed be too early to speak of the end of terrorism. But the ideology of terrorism, to the extent that it was based on vulnerability to blackmail, cowardice, lack of courage to make sacrifices and take risks, has been destroyed at its roots.[6]

This success also had two other consequences. The imprisoned RAF leaders in Stammheim prison committed suicide. The next day, October 19, Schleyer's body was discovered in the trunk of a car across the French border in Alsace. He had been garroted with piano wire. It was a dreadful murder of a distinguished German businessman, and it was especially painful to the members of the tripartite council of party and government leaders in Bonn who had taken responsibility for the decisions as to how Schleyer's kidnapping and the Lufthansa highjacking should be handled. A West German press representative explained:

> The cowardly murder of Hanns Martin Schleyer proves that the perpetrators are beyond enlightenment. . . . Giving in to these criminal fanatics could only provoke them to ever new murders. Because this is a proven fact, the state had to force them to give in. Otherwise it would have violated its obligation to the entire community.[7]

---

[6] *Relay from Bonn,* October 20, 1977.
[7] Ibid.

This was a major turning point. From that moment on, the forces of law and of the state had the upper hand, though outbreaks and killings continued. By 1980, terrorism was effectively destroyed. New upsurges emerged in 1982, but did not reach anywhere near the level of violence as those of the mid-1970s, nor did they create a similar atmosphere of public fear and intimidation. One notable difference was that, whereas in 1968–77 US military installations were only occasional targets, in the 1980s NATO and American personnel and installations became the primary targets – a sinister change.

The police methods used to combat terrorism led to a broad debate on the problem of data collection and confidentiality of personal information. In January 1978 the government passed a law to protect citizens against misuse of personal data and required the regulation of data files by official inspectors. This was an issue – privacy – that would assume increasing importance in the following years.

The murder of Schleyer catalyzed many of the feelings for and against the West German government and its democratic structure. In this respect, the terrorism debate was an exemplary forum for the struggle between the two Germanies within West Germany, in the diametrically opposed figures of Helmut Schmidt, the man of order, and Horst Eberhard Richter, the man of pain and repentance. In the interest of peace, as Schmidt saw it – and perhaps out of a certain naivete – he was tolerant, perhaps too tolerant, of Soviet violence throughout the world; but at home he was determined that terrorism should not undermine the state, either by provoking an overreaction or by intimidation. Richter, for his part, and many leftists with him, analyzed the anti-terrorist measures, although mild in historical perspective, as an excessive over-reaction to what they persisted in describing as a tiny and unrepresentative group of 50 or so extremists.

The radical argument took two tacks. Since only a small number of terrorists existed, there really should be no reason for all the alarm, the new laws, and the general increase in police powers. There must, then, be other explanations for those measures. The radicals suggested two. One, Richter's favorite, was that West German society was still psychologically crippled by Nazism, by its failure to overcome the past, and by a deep-rooted German inability to meet the world on a human level rather than on the level of power and force. The other argument asserted the existence of a sinister right wing in the West German establishment that was trying to introduce a police state via the back door.

This latter tack of the radical argument about terrorism – a position close to the beliefs of the terrorists themselves – was that West German society was so miserable, so oppressive, so deadening, that murder and mayhem were understandable, if not permissible, reactions to it (the radicals used the word "understandable," the terrorists "permissible"). As Peter Schneider (a prominent author, known for his great interest in talking to imprisoned terrorists and presenting them to the public as essentially good people, spoiled by society) asked in 1978 in an article published in the once radical chic journal *Kursbuch:* "Do we in the Federal Republic live under conditions which justify violent opposition, up to and including murder?" He went on to say that no one had dared to pose that question thus far, even though the implied answer was "yes." Schneider's point was that there were those in the Federal Republic who were free, but who were also criminals who remained unpunished for their crimes. One illustration, in his view, was Schleyer, who had been a member of the Nazi party before the party's seizure of power in 1933, and who had later joined the SS during the Third Reich.

Schneider found it ironic that such an individual had been allowed to occupy a position of high responsibility while the government focused its attention, instead, on the crimes of the anarchists of the radical left. His conclusion, which he drew after the suicides of Baader and Meinhof, led him to condemn the West German state; indeed, Schneider questioned whether Baader and Meinhof actually took their own lives voluntarily, were forced to do so, or were murdered. Because they had been closely guarded, and because it was unclear how they received the weapons to kill themselves, Schneider implied the complicity of the state. Schneider's line of reasoning reflected the conviction of the left that the state was corrupt, and only selectively pursued enemies of democracy.[8]

Schneider was, in fact, one of the more reasonable of the radical commentators. He at least admitted, if indirectly, that the West German political system was in some sense worth defending and he was, in his view, merely attacking what he saw as unnecessary and sinister official paranoia. Further to the left, the thesis that Baader, Meinhof and Ensslin, and the others had been killed by henchmen of the authorities remained uncontested. One proponent of that thesis was the radical lawyer Otto Schily, who was later to enjoy a prominent political career as a leader of the Greens in the Bundestag.

[8] Schneider, "Der Sand an Baaders Schuhen," in *Bewegung in der Republik*, eds Karsunke and Michel, 2: 265–6.

10

Party Politics and Social Trends

Stammheim prison, where the terrorists killed themselves, is in Baden-Württemberg, which in 1978 was a bastion of the CDU under the able leadership of the minister-president Hans Filbinger. To the irritation of the SPD and the radical left, Filbinger had even succeeded in increasing his party's majority while in office. Filbinger, moreover, was an articulate defender of conservative principles and a skillful opponent of the moralistic ideology of the left. Unlike many of his fellow-leaders of the CDU, he was comfortable in the world of political ideas and therefore able to engage the leaders of the left on their own ground. After the Stammheim deaths, it was not surprising that the more extreme radicals should accuse Filbinger of complicity in murdering Baader and the others. A few months later, events – whether accidental or premeditated – gave the left a welcome opportunity to attack Filbinger and, despite legal action, to force his resignation from office. If they hoped that his removal would permanently weaken the CDU in the *Land*, however, they were mistaken.

The Filbinger case, as it became known, began when Rolf Hochhuth, the leftist playwright, accused Filbinger of having acted like a "fearsome lawyer" (*furchtbarer Jurist*) when, as a military judge before and after the surrender of 1945, he was involved in maintaining discipline among German troops. In particular, Filbinger was alleged to have gone out of his way to secure death penalties for soldiers accused of nothing other than insufficient fanaticism. *Der Spiegel*, *Stern*, and, more surprisingly, *Die Zeit*, repeated these accusations without carefully verifying them. Theo Sommer of *Die Zeit* denounced Filbinger, who was never a member of the Nazi party, as worse than the Nazis and compared Filbinger's alleged behavior during the war with his zeal for law and order as minister-president of Baden-Württemberg. Clearly, an unsavory past was being invented for Filbinger in order to wage a political battle against him in 1978.

In fact Filbinger was involved, and very indirectly, in only one execution, a case that very likely would have had the same outcome in the US or the British armed forces. In early 1945, Filbinger was ordered to complete the prosecution of a deserter, a soldier who had failed to report for service on the battleship *Scharnhorst* and subsequently tried to flee to Sweden. Desertion in time of war carries the death penalty in virtually all the armies of the world. As a matter of fact, the military court at first sentenced this man to prison rather than death, because it believed him to be a courageous soldier who had been decorated for service on the eastern front. The officer commanding the German Navy in Norway, who was in charge of the court, approved the conviction for desertion but rejected the sentence and demanded death. Further investigation of the man had revealed that far from being a good soldier, he had in fact wrongfully appropriated another man's medal and carried fourteen prior convictions for crimes and insubordination. Had Filbinger been in charge of the proceedings, he might nevertheless have upheld the sentence of imprisonment, but he was not. He was simply a staff member of the court who was obliged to follow the orders of his commanding officer. Accordingly, the man was executed.

In two other cases, Filbinger, again acting as prosecuting agent for the officer commanding in Norway, passed pro forma death sentences against sailors who had escaped to Sweden, one of them after murdering a fellow-seaman. These were clear cases of mutiny, murder, and desertion, which would have entailed execution in any army or navy of the world. At the time, Filbinger and his superiors knew quite well that there was no chance that Sweden would hand over the sailors and that therefore the sentences would not be carried out. Their purpose was simply to maintain discipline at a time when the German Navy was actively making efforts to save civilians from the eastern territories. In another case, Filbinger sentenced a deserter to prison but was overruled by his commanding officer, who ordered the man executed. Like the many other cases where Filbinger went out of his way to secure milder sentences, this one was ignored by the media.

Filbinger responded to the accusations by suing Hochhuth and *Die Zeit*. His lawyer was Josef Augstein, the brother of Rudolf Augstein, publisher of *Der Spiegel* and one of the most stringent critics of Filbinger. Josef Augstein told his brother that the accusations were libelous and wholly without foundation. Rudolf Augstein responded that Hochhuth had his information from the GDR, as though this made it more reliable. In fact it merely confirmed Filbinger's suspicion that there was much more to the libel than merely an honest, if misguided, attempt to clarify a chapter of the past. He came to believe, with some reason, that elements of the West German media and political left were, knowingly or unknowingly, supporting a disinformation operation of the GDR secret services to discredit him and remove him from office because of his prominent role as an opponent of the left in the Federal Republic.

Filbinger won a judgement that Hochhuth and *Die Zeit* could no longer claim that he had only risen to his present position "because of the silence of those who knew him then [that is, in the war]," but the court declined to prohibit repetition of the most libelous accusations in the interests of freedom of the press. Not only Filbinger, but an impressive array of leading legal scholars of West Germany found this judgement puzzling, since it seemed to them that the court had accepted Hochhuth's good faith and had given his, and *Die Zeit*'s, freedom to speculate greater importance than the honor and good name of a leading citizen. Prior to the judgement Filbinger had chosen to resign as minister-president because the campaign against him (*Rufmord*, character assassination) indirectly embarrassed the CDU, that feared possible losses in the upcoming *Land* elections in Hesse and Bavaria. The very fact of the media attack made him into a liability. Filbinger therefore resigned on August 7, 1978.[1]

While party politics provided one kind of drama, social trends provided another. The late 1970s saw a number of studies of West German youth which drew conflicting conclusions. On the one hand, it was clear that a great number of young people were disillusioned with society, feared the future, and saw no grounds for optimism in the prevailing social and political conditions. On the other hand, an equal number gave favorable responses to the questions concerning belief in traditional values, work ethics, and willingness to make personal sacrifices. In 1979 the government estimated that 80,000 young people were dependent on drugs, and 150,000 on alcohol. The decline in personal ethics was notable in the rise of petty theft committed by youth, the willingness of young students to demonstrate, rather then to participate; an attitude reminiscent of the "Ohne mich" (without me) slogan of the 1950s.

One reason for the youth problems was continuing economic difficulties, associated in part with the rising costs of the welfare state. From 1970 to 1977 expenditure on social and welfare programs in West Germany rose by 117 per cent. There were three main reasons for this increase: health costs, which tripled from 1970 to 1981, pensions and unemployment, and disability compensation.

In 1979, for the first time since the mid-1960s, the trade balance was in deficit. Interest rates were relatively high, and business and government investments were low. It was estimated that one million jobs had been lost because of unmade investments. The shortage of capital hit small businesses especially hard, and the number of self-employed

[1] See Filbinger, *Die geschmähte Generation*.

Who are the "Social Partners"?

In 1985, 25.5 million or 41.8 per cent of the population of the Federal Republic of Germany were gainfully active, the greater proportion of them being employees (over 22 million wage-earners, salaried employees, civil servants and apprentices).

These include about 1.6 million foreign workers who have the same rights and duties as their German colleagues. The social system in the Federal Republic of Germany makes no distinction between German and foreign labour.

The number of self-employed is 2.4 million, together with about 860,000 assisting family members. Most self-employed also have other employees. Thus, like the joint stock companies, the government authorities, the railway and the postal authorities, the churches and associations, they are employers.

Employees and employers are partners since, in spite of their different interests, they depend on each other for their economic success.

Employees as percentage of working population

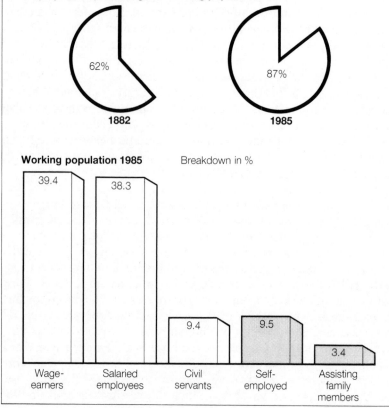

Working population 1985   Breakdown in %

Figure 2.4   Working population, 1985.
Source: **Press and Information Office,** *Employers and Unions*

Thousands

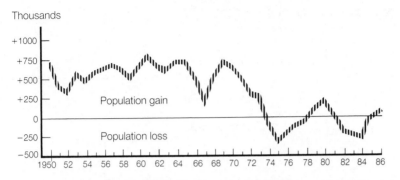

Figure 2.5   Population changes, 1950–1986.
Source: Stat. Bundesamt, *Statistisches Jahrbuch 1987*, 79

persons fell by 50 per cent between 1960 and 1980. The gradual decline in population, which was now beginning, raised questions about the future viability of pension programs, about the availability of skilled labor, and about the size of the future domestic market. Introduction of new technology brought fewer jobs and not enough job-training programs, and created widespread fear among the employed, leading to union demands that new technology not lead to dismissals. Helmut Schmidt made an effort to organize an international response to these problems by various means, including economic summit meetings and revitalization of biannual Franco-German meetings. None of the serious problems facing Western industrial nations, however, were adequately dealt with before the second oil crisis.

It should be noted, however, that despite the economic problems of the 1970s the personal incomes of Germans continued to rise, and in 1980, on average, real personal income was six times what it had been in 1949. From 1950 to 1978 the proportion of personal income needed by an average wage-earning household for basic necessities had fallen from 74 to 46 per cent. In 1973, only 51 households out of 100 had a telephone, but this number rose to 88 by 1983. In 1978, 416 of every 1,000 households lived in their own house or apartment. The most important manner of saving for large scale purchases was in the so-called *Bausparkassen* (savings institute for housing construction), where savings were treated favorably for tax purposes.[2] To promote private savings, the Schmidt government turned to new ideas to enable wage earners to share in the ownership of the businesses in which they worked; these proposals were resolved in various ways. In general, however, the unions and the SPD preferred a more organized form of

[2] Kistler, *Bundesdeutsche Geschichte*, 366, 371–4.

TABLE 2.5 INCOME DISTRIBUTION

Year	Total national income[a] (Billion DM)	National income per capita (DM)	Share of national income paid in wages & salaries[b]	Income from entrepreneurial activity[c]	Income from property[c]
1938	47.3[d]	1,216[d]	54.9[d]		
1950[e]	76.9	1,640	58.4	41.6[e]	
1951[e]	93.2	1,967	58.5	41.5	
1952[e]	105.7	2,215	57.5	42.5	
1953[e]	113.9	2,365	58.9	41.1	
1954[e]	122.5	2,515	59.9	40.1	
1955[e]	141.0	2,865	59.3	40.7	
1956[e]	156.5	3,144	59.9	40.1	
1957[e]	171.3	3,396	60.1	39.9	
1958[e]	183.3	3,590	60.9	39.1	
1959[e]	198.5	3,844	60.2	39.8	
1960[e]	222.3	4,259	60.4	39.6	
1961	260.8	4,642	62.4	34.7	2.9
1962	282.1	4,963	63.9	33.4	2.7
1963	297.8	5,189	64.9	32.2	2.9
1964	327.3	5,645	64.5	32.6	2.9
1965	358.5	6,115	65.3	31.7	3.0
1966	379.8	6,421	66.4	30.4	3.3
1967	380.7	6,422	66.1	30.6	3.3
1968	418.1	7,027	64.7	31.9	3.5
1969	462.9	7,707	65.7	30.6	3.7
1970	530.4	8,745	68.0	27.8	4.2

1971	588.2	9,598	69.6	26.5	4.0
1972	645.3	10,464	69.8	26.4	3.8
1973	721.9	11,648	70.8	24.9	4.4
1974	773.0	12,456	72.9	22.9	4.2
1975	803.6	12,997	73.1	22.8	4.1
1976	882.2	14,337	71.6	24.8	3.6
1977	938.3	15,282	72.0	24.5	3.4
1978	1,010.2	16,473	71.4	25.3	3.3
1979	1,087.9	17,730	71.5	24.9	3.6
1980	1,148.6	18,656	73.5	22.3	4.2
1981	1,187.3	19,248	74.4	20.9	4.8
1982	1,223.5	19,850	73.8	20.9	5.4
1983	1,286.2	20,941	71.6	24.0	4.4
1984	1,357.9	22,197	70.3	25.0	4.7
1985	1,420.0	23,270	69.8	25.3	4.9
1986	1,509.4	24,718	69.0	26.6	4.4
1987	1,568.3	25,626	69.0	27.1	4.0

[a] National income (net national product at factor cost), sum of all labor and capital income earned by residents.
[b] Wages and salaries as share of national income in percentage.
[c] Income from entrepreneurial activity and income from property are calculated as their respective percentage shares of national income.
[d] Federal Republic of Germany without Saarland and Berlin (West).
[e] 1950 to 1960 excluding Saarland and Berlin (West) and before the revision of the national income accounts. According to the revised data the 1960 national income amounts to 240.1 billion DM and 1960 per capita income to 4,332 DM. Additional changes due to adjustment of earlier data.

Sources: Stat. Bundesamt, *Volkswirtschaftliche Gesamtrechnungen*, Fachserie 18, Reihe 1.3; Rytlewski and Opp de Hipt, *Die Bundesrepublik Deutschland in Zahlen 1945/49–1980*, 129–30

(a) Age structure of the population as of December 31, 1960
(Federal Republic without Berlin)

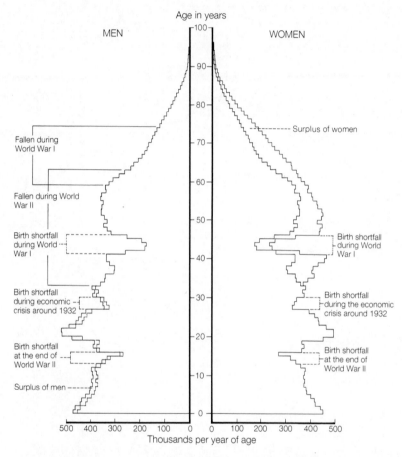

Age in years

MEN

WOMEN

Surplus of women

Fallen during
World War I

Fallen during World
War II

Birth shortfall
during World
War I

Birth shortfall
during World
War I

Birth shortfall
during economic
crisis around 1932

Birth shortfall
during the economic
crisis around 1932

Birth shortfall
at the end of
World War II

Birth shortfall
at the end of
World War II

Surplus of men

500 400 300 200 100 0   0 100 200 300 400 500
Thousands per year of age

Figure 2.6 Development of population, 1960 and 1986. The two parts
of this figure illustrate in detail why West German leaders were so
concerned with the age distribution in the Federal Republic in the 1980s.
Census data from May 1987 indicated that 9.3 million (15.2 per cent) of a
population of 61 million were older than 65. Between 1970, the previous
census, and 1987, the number of children below age six fell 40 per cent.

(b) Age structure of the population as of December 31, 1986

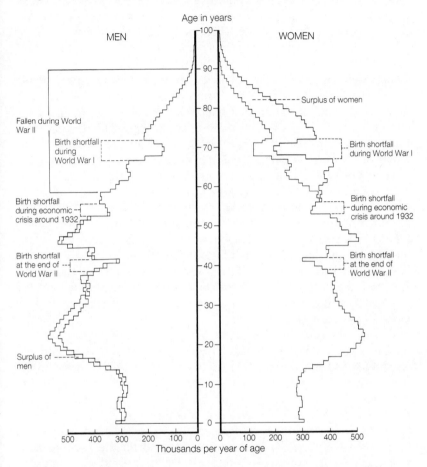

Age in years

MEN   WOMEN

Fallen during World
War II

Birth shortfall
during
World War I

Surplus of women

Birth shortfall
during World War I

Birth shortfall
during economic
crisis around 1932

Birth shortfall
during economic
crisis around 1932

Birth shortfall
at the end of
World War II

Birth shortfall
at the end of
World War II

Surplus of
men

500 400 300 200 100   0   0   100 200 300 400 500
Thousands per year of age

At the same time, the population of foreign residents nearly doubled. If current trends continued, demographers predicted in 1988 that pensioners would outnumber workers by the year 2030 (*Wall Street Journal*, December 22, 1988).

Source: Stat. Bundesamt, *Statistisches Jahrbuch 1962*, 45; and *Statistisches Jahrbuch 1988*, 63

personal investment savings, in which businesses would set aside a certain portion of cash and equity value and the employees would be entitled to receive certificates indicating their share of ownership in the thus created funds. For the unions this was decidedly a clear way to increase their influence in the economy. The difference was that the unions wanted this plan to be obligatory, whereas businesses and the CDU/CSU preferred employee participation in ownership to be on a case by case basis.

The significance of these changes, of increased affluence, of the access of ordinary wage earners to owning industry, of owning their own home, and of having their own telephone, is another example of the changes that were occurring in German society, changes that were unthinkable in the late 1940s and 1950s. Except for a small minority, the main concern was no longer where the next meal was coming from, but how to manage one's life and finances over the long term, what sorts of domestic investments to make, what kind of savings to have, and where to go on vacation. The effects of these changes on the temperaments and attitudes of the people were revolutionary. In the late 1940s most Germans feared political change, because they had experienced too much of it and longed for stability. In the 1970s they feared change because they had a lot to lose. Their exposed position on the East–West front in Europe meant that this insistence on security came to dominate political attitudes in a way that was not always compatible with West Germany's own best interests.

In 1974 the population of West Germany reached its peak of 62.1 million and then began falling. By 1980 it registered 61.4 million and was predicted to decline to 51.6 million by the year 2030.[3] Indeed, births per family in West Germany declined from an average of 2.5 in 1965 to 1.29 in 1984. This unique and unprecedented process led to intense discussion of the possible causes and remedies.[4]

In May 1976 the Bundestag debated the last budget before the federal election in October. The government insisted on the success of its policies, and the opposition attacked what it referred to as socialist illusions and lack of clear goals in foreign, economic, and welfare policy. The main issues in the election were inflation, unemployment, welfare, and the continued problems of industry in the face of the recession. The CDU/CSU candidate was, for the first time, Helmut Kohl, a former minister-president of the Rhineland-Palatinate who had replaced Barzel as leader of the opposition in 1973. The second most important

---

[3] Ibid., 374; Hübner and Rohlfs, eds, *Jahrbuch der BRD 1986/87*, 5.

[4] On causes of below-replacement fertility and possible policies see Davis et al., eds, *Below-Replacement Fertility in Industrial Societies*.

figure was once again Franz Josef Strauss, whose last post in government had been as finance minister in the grand coalition. As always, the appearance of Strauss in the federal elections challenged all the resentments of the left, for whom he represented all they disliked in West Germany, although he was immensely popular in Bavaria. The campaign differed from earlier ones in that both parties used very similar clichés, though with different emphasis, and was characterized by a high degree of polarization and mutual attacks. The SPD, in particular, charged the CDU/CSU with wanting to introduce intellectual terrorism because they did not share the SPD's views on cultural and educational policy. The influence of the New Left was becoming stronger in the SPD, and for this wing any deviation from their path could only be due to ill will and reactionary authoritarianism. For these people Strauss and Kohl were no better than neo-Nazis.

The election marked a setback for the SPD, but not enough to put it out of power. The majority of the SPD and FDP in the Bundestag fell from 46 to ten seats. The CDU/CSU did not succeed in transferring its gains in the *Land* elections of the previous four years to the federal level, and received 48.6 per cent, which was nonetheless its best result since 1957. The SPD received 42.6 per cent, almost the same result as in 1969; from a historical perspective this was a good outcome, which fell, however, short of the hopes of the party (91 per cent of the eligible voters had cast ballots). The result very clearly showed a movement away from the SPD (in 1972 the SPD received 45.8 per cent); but Schmidt himself remained extremely popular.[5] After the election Kohl made an effort to win the FDP back to a CDU coalition, since the FDP had not, as in 1972, promised beforehand to continue the government coalition with the SPD. Nevertheless, Genscher rejected Kohl's offer, and the Schmidt government continued.

The eighth Bundestag elected Schmidt chancellor once again in December 1976. In his opening policy statement he emphasized the continuity with the former SPD government. He declared that the principles of West German foreign policy would emphasize good neighborly relations and partnership, and he announced further steps in social welfare policy, specifically on pensions, and referred to problems of youth unemployment and the environment. But the period of the second Schmidt government became a difficult one. It was beset with the burdens of international economic problems, that Schmidt was on the verge of mastering in 1978, when the collapse of the dollar, followed immediately by the Iranian revolution, overturned all expectations. The entire period of the second Schmidt government was a time

[5] See Kaltefleiter, *Parteien im Umbruch*.

of increasing problems for the SPD. While domestic issues, such as economic growth, employment and inflation, occupied Schmidt's attention, so did concern with United States policy toward Europe.

The same period saw a gradual strengthening of the CDU/CSU. In late 1976 the CSU leader, Franz Josef Strauss, decided to dissolve the parliamentary alliance with the CDU by taking his own party, the CSU, to the national level. Strauss did so mainly to force the CDU to make him its candidate for chancellor in 1980; when he had achieved this goal in early 1980, he reversed the decision.

In October 1978 the CDU produced a new basic program which emphasized values, order, justice and peaceful foreign relations. Although the program asserted the importance of conservative values in a way that had not been seen in West Germany for almost ten years, it nevertheless did not denounce the Ostpolitik of the SPD nearly as strongly as had the party in the years before 1975. In the areas of broader foreign policy concerns and in development aid, the positions were close to those in the SPD. There was clearly an emerging consensus on important areas of foreign policy; a consensus based on the idea that West Germany was now a mature state with the right to take its own position in the world, and no longer a mere protectorate of the US and Europe.

Although one might question the idea of a West German state interest, distinct from that of the Western alliance in general, it is nevertheless true that an important change in the mid-1970s was the emergence of new self-confidence. The most important reasons for that change were the conclusion of the treaties with the East and the obvious competence of Helmut Schmidt in international economic policy.

All of the federal presidents, although they had little direct power, had been representative figures of great importance. Theodor Heuss (FDP), the first president, had been concerned with building bridges and with establishing consensus within Germany in the early years. Heinrich Lübke (CDU), the second president from 1959 to 1969, tried to preserve a sense of values at a time of rapid economic change. The third president, Gustav Heinemann (SPD), 1969–74, introduced the new phase of radical democracy without supporting the extremism of the New Left. Walter Scheel (FDP), president from 1974 to 1979, brought his foreign policy experience to the office, but also used his public appearances to discuss themes such as the limits of growth, the need for historical consciousness, and the responsibility of science and technology. Scheel became very popular both at home and abroad, and many hoped he would serve for a second term. However, in the Federal Assembly called in 1979, the CDU/CSU had a majority and decided to use it to elect one of their own members as president: Karl Carstens, who had served as speaker of the Bundestag since 1976. The SPD and FDP objected to Carstens, because he had been a member of the Nazi party, and because they disliked the idea of a president from the CDU who might publicly oppose the policies of the government. They tried to enlist the philosopher and physicist Carl Friedrich von Weizsäcker as a candidate, but Weizsäcker, who was making a name for himself as a philosopher of nuclear strategy and a critic of NATO arms policies, declined.

At the time of the election, Walter Scheel, as well as his wife, enjoyed great popularity, but he withdrew his candidacy when it was apparent that the FDP would not garner sufficient votes to win. Carstens' background prepared him well for the post. In 1945 Carstens was 31 years old; ten years later he became a member of the CDU and was elected to the Bundestag in 1972, as an attorney and professor of international law at the University of Cologne. He had also been the first representative to the Council of Europe in 1954, and had served as state secretary in the foreign ministry from 1960 to 1967. In office Carstens commanded respect and increasing popularity. Between 1979 and 1981 he and his wife completed a celebrated two-year weekend-walk through all *Länder* of West Germany, covering 1,129 kilometers, and accompanied by Paul Bepper, a baker from Kiel, and his wife. In the world of that time it was the kind of effort that generated popular interest, and also allowed Frau Carstens to raise DM 100,000 for charity.[6]

[6] *Relay from Bonn,* October 9, 1981.

11

National Identity and Leadership

The question of national identity arose again in the later 1970s along with the question of whether the long separation from East Germany was resulting in the loss of a common German identity. In November 1978 a conference of the cultural ministers of the *Länder* defined the task of education on the German question as one of maintaining the consciousness of the unity of the German nation and of its just demand for self-determination. These standards, set forth in the Basic Law, were difficult to preserve in schools, when daily politics clearly showed that the status quo was accepted, and no one seriously thought of trying to change it.

For the election of 1980 there was no question that Schmidt would be the candidate for his party. The CDU/CSU chose Strauss as its candidate, which doomed the party to defeat because of the violent opposition of the left, but also of the FDP, which campaigned with the slogan "For Schmidt-Genscher Against Strauss," and not against the CDU/CSU as such. In fact, a majority of the voters probably would have preferred a government of the CDU headed by Helmut Schmidt. The differences between Schmidt and his party on questions of the economy and security were not yet clear to the public, but were becoming increasingly serious. Particularly the party chairman, Willy Brandt, in his public statements, often criticised Schmidt in ways that would have been unheard of in the old SPD, where discipline and solidarity were rigorously observed.

The ability of the caucus leader, Wehner, to bridge the differences between Brandt and Schmidt in the interest of party unity was declining. Wehner mistrusted Brandt not so much because of his politics, but because of his increasingly arrogant manner, and his ill treatment of his associates. Wehner's ability to act as the SPD's grand strategist was, therefore, reduced by this conflict. The FDP faced a serious threat of losing its representation and sought support from those who wanted to see the SPD balanced by more centrist party positions, and those CDU voters who were afraid of Strauss. This tactic was successful. The FDP obtained 10.6 per cent of the vote, their best result since 1961, whereas the CDU/CSU with 44.5 per cent had their worst election since 1949. The SPD obtained 42.9 per cent of the vote, slightly more than in 1976, and the Greens failed to win representation, but did receive 1.5 per cent of the vote. Before the election Genscher had committed himself to remaining in the coalition, and following the election there was no further negotiation on this issue. The new government was born with internal disagreements, between the FDP and the SPD left on economic policy and within the SPD on defense and security issues. The left wing of the SPD now comprised 60, rather than 16, members of the Bundestag, a figure greater than the majority of the coalition vis-à-vis the CDU/CSU. As Werner Kaltefleiter, a political scientist from the University of Kiel, noted: "The march through the institutions that began at the end of the extraparliamentary period [1969] had arrived at the Bundestag caucus of the SPD."[1]

The immediate tasks of the continuing coalition government were to deal with economic problems and the execution of NATO's double track decision. The economic figures continued to deteriorate during 1980, since the second oil crisis of 1979 was only now exerting its full effects on unemployment, inflation and the government budget. The FDP, led on this issue by the economics minister, Otto Graf von Lambsdorff, insisted on balanced budgets and spending cuts, whereas the SPD insisted on welfare spending and industrial support. The first signs of a drift in the FDP toward the idea of a coalition with the CDU became clear.

Helmut Kohl, the CDU leader, had long since decided that the CDU's return to power should and would come about with, not against, the FDP. He was determined to minimize the injury of Kurt Georg Kiesinger's bitter threat to punish the FDP that the former chancellor made after the election of 1969, when the FDP declared its support for Willy Brandt. Throughout the 1970s, as Kohl gradually established himself as the most prominent *Landesfürst* of the CDU, he worked to mend fences with the liberals in the *Länder* and, finally, on the federal level.

Within the FDP, the various factions of the party watched the decline of the SPD's popularity with concern. The right wing, permanently weakened since Erich Mende's defection to the CDU, had never reconciled itself to the coalition with the SPD, but had little opportunity to change the party's line. The left wing advocated environmental, security, and welfare policies that, until the late 1970s, were to the left of

---

[1] Kaltefleiter, *Parteien im Umbruch*, 135.

most of the SPD. Its leaders were Günter Verheugen, who from 1978 to 1982 was general secretary of the party, and Hildegard Hamm-Brücher, a strong advocate of Brandt's Ostpolitik and of increased foreign aid to the Third World.

The majority of the party followed the social liberal strategy sketched out by Scheel, Genscher, Mischnick, and Lambsdorff in the late 1960s and early 1970s. This strategy required joining the FDP in order to advance the interests of industry and economic liberty within a framework of growing welfare spending, an approach that corresponded to the classical liberal element in the party's ideology. At least as important, however, was the strategy's broader ideological and cultural element. Scheel had been sympathetic to the idealized goals of the student radicals of the 1960s and believed that, to gain and keep power, his party should welcome the new permissiveness in personal, social, and cultural mores. This part of the strategy found the fervent support of the leading liberal media publishers, Rudolf Augstein of *Der Spiegel* and Henri Nannen of *Stern*. Neither had much sympathy for the classical liberalism of economic growth and personal rights. To the extent that the FDP reflected Augstein's beliefs rather than those of Lambsdorff, German liberals of the 1970s were indeed coming to resemble their American counterparts.

Supporting the free market while also welcoming modish tendencies in the intellectual and political culture was from the beginning a schizophrenic strategy, aiming at entirely different groups and destined to produce contradictory, if not incoherent results. Towards the end of the 1970s, Genscher and his followers started to doubt that this approach was still viable. They saw the SPD drifting ever more to the left, as Schmidt lost control of the apparatus to Brandt and Eppler and their supporters among intellectuals and academics. They also saw the SPD losing ground in regional politics and they recognized the possibility of a CDU victory on the federal level. The 1976 election, when the CDU/CSU failed by 1.5 per cent of the vote to gain an absolute majority, was a shock. In the aftermath of that election, the FDP strategists began planning the second *Wende*, the second strategic turn, back to alliance with the Christian democrats.

The policy of coalition with the SPD began to crack as a result of early elections in Berlin in 1981. In January of that year, the SPD mayor, Dietrich Stobbe, was forced to dismiss several members of his government who had improperly authorized loans or assumed liabilities for the city's largest housing contractor. The scandal, and Stobbe's attempt to maintain his government, provoked a public demand for early elections, and these were held on May 10.

They were a disaster for both the SPD and FDP. The social democrats suffered their poorest showing in Berlin since the war with only 38.3 per cent of the vote. The FDP barely made it into the city hall with 5.6 per cent. The victors were the CDU, who did better than ever before in Berlin with 48 per cent, and the Alternative List, combining the Greens and various extreme-left groups, who obtained 7.2 per cent. This result forced the FDP to decide whether to support a CDU government or to join the SPD in opposition. The latter course would mean yet another election, since the CDU, despite their excellent showing, had not won an absolute majority. Genscher, who followed the Berlin developments closely, judged that the voters would not forgive the FDP if it forced another election. The liberals would disappear from the city government, and the CDU might well win an absolute majority – in Berlin of all places!

The Berlin FDP opposed supporting the CDU candidate for mayor, Richard von Weizsäcker. After much soul-searching and some defections to the SPD, the party decided nevertheless to follow Genscher's advice and support the CDU. Thus ended 18 years of liberal-socialist government in Berlin. In 1963, Willy Brandt had engineered the first successful coalition of SPD and FDP, which many at the time saw, rightly, as foreshadowing the coalition on the national level that in fact came about under Brandt in 1969. In the same way, the end of the SPD/FDP coalition in Berlin in 1981 presaged the fall of the national coalition in 1982.

The Berlin outcome demonstrated that the liberals were seriously divided between the left, who wanted to pursue the policies of the left wing of the SPD, and the Genscher faction, that was leaning toward a coalition with Kohl. The left controlled the party apparatus and the party conferences, as had been clear since the late 1960s and was demonstrated again at the party's annual conference in Cologne in May 1981. Verheugen joined Genscher in condemning the SPD's fiscal policies, but the main issue of the conference was security policy, where Verheugen and the left strenuously opposed the double track decision and demanded that the FDP reject it. Like Schmidt in the SPD, Genscher was only able to hold the party to the double track decision and thus to Schmidt by insisting forcefully on his authority as party leader.

During the summer of 1981, Genscher and Lambsdorff concentrated on delivering the message that the FDP was the party of moderation and fiscal responsibility, determined either to restrain excessive spending of the SPD or to resign from the coalition. Fortunately for Genscher, he had the temporary support of his left wing and of Augstein in this strategy. He and Lambsdorff repeatedly suggested that neither of the two major parties was capable of a sound economic policy; only the liberals had the courage and the foresight necessary to construct one.

Lambsdorff's own position was weakened by the party financing scandal that erupted in 1981 with after-effects that continued into 1987. In May 1981 journalists reported that the state attorney in Bonn was investigating Lambsdorff on suspicion that he had not paid taxes on funds which he had raised and contributed to the party as treasurer of the party in the Rhineland-Palatinate. Under the German laws on party financing, as interpreted by the Federal Constitutional Court, gifts from individuals and organizations to political parties were not tax-free. The FDP did, however, maintain a party research foundation, as did the SPD and the CDU and gifts to these foundations were tax-free; thus, Lambsdorff on behalf of the FDP apparently accepted financial gifts to the FDP, but made to the party's foundation and not to the party itself. Lambsdorff was not the only figure involved; it soon emerged that the investigations found the same practice in all three parties.

In November the party financing scandal became more serious when the media reported documentary evidence that the Flick concern, one of the largest corporations in Germany, had made gifts to a number of named politicians, primarily in the FDP, during 1976–81. In those same years the SPD/FDP government had granted the Flick concern exemptions from capital gains tax on a total of 1.5 billion marks. In February 1982, the state prosecutor in Bonn reported that his office was investigating Lambsdorff, Friderichs, Maihofer and several other FDP politicians on suspicion that they had improperly approved the tax exemptions in return for gifts. (See part X, chapter 12.)

The SPD quickly distanced itself from the scandal. Schmidt ostentatiously refrained from supporting his liberal colleagues, which contributed to their sense of betrayal. The party financing scandal and its culmination in the Flick affair thus contributed to Genscher's decision, in late 1981 or early 1982, to desert the coalition and join with Kohl and the CDU at the earliest opportunity.

In 1981–2 economic prospects deteriorated. Inflation at 5 per cent was high by German standards, and unemployment at 1.7 million at the end of 1981 was a 26–year high. Rising unemployment also led to some resentment of the foreign guest workers, who in 1981 numbered 4.5 million; it was higher than 11 per cent among guest workers, as compared to 7.3 per cent nationally in December 1981. The budget for 1982 was 240.5 billion marks, a sharp increase due mainly to unemployment; the two largest items in the new budget were DM 53.8 billion (22.37 per cent) for the labor and social ministry and DM 44.2 billion (18.38 per cent) for defense.[2]

---

[2] *Relay from Bonn*, January 15 and 22, 1982.

During 1981–2 the Genscher and Lambsdorff group in the FDP argued that the failure of industry to invest was largely due to the growth of welfare spending. The state had taken over protection of individuals against risks, and thus had reduced the incentive of individuals to work and achieve. Furthermore, state control of capital, by its monetary and tax policies, was such that private business had less and less flexibility to develop. The SPD, on the other hand, saw the problems as rooted in the international economy.

For those Germans who were not unemployed or at the lower end of the scale, the early 1980s were comparatively prosperous, but nonetheless frustrating. Real income declined slightly, but there was no truth to the widespread allegations that the Germans were becoming poor. On the contrary, the social and cultural changes resulting from the affluence of the 1960s continued into the 1980s. The changes in industrial structure and society led to a debate as to whether a new society was emerging in West Germany. Some pointed to the new social movements, a phrase that included the peace movement, the anti-nuclear movement and other alternative groups, who objected to predominant values and life styles of society. Other indications that a new society was emergent were the changes in the structure of the workplace. The number of jobs in heavy industry and construction was falling, and jobs in service occupations such as health and education, or social services in various institutions were increasing. Changes in values, spurred by greater unemployment, were leading to a new social division between those with permanent or secure jobs and those who were marginally employed with no security. To solve this problem some experts proposed a redistribution of labor – a job-sharing program that would offer the unemployed an opportunity to work. Others argued that the remedy would be a 35–hour work week. Under the conditions of economic crisis, the reduction of the work week at full pay was recognized by most to be a highly ill-advised policy, although in subsequent years a somewhat reduced work week was introduced into many sectors of the economy. In early 1988 the West German Metalworkers Union (I.G. Metall) successfully negotiated a 36.5 hour work week for the industry's 140,000 workers, with an effective increase in pay, to take effect on November 1. The Iron and Steel Industry Federation characterized the metal workers as the "world leisure time champions."[3]

In the area of foreign affairs Schmidt held his party to the double track decision with adept political maneuvering between 1979 and 1981. The annual SPD party conference in 1982 concluded that the final SPD position on deployment would be made at an extraordinary party con-

[3] *Relay from Bonn*, March 4, 1988.

ference to be called in late 1983, when the results of the Geneva INF talks between the US and the USSR would be available. It was virtually certain, given the trend of opinion among party members, that the SPD, at that time, would not support a decision to deploy; the anti-Schmidt forces were gaining ground in other areas as well. In October Willy Brandt gave a speech on the tenth anniversary of the death of Willi Eichler (one of the authors of the Godesberg Program) in which he discussed the problems of radical youth. He emphasized that it was vital for the SPD to capture the new wave of youth who participated in the peace movement, and that the party should incorporate their ideals and values.

Brandt's position contrasted with that of traditional social democrats, as expressed in a memorandum, in 1981, by Richard Löwenthal, a distinguished political scientist from the Free University of Berlin, who was a long-time member of the SPD and a British citizen until 1983.[4] He concluded that the SPD must be on the side of industrial society and against those who wished to denounce it, and must support the interests of normal working people and not those of marginal outsiders. Löwenthal demanded the exclusion from the party of people who rejected the traditional values of the SPD, as reiterated in the Godesberg Program. His major concern was that Brandt's appeal, if adopted as formal party doctrine, could also isolate the SPD from the broad group of voters that had traditionally supported the party; and that, indeed, it represented an appeal to the left that could seriously divide the party internally and weaken the party's popularity among the West German electorate. Löwenthal's concern proved to be justified as events developed during the next year.

Löwenthal was echoing the convictions of Kurt Schumacher and Herbert Wehner, but he no longer represented a leading force in the SPD. A typical spokesman for these new forces was Eppler, whose rise to prominence in the SPD was due to his use of two themes: the environment and peace. He saw himself as a spokesman for all those who feared economic growth without controls, high technology, and NATO nuclear strategy. If Heinemann had been the first to introduce religious and ethical themes into SPD politics, Eppler took these a step further and without the seriousness of Heinemann. The influence of the peace movement and Eppler's moralistic arguments against technology and defense made it increasingly difficult to continue the coalition with the FDP. The FDP also included anti-nuclear and anti-NATO activists, but in the early 1980s the party was controlled largely by economic realists, who increasingly felt that the SPD was losing its credibility. In

---

[4] *Die Zeit,* December 18, 1981.

February 1982 Schmidt asked the Bundestag for a vote of confidence, an unprecedented step which showed how uncertain continuing prospects of the coalition had become. Even though Schmidt won the motion of confidence, it was a sign of weakness that he considered it necessary to ask for confidence from his own party. The patience of the left wing with Schmidt's defense policies was almost exhausted.

In the Hamburg election in the summer of 1982 the SPD, for the first time, lost the absolute majority. The Greens entered the senate of the free city with 7.7 per cent of the vote. One year earlier, the government of Berlin had changed hands for the first time in a city election since 1946, to the CDU.

In a perverse way, the SPD, which had moved from being a party of a certain milieu in early postwar Germany – that of the proletariat and the leftist intelligentsia – to being a broad-based popular party in the 1960s and 1970s, was now once again becoming a class party. Only the class it represented was no longer primarily the working class in the trade professions and the old primary industries, much reduced in size from the early postwar years, but the new class of public sector employees and intellectuals. A vivid illustration of the significance of this change was the fate of Kurt Becker, a highly regarded journalist, deputy editor-in-chief of *Die Zeit*, and long-time supporter and friend of Schmidt, who appointed him chief party spokesman after the 1980 election. Becker was not a party member and did not become one after his appointment, but Schmidt chose him because Becker understood Schmidt and his policies and was deeply loyal to both. However, Becker was not considered acceptable by Schmidt's critics, who relentlessly castigated him as incompetent. Schmidt, in his weakened position vis-à-vis his own party organization, was unable to support Becker in the long term, and consequently did not reappoint him during the cabinet reshuffle in the spring of 1982. Becker left without any public declaration of support from Schmidt. Werner Kaltefleiter commented: "This created the impression that Schmidt accepted the arguments of his critics, that Becker's public relations policies were the cause of the government's weak standing [in the polls]. Behind this development lay the fact that loyalty is an extremely bourgeois virtue which is not widespread among SPD party functionaries, who speak only of solidarity. Becker demonstrated his loyalty but he could expect no solidarity, because 'having the right smell' [*Stallgeruch*; that is, being one of them] had become the most important criterion for a SPD that was regressing toward a class party role."[5]

[5] Kaltefleiter, *Parteien im Umbruch*, 145–6.

12

The Fall of Schmidt

West Germany's foreign policy problems in 1981–2 further weakened Schmidt's position. Afghanistan, the SS-20s, Ronald Reagan, martial law in Poland, East German intransigence, American distrust: where in all this lay the road ahead? And where should that road be leading? The impossibility, for Schmidt at any rate, of finding a path that was compatible with his own ideas and opinions was the remote cause of his downfall. The direct causes, however, were to be sought in the internal politics of the coalition.

The SPD Munich party congress of April 1982 gave overwhelming support to policies unacceptable to Schmidt and incompatible with the essential orientation of the Federal Republic since the introduction of the social market economy and Western integration. The congress demanded a much greater role for the unions and the state in the control of industry, employer and employee co-determination at all levels of industry, worker participation in investment, employment, and organizational decisions, and intensified economic planning. One of the more provocative specific motions was to demand a special levy on the "wealthy," to finance job-creation schemes. With 1.8 million people out of work, the highest level since the early 1950s, the labor and union wings of the SPD rejected Schmidt's plea for moderation and demanded new income taxes on high earnings. The new taxes plus more government borrowing would theoretically finance a decision to lower the retirement age to make more jobs available to younger people, along with a reduction in the work week and government work programs. Hans Matthöfer, finance minister at that time, cautioned that it would be "sheer illusion" to expect such a tax increase to pass the Bundestag, but his admonitions went unheeded.[1]

This motion and the attitudes behind it were a powerful factor in

---

[1] *Relay from Bonn*, April 23, 1982.

convincing the FDP moderate leaders, Genscher and Lambsdorff, that the SPD was no longer a responsible party of government. But the SPD's move to the left was not confined to domestic policy. The congress charged West Germany's principal ally, the United States, with promoting the arms race and came close to rescinding the SPD's support for the double track decision. Indeed, the party took this final step in November 1983.

In the summer of 1982 the question was not whether the coalition would last until the next elections, scheduled for 1984, but for how long. The FDP was torn between a conservative group around Lambsdorff, who, on economic grounds, demanded a change in government, and a liberal group led by Hildegard Hamm-Brücher, who were sympathetic to the SPD left wing, and hoped that continuation of the coalition could be used to change, among other things, the double track decision. The conservative-radical split in the liberal party represented a re-appearance of the split during the grand coalition period when the conservatives of the day under Mende were defeated by the radicals of the day – of whom Hamm-Brücher was a leading representative – who took control of party strategy with the help of the pragmatists like Genscher and Scheel who could see which way the wind was blowing. In 1982, it was blowing in the other direction: Genscher now realized that the Lambsdorff wing was advancing. A difference between the two wings in the FDP was that the split in the 1960s was over *Deutschlandpolitik*, whereas that in the 1980s was over economic policy. On the German question, the radical victory of 1967–8 in the party still stood unchallenged.

Schmidt sensed that the coalition was moribund. But he remained firmly committed to the double track decision and to managing the inevitable coalition breakup in such a way that the FDP would look as guilty as possible and the SPD escape unscathed. Schmidt's efforts to achieve this end were an impressive display of tactical skill and demonstrated once again Kaltefleiter's point that loyalty – in this case, FDP loyalty to a party with which they had collaborated successfully for 13 years – was a bourgeois virtue, whereas the important thing for the SPD was ideological solidarity.

The late summer of 1982 was filled with rumors of conflict over economic strategy. In August 1982, Schmidt demanded that Lambsdorff explain his proposals in a formal document. On September 10, Lambsdorff handed the chancellor a confidential 34–page memorandum describing a policy of economic growth and employment which contained a proposal for drastic spending cuts, which Lambsdorff then proceeded to publish. In accordance with the spirit of the Munich party conference of the preceding spring, the SPD did not debate the

"Manchester-liberal prescriptions of the count" (Lambsdorff), but rejected Lambsdorff's paper as a provocation. Indeed, it caused an uproar, because Lambsdorff concluded that German business had lost confidence in the government, and that further public spending would paralyze economic growth.

Aware of rumors, later published in *Der Spiegel*,[2] that Lambsdorff and Genscher had discussed receiving editorial support from two large German newspaper publishers, should the FDP leave the coalition, Schmidt decided to act quickly. On September 17, he gave the FDP ministers in his cabinet a choice: either they resign or he would dismiss them. They resigned, thereby ending thirteen years of SPD/FDP coalition government. Without a majority and with Kohl waiting in the wings, Schmidt went to the Bundestag and made an unscheduled speech:

> After 13 years of work for the government I do not feel glued to my seat. But I am against the chancellorship of my colleague Kohl, because I do not want to entrust our country – neither as regards foreign or security policy, nor as regards financial, economic or socio-political policy – to another majority that so far has shown no profile at all.[3]

Schmidt proposed a vote of confidence and demanded early elections according to the procedure outlined in clause 68 of the Basic Law; namely, that if the chancellor requested a vote of confidence by the Bundestag and failed to obtain a majority in support, he could ask the federal president to dissolve the Bundestag and call elections. However, by choosing a new chancellor within 21 days the Bundestag could override the dissolution request. Schmidt thus asked the Bundestag, in effect, to deny him its confidence but also not to make use of the right to elect a new chancellor within 21 days. The CDU/CSU and FDP refused to agree, however. Schmidt then waited as the pro-SPD media unleashed a virulent public campaign denouncing the FDP as traitors.

This campaign can only be explained on ideological grounds. Coalition change between elections was not unknown either in the *Länder* or, indeed, in the federal government, where the two leading examples were the departure of the FDP in 1956 and the formation of the grand coalition in 1966. The SPD entered *Land* or federal government on five occasions by such means without ever having been denounced as traitors. Had the FDP ministers refused to resign and forced Schmidt to dismiss them, there could have been no talk of infidelity.

[2] *Der Spiegel*, October 11, 1982, no. 41.
[3] *Archiv der Gegenwart*, September 17, 1982.

As in the case of the failed attempt to overthrow Brandt and elect Barzel in his place in 1972, public as well as published opinion in 1982 did not reflect the understanding that a majority of the Bundestag has the full right to elect as chancellor whomever it chooses at any time. Many voters regarded the election of Helmut Kohl on October 1, 1982, as in some vague sense unconstitutional, while many of the same people considered Helmut Schmidt's constitutional attempt to use clause 68, asking the opposition to refrain from its rights under that clause, as morally justified and in some sense "more" legal.[4]

On October 1, 1982, the constructive vote of no-confidence was approved in a secret ballot (256 to 235) with four abstentions, the result suggesting that the FDP Bundestag members had split their votes. The preceding debate in the Bundestag was highly emotional and showed the division within the FDP, as Hamm-Brücher demonstrated in her remarks:

> It is not possible for me to give the chancellor the vote of no confidence, after I gave him my vote of confidence only a few months ago. I also cannot give him alone the vote of no confidence . . . and spare our four ministers and, as a matter of fact, myself. . . .
> I believe that neither does Helmut Schmidt deserve to be brought down without the consent of the voters, nor should you, Helmut Kohl, be made chancellor without the consent of the voters. No doubt, both devices are constitutional. But in my opinion they carry, nonetheless, the odium of damaged democratic decency. They offend the moral and ethical integrity of the change-over of power.
> Kohl called out: "That's a scandal! It's a scandal that you call the constitution immoral!"[5]

As the SPD left government, the forces of neutralism and appeasement and the forces that sought collaboration with the peace movement, gained the upper hand. Led by Brandt, Eppler, Bahr, Voigt, Lafontaine, and Gaus, this combination of old and new neutralists and optimists regarding the Soviet Union began to guide the party in a direction where its credibility as a supporter of NATO was in question. Brandt insisted that his position was not incompatible with NATO membership, but the new line contained so many reservations about the value and purpose of the alliance that it was hard to see how Brandt's views would conform with a system that depended on a great deal of common agreement on goals and means.

[4] Kaltefleiter, *Parteien im Umbruch*, 147–51.
[5] *Archiv der Gegenwart*, September 17, 1982.

13

Early Elections

When Helmut Kohl became chancellor, he had been federal chairman of the CDU since 1973 and leader of the CDU Bundestag group since 1976. Before coming to Bonn, Kohl was minister-president of the Rhineland-Palatinate from 1969 to 1976, succeeding Peter Altmeier, one of the original and most successful *Landesfürsten*, who governed from 1947 to 1969, longer than any other minister-president in the history of the Federal Republic. Altmeier turned the Rhineland-Palatinate into a bastion of the CDU and of federalist traditions, laying a solid foundation for Kohl to build on.

Kohl became member no. 246 of the CDU in the Rhineland-Palatinate in 1946, at the age of 16. Born in 1930, he was barely old enough to have served as a *Flakhelfer*, assistant to the crews of anti-aircraft batteries. He came from a pious Catholic home where Nazism had made no inroads. As soon as he joined the CDU he began taking an active part in political work. In 1947 he helped found the CDU youth organization in his *Land*, and from 1955 to 1966 he was a member of the regional party presidium. Along with his political work, he managed to complete a doctoral dissertation at the University of Heidelberg, one of the earliest accepted on postwar history. Its subject was "Political Development in the Palatinate and the Revival of Parties after 1945."[1]

In 1960, aged 30, he was elected to the *Landtag* in Mainz. As a politician, the young Kohl was already committed to two traditions. First, he was by choice and inclination a second-generation *Landesfürst*, committed to the federal structure of the republic and determined to carry on the traditions of regional authority and independence established by the great regional leaders during the occupation period. At the same time he recognized that the growth of the state and the public sector, and

[1] Filmer and Schwan, *Helmut Kohl*, 59.

the gradual centralization of authority in Bonn and in the federal agencies left the *Länder* with an ever-decreasing measure of real power. When he became minister-president in 1969, the single most important area of remaining *Land* authority was education and cultural policy. Kohl took an active part in retaining some control over education by accepting the role of the federal government in order to work with it to retain as much *Land* authority as possible, rather than to risk losing influence by opposing Bonn's reach. He also joined with his fellow-minister-presidents of the CDU in raising the profile and increasing the activity of the Bundesrat, the upper house of representatives of the *Länder*. The Bundesrat was the vehicle by which the *Land* governments exercised direct influence on federal legislation. The CDU/CSU controlled a majority of *Land* governments and therefore the Bundesrat during most of the Schmidt-Genscher era. Kohl and the other Christian democratic minister-presidents accordingly used the Bundesrat to conduct a policy of active opposition to the Bonn government by amending or delaying important legislation that required the consent of both houses. A significant example occurred in 1975, when Kohl led the Bundesrat in demanding modifications to a German-Polish trade and friendship agreement.

The other tradition that Kohl followed was the legacy of Konrad Adenauer, thus earning the nickname "Adenauer's grandson" (when Kohl was born, Adenauer was 54 years old). Like "der Alte", Kohl was a West German committed to the integration of the democratic part of Germany in Western Europe and NATO and to economic and political liberty at home. On a deeper level, Kohl was one of the very few younger politicians who resembled Adenauer in his patience and calmness in both success and adversity. In both men, this trait was founded in a genuine religious faith that, on the one hand, gave both a sense of the moral responsibility of political activity, and, on the other hand, told them that politics was neither the highest nor the most important thing in life. Both were Catholics, but unlike the political Catholics of the left who called for revolution in the name of Jesus or the conservative right who demanded the state protect their educational and moral agenda, they were pragmatists. The CDU was for Kohl, as for Adenauer, the great interdenominational party that offered Germans the choice of democracy based on the ethical value of personal liberty.

Kohl's imposing physical presence and his inevitably calm and measured demeanor gave some observers the impression that he was mentally lazy or inattentive. His enemies gleefully jumped on this trait and denounced him variously as a "wimp" (*Waschlappen*, a colloquial phrase for coward) or as a mediocre opportunist. This was a perilous misjudgement, as his success showed. One man who never learned to appreciate him was Helmut Schmidt. The two Helmuts detested each other.[2] Unlike Kurt Schumacher, who never doubted that Adenauer was a statesman of genius even while profoundly disagreeing with his policies, Schmidt apparently considered Kohl to be a sly and untrustworthy schemer without positive ideas of his own. Other social democrats were less vehement in their dislike, though still notably hostile. Few in the SPD were willing to concede that Kohl, no less than they, wanted the best for his country.

Even though regular elections were not scheduled until 1984, Kohl sought his own mandate from the voters. Therefore, as Brandt had done in 1972, Kohl used the device of a motion of confidence to force early elections. They were scheduled for March 6, 1983, and once the campaign was underway it became "the biggest and most intensive information offensive in the history of election campaigns."[3] While economic issues were of major importance (seasonal unemployment was the highest in the republic's history at 10.4 per cent or 2.5 million), national security issues dominated the rhetoric. The SPD, led by its new candidate for chancellor, Hans-Jochen Vogel, urged the United States and the Soviet Union to compromise on arms control, and Helmut Schmidt endorsed what had become known as the zero option solution, namely, the total removal of intermediate-range nuclear missiles in Europe. This goal was also supported by the FDP as "our goal to proceed from non-war through deterrence to peace through trust."[4] The CDU, on the contrary, called the NATO double track decision a schedule for disarmament and viewed the SPD position as tantamount to stepping away from the Atlantic alliance.

The leaders of the new coalition put questions of values and orientation in the foreground, and considered West Germany to be in a spiritual as well as an economic crisis, owing to more than ten years of uncertainty and confusion, deliberately provoked by the policies and attitudes of the SPD. Its policies, according to the CDU, had created doubts in the minds of Germans regarding their own history, traditional values, law and order, and confidence in their own government and legal system. The rhetoric of the campaign only exacerbated what many abroad viewed as the manifestation of instability in the West German political process. Strauss accused the SPD of "semantic deception of the citizenry" when it claimed that a victory of the coalition would endanger peace and disarmament. He continued that, should a coalition emerge between the SPD and the Greens, "a break with the United States would

[2] Ibid., 168–72.
[3] Heiner Geissler, secretary general of the CDU, on February 17, 1983, cited in *Archiv der Gegenwart*, March 6, 1983.
[4] *Relay from Bonn*, February 4, 1983.

only be a question of a relatively short time." As far as the Schmidt government was concerned, Strauss considered Schmidt himself to be a "bloody amateur and dilettante" as well as someone who had been "pulling the wool over the eyes" of his voters, and accused his government of having failed because of its "excessiveness" and "lack of standards." Vogel characterized Kohl as an "ignorant baby, if he (Kohl) believed the 2.5 million unemployed were the result of the high deficit and high social expenditure in the past, because without the policy of a government borrowing program by the social-liberal coalition the number of unemployed would even be higher."[5] The average unemployment rate for 1983 was 2.258 million or 9.1 per cent.[6]

When all was said and done, however, the CDU/CSU obtained its best results since 1957 with 48.8 per cent. The gap between the CDU/CSU and the SPD was greater than at any time since 1957. The SPD obtained 38.2 per cent and the FDP suffered from its defection to the CDU/CSU and received only 6.9 per cent, which was still more than many had feared. The most dramatic outcome, however, was the result achieved by the Greens. The party obtained representation in the Bundestag for the first time with 5.6 per cent of the vote, and thus became the first new party in the Bundestag since 1957. The Federal Republic demonstrated to its neigbors in Europe and to its friends abroad, that its political system, and its political processes, could survive the test of both time and acrimony.

Schmidt himself continued to enjoy both respect and popularity among West German citizens. Indeed, his accomplishments had been extraordinary in many ways. His vision for the future role of Western Europe was farsighted, and well conceived, as was his concept of the role the Federal Republic could play as a pillar of Western European partnership with the United States. As Kurt Becker wrote in *Die Zeit:*

Under the chancellorship of Helmut Schmidt, the Federal Republic of Germany has tremendously increased its international standing. This increase is the consequence of inner stability and economic power. Concrete results emerged from this: the biggest conventional contribution to the defense of Western Europe; steady progress in the policy of detente between East and West; and, finally, the absolute predictability of German policy in view of maintaining national interests as well as willingness to be a reliable partner. . . .

Therefore, the legacy of Chancellor Schmidt consists of the consolidation of foreign policy of a middle-sized European state, even though always aware of the division of the nation.[7]

[5] *Archiv der Gegenwart*, March 6, 1983.
[6] See Statistisches Bundesamt, *Statistisches Jahrbuch 1988.*
[7] *Die Zeit*, October 22, 1982, cited in Haftendorn, *Sicherheit und Stabilität*, 179–80.

So great was Schmidt's prestige that he was able to turn his defeat into a moral vindication and in so doing the FDP appeared to many as a group of unreliable deserters. Nevertheless the socialist-liberal coalition collapsed for serious reasons. The SPD was hopelessly split on the issue of nuclear weapons and relations with the US and the Soviet Union, as well as on many domestic policy issues. The FDP could not justify remaining in a government that refused to take elementary steps that, in its view, were required to stabilize the economy. Both factors remained after the end of the coalition to bedevil the tenure of Helmut Kohl.

PART X

The Pillar of Central Europe

There has never been an answer to the question of the political structure of Central Europe. Prussia, Bismarck's creation of the Reich, Wilhelmine attempts to break out of the confines of the European balance of power, the self-destructive reach for the status of world power [Griff nach der Weltmacht] *— all of this shows the mutability and continuing change in our part of the world. There will never be final solutions to the problem of shaping our political future in the center of Europe. In Berlin, one senses it: history goes forward.*

Richard von Weizsäcker

Introduction

In 1982 when Helmut Kohl became chancellor, there were political observers in West Germany and abroad who still viewed democracy in Germany as hanging in the balance. That feeling had not disappeared when the governing coalition of Kohl's CDU and Genscher's FDP scored an electoral triumph in the tenth national elections on March 6, 1983. But the elections symbolized another turning point – and another transition from shadow to substance. In the 1980s, unlike any other previous decade since 1945, the conduct of West Germany's national affairs had become subject to the same stresses and strains of democratic government that influenced the political fortunes of its Western European neighbors. It was, however, surviving and prospering.

In some ways, argued one commentator, the 1983 election result was the best ever for the CDU/CSU at 48.8 per cent. Only one previous election, that of 1957, had given the CDU/CSU a greater share of the second vote, namely 50.2 per cent. But at that time Adenauer was not interested in helping the FDP; in 1983, Kohl specifically urged voters to give their second vote to the FDP to guarantee its representation in the Bundestag. And there was good reason for his concern. If the FDP received less than 5 per cent and the CDU/CSU anything less than 50 per cent, a minority SPD government would have been possible with Green support, and political commentators expected the Greens to win representation as the first new party to do so in 30 years. To be absolutely sure of surviving as chancellor, Kohl therefore deliberately sacrificed the chance of an absolute majority to the interests and demands of the FDP. The strategy worked, although there were also those among the CDU voters who gave the FDP their second vote, because they feared Strauss would become foreign minister in a CDU/CSU majority government. The FDP received 6.9 per cent (1980: 10.6 per cent). Without Kohl's sacrifice, some analysts argued, the real strength of the CDU/CSU was well over 50 per cent.[1]

The major loser was the SPD, which suffered greater losses than in any previous federal election since the republic was established, at 38.2 per cent (1980: 42.9 per cent). The party's overall popularity corresponded to that at the time of the Godesberg Program in 1959, when the SPD was breaking out of the mid-thirties percentage range. In 1983, however, the question was whether the party was becoming divided and if the West German left was now permanently split between a large, moderate party, the SPD, and a radical movement, the Greens. The major reason for the defeat of the SPD was clearly the lack of confidence held by marginal voters in a party that could not make up its mind on security and economic policy and which had rejected the man who had led the country so well, Helmut Schmidt. The SPD candidate, Hans-Jochen Vogel, faced an impossible task. That he failed to win was not a surprise.

[1] Kaltefleiter, *Parteien im Umbruch*, 161–78.

1

The Nature of Party Politics

The conduct of the second Kohl government (the first having lasted only from October 1982 to March 1983) was largely determined by the same conviction that governed CDU strategy in the election, namely, the belief in the need to support the FDP and the fear that the West German electorate would never again give the CDU/CSU alone an absolute majority. This concern had been evident since the 1976 election which gave the CDU/CSU 48.6 per cent, 300,000 votes less than an absolute majority. That result, albeit a brilliant victory, contained, as Werner Kaltefleiter wrote, one flaw: it failed, in 1976, to unseat Helmut Schmidt as chancellor. Nonetheless, in view of such an accomplishment, an aggressive party leader might well conclude that a party that could garner 48.6 per cent might well hope to win a majority of seats next time. This did not happen in 1983. Rather, Helmut Kohl and his aides decided that the road to power lay in a coalition with the FDP. Hence the strategy of wooing the FDP from the coalition with Schmidt, and therefore the overwhelming leverage of the FDP leader, Genscher, who remained foreign minister and vice-chancellor through the change of government in 1982.

The defeatist view of the CDU leaders, that they were unlikely to receive an absolute majority and could not expect to gain power on their own, became a self-fulfilling prophecy. It also divided the party leadership into those who preferred the FDP alliance as a means of moderating the right wing, and the right wing leaders themselves who regarded the FDP and the moderates as obstacles to the implementation of genuine Christian democratic policies. The right wing included virtually all of the CSU, as well as the CDU leaders Manfred Todenhöfer and Alfred Dregger. They saw in the CDU/CSU government the responsibility to revise Ostpolitik and reduce the role of government and bureaucracy at home. Among the moderate group were the finance minister, Gerhard Stoltenberg, Rainer Barzel, and the general secretary of the CDU, Heiner Geissler. Among younger CDU figures was Lothar Späth, since 1978 the successful minister-president of Baden-Württemberg.

Späth (born 1937) was the one undisputed political star in a party that, though it held federal governmental power in the 1980s, seemed strangely lacking in dynamic leadership. By 1988, he was the only head of a *Land* government whose party had an absolute majority of seats in the *Landtag*. Thanks largely to his administration, the economy of Baden-Württemberg boomed in the 1980s. The powerhouse of the south-west state was its capital, Stuttgart, with the Daimler-Benz (whose chairman was Edzard Reuter, the son of the former mayor of West Berlin) and Ferdinand Porsche truck and luxury car factories and hundreds of smaller businesses supplying the larger ones. But the south-west did not rely only on the automobile industry. The entire Württemberg region and the area around Mannheim in the north and Freiburg in the south, were dotted with small electronic industries and companies catering to specialized market niches world-wide. The original external design of the familiar Apple Macintosh personal computer was the work of a Württemberg engineering and design genius who started a small company in Germany as a graduate student in 1969 and by 1988 was employing dozens of young, forward-looking, and hardworking designers in offices in the Black Forest, Silicon Valley in California, and Tokyo. So successful and so able to seize the forces of the time was the economy of the south-west *Land* that people jokingly referred to it as "*Späth-kapitalismus,*" a pun on Späth's last name and on the Marxist phrase *Spätkapitalismus*, meaning "late capitalism" with the implication that capitalism was at death's door.

The moderate group's intellectual head was the CDU leader in North Rhine-Westphalia, Kurt Biedenkopf (born 1930). He was an academic lawyer who had been the president of the University of Bochum in the mid-1970s and, after a period in the Bundestag, became one of the leading figures of the North Rhine-Westphalian CDU from 1977 to 1987. As a political intellectual he published frequently on political and social issues, advocating an environmentally conscious and ethically founded liberalism. His strategy clearly was to attract the large, moderate group of voters angry about pollution and worried about the lack of power of ordinary people in modern, technological society – people who were essentially conservative in their values, but who might be tempted to vote for the Greens if they found no spiritual home in the CDU.

Biedenkopf clearly believed that the way for the CDU to regain power was to capture voters dissatisfied with the big government philosophy of the SPD. In 1979 he nearly caused the party to oust Kohl from the chairmanship by writing a memorandum strongly critical of his leadership, although Biedenkopf claimed he never intended to threaten Kohl's position. When Kohl became chancellor in 1982 he did not invite Biedenkopf, who was his exact contemporary, to join the cabinet. Biedenkopf continued to propagate his vision of a Christian democratic future, but his influence was declining in terms of power within the party even as it rose in the public eye. In 1987 he failed to obtain reappointment as chairman of the North Rhine-Westphalian party and his influence in the party was on the wane.

Many observers formerly placed both Barzel (born 1924) and Stoltenberg (born 1928) on the right of the party. Barzel had tried and failed to unseat Brandt in 1972 over the conduct of Ostpolitik, and Stoltenberg had vociferously attacked the social-liberal coalition's economic and fiscal policies. In the Kohl era, both were clearly moderates. When Kohl came to power in 1982 he appointed Stoltenberg minister of finance and Barzel minister for inner-German relations. Barzel thus held again the same ministry he had held in 1962–3, his previous cabinet post, then known as the ministry of all-German affairs. After the election of 1983, Kohl replaced him with Heinrich Windelen (born in 1921 in Silesia), a veteran of the Bundestag since 1957 and formerly minister for expellees. Barzel became president of the Bundestag, a position he was forced to abandon in late 1984, after he became implicated in a financial scandal.

The old and the new moderates in the CDU sought rational revisions, not a revolution, in the major areas of domestic and foreign policy. Their goal was to restrain, not reduce, public spending and to continue the social-liberal Ostpolitik without essential change. They retained the upper hand throughout 1983–8. Kohl kept his own political position, however, deliberately unclear, and gave the right wing occasional reason to hope that he might support their views on important issues, such as Ostpolitik or tax policy.

In addition, Kohl and the CDU were faced with the continuing problem of Strauss. The serious defeat of Strauss in 1980 had not wholly destroyed his political hopes, although it made his political fortunes less certain. The question in 1983 was whether he should be given a ministerial post to placate him and his supporters, a possibility the FDP strenuously opposed. One of Genscher's conditions for changing coalitions was that Strauss would not be a minister in any government in which he also served. Thus Strauss remained as minister-president of Bavaria (since 1978), but continued to play an active role on the national level. He always insisted that the Union parties should seek an absolute majority without relying on the FDP, and this insistence was the reason for his temporary break with Kohl between 1976 and 1979 and his unfortunate candidacy for the chancellorship in 1980. By letting him try and fail, the CDU hoped to prove that a federal government with Strauss was unacceptable to a majority of the electorate. But proving that point was not the same as proving that an absolute CDU/CSU majority was impossible.

Within the SPD internal strife was more acute. The chancellor candidate in 1983, Hans-Jochen Vogel (born 1926), the former mayor of Munich and candidate for mayor in Berlin against Richard von Weizsäcker in 1981, did not project a strong image. His manner was schoolmasterly, he lacked charisma, and many considered him a vapid personality. Thus, a struggle began for leadership which strengthened the left wing. In 1985, the SPD chose as its candidate for chancellor Johannes Rau, a politician from North Rhine-Westphalia, who had been speaker of the Bundesrat in 1982–3 and who originally came from the circle of Gustav Heinemann. He only gradually developed a clear public identity and it remained uncertain whether he had the capacity to mount a convincing challenge to Kohl in the next election. But his selection was made with the tacit approval of Willy Brandt, who not only retained the position of party chairman, a post he held from 1964 to 1987, but who was moving to the left himself. Brandt no longer had to contend with the rivalry and criticism of Helmut Schmidt nor with the SPD's best strategic thinker, Herbert Wehner, who retired from politics in 1983, and moved to Sweden. While Brandt's influence remained dominant, his actions became increasingly erratic and contradictory, and, eventually, were of questionable value to his party and to the Federal Republic.

Brandt's views on Ostpolitik and Third World policy were continually at odds with those of the government. As chairman of the Socialist International (SI) since 1976 he became especially concerned with development in lesser-developed countries. Under Brandt's leadership the SI established a commission to study economic and social issues. It produced a report, published in 1981, entitled *North-South* but popularly known as the Brandt Report.[1] Its authors called for governmentally organized large-scale redistribution of income from industrial to Third World countries. They painted a very dismal picture of the prospects for Third World development and attributed responsibility for this state of affairs to the economic and political leaders of the industrialized countries who allegedly kept poorer nations deliberately in a condition of dependence and poverty. The report wholly ignored the role of free economic initiative in creating wealth and was based on a view of the causes of economic growth that was not shared by a majority of

[1] See Independent Commission on International Development Issues, *North-South: A Programme for Survival*.

competent economists. The issues involved were serious, but the report's conclusions were drawn so as to strengthen those forces in Third World countries who had an interest in making the industrialized nations feel guilty for their own success. In turn it strengthened those forces in the Federal Republic who also used guilt as a political tool.

Brandt's activities in the SI, culminating in the Brandt Report, irritated the moderate wing of the SPD but delighted its left wing, which admired Brandt and regarded him as a peacemaking father figure who could bring Green voters back to the SPD. The result was to complete the turn of the SPD away from the policies that produced compromise with the CDU, and toward a path of leftist sectarianism. In turn, the left wing of the SPD gradually gained control of the party apparatus in the early 1980s and began to reintroduce varieties of Marxist ideology that were incompatible with the Godesberg Program of 1959 and with most SPD policies thereafter.

Among the leaders of the SPD left were Günter Gaus, Erhard Eppler, Oskar Lafontaine, and Peter Glotz. The former head of the Jusos (Young Socialists), Karsten Voigt, became more flexible in his views as a sophisticated protégé of Egon Bahr. As Juso leader in the early 1970s, Voigt had demanded radical new initiatives in West German foreign policy and implied that Bonn's greatest foreign policy problem was not a non-existent Soviet threat but American imperialism. In the 1980s, as the SPD's chief defense spokesman, Voigt argued for gradual, not radical changes in West German defense. Unlike his contemporaries in the peace movement, Voigt did not contend that West Germany did not or should not defend itself, only that the policies of the US and of the CDU-led government were incorrect. Gaus, after leaving his position as the Federal Republic's permanent representative in East Berlin in 1981, wrote extensively, arguing for more openness toward and cooperation with the GDR and vehemently criticized the CDU government and the economic and political status quo in West Germany. Eppler, former minister for development aid in Brandt's first government, became, in the 1980s, an ideological and intellectual leader of the peace movement, and an influential public spokesman for unilateral disarmament as well as for West German opposition to US foreign policy.

Gaus and Eppler both belonged to an older generation. Lafontaine, a physicist born in 1943, was mayor of Saarbrücken from 1976 to 1985 and thereafter minister-president of the Saar. He was an able ideologue who combined demands for conventional social democratic policies against unemployment in the mining industry with grandiose plans for West German withdrawal from NATO. To expose his views to a broader public he sought the assistance of the publishing house Rowohlt, which in 1983 published his controversial analysis of West German security interests with the provocative title *Angst vor den Freunden* (Fear of one's friends). The title implied that Lafontaine believed the West Germans had more to fear politically and militarily from the US than from the Soviet Union.

In 1986 Lafontaine became deputy party chairman and clearly expected to succeed Brandt. After the Bundestag elections of January 1987 he proposed that the party move sharply leftward to capture the Green vote, implying that he was the man to do that job. He had underestimated the residual power of the moderates in the party, however, who feared losing centrist votes more than they hoped to gain Green support. They stepped up their campaign to keep Lafontaine out of the chairman's seat even as Brandt, in March 1987, announced that he would retire early as a consequence of growing criticism of his leadership within the party. Seeing his influence clearly weakening, Brandt announced his resignation on March 23 after serving as chairman for more than 20 years. His successor was Vogel. Lafontaine remained as Vogel's deputy. Whether because of his perception that moderation was a virtue or because of opportunism, Lafontaine began to express his views in more moderate terms, less likely to offend the center of his party.

All of these figures shared the view that the Soviet Union was not a threat to the West and that the challenge to maintain peace in Europe was threatened more by US actions than by Soviet intentions. They emphasized not only dialogue and negotiation as a reasonable approach to security issues, but also their unique qualifications to carry out this policy, which they viewed as vested in a special SPD relationship with the SED in East Germany. Gaus claimed that he had greatly strengthened this relationship as the FRG's permanent representative in East Berlin from 1974 to 1981. But when the SPD left government in 1982, its party leadership chose not to support the new government's Ostpolitik, which was virtually identical to its own. Rather, the SPD continued to develop bilateral contacts with the SED despite the historical memories of SED persecution of social democrats. Between 1983 and 1988 these contacts were directed by Bahr and Eppler and resulted in three SPD-SED position papers on (1) a nuclear-free zone in Germany, (2) a chemical weapon-free zone, and (3) principles of dialogue and mutual relations. The CDU/CSU found it shocking that a democratic opposition party in a Western country should seek to pursue its own foreign policy, independent of the elected West German government, with a dictatorial ruling party of a communist state; a party, moreover, which bore a great burden of guilt for oppressing its own people and denying their national right of self-determination. Bahr rejected such criticism and insisted that to demand freedom of self-determination for all Germans was to be disruptive. The special relationship continued to develop.

In the eyes of many the SPD was drifting. Gesine Schwan, a prominent SPD intellectual and professor at the Free University of Berlin, recognized this development and its potential consequences. She criticized the party's movement to the left and what she regarded as an undeclared policy that deliberately ignored the SPD's historical commitments. What she wrote about the party's current view of the Soviet Union, applied also to its view of the GDR:

> Why do so many social democratic activists close their eyes to these threats [to peace]?. . . . Because their understanding of the Soviet Union is ambivalent. They respectively trivialize and dramatize Soviet policy, two attitudes that are not contradictory. Beneath the superficial trivialization of Soviet policy lies deep fear and resignation toward Soviet military power. . . .
> The dynamic thrust in the shaping of SPD policy now comes from Oskar Lafontaine, Erhard Eppler, and Egon Bahr. Their common denominator is critical distance to the West, suspicion (verging on hostility) toward the policy of the United States and the promotion of nationalist resentments against the superpowers and especially against America. . . . This chosen course is leading directly towards making German social democracy, founded in the name of freedom, de facto into one of the most effective instruments of the Soviet policy of domination.[2]

Following Kohl's election, therefore, the SPD struggled with a choice between two strategies analogous to that faced by the CDU in 1976. One was to move toward the center, hoping to recapture the marginal vote essential for victory. Such a strategy would, in the medium term, strengthen the Greens. They could rightly say that the SPD was unable to shake off its bourgeois trappings and that they, the Greens, therefore remained the only true party of the ecological and pacifist left. Thus, they could attract more dissatisfied pacifists, egalitarians, and radicals from the left wing of the SPD. For the SPD, however, this strategy might offer the best chance of recapturing power in the longer term. Herbert Wehner himself, the master strategist who had done more than anyone else to bring the SPD to power in 1969, insisted after the 1983 election, in what was one of his last public statements, that the only road to power lay in approaching the center; in other words, a moderate strategy based on solid performance in *Land* governments to re-establish the credibility

---

[2] Schwan, "Die SPD und die westliche Freiheit," in *Wohin treibt die SPD?*, eds Maruhn and Wilke, 43, 50–1.

of the SPD as a serious party of national government. He also predicted that it would take 15 years for the SPD to return to power.

The other strategy, favored by Brandt and his younger allies, was to move left to capture the Green vote, but without losing support among traditional social democrats. It was virtually an impossible task, that was perceived as opportunistic and contradictory by definition. Brandt cleverly referred to this strategy as "finding a majority to the left of the CDU." This idea did not preclude renewal of a coalition with the FDP, but it was not clear how he proposed to embrace the Greens without offending the moderate wing of the SPD. It was nonetheless for him a desirable goal, because the combined vote of the SPD and the Greens would amount to almost 45 per cent – very nearly as much as the SPD had ever obtained on its own. If the Green vote could be absorbed and the FDP convinced to change coalition partners once again, such a strategy might conceivably return the SPD to government.

The party chose the second strategy. It was inevitable that it should do so, given the leftward momentum of the party organization under Willy Brandt and, therefore, of those who formulated party policy. The leftists in the party leadership had felt betrayed ever since Schmidt replaced Brandt, and had clearly expressed his intention to pursue a centrist policy based on fiscal responsibility and strong ties with the United States. The tension between Schmidt and the party activists was irreconcilable, since it was based on fundamental philosophical, temperamental, and ideological differences. The party activists belonged largely to the proponents of the "other Germany," exemplified in the figure of Horst Eberhard Richter, the psychiatrist and supporter of unilateral disarmament and pacifism. Indeed, the developing rift had been made clear as early as 1974 at the Juso congress, at which Schmidt illustrated his priorities by concluding that the Jusos demonstrated "a crisis of their brain," whereas he, Schmidt, was concerned with the "crisis of the world economy."[3] The Jusos did not forget this remark and took their revenge.

The activists preferred, for ideological reasons, to woo the Green vote, rather than to move to the center. Some of them preferred ideological purity to a more moderate posture, that might bring the SPD back to power. No one in West Germany outside the hard core of radicals in the Green movement – the so-called "red Greens," opposed to the ecological and rural-romantic "green Greens" – seriously considered extraparliamentary revolutionary activity to be acceptable or realistic.

Brandt, Lafontaine, Voigt and their cohorts in the SPD thus focused

---

[3] Kaltefleiter, *Parteien in Umbruch*, 46.

on wooing leftists from the Greens and on eliminating the Greens as a national movement. The Green leaders were aware of this and therefore suspicious about allying themselves with the SPD either at the state or the national level. To do so would not only be to risk *Umklammerung* (a tight, smothering embrace), but also to enter the game of party politics. The fundamentalist wing ("fundis") rejected this idea completely. For his part, Brandt repeatedly asserted in the years following 1982, that the SPD would not enter into a coalition with the Greens, even if that were the only way the SPD could assume power in the federal elections scheduled for 1987.

The Greens entered the Bundestag in March 1983 with 5.6 per cent of the vote and with only slightly fewer delegates than the FDP. Once in the Bundestag, however, the Greens were faced with the problem of operating as a party, when actually they were not a party, but a movement of diversified elements, which did not recognize the basic principle of parliamentary representation, enshrined in clause 38 of the Basic Law: that no deputy can be bound by agreement made before his election with any person or persons, but that he makes every decision as a deputy purely on his own and bound only by his own conscience.

It was perhaps not surprising that the Greens rejected this latter principle because their conception of democracy differed dramatically from that which had held sway in the West since the American revolution 200 years previously. For them, the idea that Bundestag members should decide matters as they saw fit was an example of outdated individualism. In the world view of the Greens, the truth about any issue emerges from mass consciousness and no one person can be allowed to question it. Their vision of democracy owed much to the rival tradition of Jean-Jacques Rousseau in the eighteenth and some of the socialist utopians of the nineteenth century, such as Charles Fourier and Wilhelm Weitling. They, therefore, had a rule that the deputies must vote as the leaders of the movement told them. The elected members had to resign their seats after two years, handing them over to their deputies midway through the four-year term (rotation principle). This rule caused a split between the fundis and the realists ("realos"). The realos, led by Otto Schily, a lawyer active on the extreme left since the late 1950s, insisted that the Greens would have no influence unless they followed the rules of the game. During 1983–5, a majority of Greens slowly accepted the realist position, but it was more out of opportunism and out of a desire for influence, than out of a deeper understanding or respect for parliamentary democracy. Initially, they also idealistically decided to keep only DM 1,950 of their salary of DM 12,000 per month, paid to all Bundestag representatives, putting the remaining DM 10,050 into an ecology fund.

However, the Green party itself was also undergoing transformation. On the state level, the realos were stronger, whereas on the national level the fundis seemed to be in charge. In June 1984 in Hesse the Greens agreed to "tolerate" the SPD government under Holger Börner. This was remarkable since Börner was disliked by many Greens for his support of nuclear energy and for the construction of a second runway at Frankfurt airport. Opposition to the runway, including violent demonstrations, had been one of the important symbolic issues that spurred citizens' initiatives in the late 1970s. The toleration agreement broke down when Börner refused to violate constitutional procedure in order to stop the federal ministry of the interior from licensing two nuclear power plants in the state. In December 1985 the Greens in Hesse, in spite of the opposition of the fundamentalist executive committee members Jutta Ditfurth (daughter of Hoimar Graf von Ditfurth, a popular science writer interested in environmental issues), Rainer Trampert, and Lukas Beckmann, agreed to enter a formal coalition with the minority social democrats. The most important Green member of the resulting government was Joschka Fischer, who became Hesse's minister of the environment, the first Green minister.

The coalition led an unhappy and stressful life, plagued with disagreement over environmental issues. It broke down in late 1986, and in the elections that followed, in June 1987, the CDU and FDP together obtained a majority and formed the new state government in Hesse. This debacle was viewed by the Greens, as a party, as a failed experiment that accomplished little. In turn, this judgement contributed to the victory of Ditfurth and the fundis who gained control of the party leadership on a national level, and scored an impressive victory of 8.3 per cent in the Bundestag elections in January 1987. The travails of the Greens, however, took on shades of weakness and discontent in 1988 that seemed familiar in a democratic system whose actors are real human beings. At the party convention in December, held in Karlsruhe, Ditfurth and the fundis who formed a majority of the party's executive committee were replaced following criticism for their conduct in recent financial scandals.[4] Thus, while the SPD underwent a radical transformation of internal control, and in effect expelled its more conservative members from party leadership positions, it failed to gain electoral strength from the Greens caught up in an internal feud that "endangered the continued existence of the party. . . . Eight years after its formation the party must basically form itself anew."[5]

While they lasted the struggles within the SPD and the Greens left

---

[4] *Relay from Bonn*, December 9, 1988.
[5] Horst Bieber, "Vor der Stunde der Wahrheit," *Die Zeit*, December 16, 1988.

the political field to the governing parties, the CDU/CSU and the FDP. The SPD and the Greens obtained another chance to prove that a Red–Green coalition was viable when both together gained the absolute majority in the Berlin election in March 1989, and formed a government with Walter Momper (SPD) as governing mayor of the city. Observers regarded this experiment as a test case for a possible future Red–Green coalition on the federal level, should the SPD and the Greens together win a majority in a future national election.

2

Germany and her Allies: The Missile Debate of 1983

All of West Germany's major allies welcomed the victory of the CDU/ CSU-FDP coalition in March 1983, although they without doubt regretted the departure of postwar Germany's most respected statesman after Adenauer. The total defeat of Schmidt and his few remaining supporters in the party leadership convinced many international observers that the SPD could not be relied on to carry out policies it had formerly supported, notably the double track decision. The strongest international support for the SPD came from the British Labour party, which was itself roundly defeated in the British general election of June 1983, and from the social democratic parties of some of the smaller NATO countries like the Netherlands and Denmark, where neutralist and anti-American forces were influential.

The socialist president of France, François Mitterrand, illustrated this point when he visited West Germany in January 1983, on the occasion of the twentieth anniversary of the Friendship Treaty between France and Germany, which had been signed in Paris in 1963. On one level the visit was simply another of the Franco-German summits which had taken place regularly since the 1963 treaty. When Schmidt and Giscard were in office these mini-summits had become important events which they had not been before. When Mitterrand replaced Giscard as French head of state in 1981, he continued the periodic talks with Schmidt. But the value of the Bonn–Paris relationship demanded that Mitterrand be able to collaborate with whomever was in power in Bonn. In 1983 the French president quickly moved to continue the developing Franco-German relationship with his conservative counterpart in Bonn, Kohl. On another level, the January 1983 mini-summit was used by the CDU to support the election campaign against Mitterrand's ostensible ideological ally, the SPD.

The high point of the visit was Mitterrand's strongly worded speech to a special session of the Bundestag. Observing that "the missiles are in the East, and the pacifists are in the West," he pointed to the clear and indisputable Soviet superiority in theater nuclear forces – that is to say, nuclear forces located in or targeted on Europe and intended to deter war on the European continent – and to the need for NATO to restore a credible deterrent by installing the proposed small number of accurate missiles in Western Europe capable of reaching the Soviet Union. Mitterrand took, in general, a far stronger anti-Soviet line than Giscard.

The combination of these different factors made 1983 a year of missile debate. The NATO ministers had agreed that if the US–Soviet negotiations on INF failed to produce a satisfactory result, the Pershing IIs and GLCMs (ground-launched cruise missiles) would begin to arrive at their European bases in West Germany, Italy, and Britain by the end of 1983. Indeed, every effort was made by the United States to reach a negotiated agreement. Deadlines were established and then extended several times during that year. (See the story of the negotiations in Strobe Talbott's *Deadly Gambits*.) At no time, however, did it appear very likely that the Soviet government would agree to the US "zero option" proposal, made by President Reagan in November 1981; namely, that if the Soviets dismantled their SS-20 missile launchers aimed at Western Europe, then NATO would not deploy the INF. Schmidt, according to his memoirs, first mentioned the zero option in December 1979 and repeatedly raised it thereafter in public.[1]

In the summer of 1982, the chief American negotiator on INF in Geneva, Paul Nitze, had cobbled together what he thought was a clear and satisfactory understanding with his Soviet counterpart, Yuli Kvitsinsky. It came to be known as the "walk in the woods" proposal, because it was worked out in part on a walk that Nitze and Kvitsinsky took in the Jura mountains on July 16, 1982. Its main feature was that the US would drop the plan to deploy Pershing IIs, capable of reaching the Soviet Union, in West Germany. On their part the Soviets proposed – or appeared to have proposed – deployment of fewer SS-20 launchers and suggested that the US might replace the old, inaccurate Pershing Ia missiles with extremely accurate, but shorter-range missiles. The Pershing missiles belonged to the Bundeswehr, but the nuclear warheads for them were US property and could not be released without the authorization of the American president. Washington policy-makers discussed this concept intensively throughout the summer, but what they finally might have decided was made irrelevant by the brusque Soviet condemnation of the understanding which came on September 29, 1982.[2]

---

[1]   Schmidt, *Menschen und Mächte*, 333.
[2]   Talbott, *Deadly Gambits*, 116–46.

The image of the "walk in the woods" was destined to play a much greater part in public opinion than in diplomacy. When it became known that the leading American and Soviet negotiators had apparently reached an understanding among themselves, many West Germans, particularly those close to the SPD, speculated, without justification, that a workable agreement could have been achieved if only Washington had immediately confirmed its support of the concept. The critics ignored the fact that, whatever the eventual American reaction to the proposal, the Soviets had rejected it without discussion. Thus, the legend arose in West Germany that American procrastination, intransigence, and incompetence had spoiled the chances of a significant Eurostrategic arms control agreement, therefore making the deployment of Pershing II missiles on German soil a virtual certainty.

Schmidt himself in his memoirs stated as his firm opinion that the "walk in the woods" proposal was quashed in the National Security Council by Richard Perle, the assistant secretary of defense for international security affairs, before the Soviet refusal was known. Accordingly Schmidt could state that it was "Reagan's decision to reject the . . . chance of an agreement on limitation of Eurostrategic intermediate-range nuclear weapons."[3]

With the saga of "the walk in the woods" as asserted evidence that the US was interested in deploying the Pershing IIs at any price and at the expense of arms control, the West German left prepared, in early 1983, for a hot summer and autumn of demonstrations and activism in the media. During the week of October 15–22, 1983, the largest demonstrations in West German history took place in Bonn as 300–400,000 people, mostly in their twenties, arrived from all over the country in buses and special trains to listen to Willy Brandt attack the government, and to demand that West Germany refuse to accept the new missiles scheduled for arrival by the end of the year. These and earlier demonstrations were the high-water mark of the peace movement, which embraced a variety of organizations, ideas, and people from many different professions. The Greens considered themselves part of the movement, since one of the four tenets of Green policy was pacifism. The peace movement was the coordinated action of all West Germans opposed to the double track decision. Many were members of the youthful culture of opposition that grew out of the radicalism of 1960s and the citizens' initiatives of the 1970s; others were those who felt themselves, rightly or wrongly, alienated from the established political, economic, and constitutional system of West Germany.[4] The movement

---

[3] Schmidt, *Menschen und Mächte*, 332, 334–5.
[4] See Fischer et al., *Jugend '81*; and Schmid, *Sicherheitspolitik und Friedensbewegung*.

also included a number of journalists and writers such as Günter Grass and Heinrich Böll, whose passion for peace was directed against weapons that had never been used and which, indeed, had probably ensured the very peace they considered to be in jeopardy.

The organizational framework of the peace movement was never very easy to untangle for outsiders. There did exist a coordinating committee of local organizations based in Hannover which shared an address with an organization of the DKP, the German Communist Party.[5] In general, however, communist participation in the peace movement was discreet but effective, especially concerning the logistics of the mass demonstrations. The DKP organization, suitably camouflaged, took care of renting buses and trains, directing the marchers and making sure that the banners bore innocuous slogans.[6] There were in reality several peace movements. One was manifested by the mass demonstrations and disappeared after the double track decision was implemented at the end of 1983. Another consisted of groups of professionals, such as the organization of West German Physicians Against Nuclear War; that is, of doctors who stated that they would refuse to do anything to help victims of a nuclear attack on the grounds that even preparing to offer such help made nuclear war more likely. This somewhat tortured and convoluted logic – and the implied violation of the Hippocratic oath – was surprisingly popular among West German physicians, who could be seen on the streets of West German cities throughout the early 1980s rallying support for their position.

Writers and intellectuals also took a prominent role in this kind of peace movement activity. In December 1981 the West and East German writers' associations held a meeting in East Berlin, at which a number of prominent writers signed an open letter to President Reagan and General Secretary Brezhnev calling on both to desist from further deployments of nuclear weapons.[7] In West Germany itself an especially vociferous spokesman of the peace movement was Günter Grass, "America's favorite German-language author," according to 800 American college professors and students canvassed by Boston's Goethe Institute. By the 1980s, however, much of what he wrote was pure political diatribe of little or no literary merit. On January 30, 1983, for example, the anniversary of Hitler's seizure of power 50 years earlier, Grass delivered a speech in St. Paul's Church in Frankfurt, the foremost symbol in Germany of support for democracy and independence:

---

[5] Langguth, *Protestbewegung*, 157–61.
[6] See Alexiev, *Soviet Campaign Against INF*.
[7] See Grass, *Widerstand lernen*.

Thousands of tactical nuclear weapons are stationed in the Federal Republic. . . .

Each of the two [German] states is an outpost of one or the other military bloc, and both states are confronted with the same certainty – namely, that even if "only" tactical nuclear weapons are employed, the end of the Germans is foreordained by the loyalty of both German states to a strategic pact. *Force majeure*, so to speak. The price that must be paid. The apologists of madness always have an explanation ready.

This too, I say has gone far enough. We do not know whether the Geneva conference can call a halt to the twofold madness. Already marked by failure, it holds out little hope. Moreover, the present West German government is too mindless and powerless to defend Germany's special interests against the allied superpower and our neighbor France. In place of a firm policy it offers cowardly toadying.[8]

Opposition to what the Kohl government, and the Schmidt government before it, considered to be an extremely serious national security interest, continued in various forms throughout 1983. It combined civil disobedience with an attempt to circumvent the Kohl government in the Federal Constitutional Court. The pressure from the peace movement led Kohl and Genscher to request in July that the US revive "the walk in the woods" understanding and offer unequivocally to accept an agreement excluding Pershing IIs from Europe. Once more the burden of responsibility was placed on the US, even though the Soviet government had indicated it would not accept "the walk in the woods" understanding. The US government, however, had in the meantime definitely decided to reject any arms control agreement preventing deployment of the Pershing IIs, unless the Soviet government agreed first to withdraw its SS-20 missiles.

On September 1, the Soviet Union shot down a Korean airliner, killing all 269 people on board. Though the Soviet government later claimed that it was a horrible mistake and many Western publicists professed to believe them, there was a good deal of evidence to show that the Soviet government knew very well that it was shooting down a civilian airliner and murdering people who were by no stretch of the imagination dangerous enemies of the Soviet Union. But those who believed Soviet excuses failed to consider the nature of a regime that shoots down foreign aircraft before asking questions. The American reaction was very restrained – in effect, there was no reaction – which was notable given the Reagan administration's insistence that it would hold arms control talks hostage to Soviet good behavior. In the face of murderous Soviet violence against innocent civilians, however, the

---

[8] Grass, *On Writing and Politics*, 145–6.

American government conducted itself in the same manner as the Carter administration. The White House continued talks on the grounds that, precisely at times of crisis, it was important to pursue the avenue of negotiation.

In West Germany the peace movement and its intellectual allies in the media doubted that the Korean airliner was merely a civilian flight, and within a few months an elaborate conspiracy industry had sprung up to try to prove that the plane was actually on a spy mission for US intelligence and that, while excessive, the Soviet reaction was justified. It was typical of the neurotic view of America, held by a large proportion of West German public figures on the left, that they eagerly looked for a conspiracy while refusing to accept the straightforward explanation, which, moreover, was supported by ample historical parallels; namely, the event was another example of the Soviet government's ruthlessness in demonstrating its power to potential opponents.

Although the Pershing IIs and GLCMs were US property, they could not be deployed without the official permission of the West German government. The final Bundestag debate on this issue took place on November 21–2, 1983, just after an extraordinary party conference held by the SPD in Cologne on November 18–19. Although the conference included all the themes of recent SPD history, its main purpose was to vote on a motion from the party leadership to reject the double track decision. The motion itself consisted of five pages, single-spaced. It repeated earlier party statements on the intention to deploy the Pershing IIs and claimed that the double track decision was flawed because the US administration was more interested in deploying the new missiles than in negotiating for disarmament. The motion went on to say that "the SPD does not think that all possibilities for a negotiated solution have been used." It called on the SPD to "reject the deployment of new American intermediate-range systems on the territory of the Federal Republic" and to "demand continued negotiations."

The vote on this motion came on the second and last day of the conference, after speeches by all the major party figures. On the first day, the party chose its candidates for the second direct elections to the European Parliament which were scheduled for June 1984. The party council then issued a scathing denunciation of US policy in Central America and in Grenada, a tiny Caribbean island where US forces, at the request of neighboring states, had recently overthrown a dictatorial and illegitimate communist regime. Party chairman Willy Brandt spoke at length on the need for peace and cooperation with the Third World and the Central European communist regimes. He demanded "security partnership" with the East, and insisted that "the political task is to dismantle the East–West confrontation and to transform the relationship between the alliances into a European peace order. . . . Both world powers must become partners and guarantors of such a peace order."[9] Kiesinger had coined the phrase, "European peace order," in the 1960s. In Brandt's interpretation, the phrase meant that the two "alliances" – both the democratically constituted Atlantic Alliance and the communist Warsaw Pact – were politically and morally equivalent, that both were necessary for peace and stability, and neither had aggressive designs against the other.

The vote on the motion to continue negotiations, despite the Soviet refusal to reduce the number of their SS-20s threatening Western Europe, marked the final stage of the defeat of Helmut Schmidt and all he stood for in the party. On the second day of the conference, he gave what many regarded as his finest political speech. After acknowledging the sincerity of those in the majority and requesting that they also acknowledge his, he gave a detailed analysis of the military and diplomatic situation facing West Germany and a defense of his own policies. He argued that the Soviet leaders wanted peace and wondered why, since this was so, they had built up the vast arsenal of intermediate-range nuclear weapons targeted on Western Europe. Whatever the reasons, he said, it was essential that the West remain united and modernize its defenses, because only a firm Western stance backed by credible military force could lead to a more stable and peaceful future. If NATO did not deploy INF, he warned, the Soviets could decouple Western Europe from America by implicitly threatening nuclear blackmail of Europe alone. The Pershing IIs and GLCMs would recouple European and American security by giving the West a credible response at a level lower than strategic intercontinental missiles, thus denying the Soviet Union the chance to limit nuclear war to Europe.

West Germany did not have the French option of developing its own nuclear force to replace declining American power, nor did Schmidt believe it should: "The Federal Republic must never strive for possession or use of a single nuclear weapon. . . . It is hard to endure, but it remains true: the Federal Republic remains dependent upon the nuclear protection by others, namely by the United States; at least as long as France and Britain do not commit themselves to Europe to take over this protection. . . . The Soviet Union must not have a de facto right of veto over Western Europe. . . ."[10] Schmidt used a great deal of time in his speech to stress his own commitment to detente and cooperation and won much applause when he attacked the Reagan administration for undermining economic cooperation with its attempted embargo of pipeline supplies. The delegates listened politely to Schmidt but

---

[9] SPD, *Bundesdelegierten-Konferenz*, 67–8.
[10] Ibid., 106–8.

supported the motion to reject deployment by 400 to 14, with three abstentions.

It was a sad and symbolic ending of a three-year process by which proponents of a new ideology, reminiscent in some ways of positions taken in the 1950s, had won control of the SPD. It was also the beginning of a new official social democratic outlook on security and defense, introduced by Egon Bahr in a paper presented to the conference on "alternative strategies." The phrase appeared to mean types of defense that did not rely on nuclear weapons but rather on high-technology conventional arms and militia groups. The idea behind "alternative strategies" was to reject the established institution of the Bundeswehr as well as the NATO strategy of "flexible response" which Schmidt himself had helped to introduce in the 1960s. Bahr's working group included Karsten Voigt, Oskar Lafontaine, and other members of the anti-nuclear left wing of the party. One of them, Andreas von Bülow (born 1937), became his party's leading public spokesman for "alternative strategies" in the years ahead.

Three days after the SPD rejected deployment, the Bundestag voted on November 22 to accept the new US missiles on its territory. This approval was legally necessary if the missiles were to be installed. As expected, virtually all the CDU/CSU and FDP members of the Bundestag voted for deployment. The SPD voted against it. Schmidt and his few remaining allies abstained, thus showing ultimate solidarity with the party that had rejected his policies. On November 23, Yuli Kvitsinsky announced in Geneva that the Soviet Union was walking out of the INF talks, and on the same day, the first nine cruise missiles arrived at a US Army field artillery brigade at Mutlangen in south-west Germany.

In December, however, a footnote was added to the missile debate. Although it was anticlimactic, it nonetheless illustrated the intense feeling – bordering on the irrational – that the political left devoted to its concept of peace in Europe. Shortly before Christmas, Günter Grass led a group of prominent writers, artists and scientists in a protest at Waldheide near Heilbronn (Baden-Württemberg), an alleged Pershing II site: "He called on young men to exercise their right of conscientious objection to mandatory military service as long as atomic, tactical, chemical and bacteriological weapons remained in the Federal Republic." And he told his followers that "in the future he would work to undermine the morale of the armed forces, arguing that the deployment of the Pershing II missiles in the FRG made the Bundeswehr part of an offensive strategy that perverts its mandate for defense as stipulated by the Basic Law."[11] He condemned the existence of Pershing IIs on West

[11] *The Week in Germany,* December 23, 1983.

German territory, on the ground that the Basic Law forbade any West German government to take part in plans for offensive war, and that the government, by accepting the missiles, was taking part in such plans. Allowing their presence on German soil, under American control, constituted a derogation of German sovereignty. Grass' conclusion was that the federal government was violating the Basic Law.

The "Heilbronn Declaration," as it became known, was brought before the Federal Constitutional Court, but the high court ruled in December 1984 that it was "within the federal government's jurisdiction to allow deployment of Pershing II and cruise missiles on West German soil." Manfred Wörner, Kohl's respected and often frank defense minister, testified before the high court that "deployment was the result of free and sovereign decisions by NATO members and was in line with the Basic Law provision for the securing of peace."[12]

[12] Ibid., December 21, 1984.

3

Ostpolitik:
Government and Opposition

Looking back, ten years later in 1982, at the Basic Treaty between the Federal Republic and the GDR, the consensus of the majority of the two large parties was that it had been a wise step, but some were more optimistic than others. Egon Bahr stressed his hopes that the two German states would take far more wide-reaching steps toward a neutralization of Europe. The governing mayor of Berlin, Richard von Weizsäcker, believed that the survival of West Berlin could only be ensured through negotiations with the GDR. Alois Mertes, a foreign policy expert in the CDU who became secretary of state in the foreign ministry under Kohl, was more skeptical. He acknowledged that improvements in personal contacts were important, but also stressed that the GDR could revoke at any time any concessions it had made. More stringent currency requirements and the harassment of journalists in East Berlin, and the suppression of dissident groups showed, in his view, that "change through rapprochement" was a fiction. Schmidt and Genscher believed that stabilization of the East bloc regimes, supported by trade, would lead to gradual relaxation of the systems. These opposing positions continued to provide the basis for debate on the national issue in the 1980s.

In some ways the debate became more detached, as though government and opposition were debating the issues, not among themselves, but with other audiences. The GDR was in a comparatively strong position regarding West Germany. The result of 30 years of a divided nation was still division. But the GDR had extracted diplomatic recognition, economic aid, and finally even a degree of respect from West Germans. In the 1970s, it was common for some on the West German left to refer to the GDR as the "better" Germany because whatever its faults, at least private property had been abolished, and many on the left regarded the absence of private property and free initiative as great moral qualities that made possible a morally better life.

One who expressed this philosophy in his writings was the self-proclaimed communist novelist Stefan Heym (born 1913). A Jew, he had fled the Third Reich and served with distinction in the US Army in World War II. After the war he became an information officer in occupied West Germany, but was returned to the United States for his "pro-communist stance,"[1] when US occupation policy became anti-communist. By 1952, Heym had come to believe that the US was becoming a repressive right-wing dictatorship. He accordingly returned his medals and his officer's commission, gave up his American citizenship, and went to the Soviet zone in 1952, where he lived thereafter. He quickly became disillusioned with the reality of the GDR, but never considered emigrating. As he put it: "No one is going to drive me out of this republic!" He insisted that the GDR was, in some sense, his Germany, even though its regime restricted his movements and did not, until 1988, permit any of his more critical books to be published. From the late 1970s onward, Heym's principal access to the German public was through the capitalist publisher, S. Fischer, in Frankfurt. Needless to say, it was a crime to smuggle the novels of the communist Heym into Heym's own home state in the GDR; anyone caught doing so risked prison.

Heym's best description of life in the GDR was to be found in the novel *Collin* (1979). The protagonist, Collin, is an aging apparatchik recovering from heart failure in a clinic reserved for the elite. The novel describes Collin's attempt to come to terms with his own past as someone who was willing to do anything to remain an insider, to serve the regime. The portrayal of the regime and its corrupting effect was devastating, yet Heym made various characters throughout the novel say that, despite everything, the regime had produced or at least promoted personality traits which were morally superior to those found, or permitted, in the capitalist west.

In the 1980s, this outright preference for a totalitarian dictatorship over one's own liberal democracy was not found outside the DKP. Instead, many people, such as Günter Gaus, wrote that they enjoyed the GDR because certain German qualities had been better preserved there. People were not as wealthy and had less leisure time, which in Gaus' view, made them more serious, thoughtful, and more interested in the important things in life. In addition, many people recognized that the people of the GDR had suffered and sacrificed more than Germans in the Federal Republic, since they had paid for their own reconstruction and made vast economic contributions to the Soviet Union; therefore, their accomplishments could be considered a greater achievement of German hard work and ingenuity.

---

[1] *Hamburger Abendblatt*, April 9, 1988.

While it was certainly true that East Germans worked hard, this respect for what Germans in the East had achieved *in spite of* the regime, merged easily with a respect *for* a regime that, by its very existence, prevented the Germans in the East from freely conducting their own affairs. By constantly reaffirming and never compromising its basic demands, the GDR regime had over the years brought about major reversals of West German positions vis-à-vis East Germany established under Adenauer. In the 1980s this long-term pressure on the part of the GDR continued. The slow erosion of the West German claim to being the only legitimate German state, because it was the only democratic German state, continued. No government official in the 1980s spoke of West Germany as the only legitimate German state. On the contrary, West German officials went out of their way to insist that they would never dream of interfering, or of attempting to interfere, in the internal affairs of the GDR. Michael Stürmer, a neoconservative historian at the University of Erlangen and an adviser and speechwriter to Kohl, wrote that Bonn must promote the inner stability of the GDR regime even if this meant "a certain morally dubious complicity."[2] At least Stürmer remained aware that there was something morally suspect about helping a state that was denying the basic rights of 17 million of his fellow-countrymen; but he was reluctant to distinguish between the German Democratic Republic as a state, which was an unfortunate fact of life that Bonn had to deal with, and the SED party apparatus and system of latent terror. The strategy of the GDR regime in the 1980s was to confuse the two and to make the SED, not the GDR government, the real negotiator with Bonn.

Kohl defined his concept of Ostpolitik with declarations that it would be tougher, more realistic, and less characterized by appeasement than that of the social-liberal coalition. On June 23, 1983, he gave the annual address on the state of the nation. Using the old phrase which Brandt had abandoned, the government officially termed the speech an "Address on the State of the Nation in Divided Germany."

Today we are returning once more to the true purpose of this address. It concerns Germany. It concerns self-determination, human rights, the unity of our divided nation.

We do not accept our German compatriots being denied the right to self-determination and their human rights being violated.

We Germans do not accept the division of our Fatherland.

We shall continue to strive with determination and perseverance to comply with the precept of our constitution to achieve through free self-determination the unity and freedom of Germany.

[2] Cited in Seiffert, *Das ganze Deutschland*, 213.

We shall not resign because we know that history is on our side. The existing state of affairs is not irrevocable. . . .

There are two states in Germany, but there is only one German nation. The existence of this nation is not at the disposition of governments. . . . It has evolved in the course of history, forms a part of Christian European culture, and is shaped by its position in the heart of the continent.

The German nation existed before the national [unified] state, and it survived it. . . .

Our concept of the German nation is incompatible with the concept of Germany which the officials of the GDR continue to subscribe to.

Ten years after the Treaty . . . the two states in Germany remain far from the objective of "normal, good neighbourly, relations". . . .

Normality cannot come about as long as there are the wall, barbed wire, firing order and harassment at the border which cuts through Germany. . . .

The Federal Republic of Germany has renounced violence as a political means. . . . We hope that the young generation will grow up in this spirit and we also hope that the GDR will finally stop educating its young people to hate class enemies. . . .

We need European unification, just as the peoples of Europe need the elimination of the division of Germany.[3]

In other parts of this impressive speech, the chancellor spoke of Berlin and his government's concern for the city's high unemployment rate and continuing GDR harassment of transit traffic in violation of the Quadripartite Agreement. He deplored the low number of people in the GDR, other than pensioners, allowed to visit the West, and welcomed the 13 per cent rise in intra-German trade in 1981–2.

In 1984, a number of Germans from the GDR sought refuge in the West German embassy in Prague. Under the Basic Law they were German citizens and thus entitled to protection by the West German government when on its territory. However, because the embassy was in an East bloc country, and West Germany did not want to offend Czechoslovakia or the GDR, the West German government instructed the embassy to violate its legal duty toward its citizens and send the refugees back to the GDR. They were given the explanation that the West German government could do nothing to help them, and that they must apply to GDR authorities for permission to leave the GDR for West Germany. The West German government undoubtedly took its obligation to Germans in the East seriously, but it found itself in a difficult position in the middle of a foreign country. Nonetheless, the decision seemed to represent another step in the process of recognizing GDR laws and actions as legitimate.

The breakdown of the Soviet–American arms control negotiations

[3] Dept of State, *Documents on Germany*, 1365–73.

and the deployment of new missiles in West Germany had an effect on the SPD that, in its intensity, may not have been fully anticipated. It not only greatly strengthened the left wing of the party, but in a manner of speaking, also turned the party inward. The result was increasing focus on the design of its own programs for maintaining peace and security in Central Europe. This meant developing its contacts with the SED within the framework of its changing concept of Ostpolitik.

These contacts would have been unheard of 20 years earlier when the SPD maintained an illegal party organization in the GDR, directed by the SPD *Ostbüro* in West Berlin. In the 1980s SPD leaders would have regarded any attempt to create a clandestine SPD in the GDR as an intolerable provocation, regardless of the wishes of the population. Increasingly, the SPD's policy toward the GDR resembled positions taken by the SED regime more than it resembled the position of the West German government. By the mid-1980s, the left wing of the SPD argued that the preamble to the Basic Law should be revised so that it would no longer contain the commitment to reunify the nation as a matter of national policy, that separate citizenship for the GDR be recognized in West Germany, and that the West German center monitoring human rights violations committed by GDR border guards, located in Salzgitter, be closed. The last point would constitute the abandonment by West Germany of any pretense to jurisdiction over crimes committed in the GDR against Germans by the regime. The Salzgitter monitoring center, established in 1961 when the Berlin Wall was built, was a relic of the time when Bonn asserted the *Rechtseinheit*; namely, the legal unity of Germany, which meant that German law, including the uniform German criminal code, applied to Germans living in both parts of Germany. It was this concept that had prompted the GDR citizens to seek political asylum in the West German embassy in Prague in 1984.

A major figure influencing this development in the SPD continued to be Egon Bahr. In 1983, he formulated a plan for the denuclearization of central Europe, which surfaced in Sweden as a Swedish proposal with no reference to Bahr. When it became clear that he was in fact the source of the main ideas of the plan, it caused a political uproar in Sweden where the opposition accused the social democratic government of Olof Palme of conducting a foreign policy designed by the SPD, and not by the Swedish parliament. Bahr's effort, aside from the debatable merits of the proposal's content, was the revival of a new form of the old idea, that socialists have more in common with each other than with their non-socialist fellow citizens. But it also reflected the belief of the SPD's left wing in something it called security partnership, which meant that the West and the East had a common interest in avoiding war, and that the ideological conflict between them was no longer the main issue. The CDU position, expressed by Alois Mertes, was that one had a security partnership with one's allies, but not with one's adversaries. The reason for the security partnership with one's allies was to deter one's adversaries. If one believed that one's adversaries were in fact partners, and that there was no real conflict, then the adversaries, in this case the Soviet Union, had already won, Mertes argued, a great part of their struggle because they would have convinced their enemies that they were not a threat. Within the left wing of the SPD, the Soviet Union had clearly won this struggle by the mid-1980s. Brandt and Bahr appeared to be far more concerned by the acts and policies of the United States government than by those of the Soviet Union.

4

National Identity and the Past

"The Germans and their identity" — what does being German actually mean? We are people like everyone else. We love our home country, just as they do. However, our situation, our history, our many neighbors and, last but not least, we ourselves have produced light and shade.

After the end of World War II, the French author Paul Claudel wrote the following about us Germans:

Germany does not exist to divide nations, but to gather them around herself. Her role is to create agreement, to make all the different nations surrounding her feel that they cannot live without one another.

Making them feel dependent on one another is a great and promising mission for us. Our eventful history and our division also hold out opportunities for us.

The path towards the future is not a fixed one. It is both dark and open. It is for us to influence the direction it takes. The individual is free. It is for us to give the term "German" a meaning with which we ourselves and the world as a whole can gladly live in peace.

Address by President Weizsäcker before the Twenty-first Convention of the Evangelical Church in Germany, Düsseldorf, June 8, 1985

Beginning in the late 1970s, public figures in West Germany related the debate on security, defense, and relations with the GDR to the broader issue of the national identity of Germans, the burden of the past, and how to study the past. German intellectuals rediscovered the importance and value of history that might provide a sense of identity and stability to the citizens of a modern democracy. Some among them returned to the perennial theme of National Socialism and asked whether Germany's experience was unique, or so thoroughly evil, as to be beyond the normal purview of comparative historical research. How should Germans look at their past? How should they relate the past to the political present, to East–West tensions, and to the GDR? These were some of the questions absorbing not only historians, but a wide variety of political figures and writers, culminating temporarily in the *Historikerstreit*, or historians' debate, in 1985–8, on the causes of the Holocaust, the Nazi murder of the Jews, and on whether it was a unique phenomenon.

The peculiar legacy of German history, with its moral and political encumbrances, perforce loaded these arguments and questions. The question of the Holocaust and of the legitimacy of the GDR government were intimately related, because the division of Germany was the direct consequence of the war started by Nazi Germany. Between 1985 and 1988, the frustrations of the divided nation and the guilt of the Holocaust came together in a series of political, moral, and scholarly arguments that – if often incomprehensible to outsiders – said a great deal about the spiritual condition of some elements in German culture.

These debates had a long prehistory; in fact one could well argue that they had been going on since 1945. Nevertheless they were interspersed between periods of calm, only to erupt again. One such period of anxiety was 1952–4, when attention was focused on the morality of rearmament and Western integration, and the possible price for reunification. Another occurred between 1963 and 1966, and was highlighted by the debate provoked by the Auschwitz trials, Rolf Hochhuth's play *The Deputy*, and Jaspers' book *Wohin treibt die Bundesrepublik?* Yet another was the period from 1970 to 1972, during which the Eastern Treaties and the *Grundlagenvertrag* with the GDR were debated and signed and when Brandt, as the West German head of state, knelt down at the site of the Warsaw ghetto in December 1970. In the 1980s radical intellectuals in West Germany continued to assert that their country was a fascist state, no better than the Third Reich, and reiterated the accusation first levied in the 1960s that "the power structure of existing society must be seen in its inhumanity as naked force."[1]

The debates of 1985–8 continued the recurring episodes of self-criticism and anguish. The main questions were, necessarily, the same: Were all Germans responsible for Nazi crimes? Were those crimes unique? Was discussing other examples of genocide in world history equivalent to relativizing and, therefore, to accepting Nazi crimes as another tragic episode of the human condition? Was such discussion legitimate? Had Germany in 1945 been defeated or liberated and what conclusions should be drawn from either view? Finally, what practical

---

[1] Lutheran theologian Jürgen Moltmann in a discussion in 1969, cited in Lobkowicz, *Was brachte uns das Konzil?*, 98.

consequences should follow from Germany's historical burden in the conduct of policy vis-à-vis Germany's former victims, particularly the communist states and Israel? The common denominator of these themes was the question of German identity: what was it, and what should it be – given the tragedies and the guilt of history?

The most common answer to the question of German identity was that it was no longer national or political, but cultural. Willy Brandt had begun to make this point in the 1960s. This was, however, a thin answer to give to the many who asked, in the 1970s, what the future of Germany, divided or otherwise, might be. Horst Ehmke, who had directed the chancellery under Brandt, gave a slightly different answer in an article he contributed to a collective work in 1979:

> Larger problems are bound up with the notion of the cultural nation. If it remains restricted to the cultural sphere, it is apolitical. But if it is politicized, it becomes politically dangerous. For this concept of nation would also apply to the Austrians, the Swiss-Germans, and those speaking German in many other European countries; from a political standpoint these people cannot be understood or claimed to belong to the German nation. For this reason, then, one must regard the concept of the cultural nation with critical distance.
>
> Yet in our situation this does not warrant abandoning, together with the concept of the cultural nation, the concept of nation itself; nor does it warrant the construction of two German political nations. The fact that "nation" is not simply a cultural but a political concept does not justify its truncation into a concept of state sovereignty. The opposition of cultural nation and political nation stemming from the German tradition constitutes an inadmissible tearing asunder and thus a truncation of the political concept of the nation. . . .
>
> We must attempt to influence the external and internal conditions of the German question in such a way that the GDR and the East European countries could implement reforms that would serve their own interest. This would be in agreement with the stipulations of the Helsinki accords (to which they were signatories), which called not only for good neighborly relations but also for human rights in Europe.[2]

In his article, Ehmke argued that there was German identity in both German states, defined by a mutual desire for peace and stability and by what others (not Ehmke at that time) called a "community of responsibility" (*Verantwortungsgemeinschaft*). Ehmke thus rejected Brandt's earlier notion of a purely cultural identity and tried to focus the question at the political level, although his assumption that the East German regime shared this definition of identity was dubious. As far as West Germany

---

[2] Ehmke, "What is the German Fatherland?", in *Observations on "The Spiritual Situation of The Age,"* ed. Habermas, 324–5, 332.

was concerned, Ehmke believed that the way to manifest German identity was for the Federal Republic to become less predictably loyal to the US and more willing to assert its own interests, whatever they might be.

From all this follows, finally, an insight ... that, as regards the German question, nothing is to be achieved against the will of the Soviet Union, whose power in Europe emerged with the defeat of the Nazi dictatorship. As has already been indicated, this does not mean that for its part the Soviet Union is capable of solving the German question whenever it chooses. But it does mean that we Germans have to be interested in maintaining good relations with the Soviet Union.[3]

The work to which Ehmke contributed was edited by Jürgen Habermas, a professor of philosophy and sociology, a left-liberal and leader of the so-called Frankfurt school of social science and political philosophy. It became one of the most important events in West German intellectual history. It was nothing less than the attempt, by the rational, democratic left, to reassert its control of West Germany's cultural and intellectual agenda vis-à-vis both the irrational, alienated left of the citizens' initiatives and the peace movement, and the right. As a political philosopher, Habermas believed in reason and progress, which he defined as enlightenment leading to "rule-free discourse" (*herrschaftsfreier Diskurs*; "rule" here meaning domination, power) and universal "communicative competence." These phrases described a condition of human social life in which all individuals would have absolutely equal rights of participation in all important decisions. Progress, for Habermas, meant "emancipation" from all oppression, which was conditional and could therefore be abolished. He approved highly of Brandt's domestic policies and of Ostpolitik and later condemned the Kohl government for what he saw as its repressive nature. He was also convinced, contrary to any evidence, that West Germany was sliding into a phase of reactionary conservatism which would exacerbate social tensions and perhaps even justify revolutionary action by the left. Habermas' analysis was designed to rally the forces of the moderate left against both these dangers.

The notion that West Germany had interests distinct from the common Western interest in defense and containment of the Soviet Union spread rapidly. Within several years following Ehmke's essay it became common intellectual currency, from the left of the SPD to far into the CDU/CSU. This was the first of the new ideas engendered by the debate on German identity.

[3] Ibid., 318–19.

Concurrently many scholars and public figures were also asking hard questions of the educational reforms of the 1960s and later, and their effect on the public level of knowledge of German history and culture. They noted a paradox: that there were more historians working than ever before but that Germans at large seemed less well informed about their own history; in a country, moreover, that had produced many of the most brilliant historians of the nineteenth and twentieth centuries. In the 1960s and 1970s, new study plans in several *Länder* had effectively altered the teaching of history in secondary schools to such a degree that many young people had little, if any, idea of the cultural and political forces that had shaped their world, much less of anything more remote in time or space. What this meant for Germany's students was an absence of a major building block in their educational training; namely, the omission of one of the most important tools given to any student, knowledge of history, its successes and failures, its record of the hopes and dreams of real people living in a real world in which every man is subject to human frailty. Indeed, it was the absence of a body of knowledge from which one could gain historical perspective, in the hope, for example, that one might not be condemned to repeat the mistakes of the past. Thus, it was all the more ironic that especially in the vigorous and healthy Germany of the 1970s, the teaching of history was relegated to a position of minor importance. The argument centered on whether history should be taught as an independent subject or whether it made better sense to integrate it into the social sciences.

While the merits of history were argued somewhat differently in the various German *Länder*, the case of North Rhine-Westphalia was extreme. As a separate subject the teaching of history was severely limited. Indeed, the minister of culture of this, the largest *Land*, Hanns Girgensohn (SPD), in a speech before 250 historians in June 1982 questioned whether "one can learn anything from history at all."[4] At the same time, the most influential and productive younger academic historians became obsessed with social history to the detriment of political and diplomatic history. This resulted in a great demand for historical information presented in a way that appeared innovative, because educational reforms had largely destroyed the teaching of traditional political history in favor of new types of history of society, attitudes, and structures.

The most successful school of historians in the 1970s was the Bielefeld school, led by Hans-Ulrich Wehler who, at that time, rejected traditional political history, which he saw as inherently conservative. Instead, he hoped that an emphasis on the history of social

[4] Wehler, *Preussen ist wieder chic...*, 177.

structures would contribute to a left-liberal transformation of West German society. The historian who focused on structures, Wehler held, would see that those structures functioned in the interest of a narrow ruling class even under an ostensibly democratic constitution. Once members of the thus enlightened public became more aware of these structures, Wehler and his associates hoped, they would try to change them.

Political history, however, proved more resilient than Wehler expected. In 1975 he and his colleagues had founded a new journal, *Geschichte und Gesellschaft* (History and society), to promote their ideas. One of the early issues included a scathing attack on Wehler's best-known book, a history of the Wilhelmine empire, by Thomas Nipperdey, a professor of medieval and modern history in Munich. Nipperdey had been a supporter of the Brandt–Scheel government, its Ostpolitik, and its domestic reforms; he was by no stretch of the imagination an obscurantist reactionary either as a scholar or as a citizen. Nevertheless, as the 1970s went on, he became increasingly disenchanted with the effects of political reform in higher education and society in general. He saw the reformers going beyond reform to fundamental and, in his view, disastrous change. In reviewing Wehler's book, therefore, he took the opportunity to express his views. He pointed out a number of factual errors and then addressed the underlying problem; namely, that Wehler was trying to prove that the authoritarian conservatives who ruled Germany between 1871 and 1918 were responsible for Hitler and the Third Reich because they opposed democracy. The Wehler-Nipperdey debate was the starting signal for a tremendous outburst of argument not only over what actually happened in German history, and what it meant, but over the role of history in contemporary society. By the mid-1980s this debate joined the broader debate over German identity – political, moral, cultural – which served as the harbinger of the 1985–8 arguments over Nazi crimes and their meaning.

The public demand for historical information and popularization, which the Wehler school did not and could not satisfy, manifested itself for the first time publicly in 1977 on the occasion of an excellent exhibition in Stuttgart on the subject of the Staufen period of German history (1150–1250). The Staufen was the name given to a family of regional rulers – dukes of Swabia, hence the location of the exhibition in Stuttgart – that provided the kings of Germany, who were simultaneously holy Roman emperors, for a century. Many of the threads of later German history dated from the Staufen period, the most important being the power of the territorial princes and the weakening of the central authority of the king. In the context of 1977, when many Germans were asking whether a united German state had ever been a good idea and whether the existence of two states in Germany was not, in fact, more in accord with the historical traditions of the country, the symbolic political implications of the exhibition were significant.[5] Most Germans, however, paid more attention to the artistic treasures, which were only a small part of the rich German cultural heritage that the school reforms and the burdens of industrial life had obscured.

If the Staufen exhibition focused interest on long-term cultural history and presented broad historical vistas, another exhibition a few years later pointed clearly to contemporary political concerns. This was the exhibition on Prussia in Berlin in 1981. Most West Germans associated Prussia with rigidity and authoritarianism and blamed Prussian traditions for the victory of Nazism. The exhibition did not focus on these real or imagined negative aspects of later Prussia during the period of the unified German state of 1871–1945. Rather, the organizers emphasized Prussian administrative traditions, the Prussian ethic of administrative responsibility and honesty, and the early introduction of legal guarantees and state concern for the welfare of its subjects. One of these organizers was Willy Brandt's radical son, Peter, who made a name for himself in the early 1980s as an advocate of national unification on the basis of the ideas of the left. With his colleague, Herbert Ammon, Peter Brandt argued that the left should not permit the right to monopolize the issue of national unity and that there was a legitimate leftist tradition of national unification which should be recovered and put to use.

Brandt and Ammon repeated this argument in an essay, "Patriotismus von Links" (Patriotism from the left), which appeared in 1982 in a volume edited by the leftist journalist Wolfgang Venohr under the title *Die Deutsche Einheit kommt bestimmt* (German unity is sure to come). This publication marked another stage in the debate on German identity. With two exceptions, all the contributors to Venohr's volume were leftists associated more or less closely with the Greens or the emerging peace movement.

The exceptions were Hellmut Diwald and Wolfgang Seiffert. Diwald was an eccentric historian who had published, in 1978, a controversial history of the German people, *Geschichte der Deutschen*. Following the Staufen exhibition, Diwald's book, which enjoyed impressive sales, was another good indication of the reviving interest in history. The most obvious peculiarity of Diwald's book was that it told history backwards, starting with the present and moving back to the tenth century. But this was not what caused a public outcry; rather, Diwald's essay, contained in Venohr's volume under the title "Deutschland – was ist es?"

[5] See Borst, *Reden über die Staufer*.

(Germany – what is it?), broke a number of taboos by arguing that the division of Germany was at least as much the fault of the Western Allies as of the Soviet Union and that Germans should reassert their independence from both blocs. Since West Germany was located in the West, German resistance there would have to be directed mainly against the US. Indeed, Diwald seemed far angrier at the Americans than at the Soviet Union, despite the clear and very different postwar historical relationships between these two countries and Germany. His diatribe was an example of a new political movement on the West German political landscape: the nationalist anti-American right.

Undignified, that is the condition of both German states in their total dependency upon the United States and the Soviet Union. . . .
Ever since 1949 the Western Allies reassured us that only they and their policy of commitment to the Atlantic Alliance, and nothing else, are the guarantee to reach unity for Germany. After more than three decades of political efforts by *our friends*, Germany is further away from unity than ever. Where, after all, lie the limits of our trust, on which we have built the hope that our right to unity can be realized through this policy? None of our Western partners are willing to grant us, even theoretically, those rights; but certainly any government of a democratic country would deal with an offense of those rights within hours. Only if we put an end to the foreign control (*Fremdbestimmung*) that we have been subjected to for decades, can we advance to the core of our self-assurance.[6]

Wolfgang Seiffert, who had defected from the GDR in 1978 and became a professor at the University of Kiel, was the other exception in Venohr's volume. In his article, he presented his plan for a confederation of the two Germanies. It differed from leftist proposals, however, in that it did not require prior recognition of the legitimacy of the Eastern regime. In this and later publications Seiffert repeatedly made the point that, in dealing with East Germany, one should distinguish between the government and the ideological party regime. One had to deal with the former simply because it was a fact of life and the West had failed to destroy it when it may have had the chance in 1953. To recognize the latter, to grant it legitimacy or even, as Brandt insisted, "to accept that the political systems of the two German states are of equal value" was, in Seiffert's view, absurd and unnecessary. Seiffert's calls for caution in dealing with the GDR went unheeded, not only by the left wing of the SPD but also by some members of the Kohl-Genscher coalition.

---

[6] Diwald, "Deutschland – was ist es?" in *Die Deutsche Einheit kommt bestimmt*, ed. Venohr, 16, 35, Diwald's emphasis.

To this point, the debate surrounding German identity had been inspired either by historical references and conditions, or by contemporary problems concerning how to deal with East Germany. The emotion-laden issues connected with the Holocaust, the Third Reich, and World War II had not figured prominently in the arguments. Instead, they formed a kind of natural backdrop which, by its nature, was part of the political landscape. Many thought that the left-right debate over *Vergangenheitsbewältigung* had ended in a quasi-stalemate, by which the right acknowledged that Nazi crimes were unique and called for occasional ritual displays of shame, and by which the left admitted that the Bonn republic was not really as bad as the Third Reich.

This struggle had permeated the history of the Federal Republic and had come again to the fore in 1979 on the occasion of the broadcast of the American television series, *Holocaust,* which coincided in Germany with the debate over whether to extend, once again, the statute of limitations for war crimes and crimes against humanity. The decision taken by the Bundestag, led by the SPD/FDP government, was that no limitation on the prosecution of such crimes should be imposed. Until 1985, six years later, the debate was quiescent. In that year the Holocaust reappeared with a vengeance, to such a degree that the resulting furor was entirely dominated by arguments over the meaning of what happened in Central Europe in the 1940s, who was responsible, and in what ways. The occasion was the visit of the United States president, Ronald Reagan, to a cemetery in West Germany in the town of Bitburg, in which German soldiers, killed during World War II, were buried.

Four symbolic events emerged in the Holocaust debates; that is to say, public interventions by prominent people that, each in its turn, triggered a variety of hostile or approving reactions which fed a broader stream of arguments, and in turn conditioned responses to the next event. The first symbolic event was a statement that Kohl made during a visit to Israel in January 1984. The second was the visit of Reagan and Kohl to the German military cemetery at Bitburg. The third was Richard von Weizsäcker's speech as federal president on the fortieth anniversary of the German surrender in 1945. The fourth was an article by the historian Ernst Nolte in the *Frankfurter Allgemeine Zeitung* in June 1986, in which he committed what became the ultimate sin of putting the Holocaust in perspective.

Kohl's visit to Israel was the second by a German chancellor (the first was Brandt's visit in 1973). It was uneventful in itself. Kohl argued the merits of the EC's Venice Declaration of 1980, which recognized the PLO as the legitimate political body of the Palestinian Arabs and called on Israel to do the same. The Israelis, however, told Kohl that they disagreed with the principles behind the Venice Declaration and could not recognize the PLO as long as it did not renounce its avowed intention to destroy the Jewish state. These predictable disagreements were not surprising. The reason the trip was remembered at all was a very different one. It was that Kohl, in discussing German responsibility for the Holocaust, observed that he was the first German chancellor of the postwar generation, because he was born in 1930. This made him only 15 at the end of the war and thus "someone who could not have incurred any guilt during the Nazi era, because he enjoyed the grace of late birth and the good fortune of a remarkable home."[7]

The phrase, "grace of late birth" (*die Gnade der späten Geburt*), made headlines in West Germany and gave rise to bitter attacks on Kohl from the left. Günter Gaus, the former permanent representative to the GDR and a veteran of the SPD left, led the critics. He charged Kohl with seeking to escape responsibility by claiming an alleged "grace of late birth" as evidence of innocence. Gaus argued that Kohl, in Israel, "wanted to acquit his cohort and everybody younger of German guilt, by using the stolen [from Gaus] phrase; the birth certificate as a *Persilschein*,[8] biological facts as victor over historical identity, if it helps his reputation."[9]

Gaus' attack was misdirected. Kohl's purpose was not to absolve himself, or his countrymen, from responsibility, as Germans, for dealing with the consequences of the crimes of the Third Reich. It was, on the contrary, to emphasize that he and his fellow citizens did assume a responsibility, as responsible Germans, for the path of history chosen by their country – even though they, by the grace of their age, had not been involved in the crimes of the Nazis. There is no evidence that Kohl regarded his "grace of late birth" as being due to any merits of his own. He spoke modestly about the fact that his parents were anti-Nazi and that, by accident of birth, he was probably spared from embracing, as a young boy, Nazi ideology.

Gaus was mistaken in another respect. In his attack on Kohl, he claimed that Kohl had stolen the phrase "grace of late birth" from something that he, Gaus, had written. As evidence he argued that Kohl used the phrase for the first time in January 1984, but that Gaus had formulated it some months previously in various statements, and notably in his book *Wo Deutschland liegt*, which appeared in late 1983. Gaus clearly thought that the phrase was too striking to have been invented by Kohl or his speechwriters. The facts were otherwise, since

---

[7] Presse- und Informationsamt der Bundesregierung, *Bulletin*, February 2, 1984.
[8] See footnote 7, vol. 1, part I, chapter 9, p. 77.
[9] *Stern*, no. 40, September 25, 1986.

Kohl used the phrase in a radio interview as early as February 1982, when he was still leader of the opposition.[10]

What Kohl actually meant when he used the phrase, first in 1982 and then subsequently, was to express the hope that Israel would give the members of the generation following the Nazis – that is to say, his generation – the chance for reconciliation.[11] But as so often in politics, the phrase was taken out of context by Kohl's political critics. As late as 1987, over three years after Kohl's most publicized use of the phrase, the writer and journalist Peter Schneider still accused Kohl in Die Zeit of claiming "a bonus for not having been involved," even though, as a boy, Kohl had "spent all his school years in fascist schools;" as though there had been an alternative. Schneider, like Gaus, passed over Kohl's reference to his family's anti-Nazi views. He insinuated that Kohl probably enjoyed "a splendid boyhood" and snidely suggested that when Kohl referred to the need for a sense of national solidarity he was "recalling the happy experience" of Nazism.[12] Indeed, writing about Schneider's essay in 1988, Ulrich Greiner concluded that the German left in the late 1960s and 1970s had used the concept of the "grace of late birth" as an excuse to justify its politically motivated condemnation of the West German state as well as its anti-Zionist views and support for the PLO.[13]

The tempest over the "grace of late birth" confirmed the diagnosis of Hermann Lübbe, a philosopher and astute observer of his time, in 1983; namely, that the period of Nazism was not disappearing into the archives of history as simply another of the many horrible episodes and events in the past, but was, as a terrible epoch of German history, continually resurrected for contemporary political and ideological reasons. Lübbe, like Thomas Nipperdey, had been a social democrat most of his life until what he saw as the extremism of the left in the 1970s and the attack on democratic institutions and values drove him to adopt what one might call a neoconservative position. The criticism of the phrase "grace of late birth," and the assumption by many influential West German journalists and intellectuals from Marion Dönhoff to Günter Grass and Peter Schneider that Kohl was ignorant and insensitive, was given new resonance by the Bitburg affair.

This affair resulted from Kohl's request that President Reagan, who was planning a trip to Europe in early 1985, should join him in a memorial service in Cologne Cathedral and a visit to a concentration

---

[10] Interview der Woche, February 28, 1982.
[11] Ibid.
[12] Die Zeit, April 3, 1987.
[13] Die Zeit, May 6, 1988.

camp and a German military cemetery, in this case the one at Bitburg in the Rhineland-Palatinate near the Luxembourg border. The idea was to honor the German war dead as victims of war, just as the French and German war dead had been honored in France the previous year.

According to the American journalist Hedrick Smith:

> It was to be the American analogue to Kohl's visit of reconciliation with French President François Mitterrand to the graves of the French and German World War I dead at Verdun. Photographers had framed the moving symbolism of Kohl and Mitterrand holding hands at the Verdun battlefield, with fields of white crosses as their backdrop. Kohl had also been deeply hurt by his exclusion from the Allied celebration of the fortieth anniversary of D-Day at Normandy on June 6, 1984. . . . Evidently both he and Reagan were unaware that the gesture of Verdun could not be repeated because no American soldiers were buried in German cemeteries. Thus, in agreeing, Reagan committed himself to honor the German war dead alone.[14]

When Reagan's itinerary was announced in April, "White House spokesman Larry Speakes was raked over the coals by reporters demanding whether American soldiers were buried at Bitburg and why the President was visiting a German military cemetery but not a concentration camp," since the plan to visit a concentration camp had been dropped at White House request. But it was not only the press that contributed to adverse publicity, it was also Jewish groups that were outraged: "Elie Wiesel, a 56–year-old camp survivor, world-renowned writer, and chairman of the US Holocaust Memorial Council, was declaring there could be no trade-off of a camp for Bitburg cemetery." Indeed, Wiesel considered the choice of the cemetery "unacceptable. . . . This is not just a cemetery of soldiers. This is tombstones of the SS, which is beyond what we can imagine. These are and were criminals."[15]

Neither the German government nor the White House, in fact, knew that the cemetery contained graves of several members of the Waffen-SS, who, even though they might not have been involved in acts of terror, nevertheless were identified with the SS, the most dreaded institution of Nazi Germany: "The Waffen-SS troops . . . [were] similar to regular military units, some of them press-ganged into service at early ages and not morally culpable, as the SS were, for the Holocaust atrocities."[16] But in the United States, and especially to Jewish groups, this appeared to many as a distinction without a difference. The spectrum of criticism was broad. At one end were those who said the president simply did not

[14] Smith, H., *The Power Game*, 373–4.
[15] Ibid., 376–7.
[16] Ibid., 375.

understand the implications, that Kohl was tricking him into honoring Nazi soldiers, and that he should not go. At the other were those who accused Reagan and Kohl of a conspiratorial attempt to exculpate those who had committed Nazi atrocities. Some even argued that Reagan and Kohl were part of a sinister plot to glorify the Wehrmacht and the SS in order to promote militarism and martial values in West Germany as part of a worldwide US policy of bellicose diplomacy.

Although Kohl's intention was undoubtedly well meant, as was Reagan's acceptance, the publicity preceding the visit was painful to both. The visit itself was much less traumatic. At Bitburg both leaders stood for a moment in silence before the cemetery memorial, and silently left: "At Bitburg Air Force Base, Reagan apologized. 'Some old wounds have been reopened, and this I regret very much, because this should be a time of healing,' he said. To the Germans, he offered reconciliation, and to Americans 'worried that reconciliation means forgetting,' he said, 'I promise you, we will never forget.'"[17]

After visiting Bitburg, the chancellor and the president did pay another visit, to the site of the former concentration camp at Bergen-Belsen, although the German-Jewish rabbis declined an invitation to join him. At this location, the president spoke again of the lessons of the past:

Chancellor Kohl and honored guests, this painful walk into the past has done much more than remind us of the war that consumed the European continent. What we have seen makes unforgettably clear that no one of the rest of us can fully understand the enormity of the feelings carried by the victims of these camps. . . .

Here lie people – Jews – whose death was inflicted for no reason other than their very existence. Their pain was borne only because of who they were and because of the God in their prayers. Alongside them lay many Christians – Catholics and Protestants. . . .

We're here today to confirm that the horror cannot outlast hope. . . . So much of this is symbolized today by the fact that most of the leadership of free Germany is represented here today. Chancellor Kohl, you and your countrymen have made real the renewal that had to happen.[18]

The recrimination over Bitburg had scarcely subsided when a new round of self-reproach and examination of conscience by Germans began. It took place following statements of Richard von Weizsäcker in 1985, who had been elected federal president of Germany in 1984.

---

[17] Ibid., 380.
[18] Dept of State, *Documents on Germany*, 1396–7.

His most notable speech was delivered on May 8, the fortieth anniversary of the German surrender and the end of war in Europe, and it was a tour de force.

Weizsäcker, the brother of the famous physicist Carl Friedrich von Weizsäcker, one of the signatories of the Göttingen Manifesto against nuclear arms for the Bundeswehr in 1958, was a leading CDU parliamentarian, of the liberal wing of the party. Born in 1920, he had served with distinction in World War II in the famous Ninth Infantry Regiment based in Potsdam, which was the most distinguished unit in the old Prussian and imperial army of 1871–1918. A significant number of the Prussian opponents of Hitler, who gave their lives to unseat the dictator, either had served in or had ties to the regiment.

In 1969 Kurt Georg Kiesinger wanted him to be the CDU/CSU's candidate for federal president, but he failed to secure the nomination of his party. In 1974 he did secure it, but lost the election to Walter Scheel. In 1981, the Berlin CDU, in desperation, drafted him to run for mayor, although he was not a Berliner. He won an upset election victory, defeating the SPD and its candidate, Hans-Jochen Vogel, and became governing mayor at a time when the morale and the spirit of the population in the free part of the city were at a low ebb. Most objective observers credited his administration with the remarkable turnaround in the fortunes of Berliners and, even more important, in the Berliners' faith in their future, between 1981 and 1984. By no means did he find solutions for all the city's problems, and West Berlin politics remained plagued by difficulties peculiar to an isolated city, but most Germans agreed that Weizsäcker had done an impressive job. This achievement was especially impressive in view of a hard-left, communist-dominated Green faction of over 10 per cent of the electorate in the city, and extensive and peculiar social problems stemming from the large number of Turkish guest workers and alienated youth from West Germany living in West Berlin.

Weizsäcker's success made him a logical candidate for federal president, in elections scheduled for 1984. As in 1979, the CDU/CSU candidate was sure to win since that party, now supported by the FDP, controlled a majority of votes in the Federal Assembly which elected the president. From 1979 to 1984 the president was Karl Carstens, a lawyer who had been a member of the Nazi party in his youth and was mercilessly attacked by the left for this, even though there was no evidence that Carstens had committed any crimes. Carstens, however, did not wish to stand again, and Kohl asked Weizsäcker to campaign for the post. He won as expected, and began a tenure that many considered extraordinary.

Weizsäcker, as titular head of state, had no intention of usurping the chancellor's prerogative of political leadership, but he did use his office far more than any predecessor since Heuss to focus attention on the civilization and enlightened principles of democratic Germany. Like Heuss and Heinemann, Weizsäcker was an intellectual at home with political and philosophical ideas, capable of writing well and able to engage in debate on a sophisticated level and to give his words real substance. Because he could argue forcefully and was comfortable in the arena of ideas, and because he had criticized Barzel's attempt to oust Brandt in 1972, the left may have assumed that his convictions differed from those of Kohl. Since the left disliked Kohl, they allowed the wish to be father to the thought, and concluded that there must be a rift between the president and Kohl and that the chancellor must resent the president's intelligence and prestige.

This point needs to be stressed because many saw Weizsäcker's May 8, 1985, speech as an implicit rebuke to Kohl's phrase, "grace of late birth," that the left asserted was irresponsible. Weizsäcker made a number of important points in what is one of the most straightforward and elegant speeches delivered by any postwar German leader:

Many nations are today commemorating the date on which World War II ended in Europe. Every nation is doing so with different feelings, depending on its fate. Be it victory or defeat, liberation from injustice and alien rule or transition to new dependence, division, new alliances, vast shifts of power – May 8, 1945, is a date of decisive historical importance for Europe.

We Germans are commemorating that date amongst ourselves, as is indeed necessary. We must find our own standards. We are not assisted in this task if we or others spare our feelings. . . .

For us, the 8th of May is above all a date to remember what people had to suffer. . . . For us Germans, May 8 is not a day of celebration. Those who actually witnessed that day in 1945 think back on highly personal and hence highly different experiences. Some returned home, others lost their homes, some were liberated, while for others it was the start of captivity. . . .

The 8th of May was a day of liberation. It liberated all of us from the inhumanity and tyranny of the National Socialist regime.

Nobody will, because of that liberation, forget the grave suffering that only started for many people on May 8. But we must not regard the end of the war as the cause of flight, expulsion and deprivation of freedom. The cause goes back to the start of the tyranny that brought about the war. We must not separate May 8, 1945, from January 30, 1933. . . .

May 8 is a day of remembrance. Remembering means recalling an occurrence honestly and undistortedly.

Weizsäcker continued by turning to the past:

Whoever opened his eyes and ears and sought information could not fail to notice that Jews were being deported. . . . When the unspeakable truth of the holocaust then became known . . . all too many of us claimed that they had not known anything about it or even suspected anything.

There is no such thing as the guilt or innocence of an entire nation. Guilt is, like innocence, not collective, but personal. . . . All of us, whether guilty or not, whether old or young, must accept the past.

But dealing with the burdens of the past also required recognition of the present and the future. The federal president went on to note the astonishing recovery and the cooperation of Germany's former enemies in that recovery. He also referred to the injustice that spared some who were personally guilty of atrocities and hurt others who had done no wrong.

[Some] were expelled from the lands of their fathers. We in what was to become the Federal Republic of Germany were given the priceless opportunity to live in freedom. Many millions of our countrymen have been denied that opportunity to this day. . . .

There was no "zero hour," but we had the opportunity to make a fresh start. We have used this opportunity as well as we could. . . .

The freedom of the individual has never received better protection in Germany than it does today.

There could be no "coming to terms with the past," because that is to ignore the moral burden of the past. Rather, only by facing and accepting the past, can Germans enjoy any sort of credible future at all. But perhaps most remarkable was the vision of a responsible sense of direction he gave to his countrymen:

A new generation has grown up to assume political responsibility. Our young people are not responsible for what happened over 40 years ago. But they are responsible for the historical consequences. . . . We must help younger people to understand why it is vital to keep memories alive. . . .

On this 8th of May, let us face up as well as we can to the truth.[19]

Weizsäcker's speech did not contradict what Kohl had stated in a different way several weeks earlier, except perhaps that Weizsäcker did not distinguish so clearly between guilt and responsibility. At the site of the former Bergen-Belsen concentration camp, on the fortieth anniversary of the liberation of the camp on April 21, Kohl had drawn very similar conclusions. He emphasized that "Germany bears historical responsibility for the crimes of the Nazi tyranny. This responsibility is reflected not least in never-ending shame."[20]

[19] Ibid., 1403–12.
[20] *Statements and Speeches*, April 22, 1985.

Throughout the world many hailed Weizsäcker's speech as an eloquent and moving statement by the president of the Federal Republic, acknowledging responsibility for "the historical consequences" of the Third Reich; indeed, over 1.5 million copies of the speech were distributed by request.[21] It was a courageous statement and it added to the tremendous prestige Weizsäcker enjoyed as the Federal Republic celebrated its fortieth anniversary in 1989.

Neither Weizsäcker nor Kohl supported the leftist notion of "collective guilt;" that is, that even Germans wholly unconnected with the Nazi era were in some sense guilty of its crimes. They made their views very clear, consistently and positively. It was thus a curious feature of the 1980s that the left adopted the notion of blood guilt, the idea that some people were guilty simply by virtue of being born in a certain place as members of a certain ethnic group. Such an idea was, of course, an element of Nazi ideology and of primitive ideologies everywhere; for example, in the US among those who held all whites guilty for past white racism and demanded sacrifices accordingly. For this reason both Weizsäcker and Kohl rejected the concept.

[21] *Relay From Bonn*, May 9, 1986.

5

The Politics of History and the Past

In West Germany discussion of the meaning of 1945 and of German guilt continued unabated into 1986, when it received a dramatic new impetus. It came from two more or less simultaneous events: an article by the German historian at the Free University of Berlin, Ernst Nolte (born 1923), entitled "Vergangenheit, die nicht vergehen will" (A past that will not go away), published in the *Frankfurter Allgemeine Zeitung* on June 6, 1986, and the publication in May of two essays as a book by the German historian at the University of Cologne, Andreas Hillgruber (born 1925), entitled *Zweierlei Untergang: Die Zerschlagung des deutschen Reiches und das Ende des europäischen Judentums* (Two kinds of doom: the destruction of the German Reich and the end of European Jewry). Their questions and conclusions – they did not really provide answers – provoked more anger and irritation than the "grace of late birth," and led a great number of people to suppose that German historians were now defending the Third Reich and justifying the Holocaust. Nothing was in fact further from the truth, and the misinterpretations said much more of the political views of the critics than of the content of Nolte's and Hillgruber's arguments.

Hillgruber made three simple, but historically very important points. One was that the annihilation of European Jewry by the Nazis and the destruction of the German state were simultaneous, but not causally related: Germany's wartime enemies decided to mutilate and divide Germany long before they knew of the Holocaust, so that the fate of Germany at the war's end was not intended as retribution for the Holocaust, but as a general punishment of Germany. The second point was that these two events – the genocide of European Jewry and the destruction of German political power – even if causally unrelated, were a tragedy for Europe. Middle-class Jewish and German cultures were civilizing factors in the Central European area from the Baltic states in the north to Romania in the south, Hillgruber argued, and their destruction opened the way to domination of that area by the Soviet Union and other communist regimes. The disappearance of Germany as a cultural and political factor, and the Holocaust, weakened European civilization as a whole by destroying its most important Central European component. Hillgruber's third point was that the German defeat in the East – the military events of 1944–5 and their immediate consequences – was a subject worthy of study in its own right, and one which could best be studied from the perspective of those immediately involved; that is, the soldiers of the German army and the civilians who lost their homes, their families, and friends in the course of those terrible months. Hillgruber did not deny that the German soldiers who defended to the last possible moment every inch of German territory in the East were also defending a brutal regime. But he added to this observation the equally important fact that there was an independent moral value to the defensive efforts, namely to allow as many civilians as possible to escape.

Hillgruber's book had barely appeared when Nolte's article added an additional perspective. Nolte had originally been asked to present a paper in Frankfurt at a conference on political culture. His invitation was canceled without explanation, perhaps because his hosts learned in advance of the contents of his speech, entitled "Vergangenheit, die nicht vergehen will" (A past that will not go away). Despite or because of the cancellation, the paper received enormous attention when the *Frankfurter Allgemeine Zeitung* published it on June 6, 1986. In it Nolte asked why the unique character of the Holocaust, and of German guilt, had become such a matter of faith in certain quarters – he meant the German and international academic and journalistic left – and whether this unique character was really borne out by history. He went on to note, as a matter of historical fact, that there were two examples of genocide with which the Nazis were well familiar, and which they seemed to have incorporated in their own ideology to justify their own genocidal policies. One was the massacre of the Armenians by the Turks in 1915 and the other was the Soviet massacre of kulaks, that is, of independent landowning peasants, and of Ukrainians between 1929 and 1933. In both cases millions of people were killed solely because they belonged to a certain ethnic group or social class. Max Erwin von Scheubner-Richter – who, as German consul in Erzurum, Turkey, witnessed the massacre and later worked closely with Hitler until he was shot during a march to the Feldherrnhalle in Munich in 1923 – had described the Armenian holocaust as a "reckoning 'in an Asiatic manner far from European civilization.'" Nolte asked how men (the Nazi leaders) who described one instance of political mass murder as "Asiatic," could later initiate even more gruesome mass murders themselves. He continued:

Did the National Socialists carry out, did Hitler perhaps carry out an "Asiatic" deed only because they regarded themselves and their kind as the potential or real victims of an "Asiatic" deed? Wasn't the "Gulag Archipelago" more original than Auschwitz? Wasn't class murder on the part of the Bolsheviks logically and actually prior to racial murder on the part of the Nazis?[1]

According to Nolte, both the communist and the Nazi massacres belong in the "context of those qualitative breaks in European history that began with the industrial revolution and which in each case led to an excited search for 'guilty parties' or 'those responsible' . . . Only in this context would it become clear that the biological annihilation conducted by the Nazis is qualitatively distinct from the social annihilation conducted by the Bolsheviks." He concluded that if this horrible history were to have any meaning for future generations, that meaning could not consist of constantly attacking "the Germans" or imputing collective guilt to them, but rather of "liberation from the tyranny of collectivist thought." Therewith he was making a political argument that was responded to with political counter arguments.

Several weeks later, Jürgen Habermas accused both Hillgruber and Nolte of trivializing the Nazi Holocaust and excusing it, thus either ignoring or failing to understand their condemnation of the past and their concern that history not repeat itself in the future. Habermas had been convinced since the late 1970s that there was, in West Germany, a conspiracy of right-wing intellectuals and politicians who wanted to reverse the gains, modest in his view, that the left had made in West German politics and culture since the 1960s. He regarded Nolte's arguments as part of this effort, as a "strategy of moral relativization," intended to deny guilt for the Holocaust and ultimately to deny the Holocaust itself; and he included Hillgruber and other historians associated more or less closely with the CDU, such as Michael Stürmer (born 1938) and Klaus Hildebrand (born 1941), in the conspiracy. Against this alleged cabal stood the progressive, liberal intellectuals represented by Habermas himself and his ideological allies in the historical profession. In criticizing the historians Habermas chose to do so as a defender of "Western political culture," that is, of the democracy introduced during the occupation period by the Allies. It was an unusual and somewhat paradoxical position for Habermas to take, because of his strong sympathies with the New Left of the 1960s and his frequently voiced criticism of capitalism.[2]

A number of historians, political scientists and sociologists, German

[1] Maier, *Unmasterable Past*, 29–30; Nolte's article in *"Historikerstreit,"* an anthology of virtually all the pieces written during the debate.
[2] See Habermas, "Eine Art Schadensabwicklung," in *"Historikerstreit,"* 62–76.

and foreign, agreed with Habermas' basic criticism, even though they were familiar enough with the German intellectual scene to know that Habermas' critique was, as the author of the standard German biography of Hitler and editor of the cultural section of the *Frankfurter Allgemeine Zeitung*, Joachim Fest (born 1926), pointed out, exaggerated, slightly hysterical, and outdated: Habermas was still fighting the intellectual battles of the 1960s. The issue in the 1980s was not conservative historians versus progressive liberals, but whether the political views of Habermas and those who agreed with him were blocking their recognition and acceptance of important historical facts, whose significance must be understood if democracy were to flourish. Dolf Sternberger, the highly respected publicist and political scientist, writing in the *Frankfurter Allgemeine Zeitung* on April 6, 1988, concluded that, "the senseless outrage that is described with the name 'Auschwitz,' cannot in truth be understood; it can only be reported. . . . If it is truly the purpose of scholarship to understand, then one must draw the conclusion that scholarship is useless for understanding the phenomenon of 'Auschwitz.'"

Sternberger's conclusion was surprising. Taken at face value, it represented a logical extreme. One of the primary purposes of scholarship is to be a tool that enables one to understand and learn from the past, so that the tragedies of the *Vergangenheit* will not be repeated in the future. If the validity of the tool of scholarship can be selectively discounted as useless, that is to employ a double standard in the study of history; that is to say, it is acceptable to try to understand history in some cases, but not in others. It is doubtful that Sternberger's opinion would have been shared by such eminent German historians as Ranke, Droysen, Meinecke, Ritter, or Herzfeld.

Most of Nolte's attackers had a prior political commitment to a certain view of the Holocaust and the matter of German guilt and therefore discarded or condemned Nolte's purpose, which was shared by such distinguished German historians as Thomas Nipperdey and Karl Dietrich Bracher. Habermas' view was supported in an article by Peter Schneider in *Die Zeit* (April 3, 1987). Schneider wrote that Nolte denied the unique character of the Holocaust, in obvious contradiction to Nolte's insistence that putting the Nazi Holocaust in historical perspective was not in any way to deny or excuse it. Indeed, such attacks seemed to confirm Nolte's suggestion that those who were so concerned with defending the unique character of the Holocaust and who regarded historical perspective as a denial of it, had their own political agenda which had little to do with the Holocaust itself and much more to do with influencing the cultural and intellectual agenda of West Germany in the 1980s.

Another reason to suspect this was true was that some of the critics on the far left, who attacked Nolte and Hillgruber for allegedly denying the unique character of the Holocaust, had very little sympathy for the Jews or Israel in the 1980s. Indeed, some on the far left were known for their virulently anti-Israeli position and condemnation of Israel as being "no better" than the Nazis in its treatment of the Palestinians. In 1986 a fascinating book was published by Fischer Verlag in Frankfurt, entitled *Der Ewige Antisemit* (The eternal anti-Semite). It was written by Henryk M. Broder, who had been born in 1946 in Poland, had lived in West Germany from 1958 to 1980, and who moved to Jerusalem in 1981.

Broder's book, published at an opportune time given the vehemence of the *Historikerstreit* (historian's debate), "harvested a storm of indignation," since proof of "leftist anti-Semitism" on the far political left made a bitter contrast to the assertion that threats to democratic values emanated only from the right.[3] In a chapter entitled "The Power of the Jews, or When Will This Criminal Organisation Finally Die Out?", Broder quoted from a "Green Calendar," an almanac for environmentalists printed on recycled paper, published in 1983 for the fifth consecutive year: "Jewish mercenaries are preparing 'the final solution of the Palestinian question'. . . . My ancestors have six million Jews on their conscience, and it is embarrassing for me to be a German. However, the Nazi crimes and neo-Nazi smears pale into insignificance beside the Zionist atrocities, and I am not the only one to ask myself when the Jews will be given a lesson that will make them stop murdering their fellow-men." The same almanac also raised the following point: "Many people are asking themselves when this criminal association known as Israel will finally die out."[4]

Rudolf Augstein, the publisher of *Der Spiegel*, took several contradictory positions in the argument over Nolte on the one hand and contemporary Israel and its actions on the other. In a vituperative article attacking Hillgruber and Nolte on October 6, 1986, Augstein argued in *Der Spiegel* that anyone who claimed the destruction of Germany was not an answer to the Holocaust was "a Nazi by constitution (*konstitutioneller Nazi*), who would have been one even without Hitler." Augstein continued with a blanket condemnation of all those whom he alleged were belittling or relativizing the Holocaust and, indeed, all those who had served the Third Reich in any capacity and later became honored citizens of what Augstein termed "Adenauer's Reich," such as Adenauer's aide Herbert Globke.[5] In another article, however, Augstein

---

[3] Greiner, *Die Zeit*, May 6, 1988.
[4] Cited in Broder, *Der Ewige Antisemit*, 97–8.
[5] Augstein, "Die neue Auschwitz-Lüge," in *"Historikerstreit,"* 196–202.

took the very position he was attacking so vehemently. Commenting on Weizsäcker's May 8, 1985, speech, Augstein asked "whether we really know who killed more, Hitler or Stalin," not to mention the "Allied war crimes" against Germans. The Jews had a vested interest in celebrating May 8, Augstein concluded, because they wanted money and arms from Germany.[6] Augstein was of course right that Stalin killed at least as many innocent people as Hitler, but that was precisely one of Nolte's points. Thus it was ironic that Augstein castigated Nolte and Hillgruber as Nazis "by constitution," because they had the courage to consider historical perspective of value to a democratic society, while simultaneously and disingenuously adopting Nolte's argument in order to criticize Israel.

In the June 1987 issue of *Encounter,* Josef Joffe, the foreign editor of the *Süddeutsche Zeitung* and one of West Germany's leading analysts of international politics in the 1980s, sought to place the debate itself in perspective. He addressed the question of why such different individuals as Augstein and Nolte were concerned with German national dignity. He pointed out that the burden of the Nazi past rested even on those too young to have taken part.

They had no part in the "Teutonic deed" that was Auschwitz, but they had to live with the indelible stigma of moral inferiority.

They came to adulthood without any sense of nation, continuity, or pride. . . . If anything did reach out from the past, it was the stifling, fearsome tentacle of national guilt.

It was only a matter of time before the West Germans would try to sever it. . . . During the Viet Nam War, it was the demonstrators of the New Left who raised, still unconsciously, the question of "moral equivalence." Didn't My Lai show that the "re-educators" and "liberators" were no better than their own parents? In 1982, their younger siblings drew a straight line between General Stroop's butchers murdering the last Jews of the Warsaw Ghetto and General Sharon's troops beleaguering the PLO in Beirut. . . .

With the battle against Pershing and Cruise missiles uniting Social Democrats and Greens . . . a "movement of national re-awakening" had finally appeared on the German scene. The Federal Republic is an "occupied country," thundered the former SPD mayor of West Berlin, Heinrich Albertz, and the Americans are conspiring to turn it into a "shooting gallery of the superpowers." . . .

Though separated by time and ideological colour, the Battle of the German Historians and the War against the American Missiles are clearly related – like two brothers fighting over patrimony or primogeniture. In both cases, the real object of conquest was the past that would not pass away. . . . [The left's]

---

[6] Cited in Broder, *Der Ewige Antisemit,* 110.

"progressive" purpose – national reassertion and the reclamation of moral worth – was no different from the quest of the revisionist historians. . . .[7]

The *Historikerstreit* proper ended quickly, but German writers and publicists could not so easily put an end to the debate which, as all the participants pointed out, was a struggle for political and moral power in the present as well as a debate on how interpretation of the past would affect the future. Thus, Robert Leicht, an editor for *Die Zeit*, wrote on September 18, 1987: "as long as we continue, as in the past year, the debates of the historians, in which a part of our publicists and politicians want to relativize the past and therewith make it normal intellectually, no normality will be granted us in the future." Christian Meier (born 1929), a historian from Munich, also addressed the future in an article in the *Frankfurter Allgemeine Zeitung* on November 20, 1986, but from a different perspective:

The issue in the "historians' debate" concerned and concerns less the past than the present and the future. That is the thrust of the question of how we will live with the awareness, deeply anchored in us ... of this past. Are we, historically speaking, quite different than the others? Is that an opportunity or a fate? With that, we are also debating what our federal-republican identity is and can be.

Probably it is no accident that these questions are being put anew forty years after the end of the war. The youngest of those who could have actively participated in the Nazi regime are approaching the age of grandparents. To that extent the "historians' debate" has probably raised questions whose meaning is changing in the public mind. . . .

We will make no progress if we use the Nazi past as a truncheon in partisan battles.[8]

Nolte insisted that his intention was to put the Holocaust into historical perspective, as a series of events in the fateful history of modern Europe. The article that set off the debate was in actuality the summary of the argument in the latest volume in Nolte's ambitious four-volume interpretation of modern history, which began in 1963 with the publication of *Three Faces of Fascism*. The fourth volume, *Der europäische Bürgerkrieg* (The European civil war) discussed the relationship of Nazism and Soviet communism as the two sides of a "European civil war," in which the prize was the power to impose one's own political vision on Europe. After Nolte's article appeared in the *Frankfurter Allgemeine Zeitung,* the original publisher of his fourth volume cancelled

[7] Joffe, "The Battle of the Historians." *Encounter* June 1987, 75–6.
[8] Meier, "Kein Schlusswort," in *"Historikerstreit,"* 268–73.

Nolte's contract. But because of the publicity generated by the debate he soon found another publisher, and his book was in its third printing within three months of publication.

In 1987 Nolte wrote his own conclusion to the dispute his article had generated:

> To call the comparison of the Gulag [the Soviet concentration camp system] and Auschwitz a trivialization seems to me to be in fact the oath of affirmation of a certain group of intellectuals. . . .
>
> Their counterparts are not actually "right-wing" intellectuals, but realistic intellectuals, historians, and thinkers critical of utopian ideas. I do not deny that I count myself among this group and that I am aware of the relationship between National Socialism in its beginnings and the kind of anti-utopianism that one may call anti-communism. That is why my book [*Der europäische Bürgerkrieg*] is, among other things, a detailed self-examination of anti-communism. Did it necessarily lead to the "seizure of power" of 1933, to the attack on the Soviet Union and to Auschwitz? My answer is: no. But it would be good if that group of leftists who are "constitutional patriots" and who have launched the campaign against the allegedly "neo-nationalist" historians, would ask themselves, with equal seriousness, the question whether they do not run the risk of sympathizing with the most massive annihilations, so long as they serve "progress" and "socialism." If they could free themselves from this, usually unadmitted, sympathy, they would not abandon their support of "co-existence," but would tie it to conditions, and one of these conditions ought to be that they no longer isolate National Socialism from one of its most important preconditions, and that they recognize as the best future of the present, the struggle – but not an ideological cold war and civil war – between a post-fascist "capitalism" and a post-utopian "communism."[9]

The *Historikerstreit* left no one with the last word, nor could it have been expected to. It raised new questions and old ones. Three of them were put as follows by Charles S. Maier, professor of European history at Harvard University, in a book published in 1988:

> How much polemic can history bear before it is deformed? . . . The second question involves . . . how typologies are utilized, when they are legitimate in history and social science. . . . Finally there is the issue of German identity. . . . What is the quality of identity? "Our mother country is not where we find happiness at last. Our mother country, on the contrary, is with us, in us. Germany is alive in us, we represent it, willy-nilly, in every country to which we go, in each climate. We are rooted in it." Habermas could have written those lines. . . . So of course could Michael Stürmer. They come, however, from the

[9] Nolte, *Das Vergehen der Vergangenheit*, 58–9.

youthful Leopold von Ranke [1795–1886], whose preoccupations still over-shadow much of this controversy.[10]

The *Historikerstreit* followed on and coincided with an upwelling of barely concealed anti-Semitism of the extreme left, which was part and parcel of a general attack on the West and on America, a simmering resentment curiously shared by older conservatives like Nolte. Since the victory of Israel in the Six Day War in 1967, sympathy for the PLO and Arab radicalism in general had become widespread on the European left. The Israeli invasion of Lebanon to fight the PLO in 1982 brought the rage of the far left to paroxysmic heights. Shortly after the invasion, a radical journal in West Germany, entitled *Pardon*, published the follow-ing "parody" in July:

> Massed death's-head tank units under General Moshe Guderian have over-whelmed PLO guerrilla strongholds in Beirut with layers of destructive fire, supported from the air by Stukas under Rudel Salomon. Infantry and the mobile missile battery "Shalom" under the command of Infantry General Josua "Sepp" Dietrich have levelled the suburb L'idice to the ground with accurate fire. Ten thousand partisan casualties, which enemy propaganda claims were civilians, were obtained. Since 0545 hours L'idice is an Arab-free zone. The partisan fortifications in the hills of Hol O'Caust face imminent surrender. The final solution of the Palestinian question is a matter of hours. Maj.-Gen. in the intelligence staff of the High Command of the Greater Israelite Wehrmacht, Shei-tan Wiesenthal, was convicted of collaboration with the enemy, arrested, and faces a court martial on charges of high treason. [Signed] The Führer – Menachem Begin.[11]

This "parody" was replete with thinly disguised references both to terrible events and gruesome atrocities committed during the Third Reich, and to individuals. It was a grisly satire, highly anti-Semitic in nature.

Sepp Dietrich was the name of a leading SS commander in the Third Reich. Lidice was the Czech village destroyed in 1942, with its in-habitants, by the SS in retaliation for the assassination by members of the Czech resistance of Reinhard Heydrich, one of the leaders of the Reich. Ever after, "Lidice" had been a symbol for Nazi atrocities against innocent civilians. But perhaps most macabre was the reference to the "final solution," which was Hitler's euphemism for the extermination of the Jews, and to Simon Wiesenthal, who directed the effort from Vienna following the war to locate Nazi war criminals, and after whom the Simon Wiesenthal Center for Holocaust Studies is named.

[10] Maier, *Unmasterable Past*, 64–5.
[11] Cited in Broder, *Der Ewige Antisemit*, 127.

Some on the left found it easy to pick up old Nazi denunciations of Jews as capitalists and exploiters and to combine them with Marxist and anti-American rhetoric. Hermann Gremliza, the editor of the radical Left magazine *Konkret*, made the connection when he called Israel "America's intervention commando brigade in the Middle East." By the mid-1980s the identification of Israel with the Nazis was common currency in a certain part of the radical German left. A former SPD deputy, Lenelotte von Bothmer, wrote as though it were self-evident: "Just as the Jews were persecuted where we were" – note the passive construction; she did not write: "Just as we persecuted the Jews" – "so today the Palestinians are being persecuted and murdered by the Israelis." A psychologist at the University of Mainz co-authored an "alternative travel guide" for left-wing visitors to Israel which included stereotypes that would have fitted well in Nazi propaganda leaflets: "Once again we liked Israel very much but unfortunately not its inhabitants. ... The Jews want to strangle the Arabs, get at the male tourists' money and between the female tourists' legs. That goes for all of them, from the worker to the professor. ... We continue to think humanely and give truth its due. Both are traits not common among Jews."[12]

By no means, however, did all on the left share these viewpoints. The Greens in the Bremen city government found themselves in a surprising alliance with the CDU group in denouncing a piece of supposed scholarship.[13] In 1983 the Institute for Educational Research of the Bremen city government published a "study guide" arguing that "the practices of the state of Israel repeat on the Palestinians the injustice previously done to the Jews," and attributing the blame for conflict in the Middle East exclusively to the Jews.

Another critic concerned with anti-Semitism was the highly respected head of the Jewish congregation in West Berlin, Heinz Galinski, who became head of the Central Council of Jews in Germany in 1988. Indeed, he was one of the severest critics of the Kohl-Reagan visit to the Bitburg military cemetery, as a symptom of a large reservoir of latent anti-Semitism on the right. On several other occasions, Galinski spoke out against what he termed anti-Semitic potential in as much as 20 per cent of the population. It is not at all clear how helpful Galinski's criticisms were or what purpose they served in 1985, at the time of the Bitburg visit. But in view of the radical left's virulently expressed opinions of Israel his criticisms may have been misdirected.

The German theater also contributed to the discussion of the Jew in

[12] Cited ibid., 70, 115–6, 136.
[13] Ibid., 142–6.

Germany. In late 1985, Günther Rühle, the director of the Frankfurt city theater and his company proposed to perform the play *Der Müll, die Stadt, und der Tod* (Garbage, the city, and death), written in 1975 by Rainer Werner Fassbinder, who died at the age of 37 in 1982 of a drug over-dose. Fassbinder, born in 1945, was thus the same age as postwar German society, a society whose values he rejected and wished to change. In an article in *Die Zeit*, Benjamin Heinrichs wrote: "His life was full of dramatic changes, even in the physical sense: a pimply, shy, aggressive adolescent in his early Munich years; suddenly a very slender melancholy young man in 1973 in Berlin; a fat leather-clad faun, in later years; a majestic ruin, already his own tragic legend, in the period before his death. Fassbinder was many people." But underneath his "chaos, his consuming rage for work," there was "a quiet, melancholy, sensible human being."[14]

The play described the life of a property speculator in the city of Frankfurt and his arrogant, inhuman treatment of others, culminating in his murder of a German prostitute. The basis for the play was the rapid redevelopment in the 1960s and 1970s of a large part of Frankfurt, a redevelopment much debated in the public, through which, indeed, a number of investors had become quite wealthy. This part of the play was a social critique. What enraged Fassbinder's critics, however, was the fact that his villain was Jewish and that Fassbinder deliberately drew on imagery of the typical Jew as rich, exploitative, and corrupt, as a kind of boil on society's surface. Thus, one of the characters says, "He sucks us dry, the Jew does. He drinks our blood and convicts us because he is Jewish and we bear the guilt. . . . If he had stayed where he came from or if they had gassed him I would sleep better now. They forgot to gas him. That's no joke. That's how things feel in me."[15]

This was clearly the language of Nazism, and the play was unequivo-cally condemned by Joachim Fest in the *Frankfurter Allgemeine Zeitung*. Fassbinder, however, was not simply anti-Semitic; the play also included a number of lines which attacked the very same imagery on which the plot was based. Theo Sommer, editor-in-chief of *Die Zeit*, argued that the play should be produced because "art is free and must remain so," and because it stimulated debate and was thus a "healthy imposition." He pointed out that there was no real, objective danger of an anti-Semitic movement rising to power in West Germany. His colleague, Marion Dönhoff, argued that this was irrelevant: the point was that "the past demands tribute" and that no German should permit himself, or be permitted, to publish anything that could be interpreted

[14] *Die Zeit*, November 15, 1985.
[15] Cited ibid.

as anti-Semitic propaganda. The play, in her view, had no redeeming features; "it does not present a problem for discussion but chases the most varied figures across the stage with no apparent connection between them. It is not a think-piece but a series of unrelated expressionistic fragments." She concluded that the argument for free speech was fallacious:

> The idea cannot be ... that the fewer the limits, the greater the freedom. Democracy can only last and function well if the individual sets limits for himself. That goes for the Frankfurt theater director as well. ... The damage has been done. The director has maneuvered the city [which had the authority to permit or prohibit the play's performance] into an impossible position. If the play is performed despite all protests the anti-Semites will triumph; if it is not performed then they will likewise triumph, because they will say, "There, you see how much power the Jews have."[16]

The end of the debate, on that occasion, was that the director withdrew the play from the theater schedule, but not the subject from public interest.

Another case of "the past that will not go away" concerned the well-known television host and moderator of the popular Sunday morning political round-table discussion *Der Internationale Frühschoppen*, Werner Höfer. (*Frühschoppen* is the name for a glass of wine or beer before lunch.) Höfer, who was born in 1913, had been with the West German Radio since 1946, later became its television director and, since 1952, had moderated a round table discussion consisting of four journalists from foreign countries and one German journalist. A distinguished and admired political commentator, he had at various times during his postwar career, been attacked for his pro-Nazi journalistic activities before and during the war, without any lasting damage to his career. However, in December 1987, *Der Spiegel* (No. 51/1987) published a scathing attack on Höfer, accusing him of having written, in 1943, an article for the Berlin Nazi newspaper, *12 Uhr Blatt*, that condoned and celebrated the execution of the innocent and popular concert pianist Karlrobert Kreiten, whom the Nazis denounced. *Der Spiegel* further accused Höfer of being the author of other articles – all reproduced in *Der Spiegel* – glorifying the Nazi regime, and of having been a member of the Nazi party, which was a known fact. Höfer, in the past, as in December 1987, countered that his articles, particularly the disputed Kreiten article, had been changed by the editors of the *12 Uhr Blatt* without his knowledge. He asserted that he had "written neither against the Jews nor paid homage to Hitler." And as a member of the

[16] Ibid.

Nazi party he was only a "fellow traveller (*Mitläufer*), and certainly no hero."[17]

Höfer was asked to resign by the director of the Cologne-based television station, Friedrich Nowottny, after the 41–member board of directors voted in favor of this action, with only three abstentions. The Höfer affair was hotly debated all over Germany. "Embarrassing" read the headline over an article in *Die Zeit* (January 1, 1988): "Was the end of Werner Höfer inevitable? Could it not have been more humane?" And the article questioned the fact that Höfer had not been given a chance to defend himself publicly: "The pro and contra, the weighing of arguments, could have been an informative and necessary lesson for all of us, because every problem concerning our past is extremely complicated and cannot be dismissed with a stroke of a pen."

Even though an editorial in the *Süddeutsche Zeitung* (December 16, 1987) paid tribute to the journalist Höfer, who fought for the "independence of his profession" and who knew "how to hold in check demanding politicians," it nonetheless concluded: "The name Werner Höfer was printed above the article, and we journalists have to be responsible for what is published under our name. Such is the price of freedom of the press, which even today cannot be divided into 'before' and 'after' 1945."

The Höfer case was fascinating and frustrating in every respect. The West German Radio concluded that to keep Höfer as its most distinguished television commentator would do the station's reputation more harm than good. But whatever the arguments for his summary dismissal, the station lost an individual who had made a major contribution to the arena of public debate in postwar Germany by developing a forum, respected both in Germany and abroad, for the responsible discussion of domestic and foreign policy issues. His dismissal also illustrated, once again, the continuing dilemma of how to deal with *die Vergangenheit*. Writing in the *Süddeutsche Zeitung* (December 23, 1987), Claus Heinrich Meyer cited Adenauer's approach to this problem, which the "Old Man" had explained to a group of journalists in 1951 (a number of whom had written for Nazi publications): "The machine must continue to run." Meyer continued: "Why should Höfer, whose case was one of the original sins of the republic, have worried about being questioned because of his scribbles of yesteryear or even about being hired, when, in the early years of the state and in the postwar society, he remained obviously surrounded by people of his own kind, who had formulated the same, more of it, and often worse.... It is ... an

---

[17] *Frankfurter Allgemeine Zeitung,* Dec. 23, 1987.

uncomfortable and unexplored territory. . . . There were many little Höfers, then."

In the Germany of the 1980s Claus Heinrich Meyer's question – "why should Höfer . . . have worried about being questioned" – was not only rhetorical. It was actual because the past had not gone away in Germany. Indeed, many in Europe and elsewhere would not let it go away, although few castigated the crimes of the past that took place in many other countries in Europe, such as the GDR and the Soviet Union, in equally harsh terms. It was difficult to answer because it was not clear why the German past was singled out again and again as a moral burden that required eternal restitution. Few participants in the debate asked: must restitution continue indefinitely?

In the Federal Republic of the 1980s, there were many "little Höfers," but of contemporary stripes and shades. As Nolte's supporters indicated in the *Historikerstreit*, such people pursued the past, not as a matter of principle, but as a matter of political expediency and partisanship, in order to be able to influence the agenda of West Germany's political future and self-image. In Höfer's case, they contributed to the ignominious end of the career of a man who gave much to rational political debate in the democracy of postwar Germany.

In December 1987 the Bundestag took steps to assure that the past would continue to be present for at least another three decades. It approved, more than 40 years after the war, an additional 300 million marks in restitution for victims of Nazi crimes. These funds were designated for those, such as gypsies, victims of forced sterilization, and surviving relatives of euthanasia victims, who had missed earlier deadlines for compensation and who were considered hardship cases under the original terms of the Indemnification Law of 1956. The Bundestag thus confirmed that it intended to continue to institutional-ize the past at great expense. By 1987, 80 billion marks had been paid in compensation; by the year 2020, three-quarters of a century after the war, the amount will have risen to 100 billion marks – more than 30 times the amount agreed upon in the early 1950s.[18]

Many asked if the time of atonement, in all its forms, would ever end. As long ago as 1965, the then chancellor, Ludwig Erhard, declared that "the postwar era is over," and Franz Josef Strauss demanded that Germans and foreigners draw a "final line" (*Schlussstrich*) under the arguments over the Nazi period and the moral bookkeeping involved in those arguments. But 20 years later, in the 1980s, the search for identity and the tools of history had not provided any lasting answers. Yet, if a

[18] *Relay from Bonn*, December 11, 1987.

moderate commentator like Christian Meier was right, the historians' debate and the related public events of the mid-1980s might be a sign that the past was, finally, becoming the past and not a political weapon in the present.

As the debate of the historians illustrated, the past was common to all Germans of whatever opinion or age, and one arbitrarily excerpted from it at one's own peril. Richard von Weizsäcker made this point in a speech at a banquet honoring the first visit of a president of Israel, Chaim Herzog, to the Federal Republic in April 1987:

This history of all epochs, the good and the bad, is a common legacy. We cannot and must not fade out any particular chapters of that history or see them in absolute terms. Our task is rather to accept the entire legacy, which carries over to successive generations the responsibility for its consequences for the future.

History never permits us to draw a line under the past. History is a continuous process which brings new experiences and new opportunities. The Federal Republic of Germany has stood the test as a free society based on the rule of law and social justice. It emerged as the historical response to the preceding era when a mockery had been made of human rights. The young people of this country will be more able to appreciate the meaning of our constitution the more they know about the past. Only then will they every day anew comprehend the gift of freedom and the duty it imposes. Only then will they be prepared to defend that freedom both internally and externally.[19]

One and a half years later, however, the debate generated by the *Historikerstreit* continued. On the occasion of the thirty-seventh conference of historians held in Bamberg, in Bavaria, in October 1988, President Weizsäcker addressed the participants on the subject of history:

Everything takes place in a historical framework, but every event is at the same time unique in history. It has occurred in that specific way, differently from events elsewhere. And what, after all, would it mean for us if Auschwitz could be compared with the ruthless extermination of other people? Auschwitz remains unique. It was perpetrated by Germans in the name of Germany. This truth is immutable and will not be forgotten. . . . Historical responsibility means accepting one's own history. We must do so above all for the sake of the present.

This is not changed by the passage of time. In fact, mankind's awareness of the occurrences at Auschwitz has increased in the decades since the war. But something else has also evolved: a democracy to which we are committed out of

---

[19] *Statements and Speeches*, April 7, 1987.

conviction. This democracy has proved its worth for 40 years now, not least through openness toward its history.[20]

Weizsäcker quite properly emphasized, "I feel that nobody seriously wants to raise the issue of ethical relativism." But he also concluded his speech with an observation with which Germany's distinguished historians, such as Ranke, Droysen, Meinecke, Ritter and Herzfeld, would presumably have agreed:

Coping with the unholy legacy of history is something that occurs in the heart of the entire nation. With "holy soberness" historians can help in this process. They can and must help everyone. For history, our history, does not belong to historians alone.[21]

[20] Weizsäcker, "Germany: History is Immutable," *Los Angeles Times*, October 30, 1988.
[21] Ibid.

6

The Politics of Religion and the Past

The shadows of the past continued to make their political way across West Germany not only among historians, sociologists, and political scientists, but also in other milieus. Despite the fact that many German institutions played a constructive role in resolving the struggles of reconciling the past with the present and the future, some did not. It would be logical to assume that the churches could exercise a positive influence in this process. But religion too, seemed to bear the cross of unreconciled past and present. A marked feature of the West German culture of identity in the 1980s, related to the debates on German identity and German guilt and to the peace movement, was the prominence of political religion, particularly among Protestants.

Political commitment by theologians had respectable antecedents, notably in the occupation years and in the efforts of Heinemann, Niemöller, and Helmut Gollwitzer to stop rearmament in the 1950s. The heirs of Heinemann in the 1980s, however, used religious phrases and ideas out of context to argue a very simple thesis regarding war and peace in Europe. It was that war is caused by weapons, and therefore the Germans must disarm, unilaterally if necessary; if this would not happen, nuclear war was sure to occur in the immediate future.

Beginning in 1981, the biennual Protestant assemblies (DEKT) became mass rallies of the converted who encouraged each other in their simplistic views of politics and security. In Hannover in 1983, the *Kirchentag* turned into a mass rally of the peace movement, no longer resembling a religious gathering at all. At that same meeting, the French political scientist Alfred Grosser, who had studied Germany closely for 30 years and who had a long-standing interest in religion and politics, made a speech criticizing those who, in the name of morality, demanded instant unilateral disarmament and accused the Kohl government, the US, and NATO of planning war:

I completely understand that many Germans, given their historical experience ... do not trust the power of the state when it speaks of weapons.

But exactly these Germans should understand that other people have experienced this same historical period differently, and that, seen from another perspective, different conclusions are emerging for today.

Why do so many Frenchmen not see 1939, when Hitler began the war, as the decisive year, but rather 1938? Because Daladier and Chamberlain surrendered in Munich and abandoned Czechoslovakia. France was weak-willed and badly armed. Peace was not saved that way: diplomatic surrender led to war within a year and then the humiliating defeat of the spring of 1940. One must be strong-willed in the face of a threat. . . .

That East–West talks are being held: progress! That German writers meet on this or the other side of the wall: well and good! Compared to the past, the Federal Republic, in this respect, is now more inclined towards peace. But when the West German participants carefully avoid even mentioning the constant violation of the Helsinki Agreements on the other side; when they speak only of armaments and not of the basic liberties which the arms are designed to protect; then they are doing peace a disservice because they are not telling their interlocutors clearly what the stakes are. That also applies to interviews of the press, for instance when Rudolf Augstein treats Yuri Andropov much more reverently than he would ever treat a Western politician. . . .

But competence means also expertise. On the subject of arms and strategic conflict the issues are so difficult and multifarious that one should be certain of only one thing: whoever is one hundred percent certain of anything is either ignorant of basic facts or is in the grip of a clerical attitude – or both. To be completely clear: what bothers me the most about the new German pacifism, especially in the Protestant churches, is the rebirth of spiritual intolerance.[1]

This politicization of the Lutheran church had historical roots in the guilt felt by many pastors and theologians over the accommodation with the Nazi regime by Lutherans in the Third Reich, eloquently expressed by Niemöller in the 1950s. But by the 1980s careful political judgement concerning that history and the present had not yet replaced the emotion of the early postwar years. Indeed, many Lutheran theologians continued to succumb to a profound need to atone for a perceived guilt by adopting the position of the most extreme utopians. They claimed to have found a heritage of good Lutherans in the Third Reich, Bonhoeffer, Niemöller himself, and especially the Swiss theologian, Karl Barth. They continued to reject the old Lutheran idea that one should trust one's government unless it was obviously committing evil acts, and instead maintained that the Bonn government was, by definition, immoral and that anything it did in the area of defense and security policy was automatically suspect. This new alliance of what had been a

---

[1] Cited in Reinfried and Schulte, *Die Sicherheit der BRD*, 27–8.

weak and, socially, not very significant religious force within the peace movement, gave it a great deal of social importance, but did not contribute to any genuine revival of religious feeling.

Another area where guilt of the newly revived religion flourished was in attitudes toward the Third World. On the Protestant side, the prominent SPD member Eppler had written several books arguing that the West was directly responsible for the poverty of the Third World and that an immediate change of life was required in the West to save the Third World. The best known of these was *Ende oder Wende* (End or change). On the Catholic side, the so-called theology of liberation became very popular in West Germany. One of its leading spokesmen was Norbert Greinacher of Tübingen, who combined his political activism for radical Third World causes with opposition to the INF missiles, that included his arrest along with fellow activists for obstructing deployment of these missiles.

The ease with which well-intentioned people could transform religious concerns into a political agenda was illustrated in 1983 by author Franz Alt. Alt, a popular television figure and a Catholic, wrote a short book called *Frieden ist möglich: Die Politik der Bergpredigt* (Peace is possible: the politics of the Sermon on the Mount), which, within six months, achieved the almost unprecedented sale of 600,000 copies. In it Alt explained that he had experienced a revelation when he realized that the Sermon on the Mount must be the basis for political action and that, if this could not be achieved, the world would end in nuclear war. The small book contained no practical political ideas and was based on an extreme simplification of the problems of ethics and politics. Its enormous success illustrated Grosser's remarks about the potential danger of discussion of the serious and vital issues of national survival by persons who did not grasp them or who simplified their seriousness, but at the same time publicized their simplifications with great success.

Alt's book received a response from the political scientist, Manfred Hättich, of the University of Munich and director of the Academy of Political Education in Tutzing, in the book *Weltfrieden durch Friedfertigkeit?* (World peace through peaceful intentions?). It, too, had considerable success. Hättich respected Alt's sincere fear of nuclear arms, but pointed out that fear was not a political argument, and that, as far as he was concerned, "there exists among the fears of our time, a certain fear of the many slogans of the peace movements. I am afraid that these movements, despite their good intentions, are not at all making peace safer but rather endangering our liberty." He continued, "If we demonstrate for peace against our governments and act as though we, the peacemakers, are fighting those who are against peace, then we are lying. There is no struggle here between those who want peace and those who want war."[2]

The struggle, rather, was between those who found Alt's rhetoric attractive and those who wanted to preserve both peace and freedom with realistic solutions. It was a serious mistake to try to extract political guidelines from the divine revelation of Jesus Christ and his commands to personal conversion. Alt, in Hättich's view, committed the typical mistake of the sentimental left: he failed to distinguish personal morality from political imperatives and assumed that the way for ordinary people to promote peace was to behave decently in their personal relationships while demanding unilateral disarmament from their government. Hättich argued that this was the opposite of a responsible attitude, since there was no simple correlation between personal desire for peace and international politics. Peace, he concluded, was not preserved by utopian illusions, but by realistic policies based on a sense of what one's interests are and who one's friends are, and how to defend both against one's enemies.

[2] Hättich, *Weltfrieden durch Friedfertigkeit?*, 8, 95.

7

Ostpolitik: Division, Cultural Unity, and Reunification

The Kohl government was careful to emphasize, to a greater degree than Schmidt's government, that the German question was still open. Indeed, in 1984, the new federal president, Richard von Weizsäcker, used an apt phrase when he said "the German question will remain unanswered as long as the Brandenburg Gate remains closed."[1] (The Brandenburg Gate stands at the head of *Unter den Linden* just inside the Soviet sector of Berlin. It was closed by the Wall in 1961.) In common with all governments since the grand coalition, Kohl's government did not argue, as Adenauer's government had during the 1950s, that national unity must be the primary short-term goal of its inner-German policy; rather, its purpose was to work toward a state of affairs in which all Germans could freely determine what kind of society and national political institutions they wanted. As the minister for inner-German relations, Heinrich Windelen, put it in February 1984 at a conference in Washington, DC: "The German question will be solved only in agreement with our neighbors or it will never be solved. The view expressed from time to time, that the integration of Western Europe makes the solution of the German question more difficult, is short-sighted and false."[2]

In the mid-1980s, even Windelen's conclusion was too much for the left wing of the SPD, which had publicly abandoned the goal of free national self-determination and was now primarily concerned with dialogue with the SED. In the words of the SPD in 1983, "Whoever here, now and in all seriousness declares the German question 'open' not only destroys the fragile base of Ostpolitik but also the very foundation of European postwar politics."[3] This was a view that

---

[1] Dept of State, *Documents on Germany*, 1415.
[2] Cited in Bark and Rowen, "The German Question."
[3] See SPD, *Wir informieren: Bilanz einer Wende*.

accurately reflected the changing views of the SPD, and of its chairman Willy Brandt, who had declared in December 1972, at the conclusion of the Basic Treaty between West Germany and the GDR, that the treaty kept the German question "open." The CDU/CSU, but also the more conservative members of the SPD, considered the formal position of the party's leadership in 1983 to be short-sighted and irresponsible. Indeed, they believed that at the foundation of European postwar politics was a common interest in ending Germany's and Europe's division, and in attempting to try, by peaceful means, to extend the Atlantic Charter promises of political freedom to *all* Europeans. In the Federal Republic the SPD's critics found it alarming that many left-wing social democrats seemed to ignore the political reasons for the continuing division of the continent.

One of West Germany's intellectuals who took exception to the SPD's position as unrealistic, was the political scientist Hans-Peter Schwarz, then teaching at the University of Cologne. In 1985 he wrote a short book entitled *Die gezähmten Deutschen: Von der Machtbesessenheit zur Machtvergessenheit* (The tamed Germans: from obsession with power to oblivion of power). Schwarz, a student of the leading figure of early postwar political science in West Germany, Arnold Bergstraesser, had earned great respect as an analyst of West German politics, as a historian of the Federal Republic, and as Adenauer's biographer. He wrote of the "tamed Germans" in an effort to point out the dangers of the Federal Republic's excessive self-restraint in foreign policy, which in his view was unwarranted. A country that pretended that power politics were passé was, he argued, vulnerable to blackmail by those who still conducted power politics – meaning the Soviet Union. In an earlier article, in 1979, Schwarz had written that the Schmidt government was so friendly toward the Soviet Union and so eager to declare itself committed to peace and detente because it was terrified of Soviet power, and, "in view of the decline of American power," understandably wished to "come to terms with the new lord and master."[4]

In his 1985 book Schwarz criticized followers of the dominant tradition of West German foreign policy for believing that the world was other than it was, a pretense that, in his view, was misleading and potentially dangerous. In particular, he attacked what he saw as a false moralism, expressed by many leading Bonn politicians, of all parties, since the election of Brandt and Heinemann in 1969. This position argued that morality demanded West German rejection of power politics and that it base its foreign policy on ethical principles, as though the two were mutually exclusive. Schwarz concluded that in one very

---

[4] Cited in Gress, *Peace and Survival*, 87.

important area at least, namely Ostpolitik itself, Bonn had not sufficiently respected ethical principles:

If there was ever an act of the most sober *Realpolitik* it was the recognition both of the annexation of the German Eastern provinces following the expulsion of their inhabitants and of a dictatorship on German soil. One may have fulfilled [this recognition] with sorrow in one's heart and averted eyes. Morality as a motive for the "new Ostpolitik" also played a part. But its opponents could also list moral motives in support of their case. . . . What will happen in the future to international morality if it is accepted that annexation of territory is best carried out by expelling the inhabitants and by the argument, which after thirty years cannot be refuted but which is also completely cynical, that those who were since born in those territories also have a right to live there? What will happen to morality if the crimes of a government are avenged by injustices committed against the defeated? What will happen to the moral underpinnings of a free state if, on grounds of realism, the state must recognize and celebrate a totalitarian satellite government which is oppressing eighteen million compatriots?[5]

Schwarz' criticism was not typical. A majority of the German electorate was content with the continuation of the largely unchanged Ostpolitik of the Schmidt-Genscher government. Indeed the Kohl-Genscher government made every effort to assure the GDR regime that it did not want the deployment of Pershing II and cruise missiles to affect inner-German relations and that it intended to remain predictable, a phrase that had been coined under the Schmidt-Genscher government. Predictability was a concept that Genscher gave special emphasis, and he made convincing arguments for its validity. But it also had a second, and less advantageous side, in the real world of politics. His critics asserted that he stressed predictability at the expense of exercising the power of initiative, and his supporters argued that his approach was the only way to improve relations with the GDR and Eastern Europe.

The efforts of Kohl's government to be predictable resulted in its assurance to the GDR that it would maintain and develop a policy of economic assistance and political conciliation. These efforts were joined by Franz Josef Strauss, the "Bavarian Lion" (a name referring both to his personality and to the crest of the blue and white Bavarian flag of the house of Wittelsbach), who declared in July 1987 that "the German question can no longer be solved with 'blood and iron.'"[6] In 1983–4 he helped arrange three large loans totaling approximately one

[5] Schwarz, *Die gezähmten Deutschen*, 45–6.
[6] *Die Zeit*, July 10, 1987. In 1862 Bismarck stated the German question of national unity would be solved by blood and iron.

billion marks from private West German banks on very favorable terms to the GDR; the total value of inner-German trade in 1983 was 15.2 billion marks,[7] compared to 4.5 billion in 1970.

The West German government provided economic assistance in the expectation that, in return, the GDR regime would grant humanitarian concessions; for example, improved postal and telephone communications, improvements on the autobahns in East Germany connecting West Berlin with West Germany, and more visits in both directions. Genscher explained the rationale for unprecedented economic aid as follows: "That task facing the two German states in the awareness of their joint responsibility for stability in Central Europe presupposes that they themselves are stable. A healthy economy is one of the main pillars of stability, and loans are an appropriate means of promoting economic development."[8]

The East German government did, indeed, begin to meet Genscher's expectation. Heinrich Windelen noted in the autumn of 1984:

Just over one German in three over the age of 14 who lives in the Federal Republic of Germany, including West Berlin, has relations, friends and acquaintances in the GDR.

About one in five more or less regularly sends letters, packets, and parcels. Roughly one in eight visits the GDR or East Berlin periodically. In absolute figures for 1983 there were five million visitors from the West to the East and 1.6 million visitors from the East to the West (93 per cent of whom were pensioners). Fifty-nine million letters were mailed to the GDR and 88 million came from the GDR. Between 20 and 25 million packets and parcels were mailed to the GDR and nine million sent to the Federal Republic of Germany.

There were also 23 million telephone calls from West to East, including just over ten million within Berlin.

The number of parcels sent annually from the Federal Republic of Germany to the GDR is more than twice the total number of parcels sent abroad. . . .[9]

In the "German-German Year" of 1987 these figures improved. Approximately five million visits from the GDR were registered in West Germany and West Berlin, of which 1.2 million were by persons not yet retired, an astounding number in comparison to the past. More than 60,000 young people from the Federal Republic visited the GDR, and approximately 4,000 from the GDR traveled to West Germany. Athletic teams met in one or the other part of Germany on 104 occasions, and 34 sister city relationships were agreed upon or planned. Of the 1,470

[7] Wilms, *The German Question and Inner-German Relations*, 8.
[8] *Statements and Speeches*, August 10, 1984.
[9] Windelen, "The two states of Germany," *German Tribune*, December 2, 1984.

telephone exchanges in the GDR, West Germans could dial directly 1,221, and in 1987 made approximately 30 million telephone calls to the GDR and East Berlin.[10] This was not a minor achievement. But, as one West German official noted, "whatever the Soviets and East Germans give is done unilaterally – and their concessions also can be revoked unilaterally. But what carrots West Germany gives in return – credits – are nearly impossible to get back. 'They can reverse what they are doing whenever they find it necessary, and we can't.'"[11] Yet in 1988 the number of visits continued to increase. The minister for inner-German relations, Dorothee Wilms, announced in December that by year's end more than five million people would have travelled in each direction, and that more than 1.2 million would be visitors from the GDR under the age of retirement.[12]

The construction of the Berlin Wall in 1961 benefited the GDR by drastically curtailing the flow of refugees to West Germany, since skilled workers trained in East Germany now found it virtually impossible to escape. Ironically, the Wall also generated income for the GDR once the East German government discovered that Bonn was willing to pay for the release of Germans to the West. This practice was started in 1963 by Rainer Barzel, Erich Mende's immediate predecessor in the all-German ministry during 1962 and 1963.

According to reports in the press, the GDR government made up lists with the names of persons whom the ministry of state security approved for release, so that their exit could be purchased. In the later 1960s the number of political prisoners in the GDR was reported to be 13,000, and the regime apparently kept the figure steady, arresting new people to make up for those who had left. Thus there was a steady supply of victims who could be sold to the West. The intermediary was Wolfgang Vogel, a communist lawyer in East Berlin, authorized to negotiate the sales. Vogel had the title of plenipotentiary of the GDR government for humanitarian matters. Among others, he arranged the exchange of Francis Gary Powers, the American pilot, for the Soviet spy Rudolf Abel, on the Glienecke Bridge on the border between West Berlin and East Germany in 1962.

As time passed sale and purchase became routine. The policy, according to some observers, constituted a "slave trade" and did not serve as "an active and public human-rights policy."[13] The West

---

[10] Kaiser, "Ein kleines Wunder für die Deutschen," *Die Zeit*, January 8, 1988.

[11] Frederick Kempe, *Wall Street Journal*, August 3, 1987.

[12] *Relay from Bonn*, December 9, 1988.

[13] Reinhard Gnauck, "East Germany Sells its Citizens to Freedom," *Wall Street Journal*, November 14, 1984.

German government, indeed, faced an insoluble dilemma. If this practice was the only way in which it could secure the freedom of at least some Germans living in the GDR, the question was whether it was to be condoned or condemned as a matter of principle. By 1983, more than 20,000 East German political prisoners and other applicants for emigration had been bought out for the equivalent of $949 million. By the autumn of 1984, an additional 1,710 had been purchased: "The 'goods' always cross the border at night from the East. They are unloaded in Giessen, West Germany. Payment is made two weeks in advance into an East German account in the West. The whole trans-action almost escapes notice, for the sellers demand strict secrecy from the buyers, fearing public opinion."[14] In 1985 Bonn bought more than 2,500 political prisoners, the highest number thus far, according to figures released at a press conference by Heinrich Windelen.[15] Windelen claimed that there were still 2,000 political prisoners in the GDR, and that Bonn had some leverage to ensure the GDR would not simply, as it had done in the past, arrest new prisoners as a source of hard currency.

Not just political prisoners, but anyone wishing to leave the GDR could, after applying for an exit permit (an act that often resulted in the loss of one's job), contact Vogel at his office in East Berlin. Presumably Vogel would be told by his superiors in the SED which names he could bring up at each meeting with the Bonn government, and how much he was to charge. The price was negotiable (a doctor or skilled mechanic cost more than an unskilled laborer) and the figures difficult to confirm, but in the 1980s the average price to ransom a German – to give him his native right to freedom of movement, which the GDR regime denied him – approximated 50,000 marks. The money came from the German taxpayer via the ministry of inner-German relations, where it was described as funds for "the promotion of special assistance of an all-German character." In 1988, this part of the ministry's budget amounted to 320.7 million marks and the freedom of 1,094 persons was purchased.[16]

Perhaps surprisingly, both in West and East Germany, Vogel was regarded with awe, if not affection, as a humanitarian whose work genuinely contributed to overcoming national division. Few noted the obvious fact that he was a loyal servant of his regime. By his efforts the GDR obtained considerable sums of hard West German currency, and his practices served to consolidate, and not to ameliorate, national division. It is also true, however, that the freedom of only a minority of

[14] Ibid.

[15] *Washington Post*, December 10, 1986; *Der Spiegel*, 8/1983, p. 20, 43/1983, p. 28.

[16] *Der Spiegel*, April 25, 1988, 32; *Die Welt*, April 13, 1989.

Germans moving west was actually purchased. During the first three months of 1989 the GDR permitted 15,300 residents to leave; many, but not all, retired persons whose departure reduced the regime's welfare burden, but not its productive labor power. For 1988 the number was 39,732 persons. The numbers were approximately 8,000 in 1983, 40,000 in 1984, 25,000 in 1985, 20,000 in 1986, and 12,000 in 1987.[17]

In 1987 one analysis, presenting an optimistic view of how inner-German relations were developing, was that of the social democrat Wilhelm Bruns. While much was left to be done – in the areas of law enforcement, science and technology and environmental concerns for example – much had been accomplished. Bruns divided the development into phases which put into perspective the steps taken by both German states to improve relations in a country which remains unalterably split. The first phase was that of no state-to-state relations from 1949 until 1972 when the Treaty on the Basis of Relations was signed, ending the period of "isolation and confrontation." Thereafter followed the "implementation phase," during which both states sought to find answers to "practical and humanitarian questions." By 1987 a new phase was underway, "marked by parallel efforts for humanitarian solutions, with the goal to make the division of Germany more bearable for the people involved."[18]

In 1984 the Kohl government undertook a major initiative in its inner-German policy by inviting Erich Honecker to West Germany. Honecker was born in the Saarland in 1912, but had not been to West Germany since 1948. Since Schmidt had visited him on the Werbellinsee in December 1981 in the GDR, Honecker had stressed what he called "the community of responsibility" for peace, shared by both German states. He used the old Soviet phrase of a "security partnership between East and West" which the SPD had also adopted. This rhetoric gained him a good deal of sympathy in West Germany where many in the SPD, but also in the governing coalition, interpreted his emphasis as an indication that the GDR wished to preserve inner-German detente despite the deterioration of Soviet-American relations. Honecker was clearly anxious to give the impression that he wanted to maintain good relations with Bonn, but a necessary condition was that Bonn distance itself from the United States. Honecker stressed "the responsibilities

[17] See Kaiser, "Ein kleines Wunder für die Deutschen," *Die Zeit*, January 8, 1988; *Relay from Bonn*, December 9, 1988; Press and Information Office, typewritten communication, July 1986, *Die Welt*; April 13, 1989.

[18] Bruns, "Deutsch-Deutsche Beziehungen." *Politische Bildung* 20, no. 1 (1987): 39–40.

that the two German nations have for peace" – parenthetically including a reference to the SED theory of two separate German nations.[19]

At the same time the Soviet government strenuously objected to President Reagan's announcement of March 1983 that the United States would take a "strategic defense initiative" (SDI) and seek to develop a defense against nuclear missile attack, an initiative that was quickly condemned by the USSR as an attempt to develop a new offensive strategic capability. This development, combined with INF deployment, meant that the Soviet government did not regard an improvement of East–West German relations with pleasure. As preparations for Honecker's visit continued, the Soviet Union issued official warnings that "Bonn is trying to undermine the sovereignty of the GDR" and that "West German leaders were now trying as vigorously as never before to implement their plans of undermining the German state of workers and peasants [the GDR]."[20] Indeed, an editorial in *Pravda* on August 2 concluded, "It will not be amiss to recall once again Erich Honecker's pronouncement . . . the socialist GDR and the capitalist FRG cannot be combined, just as it is impossible to combine fire and ice." Honecker finally officially postponed the trip in early September. Most commentators assumed that he wanted to come, that he sought closer relations with Bonn even at the risk of displeasing Moscow, but that the Soviet government forbade the visit.

If the West German government possessed evidence for this assumption, it was kept confidential. Wolfgang Seiffert, however, wrote that the GDR and its leadership were "instruments of Soviet German policy."[21] Honecker, as leader of the GDR, saw a clear priority in projecting the image of East Germany as a legitimate participant in a security partnership in Central Europe. To have Bonn invite him as a respected elder statesman furthered that aim, but to have gone under the conditions prevailing in 1984 would not have been advantageous. Both his display of interest and his ultimate refusal, however, served his goal of cultivating the image of a figure of moderation, irrespective of whether the decision to cancel his visit was his own or that of the Soviet government.

The GDR announcement did not blame Bonn for the postponement, in stark contrast to the attitude taken by other East European newspapers. Indeed the closer the time for the visit had come, the more

[19] See Asmus, "*Pravda* Attacks East–West German Ties," RFE-RL Background Report/145, August 8, 1984.

[20] Cited ibid.

[21] Seiffert, "Die DDR – Herrschaftsinstrument der SED und Produkt sowjetischer Deutschlandpolitik," in *Die DDR auf dem Weg in das Jahr 2000*, eds Berg et al., 13.

vitriolic the commentary by *Pravda* and East European newspapers. For example, the West German government was accused of wishing "to liquidate" the GDR and of seeking an "Anschluss" of the kind that occurred with Austria in 1938. The result was creation of an emotional climate which made a visit unacceptable.[22] A footnote to the postponed visit was reported in the September 10 issue of *Der Spiegel*. Apparently Valentin Kopteltsev, a minister at the Soviet embassy in East Berlin, in a conversation with West Germany's permanent representative in East Berlin, Hans Otto Bräutigam, outlined the objections of the Soviet government to the efforts of both Germanies to improve ties with one another. According to Kopteltsev, the Soviet government considered loans, trade and political contacts as destabilizing to the GDR, that Honecker's policy was aimed at creating greater autonomy for the GDR and that in the long term these efforts would liberalize the GDR and might eventually produce some form of German unity, in addition to isolating the Soviet Union "within its own camp."[23]

According to Peter Bender, writing in October, West Germany faced the following alternatives in the autumn of 1984: either "no trouble with the Americans," which meant there would be "no more detente," *or* an "Ostpolitik" and a "Deutschlandpolitik" which would entail quarrels with West Germany's allies.[24] But it was not evident that the alternatives were so clear cut. The West German government did recognize that there was concern in Western Europe, and in the United States about the future consequences of developing East–West German relations, such as the view expressed in France by François Mauriac: "I love Germany so much, it makes me happy to have two of them."[25]

The West German government was also legitimately committed to improving relations with East Germany, and not at the expense of weakening its ties with the West. Alois Mertes, a CDU member of the Bundestag and a senior official in the foreign ministry, explained why, in an article written for the *New York Times* in October 1984. He drew some frank conclusions:

What's troubling for us in West Germany is that many Americans show so little understanding of the moral and political substance of "the German question."

As long as Germany is divided by a most inhuman and barbed wire barrier, it remains the human and national duty of West Germany to insure the cohesion

[22] See *Die Welt*, September 6, 1984; *International Herald Tribune*, September 5, 6, 1984; *Daily Telegraph*, September 5, 6, 7, 1984.

[23] See Deutsche Presse Agentur report, September 15, 1985.

[24] Bender, "Wider die dreissigjährige Verlogenheit," *Die Zeit*, October 5, 1984.

[25] *Der Spiegel*, September 10, 1984.

of the German people by developing relations with East Germany. At the simplest level, we hope to alleviate the family or personal situations of hundreds of thousands of human beings by making possible travel, family reunions and the like. But this practical aspect of the problem is not its most important side. It is not a question of territory or borders but of national self-determination and individual human rights on both sides of the German border.

West Germany's foreign policy, particularly in relation to the Atlantic alliance, is built on the identity of German national interest with the Western democratic values of freedom and the rule of law. Whenever West Germans have been able to decide for themselves – in all free elections since 1945 – they have opted for democracy and the rule of law. From its founding onward, therefore, West Germany chose to develop the closest possible links with Western Europe and the United States. But this was a vote for the ethical values cherished and guaranteed by the West, not for the West in a geographical sense. In other words, it was not a decision against our countrymen in the other part of Germany and our other East European neighbors. . . .

Unlike many in the West, we see no contradiction between our ties with them and our overtures toward the East. On the contrary, in our view it is the moral substance of our links with the West that prevents us from abandoning the demand for the rule of law and freedom for the Germans who are arbitrarily denied these rights. This demand is part and parcel of the aspiration to lasting peace in Europe.

West Germany must continue to press this demand for freedom if democracy and the West are to have any credibility among the German generations to come. We make this demand on national and humanitarian grounds, and we must try, through dialogue with East Berlin, to ease the lot of the people affected as long as the enforced division lasts.

Unfortunately, it is likely to be a long time before the Soviet Union, too, recognizes that it has created not a cordon sanitaire but rather a cordon of political uncertainties along its western border. . . .[26]

Mertes' conclusions were shared, in general, by conservative members of the SPD. But the party's leadership also considered that "stagnation" was beginning to characterize the development of East–West German relations. It thus continued to pursue its own initiatives vis-à-vis the GDR. In the summer of 1985 the SPD and the SED published a joint statement recommending creation of a chemical-weapon-free zone in Central Europe. In Bonn the SPD announced that it would immediately enter into such negotiations with the East German government, should it be returned to government in the next elections to the Bundestag scheduled for 1987. Egon Bahr explained further that the SPD and the SED would begin talks to explore creation of a nuclear-free zone within a radius of 300 kilometers on either side of the East–

---

[26] Mertes, "Bonn Seeks Unification," *New York Times*, October 12, 1984.

West German border. He concluded that the opposition, indeed had a responsibility to "develop alternatives."[27]

Whether this reflected a policy of predictability was debatable. Its wisdom was also questioned in an editorial entitled "The Open Flank" by one of West Berlin's most respected newspapers:

> From Chancellor Schmidt comes the statement that German policy must be predictable in all directions. Chancellor Kohl has adopted it for his vocabulary; for the SPD, however, at least for the national party, it does not appear to play a role any more. It [the SPD] indeed continually emphasizes it does not want to shake loyalty to NATO, but continually discusses plans which run counter to the common policy of the alliance. It is designing treaties on chemical and atomic weapon free zones in central Europe with the SED, which in wartime (would) not protect against the effects of such weapons, but which politically would make of the Federal Republic a special area for NATO, with all of the resulting consequences for our allies. ... It is now no longer predictable what would happen in the Federal Republic, on a foreign policy level, if the social democrats were to return to government. Then, with the discussion of all such bilateral agreements the SPD is incurring vis-à-vis the SED open-ended commitments, which would remove all freedom of action in political discussions within the alliance. Every sensible party, however, keeps its options open in the event that government responsibility requires freedom to pursue a joint policy with political friends; unless it no longer believes in a connection between its own interests and those of our partners. Therewith the SPD is becoming, especially toward the West, incapable of making solutions in partnership.[28]

An additional issue was addressed by Brandt in the same month. Following a visit to all Eastern European countries except Romania and Bulgaria, Brandt met for five hours with Erich Honecker in East Berlin in the middle of September. On his return to West Berlin Brandt announced that easements in travel restrictions between both parts of Germany could be expected, if West Germany would "respect the citizenship" of Germans living in the GDR. The CDU responded to both developments very critically, pointing out that Kohl had met with Honecker in Moscow in March, and that Honecker had expressed hope that not "so much noise" – meaning, not so much publicity – would be made about the continuing development of East–West German relations.[29] The significance of these developments was analysed by Roger Thurow, writing for the *Wall Street Journal*:

[27] *Die Welt*, September 26, 1985.
[28] J.B., "Die offene Flanke," *Der Tagesspiegel*, September 25, 1985.
[29] *Der Tagesspiegel*, September 26, 1985.

The Social Democrats are hoping to create the impression among West German voters that they are the only ones capable of conducting an Ostpolitik. . . . The Kohl government, the Social Democrats contend, is capable only of dealing with its friends in the West . . . The Kohl government accuses the Social Democrats of undermining West Germany's foreign policy consensus for electoral gain. Particularly aggravating . . . was the chemical-weapons accord . . . a pact rejected by the Kohl administration because it ran counter to Western efforts to seek a global ban on chemical weapons. . . . Bonn government officials . . . maintain simply that the Soviet Union is using the Social Democrats to unsettle the foreign-policy debate within West Germany.

Thurow concluded that in the current political climate no Bonn government could do anything that might offend the East bloc regimes. Consequently those regimes had a quasi veto power over Bonn's Ostpolitik. In order to counter the SPD activities, he felt, the Kohl government had already watered down "its endorsement of the US . . . Strategic Defense Initiative, in order to avoid short-circuiting the chances for a visit by East German leader Erich Honecker. . . ."[30]

The SPD liaisons with Eastern Europe, and especially with the GDR, continued. In January 1986 *Die Zeit* noted that Honecker had met personally with several leading social democrats in the previous months, and not just social democrats of the first rank like Lafontaine or Johannes Rau, but with younger members, rising in influence, such as the head of the SPD in Lower Saxony, Gerhard Schröder, who tried and barely failed to win the state elections in June 1986. "Marxists think in the long term," *Die Zeit* commented. "When Honecker receives the young guard of SPD politicians he is doing it in the expectation that this party will govern in Bonn again some day. When that day comes it will help to have treated Schröder as a distinguished guest."[31]

In March 1986 the SPD group charged with a major responsibility within the framework of these contacts, the so-called *Grundwertekommission* or Commission on Fundamental Values, established in 1982 and chaired by Eppler, met for the fourth time with SED representatives in West Germany and issued a second joint statement on agreed positions and policies. References to uncomfortable historical facts such as the SED persecution of social democrats or to the differences in legitimacy between the dictatorship in the East and the democratically elected government in the West were not contained in the statement. In fact the SPD rejected the very idea that one should call into question the legitimacy of the GDR. The two regimes, according to the Commission, were of equal value. The SPD called on both sides to recognize the

[30] *Wall Street Journal*, December 9, 1985.
[31] *Die Zeit*, January 17, 1986.

other's right to exist and said that "mutual change through competition" was the only way forward. The SED representatives immediately defined the phrase to mean change only in the West: "Should we reintroduce capitalism?" they asked in astonishment. The Commission did not press the point and accepted the SED formulation of "peaceful coexistence;" that is to say, a situation in which the West promised not to question the legitimacy of the East, but must itself gradually change so as to become more like the East. According to this equation the East's own institutions and practices remained sacrosanct and could not be altered. Eppler's justification for this effort, certainly not shared by the right wing of the SPD, was that "I am only as secure as the person on the other side" and that security could only be achieved in collaboration with the adversary. He did not elaborate on the reasons why military forces and security arrangements existed in Europe, if the potential opponent was really a "partner" in security.[32]

The SED held its eleventh party congress and celebrated the fortieth anniversary of the forced merger of the KPD and the SPD in the Soviet zone in April 1986. Despite the fact that many members of the SPD had very mixed feelings about that anniversary, the SPD nevertheless sent an emissary to attend the party congress, where his presence was taken by the SED as passive recognition by the SPD of the legitimacy of the forced merger 40 years before. At the congress, journalists told the following joke: How have the two German states divided the inheritance of Karl Marx among themselves? Answer: The West has the capital and the East has the Manifesto.

[32] Ibid., March 14, 1986.

In January 1985, the GDR authorities dynamited the Church of the Reconciliation, which was situated immediately adjacent to the Berlin Wall, in order to improve their field of fire against persons trying to escape. [*Source*: GIC]

Top left In June 1982, President Ronald Reagan visited West Germany and gave a speech to the Bundestag that Schmidt later described as the most effective speech on Germany given by a US president since Kennedy's "Ich bin ein Berliner" speech of June 1963. [*Source*: GIC]

Below left Speaking at the Brandenburg Gate, President Reagan called on the Soviets to "tear down the Wall." In sad contrast to Kennedy's visit in 1963, many hecklers and demonstrators appeared opposing the US and NATO plans to deploy nuclear missiles in Germany to help counter a massive Soviet arms buildup. [*Source*: GIC]

Between 1979 and 1981 the federal president, Karl Carstens, walked in stages through West Germany to get to know all its regions and peoples. He is shown here (center, with hand on strap) walking in the Grunewald, a forested section of West Berlin.

In the 1980s, the SPD pursued its own relationship with the SED, organizing a series of meetings to promote disarmament and common understanding. For the SED, this recognition marked an important stage on the road to equal legitimacy with the democratic parties of West Germany. From left to right: Hermann Scheer, moderator of the SPD working group on disarmament; Egon Bahr, the SPD's chief disarmament expert and a long-time friend of the GDR; Karsten Voigt, foreign policy spokesman of the SPD; Hermann Axen, leading member of the SED Politburo; a journalist; Karlheinz Lohs of the GDR Academy of Sciences; Karl-Heinz Wagner of the SED Central Committee. [*Source*: GIC]

In 1984, the minister of economics, Otto Lambsdorff (FDP, left) resigned in connection with the Flick affair. His successor was Martin Bangemann (right), who also became chairman of the FDP in 1985. In 1988 Bangemann resigned both positions to become a member of the European Commission in Brussels, and Lambsdorff was elected chairman of the party. [*Source*: GIC]

Horst Ehmke (SPD, right), born in Danzig, was an early supporter of Ostpolitik and of a West German foreign policy distinct from that of the US. He is seen here in 1986 with the future chairman of the SPD, Hans-Jochen Vogel. [*Source*: GIC]

The ageing SPD chairman, Brandt, with his successor, Hans-Jochen Vogel (center), and the SPD's unsuccessful candidate for chancellor in 1987, Johannes Rau, former minister-president of North Rhine-Westphalia. [*Source*: GIC]

Franz Josef Strauss (right), considered Kohl (left) soft on foreign policy, but his own final bid for the chancellorship failed in 1980 and he was never again close to a government post in Bonn. [*Source*: GIC]

Richard von Weizsäcker became federal president in 1984, crowning a long career as a leading moderate of the CDU. He used the largely ceremonial office of president very effectively to present a strong positive image of West Germany and its democratic system both at home and on frequent trips abroad. A high point was his speech on the fortieth anniversary of the end of World War II. He is shown here with his wife Marianne (center) and his daughter Marianne Beatrice (left) in Red Square in Moscow during a state visit in 1987. [*Source*: Bundesbildstelle Bonn]

Top left Kohl with French President François Mitterrand in 1984 at the memorial to the bloodiest battle of World War I at Verdun. The two leaders continued and expanded the high level of cooperation established by Schmidt and Giscard, based in turn on Adenauer's 1963 treaty. [*Source*: GIC]

Below left President and Mrs Reagan and Chancellor and Mrs Kohl arriving at the Bitburg cemetery, flanked by German and American troops. From the left, with backs to camera, are Generals Steinhoff and Ridgway. [*Source*: Süddeutscher Verlag]

At Bitburg military cemetery in May 1985, two old adversaries, retired Generals Matthew B. Ridgway, US Army, and Johannes Steinhoff of the Wehrmacht and later of the Bundeswehr, shake hands, observed by President Reagan (left) and Chancellor Kohl (right). The president's visit to Bitburg caused furious controversy when it was discovered that members of the Waffen-SS, a Nazi military organization, were buried there. [*Source*: GIC]

By the early 1980s, the Berlin Wall (*left*) had become an elaborate system of fortifications and killing zones, making escape all but impossible. The picture shows the largest of the watchtowers built by the GDR along the wall, at the Heidelberger Strasse in the Berlin district of Treptow. [*Source*: GIC]

Another view of the Wall (*below*). In the left and background, the new secondary wall constructed in the 1970s to prevent anyone from coming within 100 yards of the actual sector boundary. The middle area between the secondary wall and the original barrier is controlled by watchtowers and illuminated day and night. The old Wall itself, in foreground and right, now includes a rounded top to prevent handholds and to delay anyone able to get that far long enough for the guards in the watchtowers to shoot. [*Source*: GIC]

Opposite A unit of the Federal Border Patrol at the demarcation line somewhere in northern Germany. On the left, a GDR border marker in the German colors of black, red, and gold. Not seen on this picture are the watchtowers and automatic shooting devices by which the GDR regime keeps its citizens from exercising their right of free movement. By contrast, the main role of the Federal Border Patrol is to receive and give aid to those few who make a successful escape. [*Source*: GIC]

Below The death in 1988 of Franz Josef Strauss, minister-president of Bavaria and chairman of the CSU, marked the passing of an era. Strauss was the last of the generation of politicians actively involved with establishing the Federal Republic. The picture shows his funeral cortege, surrounded by banners in the blue-white diamond pattern of the arms of Bavaria, which are those of the former ruling house of Wittelsbach. [*Source*: Bundesbildstelle Bonn]

Foreign workers, mostly from Turkey, but also from Italy, Yugoslavia, and other countries, began arriving in West Germany in the early 1960s. Despite a subsequent stop to immigration, by the mid-1980s about five million foreign workers and their families were living in Germany, mostly doing hard manual labor that many Germans were no longer prepared to undertake. The picture shows foreign workers in the BMW motorcycle factory in West Berlin. [*Source*: GIC]

The environment became a cause of serious concern in the 1980s when it became clear that the waste from burning fossil fuels was polluting streams and causing widespread "forest death" throughout Central Europe. The picture shows a coal-fired power plant in the Ruhr district. German nuclear reactors were safe and efficient, yet the accident at the Soviet reactor at Chernobyl in 1986 reignited the powerful anti-nuclear movement in West Germany and led the SPD to demand that all West German reactors be closed down, even if this meant further use of environmentally harmful fossil fuels. [*Source*: GIC]

The *Schuhplattler* is a Bavarian folk dance, here shown being performed by a group in traditional costume at the Schlier Lake. [*Source*: GIC]

Eltz castle, in a narrow valley leading to the Moselle river, is a symbol of old Germany. Such castles became the focus of a renewed interest in older history and traditions that found expression in many exhibitions and publications in the later 1970s and 1980s. [*Source*: GIC]

In October 1988, Kohl paid his first visit to the Soviet party chief Mikhail Gorbachev (right) in Moscow. Gorbachev's economic reform program found much sympathy in West Germany, and during his visit Kohl signed agreements expanding trade relations and cultural exchanges. [*Source*: Bundesbildstelle Bonn]

Kohl (*Right*) greeting Ronald Reagan in Bonn in 1986. Kohl's instincts were to draw close to the US, but he was often forced by the FDP or by public opinion to take stands critical of the US, particularly on the subjects of nuclear weapons, arms control, and Middle East policy. [*Source*: GIC]

Since the mid-1970s a variety of artists, both amateur and professional, have decorated the west side of the Berlin Wall with graffiti and painting of all kinds. This photo taken by the American photographer Leland Rice in 1984 shows a slogan reading "freedom for all." [*Source*: Leland Rice; cibachrome, 1984]

8

SDI, INF, and Gorbachev:
Changing Foreign Policy Priorities

Following deployment of the INF, the conflict over defense policy temporarily abated, but these conflicts resurfaced when discussion of the strategic defense initiative (SDI) focused on the possibility of West German participation. In fact, US politicians and scientists had been debating anti-missile defense since the late 1970s. Many worried that the Soviet government had used the anti-ballistic missile (ABM) treaty of 1972 as a means to restrain ABM research in the United States and to speed up their own, and that they were far ahead of the US in useful technologies in this area. President Reagan's announcement of the Initiative made it a policy issue for the first time, but also aroused fierce partisan opposition both in the US and Europe as allegedly a concept for "Star Wars," an emotionally loaded phrase coined by Senator Edward Kennedy in March 1983.

According to Reagan's advisers, he had become deeply concerned with the issue, when as a former governor and candidate for the Republican nomination, he visited the North American Aerospace Defense Command (NORAD) in July 1979 in Cheyenne Mountain, Colorado. Toward the end of the afternoon Governor Reagan, accompanied by a friend from Los Angeles and by Martin Anderson, who became Reagan's first chief domestic and economic policy adviser in the White House in 1981, visited the command room. Anderson later recalled the visit:

It is a very large room, several stories high, and it looks just like such command centers do in the movies. Completely covering one end of the room is a huge display screen showing an outline map of the United States and the surrounding airspace. ... The officers showing us around pointed out that attacking nuclear missiles would show up as tiny, bright, blinking lights slowly moving across the screen. Just as they finished giving us this information, I noticed several bright blinking lights moving across the display screen on the part that traced out the south-western borders of the United States. Nobody seemed to notice. Finally after ten or fifteen seconds, I cleared my throat a little and said, "Say, what are those lights down there?" I couldn't believe that this base had been operational for more than twenty years and nothing had happened until today. The officers with us seemed a little embarrassed and hesitated. Finally, one of them smiled and said, "Oh, the radar picks up small planes too. Those lights are some of the drug smugglers starting their early evening runs across the border." . . . We pressed the issue of what would really happen if the Soviets were to fire just one nuclear missile at a US city. "Well," the general replied carefully, "we would pick it up right after it was launched, but by the time the officials of the city could be alerted that a nuclear bomb would hit them, there would be only ten or fifteen minutes left. That's all we can do. We can't stop it." We didn't ask the general what would happen if the Soviet Union fired hundreds or even thousands of nuclear missiles at us.[1]

After his election to the presidency in November 1980 Reagan became determined to give a future US administration an option other than retaliation in the face of nuclear attack. This was the genesis of Reagan's interest in SDI. Outside the community of security experts, many people, both in Germany and the United States, assumed that both superpowers had some means of defense against ballistic missiles launched either by design or by accident. In fact, in the late 1980s, only the Soviet Union had any operational program of antimissile defense, whereas the United States, despite several years of research, was further from deployment of such defenses than it had been in the late 1960s.[2]

In 1985 Kohl's government and his minister of defense, Manfred Wörner, signed an agreement with the United States to take part in SDI. The agreement was confidential, but was made public by the media in 1986. It immediately became a political football because the left argued that it represented interference in West German trade and economic policy, since it would prevent the government from exporting sensitive technology to the East.

The real issue of strategic defense, however, was very different. It was, in the eyes of its proponents, a means to preserve peace. They believed that it turned upside down the concept that to be vulnerable is somehow safe, and exploded the myth that the West was safe. Reagan and Kohl agreed that the means to defend one's country must take precedence over "security partnerships" with the Soviet Union, of whatever kind. The argument on defense was colored by political controversy of the left versus the right. Both SDI and INF, as well as Ostpolitik, served as

---

[1] Anderson, *Revolution*, 81–3.
[2] See Yost, *Soviet Ballistic Missile Defense and the Western Alliance*.

catalysts providing the momentum for a reassessment of Germany's security requirements.

On March 11, 1985, Mikhail Sergeievich Gorbachev became general secretary of the CPSU. At 54, he was the youngest member of the Politburo, and the youngest man to become general secretary since Joseph Stalin, who took that post in 1922 at the age of 43. In promoting him, the Soviet leadership was clearly signaling an end to the rule of Brezhnev's generation, who was born before the Bolsheviks seized power in 1917. Born in 1931 to loyal Bolshevik parents, Gorbachev grew up in a Soviet Union marked by the twin cataclysms of collectivization (1929–32) and Stalin's purge of the party (1935–8). As a young man, he lived through the German invasion of 1941–4, the expansion of Soviet power into Central Europe in 1944–8, and Nikita Khrushchev's partial revelations of Stalin's atrocities in 1956. He became a member of the Central Committee in 1971 and of the Politburo in 1979. For him to rise so high at his age was unique at that stage of Soviet history, and was only possible because he had powerful sponsors, who were hoping that he would become the man who would renew the Soviet system and imbue it with the dynamism necessary to compete with, and defeat, the United States and the other democracies. The two most important of those sponsors were Mikhail Suslov, generally known as the chief ideologue – guardian of Marxist-Leninist orthodoxy – of the Soviet Union, and Yuri Andropov, head of the KGB in the 1970s and briefly general secretary in 1982–4.

Observers saw Gorbachev as heralding a new era both in Soviet domestic affairs and in the Soviet Union's relations with the outside world. Gorbachev himself moved quickly to confirm this impression by launching a variety of campaigns to improve the Soviet Union's domestic civilian economy and its international position, under the two slogans of *glasnost* and *perestroika*.

Western observers translated the first of these terms, *glasnost*, as "openness." The Russian word, however, had additional connotations. It meant not merely "openness" or "transparence" but "making public what everyone knows but no one dares say out loud," and described also the attitude or mentality that permitted and encouraged such openness. *Glasnost* did not mean free speech as this was understood in a democratic society. Nevertheless, Soviet citizens were able to write and speak about a broad range of social, political, cultural, scientific, and economic questions in ways that had been forbidden since the 1920s and that, until the 1980s, often entailed imprisonment or worse. These questions ranged from the corruption and inefficiency of local party organizations to Stalin's crimes or the stifling effect of communist orthodoxy on scientific and technical innovation. Many Western observers saw in

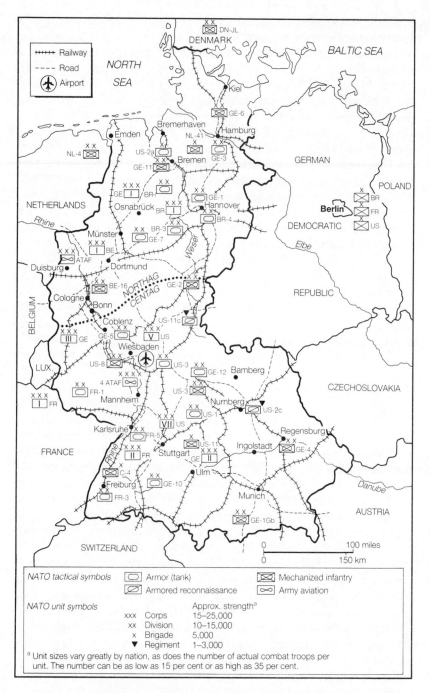

Map 2.3 NATO forces in Germany. The armies of NATO's central front were stationed throughout West Germany in the 1980s.
Source: Isby and Kamps, Jr, *Armies of NATO's Central Front*, 194

glasnost evidence that Gorbachev was permanently liberalizing public debate in the Soviet Union and making a return to Stalinist oppression impossible. Even in 1989, serious Soviet scholars were hesitant to make a final judgement on this point, though all admitted that the range of permitted discussion had grown remarkably. Some, while welcoming the new freedom, wondered how far it affected people outside the narrow class of Moscow intellectuals, and speculated that one purpose of *glasnost* might be to persuade the West that the Soviet Union was on the road to liberal democracy, that it had fundamentally changed its character and was now prepared to live in peace with the rest of the world. Gorbachev himself did much to reinforce this impression by stating repeatedly that he did not believe that any great power could or should seek unilateral advantages, that he recognized that the Soviet Union had acted in threatening ways in the past and should henceforth pursue a foreign policy of stability and disarmament.

The second term, *perestroika*, meant "restructuring" and referred primarily to economic reform. Loyal Soviet economists had been arguing, throughout the 1970s, that the civilian economy was grossly inefficient and unable to provide basic needs of the population. Gorbachev used *perestroika* to describe a range of policies and initiatives designed to remove corrupt or lazy managers, give workers and peasants a stake in production, and to unleash a new wave of industrialization and modernization. In foreign policy, he also used *perestroika* to describe what he claimed was a new Soviet approach to the world, one based on peaceful rather than military competition. Western observers differed in their view of *perestroika*. All recognized that, if successful, Gorbachev's initiatives might indeed help to make the Soviet Union more dynamic and efficient. Some, however, were skeptical of the notion of *perestroika* in Soviet foreign policy. Would a more dynamic Soviet Union be a boon or a threat to the West? Given that the supposedly stagnant and inefficient[1] Soviet Union of Brezhnev's day had surpassed the United States both in strategic nuclear weaponry and in conventional military strength, and had made geopolitical gains across the globe, some Westerners wondered, despite *glasnost* and *perestroika*, whether Gorbachev might not turn out to be a far more dangerous enemy, thanks to his undoubted diplomatic skills. Helmut Schmidt, for one, viewed the enthusiasm of many Germans and Americans for Gorbachev with some alarm and criticized those who believed the frequent Soviet claims that the Soviet Union was moving toward an exclusively defensive military posture. In his memoirs, he warned that it would be a mistake for the West to base its policy on the assumption that Soviet expansionism had come to an end.[3]

---

[3] Schmidt, *Menschen und Mächte*, 129.

Glasnost and *perestroika* were not without their own dilemmas. The history of the Soviet Union in the twentieth century teaches that change occurs much more slowly in the Soviet dictatorship than in western democracies. Therefore, the long-term significance of the changes that *glasnost* and *perestroika* were designed to bring about is much more difficult to measure. No Western commentator, in 1989, could judge whether *glasnost* and *perestroika* were more than strategic devices to mobilize public support for the regime and to modernize the Soviet civilian and military economies with the help of Western credits and diplomatic support, while the Soviet Union designed new vehicles with which to attack democratic societies. This was especially so since it became apparent that Gorbachev and his allies within the Soviet Union faced serious opposition. One veteran scholar of the Soviet scene, Michel Tatu, claimed in 1988 that "we know enough now to be able to conclude that Mikhail Gorbachev is serious when he speaks of restructuring, reform, and new thinking. Contrary to what some thought at the outset, his actions are not a trick to lull our vigilance." He continued, however, by noting that "the general secretary remains a communist, the defender of a system that is hostile to the so-called bourgeois democracies and which makes the claim that it will ultimately supplant them." On Soviet foreign policy, Tatu noted: "Dictated by geography and by geopolitical interests that go beyond regimes and succession crises, its objectives remain those of access to warm-water ports in the south and west, the isolation of Western Europe from the United States, political and, possibly, military influence in regional crises."[4]

If one of Gorbachev's goals was to separate the US militarily and diplomatically from Western Europe, he made some strides in that direction by his declarations that the era of fear and suspicion in East–West relations must give way to an era of cooperation and friendship. These announcements convinced many Germans that the Soviet military and political threat to the West had, for all intents and purposes, ended. Paradoxically, this made arms control negotiations somewhat more difficult, since it permitted the Soviet Union to play on West European feelings, arguing that they, the Russians, shared a "common European house" with the West Europeans, a house to which the Americans did not belong. Gorbachev's chief foreign policy advisor, Aleksandr Yakovlev, went much further. He argued that the Soviet Union should present itself as the true heir to European civilization in place of the Americans, whom he saw as enemies not merely of the Soviet Union, but of civilization. Yakovlev's vision also included a strategy: "As the heir to the great European tradition, the Soviet Union

---

[4] Tatu, *Gorbatchev*, 255, 258.

would win the 'decisive fight for the heads and hearts' of the [European] people, if . . . it exploited the [European] media . . . in the interests of the 'good cause.'"[5] In other words, a new, sophisticated Soviet diplomacy would use the vocabulary and the techniques of modern Western society to defeat the political forces upholding that society, which meant, above all, the United States. Yakovlev's and Gorbachev's strategy of claiming the heritage of European civilization for the Soviet Union was both audacious and remarkably successful, especially vis-à-vis many younger Germans who shared the view that Americans were superficial, uncivilized, and materialistic.

Whatever the long-range goal of Soviet diplomacy, its immediate task was to deal with the American INF missiles in West Germany. In 1985, Gorbachev agreed to resume the INF talks, thereby simultaneously confirming his reputation in Western Europe as a man of peace. These negotiations led, in 1987, to the INF treaty which determined that both sides would remove and destroy all INF missiles in or aimed at the European theater.

In April 1986 the core of the nuclear reactor at Chernobyl in the Soviet Union melted and leaked radioactive steam, causing great concern in Western Europe. In fact the amount of increased radiation was far less than the level which scientists regarded as harmful. At its highest point, several days after the accident, the level of radiation was about half of what it had been for months on end during the last years of atmospheric nuclear testing in the early 1960s. The heaviest amount of extra radiation in Germany corresponded to what one would receive naturally in five transatlantic flights. According to Heinrich Beckurts, a leading chemist and a president of Siemens, the risk of dying of cancer increased by 0.01 per cent as a result of the accident. (Beckurts was murdered by terrorists the day after he published this figure, but there was probably no connection.)[6]

Curiously, the powerful left wing in the media and the SPD did not argue that Chernobyl suggested Soviet technology was backward, but that nuclear power plants as such were dangerous. Thus, the accident at Chernobyl became another weapon in the arsenal of those who were seeking to ban the use of nuclear energy in West Germany. The Soviet government used the catastrophe to demonstrate that it was now prepared to be honest and open about failures of its own system, although it had deliberately withheld announcement of the accident, and did not make it public until scientists in Western Europe detected an unexplained increase in radioactivity.

[5] Bartel, *A. N. Jakowlew und die USA*, 87.
[6] *Die Zeit*, October 24, 1986.

During 1985–6 the SPD continued development of a "new security consensus" which it hoped would gain the support of a majority to the left of the CDU/CSU. The chief architects of this attempt, in addition to Egon Bahr, were Karsten Voigt and Andreas von Bülow. Bülow submitted a defense study to the SPD in 1986 which caused an international stir. He called for the complete denuclearization of West German defense and for a shift away from allegedly offensive weaponry such as tanks to more defensive weapons such as antitank guns, and for a general reduction in West German defense spending. Claiming that "the era of unilateral military security through deterrence must be overcome," Bülow argued that the West was not nearly as weak in conventional arms as official NATO strategists maintained, and that relying on nuclear threats increased the danger of war rather than deterring it. In any event, he went on, there was little or no threat of Soviet attack. The Soviets, rather, were afraid of the West. The tone of the document was calm, but the logic lopsided. On the one hand Bülow asserted, as a matter of fact, that the West was not weak and did not need nuclear weapons. On the other hand he argued that in order to have more security, the Soviet bloc must reduce its military forces, especially its armor. Critics asked how Bülow proposed to compel the Soviets to do this, and why he thought it was necessary if the Soviets were no threat anyway. Overall, Bülow's essay was a good illustration of the view of the rational German left of the 1980s that the main threat of war lay in the weapons and not in the policies of those who had the weapons. Few social democrats believed any more that war might result from a deliberate decision of the Soviet Union to seek domination in Europe, and that peace was preserved mainly by NATO forces, including nuclear forces. They saw little danger in Soviet power, but great danger in alleged American paranoia.[7] Bülow's views provoked debate within the SPD and the CDU/CSU, as well as the FDP. But the basic conclusion reflected the desire to have less, and not more, defense. Many FDP supporters agreed with this basic idea and the success of the FDP in federal and state elections in 1987 reflected a desire of many voters to distance themselves from the CDU on defense priorities.

The popularity of the general viewpoint, although not the specific proposals, represented by the Bülow study was influenced by simultaneous developments on arms control. In September 1986 the American president and the Soviet general secretary met in Reykjavik, Iceland. Concrete results were not expected from the summit in terms of arms control or other agreements. The world public was therefore astonished when Reagan declared that he wanted to work with the Soviet leader to

[7] See Bülow, *Das Bülow-Papier*.

abolish all nuclear weapons by the year 2000, starting with deep reductions of the numbers of intercontinental missiles held in both countries. Reagan and Gorbachev also announced new arms control talks aimed at removing nuclear missiles from Europe, the so-called double zero arms control option.

This agreement fulfilled one of the demands of the German left, but it greatly alarmed many in the conservative wing of the SPD and in the CDU/CSU, including the so-called "Stahlhelm" faction led by Alfred Dregger of Hesse and Manfred Todenhöfer, a judge by profession who was appointed spokesman for the CDU/CSU on questions concerning developing countries in 1987. The name "Stahlhelm" derived from a right-wing paramilitary organization of the Weimar years which some saw as an ally of Nazism, and it was adopted by the left to describe those CDU/CSU politicians who were skeptical of moving too far and too fast in accommodating Gorbachev and the GDR.

Kohl sympathized with this faction and was, like them, concerned that denuclearizing German defense would leave Western Europe open to Soviet domination because of superior Soviet chemical and conventional forces, thus raising the specter that had so troubled Helmut Schmidt; namely, the decoupling of American strategic nuclear defense from Europe, about which he had spoken at the International Institute for Strategic Studies in London in 1977. They also feared, with some justification, that an INF agreement might generate support for withdrawal of US forces from Europe; indeed, publication of a book in the US in 1986 by a well-known conservative American economist, Melvyn Krauss, entitled *How NATO Weakens The West*, argued for withdrawal. Their anxiety reflected their legitimate concern with how to balance superior Soviet conventional strength. If this balance could not be achieved West German foreign policy priorities vis-à-vis Western Europe and the United States, and vis-à-vis Eastern Europe and the Soviet Union, might be seriously affected. West Germany's defense minister, Manfred Wörner, expressed the point in October 1986:

A conventional balance had to *precede* zero on INF; and there would have to be nuclear compensation for cruise and Pershing II missiles – in the form of an enlarged short-range panoply and airborne or sea-based US nuclear weapons.[8]

What concerned the Europeans – especially Helmut Kohl and his predecessor Helmut Schmidt, but also the French prime minister, Jacques Chirac – prompted Kohl and Chirac to visit Washington in October 1986:

[8] Cited in Joffe, *The Limited Partnership*, 86.

In the aftermath of Reykjavik, Chancellor Kohl traveled to the United States, where he virtually repeated Helmut Schmidt to drive home an ancient German message: "The vision of a denuclearized world, which emanates from President Reagan's Strategic Defense Initiative and which is mirrored in Secretary-General Gorbachev's (Reykjavik) proposal, would fundamentally change current alliance strategy at the expense of the Europeans, unless the givens were transformed – like the enormous conventional edge of the Soviets." He was followed by ... Chirac, who demanded: "An agreement on medium-range missiles must not undercut the overall balance of nuclear forces, and must not award an advantage in short-range missiles" that would negate the value of an INF accord.[9]

[9] Ibid., 86.

9

The CDU/CSU and SPD

The CDU/CSU prevailed in the elections held for the Bundestag in January 1987. But the outcome also strengthened the Greens, the FDP, and the liberal wing of the CDU. The CDU/CSU lost two million votes compared to 1983, of which 800,000 went to the FDP, 400,000 to the SPD, and 800,000 did not vote at all;[1] it was the lowest election turnout since 1949. The CDU/CSU lost 4.5 per cent and received only 44.3 per cent of the vote, similar to the result of 1972, when, for the first and only time, the SPD became the strongest party in the Bundestag. A first in the republic's history was the large number of women who ran for office in 1987; they comprised one-fourth of all candidates, but 42 per cent of them belonged to the Greens. The 45 million electorate of 1987 was made up of 24 million eligible female voters and only 21 million male voters. When the new Bundestag began its work, it counted 81 women (15.4 per cent) among its deputies (out of a total of 519).[2]

In historical terms the 1987 result was the worst for the CDU/CSU since 1949. The voters apparently trusted the optimistic belief of the foreign minister, Genscher, in Gorbachev's sincerity and desire for more active peaceful relations, and voted for the FDP accordingly. In a speech given in the US shortly after the election, Genscher declared that he believed that Gorbachev sincerely wanted peace and arms control in order to divert resources to modernizing the Soviet economy, and that the West should help the communist leader in this task:

> If there should be a chance today that, after 40 years of East–West confrontation, there should be a turning point in East–West relations, it would be a mistake of historic dimensions for the West to let this chance slip just because it cannot escape from a way of thinking which invariably expects the worst from the Soviet Union. . . .

[1] *Economist*, October 3, 1987.
[2] *Relay from Bonn*, January 16, 1987 and January 30, 1987.

The right and absolutely imperative policy for the West today, I believe, is to take Mr Gorbachev and his "new policy" literally, with all that this implies.[3]

Genscher, along with the majority of Western politicians, argued that providing Gorbachev economic support was in the West's interest. Indeed, Genscher was supported by public opinion polls, taken in late 1986 and in the spring of 1987, that showed the West Germans regarded Gorbachev as a more responsible statesman, more committed to peace, and having a better grasp of world affairs than Ronald Reagan.[4] This was exactly the kind of development that Dregger and Todenhöfer feared, for its primary basis was emotion and not fact, and it could have serious domestic and foreign policy consequences.

This development became more pronounced in 1988. In West Germany, wrote Terence Roth in December, "few doubt that hard-line East German leader Erich Honecker will keep his guns trained on the no-man's land between the two Germanies, ready to cut down anybody who tries to escape.... But West German attitudes toward the colossus to the east, the Soviet Union, are softening. Soviet leader Mikhail Gorbachev's talk of peace and friendship has made him more popular than Ronald Reagan."[5] Josef Joffe, foreign editor of the *Süddeutsche Zeitung* of Munich, drew similar conclusions:

The most profound change . . . has taken place in the hearts and minds of the West. Gorby [Gorbachev] has cast an attractive shadow across the West because his words and promises all seem to signal that the Cold War is over. And in the West, the reaction is one of relief over the prospect of shedding the burden of protracted conflict. ... Not only the left but also the (ruling) center and center-right have begun to assume that the Cold War is indeed over. It is a profound transformation in our consensus over national security. It means that in the heart of Europe, the peace movement has lost a battle, but it may have won the war. ... The straws in the wind are as plentiful as they are significant. With the INF on the way out, left and right have jointly turned against the remaining nuclear weapons with the tidy slogan: "The shorter the ranges, the deader the Germans."[6]

The results of the federal elections were replicated in state elections in Hesse, in Rhineland-Palatinate, and Hamburg in the spring of 1987. In all cases the CDU/CSU did poorly and the FDP very well. In Hesse the CDU received fewer votes than in 1983, but was nevertheless able to form a government with FDP support. This irony, that the CDU could

---

[3] *Statements and Speeches*, February 6, 1987.
[4] *New York Times*, May 17, 1987; *Der Spiegel*, November 10, 1986.
[5] *Wall Street Journal*, December 14, 1988.
[6] *Süddeutsche Zeitung*, "World Press Review," December 1988, 25–6.

not form a state government with 48 per cent in 1983, but did do so with 42 per cent in 1987, did not pass unnoticed. In Hamburg, the election result would permit the SPD to govern only in a coalition with the Greens. After several weeks of a caretaker government and intensive negotiations, the FDP decided to join the SPD. This was the first new social–liberal coalition to be formed anywhere in the country since 1982, and some observers saw it as a sign that the SPD might be governing in Bonn again with the FDP before too long. In 1982, no one would have predicted that the two parties, who split as enemies, could join together even on the state level for many years to come.

One reason that the FDP was willing to again form a coalition with the SPD in Hamburg, and might be considering a similar move at the federal level, was that moderate elements appeared to be strengthening their position within the SPD. Another reason was that many FDP leaders, although not Genscher, had a good deal of sympathy for the ideas of the SPD left, particularly their proposals for "alternative defense." In addition, the CDU had not solved its fundamental domestic strategy problem – whether to seek a majority from the voters or to rely on a coalition with the FDP, thereby making important policy choices hostage to the influence of a small and, as some argued, an unstable party.

Heiner Geissler, the CDU's executive secretary and chief strategist, recommended a move to the left to recapture the votes lost to the FDP and the SPD. But this was a basically defeatist position, since those who held it assumed that a majority of West German voters would not support traditional CDU economic and political policies. On the other side, Strauss and his advisors repeated what they had argued since 1976; namely, that the voters would support a clear choice. In their view, the reason for the lackluster performance of January 1987 was that the CDU/CSU was not conservative enough, not that it was too conservative. In 1988 the right-wing Bavarian television personality, Franz Schönhuber, who had been an SS volunteer in the war, took the consequence of this position and founded a new conservative party, the Republicans. In 1989, to everyone's amazement, this party won 7.5 percent of the vote in West Berlin on a platform of opposition to the many Turks and other foreigners living in that city.

Another development in the spring of 1987 also affected the political landscape: the resignation of Willy Brandt from the chairmanship of the SPD. A number of factors influenced the decision, and they all reflected growing dissatisfaction within the SPD with Brandt's leadership. During the elections in January Brandt had only given half-hearted support to Johannes Rau, the SPD's candidate for chancellor, and had made what many considered uncalled-for and disparaging remarks about Rau's abilities. In turn, this led to the resignation of the party's press spokesman, Wolfgang Clement, three months before the election. On March 16 Brandt nominated a young protégé and family friend for the position. His nominee, Margarita Mathiopoulos, 31 years of age, was neither a member of the SPD nor a German citizen, and was engaged to a CDU spokesman in Weizsäcker's office.

Brandt was, under the party constitution, entitled to appoint whomever he wished as press spokesman, provided the executive secretary of the party – in this case, Peter Glotz – approved the choice. In his defense, Brandt argued that he had chosen his candidate to raise the number of women at high levels of party leadership, to give more power to the young generation, and to recognize the support he had enjoyed from people who were not party members. When he saw the outrage that his attempt provoked, he retired at age 73. On March 30, 1987, Brandt spoke to the party leadership, denouncing "lack of discipline," "ruthlessness," and "the attempt to settle old scores in an underhanded fashion." The public dispute cast a pall over Brandt's resignation similar to the pall cast over his resignation as chancellor in 1974. *Die Welt* commented on March 24, 1987, that "the real causes have deeper roots. They are related to the fact that Brandt now apparently lacks the power to effectively integrate the many political tendencies in the SPD." This conclusion was drawn not only by *Die Welt*, but by newspapers throughout Germany. It was also shared by Helmut Schmidt: "Asked by reporters how he felt following a medical checkup, Mr Schmidt said fine, adding, 'Because I knew when I should give up.'"[7]

In his resignation speech Brandt asked that the party call a special congress to consider future strategy. The congress was held in Nuremberg in April. The party delegates voted, as expected, for peace through detente, but also for an end to the use of nuclear energy. Brandt himself stepped down formally on June 20. He marked the occasion with a long farewell speech, without bitterness, in which he surveyed his commitment to political life. He recalled his flight from the Third Reich in 1933, his years of exile in Norway and Sweden, his choice to become a German citizen again in 1946, and his subsequent political career, which he saw as governed by two concerns: peace and humanitarian progress.[8] It was a moving occasion, and when he finished he received a ten-minute standing ovation from all of those present. Even his rivals in the party recognized that an era was ending and that Brandt had left his mark permanently on his party and his country. The *Deutsches Allgemeines Sonntagsblatt* wrote on March 29, 1987:

---

[7] *New York Times*, March 24, 1987.
[8] See Brandt, *Die Abschiedsrede*.

The whole affair has illustrated how much the leaders of the party have lost contact with its grass-roots, how internally insecure and incapable it is of governing the country.

Brandt personified this malaise just as much as he did the years of great triumph for the SPD at the beginning of the 70s. . . .

He often went a step ahead of his party and society. His gift was in being able to combine vision with credibility during his chancellorship and afterwards. He succeeded in giving people the feeling that it was not enough being content with just the status quo. . . .

Within the ranks of his own party his leadership ran aground because his claim to be the party's carrier of hope became more and more difficult to justify.

He wanted to adjust the party to a changing society and to make it more receptive to new problems and their solutions. But he went too far.

He was sometimes disloyal, as in the case of Johannes Rau. . . .

Whenever he went out into the crowds with those brooding eyes, then he seemed to raise himself to historical heights. In those moments he stood up there with the greats, with Lassalle, with Bebel, with Ebert and with Schumacher.

Although he often seemed to have a certain presence, and although he was often aggressive to the point of sarcasm, he nevertheless gave the impression of leading without a sense of direction. . . .

He has left behind not quite a mess but a party which is in dire need of orientation. And whose chief feature is uncertainty. . . .

The SPD elected Hans-Jochen Vogel (born 1926) as the new chairman. In January 1988 he had replaced Johannes Rau as the SPD's candidate for chancellor. Vogel was a moderate, yet this was no guarantee that the party would soon return to the positions held by Helmut Schmidt during the 1970s and early 1980s. In the late 1980s the SPD was a party in transition, with less than 20 per cent of its members younger than 35 years of age.[9] One observer noted:

It is likely that the SPD will continue its leftward drift for at least the next few years because of the nature of its emerging leadership on security issues. *Die Enkel* (the grandchildren), a new generation of leaders born and raised in post-war Germany, have replaced the old guard of Schmidt-generation reformers. *Die Enkel* came of age during the era of detente and are clearly to the left on security concerns. The moderates in the party are an isolated minority, having little influence in the development of the program on security. The key figures are all from the left and center left.

In the week after the election Lafontaine along with two other younger left leaders, Gerhard Schröder and Björn Engholm called for an opening to the Greens. . . . The party certainly will continue its strong opposition to SDI. . . . The moderates fear the implications of SDI for the future of nuclear deterrence while the left will oppose it on the grounds that it threatens to militarize space.

[9] Hellmut Herles, *Frankfurter Allgemeine Zeitung*, July 21, 1988.

The party ... will remain receptive to arms-control initiatives by both General Secretary Gorbachev and the East German SED. . . . It will continue to stress the overall theme of German interests and to criticize the Kohl government's pro-American posture. . . . The left will, at the least, continue to put substantial pressure on the government to "stand up to the Americans" and will foster a growing sense of German self-assertion in foreign policy. There seems to be little prospect that a new security consensus will soon emerge within the Federal Republic.[10]

In October 1988 an era of West German history came to an end in another sense when Franz Josef Strauss, head of the CSU, minister-president of Bavaria, and federal minister of defense and finance in the 1950s and 1960s, died after suffering a heart attack while hunting. He was 73 and the last surviving prominent member of the first generation of parliamentarians and politicians of the postwar democratic Germany. There were other retired politicians still living who were older than he was, but unlike them he had been a national political figure as early as the occupation years. He began and ended as a Bavarian leader: in 1945, he helped to found the CSU and was its chairman from 1961 until his death. His national political career began as a member of the Economic Council of the Bizone in 1947–8. He was elected to the first Bundestag in 1949 and kept his seat until 1978, when he left Bonn to become minister-president of Bavaria. After the *Spiegel* affair of 1962 perm-anently blocked his way to the highest political office, he concentrated on economic and industrial policy, but continued to offer his views on foreign relations, Ostpolitik, security policy, and military strategy. While it would be wrong to say that he was universally mourned, the more responsible among his adversaries paid him due respect. Helmut Schmidt stated: "His knowledge of details, his ability to see things in perspective and his energetic and rational way of tackling problems while many others argued emotionally were qualities I admired."[11] Curiously, Strauss' own last piece of writing was a lengthy review of Schmidt's memoirs in which the Bavarian said much the same about the northerner.[12] The *Süddeutsche Zeitung*, which as Bavaria's great liberal paper was often bitterly critical of Strauss, noted correctly that "this republic without Strauss will simply be a different one than the one we had become accustomed to in many ways: his death marks the end of the postwar period."[13]

---

[10] Szabo, "German Social Democrats," *SAIS Review* (Summer–Fall 1987): 36–7.
[11] *German Tribune*, October 16, 1988.
[12] *Die Zeit*, October 14, 1988.
[13] *Süddeutsche Zeitung*, October 4, 1988.

10

INF Resolved?
Implications for Germany

In June 1987 Kohl agreed to support the concept of the Reagan-Gorbachev arms control negotiations, which focused not only on the elimination of the INF, but also of all missiles with a range greater than 300 miles – the double zero option. That left only 72 aging Pershing Ia's with their US-controlled nuclear warheads, deployed in the early 1960s, as well as a variety of tactical nuclear weapons, including 65 Lance missiles with a range of 80 miles and some nuclear artillery with even shorter range. Even the possibility of modernizing them was opposed by the Soviet government and not pressed by the United States. In fact, many analysts argued that modernizing the Pershing Ia's and Lance missiles was the one option that would make sense from a West German security standpoint, if the Pershing IIs and cruise missiles were in fact removed, leaving West Germany without a deterrent in the area of short-range nuclear forces. Finally, in August 1987 Kohl declared that West Germany would give up the Pershing Ia's (and would expect the US to withdraw the nuclear warheads for those missiles which it controlled), if the US and the Soviet Union did indeed sign a verifiable agreement to remove all land-based INF missiles with ranges of between 300 and 3,000 miles. In 1989 the Kohl government began to pressure the US to remove rather than modernize the Lance missiles and nuclear artillery.

The US adoption of an arms control agenda, virtually identical to that of the German left, and the CDU/CSU's perception of American weakness in the face of consistent Soviet pressure in Europe, prompted many members of the CDU/CSU to doubt the US commitment to the defense of Europe. In July 1987 Dregger went so far as to say that, since the US was clearly prepared to ignore West German concerns, perhaps Bonn should make a deal with Moscow now, while it still had some protection – by using the word "deal" he was indirectly referring to the old SPD idea of neutralization and reunification.[1] Todenhöfer had similar concerns, and expressed "great bitterness" toward NATO's response to West Germany: "We are very disappointed and we feel betrayed. . . . The US is forcing us to find other security arrangements and that will strengthen neutralism." Thomas F. O'Boyle summed up the prevailing mood of some within the Kohl government as follows:

the Germans still have deep reservations because the US appears unwilling to negotiate reductions below the 300–mile range and has suggested further missile deployments might be necessary to offset the more than 15–to-1 superiority of the Warsaw Pact in this missile category. Thus, the Germans fear they are being singled out as the sole battlefield in a limited nuclear war – and that they might be asked to accept new [short-range] US missiles.

As a result, the Germans are looking to France and elsewhere for defense alternatives to safeguard their security.[2]

It was not just Dregger and Todenhöfer on the CDU/CSU right who were worrying, however. The reasons for concern were also spelled out by Josef Joffe of the *Süddeutsche Zeitung*:

The "double-zero" solution, proposing to do away with two legs of the nuclear triad in Europe [long-range and medium-range INF], was destined to trigger all of West Germany's ancient nightmares. . . .

An agreement would leave in place some 4,600 warheads the bulk of which are stationed in West Germany. And with the exception of the air-delivered munitions, all of the German-hosted warheads are destined to explode on German territory. Other things remaining equal, that outcome would amount to a momentous transformation of the Atlantic security system, which represents the very foundation of the German-American relationship.[3]

A double zero agreement to remove all INF and tactical missiles would transform the security system, because it would only leave in place short-range battlefield nuclear weapons in Germany. This would violate "a tacit condition of the Federal Republic's accession to the Atlantic Alliance;" namely "that West Germany must not serve as 'glacis' of Western defense." Furthermore, the West German understanding of security, from the time of the nuclear debate in 1958, was "that deterrence had to take absolute precedence over defense" and that "the nuclear risk had to be shared. . . . Neither the United States . . . nor

---

[1] *Die Zeit*, July 24, 1987.
[2] *Wall Street Journal*, June 2, 1987.
[3] Joffe, "Is there a German–American Question?" Paper presented at ISC Roundtable, 1987.

the Soviet Union could be allowed to think in terms of a war that began and ended in Germany." And Joffe concluded:

If the West Germans came to feel that their *supply* of security had dwindled, they would surely want to reduce their *demand* for it in order to restore equilibrium. That would entail the purchase of a good deal more "reinsurance" in Moscow than Ostpolitik and detente have already delivered. A "reinsurance-plus" strategy would receive added impetus from the long-standing quest to lighten the burden of bipolarity on the part of a nation that has paid for the contemporary system in the coinage of national unity denied. In short, the Federal Republic would face the Soviet Union as double *demandeur* – in its quest for reinsurance and for reassociation with East Germany. And the Soviet Union could profit twice because it holds the key to West Germany's security needs and to its national aspirations as well.[4]

What Joffe called the search for reinsurance by increasing accommodation with the East, could be seen not only in the alternative foreign policy of the SPD, but in the official policy of Kohl's government toward the Soviet Union and the GDR since 1985. A friendly West Germany, supplying credits and sophisticated technology, was a great prize for the Soviet Union; indeed, the largest commercial bank in West Germany, Deutsche Bank, announced in May 1988 a credit of 3.5 billion marks to the Soviet Union.[5] Earlier in the year a Swiss subsidiary of the Westdeutsche Landesbank in Düsseldorf brought to the market the first Soviet foreign bond issue since the Russian revolution of 1917, in the amount of 100 million Swiss francs. Peter Gumbel, writing in May, was clear in his interpretation of economic assistance:

the German involvement in Mr Gorbachev's economic restructuring, known collectively as *perestroika* . . . has political overtones. Chancellor Helmut Kohl, scheduled to visit Moscow in the fall, is pushing hard to mend fences with the Soviet leadership. Both sides say economic ties are a means toward that end. . . .
"Our economic ties go much deeper than is generally realized," says Martin Bangemann, the West German economics minister . . . "I'm confident that we will work well together (in economic areas) and that this will have a political impact."[6]

Since Kohl's election in late 1982, and particularly since the Bundestag voted to accept the INF missiles in November 1983, the

---

[4] Ibid. For more general analysis, see Joffe, *Limited Partnership*, chapter 1, especially pp. 23–9.
[5] *New York Times*, May 11, 1988.
[6] Gumbel, "German Banks Increase Loans to Soviets And Introduce Moscow to Bond Markets," *Wall Street Journal*, May 16, 1988.

Soviet government had attacked Kohl often and mercilessly. In 1987, however, Gorbachev decided to offer a carrot, rather than a stick. In July, Weizsäcker, the federal president, visited Moscow. The Soviets received him politely, even cordially, and told him that they "had no intention of upsetting Europe's postwar order by offering West Germany reunification in exchange for neutralization." As James Markham, *New York Times* Bonn bureau chief, commented in a piece he wrote in July just before he left his German post to go to Paris:

> Gorbachev does not appear to want a neutralized West Germany, but a pliant, self-doubting and weak-willed one in the heart of NATO. By taking a softer line toward Bonn, he seemed . . . to be already reaping dividends. The small Free Democratic Party . . . chastised Horst Teltschik, a senior aide to Chancellor Kohl, and then Defense Minister Manfred Wörner for spoiling the honeymoon with Moscow by suggesting in public that the Red Army might still harbor aggressive designs on the West. . . .
>
> In stitching together his new German policy, Mr Gorbachev and his advisers evidently hope to cash in on the Russian leader's extraordinary popularity in the Federal Republic. Gerhard Simon, a West German authority on the Soviet Union, remarked that the rush of sympathy for Mr Gorbachev was born of lingering guilt feelings for Hitler's invasion of Russia, "fear of the big neighbor to the East, uncertainty about our own future and a certain anti-Americanism."[7]

After Weizsäcker's visit the Soviets softened their public statements about Kohl considerably. Perhaps Weizsäcker convinced them of Bonn's good will, or perhaps they merely noted the astonishing success of Soviet public diplomacy in diminishing the fear of Soviet domination in the hearts and minds of Germans. A striking illustration of changing attitudes concerning the Soviet Union was the position taken by Franz Joseph Strauss. Just after Christmas 1987 he piloted his own plane to Moscow to meet with senior Soviet officials at their invitation. Following his visit he emphasized that he was "deeply convinced of the honesty of the will to change and the sincerity of joint objectives."[8]

The next step was Kohl's visit to Moscow in October 1988, that both sides declared a success. The agreements reached during the visit clearly indicated that relations of a practical nature between Bonn and Moscow would receive a new infusion of energy in 1989. Gorbachev agreed to pay a return visit to Bonn in 1989, and therefore both governments postponed issuing a political declaration. Kohl made it clear just prior to his trip that "we want to open the door wide for mutually advantageous, trusting relations."[9] On October 17 a consortium of West

---

[7] *New Tork Times,* July 19, 1987.
[8] *Relay from Bonn,* January 8, 1988.
[9] Ibid., October 21, 1988.

German banks signed an agreement providing the Soviet government a three billion DM line of credit "to stimulate and improve its consumer goods industry." On the same day the West German ministry of economics reported that thirteen joint ventures had already been set up with West German companies, and that these measures showed that the Germans wanted to pursue a variety of practical relationships.[10]

During the visit Kohl and Gorbachev concluded agreements that were designed to be of long-term value in the areas of space research, including future participation of a German astronaut in a Soviet space mission, atomic energy, a treaty dealing with future incidents between German and Soviet naval forces on the high seas, a cultural agreement expanding contact concerning academic research, education, vocational training, as well as the performing arts, an agreement on the manufacture of foodstuffs such as meat, canned goods and children's food, an agreement dealing with nuclear technology and radiation protection, and an agreement concerning joint measures to protect the environment.[11] Kohl was not able to obtain resolution of political issues, and in Germany commentators therefore concluded that nothing "dramatic" resulted from the visit on a political level. Indeed, "the much-vaunted 'new leaf' in relations has been turned over," concluded Jörg Bischoff in the *Stuttgarter Zeitung*, "but it is still a mostly blank page."[12] Nonetheless, the visit represented one more step in the developing dialogue between the Federal Republic and the Soviet Union:

It concerns nothing less than a radical political change in the world: the complete turnaround from confrontational to cooperative coexistence; to let "detente in the cold" [in the atmosphere of the cold war] grow into a "detente of warmth." To put it in another way: to transform sporadic relaxation of tension into durable detente. Only in Mikhail Gorbachev has the West been offered a Soviet partner who wants more than to set aside the old conflict, namely he wants to *overcome* [emphasis added] it. The West must make use of this chance.

It may be that it's only a slim chance. Gorbachev could fail: on the very dimension of his undertaking, on the opposition of the party machine, or because of the apathetic sluggishness of a people that, during 70 years of communist dictatorship, has lost belief and hope. We have to reinsure ourselves against this possibility, by staying with the Atlantic Alliance and by wholeheartedly participating in the expansion of the (West) European Community. But we are not the least bit interested in wishing Gorbachev's failure. His success works very much in our own interest. . . .

"The ice has been broken," says Gorbachev. "Now it's important to steer

[10] Ibid.

[11] See *German Tribune*, November 6, 1988.

[12] *Stuttgarter Zeitung*, October 27, 1988, as reprinted in *German Tribune*, November 6, 1988.

through the ups and downs of East–West politics toward new shores beyond the cold war."[13]

In the 1987–8 period, Germans worried about their country's security and its future, could choose among three viewpoints. One, advocated by Genscher and, in a somewhat different form, by Brandt and the left wing of the SPD, was that the Soviet military threat was a thing of the past and that the task of the present and future was to cooperate with the Soviets economically, scientifically, and politically, because this would contribute to greater security in Europe. Another, advocated by the conservative wing of the CDU/CSU, was that the Soviet Union remained a dangerous threat. Even though the US had demonstrated at Reykjavik and in the INF negotiations that it did not perceive West German security interests as Bonn saw them, the American alliance remained Germany's only reasonable foreign policy option. The third position, taken by former chancellor Helmut Schmidt among others, was that both Genscher and the Stahlhelm faction had part of the truth, but that the conclusion led to a strengthening of West Germany's ties within Europe, militarily, diplomatically, politically, and economically.

In 1986, while most of his party, the SPD, was devoting itself to the ideas of the Bülow study and the visions of the SPD-SED policy papers on disarmament, Schmidt began advocating "a Franco-German conventional army under a French general" as the core of a European defense force which would ultimately take the place of NATO. Schmidt agreed with Bahr that the proposed INF treaty would leave Germany at the mercy of both sides' shorter-range forces deployed in both German states – as CDU member Alfred Dregger put it on another occasion, "the shorter the range of the missiles, the deader the Germans will be." Unlike Bahr, however, Schmidt did not think the response to this situation should be disarmament in the belief that the Soviet Union was no longer a military threat. Rather, the Germans should build a joint force with the French that would be strong enough to render resort to nuclear weapons by the West to deter attack unnecessary. "The two classical military nations of Europe together are a conventional force which no Soviet marshal would ever dare take on," the former chancellor argued.[14]

In December 1987, Reagan and Gorbachev signed the INF treaty, in which their two governments undertook to dismantle and destroy all intermediate-range nuclear missiles with ranges between 300 and 3,000 miles. The advocates of detente, as well as those who distrusted its

---

[13] Theo Sommer, "Unterwegs zu neuen Ufern," *Die Zeit*, November 4, 1988.
[14] Robert Keatley, "Schmidt Would Disband NATO, Establish a Franco-German Force," *Wall Street Journal*, June 16, 1987.

promises in Europe, now found themselves in a quandary concerning how to view the defense of their own security interests. In early 1988 a West German government official emphasized that "there's no doubt Germany is the most important country in Europe for the Soviets and the second most important in the West." Indeed, one of Kohl's advisors made it clear that "'we are ready to use every opportunity to intensify contacts with the East'" – contacts which would include improved emigration and human rights in exchange for economic credits and incentives, as well as negotiations with Poland, Czechoslovakia and Bulgaria to form joint cultural institutes.[15] But there was also another perspective that the *Wall Street Journal's* Thomas F. O'Boyle captured:

> Ever since Willy Brandt knelt in 1970 at the memorial to Jews killed by the Germans in the Warsaw ghetto, Ostpolitik has had a heavy component of guilt. Germans see it as an opportunity to heal wounds. It is also a way to overcome the division of their nation by improving emigration as well as by extending civil liberties for their countrymen in the East.[16]

Schmidt's ideas for Franco-German defense cooperation received a boost toward becoming reality on the occasion of the twenty-fifth anniversary of the Franco-German friendship treaty of 1963. In January 1988, the governments of Helmut Kohl and François Mitterrand decided to create standing joint councils on military and economic policy to supplement and advise the biannual summits between the heads of government of the two countries. At the same time, they announced their intention to establish a joint military brigade, a proposal criticized by a NATO spokesman:

> The proposal for the brigade is a way of trying to come in by the back door. It will fail because such a project should be the result of European unity – it cannot be its chemistry. Europe must be built economically and politically before it can become militarily integrated.[17]

Objections of the latter variety to the contrary, however, the brigade had considerable symbolic value. It was also a beginning that reminded some of the debates for and against creation of the European Defense Community in the early 1950s. But unlike the early 1950s, the French were now eager to intensify collaboration on the military level. Indeed, Pierre Lellouche, an official of the French Institute for International

[15] Cited in *Wall Street Journal*, January 19, 1988.
[16] Ibid.
[17] Bonnart, "Franco-German Army Brigade Would Form a Weak Link," *Wall Street Journal*, August 5, 1987.

Relations, made the French perspective clear: "West Germany is playing for the long term. . . . It believes it can get East Germany back without falling under Soviet domination itself."[18] A German political analyst addressed complementary questions to the Europeans:

In the event your policy continues to nationalize itself in pure national egoism, this process will not exclude the Federal Republic. The profit of national provincialism is certainly less than the interest in working together. In addition, especially France must reconsider its security policy. Neither in its own nor in the interest of Europe can Paris afford to sink further in its twin doubt concerning the Americans as well as the Germans – and to project the resulting dilemma on the Germans.[19]

During the January meeting in Paris officials of the French government explained their concern: "There is a growing divergence between France and West Germany over German relations with the Soviet Union. . . . This is a fact, but a fact that is hidden under all these anniversary celebrations. The Germans are saying we must help Gorbachev. We are saying that we must be vigilant, and that the question of the West helping Gorbachev is unrealistic."[20] The French feared German enthusiasm for increased contacts and cooperation with the Soviet Union and the GDR, displayed increasingly clearly by the SPD. An example of this enthusiasm was the developing dialogue between the SPD and the SED that took a new direction while Erich Honecker was visiting the Federal Republic in September 1987.

---

[18] Philip Revzin, "French Fight to Anchor Germany in West," *Wall Street Journal*, January 21, 1988.
[19] Leicht, "Gute Deutsche und gute Europäer?", *Die Zeit*, September 18, 1987.
[20] Ibid.

11

Honecker in Bonn and the SPD–SED Talks

I n September 1987, "Red Erich," now 75 years of age, made his long anticipated visit to West Germany, the first Communist Party leader and head of state of the GDR to do so, and it lasted four days. (When Willi Stoph came to Kassel in 1970, he was chairman of the Council of Ministers, that is, the formal head of government, but he was neither party leader nor head of state). He was given a cordial welcome, both by the government and the public at large; however, the Bonn government took pains to avoid receiving Honecker as the head of a sovereign foreign nation. Genscher was not present to greet the East German foreign minister, Oskar Fischer, officially, instead, the Federal Republic was represented by Dorothee Wilms, minister for inner-German relations.

In all other respects, however, the visit proceeded with the usual official ceremonies accorded a head of state. President Weizsäcker, who received Honecker in the Villa Hammerschmidt, welcomed him with the words that "the people of both German states are part of the same nation, a nation that did not begin with Bismarck nor end with Hitler." Kohl, in his address, criticized the Wall, and appealed to Honecker to discontinue the "order to shoot" under which GDR border guards shoot to kill persons trying to cross the border. Honecker, in his reply, pointed to the "reality, namely the existence of two sovereign German states, independent of each other, with a different social order and opposing alliances."

The two leaders, after three meetings lasting a total of twelve hours, signed three agreements pertaining to science, technology and environmental protection. They also issued a joint communique, in which they solemnly declared that "war must never again be started from German soil." While the visit was more of symbolic than of substantive importance, it was also a meeting of two German leaders representing two very different countries of the same nation. The *Frankfurter Neue*

Presse captured its spirit: "Honecker's appearance neither made hearts beat faster nor did it fan a storm of indignation. The mentality of our society has been marked by four decades of partition."[1]

The entire visit did not take place in Bonn. On the third day Honecker met with German business leaders, including Berthold Beitz, chairman of the Krupp steel and engineering concern. The most poignant part of his visit occurred at its end. On the fourth day he visited his parents' grave in his birthplace of Neunkirchen, which he had not seen since 1935, and the village of Wiebelskirchen in the Saarland, where his sister Gertrud (70 years of age), still lived in the old family home. While in Neunkirchen, he made a remark that was without precedent. He acknowledged that the inner-German borders "are not as they should be. . . . If we work together . . . the day will come, when the borders will no longer divide us, but when they will unite us, just as the border between the German Democratic Republic and the Peoples' Republic of Poland unites us." The Bonn government welcomed his statement and called it "positive," even though critics pointed out that "the Wall still stands, the order to shoot has not yet been abolished and freedom to travel does not yet exist." Honecker concluded his visit with a meeting with Franz Josef Strauss, the CSU leader and minister-president of Bavaria, in Munich, and visited the former concentration camp at Dachau. For his part, Kohl accepted Honecker's invitation to visit East Germany.[2]

On the occasion of Honecker's visit the joint Commission on Fundamental Values, established by the SPD and SED in 1982 – and which had already produced two joint statements on a chemical-weapon-free zone in Central Europe and on common security – issued its third and most significant joint statement entitled "Principles of Dialogue." It set forth the agreement of the two parties that they would undertake common efforts to secure peace. The parties agreed, according to Marion Dönhoff of *Die Zeit*, to differ on the value of democracy as understood in the West and as understood, by the SED, in the East. And, they agreed that important differences in other areas still separated them, but that it was even more important to seek dialogue in a constructive spirit, thus making the disagreements "part of a productive competition between the systems. . . . Communists and social democrats will respect each other's basic decisions, will not establish hostile images of each other, will not sow suspicion concerning the other side's basic motives, will not distort the other side's convictions, and will not

[1] *Frankfurter Neue Presse*, September 12, 1987.
[2] *Archiv der Gegenwart*, September 11, 1987; *Facts on File*, September 11, 1987; *Relay from Bonn*, September 11 and September 18, 1987.

slander its representatives." Fourth, they agreed to work out a set of rules of the road for future dialogue.[3]

Dönhoff welcomed the document as evidence that the SED was willing to admit that it was not perfect, and did not have the final solution for all problems of society. She also drew attention to a 45-minute live appearance on GDR television, during which Erhard Eppler, the chairman of the SPD's delegation to the commission, and Thomas Meyer, director of the Gustav Heinemann Academy, discussed the document with two of their East German counterparts. She quoted Eppler as saying, "When we say that both systems are capable of reform, we are also indirectly saying that they need reform."

Dönhoff believed it extraordinary that the regime permitted its citizens to hear such words, because they represented an admission that reform was considered necessary by the SED. She also emphasized that the SPD's chairman, Hans-Jochen Vogel, and Karsten Voigt made a special effort to explain that the differences in basic values between the SED and the SPD were being set aside and that the relationship between communists and social democrats in the Federal Republic would not be affected by the statement. Of equal importance, she concluded, was that the chancellor, in a speech honoring Honecker at a state dinner in Bonn, had said the two sides should work together for peace regardless of their incompatible basic views and do what they could to increase contacts and cooperation. Thus, Dönhoff found it fortunate as well as fortuitous that the publication of the SPD-SED statement coincided with the final phase of the US–Soviet INF talks in Geneva and with the "agreement of the CDU to conduct a reasonable *Deutschlandpolitik*."[4]

Others were not as certain that the SPD-SED talks and the resulting declarations, especially the latest one, were such a wise idea. Gerd Bucerius noted that it was simply false to say, as the statement did, that "Our situation, new in world history, is that mankind can only perish collectively." Rather, Bucerius pointed out, numerous wars had occurred since 1945. A more correct wording would have been: "The frequently expected general nuclear war has not taken place. Still, it is unacceptable that a war can break out anytime and any place in the world and cause untold damage." Eppler, Bucerius noted, believed in the imminent end of the world. "If the world is about to end, then the adversary is no adversary any more and all systems are equal . . . In this way the SED succeeded in putting the discussion on a false basis."

Bucerius noted that the SPD, in setting aside its political differences

---

[3] Cited in *Die Zeit*, September 18, 1987.
[4] Ibid.

with the SED, had accepted the definition of the two social and political systems as equal in value.

Democracy for us is popular sovereignty, however imperfectly realized; in the East, it is rule over the people by a nomenklatura [narrow and self-perpetuating ruling class]. Ought one to use the same word for both in the same document? By his signature, Eppler has given permission to call the Eastern system a democracy; a system that shoots down its citizens at the Wall like rabbits, whenever they want to claim their internationally guaranteed right to emigration. . . .

That might have been acceptable if there had been two separate documents. Then the East could have spoken of "democracy" – everyone would know: *Eppler* meant a different kind of democracy. Originally, the wise Richard Löwenthal wanted two documents – one for the East, another for the West. That would have been a very different situation. But the SED knew well why it was important to insist on one document. And Eppler saw that he would not get two papers . . . and gave in, much too early.[5]

Along with many others, Bucerius was worried that the SPD no longer took seriously the real meaning of democracy, and that real threats existed to it from those who are its enemies. Many social democrats, on the conservative wing of the party, shared Bucerius' view, especially because it was increasingly apparent that the left wing of the SPD was renouncing the positions of the Godesberg Program of 1959. Bucerius' conclusion underscored this point: "Whatever may be achieved at the government level, please don't hesitate to do it. But as far as the social question is concerned, things look differently. I want to and must question the social system of the East. It is inhuman. Some say: one must begin somewhere. Certainly, but please go with Helmut Schmidt and his methods."[6]

[5] Ibid.
[6] Ibid.

12

Democracy:
Its Contents and Discontents

Our democracy has its flaws like any other. It can be argued that they are born of typical German characteristics, but that does not lead us very far. Our special experience and recollections are not only a burden on us. They have also given us insights which help and protect us. We have had more experience of dictatorship, war and tyranny than perhaps any other nation.

This is a particularly difficult part of the legacy of our history, with its bright and its dark chapters. But the better we understand it, the clearer our recollections. The more resolutely we bear the responsibility for its consequences, the less will we be faced with crises of identity resulting from the past. And the better will we understand ourselves and be understood by our neighbors.

Address by President Weizsäcker before the Twenty-first Convention of the
Evangelical Church in Germany, Düsseldorf, June 8, 1985

The reality of Germany in 1989 is that more than half of its population, approximately 54 to 55 per cent at the beginning of 1986, was born after 1945.[1] Forty years after the Basic Law, these Germans were leading lives that were not part of the past, even though they remained affected by it. The Germans of 1989 looked both forward and back, and their sorrows and frustrations, as well as their hopes and joys, were influenced by living life in a modern world, in a sophisticated country whose economic power was enormous. West Germany's trade surplus for 1987 was the largest in its history,[2] and it appeared that 1988 would produce a higher surplus still.[3]

---

[1] Statistisches Bundesamt, *Statistisches Jahrbuch 1987*, 61.
[2] *International Herald Tribune*, January 12, 1988.
[3] *Wall Street Journal*, January 4, 1989.

With Germany's coming of age also came problems that beset social, economic and political life everywhere. In the 1980s political events occurred which shook lives and allegiances, but not the fabric of society, which had been so fragile in the immediate postwar years. While these developments created headlines, and did have political consequences, they were developments which were a sign that a healthy democracy can and does deal with adversity and challenge, as the federal president, Weizsäcker, observed in December 1987: "Democracy does not create scandals, rather democracy allows a scandal to be come visible. And this is exactly what sets democracy advantageously apart from other political systems."[4]

Of the political affairs marking West Germany's graduation to normality, reflecting the imperfections in the affairs of men, five illustrated aspects of human strength and human frailty in a democratic society. The first was the Flick affair, which concerned leading FDP and CDU politicians who over the years had received major financial contributions from the Flick industrial group of companies, allegedly in return for arranging favorable tax benefits. The evidence was sufficiently serious for West German justice officials to issue indictments of Otto von Lambsdorff (FDP), the economics minister, his predecessor Hans Friderichs, who held the job of chief executive officer of the Dresdner Bank in 1984, Rainer Barzel, speaker of the Bundestag in 1983–4, Eberhard von Brauchitsch, a senior Flick company official, and several others. Lambsdorff, who had been economics minister since 1978, resigned his post after the indictment in June 1984 and was immediately replaced by Martin Bangemann (FDP). Barzel resigned in October of the same year, and was replaced by Philipp Jenninger.

The cases did not come to trial until February 1987. The federal prosecutor established that neither Lambsdorff, Friderichs nor Barzel had personally enriched themselves, but that they were instrumental in the illegal diversion of money into party funds. Lambsdorff and the others were acquitted of corruption charges; however, they were convicted of tax evasion and "aiding tax evasion on party political donations from the Flick industrial concern." Lambsdorff was fined DM 180,000, Friderichs DM 61,500. However, Eberhard von Brauchitsch, the former senior Flick manager, was fined DM 550,000 and given a two-year suspended prison sentence. The presiding judge called the Flick affair "extraordinary," since "almost all the 80 witnesses had suffered a 'conspicuous loss of memory,' making it necessary 'to depend almost exclusively on files and documents.'"[5]

[4] Cited in *Die Zeit*, December 11, 1987.
[5] *Archiv der Gegenwart*, June 17–30, 1987; *Keesing's Contemporary Archives*, March 1987, no. 3.

Lambsdorff's political career, though damaged, did not come to a halt, as a member of the party or as the economic expert of the FDP. He participated, even before the court ruling, in the campaign for the federal elections in January 1987, and did not leave any doubt that he hoped to return to the cabinet within two years. By the end of 1987, he showed great interest in becoming chairman of his party, though not economics minister. In October 1988 he was elected to succeed Bangemann as chairman of the FDP, and Bangemann himself was appointed by Chancellor Kohl as one of two representatives to the EC Commission in Brussels. By 1988 Bangemann had established a reputation in his own right. Indeed, he drew the remarkable conclusion that "the welfare state is the most inhumane state imaginable because it enslaves people more intensely than the classic slavery of the past was capable of doing," to which Anke Fuchs, the SPD executive secretary, replied, "Scandalous and offensive."[6]

A second illustration, while especially painful to the Jewish community in Germany, was nonetheless dealt with in a sophisticated and responsible manner. In the spring of 1988, Heinz Galinski, 79 years of age and the chairman of the Central Council of Jews in Germany, revealed that his predecessor Werner Nachmann had embezzled approximately 33 million marks since 1980. The funds had been taken from monies provided by the West German government as restitution to Jews. Nachmann had enjoyed a distinguished record in Germany, had fled Hitler's Reich in 1938 to France and had returned to Germany in 1945 as a French military officer. In the 1970s and 1980s he had been awarded three of the highest decorations bestowed by the West German government, was the recipient of the Theodor Heuss Prize in 1986 and was given a state funeral following his death in January 1988 at the age of 62.

The revelation of Nachmann's theft came as a shock. As Galinski put it: "This is one of the most serious situations the Jewish community has had to face since 1945. This is mainly a situation concerning moral standards. That is particularly painful."[7] It also raised moral dilemmas in judging the meaning of Nachmann's actions. On May 20 *Die Zeit* wrote:

What can we say? That Jews are human beings too? That sentence must stick in the throat of everyone who remembers that the Nazis, German Nazis, regarded and treated them as subhumans and vermin. Where there is much money there is much corruption? Surely, but should we therefore have paid less conscience money? The Jewish community must do all in its power to clear

[6] *Die Zeit*, January 22, 1988.
[7] Cited in *Deutsches Allgemeines Sonntagsblatt*, May 22, 1988.

things up and put the facts on the table. But we must guard against acting like the Pharisees. Nachmann had indeed heaped guilt upon himself. But the guilt of the Germans is not thereby reduced.[8]

Some raised the question of whether the finance ministry had failed to enforce strict adherence to proper accounting procedures. And Gerda-Marie Schoenfeld, writing in the *Deutsches Allgemeines Sonntagsblatt* (May 22) made the valid point that "compensation is a German politico-moral obligation. This idea should not be harmed because one person has conducted himself incorrectly." While the case was undoubtedly not quite like any other, it did not strike at the roots of democracy in Germany, any more than the Flick affair. Galinski clearly stated that he had "inherited a situation that I would not wish on my worst enemy," but that he would "make the unvarnished truth available to the public."[9]

The union-owned construction group of companies, the *Neue Heimat* (New Home), founded in 1951, provided the third example. *Neue Heimat* was Europe's largest construction concern in the 1980s and consisted of two separately managed entities. One, comprising four-fifths of the entire enterprise, was a nonprofit apartment house construction company, operated throughout West Germany as well as in West Berlin. The other, *Neue Heimat Städtebau* (New Home Urban Construction) was a profit-making company that built hotels and convention centers, and acted as a consultant for city and hospital planning. In 1982, at the height of the economic crisis in Germany and at a low point of union membership growth, *Der Spiegel* accused the executive directors of *Neue Heimat* of mismanagement, of having altered the books to make the finances of the group look better than they were, and of having enriched themselves by using front men. Rudolf Augstein accused the managers of "showing the ugliest characteristics of capitalism," and *Die Zeit* asked "why is it that so many companies belonging to the union . . . act more capitalist than born capitalists. . . . Power is power – and power corrupts, when it's not supervised. Power without limits corrupts capitalists and socialists alike."[10]

By 1986, after the government refused to bail out *Neue Heimat*, it was close to bankruptcy with debts exceeding 17 billion marks. At that point a Berlin bakery chain owner, Horst Schiesser, volunteered to purchase the nonprofit division of *Neue Heimat* through a newly formed company. He paid the symbolic price of one German mark, committed himself to refinancing the company, and promised to preserve its nonprofit status. A major political dispute erupted over the sale, with the CDU/CSU and

[8] *Relay from Bonn,* May 27, 1988.
[9] Ibid.
[10] *Der Spiegel,* February 8, 1982, no. 6; and February 15, 1982, no. 7.

FDP coalition accusing the trade union leader, Ernst Breit, of avoiding responsibility for the "worst economic scandal in postwar history." Schiesser, in a press conference, confirmed that he had bought 270,000 apartments from *Neue Heimat* and asked for the support by all responsible parties in "politics, administration or in the industrial sector." Fearing serious repercussions in the general real estate market in Germany should *Neue Heimat* have to declare bankruptcy, German banks initially decided to grant Schiesser financial support, even though foreign banks cancelled their credits.

It became quickly evident that Schiesser could not save *Neue Heimat* from bankruptcy, and impatient creditors turned to the union's holding company BGAG *(Beteiligungsgesellschaft für Gemeinwirtschaft)* for their money. Schiesser had to give up his newly acquired company, but was promised, and later received, compensation for his services of more than 14 million marks by the BGAG. The union tried desperately to avoid bankruptcy, but had no choice but to liquidate *Neue Heimat*. In 1986 a retired banker, Heinz Sippel, was appointed to pursue quietly the liquidation of *Neue Heimat* over a period of three years, by selling the regional *Neue Heimat* companies to the respective *Länder* in which they were located. Meanwhile the BGAG began to sell off many of its companies, including its own bank, Bank für Gemeinwirtschaft, in order to pay the accumulated debts, which were several billion marks higher than the original estimate of DM 17 billion.[11] Notwithstanding the economic implications, the real victim of the *Neue Heimat* was the credibility of the labor movement's leaders: "What really hurt the unions was not the threat of bankruptcy if the company collapsed entirely; it was the devastating effect the affair had on the confidence in the unions felt by rank-and-file members."[12]

Possibly the most tragic scandal was *Waterkantgate*, so named, with an allusion to the American Watergate scandal, because it took place "on the waterfront" in Kiel, the capital of the state of Schleswig-Holstein (*Waterkant* means waterfront in *plattdeutsch* – Low German). *Der Spiegel* of September 14, 1987, appeared on newsstands on Saturday the 12th, two days earlier than its normal Monday publication and one day before *Land* elections in Schleswig-Holstein, with a devastating article based on an affidavit by Reiner Pfeiffer, a close advisor and press aide to the CDU minister president, Uwe Barschel. Barschel, described by Kai-Uwe von Hassel, former minister-president of Schleswig-Holstein, as "a young, highly intelligent, hard-working and successful man,"[13] had

---

[11] *Der Spiegel*, nos. 45–50, 1986; *Archiv der Gegenwart*, October 12, 1986.
[12] Walter Ferchländer, *General-Anzeiger*, Bonn, July 1, 1988.
[13] *Die Zeit*, October 23, 1987.

been minister-president for five years, and had close ties to Kohl and the Bonn government. Thus, Pfeiffer's claim that the 43–year-old Barschel had ordered a campaign of "dirty tricks" to discredit his SPD opponent Björn Engholm, created a political nightmare. Barschel, according to *Der Spiegel*, feared losing the election and the 39–year-old CDU political monopoly in Schleswig-Holstein. He therefore allegedly ordered Pfeiffer to investigate Engholm's sex life, to write an anonymous letter accusing Engholm of tax evasion, to issue a flyer which stated that "the SPD approved of adults having sex with children over the age of 14," and to tap his own [Barschel's] phone and blame it on the SPD.

Barschel, in a press conference on September 18, 1987, gave his "word of honor that the accusations against me are unfounded,"[14] but resigned under pressure on September 25. An investigation was ordered, but Barschel, after his resignation, took a short vacation, which he spent in the Canary Islands, before testifying before the investigating committee. Returning from the Canary Islands, Barschel stopped in Geneva, where, on October 11, 1987, his body was found, fully clothed, in the bathtub of an expensive room at the hotel Beau Rivage in Geneva. The first accusations of "murder" by friends and CDU party members disappeared when an autopsy revealed "very serious poisoning by medication"[15] and suicide was believed to have been the cause of death. Even though the national CDU itself was not involved in the affair, it quickly became clear that a deep rift had occurred within the ranks of the party, which had earlier heavily supported its candidate Barschel. Nina Grunenberg quoted Kai-Uwe von Hassel in *Die Zeit* after Barschel's death: "Nobody can be directly 'blamed' for Uwe Barschel's death. However, that it was possible, in our political landscape, for a situation to develop in which a man such as Uwe Barschel, in spite of his youthful intellectualism and his remarkable willpower, could not survive – in the real sense as well as figuratively speaking – that is to a large extent the fault of all of us."[16]

However, not all agreed with Hassel. Many politicians, after the initial shock, called Barschel an "unscrupulous, power-hungry politician," and an "ambitious man, who, on his way to the top, walked over bodies."[17] *Die Zeit*, which originally called the *Spiegel* article "dubious," admitted after Barschel's death that *Der Spiegel* ". . . after all that we know now . . . rendered a service to the republic. It has, in the tradition of muckraking, churned up the poisonous mud which is threatening to

---

[14] *Frankfurter Allgemeine Zeitung*, September 19, 1987.
[15] *Relay from Bonn*, December 4, 1987.
[16] *Die Zeit*, October 23, 1987.
[17] Dieter Buhl, *Die Zeit*, October 25, 1987.

choke our democracy; this clears the air."[18] It was, however, patently absurd to claim, as the historian Hans-Ulrich Wehler wrote, that the scandal "opened up the anus of the republic in Schleswig-Holstein."[19]

Gerhard Stoltenberg, minister of finance in Bonn and chairman of the Schleswig-Holstein CDU, was heavily criticized for his silence in the matter. He waited three months to apologize to the SPD and to Björn Engholm in Schleswig-Holstein. Stoltenberg, speaking to journalists, admitted that Barschel "did not tell the truth," "acted irresponsibly," and that his actions had "seriously damaged respect for state politics as well as our party, and shaken confidence." He added that he regretted "the derailment of the CDU" and understood that the affair had dealt a "heavy blow" to Schleswig-Holstein and the CDU.[20] It also damaged Stoltenberg himself: "Until a few weeks ago Gerhard Stoltenberg was a potential successor to Kohl. Now he . . . is going down and under in the muddy waters of the 'Kiel Affair.' "[21] Chancellor Kohl recognized that the incident in Kiel represented a "true disaster" for his party,[22] but it was the federal president, Weizsäcker, who drew the most balanced conclusion: "In Kiel – but not only in Kiel – we have to tackle very serious problems. . . . I think everybody is not only deeply concerned, but is also dealing with the question of what can be learned from all this."[23] On May 8, 1988, a chapter in the postwar politics of Schleswig-Holstein was closed. In *Land* elections the SPD received approximately 55 per cent of the vote. Björn Engholm, 48 years old, who had served as minister of education in Helmut Schmidt's government, became the new minister-president.

If one example, more than any other, illustrated the struggle of democracy with its discontents, it was the fifth case. It occurred on November 10, 1988, the fiftieth anniversary of *Kristallnacht*, the night in Hitler's Germany of 1938 that the Nazis unleashed their first major pogrom against the Jews of Germany. Philipp Jenninger (CDU), the president of the Bundestag since 1984, delivered an address to the West German parliament as a commemoration of this infamous anniversary in German history. Jenninger, born in 1932, was only six years old on *Kristallnacht* and only 13 years of age when the war ended. In his 7,000-word text Jenninger committed what, at least for the political left in West Germany, was an unpardonable sin. He did not devote his speech to

[18] Theo Sommer, *Die Zeit*, October 25, 1987.
[19] Wehler, "Schaumschlägerei aus gestyltem Pessimismus," *Die Zeit*, June 24, 1988.
[20] *Relay from Bonn*, December 18, 1987; *Süddeutsche Zeitung*, December 16, 1987.
[21] *Der Spiegel*, no. 45, November 2, 1987.
[22] *Frankfurter Allgemeine Zeitung*, December 8, 1987.
[23] *Die Zeit*, December 11, 1987.

commemorating the memory of those who suffered on *Kristallnacht* – although he did that too – but to the guilt of the Germans, and in so doing, "the thorn in the flesh of the Germans, who must live with their history, was not removed but driven in deeper."[24] He reminded his audience that on this November night in 1938, "well over 200 synagogues were burned down or demolished, Jewish cemeteries were laid waste, thousands of shops and homes were destroyed and plundered. Some 100 Jews met death, about 30,000 were dragged off to concentration camps; many of them never came back." But before he continued much further about 50 members of the Greens, the SPD and the FDP walked out of the Bundestag. A storm of protest about the content of his speech erupted within West Germany and without, and Jenninger was forced to resign as a result of the public outcry.

What proved most remarkable about his speech, especially in the wake of the emotionally laden *Historikerstreit* of 1986, was not its content. The content was honest, forthright, and for many, brutally frank in its description of the attitudes prevailing in Nazi Germany which contributed to the circumstances that resulted in the Holocaust. What was remakable was the condemnation, verging on the hysterical, of the speech by many of Germany's leading intellectuals, journalists and political figures.

What Jenninger did, in the words of Amity Shlaes, the editorial features editor of the *Wall Street Journal* in Europe, was to detail "Hitler's racist philosophy, with which 'Germany had said goodby to all humanitarian ideas:'"

He described the murderous consequences of national support for Hitler's fevered plans. "For the destiny of the German and European Jews, Hitler's successes were perhaps even more fateful than his crimes and misdeeds. . . . The years from 1933 to 1938, even from a distant retrospective and in the knowledge of what followed, still are a fascinating thing today, since throughout history there is hardly a parallel to Hitler's triumphal procession during the first years." And Mr Jenninger offered a rendition of German feelings about Jews under the Nazis: "What concerned the Jews: hadn't they played a role that didn't suit them in the past?"[25]

Jenninger continued that Germany's past "will not rest," and in so describing that past, "criticism focused on Mr Jenninger's decision to speak – for eight paragraphs – from the point of view of Germans in the 1930s, without distancing himself from their heinous opinions. This is a

[24] Christoph Bertram, "Ein würdiges Gedenken," *Die Zeit*, November 25, 1988.
[25] Shlaes, "Germany: What the Bundestag Didn't Want to Hear," *Wall Street Journal*, November 14, 1988.

dramatic device. It's the kind of thing West Germany's Bundestag, an erudite body packed with PhDs, is sophisticated enough to recognize. ... This rage is in part [also] due to genuine sensitivity over the Nazi period. As Mr Jenninger himself reportedly commented, 'In Germany one can't call everything by its name.' But protesters also have something to gain that has nothing to do with the Jewish tragedy. The leftist Greens gain strength every time they can shake the authority of the liberal–conservative coalition. Outrage similarly serves the social democrats. The Free Democrats gain from chances to show their parliamentary muscle."[26]

What Amity Shlaes meant was illustrated by a number of responses. Marion Dönhoff wrote that Jenninger had described "Hitler's successes in an admiring tone," that his use of the dramatic device described by Shlaes did not make clear whether the views he expressed were his or those of an observer of the Third Reich, and that Jenninger had forgotten "that opposition to Hitler had formed very early" (*sic*).[27]

In pointing out that many Germans supported Hitler's propaganda, or were sympathetic with it, Jenninger was repeating what the theologian Helmut Gollwitzer had clearly expressed more than 20 years before in his commentary on the Auschwitz trials (see part VI, chapter 4, pp. 35–6), namely, that "most of us have at one time or another seen some promise in Hitler's plans; have perhaps ourselves looked down upon the groups he set out to destroy; have looked on or turned away when the atrocities began."[28]

The socialist novelist Stefan Heym, himself a refugee from Hitler's Germany and living in the GDR since 1952, put it in another way: "The plea of a man whom one would describe in literature as an advocate of the devil."[29] And Shlaes reported that one German newspaper "called his [Jenninger's] remarks 'perhaps the most unfortunate speech that was ever made in the Federal Republic.'"

The affair not only ruined the career of a prominent Christian democrat, but had wider implications:

> The ... losers are those who really care about remembering Germany's past. ... The Green Party politicians explained they were protesting the *Kristallnacht* speech in the hope that "discussion about guilt and responsibility for this recent history will take place." That is exactly what they are preventing.[30]

---

[26] Ibid.
[27] Dönhoff, "Ein verfehltes Kolleg," *Die Zeit*, November 25, 1988.
[28] Bonnhoeffer, *Auschwitz Trials*, 8–9.
[29] *Die Zeit*, November 25, 1988.
[30] Shlaes, *Wall Street Journal*, November 14, 1988.

Jeffrey Herf, an American historian of Germany, noted further:

> if, in Gertrude Himmelfarb's terms, one evokes a history with the politics, ideas, and events brought back in, if one tries, as Jenninger did, to explain how it came about, one touches the real nerves, the real shame, and unleashes rage at the return of the repressed.
> The belief that evil is never popular is a fairy tale for political children. . . . When Jews read the full text of Jenninger's speech they will recognize the friend they have in him.[31]

This is exactly the advice that the political scientist Gesine Schwan gave: "to listen as carefully as possible to what Jenninger really wanted to tell us."[32] If there is a lesson to be drawn from what was both a painful and a lamentable response, it is that while opportunism often rears its ugly head in the form of discontent, courage and truth are indispensable to the democratic process. The forced resignation of Philipp Jenninger was not a triumph for democracy in Germany – although some so alleged – nor was it a triumph for "overcoming the past." Indeed the emotionally critical reaction to his speech illustrated that human weakness and human frailty are as common to the Federal Republic as they were common to Hitler's Germany. But the speech itself illustrated another point; that moral courage is a part of the German present. Jenninger paid a price for his message. But as Gesine Schwan's advice wisely implied, his words bore a message of lasting value.

While these affairs of adversity and disgrace, frustration and discontent, generated enormous publicity, West Germany's political foundations remained firm. It was true that the Federal Republic in the 1980s, four decades after war and occupation, was "rich, bothered and divided," as journalist David Marsh wrote in the *Financial Times*.[33] And it was true, as Elisabeth Noelle-Neumann, the leading opinion analyst in a country with more pollsters and polls per capita than any other, wrote in 1987, that West Germans "tend to oscillate, more than other nations, between euphoria and depression, symptoms of what could be called, superficially, a neurotic, irritable disposition, of broken pride."[34]

But many other aspects of life and character in West Germany were equally, if not more important. They were, indeed, the rule and not the

---

[31] Herf, "Scandal is reaction to Jenninger, not speech," *Boston Globe*, December 5, 1988.

[32] Cited in Karl-Heinz Janssen, "Die Wahrheit nicht bezweifeln," *Die Zeit*, November 25, 1988.

[33] *Financial Times*, June 20, 1987.

[34] Cited ibid.

exception. Any American, or West European, or any other visitor to West Germany could not help but respect, admire, and enjoy the courage and the spirit of most Germans. The color of Bavaria, the wines of the Rhine and Mosel valleys, the artistry of German theater and music, the beauty of West Germany's villages and *Gaststätten*, the laughter of life in its restaurants, or the imagination and simplicity of human beings who are happy and proud to give visitors a warm welcome – all these remained real and valuable traits of German life and identity in 1989.

An interpretative history of West Germany would not be honest if it focused merely on problems or on symptoms of despair and legitimate frustration, such as the issue of identity or the emotion of the *Historikerstreit*. Such problems may plague those who enjoyed feasting on them and challenge those who feel a responsibility to think about them. But, fortunately, in a democratic society like that of West Germany in 1989, life did not rise and fall on the outcomes of debates that politicians, journalists, and intellectuals considered to be all-important. It is not for citizens in a democracy to await the judgement of political battles, but, on the contrary, to remind political leaders that they serve the citizens they are supposed to represent, and that journalists do not have a monopoly on the truth nor are they elected representatives of the people.

In the last years of the 1980s Bonn faced, as it had since 1949, the dual task of maintaining the faith of its allies in West Germany's commitment to peace and freedom, and at the same time upholding the special claims of the divided nation. These claims had not been satisfied by pressure or by compromise. On the other hand, if West Germany were to abandon them and try to achieve an independent status as a German state pursuing interests in Central Europe contrary to those of its NATO allies, the consequences for the cohesion and morale of German society would be unpredictable, almost certainly extremely serious. Ever since the founding of the Federal Republic, its government and its citizens have had to tread a thin line between nationalistic revivalism on the one hand, and compromise and acceptance on the other. Doing so was never easy, as the years of Adenauer, Erhard, Kiesinger, Brandt, Schmidt and Kohl showed so well. In fact, each chancellor faced the same two challenges. One was to deal with the competing political forces of the left and the right, many of which were difficult to control. The other was to give direction to German policy concerning the divided nation, and that meant dealing with the hope and anguish of the past, the present, and the future.

Where Germany was in 1989 and where it was going, was no easier to answer than it was to answer such a question for any other country.

"Wunderkind at 40 [in 1989] is a worry," wrote the *Economist*.[35] But many Germans did have a clear picture of the dilemmas and responsibilities which their divided nation presented. They believed that "the GDR Government is the only partner available with whom to seek practical advances for a forcibly separated people," and Kohl's government was "convinced that by continuing the dialogue, by pursuing cooperation and seeking to reconcile our interests, we are helping to reduce tensions and thus foster peace in Europe."[36] The Germans also continued to recognize another reality concerning their divided country:

We realize that the solution to the German question is not on the current international agenda, but it remains on the agenda of history, because history is progressive and only those systems that respect the will of the people and accept historical change rather than oppose it have a political future. We continue to feel obligated to our countrymen across the barrier ... we shall continue to stand by them, those other Germans, who through no fault of their own, have been subjected to this heavy burden in the aftermath of the Second World War.[37]

West Germany – that is to say, the Germans – recognized its own national problems, and if recognition is not synonymous with solution, it nonetheless remained a preferable alternative to ignoring them. James Markham wrote in his final report from West Germany for the *New York Times*:

On the prosperous side of a sundered Germany, in a nation that still lowers its voice because of the Nazi crimes, that is reluctant to translate its economic might into political clout and that is geographically and psychologically vulnerable to blandishments from the Communist East, a search for an acceptable homeland goes on. ...

The Federal Republic at times seems a curiously vulnerable place, a "soft state," to reapply a term once applied by the sociologist Gunnar Myrdal to certain developing nations. Its birth rate is falling so steeply that military planners are exploring the possibility of drafting foreign residents into the armed forces, and the plunging demographic curve has raised doubts about the future financing of welfare and pension benefits. ...

In international affairs, West Germany's watchwords are conciliation, compromise, even concession, but never threat or confrontation, two postures that all too readily recall the past. An American diplomat remarked that "these people have simply had power politics bred out of them."[38]

[35] *Economist*, May 7, 1988.
[36] Wilms, *The German Question and Inner-German Relations*, 8.
[37] Ibid.
[38] *New York Times*, August 2, 1987.

Markham could have added that many Germans in the late 1980s drew the same conclusion. He did add, however, that despite SPD initiatives for disarmament and Green desires for "a neutralist and bucolic utopia," Germany's voters always rejected these options by large majorities. Yet a curious contradiction persisted: on the one hand, large majorities indicated in polls that they would like reunification and would like to cooperate as much with the Soviet Union as with the US; was that true neutrality? On the other hand, official circles used the word "reunification" by 1987 only with great circumspection. The Kohl government spoke in 1987 of a right of self-determination in freedom and peace and expressed the hope that the East German government would continue to let more Germans move freely between East and West, but did so very carefully. Kohl was in some ways Adenauer's grandson, but Kohl's vision of Germany was challenged by very different circumstances, and by very different values.

In early 1988 Thomas F. O'Boyle, writing in the *Wall Street Journal*, reported that only 24 per cent of the German public viewed the Soviet Union as a military threat, "the lowest level in the 25 years since the German Defense Ministry began tracking such sentiment." O'Boyle continued that "half the German public favors unilateral disarmament as a way to achieve peace, up from 35 per cent five years ago, according to a recent Allensbach Institute poll."[39]

Such figures indicated that the Germans might change their views on security and defense more radically and more fundamentally in the 1990s than even the Greens had dared to hope in the days of the peace movement of 1980–3. Those who began by questioning whether a Soviet military threat still existed soon moved on to question the military presence and the prerogatives of Germany's Western allies, especially the US. Unlike the Greens and the pacifists, they did not question these prerogatives because they were against the military altogether, but because they no longer saw compelling reasons to justify inconvenience in the name of national defense.

By 1988, most Germans had forgotten that the allied forces had rights, inherited from the occupation period and codified in various agreements entered into by Bonn as a condition of obtaining sovereignty in 1954–5. The most important of these was the Status of Forces Agreement (SOFA) of 1955, revised in 1963. Until the 1980s, few Germans questioned these rights. The allied forces were in West Germany for a reason that almost all Germans accepted, namely to deter and, if necessary, repel a Soviet attack. When, in the 1980s, a growing number of Germans started doubting that such an attack was even

---

[39] *Wall Street Journal*, January 7, 1988.

remotely likely, they came to regard the prerogatives and activities of allied forces ever more irritating and unnecessary. At the same time, large majorities continued to believe that the allied forces helped to preserve peace and wanted the Federal Republic to stay in NATO.

Frustration with allied troop activities came to the fore in a dramatic way following two events in 1988. In July, a fighter of the Italian air force, taking part in a demonstration of aerial acrobatics at the US air base at Ramstein near Kaiserslautern in the Palatinate, crashed after failing to complete a difficult maneuver. This tragedy caused over 70 deaths and injured more than 300 people, among the many hundreds who had come to watch the show. Later in the year, a low-flying USAF F-111 Thunderbolt fighter based in Britain crashed in the city of Remscheid near Cologne, killing six. The Ramstein and Remscheid disasters also focused attention on a number of legitimate complaints by Germans of all political beliefs concerning the environmental impact of allied troop activities. Such activities included large maneuvers which harmed the landscape and disturbed the life of the countryside, low-level flights deemed necessary by military authorities to maintain combat training but regarded as "noise terror" by many Germans, and the whole range of day-to-day activities by allied troops who, collectively, occupied large tracts of land in densely populated Germany.

This wave of what one might call environmental pacifism began with the Greens but, by 1988, adherents were also found in the SPD, FDP, and CDU. It gained limited popularity, because some became impatient with the minor inconveniences of allied troop activities in the name of the greater good, which was the common defense. If there was not much need for defense, there was no reason, critics said, why any German should tolerate noise, pollution, and risky low-level flights.

To the concern about the environment critics added another, very powerful argument, which also had appeal across the political spectrum. This was the argument that the SOFA and other rights of allied troops were incompatible with West German sovereignty. Accordingly, these critics demanded that the Bonn government renegotiate these agreements to permit allied troops on West German territory only on terms of sovereign equality. A CDU deputy demanded that "these relics of the occupation era must go." [40]

This was indeed a remarkable shift. In the 1950s and 1960s, the Germans welcomed allied troops and recognized their special rights in order to protect their own sovereignty. In 1988, some, but by no means all, insisted that allied rights must go in the name of that sovereignty. The reversal of perspectives was due in part to the collapse of the threat

---

[40] Der Spiegel, December 19, 1988; Kempe, Wall Street Journal, March 13, 1989.

perception. Further, some Germans feared that West Germany's lack of independence vis-à-vis allied troop activities might entangle the German government in US military adventures against its will. Two out of three Germans had opposed the US bombing of Libya in 1986. As *Der Spiegel* noted under the provocative headline "We don't want to be occupied," the German chancellor "cannot even surrender on his own, because almost all West German troops are subject to the (American) supreme commander of NATO." Therefore, the magazine concluded, "Helmut Kohl is in no way master of his own house."[41] The news magazine did not emphasize that the former West German minister of defense, Manfred Wörner, was appointed secretary general of NATO in 1988, the first German to hold this position since 1949.[42]

There was something curiously parochial about this concern. Certainly, accidents such as those at Ramstein and Remscheid were tragic, but they were not comparable to the inconvenience and tragedy that would result as a consequence of a Soviet invasion. The outpouring of resentment at allied troop activities in 1988 might lead a cynical observer to conclude that the Germans only wanted to defend their sovereignty against their friends, but not against their enemies.

The common denominator of both the environmental attack on NATO and the argument about the SOFA and sovereignty was, once again, the lack of fear of Soviet domination, and the optimistic belief that the Soviet Union under Gorbachev was a partner in security and not a threat to security. In a short book published at the height of the furor over the Ramstein and Remscheid crashes, Egon Bahr painted an optimistic picture of a Europe living in peace and harmony with the Soviet Union and called on Western leaders to find an "appropriate answer" to Gorbachev. This answer would include accepting at face value Gorbachev's offers of disarmament and the rejection of any attempt by the West to change the political system against the will of the ruling communist parties within the Soviet empire.[43]

Perhaps that optimism was justified, perhaps not. The point was that no one could know, and certainly no one was entitled to use the words of Gorbachev to argue the case, given that Soviet leaders in the past had frequently said things for the sole purpose of influencing Western public opinion in ways favorable to themselves. Others, including Helmut Schmidt, warned against excessive optimism and noted that Gorbachev

[41] Ibid.

[42] See Dietrich Ide, *Bremer Nachrichten,* October 22, 1988, as reprinted in the *German Tribune,* November 13, 1988; see also Thomas Kielinger, *Rheinischer Merkur/ Christ und Welt,* December 2, 1988, as reprinted in the *German Tribune,* December 25, 1988.

[43] See Bahr, *Zum europäischen Frieden.*

might well be engaged, among many other things, in a vast diplomatic, political, and strategic operation to convince the West Europeans that his government was a better and more reliable guarantee of their security than the government of the United States.

In 1987, the Soviet Union, some argued, was seeking to "construct a 'European House' without US influence," and was seeking to prepare "the next generation of Germans to think of the Soviets as a basically benign, peace-seeking, European power."[44] In 1988 it was clear to some, in the United States and in West Germany, that "the US–Soviet competition is shifting from the Third World to Europe," according to an American expert.[45] At the same time, one of Kohl's principal and able foreign policy advisers, Horst Teltschik, who was an assistant to Richard Löwenthal at the Free University of Berlin in the late 1960s, concluded in April 1988 that this "'common European house' is largely still empty. . . . The concept would become interesting if the 'common European house' should mean that the Soviet Union's European policy would no longer be based on the partition on the continent but on overcoming that partition."[46] Teltschik's concern was not without justification. The attractive image of a "common house" reappeared throughout the remainder of the year, and was defined differently to serve the purposes of its advocates and critics. In Washington, DC, on December 6, 1988, it was given a definition by the new West German defense minister, Rupert Scholz, that was consistent with the view that the rationale for NATO remained valid: "The idea propagated by the Soviet Union of a 'European House' stretching from the Atlantic to the Urals is 'only conceivable with the inclusion of the USA.'"[47]

What comes of a "European house" will be the judgement of history. But Theo Sommer concluded in 1987 that a "serious crisis of identity" was facing the West Germans, and that "the recent discussion of the German Question has been marked by signs of a nationalistic neurosis." He argued that it was time the Germans – that is to say, the West Germans – chose between division and unification:

On the one hand, the contradiction between the emotionalism of a desire for reunification and political possibilities in the real world; on the other, the unsettled conflict between the objective of German unity and the objective of Western European integration. . . . We should realise today that peace in

---

[44] Kempe, "Gorbachev is Going Over Kohl's Head To Woo New Generations of Germans," *Wall Street Journal*, August 3, 1987.
[45] Cited by Frederick Kempe, "Europe Is Likely to Be New Center Stage For Confrontation Between US, Soviets," *Wall Street Journal*, May 9, 1988.
[46] *Frankfurter Allgemeine Zeitung*, April 20, 1988.
[47] *Relay from Bonn*, December 9, 1988.

Europe develops on the basis of the division of Germany rather than on the basis of its reunification. . . . Since 1969 we have been pursuing a policy of non-reunification for the sake of human beings on both sides. Isn't it time to give this policy the mark of finality?[48]

Sommer concluded that "regardless of the preamble to the Basic Law, our political aim must be to create a situation in which reunification is no longer necessary." In so doing, he drew not only on Willy Brandt's concept of cultural identity but, to give his point added legitimacy, on a famous German writer of the eighteenth century:

As Friedrich Schiller wrote 190 years ago, the "German Reich and the German nation are two different things altogether."
"German dignity . . . lives in the culture and character of a nation, irrespective of its political fate."
Let us make sure that we can say this with our heads held high in a peacefully divided Germany.[49]

Sommer argued in 1987 that "regardless of respective forms of state organization, ideological convictions and socio-political systems . . . it is essential that Germans be able to meet each other freely. . . . If the walls and border fortifications were torn down, border signs would lose their significance."[50] Sommer ignored the reasons why the walls and border fortifications existed in the first place; namely, to prevent Germans in the GDR from freely choosing dictatorship or democracy in Germany.

In 1988 Sommer's idea of embracing cultural unity, but accepting division, was taken one step further by another journalist, whose understanding of peace and freedom some might think bizarre. Writing in *Die Zeit*, Marlies Menge argued that "we should think about what we can do in order to arrive at a really peaceful partnership with a GDR, for which the free coming and going of people and ideas . . . would no longer be a problem." She suggested that perhaps the Federal Republic should not accept those from the GDR who want to come to West Germany to live, because their departure weakens social welfare in the GDR – so, for example, if they were physicians, their departure would harm the rights of those they leave behind: "One could ask whether a doctor, who leaves his GDR patients, doesn't infringe on their right to receive medical care. Especially since this patient has indirectly contributed [presumably through his labor] to the education of this doctor."[51]

---

[48] Sommer, "German identity faces a double dilemma over the wish for reunification," *German Tribune*, July 5, 1987, from *Die Zeit*, June 26, 1987.
[49] Ibid.
[50] Ibid.
[51] Menge, "Sollen die Menschen drüben bleiben?" *Die Zeit*, May 6, 1988.

Die Zeit also published a counter-argument in the same edition by Robert Leicht. He pointed out that the Basic Law of the Federal Republic guarantees freedom of profession: "Our state cannot ... tell anyone where he must exercise his responsibility, not even doctors in the GDR. ... We cannot deny any German the right to live in the Federal Republic." Indeed, Leicht concluded that the fact that differences exist between the two German states was not the fault of West Germany: "The Federal Republic cannot become the servant of the GDR, whenever and as long as it denies its citizens freedom of movement."[52] And Theo Sommer added two rhetorical questions in August of 1988: "Do we really want to erect a barrier against those who are able to come to us today, 27 years after the building of the Berlin Wall? Do we also want to transform the open Federal Republic into a closed asylum?"[53]

Perhaps the discrepancy, the lack of fit between the frustrations of division that Germans expressed and the strength of democracy in West Germany, was inevitable, rooted in the very fundamental conditions of West German politics: the perceived need to put peace above all other goals, the need to be everybody's friend and to overcompensate, if necessary, for ancient fears which were still far from dead. West Germany, and most Germans, still lived with this discrepancy. They did so, seemingly, by reserving their worries and fears, which loomed so large in German and foreign headlines, for certain times of the week or year. Only a few could sustain uncertainty and despair day in, day out, and make it the basis of an entire politicized life.

Given the appalling conditions – moral, material, and strategic, of 1945, West Germany in 1989 had clearly fared well. Time had been good to it, and had altered many perspectives. If West Germany is to continue along a constructive path without catastrophe, West Germans and others, such as the readers of this book, must look at its history of accomplishments, and not merely at its dilemmas and discontents. No history, of course, can be completely objective or satisfy everyone's idea of objectivity. But at the other extreme there are obviously partisan histories – as the version shared by the extreme right and the extreme left, who see West Germany as the victim of American manipulation and American materialism. If only the Germans were left to themselves, adherents of this version argue, they would resolve the challenges facing them, even though there is no agreement on what those challenges really are.

We believe that the basic choices the West Germans made in freedom

---

[52] *Die Zeit*, May 6, 1988.
[53] Sommer, "Mehr Angst Als Vaterlandsliebe," *Die Zeit*, August 19, 1988.

after 1945 were choices for the West, and choices that the Soviet Union, had it been able, would have denied them. In 1985 the Federal Republic's president, Richard von Weizsäcker, put it accurately in a speech in Düsseldorf:

The Federal Republic of Germany has become the East of the West, the GDR the West of the East. Thus the division of Germany cannot be ended unless the division of Europe, too, can be ended. But in spite of being in this position, Germany remains affected by the conditions inherent in its location in the Center of Europe. True, that center is divided, but it remains the center. . . .

We are part of the community of Western democracies. It is the inner system of values, the constitutional principles, that unite us with those who have the same convictions. This committment to a free democracy . . . is final and irrevocable.[54]

The same basic point was made by Robert Leicht, following Erich Honecker's visit to Bonn in September 1987. Addressing the Germans, Leicht wrote:

Europe must always remain more important for us than whatever national form the German nation may take. In the future there can be no progress for the Germans at the expense of the Europeans. The Federal Republic can only advance the *Rapprochement* of the two German states in the interest of all their citizens, if it simultaneously advances European integration, and, thereafter, advances as well the coming together of Western and Eastern Europe: vetos against the West and advances toward the East are mutually exclusive. Germany's division has made European integration difficult for a long time. It is essential now: only continuing integration will make it possible to ameliorate the consequences of the division of Germany without awakening new fears.[55]

The history of West Germany from 1945 to 1989, unlike the history of Germany during the 40 years before 1945, was a history of sacrifice, security, and stability. Marion Dönhoff, writing in *Die Zeit*, reminded her readers that the 40 years from 1905 to 1945 saw Europe engulfed by two world wars and the Nazi "Thousand-Year Reich," and concluded that the same length of time from 1945 to 1985 had been peaceful because bipolarity had replaced natural plurality.[56] In other words, it took outside control to keep Europe at peace.

But Dönhoff also argued that "all people" in Europe "and most

[54] Dept of State, *Documents on Germany*, 1414.
[55] *Die Zeit*, September 18, 1987.
[56] *Die Zeit*, March 27, 1987.

governments have enough of the costly arms race which has produced no result, which has brought no side more security and which has surely ruined the economy." She, too, showed herself to be a victim of the peculiar German double vision. She was no friend of totalitarianism or tyranny, and, throughout her career, did much to help Soviet dissidents. Surely, also, she was a loyal supporter of the free and democratic social and political order in West Germany, an order guaranteed by the military deterrent of NATO. Yet she could call defense wasteful and ruinous. But what was the alternative? Neutralism and uncertainty at best, subjugation and misery at worst. There was a middle ground and almost half a century of peace on the continent provided it.

The German nation had, in fact, survived. And prospered. Its people had regained their self-respect. The country remained divided. The empty shells of old bombed-out embassy buildings in the western sectors of Berlin have stood a silent vigil for more than 40 years to the hope for reunification. But West Germany, with West Berlin, was one of the most stable countries in the world – elegant and persuasive testimony to the courage that built democracy in a devastated land. And the continued freedom of West Berlin, wrote a German political scientist, Alexander Schwan, in 1987 – the 750th anniversary of Berlin – "ensures that we do not lose sight of the need to resolve our national problem."[57]

The division of Germany, and the Wall that divides Berlin, will not last forever. Sooner or later the postwar order in Central Europe will crumble. It is unclear what nation, or nations, will provide the leadership that change will require and whether that leadership will be conducted with statesmanship. But of one thing there is certainty. Germany will play a major role in the future of freedom and peace in the center of the European continent, just as it has in the past. And West Germany, whether it likes it or not, will be confronted with the alternatives of whether to lead, or to follow. Its history of the last forty years sends the indelibly clear message that it can provide leadership that is strong, wise and judicious.

There were still, after 40 years of democracy, choices facing Germans. It was not for foreigners to choose, but merely to understand and hope that West Germans would, at last, emerge from their self-imposed exile from world politics and take up the privileges and responsibilities their alliances and other relationships imposed on them. What was in the balance, Germany's future, had been weighed and measured. What was shadow, had become substance. And what was substance, could become leadership.

[57] *Rheinischer Merkur/Christ und Welt*, June 26, 1987.

Bibliographic Essay

The following essay is intended to help the non-specialist reader or student who wishes to pursue the study of one or more aspects of the postwar history of West Germany. In compiling it, the authors at once faced the problem of language. German ranks eighth in number of native speakers among the languages of the world, and the output of works on our subject in German is enormous. Despite the growing interest of American and British scholars and writers in the society, politics, and history of the Federal Republic, it remains true that most important writings are and will continue to be in German. We therefore direct the reader to a range of useful, informative, and authoritative works on each aspect of the subject regardless of language, although we have included English-language works when available.

Full citation of the works mentioned will be found in the bibliography.

Bibliographies, general works, and works of reference

A fairly full bibliography of works on West German history and politics through 1969 can be found in Morsey's *Bundesrepublik*, which also includes a concise narrative overview and a survey of important controversial issues. The best general bibliography on contemporary Germany is the *Bibliographie zur Zeitgeschichte*, which until 1989 appeared as a supplement in every issue of *Vierteljahrshefte für Zeitgeschichte* (1953–). Starting in 1989, the *Bibliographie* appears as a separate annual special issue of the journal rather than as a section in each regular issue. The *Bibliographie* provides a comprehensive listing by subject of books and articles on twentieth-century world history and politics with special reference to Germany. Before 1989 titles dealing with the post-1945 period were listed in even-numbered years. The Institut für Zeitgeschichte, which publishes the journal, issued the cumulative listings through 1980 (over 40,000 items) as *Bibliographie zur Zeitgeschichte 1953– 1980* (1982), and will update this with a new cumulative list (through 1990) in 1991.

The starting-point for all serious study of our subject is the *Geschichte der Bundesrepublik Deutschland*, published in the 1980s in six large tomes of close to 500 pages each, covering the period 1945–82. This is the definitive history of West Germany for the next generation. There is nothing like it in any other language or for any other country. Each volume covers politics, foreign affairs, economy, society, culture, and attitudes. The authors went to great lengths to write both clearly and accurately. In many cases, they had access to unpublished diaries or other hitherto confidential sources, so that the account is often not merely informative but original.

A short introduction, emphasizing social structures rather than individuals, is Berghahn's *Modern Germany*, which begins in 1871 but emphasizes the period since 1933. The author takes a more critical view of many aspects of the Federal Republic than do the authors of the *Geschichte*. Michael Balfour, the author of several outstanding works on German subjects, published a revised version of his *West Germany* in 1982, a lively, detailed, and well-written account of the period from occupation through the chancellorship of Schmidt. Turner's useful overview *Two Germanies*, covers two decades more than Balfour, but is intended as an introduction rather than as a comprehensive account. As the title indicates, Turner includes the GDR, which leaves even less space for West German affairs. The best account of the GDR, one of the best books on Germany altogether, is Childs' *The GDR*.

Most other German works pale into insignificance beside the *Geschichte*. Hillgruber's *Deutsche Geschichte* is a well-written, concise account, periodically updated, focusing on the national issue and Germany's place in East–West relations. It is particularly useful for the reader who wants to understand the main themes and stages of West German history. Thränhardt's book is the view of a leftist opposed at most points to Hillgruber and to the moderate world-view presented in the *Geschichte*. A leading historian of the older generation, Hans Herzfeld, left as his last work a history of *Berlin in der Weltpolitik 1945– 1970*. This is more than merely a history of Berlin politics, rather, it is an attempt to understand the course of world history since the surrender as it affected and was affected by what happened in the divided German capital.

Besson's *Aussenpolitik*, although published in 1970, remains an indispensable as well as beautifully written interpretation of the course and the rationale of West Germany's foreign policy in the first 25 years since 1945. It is one of the two or three books that anyone who really wants to know what the Federal Republic "is all about," as the phrase goes, simply *must* read. After almost two decades, Besson found a worthy successor in Hacke, whose *Weltmacht wider Willen* covers the whole story from 1945 to 1987. Hacke himself points out that he is supplementing and not replacing Besson; both works are equally important for understanding the geostrategic situation and foreign policy choices of Europe's pivotal state. Wolfram Hanrieder provided the first serious overview in English of West German foreign policy from the Basic Law to 1989 in his excellent *Germany, America, Europe*. For the history of security policy in the narrower sense, see Haftendorn's *Security and Detente*. All important government documents and treaties, as well as a selection of official statements and communiques concerning Germany are in *Documents on Germany*, published by the US Government Printing Office. Münch's *Dokumente* is a comprehensive collection of all official documents and statements dealing with the problem of divided Germany.

The student of the West German political system has a choice between introductory surveys in English and in-depth analyses, all of which are in German. The surveys are Conradt's *German Polity*, Dalton's *Politics in West Germany*, and Katzenstein's *Policy and Politics*. All three of these reliable handbooks were revised in the mid-1980s. The standard German text is Ellwein's *Regierungssystem*, first published in 1963 and known to tens of thousands of German undergraduates as "der Ellwein." It is periodically revised and updated; for the sixth edition (1987) Ellwein took a co-author and announced that he intended gradually to retire from the project. Anyone seriously interested in German constitutional law and the system of government will want to refer to Stern's *Staatsrecht*. Two of the planned five volumes were available at the time of writing.

Germany has always been a land of multivolume histories and dictionaries. One of the most outstanding is the *Staatslexikon* of the Görres society, first published in the 1890s. A seventh, entirely recast, five-volume edition of this institution of German scholarship and political culture appeared in 1985–9. In it, the reader will find detailed, concisely written, and highly informative entries (with bibliographies) on every conceivable aspect of West German politics, society, culture, and public life, as well as on political theory, constitutional law, theology, and other general subjects.

An often lively and occasionally provocative series of articles and essays on West German politics, society, and culture are found in the three volumes of *Die Bundesrepublik Deutschland*, edited by Wolfgang Benz, one of the leading historians of the postwar period of the younger generation. The reader who knows German may find these pieces a good place to start before picking up Ellwein. Burdick's *Contemporary Germany* is a similar, if less comprehensive, anthology of essays in English. The volume *Sozialgeschichte*, edited by Conze, contains articles on many aspects of social change and social policies. For culture and the politics of culture in West Germany, see Glaser's *Kulturgeschichte*, of which two volumes, covering the years 1945–67, were available at this writing and a third was promised. Glaser, himself an active journalist and politician, likes to tell stories rather than analyze structures, which makes his work fascinating and valuable as an informal introduction to postwar West Germany. A somewhat acerbic view of what the author sees as the political agenda of postwar German writers is Ross' *Mit der linken Hand geschrieben*, worth reading for its unusual and courageous, if all too brief, attempt to provide an alternative interpretation. Religion and the churches were the subject of Spotts' *Churches and Politics*, which is not only outdated (1973), but has been severely criticized in Germany. In view of the important developments in the political role and theology of both the major denominations since the early 1970s, this is clearly a subject that needs new treatment.

There is no good survey of West German education and educational policy in any language, even though these issues were highly prominent throughout our period. The relevant sections of the *Geschichte* are useful. Tent's volume on the *Free University of Berlin* is a real boon to the field and provides elements of a general history of higher education in the Federal Republic.

Abelshauser's *Wirtschaftsgeschichte* and Berghahn's *Americanisation of West German Industry* are surveys of the economy, but both emphasize the 1940s and 1950s and provide almost no in-depth information for the period after 1969. Emminger's *D-Mark, Dollar, Währungskrisen* deals with the 1970s and early 1980s, but Emminger was a banker, not a writer: his account is anecdotal, spotty, and occasionally he contradicts himself. Lampert's *Wirtschafts- und Sozialordnung* is a concise handbook full of interesting information on a broad range of issues, written from the standpoint of the defenders of the social market economy. Like Ellwein, it is frequently updated. For continuing data on the economy and competent evaluations of current and future trends, see the annual *OECD Economic Surveys: Germany*.

After the war, many people both in and outside Germany asked two questions: why did democracy fail in Germany in 1933, and what should be done to make it more secure the second time round? Conservatives blamed the problem on Germany's geopolitical position "in the middle," surrounded by enemies. Such a country could not afford democracy and was easy prey for demagogues. The American David Calleo rehabilitated this argument in *The German Problem Reconsidered*. Liberals tended to blame domestic forces for the fragility of democracy. The basic statement of this position remains Dahrendorf's *Society and Democracy*. In that book, written in the mid-1960s, he blamed the failure of democracy on the failure of political liberalism and wondered whether the new democracy was stable. Both before and after Dahrendorf, other observers tried other means of interpretation. One was to monitor public opinion intensively. As a result, West Germans answered more opinion polls on more subjects than any other people in the world, and the science and technology of public opinion surveys became one of the staples of postwar German political science and policy analysis. The leader of this movement in Germany was Elisabeth Noelle-Neumann, who founded the Allensbach Institute. The Institute's two volumes of opinion polls from 1967 and 1981, *The Germans*, provide a mass of evidence on beliefs, opinions, attitudes, and sentiments. The other method was to develop a science of "political culture" to measure and monitor underlying trends in belief and attitudes to life because, as one of the advocates of political cultural studies put it, "the evolution and persistence of mass-based democracy requires the emergence of certain supportive habits and attitudes among the general public."[1] Almond and Verba's *Civic Culture* found that Germans were democratic on the outside but authoritarian on the inside in 1960; by the 1980s, this had changed. The reasons, the course, and the significance of this change is the subject of Inglehart's *Culture Change*, which summarizes his work over the previous two decades. Taken together, these books provide important background to political and social history and give essential information for evaluating the strength of democratic sentiment in Germany.

Volume II

Wilharm's *Deutsche Geschichte* picks up where Steininger leaves off and provides interpretative essays and documents for the period 1962–83. Otherwise, the period after 1963 is not by any means as well served as the first ten to fifteen years since 1949, partly because the relevant archives were not yet open by the late 1980s. Useful memoirs by leading figures include those of Brandt, *People and Politics*, and Schmidt, *Menschen und Mächte*. The latter describes Germany's dealings with the Soviet Union, the USA, and China under Schmidt's leadership. He has promised a further volume on Europe. The American ambassador to Germany in 1963–8, George McGhee, published his recollections of

---

[1] Inglehart, "Renaissance of Political Culture," *American Political Science Review* 82 (1988): 1204.

that period, which was troubled by disputes over offset payments and the nuclear non-proliferation Treaty, under the title *At the Creation of a New Germany*.

The cultural revolution of the 1960s had many participants, but so far few historians. Source material for the New Left's world-view can be found in the anthology by Karsunke and Michel, taken from the main journal of the cultural revolution, *Kursbuch*. Nolte's *Deutschland und der Kalte Krieg* is, in part, a conservative professor's response to the political and methodological radicalism of his own students and contains useful documentation as well as provocative interpretations of what happened at the West German universities in 1965–70. Bieling's *Tränen der Revolution* is, on one level, a useful chronicle of the successive states of mind and political strategies of the student left in the later 1960s; on another level, it is the apologia of a participant who denigrates the conservative opposition. Langguth's *Protestbewegung* is a detailed and essential account of radical extremism of all types from the mid-1960s to the early 1980s; a task the same author extended to the Greens in his study *The Green Factor*.

On terrorism there are two useful works. J. Becker's *Hitler's Children*, last revised in 1979, remains the best English-language survey of the Baader-Meinhof gang and its associates, who they were, and why they chose the actions they did. Horchem's *Verlorene Revolution* describes the international and ideological context of both right- and left-wing terrorism and continues the story to the mid-1980s. A third book, Lübbe's *Endstation Terror*, links terrorism and its sympathizers to the anti-authoritarianism of the New Left and the failure of the constituted authorities to protect law and order.

The background and course of the new Ostpolitik are the subject of two good English-language studies: Stent's *Embargo to Ostpolitik* which focuses on economic relationships, and Griffith's *Ostpolitik*, which is more general. Bender's *Neue Ostpolitik* is an optimistic chronicle of the road from the Berlin Wall to the Eastern treaties. Zündorf's *Ostverträge* is an authoritative account of what the Brandt government thought it was getting in the treaties, as well as a useful analysis of the international context of Ostpolitik. Wolffsohn's *West Germany's Foreign Policy* is a sympathetic account of the years 1969–82, but is not as useful as Hacke's *Weltmacht*. An extraordinary chronicle of the Brandt years is Baring's *Machtwechsel*. Some have compared it to Kissinger's *White House Years*. Actually, it is more comprehensive, since Baring is telling the story of *all* the government's policies as well as the story of the internal struggle between radicals and moderates in the SPD.

West Germany's international position and its foreign economic and security policy in the Schmidt period are sympathetically described and interpreted in Haftendorn's *Sicherheit und Stabilität*. More detail, and somewhat more criticism, can be found in the final volume of the *Geschichte*, which also includes an important essay on the cultural revolution and its effects by Karl Dietrich Bracher. Joffe's *Limited Partnership* surveys US-European relations in the 1980s with special emphasis on Germany.

Domestic politics under Brandt and Schmidt are extensively treated in the relevant volumes of the *Geschichte*. In public debate, literature, scholarship, and intellectual life the cultural revolution sharpened the contrast between a moderate to conservative and a leftist to radical mentality, each with its own journals of opinion, publishing houses, and media apparatus. In the later Schmidt years and, *a fortiori*, under Kohl, leftists argued that West Germany was undergoing a conservative restoration, a *Tendenzwende*. Conservatives disputed this and pointed to the continuing influence of New Left ideas among students and journalists and the growing acceptance in public opinion of the moderate left's social and international political agenda as carried out by Schmidt and Genscher. The leftist arguments for where Germany stood and where it should be going in the later Schmidt years are found in Habermas' anthology *Stichworte*, which is a broad panorama of progressive opinion. For conservative criticism of progressive assumptions, see Lübbe's *Politischer Moralismus* and Stürmer's *Dissonanzen*. Lübbe, a professor of philosophy at Zürich, was a former social democrat who left the SPD in the mid-1970s.

The *Stichworte* anthology signaled, among other things, a renewed interest on the left in questions of national identity and history. This rediscovery led to intense, and sometimes emotional, debates. First in time came the concern with history, which blended into a concern with national division, documented in Venohr's *Deutsche Einheit* and Brandt and Ammon's anthology of the German left's attitude to reunification, *Die Linke und die nationale Frage*. Second came the debate over how to deal with National Socialism, an argument ostensibly provoked by Ernst Nolte, but which had in fact been simmering ever since the mid-1960s. Maier's *Unmasterable Past*, one of the more valuable English-language books on postwar Germany, is an analysis both of the arguments over national identity and of the historians' debate, by an American historian sympathetic to the left-liberal position. The main German contributions to the debate are assembled in *"Historikerstreit."* On German-Jewish relations see the useful and optimistic overview by Wolffsohn, *Ewige Schuld?* In the late 1980s, German enthusiasm for Gorbachev and for disarmament threatened to cause serious disputes in the Western camp. Arnulf Baring cogently criticized the German ambition to play a leading role in East–West relations in *Unser neuer Grössenwahn*. Harold James skilfully analyzed the long history of argument over what it meant to be a German in his *German Identity*.

Periodically, foreigners living in or dealing with Germany put their discoveries and their amazed or gratified comments into words, more or less successfully. The *New York Times* reports of James Markham in the early 1980s were a high point not only of American journalism, but of all writing on Germany; unfortunately, they had not been assembled into a book at the time of writing. Ardagh's *Germany* is a mine of useful information on most aspects of German politics, society, and culture in the 1980s, but is a less satisfying and complete work than the same author's justly renowned books on France. Two other British journalists, David Marsh of the *Financial Times* and Daniel Johnson of the *Daily Telegraph*, reportedly were preparing books on Germany for publication in 1989 or 1990.

Documents and Sources

Archiv der Gegenwart (1980–7) St Augustin (Cologne): Siegler and Co., Verlag für Zeitarchive.

Ausschuss der deutschen Statistiker für die Volks- und Berufszählung, 1946. *Volks- und Berufszählung vom 29. Oktober 1946.* Berlin: Duncker und Humblot, 1949.

Berlin Senat. *Berlin — Chronik der Jahre 1951—1954.* Vol. 5 of *Schriftenreihe zur Berliner Zeitgeschichte.* Berlin: Heinz Spitzing, 1968.

Bundeskriminalamt, "Sonderkommission Bonn," und Bundesamt für Verfassungschutz (Aus den Akten des). *Der Baader Meinhof Report.* Mainz: v. Hase und Köhler, 1972.

Bundesministerium für Arbeit und Sozialordnung (Federal Ministry for Work and Social Order). *Der Lastenausgleich.* By Peter Paul Nahm. *Sozialpolitik in Deutschland,* no. 50. Stuttgart: Kohlhammer, 1962.

Bundesministerium für innerdeutsche Beziehungen (Federal Ministry for Inner-German Relations). *DDR Handbuch.* Cologne: Verlag Wissenschaft und Politik, 1979.

— *Dokumente zur Deutschlandpolitik.* IV/1963, vols 9–12; and V/1966–7, vol. 1. Frankfurt: 1978–84.

Bundesministerium für Vertriebene, Flüchtlinge und Kriegsgeschädigte (Federal Ministry for Expellees, Refugees and War Victims). *Bundesgesetze und Leistungen für die durch Krieg und Kriegsfolgen Geschädigten.* Edited by Friedrich Panse and Edgar von Wietersheim. Mainz: Deutscher Fachschriften-Verlag, 1959.

— *Die Vertreibung der Deutschen Bevölkerung aus den Gebieten östlich der Oder—Neisse.* Edited by Theodor Schieder. Vol. 1 of *Dokumentation der Vertreibung der Deutschen aus Ost-Mitteleuropa* [1954], reprint. Munich: Deutscher Taschenbuch Verlag, 1984. A selection and translation was published as *The Expulsion of the German Population from the Territories East of the Oder—Neisse-Line.*

Bundesministerium für Wohnungsbau (Federal Ministry for Housing). *Grundsätze, Leistungen und Aufgaben der Wohnungsbaupolitik der Bundesregierung.* Bonn: 1959.

"Denkschrift des militärischen Expertenausschusses über die Aufstellung eines Deutschen Kontingents im Rahmen einer übernationalen Streitmacht zur Verteidigung Westeuropas vom 9. Oktober 1950." *Militärgeschichtliche Mitteilungen* 21 (1977): 168–90.

Department of State. "European Unity: United States will Cooperate, not Initiate." By George C. Marshall, United States Secretary of State. Delivered at meeting of Harvard University Alumni, Cambridge, MA, June 5, 1947.

—— *Documents on American Foreign Relations.* Vol. 5, 1942–1943; vol. 6, 1943–1944; vol. 7, 1944–45; vol. 8, 1945–46. Princeton, NJ: Princeton University Press, 1947.

—— *Documents on Germany 1944–1985.* Department of State Publication no. 9446. Office of the Historian, Bureau of Public Affairs [1986].

—— "Restatement of US Policy on Germany." By James F. Byrnes. Publication 2616. GPO, 1946.

Deutsche Presse Agentur report, September 15, 1985.

Deutscher Bundestag. *Verhandlungen des Deutschen Bundestages.* Stenographische Berichte. Vol 16. Bonn: 1952.

Europa-Archiv. Bonn: Verlag für Internationale Politik.

Facts on File (1955–1988). New York: Facts on File.

Federal Ministry for All-German Questions. *The Flights from the Soviet Zone and the Sealing-off Measures of the Communist Regime of 13th August 1961 in Berlin.* Bonn and Berlin: Federal Printing Works, 1961.

—— *Violations of Human Rights, Illegal Acts and Incidents at the Sector Border in Berlin since the Building of the Wall (13 August 1961–15 August 1962).* Bonn and Berlin: Federal Printing Works, 1962.

Federal Republic of Germany. *Elections, Parliament and Political Parties.* New York: German Information Center, 1986.

Federal Statistical Office. *Statistical Compass 1987.* Wiesbaden, 1987.

—— *Statistical Pocket-book on Expellees.* Wiesbaden, 1953.

Freiheit der Wissenschaft, no. 6 (July 1985).

Hauptamt für Statistik von Gross-Berlin. *Berlin in Zahlen 1947.* Berlin: Berliner Kulturbuch-Verlag, 1949.

Haute Commissariat de la Republique Francaise en Allemagne. "Naissance de la Republique Federale d'Allemagne." *Realités Allemandes* 9–10 (September/October 1949): 25–38.

Institut der deutschen Wirtschaft. *Wirtschaftstruktur der Bundesländer.* Cologne, 1986.

Institut für Zukunftsforschung. *Ausländer oder Deutsche.* Cologne: Bund-Verlag, 1981.

Interview der Woche. Archiv für Christlich-Demokratische Politik. St Augustin (Cologne): Pressedokumentation der Konrad-Adenauer-Stiftung.

John F. Kennedy. *Public Papers of the President of the United States: John F. Kennedy, 1960–1963.* GPO, 1964.

Keesing's Contemporary Archives — Record of World Events (1956–1987). Vols 25–33. England: Longman Group.

Office of the Military Government, US Sector, Berlin. *A Four Year Report* (July 1, 1945 – September 1, 1949). Civil Affairs Division (Army Dept).

Office of the Military Governor for Germany, US. *The German Press in the US Occupied Area 1945–1948.* Special Report of the Military Governor, November 1948. Prepared by the Information Services Division.

— *Monthly Report of the Military Governor.* Nos 36–50. (June 1948–September 1949).

Office of the US High Commissioner for Germany. *Elections and Political Parties in Germany, 1945–1952.* Office of Executive Secretary, 1952.

— *History of the Allied High Commission for Germany.* Office of the Executive Secretary, Historical Division, 1951.

— *Postwar Changes in German Education (US Zone and US Sector Berlin).* Office of Public Affairs, 1951.

— *Press, Radio and Film in West Germany.* By Henry P. Pilgert. Office of the Executive Secretary, Historical Division, 1953.

— *The West German Educational System.* By Henry P. Pilgert. Office of the Executive Secretary, Historical Division, 1953.

— *Quarterly Report on Germany.* (September 21, 1949–July 31, 1952).

Press and Information Office of the Federal Republic of Germany. *The Development of the Relations between the Federal Republic of Germany and the German Democratic Republic.* Bonn, 1973.

— *Employers and Unions.* (Information 16.) Bonn, 1986.

— *Erfurt, March 19, 1970: A Documentation.* Bonn, 1970.

— *Germany Reports.* 2nd rev. edn. Wiesbaden: Wiesbadener Graphische Betriebe, 1955.

— *Housing and Town Planning.* (Information 22.) Bonn, 1986.

— *Kassel, May 21, 1970: A Documentation.* Bonn, 1970.

— *Law and the Administration of Justice.* (Information 24.) Bonn, 1986.

— Typewritten communication. July, 1986.

Presse- und Informationsamt der Bundesregierung. *Bulletin.* Bonn.

Regierung der Bundesrepublik Deutschland (Government of the Federal Republic of Germany). *Gesellschaftliche Daten.* Presse und Informationsamt, 1982.

Relay from Bonn. Vols 1–15 (July 28, 1970–December 15, 1987). New York: German Information Center.

Republic of France. *Major Addresses, Statements and Press Conferences of General Charles de Gaulle.* (May 19, 1958–January 31, 1964). Press and Information Division, New York.

Senate Committee on Foreign Relations. *Hearings on United States Policy toward Europe.* Statement of Dr Henry A. Kissinger, June 27, 1966.

Statements and Speeches. New York: German Information Center.

Statistisches Bundesamt. *Lange Reihen zur Wirtschaftsentwicklung, 1986.* Cologne: Institut der deutschen Wirtschaft, 1986.

— *Statistisches Jahrbuch für die Bundesrepublik Deutschland, 1962, 1966, 1986, 1987* and *1988.* Stuttgart and Mainz: Kohlhammer, 1962, 1966, 1986, 1987, 1988.

Statistisches Bundesamt. *Volkswirtschaftliche Gesamtrechnungen,* Fachserie 18, Reihe 1.3, Konten und Standardtabellen. Wiesbaden, 1988.

Statistisches Reichsamt. *Statistisches Jahrbuch für das Deutsche Reich 1921/1922.* Berlin: Verlag für Politik und Wirtschaft, 1922.

The Week in Germany. New York: German Information Center.

Bibliography

Note: Accented letters are alphabetized along with the unaccented letter.

Abelshauser, Werner. *Wirtschaftsgeschichte der Bundesrepublik Deutschland 1945–1980*. Frankfurt am Main: Suhrkamp, 1983.

Abenheim, Donald. *Reforging the Iron Cross: The Search for Tradition in the West German Armed Forces*. Princeton, NJ: Princeton University Press, 1988.

Abraham, Henry J. *The Judicial Process*. 5th edn. New York: Oxford University Press, 1986.

Adenauer, Konrad. *Erinnerungen 1953–1955*. Stuttgart: Deutsche Verlags-Anstalt, 1966.

—— *Erinnerungen 1955–1959*. Stuttgart: Deutsche Verlags-Anstalt, 1967.

—— *Erinnerungen 1959–1963: Fragmente*. Stuttgart: Deutsche Verlags-Anstalt, 1968.

—— *Konrad Adenauer: Briefe über Deutschland, 1945–1951*. Hans Peter Mensing (ed.). Berlin: Siedler, 1986.

—— *Memoirs 1945–1953*. Chicago: Henry Regnery, 1966.

—— *Nachdenken über die Werte: Weihnachtsansprachen*. Walter Berger (ed.). Buxheim, Allgäu: Martin Verlag/Walter Berger, 1976.

Agnoli, Johannes, and Brückner, Peter. *Die Transformation der Demokratie*. Berlin: Voltaire, 1967.

Alexiev, Alexander R. *The Soviet Campaign Against INF: Strategy, Tactics, Means*. Rand Note N-2280-AF. Santa Monica, CA: RAND Corporation, 1985.

Allemann, Fritz René. *Bonn ist nicht Weimar*. Cologne: Kiepenheuer und Witsch, 1956.

Almond, Gabriel A., and Verba, Sidney. *The Civic Culture: Political Attitudes and Democracy in Five Nations*. Princeton, NJ: Princeton University Press, 1963.

Alt, Franz. *Frieden ist möglich: Die Politik der Bergpredigt*. Munich: Piper, 1983.

Anderson, Martin. *Revolution*. San Diego: Harcourt Brace Jovanovich, 1988.

Andreas-Friedrich, Ruth. *Schauplatz Berlin: Tagebuchaufzeichnungen 1945 bis 1948*. Frankfurt am Main: Suhrkamp, 1984.

Anfänge westdeutscher Sicherheitspolitik, 1945–1956. Publ. by Militärgeschicht-lichen Forschungsamt. Vol. 1, *Von der Kapitulation bis zum Pleven-Plan*, by Roland G. Foerster, C. Greiner, G. Meyer, H.-J. Rautenberg, and N.

Wiggershaus. Vol. 2, *Die Europäische Verteidigungsgemeinschaft*. Munich: Oldenbourg, 1982–9. Vols 3 and 4 in preparation.

Antonov-Ovseenko, Anton. *The Time of Stalin: Portrait of a Tyranny*. New York: Harper and Row, 1981.

Ardagh, John. *Germany and the Germans: An Anatomy of Society Today*. New York: Harper and Row, 1987.

Asmus, Ron. "The GDR and Martin Luther." *Survey* (Autumn 1984), 124–56.

—— "*Pravda* Attacks East–West German Ties." RFE-RL Background Report/145, (August 8, 1984).

Augstein, Rudolf. "Die neue Auschwitz-Lüge" in *"Historikerstreit."* Munich: Piper, 1987.

Bahr, Egon. *Zum europäischen Frieden. Eine Antwort an Gorbatschow*. Berlin: Siedler, 1988.

Baker, Kendall; Dalton, Russel J.; and Hildebrandt, Kai. *Germany Transformed: Political Culture and the New Politics*. Cambridge, MA: Harvard University Press, 1981.

Balfour, Michael. *West Germany*. London, Croom Helm, 1982.

Baring, Arnulf. *Machtwechsel: Die Ära Brandt–Scheel*. Stuttgart: Deutsche Verlags-Anstalt, 1982.

—— *Unser neuer Grössenwahn*. Stuttgart: Deutsche Verlags-Anstalt, 1988.

Bark, Dennis L. *Agreement on Berlin*. Washington: American Enterprise Institute for Public Policy Research; Stanford, CA: Hoover Institution on War, Revolution and Peace, 1974.

—— *Congressional Record*, Vol. 117, No. 1 (Jan. 21, 1971), reprinted from a speech delivered to the Commonwealth Club of California in San Francisco, Dec. 18, 1970.

Bark, Dennis L., and Rowen, Henry S. "The German Question." Unpublished paper, 1986.

Barnett, Correlli. *The Pride and the Fall*. New York: Free Press, 1986.

Bartel, Heinrich. *A. N. Jakowlew und die USA: Leitgedanken und Feindbilder eines Gorbatschow-Beraters*. Berichte des Bundesinstituts für ostwissenschaftliche und internationale Studien no. 47/1988. Cologne, 1988.

Barzel, Rainer. *Im Streit und umstritten: Anmerkungen zu Konrad Adenauer, Ludwig Erhard und den Ostverträgen*. Frankfurt am Main: Ullstein, 1986.

Becker, Hellmut. "Bildungspolitik" in *Die Bundesrepublik Deutschland*, vol. 2, Wolfgang Benz (ed.). Frankfurt am Main: Fischer Taschenbuch Verlag, 1983.

Becker, Jillian. *Hitler's Children: The Story of the Baader-Meinhof Terrorist Gang*. Philadelphia: J. B. Lippincott, 1977.

Bell, Coral. *Negotiation from Strength: A Study in the Politics of Power*. New York: Knopf, 1963.

Bender, Peter. *Neue Ostpolitik: Vom Mauerbau bis zum Moskauer Vertrag*. Munich: Deutscher Taschenbuch Verlag, 1986.

—— "Zwei neurotische Riesen." *Merkur* 34 (1980), 529–41.

Benz, Wolfgang. *Die Gründung der Bundesrepublik: Von der Bizone zum souveränen Staat*. Munich: Deutscher Taschenbuch Verlag, 1984.

—— *Potsdam 1945: Besatzungsherrschaft und Neuaufbau im Vier-Zonen-Deutschland.* Munich: Deutscher Taschenbuch Verlag, 1986.

—— *Von der Besatzungsherrschaft zur Bundesrepublik.* Frankfurt am Main: Fischer Taschenbuch Verlag, 1984.

Benz, Wolfgang, ed. *Die Bundesrepublik Deutschland.* 3 vols. Frankfurt am Main: Fischer Taschenbuch Verlag, 1983.

Berghahn, Volker R. *The Americanisation of West German Industry, 1945–1973.* Leamington Spa, England: Berg, 1986. Originally published as *Unternehmer und Politik in der Bundesrepublik.* Frankfurt am Main: Suhrkamp, 1985.

—— *Modern Germany: Society, Economy and Politics in the Twentieth Century.* 2nd edn. Cambridge: Cambridge University Press, 1987.

Bergmann, Uwe; Dutschke, Rudi; Lefevre, Wolfgang; and Rabehl, Bernd. *Die Rebellion der Studenten oder die neue Opposition.* Reinbek: Rowohlt, 1968.

Berkhahn, Karl Wilhelm; Dönhoff, Marion Gräfin; Klasen, Karl; Koerber, Kurt; Sommer, Theo; Stoedter, Helga and Rolf; and Trebitsch, Gyula, eds. *Hart am Wind: Helmut Schmidts politische Laufbahn.* Hamburg: Albrecht Knaus, 1978.

Bernstein, Barton J., ed. *Politics and Policies of the Truman Administration.* Chicago: University of Chicago Press, 1970.

Bertelsmann Lexikon-Institut. *Facts about Germany.* 1st edn; 6th rev. edn. Gütersloh: Bertelsmann Lexikon Verlag, 1979, 1988.

Besson, Waldemar. *Die Aussenpolitik der Bundesrepublik.* Munich: Piper, 1970.

Beyme, Klaus von. *The Political System of the Federal Republic of Germany.* New York: St. Martin's Press, 1982.

Beyme, Klaus von, ed. *Die grossen Regierungserklärungen der deutschen Bundeskanzler von Adenauer bis Schmidt.* Munich: Carl Hanser, 1979.

Bibliographie zur Zeitgeschichte 1953–1980. 3 vols. Publ. by Institut für Zeitgeschichte. Munich: Saur, 1982–3.

Bibliographie zur Zeitgeschichte, 1981–. Supplement to *Vierteljahrshefte für Zeitgeschichte.* Publ. by Institut für Zeitgeschichte. Munich: Oldenbourg.

Bieling, Rainer. *Die Tränen der Revolution: Die 68er zwanzig Jahre danach.* Berlin: Siedler, 1988.

Binder, David. *The Other German: Willy Brandt's Life and Times.* Washington, DC: New Republic, 1975.

Binder, Gerhart. *Deutschland seit 1945.* Stuttgart: Seewald, 1969.

Blackwell Encyclopaedia of Political Institutions. Vernon Bogdanor (ed.). Oxford: Blackwell, 1987.

Blumenwitz, Dieter; Gotto, Klaus; Maier, Hans; Repgen, Konrad; and Schwarz, Hans-Peter, eds. *Konrad Adenauer und seine Zeit.* 2 vols. Stuttgart: Deutsche Verlags-Anstalt, 1976.

Bohlen, Charles E. *Witness to History, 1929–1969.* New York: W. W. Norton and Co., 1973.

Bolesch, Hermann Otto. *Typisch Mischnick.* Munich: C. Bertelsmann, 1974.

Bonhoeffer, Emmi. *Auschwitz Trials: Letters from an Eyewitness.* Richmond, Virginia: John Knox, 1967.

Borst, Arno. *Reden über die Staufer.* Frankfurt am Main: Ullstein, 1978.

Botting, Douglas. *From the Ruins of the Reich: Germany 1945—1949.* New York: Crown, 1985.

Bracher, Karl Dietrich; Jäger, Wolfgang; and Link, Werner. *Republik im Wandel, 1969—1974, Die Ära Brandt.* Vol. 5/I of *Geschichte der Bundesrepublik Deutschland.* Stuttgart: Deutsche Verlags-Anstalt; Wiesbaden: Brockhaus, 1986.

Brandt, Peter, and Ammon, Herbert. *Die Linke und die nationale Frage.* Reinbek: Rowohlt, 1981.

Brandt, Peter; Schumacher, Jörg; Schwarzrock, Goetz; and Suehl, Klaus. *Karrieren eines Aussenseiters: Leo Bauer zwischen Kommunismus und Sozialdemokratie, 1912 bis 1972.* Berlin: Dietz, 1983.

Brandt, Willy. *Die Abschiedsrede.* Berlin: Siedler, 1987.

—— *The Ordeal of Coexistence.* Cambridge, MA: Harvard University Press, 1963.

—— *People and Politics: The Years 1960—1975.* Boston: Little, Brown and Co., 1978. Originally published as *Begegnungen und Einsichten.* Hamburg: Hoffmann und Campe, 1976.

—— *Willy Brandt Bundestagsreden.* Helmut Schmidt (ed.). Bonn: az studio, 1972.

—— *Zum sozialen Rechtsstaat: Reden und Dokumente.* Arnold Harttung (ed.). Berlin: Berlin-Verlag, 1983.

Brandt, Willy, and Lowenthal, Richard. *Ernst Reuter: Ein Leben für die Freiheit.* Munich: Kindler, 1957.

Brockhaus Enzyklopädie. Vol. 6. 17th edn. Wiesbaden: F. A. Brockhaus, 1968.

Broder, Henryk M. *Der Ewige Antisemit: Über Sinn und Funktion eines beständigen Gefühls.* Frankfurt am Main: Fischer Taschenbuch Verlag, 1986.

Broszat, Martin; Henke, Klaus-Dietmar; and Woller, Hans, eds. *Von Stalingrad zur Währungsreform.* Munich: Oldenbourg, 1988.

Brown, Anthony Cave. *The Last Hero: Wild Bill Donovan.* New York: Times Books, 1982.

Bruns, Wilhelm. "Deutsch-Deutsche Beziehungen: Vom Sonderkonflikt zum Sonderkonsens?" *Politische Bildung* 20: 1 (1987), 38–52.

Brzezinski, Zbigniew. *Power and Principle: Memoirs of the National Security Advisor, 1977—1981.* New York: Farrar, Strauss, Giroux, 1983.

Bülow, Andreas von. *Das Bülow-Papier.* Frankfurt am Main: Eichborn, 1985.

Bundy, McGeorge; Kennan, George F.; McNamara, Robert; and Smith, Gerard. "Nuclear Weapons and the Atlantic Alliance." *Foreign Affairs* 60 (1981–2), 753–68.

Burdick, Charles; Jacobsen, Hans-Adolf; and Kudszus, Winfried, eds. *Contemporary Germany: Politics and Culture.* Boulder, CO: Westview, 1984.

Calleo, David. *The German Problem Reconsidered: Germany and the World Order, 1870 to the Present.* Cambridge: Cambridge University Press, 1978.

Caro, Michael K. *Der Volkskanzler, Ludwig Erhard.* Cologne: Kiepenheuer und Witsch, 1965.

Carr, Jonathan. *Helmut Schmidt: Helmsman of Germany.* London: Weidenfeld and Nicolson, 1985.

Catudal, Honore M. *The Diplomacy of the Quadripartite Agreement on Berlin: A New Era in East—West Politics.* Berlin: Berlin-Verlag, 1978.

Charlton, Michael. *The Eagle and the Small Birds.* Chicago: University of Chicago Press, 1984.

Chaussy, Ulrich. "Jugend" in *Die Bundesrepublik Deutschland*, vol. 2, Wolfgang Benz (ed.). Frankfurt am Main: Fischer Taschenbuch Verlag, 1983.

Childs, David. *The GDR: Moscow's German Ally.* 2nd edn. London: Unwin Hyman, 1988.

Childs, David, and Johnson, Jeffrey. *West Germany: Politics and Society.* New York: St. Martin's Press, 1981.

Churchill, Winston S. *The Second World War.* Vol. 6, *Triumph and Tragedy.* Boston: Houghton Mifflin Co., 1953.

Cioc, Mark. *Pax Atomica: the Nuclear Defense Debate in West Germany during the Adenauer Era.* New York: Columbia University Press, 1988.

Clay, Lucius D. *Decision in Germany.* New York: Doubleday and Company, 1950.

— *The Papers of General Lucius D. Clay,* vol. 1. Jean Edward Smith (ed.). Bloomington, Indiana: University of Indiana Press, 1974.

— "Proconsul of a People, by Another People, for Both Peoples" in *Americans as Proconsuls,* Robert Wolfe (ed.). Carbondale, IL: Southern Illinois University Press, 1984.

Codevilla, Angelo. *While Others Build.* New York: Free Press, 1988.

Collier, Richard. *The Freedom Road, 1944–1945.* New York: Atheneum, 1984.

Conquest, Robert. *The Harvest of Sorrow: Soviet Collectivization and the Terror Famine.* New York: Oxford University Press, 1986.

Conradt, David P. *The German Polity.* 3rd edn. New York: Longman, 1986.

Conze, Werner; and Lepsius, M. Rainer, eds. *Sozialgeschichte der Bundesrepublik Deutschland: Beiträge zum Kontinuitätsproblem.* Industrielle Welt. Schriftenreihe des Arbeitskreises für moderne Sozialgeschichte, no. 34. Stuttgart: Klett-Cotta, 1983.

Cook, Don. *Charles de Gaulle.* New York: G. P. Putnam's Sons, 1983.

— *Ten Men and History.* New York: Doubleday and Company, 1981.

Craig, Gordon A. *The Germans.* New York: G. P. Putnam's Sons, 1982.

— *Germany 1866–1945.* Oxford: Clarendon Press, 1978.

Dahrendorf, Ralf. *Bildung ist Bürgerrecht: Plädoyer für eine aktive Bildungspolitik.* Hamburg: C. Wegner, 1968.

— *Law and Order.* The Hamlyn Lectures. London: Stevens and Sons, 1985.

— *A New World Order?* [Legon]: University of Ghana, 1979.

— *Society and Democracy in Germany.* New York: Doubleday, 1967.

Dalton, Russell M. *Politics in West Germany.* Boston: Scott, Foresman, 1989.

Davis, Kingsley; Bernstam, Mikhail; and Ricardo-Campbell, Rita, eds. *Below-Replacement Fertility in Industrial Societies.* New York: Cambridge University Press, 1987.

Davison, W. Phillips. *The Berlin Blockade: A Study in Cold War Politics.* Princeton, NJ: Princeton University Press, 1958.

de Gaulle, Charles. *Memoirs of Hope: Renewal and Endeavor.* New York: Simon and Schuster, 1971.

de Zayas, Alfred M. *Nemesis at Potsdam: The Anglo-Americans and the Expulsion of the Germans.* Rev. edn. London: Routledge and Kegan Paul, 1979.

Detwiler, Donald. "A Tribute to Percy Schramm." *Central European History* 4: 1 (March 1971), 90–4.

Deuerlein, Ernst. *CDU/CSU 1945–57.* Cologne: J. P. Bachem, 1957.

—— *Deutschland 1963–1970.* Hannover: Verlag für Literatur und Zeitgeschehen, 1972.

Deutsch, Karl Wolfgang, and Edinger, Lewis J. *Germany Rejoins the Powers.* Stanford, CA: Stanford University Press, 1959.

Diwald, Hellmut. "Deutschland – was ist es?" in *Die Deutsche Einheit kommt bestimmt,* Wolfgang Venohr (ed.). Bergisch Gladbach: Gustav Lübbe, 1982.

—— *Geschichte der Deutschen.* Berlin: Ullstein, 1978.

Doeker, Günther, and Brückner, Jens A., eds. *The Federal Republic of Germany and the German Democratic Republic in International Relations.* Vol. 1, *Confrontation and Co-operation.* Dobbs Ferry, NY: Oceana Publications, 1979.

Doering-Manteuffel, Anselm. *Die Bundesrepublik Deutschland in der Ära Adenauer.* Darmstadt: Wissenschaftliche Buchgesellschaft, 1983.

—— *Katholizismus und Wiederbewaffnung.* Veröffentlichungen der Kommission für Zeitgeschichte, ser. B, vol. 32. Mainz: Grünewald, 1981.

Dönhoff, Marion. *Foe into Friend.* London: Weidenfeld and Nicolson, 1982.

Dorn, Walter L. *Inspektionsreisen in der US-Zone.* Lutz Niethammer (ed.). Stuttgart: Deutsche Verlags-Anstalt, 1973.

Drummond, Gordon D. *The German Social Democrats in Opposition, 1949–1960: The Case against Rearmament.* Norman, Oklahoma: University of Oklahoma Press, 1982.

Dyson, Kenneth H. F. *Party, State and Bureaucracy in Western Germany.* Beverly Hills, CA: Sage, 1978.

Eden, Anthony. *Full Circle.* London: Cassell, 1960.

Edinger, Lewis J. *Kurt Schumacher.* Stanford, CA: Stanford University Press, 1965.

—— *West German Politics.* New York: Columbia University Press, 1986.

Ehmke, Horst. *Das Porträt: Reden und Beiträge.* Dieter Dettke (ed.). Bonn: GHM-Verlag, [1980].

—— "What is the German Fatherland?" in *Observations on "The Spiritual Situation of the Age,"* Jürgen Habermas (ed.). Cambridge, MA: MIT Press, 1984.

Eiche, Hans. *Heinrich Lübke: Der zweite Präsident der Bundesrepublik Deutschland.* Bonn: Beinhauer, [1961].

Ellwein, Thomas. *Das Regierungssystem der Bundesrepublik Deutschland.* 5th edn. Opladen: Westdeutscher Verlag, 1983.

Ellwein, Thomas, and Bruder, Wolfgang, eds. *Ploetz – Die Bundesrepublik Deutschland: Daten, Fakten, Analysen.* Freiburg/Würzburg: Ploetz, 1984.

Emminger, Otmar. *D-Mark, Dollar, Währungskrisen: Erinnerungen eines ehemaligen Bundesbankpräsidenten.* Stuttgart: Deutsche Verlags-Anstalt, 1986.

Eppler, Erhard. *Ende oder Wende: Von der Machbarkeit des Notwendigen.* Stuttgart: Kohlhammer, 1975.

Erhard, Ludwig. *Prosperity through Competition.* London: Thames and Hudson, 1958.

Eschenburg, Theodor. *Jahre der Besatzung, 1945–1949.* Vol. 1 of *Geschichte der Bundesrepublik Deutschland.* Stuttgart: Deutsche Verlags-Anstalt; Wiesbaden: Brockhaus, 1983.

Ferrell, Robert H., ed. "Truman at Potsdam." *American Heritage* 31: 4 (June/July 1980), 36–47.

Filbinger, Hans. *Die geschmähte Generation.* Munich: Universitas, 1987.

Filmer, Werner, and Schwan, Heribert. *Helmut Kohl.* Düsseldorf: Econ, 1985.

Fischer, Arthur, et al., eds. *Jugend '81.* Published by Jugendwerk der Deutschen Shell. Leverkusen: Leske und Budrich, 1985.

Fischer, Fritz. *Griff nach der Weltmacht.* 3rd edn. Düsseldorf: Droste, 1964. Published in English as *Germany's Aim in the First World War.* London: Chatto and Windus, 1967.

Flechtheim, Ossip K., ed. *Dokumente zur parteipolitischen Entwicklung in Deutschland seit 1945.* 3 vols. Berlin: Dokumenten-Verlag Dr Herbert Wendler und Co., 1962.

Forster, Karl. "Der deutsche Katholizismus in der Bundesrepublik Deutschland" in *Der soziale und politische Katholizismus,* vol. 1, Anton Rauscher (ed.). Munich: Olzog, 1981.

Foschepoth, Josef. "Adenauers Moskaureise 1955." *Aus Politik und Zeitgeschichte* B 22/86 (May 31, 1986), 30–46.

Frei, Norbert. "Presse" and "Hörfunk und Fernsehen" in *Die Bundesrepublik Deutschland,* vol. 3, Wolfgang Benz (ed.). Frankfurt am Main: Fischer Taschenbuch Verlag, 1983.

Friedberg, Aaron L. "The Making of American National Strategy, 1948–1988." *National Interest* 11 (Spring 1988), 68–75.

Frielinghaus-Heuss, Hanna. *Heuss-Anekdoten.* Munich and Esslingen: Bechtle, 1964.

Gaddis, John Lewis. *Strategies of Containment.* New York: Oxford University Press, 1982.

—— *The United States and the Origins of the Cold War, 1941–1947.* New York: Columbia University Press, 1972.

Garton Ash, Timothy. *The Polish Revolution: Solidarity.* New York: Scribner's, 1984.

Gatz, Erwin. "Caritas und soziale Dienste" in *Der soziale und politische Katholizismus,* vol. 2, Anton Rauscher (ed.). Munich: Olzog, 1981.

Gaus, Günter. *Wo Deutschland liegt: Eine Ortsbestimmung.* Hamburg: Hoffmann und Campe, 1983.

Gehlen, Reinhard. *Der Dienst.* Munich: Kindler, 1970.

—— *Verschlusssache.* Munich: Kindler, 1976.

Gelb, Norman. *The Berlin Wall.* London: Michael Joseph, 1986.

Genscher, Hans-Dietrich. *Deutsche Aussenpolitik.* Stuttgart: Verlag Bonn Aktuell, 1977.

Geschichte der Bundesrepublik Deutschland. 5 vols. Stuttgart: Deutsche Verlags-Anstalt; Wiesbaden: Brockhaus, 1981–7.

Gillessen, Günther. "Konrad Adenauer und der Israel-Vertrag" in *Politik, Philosophie, Praxis,* Hans Maier , Ulrich Matz, Kurt Sontheimer, and Paul-Ludwig Weinacht (eds). Stuttgart: Klett-Cotta, 1988.

Gimbel, John. *The American Occupation of Germany: Politics and the Military, 1945– 1949.* Stanford, CA: Stanford University Press, 1968.

—— "Governing the American Zone of Germany" in *Americans as Proconsuls,* Robert Wolfe (ed.). Carbondale, IL: Southern Illinois University Press, 1984.

Glaser, Hermann. *Kulturgeschichte der Bundesrepublik Deutschland.* 2 vols. Munich: Carl Hanser, 1985-6.

Glaser, Hermann, ed. *Bundesrepublikanisches Lesebuch*. Frankfurt am Main: Fischer Taschenbuch Verlag, 1980.

Golay, John Ford. *The Founding of the Federal Republic of Germany*. Chicago: University of Chicago Press, 1958.

Goldman, Guido. *The German Political System*. New York: Random House, 1974.

Gollancz, Victor. *In Darkest Germany*. Hinsdale, IL: Henry Regnery Company, 1947.

—— *Our Threatened Values*. Hinsdale, IL: Henry Regnery Company, 1948.

Gottlieb, Manuel. *The German Peace Settlement and the Berlin Crisis*. New York: Paine-Whitman, 1960.

Gotto, Klaus. "Adenauers Deutschland- und Ostpolitik 1954–1963" in *Adenauer-Studien*, vol. 3, Rudolf Morsey and Konrad Repgen (eds). Mainz: Mathias Grünewald, 1976.

Gotto, Klaus, ed. *Der Staatssekretär Adenauers: Persönlichkeit und politisches Wirken Hans Globkes.* Stuttgart: Klett-Cotta, 1980.

Gradl, Johann B. *Anfang unter dem Sowjetstern: Die CDU 1945–1948 in der sowjetischen Besatzungszone Deutschlands.* Cologne: Verlag Wissenschaft und Politik, 1981.

Graml, Hermann. *Die Alliierten und die Teilung Deutschlands: Konflikte und Entscheidungen 1941–1948.* Frankfurt am Main: Fischer Taschenbuch Verlag, 1985.

—— "Die Legende von der verpassten Gelegenheit." *Vierteljahrshefte für Zeitgeschichte* 29 (1981), 307–41.

Grass, Günter. *Aus dem Tagebuch einer Schnecke.* Neuwied: Luchterhand, 1972.

—— *On Writing and Politics 1967–1983.* Orlando, FL: Harcourt Brace Jovanovich, 1985.

—— *Widerstand lernen.* Darmstadt: Luchterhand, 1984.

Grebing, Helga; Pozorski, Peter; and Schulze, Rainer. *Die Nachkriegsentwicklung in Westdeutschland 1945–1949.* 2 vols. Stuttgart: J. B. Metzler, 1980.

Greiner, Christian. "The Defence of Western Europe and the Rearmament of West Germany, 1947–1950" in *Western Security: The Formative Years,* Olav Riste (ed.). Oslo: Norwegian University Press, 1985.

Gress, David. *Peace and Survival: West Germany, the Peace Movement, and European Security.* Stanford, CA: Hoover Institution Press, 1985.

Grewe, Wilhelm G. *Rückblenden 1976–1951.* Frankfurt am Main: Propyläen, 1979.

Griffith, William E. *The Ostpolitik of the Federal Republic of Germany.* Cambridge, MA: MIT Press, 1978.

Grosser, Alfred. *Germany in Our Time.* New York: Praeger, 1971.

— *L'Allemagne en Occident.* Paris: Fayard, 1985.

— *The Western Alliance.* Rev. edn. New York: Viking, 1982.

Grosser, Alfred, and Seifert, Jürgen. *Die Staatsmacht und ihre Kontrolle.* Vol. 1 of *Die Spiegel-Affäre,* Jürgen Seifert (ed.). Olten: Walter- Verlag, 1966.

Günther, Klaus. *Der Kanzlerwechsel in der Bundesrepublik: Adenauer-Erhard-Kiesinger.* Hannover: Verlag für Literatur und Zeitgeschehen, 1970.

Guttenberg, Karl Theodor Freiherr von und zu. *Fussnoten.* Stuttgart: Seewald, 1971.

Habermas, Jürgen. "Eine Art Schadensabwicklung" in *"Historikerstreit."* Munich: Piper, 1987.

Habermas, Jürgen, ed. *Observations on "The Spiritual Situation of the Age": Contemporary German Perspectives.* Cambridge, MA: MIT Press, 1984. Partial translation of *Stichworte zur "Geistigen Situation der Zeit."* Frankfurt am Main: Suhrkamp, 1979.

Hacke, Christian. *Weltmacht wider Willen: Die Aussenpolitik der Bundesrepublik Deutschland.* Stuttgart: Klett-Cotta, 1988.

Haftendorn, Helga. *Security and Detente.* New York: Praeger, 1985.

— *Sicherheit und Stabilität: Aussenbeziehungen der Bundesrepublik zwischen Ölkrise und NATO-Doppelbeschluss.* Munich: Deutscher Taschenbuch Verlag, 1986.

Hahn, Walter F. "West Germany's Ostpolitik." *Orbis* 16 (1973), 859–80.

Hallett, Graham. *The Social Economy of West Germany.* London: Macmillan, 1973.

Hallstein, Walter. *United Europe: Challenge and Opportunity.* Cambridge, MA: Harvard University Press, 1962.

Hanrieder, Wolfram F. *Germany, America, Europe: Forty Years of German Foreign Policy.* New Haven, CT: Yale University Press, 1989.

Hartrich, Edwin. *The Fourth and Richest Reich.* New York: Macmillan, 1980.

Hattenhauer, Hans. *Geschichte des Beamtentums.* Cologne: Carl Heymanns Verlag, 1980.

Hättich, Manfred. *Weltfrieden durch Friedfertigkeit?: Eine Antwort an Franz Alt.* Munich: Olzog, 1983.

Heidenheimer, Arnold J. *The Governments of Germany.* 4th edn. New York: T. Y. Crowell, [1975].

Heinrich, Gerd. *Geschichte Preussens.* Frankfurt am Main: Propyläen, 1981.

Heller, Michel, and Nekrich, Aleksandr. *L'utopie au pouvoir: Histoire de l'URSS de 1917 a nos jours.* Paris: Calmann-Levy, 1982.

Herzfeld, Hans. *Berlin in der Weltpolitik 1945—1970.* Berlin: Walter de Gruyter, 1973.

— *Der Erste Weltkrieg.* Munich: Deutscher Taschenbuch Verlag, 1968.

Hilberg, Raul. *The Destruction of the European Jews.* Rev. edn. New York: Holmes and Meier, 1985.

Hildebrand, Klaus. *Von Erhard zur Grossen Koalition, 1963—1969.* Vol. 4 of *Geschichte der Bundesrepublik Deutschland.* Stuttgart: Deutsche Verlags-Anstalt; Wiesbaden: Brockhaus, 1984.

Hildebrandt, Horst, ed. *Die deutschen Verfassungen des 19. und 20. Jahrhunderts.* Paderborn: Ferdinand Schöningh, 1983.

Hilgemann, Werner. *Atlas zur Deutschen Zeitgeschichte, 1918–1968.* Munich: Piper, 1984.

Hillgruber, Andreas. *Deutsche Geschichte 1945–1982: Die "deutsche Frage" in der Weltpolitik.* 5th edn. Stuttgart: Kohlhammer, 1984.

— *Zweierlei Untergang: Die Zerschlagung des deutschen Reiches und das Ende des europäischen Judentums.* Berlin: Siedler, 1986.

"Historikerstreit": Die Dokumentation der Kontroverse um die Einzigartigkeit der nationalsozialistischen Judenvernichtung. Munich: Piper, 1987.

Horchem, Hans. *Die verlorene Revolution: Terrorismus in Deutschland.* Herford: Busse Seewald, 1988.

Howard, Michael. *The Causes of Wars and other Essays.* 2nd edn. Cambridge, MA: Harvard University Press, 1984.

Hübner, Emil, and Rohlfs, Horst-H., eds. *Jahrbuch der Bundesrepublik Deutschland 1986/87.* Munich: Beck/dtv, 1987.

Independent Commission on International Development Issues. *North–South: A Programme for Survival.* Cambridge, MA: MIT Press, 1981. Published in German as *Die Zukunft Sichern.* Bericht der Nord–Süd Kommission.

Inglehart, Ronald. *Culture Change in Advanced Industrial Societies.* Princeton, NJ: Princeton University Press, 1989.

— "The Renaissance of Political Culture." *American Political Science Review* 82 (1988), 1204.

— *The Silent Revolution.* Princeton, NJ: Princeton University Press, 1977.

Isby, David C., and Kamps, Charles, Jr. *Armies of NATO's Central Front.* London: Jane's, 1985.

Jäger, Wolfgang, and Link, Werner. *Republik im Wandel, 1974–1982, Die Ära Schmidt.* Vol. 5/II of *Geschichte der Bundesrepublik Deutschland.* Stuttgart: Deutsche Verlags-Anstalt; Wiesbaden: Brockhaus, 1987.

James, Harold. *A German Identity: 1770–1990.* London: Weidenfeld and Nicolson, 1989.

Jaspers, Karl. *Antwort: Zur Kritik meiner Schrift "Wohin treibt die Bundesrepublik?"* Munich: Piper, 1967.

— *Die Atombombe und die Zukunft der Menschen.* Munich: Piper, 1958. Published in English as *The Atom Bomb and the Future of Man.* Chicago: Chicago University Press, 1961.

— *Die geistige Situation der Zeit.* Berlin, Leipzig: Walter de Gruyter, 1931.

— *Hoffnung und Sorge: Schriften zur deutschen Politik, 1945–1965.* Munich: Piper, 1965.

— *Wohin treibt die Bundesrepublik?* Munich: Piper, 1966. An English translation, *The Future of Germany*, contains parts of *Wohin treibt die Bundesrepublik?* as well as parts of *Antwort: Zur Kritik meiner Schrift "Wohin treibt die Bundesrepublik?"* Chicago: University of Chicago Press, 1967.

Joffe, Josef. "The Battle of the Historians." *Encounter* (June 1987), 72–7.

— *The Limited Partnership: Europe, the United States, and the Burdens of Alliance.* Cambridge, MA: Ballinger, 1987.

—— "Is there a German-American Question? Defense, Detente, Neutrality, Reunification." Paper presented at the International Security Council Roundtable on "The Future of German-American Relations," Berlin, FRG, (June 8–10, 1987).

Junker, Detlef. "Die 'revisionistische Schule' in der US-Historiographie" in *Die Deutschlandfrage und die Anfänge des Ost-Westkonflikts 1945—1949*. Studien zur Deutschlandfrage, vol. 7. Publ. by Gottinger Arbeitskreis. Berlin: Duncker und Humblot, 1984.

Kaiser, Bruno. *Notstandsgesetzgebung in der Grossen Koalition*. Unpublished manuscript in Archiv K. G. Kiesinger, Bonn.

Kaltefleiter, Werner. *Parteien im Umbruch*. Düsseldorf: Econ, 1984.

Karsunke, Ingrid, and Michel, Karl Markus, eds. *Bewegung in der Republik 1965 bis 1984: Eine Kursbuch-Chronik*. 2 vols. Berlin: Rotbuch, 1985.

Katzenstein, Peter J. *Policy and Politics in West Germany*. Philadelphia: Temple University Press, 1987.

Kelleher, Catherine McArdle. *Germany and the Politics of Nuclear Weapons*. New York: Columbia University Press, 1975.

Kempf, Udo. "Die Deutsch-Französischen Beziehungen seit October 1982: Versuch einer Bilanz." *Zeitschrift für Politik* 34 (March 1987), 31–55.

Kennan, George F. *Memoirs 1925—1950*. Boston: Little, Brown and Company, 1967.

—— *Russia and the West under Lenin and Stalin*. Boston: Little, Brown and Company, 1961.

—— *Russia, the Atom and the West*. New York: Harper and Brothers, 1958.

—— "The Sources of Soviet Conduct." *Foreign Affairs* 65 (1986-7), 852–68.

Kennan, George F.; Urban, George; Seton-Watson, Hugh; Pipes, Richard; Novak, M.; Weiss, S.; Luttwak, E. N.; Rostow, E. V.; Gaddis, J. L.; and Mark, E. *Decline of the West?* Washington, DC: Ethics and Public Policy Center, Georgetown University, 1978.

Kershaw, Ian. *Der Hitler-Mythos*. Schriftenreihe der Vierteljahrshefte für Zeitgeschichte, no. 41. Stuttgart: Deutsche Verlags-Anstalt, 1980.

—— *Popular Opinion and Political Dissent in the Third Reich: Bavaria, 1933—1945*. Oxford: Clarendon Press, 1983.

Kissinger, Henry. *The Troubled Partnership*. New York: McGraw-Hill, 1965.

—— *White House Years*. Boston: Little, Brown and Company, 1979.

—— *Years of Upheaval*. Boston: Little, Brown and Company, 1982.

Kistler, Helmut. *Bundesdeutsche Geschichte*. Stuttgart: Bonn Aktuell, 1986.

Klarsfeld, Beate. *Wherever They May Be*. New York: Vanguard Press, 1975.

Klessmann, Christoph. *Die doppelte Staatsgründung: Deutsche Geschichte 1945—1955*. Göttingen: Vandenhoeck und Ruprecht, 1982.

Klimow, Gregory. *Berliner Kreml*. Cologne: Kiepenheuer, Witsch and Co., 1952.

Koch, H. W. *A Constitutional History of Germany in the Nineteenth and Twentieth Centuries*. London: Longman, 1984.

Kocka, Jürgen. *Die Angestellten in der deutschen Geschichte, 1850—1980*. Göttingen: Vandenhoeck und Ruprecht, 1981.

Koerfer, Daniel. *Kampf ums Kanzleramt: Erhard und Adenauer.* Stuttgart: Deutsche Verlags-Anstalt, 1987.

Kohl, Helmut. *Helmut Kohl: Bundestagsreden und Zeitdokumente.* Horst Teltschik (ed.). Bonn: az studio, 1978.

Kolko, Gabriel. *The Politics of War.* New York: Random House, 1968.

Kommers, Donald P. *Judicial Politics in West Germany: A Study of the Federal Constitutional Court.* Beverly Hills: Sage Publications, 1976.

Kopelev, Lev. *To Be Preserved Forever.* Philadelphia: Lippincott, 1977.

Körner, Heiko; Meyer-Dohm, Peter; Tuchtfeldt, Egon; and Uhlig, Christian, eds. *Wirtschaftspolitik — Wissenschaft und politische Aufgabe: Festschrift zum 65. Geburtstag von Karl Schiller.* Bern: Paul Haupt, 1976.

Kortmann, Erhard, and Wolf, Fritz, eds. *Die Lage war noch nie so ernst!: Doctor Adenauers geflügelte Worte.* Bergisch Gladbach: Gustav Lübbe, 1966.

Krauss, Melvyn. *How NATO Weakens the West.* New York: Simon and Schuster, 1986.

Krisch, Henry. *German Politics under Soviet Occupation.* New York: Columbia University Press 1974.

Krockow, Christian Graf von. *Die Stunde der Frauen: Bericht aus Pommern 1944–1947.* Stuttgart: Deutsche Verlags-Anstalt, 1988.

Kuklick, Bruce. *American Policy and the Division of Germany.* Ithaca: Cornell University Press, 1972.

Lacouture, Jean. *De Gaulle.* Vol. 3, *Le Souverain 1959–1970.* Paris: Seuil, 1986.

Lafontaine, Oskar. *Angst vor den Freunden.* Reinbek: Rowohlt, 1983.

Lahr, Rolf. *Zeuge von Fall und Aufstieg.* Hamburg: Albrecht Knaus, 1981.

Lampugnani, Vittorio. "Architektur und Stadtplanung" in *Die Bundesrepublik Deutschland,* vol. 1, Wolfgang Benz (ed.). Frankfurt am Main: Fischer Taschenbuch Verlag, 1983.

Lampert, Heinz. *Die Wirtschafts- und Sozialordnung der Bundesrepublik Deutschland.* 8th edn. Munich: Olzog, 1985.

Langguth, Gerd. *Protestbewegung: Entwicklung, Niedergang, Renaissance.* Cologne: Verlag Wissenschaft und Politik, 1983.

—— *The Green Factor in German Politics: From Protest Movement to Political Party.* Boulder, Colorado: Westview, 1986. Originally published as *Der Grüne Faktor: Von der Bewegung zur Partei?* Osnabrück: Fromm, 1984.

Lasky, Melvin. "Journey among the 'Ugly Germans.'" *Encounter* Pamphlet No. 17 (1987), 56–63.

Lehmann, Hans Georg. *Öffnung nach Osten.* Bonn: Neue Gesellschaft, 1984.

Leonhard, Wolfgang. *Child of the Revolution.* Chicago: Henry Regnery Company, 1958. Originally published as *Die Revolution entlässt ihre Kinder.* Cologne: Kiepenheuer und Witsch, 1955.

Lippmann, Walter. "The Cold War." *Foreign Affairs* 65 (1986–7), 869–84.

—— "Rough-hew Them How We Will." *Foreign Affairs* 15 (1936–7), 587–94.

Lobkowicz, Nikolaus. *Was brachte uns das Konzil?* Würzburg: Naumann, 1986.

Loewenberg, Gerhard. *Parliament in the German Political System.* Ithaca: Cornell University Press, 1967.

Löwenthal, Richard. "Vom kalten Krieg zur Ostpolitik" in *Die zweite Republik*, Richard Löwenthal and Hans-Peter Schwarz (eds). Stuttgart: Seewald, 1974.

Löwenthal, Richard, and Schwarz, Hans-Peter, eds. *Die zweite Republik: 25 Jahre Bundesrepublik Deutschland — eine Bilanz*. Stuttgart: Seewald, 1974.

Lukacs, John. "The Soviet State at 65." *Foreign Affairs* 65 (1986–7), 21–36.

—— *A New History of the Cold War*. New York: Doubleday, 1966.

Lübbe, Hermann. *Endstation Terror: Rückblick auf lange Märsche*. Stuttgart: Seewald, 1978.

—— *Politischer Moralismus*. Berlin: Siedler, 1987.

McAdams, A. James. *East Germany and Detente*. Cambridge: Cambridge University Press, 1985.

McCloy, John J. "From Military Government to Self-Government" in *Americans as Proconsuls*, Robert Wolfe (ed.). Carbondale, IL: Southern Illinois University Press, 1984.

McGhee, George. *At the Creation of a New Germany*. New Haven: Yale University Press, 1989.

Macmillan, Harold. *Riding the Storm*. New York: Harper and Row, 1971.

—— *Tides of Fortune: 1945–1955*. New York: Harper and Row, 1969.

Maier, Charles S. "The Two Post-War Eras and the Conditions for Stability in 20th Century Western Europe." *American Historical Review* 86 (1981), 327–52.

—— *The Unmasterable Past: History, Holocaust, and German National Identity*. Cambridge, MA: Harvard University Press, 1988.

Malia, Martin. *Comprendre la revolution russe*. Paris: Seuil, 1980.

Mann, Golo. *History of Germany since 1789*. New York: Praeger, 1968. Reprinted London: Penguin Books, 1988.

Mann, Thomas. *Thomas Mann's Addresses Delivered at the Library of Congress, 1942–1949*. Washington: Library of Congress, 1963.

Marcuse, Herbert. *An Essay on Liberation*. Boston: Beacon Press, 1969.

—— *One-Dimensional Man*. Boston: Beacon Press, 1964.

Massing, Peter. "Die Bildungspolitik" in *Die Bundesrepublik in den siebziger Jahren*, Gert-Joachim Glaessner, Jürgen Holz, and Thomas Schlüter (eds). Opladen: Leske und Budrich, 1984.

Mastny, Vojtech. *Russia's Road to the Cold War*. New York: Columbia University Press, 1979.

Mayne, Richard. *Postwar: The Dawn of Today's Europe*. London: Thames and Hudson, 1983.

Mehnert, Klaus, and Schulte, Heinrich, eds. *Deutschland-Jahrbuch 1949*. Essen: West, 1949.

Meier, Christian. "Kein Schlusswort" in *"Historikerstreit."* Munich: Piper, 1987.

Meinecke, Friedrich. *The German Catastrophe*. Cambridge, MA: Harvard University Press, 1950.

Meissner, Boris. *Russland, die Westmächte und Deutschland: Die sowjetische Deutschlandpolitik 1943–1953*. Hamburg: H. H. Noelke, 1953.

Mende, Erich. *Die neue Freiheit, 1945–1961*. Munich: Herbig, 1984.

Merkl, Peter H. *German Foreign Policies, West and East.* Santa Barbara: ABC Clio, 1974.
— *The Origin of the West German Republic.* New York: Oxford University Press, 1963.
Merritt, Anna J., and Merritt, Richard L., eds. *Public Opinion in Occupied Germany: The OMGUS Surveys, 1945–1949.* Urbana, IL: University of Illinois Press, 1970.
— *Public Opinion in Semisovereign Germany: The HICOG Surveys, 1949–1955.* Urbana, IL: University of Illinois Press, 1980.
Mertz, Peter. *Und das wurde nicht ihr Staat: Erfahrungen emigrierter Schriftsteller mit Westdeutschland.* Munich: Beck, 1985.
Milward, Alan S. *The Reconstruction of Western Europe, 1945–1951.* Berkeley: University of California Press, 1984.
Mitchell, B. R., ed. *European Historical Statistics 1750–1975.* 2nd rev. edn. New York: Facts on File, 1981.
Mitscherlich, Alexander. *Society Without the Father.* New York: Schocken, 1970. Originally published as *Auf dem Weg zur vaterlosen Gesellschaft.* Munich: Piper, 1963.
Mitscherlich, Alexander, and Mitscherlich, Margarete. *The Inability to Mourn: Principles of Collective Behavior.* New York: Grove Press, 1975. Originally published as *Die Unfähigkeit zu trauern, Grundlagen kollektiven Verhaltens.* Munich: Piper, 1967.
Mont Pelerin Society Records, 1945–1981. Hoover Institution Archives, Stanford, California.
Morgan, Roger P. *The United States and West Germany, 1945–1973.* London: published for the Royal Institute of International Affairs and the Harvard Center for International Affairs by Oxford University Press, 1974.
Morgenthau, Henry, Jr. *Germany Is Our Problem.* New York: Harper and Brothers, 1945.
Morsey, Rudolf. *Die Bundesrepublik Deutschland: Entstehung und Entwicklung bis 1969.* Oldenbourg-Grundriss der Geschichte, vol. 19. Munich: Oldenbourg, 1987.
Mühlfenzl, Rudolf, ed. *Geflohen und vertrieben.* Königstein: Athenaeum, 1981.
Münch, Ingo von. *Dokumente des geteilten Deutschland.* 2 vols. Stuttgart: Alfred Kröner, 1968–74.
Naumann, Bernd. *Auschwitz.* New York: Frederic A. Praeger, 1966.
Negt, Oskar. "Studentischer Protest – Liberalismus – 'Linksfaschismus'" in *Bewegung in der Republik 1965 bis 1984: Eine Kursbuch-Chronik,* vol. 2, Ingrid Karsunke and Karl Markus Michel (eds). Berlin: Rotbuch, 1985.
Nelson, Daniel J. *Wartime Origins of the Berlin Dilemma.* University, AL: University of Alabama Press, 1978.
Nicholson, Frances, and East, Roger. *From the Six to the Twelve: The Enlargement of the European Communities.* Keesing's International Studies. Harlow: Longman, 1987.
Niethammer, Lutz. *Die Mitläuferfabrik: Die Entnazifizierung am Beispiel Bayerns.*

Berlin: Dietz, 1982. Originally published as *Entnazifizierung in Bayern.* Frankfurt am Main: S. Fischer, 1972.

Niethammer, Lutz, and Plato, Alexander von, eds. *Lebensgeschichte und Sozialkultur im Ruhrgebiet 1930 bis 1960.* Vol. 3, *"Wir kriegen jetzt andere Zeiten."* Berlin: Dietz, 1985.

Noelle, Elisabeth, and Neumann, Erich Peter, eds. *Jahrbuch der Öffentlichen Meinung, 1947—1955.* Allensbach am Bodensee: Verlag für Demoskopie, 1956.

Noelle-Neumann, Elisabeth. "Who Needs a Flag?" *Encounter* 60, no. 1 (January 1983), 72–80.

Noelle-Neumann, Elisabeth, ed. *The Germans: Public Opinion Polls 1967—1980.* Allensbach Institut für Demoskopie. Westport, CT: Greenwood, 1981.

Noelle-Neumann, Elisabeth, and Köcher, Renate. *Die verletzte Nation.* Stuttgart: Deutsche Verlags-Anstalt, 1987.

Noelle-Neumann, Elisabeth, and Neumann, Erich Peter, eds. *The Germans: Public Opinion Polls 1947—1966.* Allensbach am Bodensee: Verlag für Demoskopie, 1967.

Nolte, Ernst. *Das Vergehen der Vergangenheit.* Frankfurt am Main: Ullstein, 1987.

—— *Der europäische Bürgerkrieg, 1917—1945.* Berlin: Propyläen, 1987.

—— *Deutschland und der Kalte Krieg.* 2nd edn. Stuttgart: Klett-Cotta, 1985.

—— *The Three Faces of Fascism.* New York: Holt, Reinhart and Winston, 1963.

—— *Universitätsinstitut oder Parteihochschule?* Cologne: Markus-Verlagsgesellschaft, 1971.

—— "Zusammenbruch und Neubeginn." *Zeitschrift für Politik* 32 (1985), 296–303.

Oberndörfer, Dieter, ed. *Begegnungen mit Kurt Georg Kiesinger.* Stuttgart: Deutsche Verlags-Anstalt, 1984.

OECD Economic Surveys: Germany, 1969–. Paris, Organization for Economic Cooperation and Development.

Olson, Mancur. *The Logic of Collective Action.* Cambridge, MA: Harvard University Press, 1965.

Ostwald, Thomas. *Karl May: Leben und Werk.* 4th edn. Braunschweig: Graff, 1977.

Overesch, Manfred. *Das besetzte Deutschland 1948—1949.* Vol. 3/II of *Chronik deutscher Zeitgeschichte* (Droste-Geschichts-Kalendarium). Düsseldorf: Droste, 1986.

Parkes, K. Stuart. *Writers and Politics in West Germany.* London: Croom Helm, 1986.

Picht, Georg. *Die Deutsche Bildungskatastrophe.* Olten and Freiburg: Walter-Verlag, 1964.

Pincher, Chapman. *The Secret Offensive.* New York: St. Martin's Press, 1985.

Plischke, Elmer. "Denazification in Germany: A Policy Analysis" in *Americans as Proconsuls,* Robert Wolfe (ed.). Carbondale, IL: Southern Illinois University Press, 1984.

Poppinga, Anneliese. *Meine Erinnerungen an Konrad Adenauer.* Stuttgart: Deutsche Verlags-Anstalt, 1970.

Pridham, Geoffrey. *Christian Democracy in Western Germany*. New York: St. Martin's Press, 1977.

Prittie, Terence. *Konrad Adenauer*. Stuttgart: Bonn Aktuell, 1983.

—— *Willy Brandt: Portrait of a Statesman*. New York: Schocken, 1974.

Putnam, Robert G., and Bayne, Nicholas. *Hanging Together: The Seven-Power Summits*. London: Heinemann, 1984.

Raddatz, Werner. *Das abenteuerliche Leben Karl Mays*. Gütersloh: Sigbert Mohn, 1965.

Reinfried, Hubert, and Schulte, Ludwig. *Die Sicherheit der Bundesrepublik Deutschland*. Vol. 1, *Die Bundeswehr*. Regensburg: Walhalla und Praetoria, 1985.

Richter, Horst Eberhard. *Die Chance des Gewissens: Erinnerungen und Assoziationen*. Hamburg: Hoffmann und Campe, 1986.

Riste, Olav, ed. *Western Security: The Formative Years*. Oslo: Norwegian University Press, 1985.

Roellecke, Gerd. "Entwicklungslinien deutscher Universitätsgeschichte." *Aus Politik und Zeitgeschichte* B 3–4/84 (January 21, 1984), 3–10.

Ross, Werner. *Mit der linken Hand geschrieben . . .: Der deutsche Literaturbetrieb*. Zürich: Edition Interform, 1984.

Rothenberger, Karl Heinz. *Die Hungerjahre nach dem Zweiten Weltkrieg*. Boppard: Boldt, 1980.

Rovan, Joseph. *Geschichte der Deutschen Sozialdemokratie*. Frankfurt am Main: Fischer Taschenbuch Verlag, 1980.

Rückerl, Adalbert. *NS-Verbrechen vor Gericht*. Heidelberg: C. F. Müller, 1982.

Ruhl, Klaus-Jörg, ed. *"Mein Gott, was soll aus Deutschland werden?": Die Adenauer Ära 1949—1963*. Munich: Deutscher Taschenbuch Verlag, 1985.

Rumpf, Helmut. "Die deutschen Reparationen nach dem Zweiten Weltkrieg" in *Handbuch zur Deutschen Nation*, vol. 1, Bernard Willms (ed.). Tübingen: Hohenrain, 1986.

Rutschky, Michael. "Neues aus der Strauss-Forschung." *Merkur* 41 (January 1987), 78–82.

Rytlewski, Ralf, and Opp de Hipt, Manfred. *Die Bundesrepublik Deutschland in Zahlen, 1945/49—1980*. Munich: Beck, 1987.

Salomon, Ernst von. *Der Fragebogen*. Hamburg: Rowohlt, 1952.

Schick, Jack M. *The Berlin Crisis, 1958—1962*. Philadelphia: University of Pennsylvania Press, 1971.

Schickling, Willi. *Entscheidung in Frankfurt: Ludwig Erhards Durchbruch zur Freiheit, 30 Jahre Deutsche Mark, 30 Jahre Soziale Marktwirtschaft*. Stuttgart: Seewald, 1978.

Schillinger, Reinhold. *Der Entscheidungsprozess beim Lastenausgleich, 1945—1952*. Sankt Katharinen: Scripta Mercaturae, 1985.

Schlesinger, Arthur Meier. *A Thousand Days*. New York: Houghton Mifflin, 1965.

Schmid, Carlo. *Erinnerungen*. Bern: Scherz, 1979.

Schmid, Claudia. "Staatliche Hochschulpolitik in der Bundesrepublik: Daten,

Strukturen und Tendenzen." *Aus Politik und Zeitgeschichte* B 3–4/84 (January 21, 1984), 11–23.

Schmid, Günther. *Sicherheitspolitik und Friedensbewegung.* Munich: Olzog, 1983.

Schmidt, Helmut. *The Balance of Power: Germany's Peace Policy and the Super Powers.* London: William Kimber, 1971. Originally published as *Strategie des Gleichgewichts.* Stuttgart: Seewald, 1969.

— *Defense or Retaliation: a German View.* New York: Praeger, 1962. Originally published as *Verteidigung oder Vergeltung.* Stuttgart: Seewald, 1961.

— *Der Kurs heisst Frieden.* Düsseldorf: Econ, 1979.

— *Helmut Schmidt: Perspectives on Politics.* Wolfram F. Hanrieder (ed.). Boulder, Colorado: Westview, 1982.

— *Menschen und Mächte.* Berlin: Siedler, 1987.

Schmückle, Gerd. *Ohne Pauken und Trompeten: Erinnerungen an Krieg und Frieden.* Stuttgart: Deutsche Verlags-Anstalt, 1982.

Schneider, Peter. "Der Sand an Baaders Schuhen" in *Bewegung in der Republik 1965 bis 1984: Eine Kursbuch-Chronik,* vol. 1, Ingrid Karsunke and Karl Markus Michel (eds). Berlin: Rotbuch, 1985.

Schoenbaum, David. *The Spiegel Affair.* Garden City, New York: Doubleday, 1968.

Scholz, Günther. *Herbert Wehner.* Düsseldorf: Econ, 1986.

Schrenck-Notzing, Caspar. *Charakterwäsche: Die amerikanische Besatzung in Deutschland und ihre Folgen.* Stuttgart: Seewald, 1965.

Schrenck-Notzing, Caspar von. "Die Umerziehung der Deutschen" in *Handbuch zur Deutschen Nation,* vol. 1, Bernard Willms (ed.). Tübingen: Hohenrain, 1986.

Schröder, Gerhard. *Decision for Europe.* London: Thames and Hudson, 1964.

Schumpeter, Joseph A. *Capitalism, Socialism, and Democracy.* 3rd edn. New York: Harper, 1950.

Schwan, Gesine. "Die SPD und die westliche Freiheit" in *Wohin treibt die SPD?: Wende oder Kontinuität sozialdemokratischer Sicherheitspolitik,* Jürgen Maruhn and Manfred Wilke (eds). Munich: Olzog, 1984.

Schwarz, Hans-Peter. *Adenauer: Der Aufstieg, 1876–1952.* Stuttgart: Deutsche Verlags-Anstalt, 1986.

— *Die Ära Adenauer, 1949–1957.* Vol. 2 of *Geschichte der Bundesrepublik Deutschland.* Stuttgart: Deutsche Verlags-Anstalt; Wiesbaden: Brockhaus, 1981.

— *Die Ära Adenauer, 1957–1963.* Vol. 3 of *Geschichte der Bundesrepublik Deutschland.* Stuttgart: Deutsche Verlags-Anstalt; Wiesbaden: Brockhaus, 1983.

— *Die gezähmten Deutschen: Von der Machtbesessenheit zur Machtvergessenheit.* Stuttgart: Deutsche Verlags-Anstalt, 1985.

Seifert, Jürgen. "Die Verfassung" in *Die Bundesrepublik Deutschland,* vol. 1, Wolfgang Benz (ed.). Frankfurt am Main: Fischer Taschenbuch Verlag, 1983. Munich: Piper, 1986.

Seiffert, Wolfgang. *Das ganze Deutschland: Perspektiven der Wiedervereinigung.* Munich: Piper, 1986.

— "Die DDR – Herrschaftsinstrument der SED und Produkt sowjetischer Deutschlandpolitik" in *Die DDR auf dem Weg in das Jahr 2000,* Hermann von Berg, Franz Loeser and Wolfgang Seiffert (eds). Cologne: Bund, 1987.

Seton-Watson, Hugh. *The East European Revolution*. London: Methuen, 1956.

Sharp, Tony. *The Wartime Alliance and the Zonal Division of Germany*. Oxford: Clarendon Press, 1975.

Sherwood, Robert E. *Roosevelt and Hopkins: An Intimate History*. New York: Harper and Brothers, 1950.

Shirer, William L. *20th Century Journey*. Vol. 2. Boston and Toronto: Little, Brown and Company, 1984.

Slusser, Robert M. *The Berlin Crisis of 1961*. Baltimore: Johns Hopkins University Press, 1969.

Smith, Bradley F. *The Road to Nuremberg*. New York: Basic Books, 1981.

Smith, Gordon R. *Democracy in Western Germany*. 2nd edn. New York: Holmes and Meier, 1982.

Smith, Hedrick. *The Power Game: How Washington Works*. New York: Random House, 1988.

Solzhenitsyn, Aleksandr I. *The Gulag Archipelago, 1918–1956*. 2 vols. New York: Harper and Row, 1974.

Sonnenhol, Gustav Adolf. *Untergang oder Übergang? Wider die deutsche Angst*. Stuttgart: Seewald, 1983.

Sontheimer, Kurt. *Antidemokratisches Denken in der Weimarer Republik*. Munich: Nymphenburger Verlagshandlung, 1962.

—— *The Government and Politics of West Germany*. London: Hutchinson, 1972.

Sozialdemokratische Partei Deutschlands. *Bundesdelegierten-Konferenz und Ausserordentlicher Parteitag, 18.-19. November 1983*. Bonn: Vorstand der SPD, 1983.

—— *Wir informieren: Bilanz einer Wende*. Bonn: Vorstand der SPD, 1983.

Speer, Albert. *Spandau: The Secret Diaries*. New York: Macmillan, 1976.

Spotts, Frederic. *The Churches and Politics in Germany*. Middletown, Connecticut: Wesleyan University Press, 1973.

Staatslexikon. Publ. by Görres-Gesellschaft. 5 vols. 7th rev. edn. Freiburg: Herder, 1985–9.

Steinberg, Rudolf, ed. *Staat und Verbände zur Theorie der Interessenverbände in der Industriegesellschaft*. Wege der Forschung, vol. 298. Darmstadt: Wissentschaftliche Buchgesellschaft, 1985.

Steininger, Rolf. *Deutsche Geschichte 1945–1961*. 2 vols. Frankfurt am Main: Fischer Taschenbuch Verlag, 1983.

—— *Eine Chance zur Wiedervereinigung?: Die Stalin-Note vom 10. März 1952*. No. 12 of *Archiv für Sozialgeschichte*. Bonn: Neue Gesellschaft, 1985.

Stent, Angela. *From Embargo to Ostpolitik*. Cambridge: Cambridge University Press, 1981.

Stercken, Hans, ed. *De Gaulle hat gesagt . . .* Stuttgart: Seewald, 1967.

Stern, Carola. *Willy Brandt in Selbstzeugnissen und Bilddokumenten*. Reinbek: Rowohlt, 1975.

Stern, Fritz. *Dreams and Delusions*. New York: Alfred A. Knopf, 1987.

Stern, Klaus. *Das Staatsrecht der Bundesrepublik Deutschland*. Vol. 1, *Grund-*

begriffe und Grundlagen des Staatsrechts, Strukturprinzipien der Verfassung. 2nd edn 1984. Vol. 2, *Staatsorgane, Staatsfunktionen, Finanz- und Haushaltsverfassung, Notstandsverfassung.* Munich: Beck, 1980. Vols 3–5 in preparation.

Sternberger, Dolf. "Die deutsche Frage" in *Bundesrepublikanisches Lesebuch*, Hermann Glaser (ed.). Frankfurt am Main: Fischer Taschenbuch Verlag, 1980.

Stürmer, Michael. *Dissonanzen des Fortschritts: Essays über Geschichte und Politik in Deutschland.* Munich: Piper, 1986.

Szabo, Stephen F. "The German Social Democrats after the 1987 Elections." *SAIS Review* (Summer/Fall 1987): 36–7.

Talbott, Strobe. *Deadly Gambits.* New York: Alfred A. Knopf, 1984.

Tatu, Michel. *Gorbatchev.* Paris: Le Centurion, 1987.

Tenbruck, Friedrich. "Alltagsnormen und Lebensgefühle in der Bundesrepublik" in *Die zweite Republik*, Richard Löwenthal and Hans-Peter Schwarz (eds). Stuttgart: Seewald, 1974.

—— "Frieden durch Friedensforschung?" in *Friedensforschung: Entscheidungshilfe gegen Gewalt*, Manfred Funke (ed.). Munich: List, 1975.

Tent, James F. *The Free University of Berlin.* Bloomington, IN: Indiana University Press, 1988.

—— *Mission on the Rhine.* Chicago: University of Chicago Press, 1982.

Terjung, Knut, ed. *Der Onkel: Herbert Wehner in Gesprächen und Interviews.* Hamburg: Hoffmann und Campe, 1986.

Thayer, Charles W. *The Unquiet Germans.* New York: Harper and Brothers, 1957.

Thomas, Hugh. *Armed Truce: The Beginnings of the Cold War, 1945—46.* New York: Atheneum, 1987.

Thomas, Michael. *Deutschland, England über alles.* Berlin: Siedler, 1984.

Thränhardt, Dietrich. *Geschichte der Bundesrepublik Deutschland.* Frankfurt am Main: Suhrkamp, 1986.

Tilford, Roger, ed. *The Ostpolitik and Political Change in Germany.* Westmead, England: Saxon House; Lexington, MA: Lexington Books, 1975.

Tindall, George Brown. *America: A Narrative History.* New York: W. W. Norton, 1984.

Topitsch, Ernst. *Stalin's Krieg.* Munich: Olzog, 1985.

Treverton, Gregory F. *The Dollar Drain and American Forces in Germany.* Athens: Ohio University Press, 1978.

Tüngel, Richard, and Berndorff, Hans Rudolf. *Auf dem Bauche sollst Du kriechen . . .: Deutschland unter den Besatzungsmächten.* Hamburg: Christian Wegner, 1958.

Turner, George. "Hochschulreformpolitik: Versuch einer Bilanz." *Aus Politik und Zeitgeschichte*, B 3–4/84 (January 21, 1984), 24–35.

Turner, Henry Ashby, Jr. *The Two Germanies since 1945.* New Haven: Yale University Press, 1987.

Ulam, Adam B. *Expansion and Coexistence: Soviet Foreign Policy, 1917—73.* 2nd edn. New York: Praeger, 1974.

—— *A History of Soviet Russia.* New York: Praeger, 1976.

—— *The Rivals: America and Russia Since World War II.* New York: Viking Press, 1971.

Van Cleave, William R. *Fortress USSR: The Soviet Strategic Defense Initiative and the U.S. Strategic Defense Response.* Stanford, CA: Hoover Institution Press, 1986.

Vassiltchikov, Marie. *Berlin Diaries, 1940–1945.* New York: Alfred A. Knopf, 1987.

Vaubel, Ludwig. *Zusammenbruch und Wiederaufbau: Ein Tagebuch aus der Wirtschaft, 1945–1949.* Wolfgang Benz (ed.). Munich: Oldenbourg, 1984.

Venohr, Wolfgang, ed. *Die Deutsche Einheit kommt bestimmt.* Bergisch Gladbach: Gustav Lübbe, 1982.

Vogel, Angela. "Familie" in *Die Bundesrepublik Deutschland,* vol. 2, Wolfgang Benz (ed.). Frankfurt am Main: Fischer Taschenbuch Verlag, 1983.

Wallich, Henry C. *Mainsprings of the German Revival.* New Haven: Yale University Press, 1955.

Weber, Hermann. *Die DDR 1945–1986.* Munich: Oldenbourg, 1988.

—— *Geschichte der DDR.* Munich: Deutscher Taschenbuch-Verlag, 1985.

Weber, Hermann, ed. *DDR: Dokumente zur Geschichte der Deutschen Demokratischen Republik 1945–1985.* Munich: Deutscher Taschenbuch Verlag, 1986.

Weber-Fas, Rudolf. *Das Grundgesetz.* Berlin: Duncker und Humblot, 1983.

Wehler, Hans-Ulrich. *Preussen ist wieder chic. . . .* Frankfurt am Main: Suhrkamp, 1982.

Wehner, Herbert. *Wandel und Bewährung: Ausgewählte Reden und Schriften, 1930–1975.* Gerhard Jahn (ed.). Frankfurt am Main: Ullstein; Hannover: Dietz, 1976.

Weizsäcker, Carl Friedrich von. *Mit der Bombe leben.* Hamburg: Die Zeit, 1958.

Weizsäcker, Richard von. *Die deutsche Geschichte geht weiter.* 3rd edn. Berlin: Siedler, 1983.

Wesel, Uwe. *Juristische Weltkunde.* Frankfurt am Main: Suhrkamp, 1984.

Wettig, Gerhard. *Entmilitarisierung und Wiederbewaffnung in Deutschland, 1943–1955.* Munich: Oldenbourg, 1967.

Whetten, Lawrence L. *Germany East and West.* New York: New York University Press, 1980.

Wiggershaus, Norbert. "The Decision for a West German Defence Contribution" in *Western Security: The Formative Years,* Olav Riste (ed.). Oslo: Norwegian University Press, 1985.

Wilharm, Irmgard, ed. *Deutsche Geschichte 1962–1983.* 2 vols. Frankfurt am Main: Fischer Taschenbuch Verlag, 1985.

Willis, F. Roy. *France, Germany and the New Europe, 1945–1967.* Rev. and exp. edn. London: Oxford University Press, 1968.

Wilms, Dorothee. *The German Question and Inner-German Relations.* Occasional Paper Series, no. 8–87. St Augustin bei Bonn: Konrad Adenauer Stiftung, 1987.

Windsor, Philip. *Germany and the Western Alliance.* London: International Institute for Strategic Studies, 1981.

Wolfe, Robert, ed. *Americans as Proconsuls: United States Military Government in Germany and Japan, 1944–1952*. Carbondale, IL: Southern Illinois University Press, 1984.

Wolffsohn, Michael. *Ewige Schuld? 40 Jahre deutsch-jüdisch-israelische Beziehungen*. Munich: Piper, 1988.

—— *West Germany's Foreign Policy in the Era of Brandt and Schmidt, 1969–1982*. Frankfurt am Main: Lang, 1986.

Wunder, Bernd. *Geschichte der Bürokratie in Deutschland*. Frankfurt am Main: Suhrkamp, 1986.

Yost, David M. *Soviet Ballistic Missile Defense and the Western Alliance*. Cambridge, MA: Harvard University Press, 1988.

Ziemke, Earl F. "Improvising Stability and Change in Postwar Germany" in *Americans as Proconsuls*, Robert Wolfe (ed.). Carbondale, IL: Southern Illinois University Press, 1984.

Zink, Harold. *The United States in Germany, 1944–1955*. Princeton, NJ: Van Nostrand, 1957.

Zöllner, Detlev. "Sozialpolitik" in *Die Bundesrepublik Deutschland*, vol. 2, Wolfgang Benz (ed.). Frankfurt am Main: Fischer Taschenbuch Verlag, 1983.

Zuckmayer, Carl. *Des Teufels General*. Stockholm: Bermann-Fischer Verlag, 1946.

Zündorf, Benno. *Die Ostverträge: Die Verträge von Moskau, Warschau, Prag, Das Berlin-Abkommen und die Verträge mit der DDR*. Munich: Beck, 1979.

Index